**Florida Real Estate
Principles, Practices, and Laws**

Sam Irlander

Executive Editor: Sara Glassmeyer

Project Manager: Elizabeth King, KnowledgeWorks Global Ltd.

Product Specialist: Deborah Miller

Manager, Creative Services: Brian Brogaard

Cover Image: typhoonski/iStock/GettyImages

Chapter Opener Image Credits:

Chapter 1: © Photographer/Collection/Thinkstock 83066306
Chapter 2: © Photographer/Collection/Thinkstock 492548403
Chapter 3: © Photographer/Collection/Thinkstock Dv1248011
Chapter 4: © Photographer/Collection/Thinkstock 79073965
Chapter 5: © Photographer/Collection/Thinkstock 480297303
Chapter 6: © Photographer/Collection/Thinkstock 152022227
Chapter 7: © Photographer/Collection/Thinkstock AA014353
Chapter 8: © Photographer/Collection/Thinkstock 484579397
Chapter 9: © Photographer/Collection/Thinkstock 462268195
Chapter 10: © Photographer/Collection/Thinkstock 76800092
Chapter 11: © Photographer/Collection/Thinkstock 155327573
Chapter 12: © Photographer/Collection/Thinkstock 99829892
Chapter 13: © Photographer/Collection/Thinkstock 468473951
Chapter 14: © Photographer/Collection/Thinkstock 83404793
Chapter 15: © Photographer/Collection/Thinkstock 101418143
Chapter 16: © Photographer/Collection/Thinkstock 86533751
Chapter 17: © Photographer/Collection/Thinkstock 140465661
Chapter 18: © Photographer/Collection/Thinkstock 492222398
Chapter 19: © Photographer/Collection/Thinkstock 455640647
Chapter 20: © Photographer/Collection/Thinkstock Dv1662073

Copyright © 2021, 2018, 2009 Mbition LLC

ALL RIGHTS RESERVED. No part of this work covered by the copyright hereon may be reproduced or used in any form or by any means—graphic, electronic, or mechanical, including photocopying, recording, taping, Web distribution, information storage and retrieval systems, or in any other manner—except as permitted under Section 107 or 108 of the 1976 United States Copyright Act, without the prior written permission of the publisher.

For product information and technology assistance, contact us at
Mbition Customer Support, 800-532-7649.
For permission to use material from this text or product, please contact **publishingsupport@mbitiontolearn.com.**

Library of Congress Control Number: 2018943460
ISBN-13: 978-1-62980-956-4
ISBN-10: 1-62980-956-X

Mbition, LLC
18500 W Corporate Drive, Suite 250
Brookfield, WI 53045
USA
Visit us at **www.mbitiontolearn.com**

Printed in the United States of America
1 2 3 4 5 6 7 20 19 18

Florida Real Estate: Principles, Practices, & License Laws

Fourth Edition

Sam Irlander

BRIEF CONTENTS

	Preface	*xxix*
1	The Real Estate Business	1
2	License Law and Qualifications for Licensure	25
3	Real Estate License Law and Commission Rules	56
4	Law of Agency–Relationships and Disclosures	77
5	Real Estate Brokerage Activities and Procedures	108
6	Violations of License Law, Penalties, and Procedures	133
7	Federal and State Laws Pertaining To Real Estate	155
8	Property Rights: Estates and Tenancies: Condominiums, Cooperatives, Community Development Districs, Homeowners Associations, and Time-sharing	180
9	Title Deeds and Ownership Restrictions	216
10	Legal Description	254
11	Real Estate Contracts	268
12	Residential Mortgages	301
13	Mortgage Market Operations	327
14	Real Estate Related Computations and Closing of Transactions	382
15	The Real Estate Markets and Analysis	434
16	Real Estate Appraisal	447
17	Real Estate Investments and Business Opportunity Brokerage	500
18	Taxes Affecting Real Estate	520
19	Planning, Zoning and Environmental Hazards	556
	Addendum: Introduction to Residential Product Knowledge	576
	Math Busters Guide to Real Estate Math	606
	Answers to Chapter Review Questions	614
	Practice End-of-Course Exam	621
	Answers to Practice End-of-Course Exam	641
	Example Real Estate Forms	647
	Glossary	667
	Index	685

CONTENTS

Preface	*xxix*

1 The Real Estate Business — 1
Introduction to the Real Estate Business — 1
Overview of the Real Estate Business — 3
The Real Estate Industry's Role in the Nation's Economy — 4
Other Professions that Rely on the Real Estate Business — 4
Real Estate: A Business of Many Specialties — 5
Real Estate Brokerage: Sales and Leasing — 6
   The Broker as Agent/Intermediary—The Sales Associate's Role with the Broker — 7
   Efficiency of Utilizing a Real Estate Agent — 7
   Specialization in a Geographic Area or Property Type — 8
   Nonfiduciary Relationship — 8
   Fiduciary Relationship — 9
   Real Estate Brokerage — 9
   Brokerage Specialty Types — 11
The Sales Process and the Sales Licensee — 12
   Step 1—Farming/Canvassing for Product — 12
   Step 2—Canvassing for the Product Buyer/User — 12
   Step 3—Showing the Property — 13
   Step 4—Submitting and Negotiating the Offer — 13
   Step 5—Execution of a Sales Contract — 13
   Step 6—Closing of the Sales Contract — 13
   Step 7—Recording Activities — 13
Property Management — 14
   Need for Property Management and the Typical Services Provided by a Property Manager — 14
   Community Association Manager (CAM) — 15

Appraisal ... 15
  The Process of Estimating the Value of Real Estate ... 15
  Types of Real Estate Activities That Require Appraisal Services ... 15
  State-Certified Licensed and Registered Appraisers are Regulated by the Florida Real Estate Appraisal Board ... 16
  Comparative Market Analysis (CMA) ... 16
  Broker Price Opinion (BPO) ... 17
  Ethics Rules Governing Appraiser Compensation ... 17
Financing and the Real Property Transaction ... 17
  Sources of Funds Used to Finance Real Property ... 18
  Importance of Expertise in Financing Matters/ Problem-Solving Skills ... 18
  Counseling ... 18
Development and Construction ... 18
  Land Acquisition/Subdividing and Construction ... 18
Government's Role ... 19
  Federal Government ... 19
  State Government ... 20
  Local Government ... 20
Professional Organizations ... 20
Summary ... 21
Review Questions ... 22

2 License Law and Qualifications for Licensure ... 25
Historical Purposes of Real Estate License Laws ... 25
  History of Florida Real Estate License Law ... 25
  Department of Business and Professional Regulation (DBPR) ... 26
  Division of Real Estate (DRE) ... 26
  Florida Real Estate Commission ... 27
  Need For Regulation ... 27
Important Real Estate Statutes and Rules ... 28
  Florida Statutes ... 28
  Federal Regulations/United States Code ... 29
License Categories ... 30
General Licensing Provisions (Sales Associate Candidate) ... 30
  Application Requirements ... 33

Application Form: Responding Accurately and Completely to Background Information	33
Period to Check for Errors and Omissions/ Period to Inform Applicant of Approval or Denial of Application/Rights of the Applicant	34
Length of Time a Licensure Application is Valid/Initial Application/Exam Eligible	34
Nonresident Application Requirements	35
Regulations Pertaining to Pre-License Courses	37
Public Record	37
Sales Associate License Requirements	38
Education Exemptions	38
Sales Pre-License Course	38
State Licensure Examination	38
Examination Content	39
Broker and Broker Associate License Requirements	39
Education Exemptions	39
Experience Requirement for Broker Pre-License Course	39
Examination Content: Broker	40
Mutual Recognition Agreements with Other States	41
Florida Resident Defined	42
Distinguishing Between Mutual Recognition and Reciprocity	43
Information Included on the Real Estate License	43
Prima Facie Evidence	43
Registrations Vs. Licenses	43
License Renewal Education	44
Post license Requirement (Sales Associate)	44
Post-license Requirement (Broker)	44
Continuing Education	45
Reactivation Education	47
Licensure, License Renewal, Post-Licensing, and Continuing Education Exemptions	47
Real Estate Services	48
Individuals Who Are Exempt from Licensure	49
Unauthorized Practice of Law	51
Summary	52
Review Questions	52

3 Real Estate License Law and Commission Rules — 56

Regulation by Department of Business and Professional Regulation — 56
- *Organizational Structure, Governing Body, and Enforcement* — 56

Licensing Examinations — 60
- *Licenses, Fees, Statuses, and Renewals* — 60
- *Renewal* — 63
- *License Renewal/Military Exemptions (F.S. 455.02)* — 63

Types of Real Estate Licenses — 64
- *Multiple and Group Licenses* — 64

Registration Of Proprietary Real Estate Schools — 65

Division of Real Estate — 65
- *Organizational Structure* — 65
- *The Division of Real Estate (DRE) Address Requirements* — 66

Functions of the Florida Real Estate Commission and the Division of Real Estate — 66
- *Chapter 61J2-20—Rules Governing Internal Organization and Operation* — 68

Composition and Qualifications of FREC Members — 71
- *Meetings and Minutes* — 71
- *Duties and Powers of the Commission* — 72

The Real Estate Education and Research Foundation — 73

Summary — 73

Review Questions — 74

4 Law of Agency–Relationships and Disclosures — 77

Law of Agency–Authorized Relationships, Duties, and Disclosures — 78
- *Concept of Agency* — 78

Statutory and Common Law — 80
- *Statutory Law* — 80
- *Common Law* — 80

Types of Agents — 80
- *Universal Agency* — 80
- *General Agency* — 81
- *Special Agency* — 81

Fiduciary Relationships	82
Responsibilities to the Principal: Fiduciary Responsibilities	83
Dual Agency	87
Subagency	87
Customer vs. Principal: Responsibilities to the Customer	88
Agency Relationships Determined by Broker	91
Disclosure Requirements and the Florida Brokerage Relationship Disclosure Act	92
Exemptions to Disclosure Requirements	92
Authorized Brokerage Relationships	92
Transaction Broker Relationship	92
Single Agent Relationship	94
Nonrepresentation (No Brokerage Relationship)	96
Transitioning To Another Authorized Relationship	99
Designated Sales Associate	100
Discipline: Violations and Penalties	101
Record Keeping and Retention	102
Termination of Agency	102
Summary	104
Review Questions	105

5 Real Estate Brokerage Activities and Procedures — 108

Brokerage Offices and Sales Associates	109
Signage	109
Temporary Shelters	110
Guidelines for Advertising: False or Misleading Advertising/Penalties for False Advertising	110
Internet Advertising/Point of Contact Information	111
Handling of Deposits: Escrow (Trust) Accounts in Florida	112
Escrow Accounts Held by a Title Company or Attorney	113
Management of Escrow Accounts	113
Management of Escrow Accounts: Escrow Dispute and Disposition of Funds	115
Good-Faith Doubt	116
Mediation	117

Arbitration	117
Litigation	117
Rental Lists or Rental Companies	118
Inaccurate Rental Lists	118
Broker/Sales Associate: An Expert in Certain Areas of Property Transfer	119
Fixing of Commissions or Fees	119
Kickbacks	120
Broker's Policy Manual	120
Change of Employer: Notice of Change/Duplication of Records	121
Sales Associate Obligation to a Principal Following Termination of Employment	121
Unauthorized Use of Names and Insignias of Real Estate Organizations	121
Change of Address: Procedure and Penalty for Failure to Notify the FREC	121
License Versus Registration	122
Types of Business Entities: Permitted Registrations	122
Entities That May Not Register as a Brokerage	127
Officers and Directors of Real Estate Firms	129
Trade Names	129
Summary	129
Review Questions	130
6 Violations of License Law, Penalties, and Procedures	**133**
Procedures for Disciplining Licensees	134
The Complaint	134
The Complaint Process, Procedures, and Appeal	135
Complaint and Investigation	135
Probable Cause Panel	136
Formal Complaint	137
Formal or Informal Hearing	138
Final Order	139
Appeal Process	139
License Law Violations and Penalties	140
Revocation/Suspension of Broker's License	142
Violations and Penalties	143

Violations and Recommended Penalties	144
The Real Estate Recovery Fund	149
Summary	151
Review Questions	152

7 Federal and State Laws Pertaining To Real Estate — 155

Introduction to Fair Housing	155
The Civil Rights Act of 1866	156
The Civil Rights Act of 1964	156
The Civil Rights Act of 1968	157
Equal Housing Opportunity Poster	162
Enforcement	162
State Law	162
Introduction to Fair Housing Violations	162
Fair Housing Violations: Responsibility and Liability of Real Estate Licensees	163
Blockbusting	163
Improper Listings	164
Refusal to Show Property to Minorities	165
Steering	165
Advertising	166
Less Favorable Treatment of Minority Buyers	166
Redlining	167
Fair Housing Act—Enforcement	167
Americans with Disabilities Act of 1990 (ADA)	168
Interstate Land Sales Full Disclosure Act	169
Florida Housing Laws	170
The Florida Fair Housing Act	170
The Florida Residential Landlord and Tenant Act	170
Leases Covering Residential Dwelling Units	171
Landlord's Access to Premises	174
Vacating Premises	174
Summary	176
Review Questions	176

8 Property Rights: Estates and Tenancies: Condominiums, Cooperatives, Community Development Districs, Homeowners Associations, and Time-sharing — 180

Introduction and Historic Perspective of Property Ownership — 181
Real Property Composition: Land Real Estate and Real Property — 182
- *Physical Components of Real Property* — 183
- *Real Versus Personal Property* — 185

Fixtures — 186
- *Plants, Trees, and Crops* — 186
- *Legal Determination of a Fixture* — 187
- *Trade Fixtures* — 188
- *Basic Property Rights: Bundle of Rights* — 189

Types of Estates — 190
- *Freehold Estate* — 190
- *Nonfreehold Estates or Estates Less Than Freehold* — 194

Forms of Ownership — 196
- *Sole Ownership: Ownership in severalty* — 197
- *Concurrent Ownership or Co-ownership* — 197
- *Community Property* — 200
- *Partitioning of Ownership* — 200
- *Special Ownership Interests* — 201

Community Ownership — 203
- *Condominiums* — 203
- *Cooperatives* — 207
- *Planned-Unit Development (PUD)* — 210
- *Resort Developments: Time-Share* — 210
- *Homeowner Associations* — 211
- *Community Development Districts (CDDs)* — 213

Summary — 213
Review Questions — 214

9 Title Deeds and Ownership Restrictions — 216

Concept of Title: Ownership in a Bundle of Rights — 217
- *Equitable Title* — 217
- *Transfer by Voluntary Alienation* — 218

Transfer by Descent — 219

Deeds	220
Requirements of a Valid Deed	221
Nonessential Element	224
Types of Statutory Deeds	224
General Warranty Deed	224
Special Warranty Deed	225
Bargain and Sale Deed	225
Quitclaim Deed	225
Deed Clauses	226
Preparation of Deeds	227
Titles	228
Public Records	228
Constructive Notice	229
Actual Notice	229
Recording	230
Torrens Land Titles	230
Title Insurance	230
Owner's Title Insurance	231
Mortgagee's Title Insurance	231
Easements	232
Easement Appurtenant	232
Easement in Gross	232
Example	233
Party Wall Easement	233
Licenses	234
Creation of Easements	234
Termination of Easements	235
Encroachments	236
Leases	236
Basic Principles of Leases	237
Types of Leases	238
Example	240
Example	242
Contract versus Economic Rent	243
Security Deposits	243
Essentials of a Valid Lease	243
Example	244

Termination of a Lease	244
Assignment and Subletting	245
Liens	245
Mortgage Liens	246
Tax Liens	246
Special District Assessment/Tax Liens	247
Federal Income Tax Liens	247
Estate/Inheritance Tax Liens	247
Corporate Tax Liens	247
Mechanic's Liens	248
Judgment Liens	248
Deficiency Judgment Liens	248
Categories of Liens	249
Priority of Liens	250
Transfer of Encumbered Title	251
Summary	251
Review Questions	251

10 Legal Description — 254

Purpose of Legal Descriptions	254
Types of Descriptions	255
Metes and Bounds	255
Government Survey System	257
Basic Facts	260
Introduction	260
Lot and Block Survey Method (Recorded Plat Method)	264
Summary	265
Review Questions	265

11 Real Estate Contracts — 268

Definitions	269
The Statute of Frauds	269
Statute of Limitations	270
Valid Versus Void and Voidable	270
Valid Contract	270
Void Contract	271
Voidable Contract	271
Contract Validity and Enforcement Requirements	271
Consideration	272
Agreement	273

Legal Objective	273
Legally Competent Parties	273
Authority of Real Estate Licensees to Prepare Contracts	274
Classifications of Contracts	275
Expressed versus Implied	275
Bilateral versus Unilateral	276
Executed versus Executory	277
Formal and Informal Contracts	278
Contract Negotiation	278
Intentional Misrepresentation	279
Innocent (Unintentional) Misrepresentation	279
Termination of Contracts	281
Methods of Terminating Contracts	281
Rescission of a Voidable Contract	283
Operation of Law	283
Breach of Contracts	284
Remedies for Breach	284
Liquidated Damages	285
"Time Is of the Essence"	285
Contracts Important to Real Estate	285
Employment Contracts (Listing Contracts/Agreements)	285
Buyer Broker Agreements	287
Sales Contracts	287
Equitable Title	289
Disclosure of Defects That Materially Affect the Value of Residential Property	290
Duty of Disclosure by Licensees	291
Building Code Violation Disclosure	293
Time Limits	293
Acceptance	293
Back-up Contract	293
Binder	293
Option Contracts	294
Example	294
Miscellaneous Characteristics of Options	295
Installment Sales Contract	296
Miscellaneous Real Estate Contract Considerations	297
Procuring Cause	297
Telephone Solicitation Laws	297

	Multiple Listing Service (MLS)	297
	Ethical Practices	297
	Summary	298
	Review Questions	298
12	**Residential Mortgages**	**301**
	Mortgage Concepts: Mortgage Law	302
	Title Theory	302
	Lien Theory	305
	Loan Instruments: Lien Theory	305
	Subordination Agreements	308
	Essential Elements of the Mortgage	308
	Essential Elements	310
	Other Mortgage Provisions	310
	Common Mortgage Features	312
	Estoppel Certificate	316
	Methods of Purchasing Mortgaged Property	317
	Subject to the Mortgage	317
	Changing Loan Balance: Assumed Mortgages	318
	Effects of the Due on Sale Clause	319
	Novation	319
	Contract for Deed (Land Contract or Installment Sales Contract)	320
	Default: Consequences of Default	321
	Foreclosure	321
	Judicial Foreclosure	321
	Deficiency Judgment	322
	Excess from Sale	323
	Statutory Equity of Redemption	323
	Deed in Lieu of Foreclosure (Non-Judicial Foreclosure)	323
	Lis Pendens	323
	Short Sales	323
	Summary	324
	Review Questions	324
13	**Mortgage Market Operations**	**327**
	Federal Reserve System	328
	Federal Home Loan Bank System	328

Federal Deposit Insurance Corporation	328
Intermediation	329
Disintermediation	329
Primary and Secondary Mortgage Markets	329
Primary Mortgage Market	329
Secondary Mortgage Market	332
The History of Loans	335
Amortized Loans	335
Federal Agencies	336
Loan Discounting	338
Loan-To-Value Ratio	339
Conventional Loans	340
Types of Conventional Loans	340
Interest Rate	341
Assumption	342
Prepayment	342
Adjustable Rate Mortgage	342
Adjustments	342
Interest Rate Caps	342
Payment Cap	343
Teaser Rate	343
Partially Amortized Loans	343
Biweekly Mortgage	343
Package Mortgage	343
Down Payments	344
Private Mortgage Insurance Payments	346
FHA Loans (Nonconventional)	348
Loan Insurance Programs	348
203(B)—Standard Loan Program	350
Loan Insurance	350
Cash Investment	350
Qualifying Ratios	351
Loan Amount	351
Interest Rate	352
Discount Points	352
Maximum Term	352
Closing Costs	352
Escrow Accounts	352

Loan Processing	352
Appraisal	353
Restrictions	354
Condominium Units	354
Qualifications	355
Eligibility	355
Loan Origination Fee	355
Prepayment	355
VA Loans (Nonconventional)	355
Qualifications	355
Eligibility	356
Maximum Loan Amount	357
Down Payment	357
Term and Interest Rate	357
Discount Points	358
Closing Costs	358
Funding Fee	358
Escrow Account	359
Veteran's Liability	359
Appraisal	359
Eligible Properties	360
Assumption Methods	361
Assuming and Agreeing to Pay a Loan	361
Taking Subject to an Existing Loan	361
Limitations from Other Clauses	362
Changing Loan Balance	362
When to Use an Assumption	363
Closing Requirements	365
Advantages and Disadvantages	365
Qualifying the Buyer	366
Underwriting	366
Loan Charges	372
Variable Costs	373
Fixed Costs	373
Discount Points	374
Seller Financing	375
Mortgage Bond Financing	375
Mortgage Fraud	375

No Document Loans	375
Equal Credit Opportunity Act	376
Consumer Credit Protection Act/Truth-in-Lending Act	376
Annual Percentage Rate (APR)	377
Real Estate Settlement and Procedures Act	377
Summary	378
Review Questions	379

14 Real Estate–Related Computations and Closing of Transactions — 382

Basic Real Estate Computations	382
Sales Commissions	383
Calculating Selling Price, Cost, and Profit	383
Calculating Price and Commissions	383
Commission Problems	384
Investment Problems	387
Value Problems	389
Loan Problems	393
Calculating Cost and Price	395
Cost Problems	395
Price Problems	396
Preliminary Steps to a Closing	399
Sales Contract to Closing	399
Sale Pending Sign and Sold Sign Rule	399
Notice of "Under Contract" to MLS	399
Earnest Money Deposited	400
Preparing for Closing	405
New TILA-RESPA Requirements	406
Preclosing Inspection	407
Prorated Expenses and Title Closing	407
Prorating	407
Property Taxes	410
Practice Exercises	412
Calculating the Number of Days Prior to the Month of Closing	412
Calculating the Total Number of Days the Seller Is Responsible for Property Taxes	412
Calculating the Amount of Property Tax	

	Due for Each Day of the Year	413
	Calculating the Amount of the Seller's Tax Payment at Closing	413
	Other Charges	415
	Preparation of Document—Closing Statements	415
	State Transfer Taxes	421
	Summary	431
	Review Questions	432
15	**The Real Estate Markets and Analysis**	**434**
	Physical Characteristics of Real Estate	434
	Economic Characteristics of Real Property	436
	Demand	437
	Supply	440
	Interpreting Market Conditions	441
	Price Levels	442
	Vacancy Rates	442
	Sales Volume	443
	Area Preference—Situs	443
	Summary	443
	Review Questions	444
16	**Real Estate Appraisal**	**447**
	Regulation of Appraising–FIRREA	448
	Appraisal Foundation	449
	Appraisal Standards Board	449
	Appraisal Qualifications Board (AQB)	449
	State-Licensed and -Certified Appraisers	450
	Requirements for Federally Related Transactions	450
	Certified Appraisal Reports	451
	Appraisal Service of Real Estate	451
	Part 1, Chapter 475	452
	Appraisal versus CMA	452
	Broker Price Opinion (BPO)	453
	Concept of Value	453
	Market Value	455
	Valuation at a Glance	455
	Cost/Price/Value	455
	Elements of Value	455

Principles (Theorems) of Value	457
Principle of Anticipation	457
Principle of Substitution	458
Principle of Highest and Best Use	458
Principle of Competition	459
Principle of Supply and Demand	459
Principle of Diminishing and Increasing Returns	460
Principle of Conformity	460
Other Valuation Terminology	460
Assemblage versus Plottage	461
Regression versus Progression	461
Sales Comparison Approach	462
Steps in the Appraisal Process	463
Step 1: Define the Problem	463
Step 2: Data Selection and Collection	463
Step 3: Determining the Highest and Best Use	463
Step 4: Estimate the Value of the Land	464
Step 5: Application of the Three Approaches and the Adjustment Process	464
Step 6: The Reconciliation Process	465
Step 7: Reporting the Value	465
Cost Approach (Reproduction)	465
The Square Foot Method	467
The Unit-in-Place Method	467
The Quantity Survey Method	467
Depreciation	468
Physical Deterioration	468
Functional Obsolescence	469
Economic (External) Obsolescence	469
Calculating accrued depreciation	470
Gross Rent Multiplier	476
Reconciliation	476
Preparing a Comparative Market Analysis (CMA)	477
Gathering Appropriate Data	485
Completing the Market Analysis	487
Replacement Cost Pricing	490
Step 1: Estimate Land Value	491
Step 2: Estimate Replacement Cost	491
Determine Replacement Cost	493

	Step 3: Add Replacement Cost and Land	494
	Step 4: Deduct Depreciation	494
	Automated Valuation Model (AVM)	496
	Summary	496
	Review Questions	497
17	**Real Estate Investments and Business Opportunity Brokerage**	**500**
	Investment Real Estate Terminology	500
	Introduction	500
	Cash Flow	501
	Leverage	501
	Capital gain or loss	502
	Basis	502
	Appreciation	502
	Equity	503
	Liquidity	503
	Risk	503
	Tax Shelter	503
	The Licensee Regarded as an Expert	503
	Types of Investments: Property Types and Subtypes	504
	Residential Property	504
	Commercial Property	505
	Industrial Property	506
	Agricultural Property	506
	Mixed-Use Property	507
	Business Opportunities	507
	Goals of Investments	508
	Advantages of Investing in Real Estate	508
	Disadvantages of Investing in Real Estate	509
	Property Investment Analysis	512
	Nature of Business Brokerage	513
	Comparison to Real Estate Brokerage	513
	Differences From Real Estate Brokerage	514
	Steps in the Sale of a Business	515
	Valuation of a Business	516
	Summary	517
	Review Questions	517

18 Taxes Affecting Real Estate ... 520
- Real Property Taxation–Local Importance ... 520
  - *Determination of "Just Value"* ... 521
  - *Grievance Process for Contesting Property* ... 523
  - *Overview of Establishing the Real Property Tax* ... 528
  - *Nonpayment of Real Property Tax and Tax Certificates* ... 531
- Federal Income Tax ... 531
  - *Active Income* ... 531
  - *Passive Income* ... 532
  - *Portfolio Income* ... 532
- Federal Income Tax and Real Property ... 533
  - *Deductions* ... 533
  - *IRA Withdrawal* ... 533
- Investment Real Estate ... 535
  - *Calculating the Net Operating Income (NOI)* ... 536
  - *Determining Taxable Income* ... 537
  - *Deductions on Business/Investment Property* ... 538
  - *Tax on Sale of Property* ... 541
  - *Exclusion of Capital Gains* ... 543
  - *Capital Gains Tax Rates* ... 544
  - *Installment Sales* ... 545
  - *Real Estate Exchanges* ... 545
- 2018 Tax Reform Act ... 546
  - *Tax Cuts and Jobs Act of 2017* ... 547
  - *What has Changed and What Remains the Same* ... 547
  - *A Breif Overview of Business Taxes Under the Act* ... 550
- Summary ... 552
- Review Questions ... 552

19 Planning, Zoning, and Environmental Hazards ... 556
- The History of Urban (City) Planning and Zoning ... 556
- Master Plan ... 558
- The Process of Planning ... 558
  - *Local Planning Agency* ... 559
- Florida's Comprehensive Plan ... 560
  - *Optional Elements* ... 561
- Zoning Land Use Restrictions and Building Codes ... 562
  - *Zoning Ordinances* ... 562

Building Codes	564
Health Ordinances	564
Appeals and Exemptions	565
Zoning Board of Adjustment	565
Variance	565
Indoor and Outdoor Environmental Hazards	568
Water Supply	568
Septic Tank	569
Asbestos	569
Radon	569
Toxic Waste in Soil	570
Underground Storage Tanks	570
Lead Paint	570
Mold	571
Chemical Contamination	571
Structural Damage and Wood-Destroying Organisms	571
Comprehensive Environmental Response, Compensation, and Liability Act (CERCLA)	572
Summary	573
Review Questions	573
Addendum: Introduction to Residential Product Knowledge	**576**
Introduction	576
Building Construction Standards	577
Local Regulations	577
Lot Types	577
Corner Lots	577
Interior Lots	578
T Lots	578
Cul-de-sac Lots	578
Key Lots	578
Flag Lots	578
Zero Lot Line	578
Product Knowledge–Basic Residential Design, Materials, and Systems	579
Roofs	579
Type of Materials	581

Shingles	581
Walls: Bearing and Nonbearing	582
Exterior Wall Covering	582
Ceiling/Walls: Joist	583
Windows	583
Insulation	584
Mechanical Systems and Equipment	585
Heating Systems	585
Cooling Systems	587
Framing and Construction	590
Platform Framing	590
Balloon Framing	590
Post-and-Beam Framing	590
Damage by Wood-Destroying Organisms	591
Indoor and Outdoor Environmental Hazards	591
Radon	592
Formaldehyde Gas	592
Asbestos	593
Lead	593
Groundwater Chemical Contamination	594
Disclosure Statement	595
Due Diligence Investigation	596
The Construction Dictionary	596
Backfill	596
Commercial Acre	596
Conduit	597
Deciduous	597
Drywall	597
Elevation Drawing	597
Energy Efficiency Ratio (EER)	597
Flashing	597
Footing	598
Foundation	598
Header	598
Percolation Test	598
Plot Plan (Plot Map)	600
Potable Water	600
R Value	600

Rafter	600
Ridgeboard	600
Sill	600
Soil Pipe	600
Additional Dictionary of Construction Terms at a Glance	600
Summary	603
Review Questions	603
Math Busters Guide to Real Estate Math	606
Answers to Chapter Review Questions	614
Practice End-of-Course Exam	621
Answers to Practice End-of-Course Exam	641
Example Real Estate Forms	647
Glossary	667
Index	685

PREFACE

Welcome to the fascinating world of real estate. Making career decisions in life is never easy. Decisions are usually filled with questions. In fact, you may even question whether this career decision was appropriate. Relax, you are not alone. If you are the type of person who is looking for a career that is highly lucrative, provides excitement, and involves problem solving, you have come to the right industry. I am pleased to report that after 47 years of transactional real estate experience, no two days have ever been the same for me. How many folks get to say that about their career?

As is the case with learning of any new subject matter, questions will arise. This book was written to provide you with the answers. This edition provides the reader with direct and simple answers to real estate questions. You will be faced with industry terms that at times seem as if you are learning a foreign language. Let this book be your guide and interpreter. Learning does not have to be a difficult or unpleasant experience. It should always be rewarding. Every effort went into this publication to ensure that your learning experience is a pleasant one.

This book was written with you in mind. During your career in real estate, you will be faced or challenged with a variety of transactional issues. It would be difficult to imagine that any one book could provide all the answers or solutions. However, this book provides the reader with the necessary essentials required for one to practice real estate in Florida. This edition has been written and organized to help the real estate license applicant to better prepare for the state exam.

As your journey begins through the learning process, we will first examine the various sectors of the real estate industry. Later, we will learn about the regulatory agencies, license law, and the licensing process. As we progress through the remaining sections of this book, you will learn about the principles and practices of the real estate field. In order to help with your learning experience, an addendum on industry specialty items and terminology was included in this edition.

I created what is believed to be a fresh, new, comprehensive Florida real estate book that provides up-to-date content in a crisp and efficient format punctuated with realworld examples. Key terms, summaries and extensive review questions for each chapter allow users to check their understanding. A 100-question practice exam at the end of the book tests student knowledge of key concepts.

Two additional online practice exams simulate the actual Florida real estate exam providing critical exam preparation.

Most notably, users will appreciate the *"Coaching Tips"* throughout each chapter enabling them to master the material and confidently pass the Florida real estate salesperson license exam. The book incorporates engaging learning features such as:

- **Crisp, uncluttered format** will engage learners enhancing their success on the Florida real estate salesperson license exam.
- ***"Math Buster"* appendix** provides keen insights to learning and using fundamental math formulas used on the real estate exam.
- ***"Coaching Tips"* highlight** practical application of the key principles using reallife scenarios to fully prepare users for their new real estate careers.
- **Two online practice exams** match the question format used on the actual Florida real estate salesperson license exam.
- **Learning tools** like key terms, chapter summaries and extensive review questions help users successfully master the material.

This preface would not be complete without personally reaching out to thank those whose contributions to this publication were just so valuable. My heart-felt thanks goes out to Sara Glassmeyer whose belief in me resulted in the opportunity to write this book. Finally, I would like to thank the following real estate professionals who provided valuable insights as previous reviewers: James P. Christie, Christie's School of Real Estate; Joseph R. Ponds, Jr., MemoryQuest, Inc.; Glenn Sudnick, Palm Beach School of Real Estate; and Don Widmayer, American Business College, Inc. Their reviews were invaluable and their comments were incorporated to make this a quality publication.

I close with the following: may the real estate practice that has rewarded and enriched my life over the years be as rewarding to you and yours.

Samuel Irlander
CDEI
President
Parker Madison Partners, Inc.
Email: sirlander@parkermadisonpartners.com

NEW TO THIS EDITION

Chapter 1 – The Real Estate Business

This chapter has been updated to reflect current conditions within the real estate industry. New to this chapter includes a brief overview of financing (mortgage broker and mortgage banker) and counseling (consulting services).

Chapter 2 – License Law and Qualifications for Licensure

This chapter has been updated to reflect current coverage on this subject.

Chapter 3 – Real Estate License Law and Commission Rules

This chapter has been updated to reflect current coverage on this subject.

Chapter 4 – Law of Agency–Relationships and Disclosures

This chapter has been updated to reflect current coverage on this subject.

Chapter 5 – Real Estate Brokerage Activities and Procedures

This chapter features restructured and consolidated information concerning operating a real estate brokerage office and procedures to remain in compliance with state license laws.

Chapter 6 – Violations of License Law, Penalties, and Procedures

This chapter has been updated to reflect current coverage on this subject.

Chapter 7 – Federal and State Laws Pertaining to Real Estate

This chapter has been updated to reflect current federal and state housing and accessibility laws. Featured in this chapter are case examples of contemporary issues regarding fair housing that the real estate practice must face. This includes but is not limited to issues such as consistency of services that come out of a real estate brokerage.

Chapter 8 – Property Rights: Estates and Tenancies

This chapter features restructured and consolidated information concerning the different forms of real property ownership and vesting options. In addition, this chapter includes information about creation of and requirements of multi-family housing and communities such as condominiums, cooperatives, community development districts, homeowners associations, and time-sharing. Please also note that in this chapter, each form of multi-family housing and community are included as key terms.

Chapter 9 – Title Deeds and Ownership Restrictions

This chapter has been restructured and consolidated to better reflect the subject matter. All information has been updated to reflect current coverage on this subject.

Chapter 10 – Legal Descriptions

This chapter has been updated to reflect current coverage on this subject.

Chapter 11 – Real Estate Contracts

This chapter has been updated to reflect current coverage on this subject.

Chapter 12 – Residential Mortgages

This chapter has been restructured and consolidated to better reflect the subject matter. All information has been updated to reflect current coverage on this subject.

Chapter 13 – Mortgage Market Operations

This chapter has been restructured and consolidated to better reflect the subject matter. All information has been updated to reflect current coverage on this subject.

Chapter 14 – Real Estate–Related Computations and Closing of Transactions

This chapter has been restructured and consolidated to better reflect the subject matter. All information has been updated to reflect current coverage on this subject.

Chapter 15 – The Real Estate Markets and Analysis

This chapter has been renamed, restructured, and consolidated to better reflect the subject matter. All information has been updated to reflect current coverage on this subject. New in this chapter includes information on households and related topics.

Chapter 16 – Real Estate Appraisal

This chapter has been restructured and consolidated to better reflect the subject matter. All information has been updated to reflect current coverage on this subject.

Chapter 17 – Real Estate Investments and Business Opportunity Brokerage

Chapter number has changed from previous edition. This chapter has been restructured and consolidated to better reflect the subject matter. All information has been updated to reflect current coverage on this subject.

Chapter 18 – Taxes Affecting Real Estate

This chapter features a restructured and consolidated information concerning tax issues that affect real property ownership. All information has been updated to reflect current coverage on the subject of taxes and their effect on ownership. The chapter also features added terminology commonly used in this subject.

Chapter 19 – Planning, Zoning, and Environmental Hazards

This chapter features restructured and consolidated information concerning planning, zoning, and environmental hazards previously contained in various chapters and now all in one chapter. The format of this chapter provides the student with a greater understanding as to how today's planning can affect the future of a municipality.

Other Changes

Other changes in this edition include the elimination of the construction chapter from the state syllabus. Rather than eliminate this information from the book, we added this previous chapter as an informational addendum for the reader.

CHAPTER 1

THE REAL ESTATE BUSINESS

KEY TERMS

absentee owners
agricultural areas (target market)
appraisal
appraiser
business opportunity
Broker Price Opinion (BPO)
comparative market analysis (CMA)
dedication
follow-up
Multiple Listings Service (MLS)
property management
real estate brokerage
special purpose property
subdivision plat map
Uniform Standards of Professional Appraisal Practice (USPAP)

LEARNING OBJECTIVES

After completing this lesson, you will be able to:

- describe the various activities of real estate brokerage
- distinguish among the five major sales specialties of real estate practice available to you
- identify the role of property managers
- explain the appraisal process and role of the appraiser
- understand the mortgage process and the role of mortgage loan originator
- explain the three phases of development and construction
- distinguish among the three categories of residential construction

INTRODUCTION TO THE REAL ESTATE BUSINESS

This chapter is intended to familiarize the student with the real estate business as a career. It will also provide the student with a clear understanding of the different choices and areas (including required expertise) for entry into real estate practice.

CHAPTER 1 The Real Estate Business

The practice of real estate includes many areas of consideration. Some of the areas include but are not limited to:

- **Brokerage**—includes assisting others in the buying/selling or leasing of the following types of properties:

  1. Commercial—the sale or lease on property usually held for investment purposes
  2. Residential—the sale or lease of properties that contain 1–4 units intended for dwelling purposes. In Florida, the definition of a residential transaction also includes up to 10 acres of agricultural land
  3. Manufacturing—sale or lease of heavy industrial, light industrial, or warehouse/storage properties (sometimes referred to as loft space)
  4. Mixed-use properties—sale or lease of properties utilizing two or more legal uses to the property (i.e., residential and retail)
  5. Agricultural—the sale or long-term leasehold of farm lands for future potential development opportunity

- **Property management**—the business of handling and administrating real property (normally on property belonging to others). Aside from collecting rents and paying bills, a property manager's job starts with maximizing income while maintaining the value of the property. The management business consists of two primary services:

  1. Operational duties—the oversight and administration of day-to-day issues necessary to run real property. This specifically deals with:
     - ensuring public safety
     - supervising building staff
     - complying with all local laws
     - correcting property violations
     - effectuating repairs
     - instituting capital improvement programs

  2. Financial reporting—involves:
     - the budgeting and controlling of operating expenses (expenses required to run building operations)
     - keeping appropriate bank and service accounts
     - reporting income and expense activity
     - conducting income/expense analysis
     - planning and maintaining an appropriate reserve to fund major capital improvements

- **Appraisal**—the business of valuing real property and/or business enterprises. The sole focus of appraisal is for the establishment of valuation.

- Real estate finance—the business of investment property analysis and/or origination of borrowed funds to complete the acquisition of real property investments. In most cases, origination of borrowed funds (leveraging) is accomplished by the use of mortgage brokers and mortgage bankers.
- Subdivision—the business of legally dividing a larger parcel of land (or air-lots in high-rise construction) into smaller units or lots. In essence, the investor maximizes investment profit by buying by the acre while selling by the lot.
- Development—the business of creating or retrofitting an improvement on improved or unimproved land.
- Construction—the business of building improvements to real property. In order to legally construct the improvement, one must receive a permit from the local municipality that issues same. Issuance of a permit is based on submission of blueprints (rendering plans) and specifications (written narrative as to how you will build the improvement).
- Consulting—the business of providing professional transactional guidance and advice.

OVERVIEW OF THE REAL ESTATE BUSINESS

Real estate as a profession is a clear and direct response to society's demand for housing, commercial space, manufacturing facilities, and institutional use. Each category of property contains subcategories of the different variations to the same theme.

For example, housing or residential property can be categorized as:

- single-family
- multi-family
- cooperative (co-op)
- condominium (condo)

Commercial space would include:

- office
- retail
- hotel/motel
- parking

Industrial would include:

- heavy industrial
- light industrial
- loft/storage and delivery

Institutional needs or **special purpose properties** (properties that are not income producing or used for owner-occupant use) include:

- hospitals
- libraries

- property used by
- municipalities

In previous years, population trends have grown and expanded into different areas of the country as well as the state of Florida. Colder, harsh winters in other parts of the country have also contributed to Florida's population growth. Therefore, the ongoing need for qualified and competent industry service providers has increased as well.

The Residential real estate arena remains the largest and most active market. For a licensee wishing to specialize in this area, residential brokerage offers many opportunities. (This subject is covered later in this chapter.)

THE REAL ESTATE INDUSTRY'S ROLE IN THE NATION'S ECONOMY

The real estate industry plays a key and important role in our nation's economy. As a result of an active industry, the business of real estate contributes many jobs to the financial system as well as to the local economy. The real estate industry provides:

1. housing for the individual
2. a vehicle that houses and generates cash flow for the investor (in addition to other similar cash flow vehicles like stocks, bonds, and treasuries)
3. tax revenues for the government from property taxes

OTHER PROFESSIONS THAT RELY ON THE REAL ESTATE BUSINESS

Where federal, state, and local laws can directly affect the procedural considerations of most real estate transactions, there are many other industry nuances that sellers and buyers experience. Therefore, sellers, buyers, landlords, and tenants most likely will have a need for professional assistance.

Due to society's litigious overtones, property transactions have become more sophisticated and complex. The transactions' sophistication and complexity must be addressed and answered. Therefore, the real estate business has expanded to provide these answers. The need for expertise is addressed by various types of service providers. Today, property transactions will probably include a team of professionals whose sole purpose is to assist in completing the transaction. Within any property transaction, you could expect to see one or more service providers assisting with the transaction.

The following are just a few examples of transaction-oriented professionals involved with a purchase/sale or lease transaction:

- Attorney—reviews legal documents and renders legal advice primarily for the direct protection of a buyer, seller, landlord, or tenant (as the case may be).
- Certified public accountant (CPA)—renders tax advice to a buyer, seller, landlord, or tenant as to the income tax ramifications of any transaction.

- Title company—charges a premium for issuance of title insurance coverage. This policy protects a buyer from covered defects to the title transferred by the selling party.
- Architect/engineer—assists the buyer with:
    - construction/structural design services
    - decorative services
    - municipal property violation correction services
    - variances
    - certificate of occupancy and property issues
    - compliance with all local laws and ordinances
- Expediter—helps in obtaining building permits through the municipality. Expediters are hired and paid by the owner or user (in a lease) because they understand local building codes and advise the hiring party as to how to successfully get their project approved.

While there may be an array of other service providers involved in any one transaction, the above highlights the most common transactional players found in any given deal.

In order to protect the general public from potential loss caused by the acts of others performing certain transactional duties, many of these industries are regulated in some manner or form. For example, any service providers in a regulated industry are required to responsibly discharge their role within a transaction. The service providers can and will be held accountable for their actions or for failing to deliver the appropriate service within their job role. This may be enforced by the industry's regulatory agency or by the damaged party's rights under a civil lawsuit.

REAL ESTATE: A BUSINESS OF MANY SPECIALTIES

Today, most real estate transactions are performed by licensed real estate professionals. Although real estate involves a variety of different activities and transactions, the most common and active market is residential housing. Some of the specialty areas of real estate include but are not limited to:

1. brokerage/consulting
    a. commercial—includes retail, offices, and all property not considered residential
    b. residential—properties consisting of four or fewer units intended for dwelling purposes to also include up to 10 acres of agricultural property (**agricultural areas** in particular have become **target markets** for new development)
    c. industrial—can be heavy, light, or storage/distribution

2. **property management**—the business of maintaining and operating a property
3. loan originating/financing—involves lending of money to qualified borrowers
4. appraisal—the business of valuation
5. business brokerage—the purchase or sale of **business opportunities**

With the exception of a federally related transaction involving an appraisal, the aforementioned services are normally performed by a real estate broker or sales associate. As a direct result of a regulated profession, expert information is the ultimate product that a broker or sales associate will market. In performance of their role in any transaction, real estate licensees must be knowledgeable and proficient in some of the following areas:

1. market conditions
2. marketing real property
3. nuances of property transfer

REAL ESTATE BROKERAGE: SALES AND LEASING

Real estate activities are performed under the authority of a real estate broker. Of all the different areas of the real estate industry, the brokerage end of the business contains the majority of real estate licensees. Brokerage can be defined as the business of bringing together buyers and sellers or landlords and tenants who are interested in concluding a transaction where the licensee is engaged for a fee. The fee is generally paid in the form of a commission. The fee is always paid to the broker and never to the sales associate or broker associate. In fact, a sales associate or broker associate may only receive compensation from his/her registered sponsoring broker.

Real estate agents are no different from other business people. They perform acquisition and disposition services in exchange for a fee. These services are generated for either a sale or a lease. Whether one is involved in the selling or leasing of real property, each service is performed under the direct authority of a real estate broker. The broker is responsible for supervising the activities of all licensees under his or her registration. This involves constant supervision and oversight of all licensees under the broker's registration, as well as knowledge of all transactions conducted by the licensees of the brokerage. Success in the brokerage field requires follow-up on the part of the licensee. This is particularly true as it applies to new and existing clientele. In addition, some firms provide property management services. In particular, this field has grown over the years in response to the need for professionals qualified to run and manage properties. The majority of the need for property management services comes from **absentee owners**. Absentee owners own property but are not considered "hands-on owners."

In many cases, agents are compensated in the form of commission. This will usually result in the broker receiving an agreed-upon percentage of the final sales price on a sale and an agreed-upon percentage of the annual rent paid on a lease. However, please note that although the amount of compensation is derived via negotiation, between the principal (the party that hires the agent) and the agent (the party that transacts business on behalf of the principal), this does not preclude the parties from entering into:

- flat fee arrangements (a mutually agreed upon amount/fee as full compensation)
- fee for service, as provided (a fee commensurate with specific non-representation services requested and agreed to)
- any other legal or valuable consideration exchanged for services

The Broker as Agent/Intermediary—The Sales Associate's Role with the Broker

In Florida, when one performs a real estate act (as defined under the Florida Statutes) for another, for compensation or in anticipation of compensation or any other valuable consideration, he or she must be licensed as one of the following:

- broker
- sales associate (within the employ of a broker)

Broker

The broker acts as the agent to the principal. The broker also acts as an intermediary between two or more parties in a negotiation for the sale and/or lease of real property.

Sales Associate

The sales associate acts as an agent of the broker, and as such, the sales associate acts as a sub-agent of the broker's clients. In essence, the sales associate is not conducting his/her own business and is assisting in the disposition of the broker's day-to-day business responsibilities on any given transaction. Due to the fact that the real estate business requires expert information that the average layperson does not possess, the sales associate requires constant and frequent supervision by the registered sponsoring broker. This is to insure that the broker's business is conducted in conjunction with all laws, rules, and regulations promulgated by the Florida Real Estate Commission (FREC) and/or the Department of Business and Professional Regulation (DBPR). In particular, these two bodies of Florida government regulate the profession.

Efficiency of Utilizing a Real Estate Agent

Due to the information and knowledge required to conclude a real estate transaction, the general public has traditionally turned to the real estate agent to provide these services. This provides consumers with a more efficient use of their time and money. Although the internet has made it easier for the consumer to find certain types of information, websites provide the consumer with only general information. The knowledge base required to complete a real estate transaction is vast and complicated, and, as a result, consumers will still turn to the real estate licensee for their solutions.

Specialization in a Geographic Area or Property Type

Real estate brokers and sales associates will often specialize in certain types of properties. This will also be a function of the geographic area that they specialize in. This method of target marketing is often referred to as "farming." Farming requires licensees to obtain and maintain pertinent property information that will assist them in obtaining customers and listings. This may include but not be limited to:

1. property criteria
2. property tax information
3. property sales history
4. legal use(s)

Smaller firms tend to specialize in property located within the neighborhood where they are located; while medium-sized firms expand to areas that also surround their core market. Larger companies will expand their operations to other cities, towns, or villages throughout the state or union. In either case, it is important that licensees earn and adopt a reputation for honest dealing within their target community as specialists for the property type being handled.

In any Florida residential transaction (sale or rental of 1–4 dwelling units), a licensee may be employed by a buyer, seller, landlord, or tenant as any one of the following legal relationships:

1. transaction broker (Florida law presumes this role and relationship at first meeting.)
2. no representation
3. single agent (Of the three, this is the only fiduciary relationship in Florida.)

Nonfiduciary Relationship

A transaction broker is a broker that provides a customer with limited representation. A customer can be a buyer, a seller, landlord, or tenant. Until another relationship is arranged, under Florida law, it is presumed that all licensees operate as transaction brokers.

No brokerage relationship occurs when neither party wishes to engage a real estate licensee to represent him or her. However, they require services such as the facilitating of a real estate transaction.

Fiduciary Relationship

A single agent is a broker who must provide fiduciary responsibilities to the principal (party that hires the agent). In a single agent relationship, a broker may be working for a seller, buyer, landlord, or tenant (but never more than one party within any residential transaction as defined under Florida law).

Coaching Tips

Although this will also be addressed in more detail later, it is important for the reader to understand that in Florida, a *residential transaction* is defined as any transaction involving the sale or leasing of a property that contains *four or fewer units* intended for dwelling purposes. This definition is expanded to include *10 acres or less* of agricultural property.

Any transaction for the sale or lease of real property containing greater than four units or more than 10 acres of agricultural property is considered to be a commercial transaction. The purchaser of the property is deemed to be holding same for investment purposes rather than as an owner-occupant transaction.

Example Consider a five-unit residential property where the buyer intends to live in one of the units while leasing out the other four. Regardless of the buyer residing in one unit, this example would still be considered investment property and, as such, is a commercial transaction.

The reader should not confuse the definition of residential property provided within zoning regulations. Under zoning, residential property is a class or category type that defines and determines the property's lawful use.

The reader should also note that from state to state (with some variation), the definition of a residential transaction is used extensively by lending institutions. This enables the lender to determine whether or not the property will be used for owner-occupant purposes. Pursuant to the loan origination process, this enables the lender to determine and underwrite risk. This enables the lender to arrive at the appropriate interest rate to charge the borrower. This may be in addition to any other loan underwriting technique that the lender may use.

Real Estate Brokerage

The **real estate brokerage** (the business of bringing together buyers and sellers and landlords and tenants for a fee) business consists of two primary services:

- sales
- leasing

We all need a roof over our head. It is for that reason that residential real estate tends to be the more active of markets. Real property sales are generated by two driving forces:

- the owner-occupant
- the investor

Some people purchase residential property for the sole purpose of becoming an owner-occupant of the property. The property may be used as a primary residence or as a secondary residence (weekend or vacation home). Others may find an investment haven through real property ownership.

There are many specialties in the real estate brokerage business. A licensee might choose to specialize in any of the five following areas:

1. Residential—This part of real estate practice contains the most licensees. Chapter 475, Florida Statutes (F.S.), defines residential property transactions as any transaction involving the sale or leasing of a property that contains four or fewer units intended for dwelling purposes. This would include unimproved land or lots to be improved to contain four or fewer units intended for dwelling purposes. The definition is expanded to include 10 acres or less of agricultural property. Knowledge in this area will warrant a local awareness of demographics, infrastructure, services and amenities, property taxes, utilities, and countless other items essential in concluding a transaction.

2. Commercial—These transactions usually involve investment properties and/or enterprises seeking space. Participating in commercial transactions requires the sales associate be well educated and versed in a variety of other subjects. The licensee must possess an expertise that may or may not arise in a residential transaction. In order to achieve success in this arena, the licensee must have an acute awareness of the valuation process, finance, and leasing markets. Simply put, any licensee involved in this facet of the business must have problem-solving skills.

3. Industrial—This field requires a licensee to be familiar with the needs of industry. This includes the understanding of transportation issues, availability of raw materials, and utilities necessary for manufacturing of goods and products. Activity within this area may include independent sites, industrial parks, and unimproved land for future development and expansion. As a result of certain land uses, Brownfields (contaminated land) have become a growing concern.

4. Agricultural/Farm area—This specialty area requires skills from the licensee that the previous property types may not require. To best communicate with the constituency in this field, a licensee may need direct knowledge of farming operations and costs. Chapter 475, F.S., defines agricultural property as any property consisting of greater than 10 acres.

5. Business brokerage—This area of brokerage can be highly lucrative and complicated and involves a valuation process based upon the income attributable to the business in question. This includes valuing tangible and/or intangible assets (i.e., goodwill). Knowledge and understanding in the use of financial

statements becomes critical in achieving success. In Florida, business brokerage requires the individual collecting a fee to possess a real estate license.

Depending on staff size, market, and geographic location, a brokerage firm can take on many forms of operation. Here are some examples:

- Small firms consist of 1–5 licensees.
- Boutique firms consist of 6–19 licensees.
- Mid-size firms consist of 20–100 licensees.
- Larger institutional firms consist of greater than 100 licensees.

As the business realizes its specialty area of expertise, it will simultaneously focus its sales promotion and efforts toward that core direction. It is the core business that enables the real estate firm to evolve into a diverse-services organization. In order to accomplish this (not so easy) feat, the brokerage firm needs to identify:

- their geographic area of coverage
- specialty services
- an appropriate marketing campaign

It is the geographic area and types of specialty services that a firm will provide that enable its sales associates to succeed. Careful selection is required to ensure success. Not all brokers choose urban or central business areas as their primary focus. In rural sections, agriculture and farming fuel both micro and macro-economies. Regardless of location or primary area of expertise and servicing, knowledge of the product market becomes essential. Expert information is the product that a licensee should market. This would include assembling and maintaining databases of properties within the selected area as well as information critical to marketing to that area. It is market knowledge that affords the broker the ability to market his/her services to others seeking those services. Although market knowledge and name recognition through branding become critical to the success of an organization, the business tends to be more of a "who you know before you get to show what you know." It is critical to become familiar with individuals or clientele within a constituency. This is usually achieved via networking or actual market activity on the part of the organization.

Brokerage Specialty Types

The future use of a property determines its type and category. Conventional real property (non-single-purpose/nongovernmental) can be broken down into four basic property group types. Each property group has various subgroupings. The following best describes how properties are categorized and subcategorized:

- residential
    - single-family homes
    - townhouses
    - multifamily

- - - cooperative
    - condominium
    - rental income producing
  - commercial
    - office
    - retail
    - professional/medical
    - garage/parking
  - manufacturing
    - heavy industrial (factories)
    - light manufacturing
    - loft/storage (warehouses)
  - agricultural
  - mixed-use
    - flex properties
  - businesses (business brokerage)

THE SALES PROCESS AND THE SALES LICENSEE

Real estate is a complicated and sophisticated business. As stated earlier in this chapter, an agent acts as an intermediary between the parties and performs duties on behalf of the party that the agent has been hired to represent. The term agent is defined as one who transacts business on behalf of another within a relationship of trust and normally for a fee. Sales associates work for the broker. They assist the broker in the disposition of the broker's responsibility on that assignment. This is accomplished by providing services to buyers, lessees, landlords, and sellers. This requires expert knowledge. It is essential that the sales associate have a clear understanding of the steps associated with a sales transaction. Therefore, it is important to illustrate the steps associated with a typical sale.

Step 1—Farming/Canvassing for Product

As in any sales arena, one needs to match a product to someone who needs the product. This may include the listing of properties for sale or lease or businesses for sale.

Step 2—Canvassing for the Product Buyer/User

This part of the process tends to be a little more challenging. The sales associate must find the "right lid to fit the right barrel." This is a process of hard work and good marketing skills. Today, social media plays a major role in marketing and reaching a larger audience.

NOTE: When a licensee is marketing property, and this involves contacting members of the general public, it is important to observe all local, state, and federal laws (i.e., consult the "do not call registry").

Step 3—Showing the Property

The sales associate requires appropriate knowledge of the product as well as good people-handling skills. The licensee should be trained to discover defects that are visible and require disclosure of same. The licensee should know when a further detailed inspection may be required.

Step 4—Submitting and Negotiating the Offer

This step can be critical to the success of any transaction. Regardless of the agent's opinion of an offer, all offers as directed must be submitted for the other party's consideration.

Step 5—Execution of a Sales Contract

If all has gone well, both parties will sign a sales contract.

Step 6—Closing of the Sales Contract

In this step, the parties to the contract may be charged with the execution of various tasks and responsibilities. Examples include but are not limited to the following:

<u>The buyer</u>
- arranging for necessary financing to conclude the transaction including:
    - credit approval and underwriting
    - property appraisal
    - property survey
    - any other item that the lender requires prior to extending a financing commitment

<u>The seller</u>
- ensuring that they have marketable title
- deed preparation and any other item required for the closing to occur

Step 7—Recording Activities

If all goes well, the closing takes place, and the deed issued to the buyer is usually recorded with the county clerk to provide protection (for the buyer) against any future claims by others to the property.

PROPERTY MANAGEMENT

Need for Property Management and the Typical Services Provided by a Property Manager

The way a property is managed determines the appearance and ultimate success of an investment project. Management represents the personality that the property takes on. It is truly a hands-on activity. Not all investors who own income-producing properties have the time or the expertise to devote to a project. As a direct result of these *absentee owners*, the need for professional management services has grown dramatically with the popularity of investing in income-producing property.

There are two primary service functions within the property management field:

1. Operations—This includes the day-to-day operation of the property. It includes knowledge of mechanical systems, the ability to make repairs, implementing preventative-maintenance measures, and remodeling and decorative upgrades to enhance the property's appearance and desirability to renters. Maximizing income while maintaining the value of a property is the main role and focus of the property manager/management firm.

2. Financial reporting—Investors in income-producing real property do not invest in "brick and mortar." They purchase and invest in cash-flow operations. It is the property's cash flow that generates the investor's return on the invested capital. *Therefore* (as previously stated earlier in this chapter), *real property, such as stocks and bonds, act as mere vehicles that house cash flow.* As such, the property manager is charged with the responsibility of reporting the property's financial activity. This may be as often as monthly or bimonthly reports. Financial reporting includes submitting accounting records in the form of general ledger reports. This activity includes collecting rents, annual budgeting, financial analysis, setting profit goals, and recognizing financing opportunities. Financial reporting offers the ownership the ability to make educated and informed decisions concerning the property.

Property management services are compensated in a variety of ways. In most cases, the management firm receives a percentage of the effective gross income (actual income collected after taking into account any vacancy and/or collection loss) attributable to the property. Other fee arrangements might include flat fees, annual per square foot amount, or increased income performance requirements. The type of compensation is determined by the property owner and the management firm. The scope of work and how the manager will be compensated is always detailed in the management contract.

NOTE: The relationship between a property owner and a property manager is typically found to be a general agent relationship. In this type of relationship the agent has a broader scope of authority. The actual scope of authority is defined by the terms of the management contract.

Community Association Manager (CAM)

In Florida, a community association manager's license is required when a property contains 10 or more units or the annual budget of the property is greater than $100,000. This subject will be covered in greater detail later in this book.

Scope of Work Detailed in Management Agreements

When income-producing property is involved, usual management duties will include but not be limited to:

- collecting rents
- paying property operating expenses
- effectuating repairs
- preventative maintenance
- corrective maintenance
- financial reporting

However, regardless of the management assignment, when performing property management services, the assignment will always require the manager to protect the owner's investment while working to maximize the property's income. In doing so, the owner's returns on invested capital are maximized.

APPRAISAL

The Process of Estimating the Value of Real Estate

The process of estimating the value of real estate is known as appraising. Appraisal is one of the most vital areas of real estate practice. **Appraisal** can be defined as an opinion of value that is based upon certain facts as of a given date. That date is referred to as "the effective date" or "as of date."

It should be noted that in Florida, appraising services are part of the real estate services that a real estate licensee provides to a consumer (see Chapter 475.01, F.S.). When providing this service, the licensee must adhere to the rules as prescribed by the **Uniform Standards of Professional Appraisal Practice (USPAP)**. USPAP are considered the method, ethics, and quality control standards applicable to real property and other appraisal assignments in the United States. Furthermore, only a general, certified, or licensed appraiser may conduct appraisals for a federally related transaction. Unless licensed as an appraiser, real estate licensees may not refer to their findings as an appraisal. They must refer to it as an opinion of value or a price opinion.

Types of Real Estate Activities That Require Appraisal Services

An **appraiser** is usually hired for the purpose of valuing a property. There are many driving reasons why appraisals are conducted; however, most appraisals are conducted for the purposes of sale or purchase agreements. Financing of all types of real property transactions will generally require the use of an appraisal toward value/loan determinations. The driving force of appraising is always for establishing value.

State-Certified Licensed and Registered Appraisers are Regulated by the Florida Real Estate Appraisal Board

In Florida, appraisers are regulated by the Florida Real Estate Appraisal Board. Appraisers are also required to abide by the **Uniform Standards of Professional Appraisal Practice (USPAP)**. Where the Appraisal Board is empowered to regulate the activities of all state-certified, licensed, and registered appraisers, USPAP provides standards for how appraisers accomplish their assignments. When performing an appraisal, many factors come in to play. The different types of properties create challenges in deriving the appraised value. For example, in the sales comparison approach, previous sales are examined and compared with the subject property for similarities in transactional, locational, and physical differences. For income-producing property, sales are not used to gauge or establish value. The income stream is used to determine value for the investor. Single-purpose, non-income-producing properties such as schools, government buildings, and libraries are valued using replacement/construction cost tables (along with other factors) for measurement. This subject is discussed in greater detail in Chapter 15.

Appraisers are generally compensated by type, time, and complexity of an assignment. USPAP is clear concerning how compensation may never be tied in or geared to the value of the property. This practice would create a direct conflict of interest on the part of the appraiser while performing service on behalf of the client/principal.

Comparative Market Analysis (CMA)

Although the definition of a real estate broker under the Florida Statutes includes the right to appraise real property for compensation, unless licensed as an appraiser, a real estate broker may not present him/herself as a state-certified, licensed, or registered appraiser. More importantly, only state-certified, licensed, and registered appraisers may render appraisals on federally related transactions. This minimizes the types of transactions that a real estate licensee may be involved in. A federally related transaction (as defined by the Federal Institutions Reform Recovery and Enforcement Act of 1989 [FIRREA]) is defined as a real property transaction involving a lending institution insured or regulated by the federal government where preparation of an appraisal is required as a precursor for loan consideration and underwriting. This type of transaction includes transaction values of greater than $250,000 where real property is hypothecated (pledged) as security for the repayment of a loan.

In the normal course of conducting business, a real estate broker is often asked by a seller to render an opinion of value by examining recently sold properties, listings of properties currently on the market, and previous expired-listing information. The preparation of a **comparative market analysis (CMA)** provides the seller with vital market information. CMAs differ from a broker's price opinion. The type of information contained in a CMA helps the seller when setting the selling price of his/her property. Even though the licensee may use similar techniques as an appraiser to determine the value of a property, the two are different. As previously stated, a CMA will primarily focus on the marketing/price setting of a particular property while an appraisal will strictly focus on the specific value of the subject property. This is critical to lenders, sellers, and buyers. This is the primary reason a CMA may never be referred to or represented as an appraisal. Most real estate brokerage firms offer CMAs for free as a selling tool to obtain a listing; however, firms are not prohibited from charging a fee for a CMA.

Appraisers are governed by the rules of ethics covered within USPAP. An appraiser should not have any ownership interest in the appraisal assignment. It should always be an arm's-length transaction.

Broker Price Opinion (BPO)

It is not uncommon for a licensee to provide a **Broker's Price Opinion (BPO)**. A BPO is an estimate of value usually provided in written form.

It is important to note that when used for setting a market price, the price opinion is called a CMA and not a BPO. When providing a price opinion of value for or without a fee being paid, the common term used to describe this act is a BPO.

For example, and for income tax purposes, a BPO may aid an estate to transfer real property to an heir. Upon transfer, the BPO supports the setting of the new tax basis for the heir.

Although USPAP will not apply to a real estate licensee who provides a BPO or a CMA, a real estate licensee should take caution not to violate USPAP when providing opinions of value. As previously mentioned within this chapter, real estate licensees conducting appraisals (unless licensed as an appraiser) must remember to never identify themselves as being an appraiser or call the valuation report an appraisal.

Whereas a sales associate may perform a BPO, it must be performed under the direct supervision and control of the registered sponsoring or supervising broker. Sales associates may only accept compensation from their registered sponsoring employing broker and from no other.

Ethics Rules Governing Appraiser Compensation

Unlike real estate licensees whose compensation is derived via commission, appraisers are compensated based upon time and complexity of an assignment. USPAP rules would deem compensation based on value as an unethical act. As a result of a conflict that may arise, the probability of valuation bias would be compromised.

FINANCING AND THE REAL PROPERTY TRANSACTION

If every purchaser of real property could pay cash for the purchase, transactions would be simplified. However, that is not realistic or probable. A majority of purchase and sales transactions involve financing of the property in one way or another. It is critical that the licensee has a good understanding of how financing works. Whereby mortgage loan originators in Florida must hold a current and valid mortgage broker license to engage in that practice, a sales associate should know the costs associated with borrowing funds. This can only aid the licensee in successfully concluding a sale.

Sources of Funds Used to Finance Real Property

There are a variety of sources available to finance the different types of real estate transactions. Some of these sources include but are not limited to:

1. government programs (include but are not limited to FHA and VA loans)
2. commercial banks (generally originate conventional loans)
3. credit unions (they accept deposits, originate loans, and provide a broad scope of general financial services)
4. pension funds (prefer owning and financing large institutional income-producing properties)
5. life insurance companies (prefer large institutional ownership and financing of income-producing property)
6. private individuals (utilizing their own funds, they originate first and second mortgages for qualified borrowers)

Importance of Expertise in Financing Matters/Problem-Solving Skills

Having knowledge in the area of finance is a critical tool toward achieving success in real estate. Understanding how the financing of property works can aid the licensee in solving problems that arise on transactions. Having direct knowledge of the mechanics of lending will surely assist the licensee in providing reasonable solutions.

Counseling

Real estate licensees should obtain constant training and education to further their knowledge base. From time to time, a property owner may require the advice of a professional consultant. This type of service requires a vast knowledge of real estate investment, financing, and valuation.

DEVELOPMENT AND CONSTRUCTION

Land Acquisition/Subdividing and Construction

To quote one of our nation's earliest and wealthiest real estate entrepreneurs, John J. Astor, "Buy by the acre and sell by the lot."

This quote reflects the business of subdividing large parcels of land into smaller ones for sale. There are subdividers and there are builders. Where all subdividers may be builders, not all builders are involved in the subdivision process. This process requires the division and planning (zoning permitting) of larger parcels of land into smaller buildable lots. The ability to create streets and the availability of utilities to the area are prime essentials for any subdivider. It is no secret that development costs exceed the original cost for land. We refer to the costs associated with land acquisition and development as hard costs. Before a subdivision is created and sold, it must be approved by the local municipality. This requires the subdivider to prepare and submit a plat map of subdivision for review by the municipality. The subdivision plat map acts as a visual rendering of the proposed development. Streets, building lots, water, sewer, and public utilities are often the subject of the rendering. In order to provide municipal service to the common areas (i.e., sanitation, street cleaning)—namely, the streets—the subdivider will grant the municipality ownership of the streets through a process called dedication. Dedication can be defined as private property given by an owner for the public's use. It is important to know that not all dedication of private property is accepted by the municipality. Acceptance by the municipality obligates the public body to provide vital services to that area. In certain places throughout the country, municipalities are only required to accept dedications for mapped streets.

When a subdivision reaches the development stage, developers will most often include and record restrictive covenants. These covenants are designed to create a means of conformity within a particular subdivision. Examples include setback requirements, size minimum square footage requirements, property use(s), and in most cases the architectural design of the improvement. These restrictive covenants assure the developer that property values for the sale of the last available lots will not be less than the first one that was sold.

It is at this point that the construction process begins. Construction is performed by a licensed contractor. Residential construction can be seen in three types of residential construction:

1. Speculative homes—The builder constructs these homes in anticipation of an active market without having buyers in hand. Where the spec home may act as a marketing tool for the builder (a model), this tends to be a risky area of the construction business.
2. Tract homes—These are similar to spec buildings. Numerous models are finished with size and design differences intentionally created.
3. Custom homes—These homes contain custom designs and usually include the input of either the buyer or the architect.

With the exception of custom houses, timing is crucial to the developer. The outlay of cash combined with the carrying costs of loans to construct requires a massive marketing campaign to sell these homes. This may call for the developer to enlist and engage the services of outsourced real estate licensees. Not all developers employ in-house sales staff to complete the sale of their inventory.

GOVERNMENT'S ROLE

Federal Government

Real property transactions are influenced by the federal government's activities. There are two direct factors that affect purchase considerations. Interest rates and income tax policies in particular will influence real estate markets nationally. In forthcoming chapters we will learn more about the federal government's influence. We will also take a closer look at some of its agencies—namely, the Internal Revenue Service (IRS), the Department of Veterans Affairs (VA), and the Department of Housing and Urban Development (HUD).

State Government

State government activities range from being vast owners of public property to custodians of coastal property. In addition, the state occupies leased space in privately owned properties. There are three types of transfer taxes paid on the sale of real property. This includes all transfers of property. These taxes are paid to the state. They include:

1. documentary stamps on the deed
2. documentary stamps on the note
3. intangible tax on (new) mortgage money introduced to the transaction

We will discuss these in greater detail in later chapters.

Local Government

Local government's role in real property transactions includes the right to:

1. assess or reassess property taxes
2. limit the bulk and use of property through zoning regulations
3. issue building permits
4. exercise the use/right of eminent domain

PROFESSIONAL ORGANIZATIONS

Professional organizations provide services to their constituents. In most cases, they provide and promote seminars for career building, print and circulate newsletters to their members, and conduct courses in ethics practice as well as other necessary continuing education for the real estate professional. Additionally, organizations like the National Association of REALTORS® (NAR) and the Florida Realtors and local boards provide a **Multiple Listings Service (MLS)** for their subscribing members. This service allows the member licensee to access available properties for sale or lease by creating certain parameters of search. The NAR and Florida Realtors further provide very important government-lobbying services. It is these services that protect the nature, interests, and integrity of the real estate licensee. Florida Realtors, local boards, and NAR also provide valuable education services to their memberships.

NAR is a national association that on a local basis comprises the board of REALTORS®. One must apply to become a member. Unfortunately, membership is company based. Therefore, if a company or brokerage is accepted for membership, the licensees of that company or brokerage are required to join as well. Individual membership without company or brokerage membership is currently unavailable. As a large national organization, NAR also has the ability and clout to create affinity group programs. This may include group health coverage, car rental discounts, and many other perks.

The NAR's primary focus is to provide education and ethic guidelines for the real estate practice. The genesis for the NAR's code of ethics dates back to 1913. There are three major areas of conduct focus that the code addresses:

1. dealings with licensees outside the employ of their sponsoring broker
2. dealings with consumers or the general public
3. working relationships with clients

Other organizations include the ICSC (International Council of Shopping Centers) and CoreNet Global whose constituents consist of those licensees engaged in the practice of retail or commercial office space. It is important to note that by being a member in the NAR, each member may use the trademarked name "REALTOR®" and logo.

In order to refer to oneself as a REALTOR® or to use the NAR trademark "R" on stationery or a business card, the individual must be a member of the NAR.

Regardless of membership within a professional organization, obtaining and holding a real estate license are always dealt with separately. Licensing and membership have no bearing or relationship with each other. Where licensing is obtained and issued by the State of Florida, participation in a professional organization is always via private membership.

Coaching Tips

Throughout this course, you will encounter terminology involving parties to a transaction. You may or may not be familiar with the identity of the party being referenced. A helpful tool to resolve that problem is

The "OR" "EE" Rule.

A good way to remember which party is which in a transaction would be to use the "OR" "EE" rule. Words that end in "OR" are the owners or givers of whatever is owned or being given. Words that end in "EE" are the receivers of whatever is owned and being given.

There are no exceptions to this rule other than one spelling exception. The word employer falls under the category of "OR" because it ends in the letter "r." Employers are still the provider of employment.

Summary

The real estate business contains other areas of the trade outside of sales. Even though the sales market tends to be the most active and thereby the most populated part of the real estate industry, an applicant for a real estate license should also be aware of other specialty areas of the real estate profession. Due to absentee ownership, property management is a growing business. In Florida, an individual may require a Community Association Manager's license to manage property. Valuation is another aspect of the real estate business. Only a licensed, certified, or general appraiser may call an estimation of value an appraisal. Under Chapter 475, F.S., Part I, a real estate licensee may conduct an appraisal but must at all times comply with USPAP. Remember, only licensed appraisers can legally conduct appraisals on a federally related transaction. Real estate licensees conduct CMAs in their normal course of business. Even though CMAs resemble appraisals, there is a difference. Appraisals focus strictly on value while a CMA will focus on pricing for marketing purposes. Government plays a large role in real property ownership. In addition, professional organizations are created to service their constituents and strive to enhance the information pool provided on an industry level. They also provide education to licensees. This enables licensees to stay on top of day-to-day nuances and changes that arise.

Review Questions

1. A Florida real estate licensee is employed to appraise a property for an FHA loan. Which of the following is true?
    a. The licensees can do this only if it is a federally related transaction.
    b. Under Chapter 475, F.S., real estate licensees cannot appraise property with a real estate license.
    c. The licensee must hold an appraiser's license for this activity.
    d. When performing an appraisal, a licensee is not required to follow the Uniform Standards of Professional Appraisal Practice (USPAP).

2. Which of the following is NOT considered a residential property transaction?
    a. sale of a duplex
    b. sale of three agricultural acres
    c. sale of a vacant lot in a subdivision
    d. sale of a ten-unit residential apartment building

3. Which of the following correctly describes the reason why property management in Florida has grown dramatically?
    a. only from an increase in the state's population
    b. the popularity of the internet
    c. the rising sale of single-family homes
    d. absentee ownership and the popularity of investments in income-producing property

4. The purpose of subdivision restrictive covenants is to:
    a. control the quality of the homes in order to maintain values within the subdivision
    b. limit the maximum of square feet allowed for improvements
    c. define the numbers of household composition
    d. set the ratio of land cost to development for income tax purposes

5. Concerning a comparative market analysis (CMA), which of the following statements is FALSE?
   a. A CMA may never be referred to as an appraisal.
   b. Licensees use CMAs as marketing tools.
   c. No one may charge for a CMA.
   d. A CMA focuses on the market value of a property.

6. The process by which a developer turns over the common areas of a subdivision such as streets is referred to as:
   a. restrictive covenants
   b. land acquisition
   c. subdividing
   d. dedication

7. The purpose of recording a deed is to:
   a. fulfill legal requirements
   b. protect the rightful property owner against present and future claims of ownership by others
   c. prevent liens
   d. ensure the title is marketable

8. A state-licensed appraiser charged a seller "1% of the appraised value of the property" as part of the agreement. This action is:
   a. a conflict of interest
   b. not legal
   c. standard practice in Florida
   d. a USPAP requirement

9. ABC Development builds homes and advertises the properties in brochures and newspapers and on billboards. This is an example of:
   a. custom building
   b. tract building
   c. spec building
   d. primary market activity

10. State government affects the real estate industry by establishing:
    a. zoning laws
    b. transfer taxes
    c. building moratoriums
    d. air-quality standards

11. A builder wants to find if Mediterranean-style homes are allowed in an existing subdivision. The builder could find this information in the:
    a. zoning requirements
    b. building codes
    c. restrictive covenants
    d. commerce codes

12. A real estate licensee can appraise property for compensation for a nonfederally related transaction:
    a. only as long as they call the appraisal a CMA
    b. only if licensed as an appraiser
    c. if the licensee is listing the property
    d. if he/she does not refer to him/herself as an appraiser

13. A business broker in Florida:
    a. must hold a real estate license
    b. holds a business broker license
    c. focuses on sales promotion and advertising
    d. cannot deal in residential property for others

14. Teresa just received her first license as a sales associate, and she wants to join the local board of realtors. Teresa:
    a. can join by paying a membership fee and quarterly dues
    b. can join when her license is activated
    c. must be a broker to join the board of realtors
    d. must work for a firm that is a board member

15. Which of the following is a function of local government?
    a. property tax
    b. interest rates
    c. transfer taxes on the deed
    d. intangible tax

16. A company that reports the financial activity for a particular property and bears the responsibility for maximizing the profit for the property owner is engaged in:
    a. "farming" the area
    b. industrial development
    c. property management
    d. public accounting

17. Maria's dad owns four lots in Florida and has moved to another state. The dad asked Maria to sell his lots and promised if she sold three, he would give her the remaining lot. She quickly accepted. She sold two of the lots but could not sell the third lot. Her dad did not give her the fourth lot. Which of the following is true?
    a. If Maria receives a lot, a license is not required.
    b. Maria did this for her dad, so no license is required.
    c. There was no compensation so no license is required.
    d. Maria has broken Florida real estate laws.

18. A real estate licensee who is well versed in transportation issues could specialize in dealing with which of these properties?
    a. commercial
    b. industrial
    c. business
    d. residential

19. Most firms engaged in the real estate profession in Florida deal with:
    a. residential properties because it is the most active market
    b. industrial properties as more and more industries relocate to Florida
    c. commercial properties because this is where the big money is
    d. agricultural properties because agribusiness is the largest industry in Florida

20. A licensed mortgage broker:
    a. originates loans directly
    b. services loans
    c. sells loans in the secondary mortgage market
    d. acts as a financial intermediary who brings borrowers and lenders together for a fee

LICENSE LAW AND QUALIFICATIONS FOR LICENSURE

2

KEY TERMS

adjudication withheld
broker
broker associate
caveat emptor
compensation
expungement

Florida resident
license/registration
nolo contendere/no contest
prima facie evidence
real estate services
sales associate

LEARNING OBJECTIVES

After completing this lesson, you will be able to:

- identify the qualifications for a sales associate's license
- describe the application requirements for a license, including nonresident application requirements
- explain the importance of responding accurately and completely to the background information questions on the licensure application
- illustrate the background check procedure conducted by the Department of Business and Professional Regulation
- describe the requirements for pre- and post-license education and continuing education
- distinguish the various license categories
- identify services of real estate where licensure is required
- recognize actions that constitute unlicensed activity
- recognize exemptions from real estate licensure
- distinguish between registration and licensure
- explain mutual recognition agreements

HISTORICAL PURPOSES OF REAL ESTATE LICENSE LAWS

History of Florida Real Estate License Law

Before the turn of the 20th century, it would not have been uncommon to find the existence of fraud in real estate transactions. In some cases, these acts occurred by those transacting on behalf of others. Therefore, as a direct result of public safety and welfare, in 1923 many states, including Florida, enacted license laws governing real estate activities.

Department of Business and Professional Regulation (DBPR)

The Department of Business and Professional Regulation (DBPR) is the Florida governmental agency responsible for licensing and regulating professions in the State of Florida. Some of these professions would include but not be limited to:

- cosmetologists
- veterinarians
- real estate agents

The DBPR is governed by Chapter 120, F.S. (Florida Statutes). It is also structured according to Section 20.165, F.S. Most importantly, it is under the executive branch of the governor. The secretary is the person who heads the department. The secretary of the DBPR is an appointed position. The appointment is given by the governor. The governor's appointment alone is not enough as the appointee must also be confirmed by the Senate. While there are no term limits, the secretary will normally serve until the next appointee.

Division of Real Estate (DRE)

As you learned earlier, real estate license laws were passed by Florida state legislature in 1923. Chapter 475 of the Florida Statutes governs the activities of real estate licensees. Pursuant to Chapter 475, F.S., the Division of Real Estate (DRE) is charged with the protection of the general public. This is accomplished by and through the regulation of:

- real estate
- appraisal licensees

The DRE is responsible for:

- examination
- licensing
- regulation of
  - individuals
  - corporations
  - real estate schools
  - instructors

Florida Real Estate Commission

In 1925, Florida lawmakers created and empowered what is known today as the Florida Real Estate Commission (FREC). The structure and function of FREC will be discussed in Chapter 3.

The FREC is headquartered in Orlando. The FREC is made up of seven members (five real estate licensees and two persons never licensed in real estate). Members of the FREC are appointed by the governor. They must also be confirmed by the Florida Senate.

In disposing of their duties, the FREC is assisted by the DBPR's DRE. The DRE assists the FREC in the role of an investigative unit while the FREC prosecutes based upon the DRE's findings and recommendations.

Need For Regulation

Caveat Emptor

Prior to the aforementioned enactment of license laws, the expression **caveat emptor**, the Latin term for "let the buyer beware," was prevalent in the real estate marketplace. Today, seller property condition disclosure requirements and case law governing same suggests, "let the seller beware."

Purpose of Regulation/Consumer Protection

Generally speaking, licensing laws were originally created primarily to protect the general public (consumer) against financial losses resulting from acts involving:

- fraud
- dishonesty
- incompetency of individuals transacting on behalf of others

Today, each state in the United States has adopted and enacted its own license law.

License law requires any licensee representing another in a real estate transaction (particularly where compensation is involved) to be held at a higher standard than that of the general public. **Compensation** is defined as a payment, something of value that is tangible or intangible. In essence, the licensee is held accountable for any infraction of the license law. This process is policed through the governing body regulating and enforcing the license law. If necessary, this enforcing body administers disciplinary action on any licensee. Where license law was designed primarily to protect the public against fraud, dishonesty, and incompetency, it is not used to prescribe or regulate commission rates charged by service providers such as brokers. In fact, compensation is derived solely through negotiation between the licensee and a seller, landlord, buyer or renter (as the case may be). In addition, license law does not protect buyers from sellers.

IMPORTANT REAL ESTATE STATUTES AND RULES

In order to prepare for both the licensing exam and real estate practice, there are various state and federal laws that the reader will need familiarity with. These laws are in the form of statutes and rules that directly affect and impact the activities of the real estate licensee. For example, the following are just a few of the areas of law that the reader will need to be familiar with.

Florida Statutes

1. Chapter 475, Part I, Florida Statutes, Real Estate Brokers, Sales Associates, and Schools
2. Chapter 455, Florida Statutes: Business and Professional Regulation: General Provisions
3. Chapter 61J2, F.A.C., Division of Real Estate, Florida Real Estate Commission (FREC)
4. Chapter 20, Florida Statutes: Organizational Structure—Executive Branch
5. Chapter 83, Florida Statutes: Landlord and Tenant—Nonresidential Tenancies, Residential Tenancies, and Self-Service Storage Space
6. Chapter 95, Florida Statutes: Limitations: Limitations of Actions; Adverse Possession
7. Chapter 120, Florida Statutes: Administrative Procedure Act
8. Chapter 163, Florida Statutes: Intergovernmental Programs
9. Chapter 173, Florida Statutes: Foreclosure of Municipal Tax and Special Assessment Liens
10. Chapter 193, Florida Statutes: Assessments (Florida Green Belt Law of 1959)
11. Chapter 196, Florida Statutes: Exemptions (Homestead Exemptions, etc.)
12. Chapter 197, Florida Statutes: Tax Collections, Sales and Liens
13. Chapter 201, Florida Statutes: Excise Tax on Documents
14. Chapter 501, Florida Statutes, Part II: Deceptive and Unfair Trade Practices
15. Chapter 553, Florida Statutes: Building Construction Standards
16. Chapter 542, Florida Statutes: Combinations Restricting Trade or Commerce
17. Chapter 607, Florida Statutes: Corporations
18. Chapter 608, Florida Statutes: Limited Liability Companies
19. Chapter 609, Florida Statutes: Common Law Declarations of Trust
20. Chapter 617, Florida Statutes: Corporations Not For Profit
21. Chapter 619, Florida Statutes: Nonprofit Cooperative Associations
22. Chapter 620, Florida Statutes: Partnership Laws

23. Chapter 621, Florida Statutes: Professional Service Corporations and Limited Liability Companies
24. Chapter 673, Florida Statutes: Uniform Commercial Code: Negotiable Instruments
25. Chapter 689, Florida Statutes: Real and Personal Property: Conveyances of Land and Declarations of Trust
26. Chapter 695, Florida Statutes: Record of Conveyances of Real Estate
27. Chapter 701, Florida Statutes: Assignment and Cancellation of Mortgages
28. Chapter 712, Florida Statutes: Marketable Record of Titles to Real Property
29. Chapter 718, Florida Statutes: Condominiums
30. Chapter 719, Florida Statutes: Cooperatives
31. Chapter 720, Florida Statutes: Homeowners' Associations
32. Chapter 721, Florida Statutes: Vacation and Timeshare Plans
33. Chapter 725, Florida Statutes: Unenforceable Contracts
34. Chapter 726, Florida Statutes: Fraudulent Transfers
35. Chapter 732, Florida Statutes: Probate Code: Intestate Succession and Wills
36. Chapter 733, Florida Statutes: Probate Code: Administration of Estates
37. Chapter 760, Florida Statutes: Florida Civil Rights
38. Chapter 865, Section 865.09: Florida's Fictitious Name Act

Federal Regulations/United States Code

1. Title 12, Chapter 27, Sections 2601 through 2617, United States Code: Real Estate Settlement Procedures
2. Title 15, Chapter 41, Subchapter I, Part A, Sections 1601-1615, United States Code: Consumer Credit Cost Disclosure (Truth-In-Lending Act)
3. Title 15, Chapter 41, Subchapter IV, Sections 1691 through 1691f, United States Code: Equal Credit Opportunity Act
4. Title 15, Chapter 42, Sections 1701-1720, United States Code: Interstate Land Sales Full Disclosure
5. Title 42, Chapter 21, Sections 1981 through 2000h-6, United States Code: Civil Rights (Civil Rights Act of 1964, Civil Rights Act of 1991, etc.)
6. Title 42, Chapter 45, Sections 3601 through 3631, United States Code: Fair Housing (amended in 1988) (Title VIII, Civil Rights Act of 1968)
7. Title 42, Chapter 63A, Sections 4851 through 4856, United States Code: Residential Lead-Based Paint Hazard Reduction
8. Title 42, Chapter 126, Sections 12101 through 12213, United States Code: Equal Opportunity for Individuals with Disabilities
    (American Disabilities Act of 1990 and Rehabilitative Act of 1973)
    http://www.usdoj.gov/crt/ada/adahom1.htm

> Laws to remember that affect the real estate industry:
> - Chapter 455, F.S.
> - Chapter 475, Part 1, F.S.
> - Chapter 61j2, Florida Administrative Code
> - Chapter 120, F.S.

LICENSE CATEGORIES

Although there are officially two categories of real estate licenses in Florida, there is a third hybrid category. The three categories are:

1. broker—any person who, for another, performs a real estate act (as prescribed by law) for, or in anticipation of, compensation or other valuable consideration
2. sales associate—any person who assists a broker in the disposition of the broker's business.

    It should be noted that regardless what sales associate is responsible for bringing in new customers or clients, all business conducted on behalf of the brokerage belongs to the broker. This includes individual sales associate listings for lease or sale as well as all buyers and renters.
3. broker associate—any person who has otherwise qualified to be a broker but has opted to remain within the employ and direct supervision of another broker. (This usually occurs when a sales associate working within the employ of a brokerage obtains his/her broker's license and chooses to remain within that brokerage's employ.)

GENERAL LICENSING PROVISIONS (SALES ASSOCIATE CANDIDATE)

In order to qualify for a license as a sales associate (one who assists a broker in the disposition of the broker's business duties) in the state of Florida, at a minimum, you must:

1. be at least 18 years of age
2. hold a high school diploma or equivalent
3. submit a fingerprint card (for performance of a background check)
4. be honest and of trustworthy character
5. successfully complete a FREC-approved 63-hour qualifying course (entitled FREC Course I) through any Florida-accredited school authorized by the FREC to administer prelicense courses. The education requirement can be completed in a classroom environment or via distance learning. In either case, the applicant must pass an end-of-course exam.
6. pass the state sales associate license exam with a grade of at least 75%
7. complete form DBPR RE 11 if you are a broker, in order to become active
8. pay the required license fee

Let's examine one of these sales associate requirements in more detail—being honest and trustworthy. In order to be considered honest and of trustworthy character, certain disclosures are required. For example, if the applicant had a problem in the past (e.g., convicted of a crime), honest and trustworthy character can be demonstrated to the licensing body by the applicant's full cooperation and disclosure of all facts that would normally affect the ability to qualify as a licensee. Depending on the applicant's past, the level of cooperation through the applicant's disclosure may be viewed by the regulatory body as an act or sign of that person's character. This may or may not be a mitigating factor in successfully obtaining a real estate license. It is important to note that an **expungement** of record is defined as the destruction or sealing of a previous criminal record. The reader is cautioned to check with the necessary authorities to confirm if records in fact have been sealed/expunged, as same is not an automatic event and it is up to the applicant to determine.

1. The applicant must disclose if:
   a. under investigation
   b. convicted of a crime

2. An applicant must make full disclosure if the applicant has ever:
   a. been convicted of a crime
   b. pleaded guilty or nolo contendere to a charge (nolo contendere means the person does not dispute the charges but does not admit any guilt)

The aforementioned disclosure applies to any felony, misdemeanor, or traffic offenses (except traffic signal, parking, speeding, or inspection violations). This disclosure is required without regard to whether the applicant was placed on probation, had adjudication withheld, was paroled, or was pardoned. (**Adjudication withheld** means that the person is placed on probation; if probation is successfully completed, the conviction is not entered into the records.) Failure on the part of the applicant to fully disclose such events may render the applicant ineligible to receive a license. If the applicant has fraudulently received a license, failing to make the appropriate disclosures would be grounds for immediate revocation of the license. This type of behavior may subject the individual to other civil or criminal liability, as well as disciplinary action by the appropriate regulatory body.

3. If the applicant has ever been known under any other name or alias, the applicant must disclose:
   a. if he/she was ever denied a license, or
   b. had a license disciplined or pending discipline in any other jurisdiction.

4. The applicant must disclose if the applicant has ever had a license:
   a. denied;
   b. surrendered;
   c. revoked; or
   d. registration to practice a regulated profession in any other jurisdiction.

5. The applicant must disclose if he/she was guilty of any conduct or practice that would have been grounds for suspension or revocation under Chapter 475.
6. Qualification of immigrants for examination Chapter 455.11:
    a. This section of the Florida Statutes was enacted to encourage the use of foreign-speaking Florida residents who are duly qualified to become actively qualified in their professions. This is so that all Florida citizens may receive better services.
7. Requirement for United States Social Security number per Chapter 559. The individual applicant must also have and provide their social security number.

Coaching Tips

Applicants for licensure should disclose whether or not:
1. any criminal charge(s) are pending against applicant
2. applicant has had any previous felony or misdemeanor convictions
3. applicant has ever entered a plea of "nolo contendere" (no contest)
4. applicant has ever been known by any other name (i.e., an alias/aka)
5. applicant has ever been denied or has had a license suspended or revoked in another state or jurisdiction
6. applicant has ever been denied a license or registration to practice a regulated profession in Florida or any other state or jurisdiction
7. applicant has been found guilty of any practice or conduct that would have been grounds for suspension or revocation under F.S. 475
8. applicant must be a citizen of the United States (F.S. 455.10) or a qualified immigrant (F.S. 455.11)
9. applicant has ever had a license, permit, or other registration revoked in Florida or any other jurisdiction
10. applicant is currently residing in a mental health facility or similar institution

Coaching Tips

Completion of FREC Course I can be done in a variety of ways:
- online approved course
- classroom
    - in English with the class final and state exam in English
    - in Spanish with the class final and state exam in Spanish

Application Requirements

Any person who wishes to receive a license must submit a fully completed application. After the application is submitted, a 30-day period is allowed to check for any deficiencies, errors, or omissions on the application. The applicant will be notified that the application was either approved or denied within 90 days. Currently, an approval notification is given to the applicant by Pearson VUE (http://www.PearsonVue.com). This notification will also describe the process required for the applicant to sit for the exam. The student should refer to the Candidate Information booklet available on line

Fees

The FREC charges various licensure fees, such as:

- initial license fees
- subsequent renewal fees
- exam fees that are paid directly to the testing vendor (currently Pearson VUE)

Because fees are subject to change at any time, please consult the DRE and the testing vendor at the time of application for the current amount.

Coaching Tips

Currently the fee for an initial license is $89. However, as fees do change over time, it is recommended that the applicant check with the appropriate department to determine the correct amount.

Application Form: Responding Accurately and Completely to Background Information

An applicant must have a background check as part of the licensing process. The application form can be downloaded from the internet by visiting myflorida.com or by contacting the DBPR and requesting same. You can also complete the application by clicking on the "Online Services" link or the "Printable Application" link at the bottom of the page where the application can be found.

Once the applicant has the required package, it is imperative that the applicant answer all questions concerning background information truthfully and honestly. Failure to do so can result in a delay or denial of the applicant to qualify for licensure.

Background Check Procedure

When applying for a real estate license in Florida, applicants will be asked whether they have ever been convicted of:

- a criminal offense
- entered a plea of guilty
- have entered a plea of **nolo contendere/no contest** (a legal term that comes from the Latin for "I do not wish to contend") to a criminal charge. This is

pertinent whether or not the applicant received a withhold of adjudication. A withhold of adjudication is when the court stops or refrains from imposing a sentence on the defendant. When this occurs, it would not be uncommon to place the individual on probation. Regardless of the aforementioned, applicants are required to disclose such on their application.

Along with the application, each applicant is required to also submit fingerprints electronically (discussed next) or a fingerprint card that will be used to perform a background check on the applicant. The purpose behind this requirement is to determine whether or not the applicant has any criminal background. The fingerprints will be sent to the FBI and other law enforcement agencies for the sole purpose of determining the applicant's criminal history.

Currently in Florida, fingerprints are taken electronically through a scanning process by the test vendor. For out of state residents where scanning is not available, applicants will need to furnish the DRE with the hard copy of their fingerprint card. This card and application must be sent to a special address (see Coaching Tips below for the current address).

Period to Check for Errors and Omissions/Period to Inform Applicant of Approval or Denial of Application/Rights of the Applicant

A fully complete application would include but not be limited to:

- the filled out application with background information
- a fingerprint scan (resident) or hard fingerprint card (nonresident) as well as the irrevocable consent to service section for nonresident applicants
- the required fee and/or any other required documentation (i.e., license certification from another state)

Upon receipt of the aforementioned, the DBPR has 30 days in order to check for deficiencies, errors, or omissions. Should the application contain either an error or omission, the applicant will receive a notice of deficiency. This notice will list the required information necessary toward approval of the application.

Furthermore, no later than 90 days from receipt of a fully completed application, all applicants must be notified as to approval or denial of their application for licensure. If the FREC denies an application, the applicants will receive a notice of the denial as well as the reasons for same. The notice will also inform the applicants that they have 21 days from receipt of the FREC order denying an application for licensure to request a hearing in conjunction with Chapter 120, F.S.

Length of Time a Licensure Application Is Valid/Initial Application/Exam Eligible

Applications for licensure are good for two years. However, the applicant must take the test at least once within one year from the time that the application was approved. Failure to do so will require the applicant to reapply and for the reapplication to be approved before sitting for the state exam.

Nonresident Application Requirements

Any person considered a nonresident of Florida may apply for a Florida real estate license. A nonresident is anyone who does not physically reside in Florida for the statutory period required to create Florida residency. The establishment of Florida residency is covered by Rule 61J2-26.002. This rule states that one is a *Florida resident* after residing in Florida continuously for four calendar months or more within a calendar year. This definition would also include one's intent to reside for four calendar months or more within a calendar year. Residency can be established irrespective of residing in a:

- hotel
- rental unit
- mobile home/recreation vehicle

In order to receive a Florida real estate broker or sales associate license, every nonresident applicant must meet the same requirements as a resident applicant, including:

- completion of all pre-license requirements
- passing the state exam
- paying the required license fee

In addition, a nonresident applicant must file a completed irrevocable consent to service form. Consent to service means that the nonresident applicant designates the director of the Florida DRE as the recipient of any legal notices against the nonresident. In the event that a legitimate complaint is filed against the nonresident licensee, a copy of the legal notice will be sent to the nonresident at the address kept on file. This form also states that any lawsuits against the nonresident licensee may be filed in any county in Florida in which the plaintiff resides. The irrevocable consent to service form is included in the Forms Appendix.

Important tip to remember: To avoid disciplinary action against one's license, any Florida resident licensee who relocates to another state and becomes a nonresident of Florida needs to do the following:

1. Notify the DBPR within 10 days of the change of address; and
2. Comply with all other nonresident requirements within 60 days of nonresidency.

Coaching Tips

As companies do relocate from time to time, the nonresident applicant should contact either the DBPR in Tallahassee or Pearson VUE to confirm his/her current address prior to submission of the fingerprint card and application. The required fee (currently it is $89 for the initial application for sales associate license) should be submitted with the fingerprint card. Due to the constant change in fees, the applicant should check in advance to confirm the fee charged at the time of application.

Application policies and fees
Currently the law requires electronic fingerprinting. However, an applicant who is a nonresident of Florida can send the DRE fingerprint card and application to the following address:

FLDBPR, Florida Fingerprinting Program, Prints Inc.
Tallahassee, FL 32301

(Because the current location can change, the applicant should confirm the correct address before submitting their application and fingerprints.)

Those applicants who are able to provide an electronic fingerprint would send their application to the following address:

Customer Contact Center
1940 North Monroe Street
Tallahassee, FL 32399-0783
850-487-1395

Scheduling, Grade Notification, and Reviews
Pearson VUE Inc.
Customer Care at 888-204-6230
Fax-back system at 800-274-8920
Website: www.PearsonVue.com

Formal Hearings
DBPR Bureau of Education & Testing—Review Office
1940 North Monroe Street
Tallahassee, FL 32399-0783
850-487-9762

Request for Special Testing Accommodations
Examination Administration Unit—Special Testing
DBPR Bureau of Education & Testing
1940 North Monroe Street
Tallahassee, FL 32399-0783
850-487-9755

Regulations Pertaining to Pre-License Courses

Every applicant for a real estate license in Florida must complete the required prelicense education. For the sales associate, the course breaks down into 60 hours of instruction plus a 3-hour final exam. The passing grade for the state exam is 75%, but the passing grade for the course exam is 70%. In the event the student fails the final exam, the student is entitled to a one-time retest. The exam (which must be a different exam from that of the first failed exam) must be retaken no later than one year from the time of the original exam. If the student does not take the make-up exam within this 1-year period, or takes and fails the make-up exam, the student must repeat FREC Course I.

Furthermore, the student enrolled in a classroom pre-license course may not miss more than the prescribed classroom hours. Should the student miss more than the allowable course hours (currently 8 hours), he/she will be required to make up the exact time and course material missed. For example, a student misses a total of 16 hours of course time. The student will have to make up (at a minimum) 8 hours. Doing so will place the student back in good standing with course completion requirements.

The pre-license course may be completed in any of the following ways:

- in a classroom
- a timed distance learning course
- a correspondence course for applicants who cannot attend a classroom or do not have access to distance learning courses

PUBLIC RECORD

Under current Florida law, all communications received by the DBPR are of public record unless a specific exemption applies in a statute (see Chapter 455). For example, the email addresses of licensees are of public record. In addition, licensing information or status concerning any licensee is available online on the DBPR website. Some of the other areas of public record include, but are not limited to, the ability to:

- search for a licensee
- apply for a license
- view license application status
- find exam information
- file a complaint

SALES ASSOCIATE LICENSE REQUIREMENTS

Education Exemptions

Although all applicants for a sales associate license must complete pre-license education, the following individuals are exempt from FREC Course I:

1. attorneys admitted to the Florida Bar (only exempt from FREC Course I)
2. any person holding a 4-year degree in real estate from an institution of higher learning

Sales Pre-License Course

All applicants that are not exempt from the sales associate prelicense course must complete FREC course I or other approved equivalent course work. The course will prepare the applicant in the following subjects:

- real estate license law
- principles and practices
- real estate law
- real estate math

The course consists of 60 hours of classroom instruction plus a 3-hour final end-of-course school exam. The sales associate exam consists of 100 multiple-choice questions worth 1 point each. The exam is broken down by category in the following manner:

- 45 questions test Florida real estate law
- 45 questions test principles and practices of real estate
- 10 questions test calculation skills

State Licensure Examination

As mentioned earlier, any applicant for a broker, broker associate, or sales associate's license must pass an examination administered by the state. There is an exam fee, which is paid to the approved testing agency (currently Pearson VUE). It is the approved testing agency that will arrange for the individual to sit for a computer-based test. If the applicant fails the exam, the applicant may retake the exam as many times as necessary in order to pass. However, the exam must be passed within the EARLIER of either:

- two years from when the applicant was issued a transcript for the successful completion of the pre-license requirements from the approved school
- two years from the time of receiving, from FREC, an approved application permitting the applicant to sit for the state exam

Each time an applicant retakes the exam, the required examination fee must be paid. There are two types of state exams:

1. the sales associate exam
2. the broker exam

In both cases, passing grades are 75% or higher. Notification of exam results is communicated as a Pass/Fail notice.

Examination Content

Sales associate state exam consists of a hundred multiple choice questions; the break-down is in the following manner:

- 45 questions test Florida real estate law
- 45 questions test principles and practices of real estate
- 10 questions test math skills

BROKER AND BROKER ASSOCIATE LICENSE REQUIREMENTS

Education Exemptions

Although all applicants for a broker or broker associate license must complete prelicense education, the following is exempt from FREC Course II:

1. any person holding a 4-year degree in real estate from an institution of higher learning.

> **Coaching Tips**
>
> Unlike FREC Course I for a sales associate license, attorneys admitted to the Florida Bar are not exempt from FREC Course II. They are only exempt from FREC Course I and any real estate continuing education.

Experience Requirement for Broker Pre-License Course

In addition to meeting all of the requirements to obtain a sales associate's license, a broker or broker associate applicant must also successfully complete FREC Course II. FREC Course II:

- is an approved 72-hour qualifying course
- can be administered by or through any Florida-accredited school authorized by FREC to administer pre-license courses
- can be administered in a classroom or online

The passing grade for Course II is 70%. The course content covers the 12 content areas of testing (covered areas of testing listed below).

Examination Content: Broker

The broker exam consists of 100 multiple-choice questions. The exam is also broken down by category in the following manner:

- 43% of the exam questions test Florida real estate law
- 9% of the exam questions test Valuing Real Property
- 11% of the exam questions test Contracts
- 4% of the exam questions test Financing
- 12% of the exam questions test Closing Transactions
- 5% of the exam questions test Federal Income Tax Laws
- 4% of the exam questions test Investments
- 1% of the exam questions test Zoning & Planning
- 1% of the exam questions test Environmental Issues
- 1% of the exam questions test Property Management
- 3% of the exam questions test the Real Estate Market
- eight questions test knowledge of a closing disclosure document

For any individual who has not held a previous real estate license, this 72-hour course is in addition to the 63-hour sales associate's qualifying course and the mandatory 45-hour sales associate's post-license course (discussed in greater detail later in this chapter). However, it is important to note that if an applicant has previously held a real estate license in another state, jurisdiction, or country, and if an applicant can prove at least two years of active licensing within the previous five years from that state, jurisdiction, or country, the applicant is exempt from taking FREC Course I and the salesperson post-licensing courses. To obtain a broker or broker associate license, the applicant must:

- successfully pass FREC Course II
- successfully pass the state broker's license exam with a grade of at least 75%
- complete the sales associate's post-license education (45 hours) as well as hold a current and valid license—if the applicant is a sales associate licensed in Florida

In addition, an applicant for a broker or broker associate's license must meet a certain experience requirement. This experience requirement is considered satisfied by the FREC when the applicant has achieved one of the following:

- has held a valid and active sales associate's license under a broker for at least two years within the preceding five years
- has held a valid and active broker's license for at least two years within the preceding five years in another state
- has held a valid and active real estate sales associate's license for at least two years during the preceding five years while in the employ of a governmental agency for a salary and performing the duties as authorized in Chapter 475, F.S.

As just mentioned, to obtain a broker's license, an applicant must have held a valid and active real estate license for at least two years during the previous five years.

Coaching Tips

Florida recognizes and accepts the experience of any person who has previously held or is the holder of an active sales associate, broker associate, or broker's license in Florida or any other state for at least two years within the preceding five years.

MUTUAL RECOGNITION AGREEMENTS WITH OTHER STATES

If an applicant already possesses a real estate license in another state that shares mutual recognition with Florida, a nonresident may be able to obtain a Florida license without taking the prelicense education. This is true for licensees who reside in a state where Florida shares a mutual recognition agreement with that state. Under such an agreement, Florida will mutually recognize the education and experience that a licensee has obtained by holding a real estate license in another state.

Currently, Florida shares mutual recognition agreements with seven other states:

1. Alabama*
2. Arkansas*
3. Connecticut
4. Georgia
5. Illinois
6. Mississippi
7. Nebraska

Must meet additional requirements

Please take note of the following:

- As of July 15, 2009, Florida no longer shares mutual recognition with Kentucky.
- As of January 31, 2009, Florida no longer shares mutual recognition with Colorado.
- As of September 30, 2012, Florida no longer shares mutual recognition with Tennessee.

Mutual recognition is possible only for residents of states that offer Florida residents the same license privileges in exchange. If a licensee from a mutual recognition state wishes to obtain a Florida real estate license, the licensee must:

- pass a 40-question exam (each question worth 1 point each) covering Florida real estate law with a grade of 75% or higher (30 points or higher)
- complete an irrevocable consent to service form
- submit a fully completed application, fingerprint card, or scan of same
- pay the required license fee
- submit a certification of license history from the home state, which:
    - acts as proof of licensure within that state
    - indicates how one obtained a license in that given state
    - states how long one has held a license (taking into consideration that in some states, records are destroyed after approximately seven years)
    - indicates to the DRE whether or not the licensee has had any previous disciplinary action assessed to his/her license

Florida Resident Defined

As previously discussed in this chapter, a Florida resident is defined as any person who physically resides in Florida for the statutory period required to create Florida residency. The establishment of Florida residency is covered by Rule 61J2-26.002. This rule states that one is a **Florida resident** after residing in Florida continuously for four calendar months or more within a calendar year. This definition would also include one's intent to reside for four calendar months or more within a calendar year. Residency can be established irrespective of residing in a:

- hotel
- rental unit
- mobile home/recreation vehicle

Distinguishing Between Mutual Recognition and Reciprocity

The primary difference between mutual recognition and reciprocity is:

- Mutual recognition always requires applicants to complete some act (education and/or testing) for the state they are applying for.
- Licensure in a reciprocal state requires no further action on the part of the licensee (other than submission of an application and other required documents) such as education or testing.

INFORMATION INCLUDED ON THE REAL ESTATE LICENSE

A real estate license contains the following information on the license:

- name of the license holder
- issuance date
- expiration date
- unique licensee identification number

Prima Facie Evidence

Prima facie evidence is a legal term that is defined as valid on its face value unless proven to be invalid. A real estate license that is issued by the state becomes prima facie evidence of the individual holding a valid license.

REGISTRATIONS VS. LICENSES

Real estate licenses and registrations are similar to those of motor vehicles licenses. For example, a driver's license is issued only to an individual who has successfully completed all education and exams (written and driver's test) to drive a motor vehicle; a registration is thereby issued to the vehicle itself. The driver's license allows the individual to operate the vehicle while the registration allows the vehicle to be driven on the roadways.

Real estate **licenses** (permission from the state to operate as a real estate agent) are given only to individuals. As we have discovered earlier, in order to obtain a real estate license in Florida, one must complete necessary education as well as qualify to sit for and pass an exam. Therefore, **registrations** are given to business entities. A registration can be defined as the official placement of a real estate brokerage business or practice within the records of the Florida DBPR. Think of the business entity as the vehicle that houses or holds the license for the licensee.

Registrations can include but are not limited to some of the following:

- business entities
- offices and branch offices

- persons registered as officers and directors of real estate corporations
- persons registered as partners in real estate
  - general partnerships
  - limited partnerships

Office and branch office registrations result in the issuance of a license to perform activities only at the registered location. Any change in address would require notification to the DRE and require a new registration. Issued licenses resulting from a registration are not transferable. A licensee has 10 days to report any change of address. This includes an office or a branch office.

LICENSE RENEWAL EDUCATION

Post license Requirement (Sales Associate)

Within the first license cycle following issuance (which may be no less than 18 months or more than two years after initial licensure), a licensed sales associate must complete additional FREC-approved education. The licensee is issued a conditional license that is subject to the completion of additional post-license education. This education must equal a total of 45 hours in order for the sales associate to renew the license. The course can be completed in:

- a classroom
- online

In either case, the licensee must also pass an end of course examination covering the post-license course material with a grade of 70% or higher. If the student fails the final exam, a one-time retest can be taken. The retest must be taken no later than one year from the time of the original exam. As another option, the student may choose to retake the post-license course.

If the licensee fails to complete the course by the end of the first license renewal period, their license becomes null and void. To return to real estate practice, the individual must retake the sales associate's pre-license course (FREC Course I) and pass the state exam.

Post-license Requirement (Broker)

Within two years after initial licensure, a licensed broker must complete additional FREC-approved education. This education must equal a total of 60 hours in order to renew the broker's license. The course can be completed in:

- a classroom
- online

In either case, the licensee must also pass an exam covering the post-license course material. In the event the student fails the final exam, a one-time retest can be taken. The retest must be taken no later than one year from the time of the original exam. As another option, the student may choose to retake the post-license course.

If the licensee fails to complete the course by the end of the first license renewal period, the licensee's broker's license becomes null and void (this term will be discussed in Chapter 3 in greater detail). If the broker's license becomes null and void and the licensee wishes to act as a sales associate, the licensee may do so but only after providing proof of completion of 14 hours of continuing education (described later) within six months following expiration of the broker's license. If the licensee wishes to act as a broker, the licensee must retake the broker's pre-license course and pass the state broker exam.

> ### Coaching Tips
>
> The 60-hour broker post-license education is offered in two separate 30-hour courses.

CONTINUING EDUCATION

After a real estate license has been issued, the license must be renewed periodically. The license renewal period is two years.

In Florida and in any calendar year, there are two license issuance/expiration dates:

1. March 31
2. September 30

When an original license is issued, the license will expire on the nearest renewal date under two years. In most cases, the initial license when issued will be for a term of no less than 18 months and no more than 24 months. This will be dependent on the issuance date. After that, the license renewal period is every two years. For example, an initial license issued on November 1, 2017, will expire on September 30, 2019. Thereafter, the license will expire every two years on September 30. License renewal will be covered in greater detail in Chapter 3.

As mentioned earlier, the license period is two years for brokers, broker associates, and sales associates (with exception to the initial license). Before the end of the first renewal period after initial licensure, a licensee must complete post-license education (45 hours for sales associates and 60 hours for brokers). Post-license education requires either the sales associate or broker to pass an end-of-course final exam with a grade of 75% or higher. Course material consists of preapproved subject matter to include core law as well as other approved topics.

However, please take note that after completing the required post license education and during the second and all subsequent renewal periods, the licensee has the responsibility to complete all continuing education requirements. Prior to renewing or being eligible to renew the license, a licensee must complete at least 14 hours of FREC-approved continuing education courses (unless otherwise exempt under the law).

The continuing education requirement may be accomplished in several ways:

- 14 in-class hours of prescribed and approved education—no end-of-course exam required.
- 14 hours of prescribed and approved education satisfied by completing an approved correspondence/distance learning course containing an end-of-course exam with a passing grade of 80% or better.

Beginning October 2017, the 14 hours of prescribed education break down as follows:

1. three hours of core law (Core law includes a review of real estate law as well as updates to current law.)
2. eight hours of FREC-approved specialty courses (This section is offered by local boards and a variety of real estate schools. If licensees attend a FREC meeting, they can earn three hours [specialty course hours and not core law hours] of continuing education credit toward their 14-hour requirement.)
3. three hours covering ethics (Ethics covers permitted activities when in a legal relationship with others in a real estate transaction.)

It should be noted that the National Association of REALTORS® (NAR) Code of Ethics can meet the ethics requirement.

Coaching Tips

Providers of continuing education courses are required to electronically report to the DRE a student roster of those who have successfully completed the course(s). Reporting must occur:

- within 30 days from the date of course completion, or
- by month's end if it is a renewal month.

Currently, the DRE will not issue a renewal unless the licensee has successfully completed the required education. Presently, the DRE will issue the licensee a letter stating that renewal is denied due to insufficient education. In addition, any licensee who has not successfully completed the required continuing education will be issued a deficiency letter. This letter informs the licensee that he/she has not completed the required continuing education prior to license renewal.

Reactivation Education

Licensees who have not completed their continuing education will not be able to renew their license until the education has been completed for the respective license cycle. Until that time, the license reverts to involuntary inactive status should the license expire, and the licensee has one license cycle to reactivate the license. In order to accomplish reactivation and to reinstate the license, the licensee must complete either:

1. 14 hours of approved continuing education (if expiration is less than 12 months into the next cycle), or
2. 28 hours of approved reactivation course(s) (if expiration is greater than 12 months but less than 24 months).

LICENSURE, LICENSE RENEWAL, POST-LICENSING, AND CONTINUING EDUCATION EXEMPTIONS

Some individuals are exempt from continuing education requirements:

- A licensee who is currently a member of the U.S. Armed Forces is exempt from license renewal requirements, including continuing education, while serving on active duty. The licensee has up to six months from release of duty to renew the license without penalty or loss of license. In addition, if the spouse of any active member of the military (particularly one who is serving active duty in a place outside Florida) is also a current holder of a valid real estate license, both licensees will have six months after release from active duty to fulfill all renewal requirements in order to renew their licenses without loss or penalty. The aforementioned exemption will only hold true if the licensee is not active in the practice of real estate during this period.
- Active members of the Florida Bar are exempt from continuing education requirements. However, they are not exempt from the post-license education requirements.

If a sales associate or a broker applicant has previously earned a four-year degree in real estate from an accredited college/university or other institution, the applicant is exempt from pre-license and post-license education. In Florida, members in good standing accepted to the Florida Bar are exempt only from the sales associate prelicense course.

Coaching Tips

Important State Laws

Florida law clearly defines who must be licensed. The student should know that:

- Chapter 455 of the Florida Statutes (455, F.S.) regulates professions and occupations.
- Chapter 475 of the Florida Statutes (475, F.S.) is known as the real estate license law.

> - Chapter 61J2 of the Florida Statutes (61J2, F.S.) provides the rules of the Florida Real Estate Commission as to how real estate activities by a licensee may lawfully occur.
> - Chapter 120 of the Florida Statutes (120, F.S.) is the Administrative Procedures Act.
>
> Where 61J2, F.S., provides the rules for the disposition of a licensee's duties, the licensing and disciplinary process is outlined in Chapter 120.

REAL ESTATE SERVICES

There are certain individuals who are required to be licensed. At the same time, there are individuals who are also exempt from licensure. The following describes who must be licensed as well as who is exempt.

Broker

A real estate **broker** performs real estate services that are defined as any person, corporation, partnership, limited liability partnership, or limited liability company who performs a real estate act for another, in exchange for or in anticipation of compensation or other valuable consideration.

The following **real estate services** or activities require a real estate broker's, broker associate's, or sales associate's license:

- buying, selling, leasing, renting, or exchanging real property
- buying, selling, leasing, renting, or exchanging business enterprises or business opportunities
- buying, selling, leasing, renting, or exchanging mineral rights
- soliciting prospects for any of these functions
- negotiating for any of these functions
- advertising for any of these functions
- appraising real property
- auctioning real property
- providing rental lists or rental information

A broker may operate a business under a trade name (fictitious name) by registering that name with the FREC. All real estate brokers are responsible for the activities of the broker sales associates and sales associates within their employ. It is the principal broker's responsibility to continuously supervise all licensees engaged in real estate activities within his/her employ. This responsibility is applicable whether the individual is categorized as an independent contractor or as an employee. Independent contractor versus employee status only refers to how income is taxed by the Internal Revenue Service (IRS).

Broker Associate

A **broker associate** is a person who is licensed as a real estate broker but, rather than forming his/her own business, chooses to work under the name and supervision of another broker. Although the licensee holds a real estate broker's license, the licensee operates within the organization performing sales associate duties and activities on behalf of the broker. A broker associate or sales associate may be issued a license as a professional corporation if the licensee provides the FREC with proper authorization from the Department of State. However, this election is for tax and liability purposes and is not intended for the broker associate to run a brokerage company and/or hire other sales associates.

Sales Associate

A **sales associate** is a person associated with a licensed real estate broker who assists in performing services offered by the broker. A sales associate is licensed to work for and act as a representative of the broker. A sales associate may be issued a license as a professional corporation if the licensee provides the FREC with proper authorization from the Department of State. As stated above, this election is for tax and liability purposes and is not intended for the sales associate to run a brokerage company and/or hire other sales associates. A sales associate performs real estate activities previously described within the definition of a real estate broker. A sales associate must be under constant supervision by a principal broker who is responsible for the sales associate's activities while engaged and registered within the broker's employ. A sales associate:

- may assist in any of the services performed or to be performed by a licensed broker
- may only work in the name of the licensed principal employing broker, an owner/developer, or a governmental agency. However, if the sales associate wishes to become a broker, only employment by a broker counts toward the 2-year experience requirement
- may only work while under the supervision of a licensed principal employing broker
- may never accept compensation or any valuable consideration of any type directly or indirectly from anyone other than her principal employing broker

Reminder: In Florida, an applicant who has received a 4-year degree in real estate is exempt from pre- and post-licensing requirements. In addition, accepted members into the Florida Bar are exempt only from taking the sales associate pre-licensing course.

Individuals Who Are Exempt from Licensure

We just looked at the activities that require a real estate broker's license. However, some individuals are exempt from licensing requirements even though they may perform the services of a broker. Under Florida license law, the following persons are exempt from license law requirements:

- owners of real property transacting in real estate strictly for their own account
- a corporation, partnership, or other entity when selling, exchanging, or leasing its own property
- this exemption does not exist if an agent, employee, or independent contractor receives compensation (other than a salary) in the form of commission or the individual is compensated on a transactional basis
- anyone who sells cemetery lots
- an attorney-in-fact under a duly authorized power of attorney to carry out a specific real estate transaction
- those persons appointed or acting under a court order while disposing of those duties under the order (i.e., receiver, trustee in a bankruptcy, etc.)
- a person who is authorized to act as an executor or administrator of a will
- a trustee under a deed of trust or trust agreement
- authorized employees of a government agency, utility company, or railroad, while acting in the conduct of official business
- a salaried employee of an owner of an apartment (or the owner's registered broker) who is employed on the premises to lease the property
- anyone who rents rooms in public lodging establishments (e.g., hotels and motels) for temporary occupancy
- a salaried employee acting as a manager for a condominium or cooperative who rents individual units, if the units are rented for periods of one year or less
- a property management firm or owner of an apartment complex who pays a finder's fee or referral fee to a tenant, if the value does not exceed $50. The finder's fee or referral fee may be cash, credit toward the tenant's rent, or another item of value
- the owner of a time-share, for the owner's own use and occupancy, who later resells the time-share
- certified public accountants performing services within the scope of the accounting profession
- a depository institution selling, exchanging, buying, or renting a business enterprise to or from an accredited investor
- an appraiser who is registered, licensed, or certified under Part II of Chapter 475 of the Florida Statutes (the portion addressing appraisers) and who performs appraisals in accordance with that statute
- a full-time graduate student in a FREC-approved college or university program, who is acting under direct supervision of a broker or appraiser and is performing tasks related to the educational program

- attorneys performing services within the scope of the legal profession
  - In Florida, any attorney who seeks to engage personally or employ other sales associates under his/her supervision must comply with the license law by obtaining a real estate broker's license. To do so, the attorney must meet experience requirements, complete education requirements, pass the state exam, and pay the required fees.
  - Any attorney wishing to operate under any name other than that of the individual must also comply with the Florida Fictitious Name Act by:
    - paying the appropriate license fees
    - registering and clearing any fictitious name(s) with the DRE
    - having the license issued under the registered fictitious name or entity

Unauthorized Practice of Law

Real estate licensees must exercise extreme caution to avoid performing duties that could otherwise be construed as the unauthorized practice of law. The unauthorized practice of law will expose the licensee to:

- disciplinary action by the FREC
- civil and/or criminal liability (depending on the severity of the offense)

For example, a buyer and seller have entered into a contract for purchase and sale that a real estate licensee has prepared. The buyer and seller agree to a change in terms, and the licensee crafts language in the rider to reflect the change. This is not okay; the licensee should not craft language, as doing so is considered the unauthorized practice of law.

FREC Rule Legal Update

The FREC has amended Rule 61j2-3.009(2), Florida Administrative Code. This rule change takes effect October 1, 2017, and now mandates 14 hours of continuing education to include:

1. three hours of core law
2. eight hours of specialty education
3. three hours of ethics and business practices

This rule is applicable to all licensees whose license expires on or after September 30, 2018.

House Bill 927 was signed by the governor into law and takes effect October 1, 2017. House bill 927 contains minor changes made to 475.451, F.S., concerning distance learning courses.

Repealed Rules

1. 475.6175, F.S.—the post-license education previously required for the registered trainee appraisers—is repealed.
2. Rule 61J2-4.009, F.A.C.—post-license education for registered trainee appraisers—is repealed.

Summary

License laws came about in the early 1920s in order to protect the general public. In order to be a holder of a real estate license in Florida, and in conjunction with all applicable laws, every applicant (unless exempt by law) must qualify through education and testing requirements. Once an individual receives a license, each licensee is charged with the responsibility of completing the required post-license education. Nonresidents are able to achieve licensing in Florida; however, in addition to all other requirements, the applicant must complete an irrevocable consent to service form, which designates the director of the Florida Division of Real Estate as the recipient of any legal notices against the nonresident. Mutual recognition is an agreement entered into between states allowing residents of one state to receive licenses in the other state. Finally, anyone who performs a real estate act for another and for compensation or the expectation of compensation (as defined by state law) must be a holder of a valid real estate license.

Review Questions

1. Florida real estate laws are passed by legislature primarily to:
   a. limit the number of licensees
   b. protect brokers from sellers
   c. protect the general public
   d. protect licensees from fraudulent actions

2. If applicable, which of the following would an applicant for a real estate license be required to reveal?
   a. maiden name
   b. speeding tickets
   c. parking tickets
   d. proof of citizenship

3. Max is licensed in a mutual recognition state and is applying for a Florida real estate license. In order to qualify he must:
   a. successfully pass a prelicense course
   b. complete the salesperson post-licensing class
   c. pass a 40-question test about Florida laws
   d. become a resident of Florida

4. Ian is registered as a broker associate. Which statement is true about Ian?
   a. Ian holds a broker associate license.
   b. Ian is inactive.
   c. A broker associate license is used to operate a real estate business.
   d. Ian owns and has his own real estate brokerage.

5. Which of the following would require a real estate license?
   a. Ruth sells cemetery lots for a cemetery association.
   b. Herman receives a salary to manage an apartment complex.
   c. Ben brokers the sales of businesses.
   d. Janet suggests in a conversation that the buyers finance the purchase of condos.

6. Jim is licensed and works for ABC Realty. Jim worked especially hard to sell Ms. Smith's home and she was very grateful. To show her appreciation, Ms. Smith gives and Jim accepts $100 to take his wife out to dinner. According to Florida laws:
   a. This is fine as long as Jim tells his broker.
   b. Jim has violated Chapter 475, F.S.
   c. Ms. Smith is the seller. She can compensate Jim.
   d. Jim must keep written records and report gifts received from clients.

7. A sales associate wants to apply for a broker's license. The associate:
   a. can do this at any time after receiving a sales license
   b. can apply after completing a minimum number of transactions
   c. cannot apply until one year passes after being licensed
   d. can apply after working for a broker for at least two years out of the previous five years

8. Diane lives in Tampa and sells homes for XYZ Development Corp. If Diane moves to Georgia and continues to work for the developer, Diane must:
   a. stop working for the developer in Florida
   b. hold a Georgia license to work for the developer
   c. do nothing because a license isn't needed to work for a developer
   d. within 60 days send the irrevocable consent to service form to the DRE and conform to all nonresident requirements

9. Fred received his first sales license November 29, 2017. His license expires:
   a. November 30, 2019
   b. September 30, 2019
   c. March 31, 2019
   d. January 31, 2019

10. A sales associate works during the week for Acme Realty and shows model homes on weekends for an owner-developer.
    a. This is legal only if both employers are not licensed or registered with the FREC.
    b. Only broker sales associates can have more than one employer.
    c. The associate is engaged in illegal activity.
    d. If salaried, a license is not required to work for an owner-developer.

11. To qualify as a resident for a real estate license, an applicant must:
    a. live in Florida for one year prior to applying
    b. have a Florida mailing address
    c. have a Florida driver's license
    d. intend to live in Florida for at least four months in any calendar year

12. A sales associate failed to complete the 45-hour post-licensing class. The associate wants to continue to practice real estate in Florida. The associate:
    a. does not have a license and must start over
    b. can pay a $1,000 fine and complete the class after renewal
    c. must pay a late fee in order to renew
    d. will be disciplined by the FREC

13. In order to renew an initial broker's license, the broker:
    a. must complete 60 hours of broker post-licensing classes and successfully pass the exams
    b. can complete 14 hours of continuing education in order to renew
    c. must pass another state exam and have an active license
    d. cannot have a nonresident license

14. Julio is an active real estate licensee in another state, and he wants to acquire a broker's license in Florida. Julio:
    a. must acquire a Florida sales license before applying for a broker's license in Florida
    b. must prove he has been actively licensed for at least 24 months in the past five years within the state where he is licensed when applying for a Florida broker's license
    c. cannot apply for a broker's license in Florida under any circumstances
    d. is a broker in another state so he can apply for a broker's license in Florida

15. Which of these persons is NOT exempt from FREC Course I?
    a. a practicing Florida attorney
    b. a person with a 4-year degree in real estate
    c. persons paid on commission for renting motel rooms
    d. anyone who advertises rentals for others

16. Rules and regulations passed by the FREC can be found in:
    a. F.S. 455
    b. Chapter 475, F.S.
    c. Chapter 61J2, FAC
    d. Florida Statute 83

17. A California real estate licensee sold two lots she owned in Florida.
    a. The licensee has broken Florida real estate laws.
    b. A real estate license to sell your own property is not required.
    c. Mutual recognition agreements allow this practice.
    d. Sales associates from other states must have a real estate license in Florida. Brokers from other states do not.

18. Jacob has an uncle who helped him sell a vacant lot Jacob owned. This is the second time his uncle has helped him market a property. Jacob's uncle refuses all compensation. What is true about this situation?
    a. No compensation is involved therefore no license is required.
    b. Jacob's uncle must have a real estate license.
    c. Relatives can help other relatives with properties, for a fee without a real estate license.
    d. Both Jacob and his uncle are practicing real estate without a license.

19. Harold failed the exam for FREC Course I a second time. In order to take the exam again, Harold must:
    a. reapply for the sales license
    b. retake the class
    c. pay the state an additional fee
    d. wait 1 year in order to retest

20. The decision regarding the acceptance of a licensee's application for licensure is made by the:
    a. Division of Real Estate
    b. Department of Business and Professional Regulation
    c. Division of Licensure and Testing
    d. Florida Real Estate Commission

3 REAL ESTATE LICENSE LAW AND COMMISSION RULES

KEY TERMS

active/inactive
canceled
cease to be in force
group license
involuntarily inactive

license authority voided
multiple licenses
null and void
voluntarily inactive

LEARNING OBJECTIVES

After completing this lesson, you will be able to:

- describe the composition, appointment, and member qualifications of the Florida Real Estate Commission
- define the powers and duties of the Florida Real Estate Commission
- explain the different licensure status
- distinguish between active and inactive license status
- describe the regulations regarding involuntarily inactive status
- distinguish between multiple and group licenses

REGULATION BY DEPARTMENT OF BUSINESS AND PROFESSIONAL REGULATION

Organizational Structure, Governing Body, and Enforcement

There are two key regulatory agencies related to real estate licensing in Florida. They are the Florida Real Estate Commission (FREC) and the Division of Real Estate (DRE). The FREC is the regulatory body whose purpose is to protect the general public by regulating:

- real estate brokers
- broker associates
- sales associates
- real estate schools
- real estate instructors

The DRE performs ministerial, administrative, and all functions concerning the regulation of the real estate industry. The DRE performs investigative duties that assist the FREC in disposing of their responsibilities as the body of government that acts as the licensing prosecuting unit.

> ## Coaching Tip
>
> Concerning license law, the DRE acts as the investigative unit while the FREC acts as the prosecuting unit.

Today, both the FREC and the DRE are administratively part of the Department of Business and Professional Regulation (DBPR). The DBPR is charged with regulating licensed professions and professionals within the state of Florida. There are many other departments that fall within the auspices of the DBPR ("Department").

Other divisions contained within the DBPR include:

- The Division of Technology—an outsource provider for exam development
- The Division of Professions and Regulation—responsible for administering and regulating professional boards. This division is also charged with the enforcement of regulated businesses

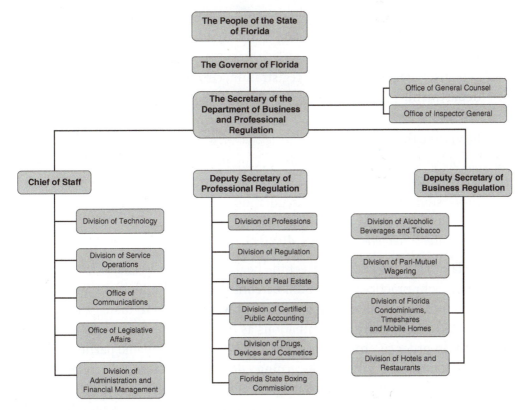

FIGURE 3.1 Florida Department of Business Professional Regulation Chart
Source: www.myfloridalicense.com

- The Division of Service Operations and Licensure—includes units such as:
  - The Bureau of Education and Testing—oversees education course content and exams for the various regulated professions
  - Central Intake Unit—responsible for license application processing
  - Central Customer Contact Center—handles public inquiries from the general public

Let's look at the functions of the FREC and the DRE.

Definitions: 455.01 F.S. (Excerpt of This Chapter of Law)

The definition of terms contained and used in 455.01 F.S. are:

1. "Board" means any board or commission, or other statutorily created entity to the extent such entity is authorized to exercise regulatory or rulemaking functions, within the department, including the Florida Real Estate Commission; except that, for F.S. 455.201-455.245, "board" means only a board, or other statutorily created entity to the extent such entity is authorized to exercise regulatory or rulemaking functions, within the Division of Certified Public Accounting, the Division of Professions, or the Division of Real Estate.
2. "Consumer member" means a person appointed to serve on a specific board or who has served on a specific board, who is not, and never has been, a member or practitioner of the profession, or of any closely related profession, regulated by such board.
3. "Department" means the Department of Business and Professional Regulation.
4. "License" means any permit, registration, certificate, or license issued by the department.
5. "Licensee" means any person issued a permit, registration, certificate, or license by the department.
6. "Profession" means any activity, occupation, profession, or vocation regulated by the department in the Divisions of Certified Public Accounting, Professions, Real Estate, and Regulation.

Legislative Intent: Requirements (F.S. 455.02)

License law was legislated to protect the health, safety, and general welfare of the consumer from practices that would be considered fraudulent by regulating the real estate profession. Bodies of government were created to manage the regulatory process and to make determinations as to whom a real estate license should be issued. In order to protect the general public from incapable parties transacting on behalf of others, rules concerning education and testing were enacted to ensure minimum competency on the part of the applicant.

Next, let's examine the responsibilities of a licensee who is a member of the armed forces (and his/her spouse) serving the country on active duty (455.02).

455.02 Licensure of members of the Armed Forces in good standing and their spouses with administrative boards.

Under Chapter 455.02, F.S., the following apply for any real estate licensee in good standing at time of service who is a member of the Armed Forces serving on active duty:

- Licensee is exempt from registering, paying dues or fees, or performing any other act on his or her part (such as completing continuing education), as long as he or she is a member of the Armed Forces and on active duty.
- Exemption will continue for a period of six months following discharge from active duty.
- Exemption will only apply if the licensee (while a member of the Armed Forces) does not engage in transactions in the private sector for profit.
- If the service is outside the state of Florida, the same exemption will apply to a licensed spouse.
- In essence, following the release from the Military, both licensees are issued temporary licenses that will expire six months after the date of issuance and are not renewable. The purpose is to allow the licensees time to complete the required education to renew their licenses.

Department Power and Duties (F.S. 455.203)

The Department of Business and Professional Regulation (DBPR or the Department) is responsible for regulating businesses and professions that fall under its jurisdiction. Chapter 455, F.S., created the authority for the DBPR to:

1. approve applications for professional licenses that meet all statutory and rule requirements for licensure
2. adopt rules for the biennial renewal and issuance of licenses (Please note that notwithstanding any law to the contrary the department is able to extend the license term to a 4-year license to certain licensees)
3. investigate complaints
4. issue subpoenas when conducting investigations
5. issue cease and desist orders
6. issue citations to licensed individuals

As we previously learned in Chapter 2, the DBPR is governed by Chapter 120, F.S. It is also structured according to Section 20.165, F.S. Most importantly, it is under the executive branch of the governor. Furthermore, the secretary is the person who heads the department. The secretary of the DBPR is not an elected position. It is an appointment. The appointment is given by the then presiding governor. The governor's appointment alone is not enough as the appointee must also be confirmed by the state's Senate. While there are no term limits, the secretary will normally serve until the next appointment.

There are a variety of divisions housed under the department. The divisions that bear the most relevance to real estate profession would be the following:

- Division of Service Operations
- Division of Professions
- Division of Real Estate
- Division of Florida Condominiums, Timeshares, and Mobile Homes

LICENSING EXAMINATIONS

Licensing exams are administered in Florida through the efforts of a testing vendor. Currently, that vendor is Pearson VUE. License exams are created in conjunction with a syllabus of subjects that will test the applicant's ability to practice real estate. Florida law provides that exams must be kept of each applicant who has previously sat for same for a minimum of two years. In addition to the exam, grades are not of public record. Statistics of applicants who have taken the exams, as well as pass/fail rates, are shared with schools and instructors of prelicensing courses. It is important to note that copying or stealing a state license exam is a third-degree felony in Florida.

Licenses, Fees, Statuses, and Renewals

License Fees

Applicants with existing licensing will be charged a fee for the biennial license. New applicants who have not previously held a license in Florida will be charged the same biennial fee plus the initial license application fee. The fees received from licensees, when required, fund the Real Estate Recovery Fund (the Recovery Fund will be discussed in greater detail in Chapter 6). In addition to the licensing fee, late renewals will be assessed a late fee. As all of the aforementioned subject fees can change from time to time, the reader is advised to contact the appropriate party to determine the current required amount(s).

Active License vs. Inactive License

In addition to the categories of licensure in Florida, licensees may also place their license in one of the following two types of statuses:

1. active status
2. inactive status

An **active** license is where the licensee is actively engaged in real estate activities as defined by the Commission. An **inactive** license is where the licensee is not actively engaged (or is not permitted to engage) in real estate activities.

There are two forms of inactive licensing:

1. Voluntary inactive
2. Involuntary inactive

Voluntary Inactive

Voluntary inactive status exists when a licensee chooses this status. In doing so, the licensee:

- may not engage in any real estate activity defined as requiring an active license during this voluntary inactivity
- may remain voluntary inactive indefinitely (This may be done as long as the licensee completes all required postlicense and continuing education, as the case may be, for the period necessary for the licensee to renew the license.)
- may reactivate the license at any time by notifying the FREC in writing by completing the required form

Involuntary Inactive

Involuntary inactive status occurs automatically when licensees fail to renew their license in a timely manner (the procedures for renewing a license will be discussed later in this section). This may also occur when a case for summary suspension is brought against a licensee. (Summary suspension will be discussed further in Chapter 6.) The following applies when a licensee's status is involuntarily inactive:

- The licensee may not engage in any real estate activity that requires an active license.
- The licensee may not remain in the involuntary inactive status indefinitely.
- The licensee must reactivate the license within two years following entry into the involuntary inactive status or subsequently face the license's becoming null and void.
- Due to the severity of this implication, 90 days prior to the expiration of an involuntary inactive license, the licensee is notified by the DBPR as to this important deadline.
- Depending on the amount of involuntary inactivity time that has passed, the licensee can redeem and/or reactivate the license by completing the required continuing education as follows:
  - 12 months and fewer—The licensee must complete 14 hours of approved education.
  - Greater than 12 months and up to 24 months—The licensee must complete a 28-hour FREC-approved reactivation course.
- If the license becomes null and void and the licensee wishes to remain within the real estate industry, he/she would be required to repeat the entire prelicensing process.

Other than the common cause of involuntary inactivity (not completing required continuing education), as previously mentioned, a licensee can be placed in an involuntary inactive status when emergency suspension actions against a licensee are necessary.

License That Ceases to Be in Force (F.S. 475.23)

Licenses that are issued by FREC, **cease to be in force** when required notification (within 10 days from either event below has occurred) has not been received by the FREC as a result of:

- any relocation requiring notification of a change of address occurs
- a change of association occurs

Void and Ineffective Licenses

A license is void when one of the following has occurred:

- The license has been expired for more than 24 months.
- The license has been revoked following a disciplinary action.

Whereby, void means that the action was involuntary in nature (i.e., failing to renew one's license on a timely basis, rendering the license involuntary inactive, and taking no action to activate the license within two years subsequent to the inactivity renders that license **null and void**). In addition, failure to complete sales or broker postlicense education requirements in a timely manner will render the license null and void.

Revocation is an act that always occurs as a result of disciplinary action taken against the licensee. This act permanently removes the individual from the real estate profession as a licensed party. However, licenses are not permanently revoked in the following two exceptions:

1. an applicant for licensure files an application containing false information
2. failing to complete continuing education requirements prior to executing a renewal for the forthcoming cycle

A license that is **canceled** is considered **license authority voided.** This may occur when a licensee chooses to no longer conduct real estate activities or merely because the licensee did not complete the required continuing education to renew the license and same expires. Cancelation of a license does not occur as a result of any disciplinary action.

A license is said to be ineffective under certain circumstances. This is not to say that a license does not exist; however, predicated on the circumstances specific to that individual, the licensee may not use it. The following are examples of an ineffective license:

- voluntarily inactivity
- involuntarily inactivity
- revocation of license
- suspension of license

Renewal

License Periods

Unlike other states, Florida has two license issuance/expiration periods. A license will bear an issuance/expiration date of either one of the following:

1. March 31
2. September 30

In either of these two cases, the license period is for two years with the exception of the initial license issuance. Currently, the initial issuance term may be no less than 18 months and no greater than 24 months. This is primarily due to the applicable date of license issue. That date will be March 31 or September 30 of any given year.

License Renewal/Military Exemptions (F.S. 455.02)

In order to renew a license, the required education applicable to that license must be completed. For example:

- A first-time renewal requires the licensee to complete the necessary *postlicense* education *prior to the submission* of a renewal form (45 hours for sales associate and 60 hours for broker postlicense education).
- For all subsequent renewals (following the initial renewal), the licensee must complete 14 hours of prescribed FREC-approved continuing education.
- As in the initial license renewal above, all education must be completed *prior to the submission* of a renewal form.

The licensee's signature on the renewal form acts as an oath that the licensee has completed his/her education requirement in conjunction with state requirements. Any renewal that occurs after the license has expired subjects the licensee to a late fee. It should be noted that licensees who do not complete their continuing education will not receive a renewal notice.

Some individuals are exempt from renewal requirements. As you learned earlier in this chapter, a licensee who is currently a member of the U.S. Armed Forces is exempt from license renewal requirements, including continuing education, while serving on active duty. The licensee will have up to six months from release of duty to renew the license without penalty or loss of license. In addition, if the spouse of any active member of the military (particularly one who is serving active duty in a place outside Florida) is also a *current* holder of a valid real estate license, both licensees will have six months after release from active duty to renew their licenses without loss or penalty. The aforementioned exemption will hold true only if the licensee is not active in the practice of real estate during this period.

TYPES OF REAL ESTATE LICENSES

Florida currently has two categories of licensure:

1. sales associate
2. broker

When sales associates become a broker candidate, they are faced with the decision of either:

1. remaining within the employ of their current sponsoring broker, or
2. starting their own brokerage company as a sponsoring broker.

However, it is important to note that by meeting all the qualifications to otherwise be a broker, if the candidate chooses to remain as a licensee under the supervision of another broker, a third category of licensing exists. This individual falls under the banner of a broker associate. It is important to note that this category is a hybrid between a sales associate and broker. Simply put, the individual operates as a sales associate with a broker's license. This is regardless of qualifications to be a broker. However, at any time the licensee elects, he/she can file with the department to operate his/her own brokerage.

Multiple and Group Licenses

An owner-developer who owns property in the name of several entities may submit proof that such entities are so connected or affiliated and that ownership is essentially held by the same individual(s). Any sales associate or broker associate working for the owner-developer may be issued a **group license**. In this situation, the licensee is considered to hold one license and to be working for one employer.

For example, a developer has five developments located in various parts of Florida, and each development operates under a different entity name. Each development utilizes local in-house sales staff for selling out the project. In order for the various in-house sales staff to work on all five development projects, the developer would need a group license issued.

Florida allows a broker, but not a broker associate or sales associate, to hold more than one license at any one time. In Florida, any broker who holds more than one broker license at one time is called a holder of **multiple licenses**. A sales or broker associate may *not* work for more than one broker at any one time or hold more than one Florida license. It should be noted that any licensee may hold licenses issued by other states.

For example, a broker has a brokerage company in South Florida where he/she is the principal broker. In another part of the state the same broker is offered an opportunity and wishes to be licensed under a different registration. The broker would then apply for multiple licensing.

REGISTRATION OF PROPRIETARY REAL ESTATE SCHOOLS

In addition to the aforementioned categories of real estate licensing, in Florida, all schools that intend on offering any type of prelicense curriculum must be registered and issued a permit. Exceptions to this rule include the following accredited institutions:

- universities
- colleges
- community colleges

An owner of a proprietary real estate school must exercise caution when advertising. Any inappropriate advertising may subject the school owner's permit to suspension. Some of these include:

- inaccurate, false, or misleading statements
- promises or guarantees of employment where none is provided by the school
- providing a student with questions from previous state exams
- offering refunds to a student who has failed the exam
- offering a guarantee program for the passage of the state exam if the student enrolls in the school

A school permit holder must be careful to observe Rule 61J2-17.015. This rule prohibits recruiting of students during classroom time.

DIVISION OF REAL ESTATE

Organizational Structure

Whereas the FREC is composed of appointees (individuals appointed by the governor), the Florida DRE is composed of state employees. The DRE is funded by fees assessed by the commission. Aside from key investigative functions, the DRE also:

- acts as the record keeper/file cabinet of the DBPR (e.g., maintaining records of each applicant exam, which is required to be kept and may not be disposed of for a period of two years subsequent to taking the examination, etc.)
- provides exams necessary for licensure

- Provides support services to FREC, such as:
  - legal services
  - administrative services

Although the state capital of Florida is Tallahassee, the primary offices of both the DRE and FREC are located in Orlando. The DRE makeup consists of the following:

- Whereas Commission members are appointed by the governor, the director of the DRE is appointed by the Secretary of the Department.
- DRE workers are employed by the Department as ancillary to the support of the FREC.

The DRE provides the FREC with the information critical to its ability to carry out, administer, and enforce the license law. Enforcement of the law is an essential procedure to protect the general public. It is for this basic and primary reason that license law came into effect throughout the nation.

As mentioned previously, the DRE represents one of the divisions within the DBPR. The DRE performs various functions essential for the FREC to carry out its duties. The DRE's primary and most important function that assists the FREC in carrying out its duties is that of investigative-related services.

The investigative function of the DRE involves screening applicants when the FREC is making a determination of license issuance, as well as investigation of potential violations by licensees. The DRE does *not* regulate commission rates.

The Division of Real Estate (DRE) Address Requirements

Although one does not need to be a Florida resident to hold a Florida real estate license, Chapter 455.275(1) requires that all licensees maintain an accurate and current mailing address with the DBPR. Post office boxes are deemed acceptable by the DBPR as a valid address. Licensees are required to immediately notify the DBPR of any change in their mailing address. Notification must be sent or received by the DBPR within 10 days from the change of address (Rule 61J2-10.038). Failure to do so in a timely manner subjects the licensee to disciplinary action. This would include a citation and a $100 fine. In addition, licensees who do not reside in Florida must execute an irrevocable consent to service. A resident who relocates outside of Florida (becomes a nonresident) has 60 days to comply with all nonresident requirements (see Chapter 2).

FUNCTIONS OF THE FLORIDA REAL ESTATE COMMISSION AND THE DIVISION OF REAL ESTATE

In order to simplify the reader's understanding of the functions of the FREC and the DRE, it should be noted that they work in tandem with each other. A description of each one's role in the licensing of professionals can be explained in the following way.

The FREC is empowered by the Florida Statutes to protect the general public. This is accomplished by regulating:

- real estate brokers and real estate brokerage firms
- broker associates
- sales associates
- real estate schools and instructors

The purpose is to foster the education of:

- real estate licensees
- permit holders

The powers and duties of the FREC fall into three general areas of responsibilities:

1. *executive powers* to regulate and enforce the license law
2. *quasi-legislative responsibilities* that include the power to:
   - enact and revise administrative rules and regulations
   - interpret questions regarding the practice of real estate
3. quasi-judicial responsibilities that include the power to:
   - grant or deny license applications
   - determine license law violations
   - administer penalties

Although the DRE performs various functions that are related to the regulation of real estate in Florida, the DBPR employs all DRE personnel to support FREC activities.

In essence, the FREC performs the administrative functions required to protect the general public. The functions of the FREC include regulating licensees through its ability to:

- grant or deny a license or registration
- suspend or revoke a license or registration
- administer disciplinary action including but not limited to:
  - fines
  - other forms of disciplinary action, such as requiring the licensee to sit for education course work in addition to a fine (This may be a necessary imposed action on the part of the FREC in order to educate the licensee to avoid future infractions of license law.)

In addition to the aforementioned, the FREC has a duty to educate members of the real estate profession. They decide on questions and rules of practice. Furthermore:

- The FREC may inspect and audit real estate licensees and permitted schools.
- They also possess the power to discipline licensees.

- When criminal violations occur, the FREC has the duty to inform the state attorney.
- When a disciplinary action occurs against a licensee, the FREC is further required to notify the Florida Division of Land Sales, Condominiums, and Mobile Homes.
- The Department of Legal Affairs provides the legal counsel necessary for the FREC to administer license law.

Chapter 61J2-20—Rules Governing Internal Organization and Operation

Chapter 61j2-20 covers some of the following areas of organization and operation of the FREC:

1. 61J2-20.009 Probable Cause Panel
2. 61J2-20.040 Membership
3. 61J2-20.048 Principal Office
4. 61J2-20.049 Commission Member Compensation
5. 61J2-20.051 Authorized Signatures on Final Orders
6. 61J2-20.052 Designation of Official Reporter
7. 61J2-20.054 Public Comment

Coaching Tips

Below are actual excerpts from 61j2-20

61J2-20.009 Probable Cause Panel.
A probable cause panel shall determine if probable cause exists that a licensee, registrant, a permit holder, or the subject of the investigation violated Chapter 475, Part I, F.S., or any of the Commission's rules. A probable cause panel shall consist of at least one present member of the Commission. As provided in Section 455.225(4), F.S., one of the panel members may be a former member of the Commission.

Rulemaking Authority 475.05 FS. Law Implemented 455.225 FS. History– New 11-21-79, Amended 3-15-82, 11-16-83, Formerly 21V-20.09, Amended 6-28-93, Formerly 21V-20.009, Amended 11-8-12.

61J2-20.040 Membership.

- The Florida Real Estate Commission, created by Chapter 475, Part I, F.S., is a regulatory agency and performs its functions pursuant to Chapter 475, Part I, F.S., and such other functions as may be delegated by law. The Commission's membership as set forth in Chapter 475, Part I, F.S., shall consist of seven members who shall elect from the members a chairperson and vice chairperson.

- Three consecutive unexcused absences or absences constituting 50% or more of the Commission's meetings within any 12-month period shall cause the membership in question to become void, and the position shall be considered vacant. An unexcused absence is one where no advance notice of an absence is given to the chairperson, vice chairperson or Director of the Division or, if there is advance notice of an absence, no explanation of the absence is given.

Rulemaking Authority 475.05 FS. Law Implemented 455.207(3), 475.02 FS. History–New 1-1-80, Formerly 21V-20.40, Amended 11-8-92, 7-20-93, Formerly 21V-20.040.

61J2-20.042 Chairperson.
Rulemaking Authority 475.05 FS. Law Implemented 120.53, 455.207 FS. History–New 1-1-80, Formerly 21V-20.42, Amended 6-28-93, Formerly 21V-20.042, Repealed 9-6-07.

61J2-20.047 Official Records.
Rulemaking Authority 475.05 FS. Law Implemented 120.53, 475.021 FS. History–New 1-1-80, Formerly 21V-20.47, Amended 6-28-93, Formerly 21V-20.047, Amended 11-10-97, Repealed 10-7-12.

61J2-20.048 Principal Office.
The principal office of the Commission shall be located at 400 West Robinson Street, Orlando, Florida 32801-1757. The Commission may also be contacted through the Department of Business and Professional Regulation, 1940 North Monroe Street, Tallahassee, Florida 32399-0750.

Rulemaking Authority 475.05 FS. Law Implemented 120.53, 455.205 FS. History–New 1-1-80, Formerly 21V-20.48, Amended 7-20-93, Formerly 21V-20.048.

61J2-20.049 Commission Member Compensation.
Unless otherwise provided by law, a Commission member shall be compensated $50.00 for each day in attendance at an official meeting of the Commission, including Probable Cause Panel Meetings, and for each day the member participates in any other business involving the Commission. "Other business involving the Commission" shall be defined as:

1. Attendance at instructors' seminars sponsored by the Commission.
2. Appearances before a legislative committee, upon direction of the chairperson of the Commission or the chairperson of the Committee.
3. Attendance at a meeting with the staff or contractors of the BPR at the request of the Secretary of the BPR or the Division Director.
4. Attendance at a conference or trade association meeting in the capacity of a member of the Commission.

5. Attendance at the Florida Realtor's Legislative Days in Tallahassee in the capacity of a member of the Commission regarding legislation being promoted by the Commission.

Rulemaking Authority 475.05 FS. Law Implemented 455.207(4) FS. History–New 9-17-81, Amended 10-19-83, Formerly 21V-20.49, Amended 10-15-91, 7-20-93, Formerly 21V-20.049, Amended 6-5-96.

61J2-20.051 Authorized Signatures on Final Orders.

A Final Order of the Commission may be signed by either the chairperson or vice chairperson of the Commission or the Division Director. Serving on a probable cause panel does not preclude the chairperson or the vice chairperson from signing a Final Order of the Commission.

Rulemaking Authority 120.53(1)(a),(b), 475.05 FS. Law Implemented 455.225(6), 475.03(1), 475.10 FS. History–New 5-22-83, Formerly 21V-20.51, Amended 6-28-93, Formerly 21V-20.051.

61J2-20.052 Designation of Official Reporter.

1. The Commission designates the Department of Business and Professional Regulation (BPR) as its official reporter for the purpose of publishing and indexing by subject matter, after a proceeding has been held, all orders rendered which affect substantial interests.

2. The BPR maintains and stores such orders in the offices of the agency clerk at the Northwood Centre, 1940 North Monroe Street, Tallahassee, Florida 32399-0750. The agency clerk's office is open to the public between the hours of 9:00 a.m. and 4:00 p.m., excluding holidays and weekends. For further information regarding the indexing of orders by the BPR, refer to Rule Chapter 61-14, F.A.C.

Rulemaking Authority 475.05 FS. Law Implemented 120.53(2) FS. History– New 8-23-93, Amended 4-19-94.

61J2-20.054 Public Comment.

The Florida Real Estate Commission invites and encourages all members of the public to provide comment on matters or propositions before the Commission or a committee of the Commission. The opportunity to provide comment shall be subject to the following:

1. Members of the public will be given an opportunity to provide comment on subject matters before the Commission after an agenda item is introduced at a properly noticed Commission meeting.

2. Members of the public shall be limited to three (3) minutes to provide comment. This time shall not include time spent by the presenter responding to questions posed by Commission members, staff or Commission counsel. The chair of the Commission may extend the time to provide comment if time permits.

> **3.** Members of the public shall notify Commission staff in writing of their interest to be heard on a proposition or matter before the Commission. The notification shall identify the person or entity, indicate its support, opposition, or neutrality, and identify who will speak on behalf of a group or faction of persons.

COMPOSITION AND QUALIFICATIONS OF FREC MEMBERS

The FREC is comprised of seven members. The seven members receive minimal compensation in the form of a minimal per diem amount plus any expense reimbursement relating to direct service performed on behalf of the Commission. The makeup of the seven-member FREC consists of:

- four members who must hold or have held active Florida real estate brokers' licenses. An active license must be validly held by each member for a period not less than five years prior to serving on the Commission
- two members who must be individuals from the general public who have never held or been licensed as either a broker or sales associate
- one member who must be either an active broker or sales associate. The active license status must be held by this member for at least two years prior to serving on the Commission

At least one of the seven members of the Commission must be 60 years of age or older. The seven members of the Commission are appointed by the governor and serve a 4-year term. Term limits consist of not more than two consecutive terms. Commission meetings are held no fewer than 12 times per year. Of the seven Commission members, a Chairperson and Vice Chairperson is appointed.

The Commission and its members are accountable to the office of the presiding governor. The governor bears the responsibility of supervising the Commission and its members. As a result of their Commission responsibilities and activities, all seven Commission members receive total exculpation (release from blame or liability) from any civil claims that may result while in office and performing Commission service.

Meetings and Minutes

As previously mentioned, the FREC meetings occur not less than 12 times per year. FREC meetings are open to the public. In certain cases, attending a FREC meeting may qualify a licensee for continuing education credit. Minutes of each meeting are kept and archived. These minutes are available to the public.

Duties and Powers of the Commission

Specific Areas of Responsibility, Rule Making, Education, and Discipline

In addition to the previously mentioned activities, the FREC has the following powers and duties:

- adopt a seal that when placed on official documents will act as prima facie (on face value) evidence of the documents' authenticity (Chapter 475.10, F.S.)
- create or change (as the case may be) the rules and regulations that affect brokers, broker associates, sales associates, and authorized licensed real estate instructors (Chapter 475.05, F.S.)
- create and mandate the required syllabus identifying the minimal and acceptable course content required for a person to hold a real estate license. In addition, the FREC has the ability to create rules and regulations as to what schools may offer within approved course content (Chapter 475.04, F.S.)
- create rules and regulations pertaining to license law that dictate the allowed practices and activities of a licensee. They have the power to discipline licensees (Chapter 475.25, F.S.). The FREC is an administrative regulatory body that governs all licensees under its jurisdiction. It has the power to inspect and audit brokers, broker associates, sales associates, and authorized licensed real estate schools and instructors (Chapter 475.5016, F.S.). However, it is the DRE that actually carries out the rules, regulations, and policies of the FREC.
- administer the FREC Education and Research Foundation. The purpose of this foundation is to promote projects that educate licensees and the public in real estate matters.
- create license fees and/or other miscellaneous fees associated with the holding of a Florida real estate license. Such fees include exam fees, initial license fees, and any Real Estate Recovery Fund assessment, if necessary. (The Real Estate Recovery Fund will be discussed in greater detail in Chapter 6.)

Coaching Tips

Because fees are subject to change at any time, please consult the DRE when you apply for a real estate license for the most updated amount.

As mentioned previously within this chapter, the FREC is required to report all known or suspected criminal activities to the appropriate agencies for further investigation and/or prosecution. As a commission, the FREC merely administers the license law (as it applies to all licensees). It is not permitted to impose criminal penal sanctions, such as prison sentencing.

While the FREC has the power to create or change the rules and regulations that affect brokers, broker associates, sales associates, and authorized licensed real estate instructors, the DRE actually carries out the rules, regulations, and policies of the FREC.

THE REAL ESTATE EDUCATION AND RESEARCH FOUNDATION

The Real Estate Education and Research Foundation was created to develop and fund programs directly designed to further real estate research and education to both the general public and real estate licensees.

Created in 1985 by the state legislature, this foundation fell under the direct control of the FREC. To further the education of the real estate issues pertaining to Florida, the foundation seeks information from various people to accomplish its goal. This includes:

- real estate schools
- colleges and universities
- real estate licensees
- the general public

Summary

The Florida DRE provides investigative, record-keeping, and exam services, and as a result of its functions, the DRE provides the FREC with the information critical to their ability to carry out, administer, and enforce license law.

Enforcement of the law is a critical and necessary procedure to protect the general public. It is for this primary reason that license law came into effect throughout the nation. Today, each state in the United States has enacted its own license laws.

The FREC in essence performs the required administrative functions to protect the general public that include regulating licensees through the ability to:

- grant or deny a license or registration
- suspend or revoke a license or registration
- administer fines
- impose other forms of disciplinary action that may include but not be limited to:
    - requiring the licensee to sit for education course work in addition to a fine. (This may be a necessarily imposed action on the part of FREC in order to educate the licensee to avoid future infractions of license law.)

Review Questions

1. Sal works for ABC Realty in Tampa, Florida, but lives in Palm Harbor. Recently, Sal moved to Lutz but still works for ABC Realty. Sal:
   a. has 10 days to register his new address with the DBPR
   b. works in the same location. There is no paperwork
   c. must register the employer within 10 days
   d. has 60 days to notify the DBPR of an address change

2. John is registered as the broker of record for three different companies. John:
   a. is in violation of F.S. 475
   b. has a group license
   c. holds multiple licenses
   d. can have only one real estate license in Florida

3. Jake has legally obtained a group license. This means Jake:
   a. works for an owner-developer
   b. owns and operates more than one business
   c. supervises others in real estate matters
   d. is the broker of record for several employees

4. Which of the statements below is FALSE about the FREC?
   a. Commissioners only work for the Florida governor.
   b. Four commissioners must own and operate real estate businesses.
   c. One commissioner can work as a sales associate.
   d. Commissioners are employed by the state of Florida.

5. Kim and Kelly are married, and both are real estate licensees. Kim was called to active duty with the National Guard, and Kelly left the state as a result. Which statement is true about their license renewals?
   a. Kim is exempt from renewal requirements, but Kelly is not.
   b. They must renew their licenses within six months of Kim's discharge.
   c. There are no legal exceptions from license renewal requirements.
   d. The licenses are automatically canceled.

6. Sonia is going to take a break from practicing real estate and informs her broker she will no longer be an employee.
   a. Her sales license will be canceled.
   b. The license is involuntarily inactive.
   c. The broker must report the change in employment.
   d. Sonia must inform the DRE within 10 days of the change.

7. Tyrone let his third license expire but changed his mind seven months later. In this situation, Tyrone:
   a. must take FREC Course I and begin again
   b. may complete a 28-hour continuing education course and reactivate his license
   c. has a license categorized as voluntary inactive
   d. holds an involuntarily, inactive license

8. Kaitlyn let her third license expire but reconsidered 13 months later. Kaitlyn:
   a. must take FREC Course I and begin again
   b. may complete a 28-hour course and reactivate her license
   c. has a license labeled voluntary inactive
   d. has a canceled license

9. George is the only broker for ABC Realty. George's license is suspended. The licenses of the associates registered as George's employees are:
   a. involuntarily inactive
   b. automatically canceled
   c. null and void
   d. effective

10. The offices of the DRE, part of the Department of Business and Professional Regulation, are located in:
    a. the various real estate districts
    b. Tallahassee
    c. Orlando
    d. Miami

11. The content of all real estate exams is mandated by the:
    a. DBPR
    b. DRE
    c. Bureau of Education and Testing
    d. FREC

12. Frank's broker's license expired 26 months ago. As a result, Frank:
    a. has a null and void license
    b. can reactivate by completing a prescribed 28-hour course
    c. lost the broker's license but can practice as a sales associate
    d. must pay a late fee as well as the license fee to bring the license up-to-date

13. Lila changed her address and has not notified the FREC. Lila's license:
    a. no longer exists
    b. is involuntarily inactive
    c. has been canceled
    d. is an effective license

14. Members of the FREC are appointed by the governor for a period of:
    a. 1 year
    b. 2 years
    c. 4 years
    d. 8 years

15. Members of the FREC are currently paid:
    a. $51,000
    b. nothing
    c. on a per diem basis
    d. expenses plus $50 a day when on Commission business

16. One exception to permanent revocation of a license occurs when:
    a. a license was renewed prior to completing the required education
    b. the cause of revocation was unlawful activity in another state
    c. the individual can prove a change of character
    d. a pardon and restoration of voting rights are obtained

17. Osvaldo's broker lost her license and Osvaldo's license is involuntarily inactive. In order to have a valid real estate license at this point, Osvaldo:
    a. must take the state-licensing exam again
    b. can reassociate with a new broker as an employer
    c. must wait 30 days for a new broker to be appointed
    d. must file an exception before 30 days pass

18. The FREC's powers and duties would include all these activities EXCEPT:
    a. adopting a seal that is evidence in court that a document is legal
    b. writing rules that become legal requirements for real estate practitioners
    c. revising administrative rules about the practice of real estate
    d. keeping the Commission's records

19. FREC meetings require the presence of a quorum of members and must occur:
    a. biannually
    b. quarterly
    c. monthly
    d. bimonthly

20. Susan was so busy moving to her new house that she forgot to notify the DBPR of her change of address. When she realized her lapse, she sent in her new address with a sincere letter of apology.
    a. A citation with a $100 fine will be issued.
    b. This is OK because it was an accident.
    c. Susan's license is subject to a 60-day suspension.
    d. The license is involuntarily inactive.

CHAPTER 4

LAW OF AGENCY—RELATIONSHIPS AND DISCLOSURES

KEY TERMS

- agent
- consent to transition to transaction broker
- customer
- dealing at arm's length
- designated sales associates
- dual agency
- fiduciary
- general agent
- limited representation
- nonrepresentation
- principal
- residential sale
- single agent
- special agent
- subagency
- transaction broker

LEARNING OBJECTIVES

After completing this lesson, you will be able to:

- describe which provisions of the Brokerage Relationship Disclosure Act apply only to residential real estate sales and list types of real estate activities that are exempt from the disclosure requirements
- define a residential transaction
- distinguish among nonrepresentation, single agent, and transactional broker
- list and describe the duties owed in the various authorized relationships
- compare and contrast the fiduciary duties owed in a single agent relationship and the duties owed in a transaction broker relationship
- describe the disclosure procedures for the various authorized relationships
- describe the required consent and format of the various disclosure forms
- explain the procedure for transition from a single agent to a transaction broker
- describe the disclosure requirements for nonresidential transactions where the buyer and seller have assets of $1 million or more
- list the events that will cause an agency relationship to be terminated
- distinguish between and explain the disclosure requirements and forms pursuant to Florida Statute
- identify information that is subject to public record

LAW OF AGENCY—AUTHORIZED RELATIONSHIPS, DUTIES, AND DISCLOSURES

Concept of Agency

Historical perspective of agency relationships

Due to wide confusion by the general public when engaging the services of a real estate licensee, all states in the union enacted laws governing how working relationships would be treated and administered. Although each state has its own set of laws regarding these working relationships, they are universally similar in nature. In short, some of the common problems that arose on the part of the consumer stemmed mostly from:

- representation
- issues concerning disclosure

For many years, it was unclear to the consumer as to which party an agent was working for. This led to the use of the term *caveat emptor* (let the buyer beware). This concept will be discussed later in this chapter. As a result of this confusion, caveat emptor contributed further to a lack of disclosure(s) made to the consumer in a real property transaction.

Based on the aforementioned, on October 1, 1997, Florida enacted the Florida Brokerage Relationship Disclosure Act. The act has since been modified and amended several times. The Florida Brokerage Relationship Disclosure Act was created to provide clarity to the consumer about the relationships between licensees and buyers and sellers in real estate transactions. This was achieved via required disclosures on the part of a licensee.

Any person who transacts business activities on behalf of another (normally for compensation) is commonly referred to as an **agent**. The activities of an agent are regulated and governed by the law of agency.

In Florida, a buyer, seller, landlord, or tenant has only three choices concerning representation. A real estate licensee may only transact as one of the following:

1. a nonrepresentative (no brokerage relationship)
2. a single agent for either a buyer or a seller
3. a transaction broker

The buyer or seller, in conjunction with the broker, must decide which option best serves the parties. We will look at each of these options individually in greater detail later in this chapter.

As of October 1, 1997, dual agency relationships are no longer permitted within the state of Florida. A dual agency relationship is defined as a relationship in which the agent (broker) represents both the buyer (or lessee) and the seller (or lessor) within the same transaction. Therefore, the licensee (a dual agent) has an agency relationship with both the buyer (lessee) and seller (lessor). In essence, the broker is representing two principals in the same transaction. Dual agency results in a very dangerous situation for the licensee because of the inability on the licensee's part to provide certain responsibilities to both parties within the transaction at the same time. To say the least, "No one can serve two masters." That is, in a dual agency relationship, it is highly improbable that the licensee can serve both parties with the same undivided loyalty and confidentiality. It is for these reasons that the Florida legislature and regulators have passed laws that have totally *outlawed dual agency* as an authorized and acceptable type of relationship in Florida. In fact, Florida is the first state in the union to totally outlaw this type of agency relationship. Therefore, dual agency is never legal in Florida. It is illegal for any agent to represent both parties in the same transaction as a single agent. However, a real estate licensee can serve both sides as a transaction broker. The licensee can also work with one side as a single agent and another in a no representation relationship.

Later, we will go over the features the three types of relationships (nonrepresentation, single agency, and transaction broker) and the disclosures that licensees must make in each situation. Keep in mind that these disclosures apply to residential sales transactions only. In these types of transactions, disclosure forms are issued in writing; however, the signature of the party receiving the disclosure is preferred but not required. In the event that the recipient of the disclosure form refuses to sign, the licensee should make a note of the party's refusal to sign the form, write the party's name(s) and the date, and save in his/her files for a period of not less than five years. This would apply regardless of if a contract was formed. The only disclosure form that requires the principal's signature at all times is the *consent to transition to transaction broker*. From time to time the need may arise for a licensee to change his/her relationship with a principal; therefore, the consent to transition form is used to apprise a principal of the agent's need to transition to another authorized form of agency relationship. Prior to any transition on the part of a licensee, the written consent of the principal is required.

Coaching Tips

- An agent is one who transacts business on behalf of another usually for a fee.
- A principal or client is the party that hires the agent under a working agreement.
- Agency is the term for the working relationship created by employment
- Customer is the party that the agent is hired to bring to the principal. The customer can be a buyer, seller, landlord, or tenant. That will depend on who is the principal/client.
- Fiduciary is the role an agent takes on when hired under a single agent relationship. It is a relationship of the highest form of trust.

STATUTORY AND COMMON LAW

Most of our real estate terminology is derived from the old English feudal system. As a result of time and progress, laws concerning how agency relationships (working relationships) are derived and treated stem from two primary types of prevailing law:

1. statutory law
2. common law

Statutory Law

Statutory law is a derivative of the legislative procedure toward creation of law. It is law that is enacted via state legislature. Any person working on behalf of another, as an agent, will fall under the auspices of the state law of agency. In addition to the aforementioned, Florida Real Estate Commission (FREC) rules will also come into play and will dictate how an agent may operate within an agency relationship in Florida.

Common Law

Where statutory law is legislatively enacted and created, common law is derived from case law or, in other words, from the courts. Cases heard by the courts resulted in judgments. Today, it is these judgments that guide us in interpreting agency activities as well as dispute resolution. Irrespective of common law, the student should be aware that statutory law can supersede that of common law.

TYPES OF AGENTS

When we examine the various types of agents, it is important to note that the level or scope of authority extended to an agent is the sole determining factor as to which type of agency category the relationship falls within. Therefore, there are three major types of agencies:

1. universal
2. general
3. special

Universal Agency

In a universal agency, the agent is given the legal authority to transact matters of all types on all transactions for the principal. Universal agencies are extremely rare and discouraged by the courts because the agent's powers are so broad. One of the few examples of this type of agency has become more visible recently in professional sports. Many athletes are hiring universal agents who have the authority to:

- negotiate salary with a team owner
- select and manage all the player's investments
- negotiate endorsement contracts

Another example of a universal agent is a person responsible for taking care of an elderly family member who no longer can look after himself/herself. This may include:

- handling of bank accounts
- sale of real and/or personal property
- any other matter requiring decision or action

General Agency

The second type of agency is a general agency. A **general agent** is authorized to act for the principal in a specific business or trade. Unlike a universal agency where the universal agent transacts on all matters related to all transactions for the principal, a general agency allows the agent to transact on all matters concerning one or more (but not all) matters. A general agent operates on a narrower scope of authority to that of a universal agent. Some examples of general agency include:

- a property manager who manages property for the owner
- a real estate sales associate who is a general agent for the broker in the real estate business
- a sales representative in any field who sells products for a company

Based on the type of agreement between the parties, a general agent would have the ability to bind their principal. Next, let's look at an example of how this would work:

> **Example** A property manager experiences a water main break in the property. The owner is away on vacation and is unreachable. The repair will cost $5,000. As this would most probably be deemed an emergency repair, the manager calls the plumber to effectuate the repair without obtaining or discussing same with the owner. Upon return, the property owner is now bound (by the managing agent's action) to pay for this repair.

Special Agency

The third type of agency is a special agency or agent. In a special agency, the **special agent** is merely authorized to perform a specific act or transaction. A very narrow scope of authority is granted to the agent. Some examples of special agency include:

- a real estate broker who is authorized to facilitate a sale for a home
- a person who has power of attorney to sign a deed for someone

In the first example, the agent merely receives the assignment of bringing prospective buyers to the table for the seller/principal. Unlike the universal and the general agent, a special agent may not bind the principal within this relationship. Special agents operate within the narrowest scope of authority. This agency relationship is created by the listing agreement. It also is limited to one transaction—facilitating the selling of the property.

Coaching Tips

There is a fourth type of agency category that exists called an agency coupled with an interest. Although this agency is not as common as the previous three, the student should have a practical understanding of its existence as well as its meaning. This type of relationship exists when an agent has some form of interest within the property in question.

For example, a developer wishes to construct an office building for income-producing purposes. Whereby construction and completion dictate the project obtain some form of financing, the developer engages the agent to procure financing in exchange for the exclusive right to lease and manage the property upon its completion. Obviously, the appointment cannot legitimately commence prior to construction and completion of the building. Provided that the agent is successful in arranging financing of the project, this type of agency relationship:

- is nonterminable by the death of the developer/principal
- may not be revoked by the principal

Coaching Tips

- A universal agency is the broadest in scope of the different agency types.
- A general agency is more limited in scope of authority than a universal agency. A property manager is a good example of a common general agent relationship.
- A special agency provides the narrowest scope of authority when compared to that of a general or universal agency.
- Power of attorney can create a universal or general agency.
- A broker under a listing agreement has a special agency with the principal.

FIDUCIARY RELATIONSHIPS

A fiduciary relationship is created when the agent is employed under an agreement. The agent is then referred to as a fiduciary. A fiduciary is anyone appointed to represent or transact business on another's behalf. This appointment bears the highest form of a trust relationship. A fiduciary or fiduciary relationship is created when a principal engages the services of a real estate licensee under a single agent relationship. Other examples of fiduciaries consist of banks and attornies. For example, with banking, the trust relationship begins with the deposits of funds. In conjunction with this, it is likely that any person would rely on those funds being available on demand.

Responsibilities to the Principal: Fiduciary Responsibilities

When a single agency relationship is created, the agent takes on fiduciary responsibilities to the principal. It is important to note that in Florida, the only fiduciary real estate relationship is a single agent relationship. As a result of these fiduciary responsibilities, the agent is often referred to as a **fiduciary**. This means that the agent:

- owes loyalty to the principal
- must act in the principal's best interest

An agent's responsibilities to the principal consist of the following:

- loyalty
- obedience
- disclosure
- accountability
- care
- confidentiality

Let's look at these responsibilities in more detail.

Loyalty

In an agency relationship, the agent's fiduciary responsibilities include providing the principal with undivided loyalty. This means that the interests of the principal come before all others. The interests of the agent are secondary to those of the principal. Let's examine this duty of loyalty as it applies to a real estate agent.

If an agent works for a seller, the agent occupies a position of trust that requires loyalty to the seller. This means that the agent must always act in the best interests of the seller. It further requires placing the seller's interests above all others including those of the agent. To safeguard the interests of the seller, the law prohibits several specific acts that would represent a failure to be loyal to the seller. An agent is prohibited from:

- making a secret profit
- violating the seller's confidence
- failing to disclose the purchaser's identity
- acting as a dual agent
- acting in an undisclosed dual capacity
- holding, not immediately submitting and communicating an offer to purchase

An agent is prohibited from receiving any additional fee or profit over and above the commission *unless* it is done with the knowledge and consent of the seller.

Example A seller lists a house for sale for $100,000 with a broker. A purchaser wants to buy the house for a lower price and offers the broker $500 if the broker convinces the seller to sell the house for $95,000. The broker may not legally accept such an offer.

Obedience

The agent must follow all of the principal's instructions as long as the instructions are:

- legal
- ethical
- reasonable

As an example of illegal instructions, a principal/seller of property instructs the single agent to exclude members of protected classes as potential purchasers. As the statement and act violate federal fair housing laws, the single agent is directed to withdraw from the relationship.

> **Coaching Tips**
>
> When a principal insists that an agent obey the performance of an illegal act, the agent is directed to withdraw completely from the relationship. In addition, the agent may not substitute his/her judgment or opinion for that of the principal.

Disclosure

The agent is required at all times to fully disclose to all interested parties within a transaction all material facts concerning or affecting (adversely or otherwise) the value of the property in question. The presenting of all offers and counteroffers must be made in a timely manner. This disclosure must take place prior to the parties' entering into a contract of sale and purchase. Failure to disclose will result in disciplinary action against the licensee committing the violation. All offers, written or otherwise, must be submitted promptly. When more than one written offer is received, all offers must be submitted in one sitting. The agent may present the offers in any order he/she deems fit for the principal. The agent is not allowed to hold one offer in the expectation of receiving another offer later, even if it would be a better offer. The agent always owes full disclosure to the principal.

Accountability (accounting for all funds entrusted in the holder's possession)

In Florida, a real estate broker entrusted with funds belonging to others must place these funds in a separate account known as an escrow, special, or trust account. An agent is responsible for an accounting and/or the remittance of all valuable consideration belonging to others that is entrusted to the agent. This further includes maintaining:

- appropriate books and records
- evidence of all receipts or expenditures from an agent escrow (trust) account

Care (Skill, Care, and Diligence)

Agents should not be negligent in the disposition of their obligations within the relationship. The broker is a licensed professional and, as such, is expected to exert due diligence in performing on the principal's behalf. Failure to do so is considered negligence. When a licensee is acting on behalf of a principal, the licensee must exercise extreme care when disposing of his/her duties. The agent must possess skill while simultaneously exercising required diligence.

Confidentiality

When information concerning the principal is entrusted with the agent, the agent may not divulge to another party any information that would be deemed sensitive or damaging in nature to the principal without the principal's prior consent. In particular, this would include any information that could or would adversely affect the principal's position within a transaction.

> **Coaching Tips**
>
> A good rule to follow is to never mention anything concerning the principal in his/her absence that you would not say in his/her presence.

One convenient memory device for the fiduciary responsibilities that an agent owes to a principal under an agency relationship is to remember the mnemonic LOW PAIN:

- *L*oyalty to the principal
- *O*bedience to the principal
- *W*ritten offers must be submitted
- *P*ersonally act for the principal
- *A*ccount for all monies
- *I*nform the principal of all material facts
- *N*ot be negligent

Dealing at Arm's Length

In any real estate transaction, it is important that the parties are dealing at arm's length. **Dealing at arm's length**, or an arm's length transaction, can be defined as any transaction where buyers and sellers or landlords and tenants have no relationship to each other. In other words, they are unrelated parties. The purpose behind an arm's length transaction is to ensure that all interested parties to a transaction are acting in their own interest and are not subject to any influences from the other opposing party. When the parties are negotiating, this concept enables all interested parties to deal from equal positions of strength. It should be noted that any interest in property must be disclosed.

Caveat Emptor (Let the Buyer Beware)

Prior to the early 1920s and creation of state license laws regulating the real estate profession, many transactions experienced acts that today would most likely be defined or considered as fraud. During these times, the purchasing party was warned using the expression *caveat emptor*. Caveat emptor is a Latin phrase for "let the buyer beware." This term is most commonly associated with a purchaser or renter of real property. The purpose behind its use and meaning is to warn the consumer/buyer/renter to perform due diligence (homework) before consummating the transaction.

For example, when purchasing a home, a buyer would engage a team of professionals to assist them with the closing (see Chapter 1). This would probably include a full physical inspection of the property by a home inspector. This process will provide the buyer with latent defects that might be contained in the property. A latent defect is any defect not visible to the human eye without further inspection. Prior to the closing, the buyer is no longer just relying on the seller's statement as to the condition of the subject property. Today and as a result of cases such as *Johnson v. Davis*, disclosure of the property condition is an obligation that falls on the seller.

In the past, the real estate brokerage profession operated in a legal environment that can be succinctly described by the legal phrase caveat emptor. Caveat emptor describes a general legal environment in which the burden of obtaining information about a property was almost entirely the buyer's responsibility, not the seller's or the seller's agent's. Under caveat emptor, for example, an agent working for the seller was under no obligation to voluntarily disclose pertinent information about a property to the buyer. The agent was bound only to tell the truth when he/she said anything about the property but was not obligated to say anything. If buyers wanted to obtain pertinent information about the property, it was their responsibility to get it themselves. During the last half of the twentieth century, caveat emptor was gradually replaced by an environment that was much more favorable to the buyer. In today's environment, the broker has a much greater responsibility to safeguard the interests of the buyer as the customer, even if the broker represents the seller as the principal.

Dual Agency

In Florida, dual agency relationships are not permitted. This illegal practice is covered under the Florida Brokerage Relationship Disclosure Act of 1997. **Dual agency** is defined under the Act as when any agent (individual or business entity) represents or attempts to represent both parties (buyer and seller or landlord and tenant) in the same transaction. This practice (while perfectly legal in certain states within the nation) is not allowed in the state of Florida. In Florida, an agent may only represent:

- a seller
- a buyer
- a landlord or tenant but never both in the same transaction

It is also a common fallacy to believe that two (2) separate agents within the same broker or brokerage may safely handle each party separately without creating a dual agency. This is not the case. In fact, a dual agent or agency is created when the broker or brokerage represents or attempts to represent both parties to a transaction. Simply put, a dual agency is created when the broker has two principals within the same transaction.

It is important to further note to the student that all agency relationships (the employment relationship) are created between the principal supervising broker or brokerage and never by the sales associate or broker associate within that broker or brokerage's employ.

SUBAGENCY

In the normal course of business when a broker accepts a listing from a principal seller or a landlord, the agency relationship and duties therein are clear. In this situation it is clear that:

- the broker or brokerage acts as the seller's or landlord's agent (as the case may be), and
- all licensees in the employ of that broker are
  - agents of the broker, and
  - subagents of the principal seller or landlord.

However, the aforementioned becomes less clear when another broker not in the employ of the listing broker procures either a buyer or tenant for that property. The question become whether the outside broker is acting as:

- a subagent of the seller, or
- an agent of the buyer (buyer's agent).

A subagent relationship or **subagency** occurs when:

1. An outside broker (not in the employ of the listing broker) procures the buyer or tenant but owes fiduciary responsibilities to only the seller or landlord rather than to the buyer or tenant

2. When an agent in the employ of the listing broker procures a buyer or tenant

In either situation, the aforementioned is accomplished by the acceptance of the invitation to subagency or to act as a subagent. In essence, the seller receives fiduciary responsibilities undertaken by the licensee accepting this invitation to subagency.

CUSTOMER VS. PRINCIPAL: RESPONSIBILITIES TO THE CUSTOMER

While engaging the use of a real estate licensee in a real estate transaction is not required by law, when discussing the law of agency, it is first important to learn certain terminology to understand the different roles and responsibilities such as:

- consumer—member of the general public
- customer—the party the agent is hired to bring to the principal
- principal—describes the party that hires the agent (can be a landlord, tenant, seller, or buyer)
- agent—the person hired by the principal

For example, with understanding the aforementioned, think of it in the following context:

1. When a person walks into a shopping center, that person is considered a consumer.
2. When the consumer enters a department or other store in the center, that person now becomes a customer of that store.
3. When that customer makes a purchase from a particular establishment, that person is now a client of that store.

A **customer** in a real estate transaction is the party that the agent is hired to bring to the principal. Under a listing agreement to sell or lease a property, the customer is all buyers or tenants. Under a buyer agent relationship, the customer is all sellers and landlords. Customers are third parties that are not owed fiduciary duties by a licensee. However at a minimum, the customer is owed care/fair and honest dealing, accountability, and disclosure of material facts that affect the value of a property (discussed next).

The customer in a transaction:

- may be a potential buyer or seller of real property
- may or may not be represented by a real estate licensee

As you learned earlier, the agent always has a fiduciary responsibility to the principal. In addition to the responsibilities to the principal, the agent (broker) is bound by certain duties to third parties. When dealing with third parties, also termed customers, the agent's responsibilities are more limited than those owed to the principal. This is primarily due to the agency relationship that exists between the principal and the agent. As you will learn shortly, an agent must provide undivided loyalty to the principal. However, the agent also owes the following primary responsibilities to the customer:

- honesty
- fair dealing
- accountability
- full disclosure of all material facts that affect the value of the property

These responsibilities are always required of an agent in dealing with a third party. The third party is usually a prospective buyer with whom the broker deals. When dealing with a buyer, the seller's agent should:

- deal honestly, fairly, and in good faith
- account for all funds that are entrusted to him/her
- disclose all material facts known to the agent concerning:
    o the value of the property
    o the desirability of the property

In Florida, the precedent-setting court case *Johnson v. Davis* provides that a *seller* of residential property (property that includes one- to four-family units) is required to disclose to a buyer any known defects to or within the property that would affect the value of that property. In addition, Florida statutes require that a real estate *licensee* disclose to all interested parties within the transaction any known or suspected defects to the property or its condition that would affect the value of that property. This disclosure must take place prior to the parties entering into a contract of sale and purchase.

As just mentioned, all material facts about the subject property must be communicated to the prospective buyer. Facts must be disclosed even if they are detrimental to the principal (the seller). This applies to all material facts that are known to the broker or should have been known to the broker (i.e., presumption of knowledge). Some sellers have the mistaken notion that selling a property "as is" relieves them of any obligation to disclose defects. This is not the case.

Selling "as is" does *not* mean that the seller or the agent has the right to withhold any information about known defects that might affect the buyer's decision to buy. When a property is sold "as is," it only means that the seller is selling without agreeing to correct any known defects that exist.

As previously stated, when a licensee enters into an authorized agency relationship:

- the licensee is referred to as an agent who is hired to transact business on behalf of another
- an agent is governed by strict laws and rules concerning that relationship

- a customer may or may not be represented by a real estate licensee
- a principal is always represented by a licensee

> ## Coaching Tips
>
> - An agent transacts on behalf of the principal and no one else within the same transaction.
> - The principal employs the agent to bring the customer to the bargaining table.
> - The customer is the third party to the transaction that the agent is hired to bring to the principal.
> - If the principal is the buyer, the customer is the seller.
> - If the principal is the seller, the customer is the buyer.
> - All of these statements apply to transactions involving leased spaces as well.

When an agency relationship is created, the agent takes on what are referred to as fiduciary responsibilities. These responsibilities will be discussed in greater detail later in this chapter. A fiduciary is best defined as someone within an agency relationship who is granted a position of the highest form of trust. The agent is then considered a fiduciary. Because an agent is defined as one transacting business on behalf of another (usually for compensation of some sort), the term *fiduciary* is synonymous with *agent*. Therefore, it is safe to conclude that all agents are fiduciaries. It is the fiduciary's job to ensure that the interests of the principal are maintained when dealing with others. It is for this reason that an arm's length relationship should exist with third parties. In this type of situation, the term *caveat emptor* certainly applies to those third parties.

Principal

We have previously learned that an agent is someone who is hired to transact business on behalf of another.

An agent:

- is employed by another person
- in some cases, has the legal authority to act on behalf of and bind that person
- has the authority to exercise some degree of discretion while acting for the other person
- some examples of agents would include:
    - a real estate broker acting for a homeowner to sell a home
    - a lawyer representing a client
    - an investment manager who invests someone else's money

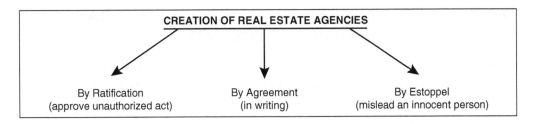

FIGURE 4.1
Source: © 2021 Mbition LLC

FIGURE 4.2
Source: © 2021 Mbition LLC

The person who hires or appoints an agent to act on his/her behalf is called the **principal**. Previously, we defined the customer as the third party in a transaction. We also defined agency as the name for the working relationship created between the agent and the principal/client. An agency relationship is created by employing the agent under a contract (see Figure 4.1). For example, when a real estate broker obtains a listing to sell a home, the broker has an agency that allows him/her to act for the homeowner. Please note that the term *agency* does not refer to a business but to the actual working relationship between the agent and the principal/client (see Figure 4.2).

The principal/client is:

- the party who hires the licensee
- the party with whom the licensee enters into an authorized brokerage relationship

AGENCY RELATIONSHIPS DETERMINED BY BROKER

We have previously learned that the agency relationship occurs between the principal and the broker/brokerage. As a result, some firms choose to focus on sales with seller representations. They prefer to work on the listing property side while other brokers/brokerages focus on buyer brokerage/buyer representation. In other words, they prefer working with buyers or end users of property. There are no laws that guide or dictate which avenue a broker or brokerage must pursue. Therefore, it is solely up to the principal broker to determine his/her specialty market and business focus. In any of the aforementioned cases, the broker is cautioned to observe all necessary laws and rules in the disposition of his/her business.

DISCLOSURE REQUIREMENTS AND THE FLORIDA BROKERAGE RELATIONSHIP DISCLOSURE ACT

Practically speaking, there has been confusion on the part of the general public as to whose interests are being served in any given real property transaction. Anyone who has previously engaged the services of a real estate agent may at some point have felt that same confusion. As a result of this confusion and to meet the needs of the general public, Florida enacted laws that clearly define the responsibilities of agents within an authorized agency relationship. When a licensee is engaged in any type of authorized brokerage relationship, Chapter 475 imposes definite duties and obligations on the part of a licensee to make adequate disclosures concerning the relationship and duties afforded to the parties in a transaction. Although the aforementioned applies to all transactions, disclosure requirements apply only to residential transactions as defined by Florida law. Next, we will define some of the important terms concerning the Florida Brokerage Relationship Disclosure Act. The act covers agency and nonagency relationships as they pertain to a residential sale in Florida.

A **residential sale** is defined as any of the following:

- the sale of improved land used as one- to four-family dwelling units
- the sale of unimproved land intended for use as one- to four-family dwelling units
- the sale of farm/agricultural land of up to 10 acres

Exemptions To Disclosure Requirements

As mentioned previously, the disclosure requirements of the Florida Brokerage Relationship Disclosure Act (which were just described) apply to residential sales only.

The disclosure requirements do not apply to:

- nonresidential transactions
- transactions involving the rental or leasing of property, unless an option to purchase property with one to four residential units is given
- auctions
- appraisals
- transactions involving business enterprises or business opportunities, unless the property has one to four residential units

AUTHORIZED BROKERAGE RELATIONSHIPS

Transaction Broker Relationship

The first type of authorized relationship in Florida is the transaction broker relationship. In a **transaction broker** relationship, the broker provides **limited representation** to one or both parties to the transaction. The broker does not represent either party in a fiduciary capacity or as a single agent. In fact, either party or both are treated as customers. Rather, the broker provides a limited form of nonfiduciary representation to the buyer, seller, or both. *Since July 1, 2003, under Florida law, it is presumed that a licensee is acting as transaction broker unless a single agent or no brokerage relationship is established in writing with a customer.* In a transaction broker relationship, a buyer or seller is not responsible for the acts of the licensee. In other words, the buyer or seller does not have vicarious liability resulting from the acts of a licensee. In addition, within this relationship, the parties to the real estate transaction give up their rights to the undivided loyalty of a licensee. This aspect of limited representation allows the licensee to facilitate a real estate transaction by assisting both the buyer and the seller, but the licensee will not work to represent one party to the detriment of the other party when acting as a transaction broker to both parties.

Consumers are not required to hire agents or enter into fiduciary relationships. If either a buyer or a seller hires an agent, he/she may not require a relationship that bears full fiduciary responsibilities like those of a single agent relationship. That is, the buyer or seller may be in need of only limited services. In this case, the transaction broker relationship may be appropriate. A transaction broker relationship imposes only limited representation responsibilities on the part of the licensee. In this type of relationship, there is *no* fiduciary relationship created; therefore, both the buyer and seller become *customers* of the transaction broker. There are no principal in a transaction broker relationship. In other states, a transaction broker is more commonly known and referred to as a *facilitator*. Compensation for services may or may not be equivalent to a brokerage commission. A broker may only be compensated for the agreed-upon service being provided.

In the transaction broker relationship, the transaction broker is not totally relieved of responsibilities to both parties. In fact, the transaction broker has several duties including:

- *Accountability (accounting for all funds)*—Licensees are responsible for a full accounting of all funds belonging to others that are entrusted to their possession.
- *Care (skill, care, and diligence)*—Licensees are considered professionals and, as such, must dispose of their responsibility with the utmost skill, care, and diligence.
- *Disclosure of property defects*—Licensees are compelled and required to fully disclose any fact known to them that could materially affect the value of the property. In addition, licensees may not withhold information that would be considered to materially affect the value of the property or could materially affect or sway the decision-making process of the customer had the information been disclosed or made readily available prior to a decision. This includes the disclosure of material facts that are not readily observable to the customer.
- *Fair and honest practice*—Licensees must be fair and honest in the manner that information is exchanged to a customer.

- *Submitting all offers and counteroffers in a timely manner*—Licensees must promptly present any and all offers and counteroffers.
- *Limited confidentiality*—Licensees' duty of confidentiality is limited. They may not disclose to one party what they know about the other. Specifically, licensees cannot disclose that the seller will accept a lower price than the list price, that the buyer will pay a greater price than offered, that either party will agree to financing terms other than those offered, or the motivation of either party for buying or selling the property.

Any other duties required by the parties may be created by agreement with the transaction agent.

Today, in Florida, in the absence of any other relationship, a real estate licensee is presumed to be a transaction broker. Due to this presumption, no disclosure regarding this relationship must be given.

Coaching Tips

As of July 1, 2008, changes in Florida law expanded the definition of a transaction broker. The law now states:

- A buyer or seller (within this relationship) is not responsible for acts committed by a licensee.
- The parties relinquish their rights as it applies to the duty of the agent to provide undivided loyalty.
- Any licensee working in this capacity may not favor one party to the detriment of the other party within that transaction.

Single Agent Relationship

In a **single agent** relationship, a licensee represents either a buyer or a seller *but never both* within the same transaction. The seller-broker agency (single agent for the seller) was the first kind of agency to develop. The buyer-broker agency (single agent for the buyer) was developed more recently and is becoming increasingly common. Florida recognizes both types of agency relationships. In Florida, a single agent relationship is defined as a relationship *bearing full fiduciary* responsibilities on the part of a licensee. When a licensee has full fiduciary responsibilities, the highest form of trust should exist between the principal and the agent. An agent who is not careful in the disposition of duties under this type of relationship may be the subject of disciplinary actions, civil suits, and penalties. When a single agency relationship is created and ultimately entered into, the person hiring the licensee is called the principal, and the licensee is referred to as the single agent. Remember, in Florida, a real estate licensee should never have two principals in the same transaction.

> **Coaching Tips**
>
> It is actually the broker or the legally registered brokerage firm that is the agent for the principal (buyer or seller). Any sales associate or broker associate registered under the broker is an agent for the broker and a subagent for the principal (buyer or seller). All such licensees have a fiduciary duty to the principal and must represent the principal's best interests. It should also be noted that under a single agent relationship, the principal is responsible for the acts of the agent/licensee.

When an authorized single agent relationship is created and entered into, the licensee owes the principal the following fiduciary duties:

- *Fair and honest practice*—The licensee must be fair and honest in the manner that information is exchanged and/or communicated to a principal.
- *Care (skill, care, and diligence)*—A licensee is considered not only a professional but also an expert and, as such, must dispose of his/her responsibility with the utmost skill, care, and diligence.
- *Confidentiality*—The licensee must at all times keep the confidence of any sensitive information that is entrusted to the licensee by the principal and should avoid at all costs any relationships that would adversely affect the principal.
- *Loyalty*—The licensee must place the needs and interest of the principal above those of all others including those of the agent.
- *Obedience*—The agent should always obey the legal and reasonable instructions of the principal.
- *Accountability*—The licensee must account for all funds belonging to others entrusted to his/her possession.
- *Full disclosure*—The licensee must fully disclose to the principal all facts and information that could materially affect the transaction or the value of the property. This includes the disclosure of material facts that are not readily observable.
- *Submitting all offers*—The licensee must promptly present any and all offers and counteroffers in a timely manner.

As you have already learned, a real estate licensee has three relationship choices in Florida. The licensee will either work as a transaction broker, a single agent, or in a no representation relationship.

Disclosure forms must contain all required information such as the licensee duties that are expected under the respective relationship. These forms must be presented at first substantive contact.

For example, prior to, or at the time of, entering into a single agent relationship with a principal, a licensee must provide the principal with a Single Agent Notice disclosure form, the contents of which are prescribed by law. (A copy of this form is included in the Forms Appendix at the end of the book.) This disclosure may be a separate disclosure document, or it may be included as part of another document, such as a listing or an agreement for representation. When it is included within another document, the notice must be of the same size type, or larger, as other provisions of the document and must be conspicuous in its placement to advise customers of the duties of a single agent. Also, the first sentence must be printed in uppercase bold type.

The Single Agent Notice disclosure form must be given at the earlier of:

- the time of entry into a single agent relationship with a principal
- the showing of the property

Nonrepresentation (No Brokerage Relationship)

In Florida (as in other states), buyers, sellers, landlords, and tenants are not required to employ and engage the services of a real estate licensee. Therefore, if any of the above parties chooses not to employ the services of a licensee under a single agent or transaction broker relationship (discussed later in this chapter), the licensee takes on the role of a facilitator to the transaction. In this role, the licensee only has customers and no principal and is free to enter into any compensation agreement with any party without fear of creating a single agent or transaction broker relationship.

At this point, it would be important to note that compensation or a compensation agreement neither constitutes an agency relationship nor dictates that the paying party is owed any fiduciary responsibilities by the licensee. Agency relationships are created via agency agreements. Those agreements may be implied or expressed (this subject will be covered in greater detail in Chapter 11).

In essence, compensation does not dictate who the licensee works for or owes allegiance to. A licensee's responsibility is to dispose of his/her obligations as prescribed by or under an agency agreement he/she enters into.

> **Example** You are hired as a buyer's broker under a single agent relationship agreement. Within the compensation paragraph of the single agent agreement, the buyer requires that "all compensation resulting from any transaction under that agreement is to be paid by the seller of the property that the buyer ultimately selects."

In this scenario, the buyer hires the licensee to procure the new premises on his/her behalf under a buyer broker/single agent relationship agreement. However, within the agreement, the buyer requires that the licensee seek compensation from the selling party. Assuming the selling party ultimately pays the fee, the licensee is hired by the buyer and therefore is required to deliver to the buyer no less representation than that called for within the single agent relationship. The licensee would owe the selling party nothing other than what is required of a broker in a nonrepresentation relationship.

In a nonrepresentation relationship, the broker owes the party the following duties:

- accountability (accounting for all funds)—Licensees are responsible for a full accounting of all funds belonging to others that are entrusted to their possession.
- care/fair and honest practice—Licensees must exercise care in the disposition of responsibilities and be fair and honest in the manner that information is exchanged to a customer. Licensees may not act in any way that would otherwise defraud the customer.
- disclosure of property defects—Licensees are compelled and required to disclose any known fact that could materially affect the value of the property. In addition, the licensee may not withhold information that would be considered to materially affect the value of the property or could materially affect or sway the decision-making process of the customer had the information been disclosed or made readily available prior to a decision. This includes the disclosure of material facts that are not readily observable to the customer without further inspection (latent defect). For example, a defective boiler system or defective septic system are considered latent defects.

In a nonrepresentation relationship, the broker is not obligated to provide loyalty, which is considered one of the fiduciary duties that a broker owes to a principal under a single agency relationship. For example, a broker is a single agent to a seller. A buyer calls wanting to buy the home. In this situation the broker would either have to transition to transaction broker or serve the buyer as a nonrepresentative. Under a single agency relationship, a broker would owe full fiduciary duties to a principal.

To summarize, in a nonrepresentation (no brokerage) relationship, the broker owes the party the duties of accountability, fair and honest practice, and full disclosure of facts that could materially affect the value of the property. The broker is not obligated to provide loyalty or confidentiality, which are considered fiduciary duties a broker owes to a principal under a single agency relationship.

Nonrepresentation (No Brokerage) Relationship Disclosure Requirements

In Florida, prior to showing a property and when no brokerage relationship/ **non-representation** exists, a licensee is required to provide the customer (either a buyer or seller) with a disclosure form entitled No Brokerage Relationship Notice. This important notice informs the potential buyer or seller that he/she is not being represented, nor will he/she be represented, by the licensee providing the notice until the parties enter into an agreement creating an authorized agency relationship. At inception of this relationship, this disclosure form must be provided to a buyer or a seller at the earlier of:

- at first substantive contact (where confidential information about the buyer or seller is given or exchanged)
- prior to showing the property

When a brokerage relationship exists, all licensees are required to provide a buyer or seller with a written No Brokerage Relationship Notice disclosure form, the contents of which are prescribed by law. (A copy of this form is included in the Forms Appendix at the end of the book.) After receiving the No Brokerage Relationship Notice, should the consumer prefer a fiduciary relationship, the licensee must then provide the consumer with a Single Agent Notice disclosure form (Single Agent Relationship will be discussed next).

The disclosure itself is not required if:

1. It has been determined that the buyer or seller is being represented by another broker as one of the following:
   a. a single agent
   b. a transaction broker

2. Any of the following does not occur at an open house:
   a. negotiations of any type concerning the subject property
   b. exchanging of any confidential information
   c. obtaining a submission of an offer to purchase by the purchaser
   d. entry into an agency agreement
   e. meetings with buyers or sellers where no discussions concerning any of the above open house issues arise or enter the discussion
   f. responding to questions concerning an advertised listing(s)

A licensee who is an agent of a seller must disclose the agency relationship in writing to any potential buyers with whom he/she is working. This may be accomplished by the licensee giving a copy of the No Brokerage Relationship Notice to the buyer. The disclosure must be in writing. Verbal disclosure may prove adequate in court in some cases, but written disclosure is always a better and safer approach. When speaking on the telephone, it is best to make an immediate verbal disclosure followed by a written disclosure prior to showing property. Although a nonrepresentation relationship bears duties and responsibilities on the part of the licensee, these responsibilities will differ from those of a fiduciary relationship (which will be discussed next).

TRANSITIONING TO ANOTHER AUTHORIZED RELATIONSHIP

In Florida, a broker or legal registered brokerage entity may transition from a single agent relationship with either a buyer or a seller to a transaction broker at any time as long as the following are true:

- The broker provides the proper disclosure form entitled **Consent to Transition to Transaction Broker.**
- The principal to whom this situation applies (either the buyer or the seller as the case may be) has fully consented to the transition prior to the agent's making the actual transition.
- The principal's permission is evidenced by his/her signature on the Consent to Transition to Transaction Broker disclosure form.

The licensee will be disciplined if he/she transitions to a different relationship before the events listed above have occurred.

The Consent to Transition to Transaction Broker disclosure form may be a separate disclosure document, or it may be included as part of another document, such as a listing or an agreement for representation. (A copy of this form is included in the Forms Appendix at the end of the book.) When it is included within another document, the notice must be of the same size type, or larger, as other provisions of the document and must be conspicuous in its placement to advise customers of the duties of limited representation. Also, the first sentence must be printed in uppercase bold type. The disclosure form must include the name of the real estate firm, a list of duties associated with this relationship, and the signature of the principal.

Let's look at an example of a transition to another authorized relationship. This example involves an in-house transaction.

Example Potential Situation—XYZ Realty is a single agent for Seller Ian. XYZ Realty is also a single agent for Buyer Max. Buyer Max is interested in Seller Ian's property. Although this type of situation may seem innocent, it can be very dangerous if not handled lawfully. The danger specifically lies in the creation of an *unlawful* dual agency. In this situation, a sales associate employed by XYZ Realty *cannot* show Seller Ian's property to Buyer Max because a broker cannot represent both the buyer and the seller in the same transaction (dual agency). As previously mentioned, dual agency is illegal in Florida.

Lawful Solution—One way for the broker to proceed with this transaction legally would be for the broker/brokerage entity to transition from a single agent relationship to that of a transaction broker. The broker would be required to transition from a single agent relationship to that of a transaction broker with both the buyer and seller *prior* to the buyer inspecting the property. Any attempt to show the property to the buyer prior to a lawful transition occurring would be an infraction of the license law. Doing so would create a dual agency and subject the licensee to severe disciplinary action.

DESIGNATED SALES ASSOCIATE

We have already looked at the authorized brokerage relationships that apply to *residential sales* transactions. Now let's look at a special agency situation that is permitted in *nonresidential* transactions.

Earlier in this chapter, you learned that a residential sales transaction is defined as one of the following:

- the sale of improved land used as 1- to 4-family dwelling units
- the sale of unimproved land intended for use as 1- to 4-family dwelling units
- the sale of farm/agricultural land of up to 10 acres

If a transaction does not fall under these definitions of a residential sales transaction, it is considered a *commercial* or *nonresidential sales transaction even if it involves residentially zoned property*. This would be the case in a property containing greater than four dwelling units.

In a *nonresidential* sales transaction, if the buyer and the seller desire the services of the same real estate broker to act as a fiduciary single agent to both parties, the broker may appoint **designated sales associates** to act as single agents for the parties. That is, the broker may designate one sales associate to act as a single agent for the buyer and a different sales associate to act as a single agent for the seller. In this case, the broker is not considered a dual agent but a neutral party.

The designated sales associate relationship is only permitted if and when the following disclosure requirements are met:

- A request for such representation is made by both parties.
- Both parties can demonstrate that their asset holdings are valued in excess of $1,000,000.
- The broker acts strictly on an advisory level to both designated sales associates within the organization.
- The broker only uses any confidential information disclosed by either designated sales associate in order to properly advise the sales associates on how to proceed in a lawful and appropriate manner.

A designated sales associate has the same duties as a single agent, including the disclosure requirements (described earlier in this chapter). In addition, a Designated Sales Associate Disclosure Notice must be provided.

Duties Owed Under Lawful Relationships

Duty Owed	Single Agent	Transaction Broker	No Brokerage Relationship
Fiduciary relationship	yes	no	no
Care (skill, care, and diligence)	yes	yes	yes
Full confidentiality	yes	no	no
Loyalty	yes	no	no
Obedience	yes	no	no
Accountability (accounting for all funds)	yes	yes	yes
Full disclosure	yes	yes	yes
Presenting all offers/counteroffers	yes	yes	yes
Fair and honest dealing	yes	yes	yes
Limited confidentiality	no	yes	yes
Perform additional duties that are agreed to	yes	yes	yes

DISCIPLINE: VIOLATIONS AND PENALTIES

Violation of state license laws rules and regulations can result in administrative penalties. Penalties include but are not limited to:

- denial of an application for licensure
- refusal to renew a license
- revocation of a license
- suspension of one's license for a period not to exceed 10 years
- fines of up to $5,000 for each violation of Chapter 475 (or separate offense) of the Florida Statutes (475, F.S., which applies to the regulation of real estate brokers, sales associates, and schools)
- fines of up to $5,000 for each violation of Chapter 455 of the Florida Statutes (455, F.S., which applies to business and professional regulation)

In addition to administrative/monetary fines, criminal assessments may be applied for a first-degree misdemeanor. There is one offense that would fall into this category:

- failing to provide accurate and current rental information

The penalty for these offenses consists of one or both of the following:

- punishment of up to one year in jail
- a $1,000 fine

In addition, any violation of Chapter 475, or any lawful order, regulation, or rule is a second-degree misdemeanor. The penalty for a second-degree misdemeanor is one or both of the following:

- a fine not exceeding $500
- a prison term not to exceed 60 days

In addition to the aforementioned, it should be noted that practicing real estate without a license is a very serious violation of license law. The student should know these things:

- Performing unlicensed real estate activities in Florida is a third-degree felony.
- The DBPR may issue fines of up to $5,000 per count.
- Violators may also have a cease and desist order issued to them by the DBPR when any statute pertaining to real estate has been violated.
- Under Florida license law, any infraction of the law is deemed a misdemeanor.
- A jail sentence as a result of an infraction may only be administered by a court of law.
- The FREC cannot impose a jail sentence. It is, therefore, the FREC's responsibility to inform the attorney general's office if it knows or suspects a crime has been committed.

RECORD KEEPING AND RETENTION

If a transaction results in a written sales contract, the broker is required to maintain copies of the disclosure forms in a transaction file for at least five years. In the event of litigation concerning the books or records of a transaction, the broker is required to keep the records for a period of two years following the conclusion of litigation but not less than five years.

Record maintenance requirements apply to:

- all residential transactions (as defined by 475, F.S.) to include:
  - closed transactions
  - transactions that do not close; the following should be included in the broker's files:
    - the purchase contract
    - any escrow documents and bank statements referencing the purchase contract
    - agency disclosure forms
- all nonresidential transactions that utilize designated sales associates

TERMINATION OF AGENCY

The agency relationship created by a listing agreement is automatically terminated when a sale of the property is completed. In addition, there are several other ways in which a listing agreement can be terminated (see Figure 4.3). One good way to remember the methods by which an agency can be terminated is to remember the mnemonic READIE:

- *Revocation* or renunciation
- *Expiration* of the listing period
- *Agreement* of the parties

- *Death* of either party
- *Incapacity* of either party
- *Extinction* of the property

Revocation or renunciation—The principal may decide to revoke the agency and terminate the listing. However, this does not relieve the principal from the obligation to pay a commission if the property is sold during the original listing period. For example, the owner may "take the property off the market" and terminate the agency, but the principal must pay a commission if it is sold during the listing period.

Expiration of the listing period—If the property does not sell during the listing period, the listing agreement automatically terminates.

Agreement of the parties—If both parties mutually agree, the listing agreement can be terminated.

Death of either party—If the principal or broker dies, the listing agreement is automatically terminated.

Incapacity of either party—The listing agreement is terminated if either party is declared legally incompetent, declares bankruptcy, or if the broker loses his/her license.

Extinction of the property—If the property is destroyed, the listing agreement is terminated.

These six ways of terminating a listing can be classified as occurring through one of the following:

- acts of the parties
- acts of law

To remember which method of termination falls into which category, use the following graphic illustrations:

The first three categories are classified as "acts of the parties":
- revocation or renunciation
- expiration of the listing period
- agreement of the parties

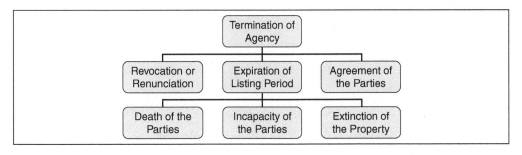

FIGURE 4.3

Source: © 2021 Mbition LLC

> The remaining three categories are classified as "acts of law":
>
> - death of either party
> - incapacity of either party
> - extinction of the property

> To remember which category is which, remember that the "D" in "DIE" stands for "death" of either party, which is termination by an "act of law."

Summary

There are three types or categories of agents: universal, general, and special. Under Florida law, it is presumed that a licensee is acting as a transaction broker unless a single agent or nonrepresentation relationship is established in writing with a customer.

- In a single agency relationship, an agent represents one party.
- An agent who represents only buyers is a single agent for the buyer (a buyer's agent).
- An agent who represents only sellers is a single agent for the seller (a seller's agent).
- Full fiduciary duties are owed to the principal.
- In a single agency relationship, a licensee represents either a buyer or seller or a landlord or tenant—but never both in the same transaction.
- Dual agency refers to a relationship in which the agent represents both the buyer (or lessee) and the seller (or lessor) within the same transaction.
- Dual agency is never legal in Florida.
- In a nonrepresentation relationship, the broker owes the party:
  - the duties of accountability (accounting for all funds)
  - care/ fair and honest practice
  - disclosure of facts that could materially affect the value of the property
- Neither a buyer nor a seller is obligated or required to enlist the efforts or services of a real estate licensee.
- Therefore, in this situation, the licensee merely acts as a facilitator in concluding the sale.
- In a transaction broker relationship, the duty of confidentiality is limited.
- The broker provides limited representation to one or both parties to the transaction.

Review Questions

1. The brokerage relationship disclosure requirements are relevant to the:
   a. sale of a business
   b. lease of a single-family home
   c. sale of a residential apartment complex
   d. sale of three agricultural acres

2. Only a transaction broker would owe customers:
   a. loyalty
   b. limited confidentiality
   c. obedience
   d. full disclosure

3. A seller listed a lot with Jones Real Estate for $100,000. A buyer calls the company and asks if the seller will take $30,000. The company:
   a. should tell the buyer to raise the offer
   b. doesn't have to present verbal offers
   c. must present all offers to the seller
   d. can use its own discretion in the matter

4. A company represents a buyer and a seller as a transaction broker. As an associate presents a low offer to the seller, the associate tells the seller the buyer would pay more. The company:
   a. has violated limited confidentially and can be sued
   b. is obligated to reveal this to the seller
   c. must be loyal to the seller
   d. has violated the duty of confidentiality to the buyer

5. In a nonrepresentation relationship with a buyer, which of the following duties does the company NOT owe?
   a. undivided loyalty
   b. accounting for all funds
   c. skill, care, and diligence
   d. presenting all offers in a timely manner

6. Written disclosures regarding the duties in each type of brokerage relationship apply to:
   a. all real estate transactions
   b. all residential transactions
   c. residential leases and sales
   d. residential sales as defined by Florida law

7. A signature on the written disclosure forms is:
   a. important but not required
   b. only required on the Consent to Transition forms
   c. only required on Single Agent Notice forms
   d. always required

8. Under Florida law, it is presumed that all licensees are transaction brokers unless a single agent or nonrepresentation relationship notice is established in writing. Based on this, which of the following is correct?
   a. The written Transaction Broker Notice is obligatory.
   b. The written Transaction Broker Notice must be given in all residential transactions.
   c. No written Transaction Broker Notice is required in residential sales.
   d. If the firm advertises "Transaction Broker (Brokers)," the written notice is not mandatory.

9. When buyers and sellers have $1,000,000 or more in assets, a designated sales associate:
   a. represents the broker's interest in residential sales
   b. is a subagent for the broker
   c. may be appointed as a single agent by single agent brokers
   d. is appointed by the broker, at the request of the parties to the transaction, as a single agent for the buyer or seller in a nonresidential transaction

10. Which of these will NOT terminate a brokerage relationship?
    a. The offer is withdrawn.
    b. The broker renounces the relationship.
    c. The principal renounces the relationship.
    d. The broker dies.

11. Broker Beth is a single agent for the seller. The seller tells Broker Beth the garage roof leaked in the last rain, but there is no visible evidence. The seller asks Broker Beth not to mention the leak. Beth's legal obligation is to tell buyers:
    a. The roof does not appear to leak.
    b. Nothing unless someone asks about leaks.
    c. The roof has developed a leak.
    d. Nothing because licensees in a single agent relationship owe principals obedience.

12. A real estate licensee has a legal obligation to tell all prospective buyers before or at the time of showing a property that:
    a. Two owners ago, there was a murder in the house.
    b. The residents in the neighborhood are predominantly Hispanic.
    c. The shutters do not meet the Miami-Dade wind codes.
    d. The seller allegedly has AIDS.

13. A transaction broker for a customer owes all of the following duties EXCEPT:
    a. using skill, care, and diligence in the transaction
    b. dealing honestly and fairly
    c. limited confidentiality, unless waived by a party
    d. full disclosure

14. A real estate firm is the single agent for a seller. A buyer offers to purchase the seller's property for more than the listing price and will pay in cash. The buyer insists on an answer today, or the buyer will buy a different property. The seller can't be found. In this situation, the broker:
    a. must accept the offer because it is in the seller's best interest
    b. cannot say yes, no, or maybe
    c. can accept the offer, conditional to the seller's signature
    d. legally must reject the offer

15. As a single agent broker, Acme Realty can represent:
    a. buyers only
    b. sellers only
    c. both buyers and sellers if they are in the same transaction
    d. both buyers and sellers, but not if they are in the same transaction

16. Sherman Homes is the single agent for Seller Jim and Buyer Mary. Jim's home is perfect for Mary. How can Mary see Jim's house?
    a. Jim can sign a waiver allowing Mary to see the house.
    b. Mary can sign a waiver allowing herself to see the house.
    c. Before Buyer Mary may see the home, both Jim and Mary must sign the consent form to allow Sherman Homes to transition from a single agent relationship to a transaction broker.
    d. Mary can't see Jim's house under any circumstances.

17. It would be appropriate to give the No Brokerage Relationship Notice to:
    a. sellers who are represented by other companies
    b. persons attending an open house
    c. all persons who ask about the price of the house
    d. a for-sale-by-owner when showing your buyer the home

18. Vivian has signed a listing agreement with your company to sell her house, but Vivian doesn't want to sign the Transaction Broker Notice. What are you going to do?
    a. Be polite, but insist on a signature.
    b. Put a note in the office files that Vivian accepted the relationship but didn't want to sign.
    c. You can accept the listing, but you can't be Vivian's transaction broker.
    d. You can sign the notice; this will suffice.

19. Brokerage relationship disclosure documents that result in a written contract to buy or sell residential property, even if the transaction didn't close, must be:
    a. kept for a period of three years
    b. kept for a period of five years
    c. replaced with electronic files or CDs
    d. kept confidential

20. A transaction broker for buyers or sellers:
    a. must represent either a buyer or seller but not both in the same transaction
    b. does not represent either party in a fiduciary capacity
    c. represents principals in residential transactions
    d. can work for one party's interest over the other

5 REAL ESTATE BROKERAGE ACTIVITIES AND PROCEDURES

KEY TERMS

arbitration
blind advertisement
commingling
conflicting demands
conversion
corporation
deposit
earnest money
escrow (trust) account
escrow disbursement order (EDO)
general partnership
good-faith doubt
interplead
kickback
limited liability company
limited liability partnership
limited partnership
litigation
mediation
ostensible partnership
professional association (PA)
point of contact information
sole proprietorship
trade name

LEARNING OBJECTIVES

After completing this lesson, you will be able to:

- identify the requirements for a real estate brokerage office(s) and the types of business entities that may register
- explain what determines whether a temporary shelter must be registered as a branch office
- list the requirements related to sign regulation
- describe the obligations placed on a sales associate who changes employers and/or address
- list the requirements related to the regulation of advertising by real estate brokers
- explain the term *immediately* as it applies to earnest money deposits
- describe the four settlement procedures available to a broker who has received conflicting demands or who has a good-faith doubt as to who is entitled to disputed funds
- explain the rule regarding the advertisement of rental property information or lists or negotiation of rentals

BROKERAGE OFFICES AND SALES ASSOCIATES

All Florida brokers must establish and maintain a principal place of business that must be registered with the Division of Real Estate (DRE). Florida law defines and requires the broker's principal office to be contained or housed within a stationary building containing one or more enclosed rooms. Therefore, a mobile home does not qualify under these definitions. However, a mobile home resting on a permanent foundation does qualify and fall within the guidelines.

Furthermore, all sales associates with a brokerage must be registered with the DRE and work under the direct control and supervision of their sponsoring broker. As the case may be, this can be accomplished in the broker's office or branch office(s).

SIGNAGE

The broker's place of business must have a sign. This includes the broker's principal office as well as any branch offices. The sign must be easily observed and read by anyone who is about to enter the office. Each sign must contain, at a minimum, the following information:

- the name of the broker
- any fictitious name or trade name, as registered with the Florida Real Estate Commission (FREC) (A **trade name** is a fictitious name other than one's own name used to conduct one's business.)
- the words "licensed real estate broker" or "lic. real estate broker" following the broker's name

If the firm is a partnership or corporation, the sign must also include the name of the partnership or corporation and at least one of the brokers. The inclusion of any broker associates' or sales associates' names is the broker's decision and is optional. Should the broker opt to list either one or both classes of licensed individuals, the broker is cautioned to make a clear distinction between the broker and any affiliated licensees.

Example

Sunshine State Real Estate Services
Theodore Sunshine—Licensed Real Estate Broker
Wilma Morrison—Broker Associate
Harry Thompson—Sales Associate

You should be aware that the broker's address is *not* required on the sign.

The licensee is cautioned to observe both zoning and license laws governing the operation of a real estate brokerage business from a residence. In this type of situation, the signage requirements are not relaxed or excused. In addition to any signage requirements, the licensee is cautioned to adhere to accessibility laws such as the Americans with Disabilities Act (ADA). This would apply to any principal office, branch office, and any office within a residence. Any violation can and most probably will result in disciplinary action against the licensee.

TEMPORARY SHELTERS

If a broker operates more than one office, each additional location must be registered as a branch office. A temporary shelter, located on the grounds of a subdivision being sold by the broker, is not considered a branch office if the purpose of the shelter is strictly protection from the weather. However, the shelter is considered a branch office and must be appropriately registered if one or both of the following occurs:

- Transactions are closed in the shelter (this includes conducting negotiations).
- Sales associates are permanently assigned to the shelter.

GUIDELINES FOR ADVERTISING: FALSE OR MISLEADING ADVERTISING/PENALTIES FOR FALSE ADVERTISING

A broker is prohibited from placing any advertisement that is false or misleading. This applies to all types, methods, and vehicles of advertising, including but not limited to:

- newspapers
- magazine ads
- fliers
- television
- radio
- internet
- billboards
- yard signs
- benches

Furthermore, it is unlawful for a broker to place an ad without indicating that the advertiser is a licensed real estate broker. That is, all ads must contain the name of the brokerage firm. An ad that does not include the brokerage firm name is called a **blind advertisement**. Blind advertisements are not only unlawful; they also subject the licensee to disciplinary action. Blind ads mislead the general public by lacking disclosure that the advertiser is a real estate licensee. All advertising must be worded in such a manner that a reasonable person would know the ad was placed by a real estate licensee. If the name of any contact person appears within an ad, the ad must *always* include the person's surname. Ads with only a contact person's first name are prohibited. The licensee's last name must appear as it appears on his/her license and as it is registered with the DRE. Failure to observe rules governing advertisements will subject the licensee to disciplinary action. As a result of the severity of the infraction, penalties will vary.

It should be noted that blind advertising can also occur when a licensee places an ad in a periodical or on the internet for the sale of the licensee's own property. This occurs by placing the ad while in the employ of a real estate broker or brokerage "for sale by owner" without identifying the broker or brokerage's name and/or that the advertiser is a licensee. The licensee is also cautioned to check for rules and restrictions within their employment/independent contractor agreement before placing ads for the sale of their own property.

Internet Advertising/Point of Contact Information

When advertising on the internet, the name of the brokerage firm must appear immediately above, below, or adjacent to the name of the point of contact information. The **point of contact information** means the method by which the brokerage firm or licensee may be contacted and includes any of the following:

- e-mail address
- mailing address
- street address
- phone number
- fax number

When licensees are soliciting by telephone or fax transmission, they should observe all federal and state laws governing same. This will require the licensees to check the National and Florida Do Not Call Registry. Under the Florida Solicitation Act, those who violate the National Do Not Call Registry or place an illegal robo-call can be fined up to $11,000 per call. Violations are subject to civil penalties of up to $10,000 per violation and injunctive relief through the courts.

Coaching Tips

Many brokers like to place "sold" signs on properties as a means of advertising. There was a time when a "sold" sign could not be placed on a property prior to closing without the seller's consent. That rule was repealed in October 2002. Currently, a licensee may place any of the following types of signs:

- sold
- sale pending
- contract pending
- under contract

It is important to note that in Florida, any person or entity that advertises real estate services and/or property for sale or lease is acting as a broker and, as such, must be duly licensed as same. Furthermore, sales associates or broker associates may never advertise in their own name or without including the name of their broker or brokerage in the advertisement. Licensees should exercise caution when self-dealing in the sale of their own property. Licensees should take further caution in observing all agreements (independent contractor agreement or employment agreement) with their broker. Most agreements require that agents advertise only in the name of the broker. This may also include situations where a licensee is self-dealing for his/her own account. This subject was just covered in greater detail earlier in this chapter.

HANDLING OF DEPOSITS: ESCROW (TRUST) ACCOUNTS IN FLORIDA

Licensees are often entrusted with **deposits**, which is defined as money or other valuable consideration belonging to others. We will now take a look at the laws and requirements that must be followed in such situations. It is important to note that the single most common license infraction leading to cancelation or revocation of one's license occurs while mishandling other people's money.

The purpose of an escrow or trust account is to hold the funds of others that have been entrusted to the broker. In Florida, when a licensee handles funds belonging to others in the normal course of business, the licensee must immediately deposit those funds in the broker's **escrow (trust) account**. Let's look at what is meant by *immediately*.

In Florida, *immediately* means the following:

- To the sales associate—When funds belonging to others are entrusted to a sales associate or broker associate, the licensee must immediately place those funds in the possession of his broker. In this case, *immediately* means within the next business day following receipt.
- To the broker—When funds belonging to others are received by the broker, the broker must immediately deposit the funds into her escrow (trust) account. In this case, *immediately* means no later than the close of banking business on the third business day following receipt of the money. This time period begins on the day the *sales associate* or *broker associate* received the funds.

Example On Monday, a sales associate receives an earnest money deposit from a buyer. **Earnest money** refers to a deposit paid by a prospective buyer to show his intention to go through with the sale. The sales associate must turn the funds over to her broker by Tuesday (assuming there are no holidays). The broker must deposit the funds into an escrow (trust) account by the close of banking business Thursday—the third day after the funds were received by the sales associate (again, assuming there are no holidays). Failure to do so will result in a citation, fine, and/or other administrative penalty assessed to the licensee.

Escrow Accounts Held by a Title Company or Attorney

Under Florida law 61J2-14.008, a real estate licensee is required to do all of the following when an earnest money deposit is placed and held with either an attorney or a title company:

- A licensee who has prepared or presented a sales contract shall clearly indicate on that contract:
    - name,
    - address, and
    - telephone number of such title company or attorney.
- Unless the deposit is being held by a title company or by an attorney who has been nominated in writing by either a seller or seller's agent, and in order to provide written verification of receipt of the deposit, the licensee's broker shall cause to effect and make a written request to the title company or attorney. The verification request must occur within ten (10) business days after each deposit is due under the sales contract,
- Within 10 business days of the date the licensee's broker made the written request for verification of the deposit, the licensee's broker shall provide to the interested parties the following:
    - either a copy of the written verification (to seller's broker) or, if no verification is received by licensee's broker, written notice that licensee's broker did not receive verification of the deposit
    - if the seller is not being represented by a broker, then the licensee's broker shall notify the seller directly in the same manner as if seller was represented by a broker above

It is important to note that the commission has no jurisdiction over the title company or the attorney that holds escrowed funds as an escrow agent. Furthermore, under Chapter 475 a broker is required to deliver escrow funds to the escrow agent within the same time frame prescribed by law (three business days following receipt of funds). This must be handled in the same manner as if the funds were being deposited within the broker's escrow/trust account. Although the broker is not handling the escrow funds, failure to observe the rules associated with the aforementioned can result in the licensee being disciplined and ultimately receiving an administrative penalty.

Management of Escrow Accounts

When a broker receives funds belonging to others in a real estate transaction, the broker must *not* commingle the funds. **Commingling** refers to mixing funds belonging to others with the broker's personal funds or business funds. If the broker deposits such funds into a business operating account, it would be considered commingling. There is one exception permitted under the license law. A broker is permitted to maintain up to:

- $5,000 of personal or brokerage funds in the broker's property management escrow account; and up to
- $1,000 in the sales escrow account. (In the event of any legal proceeding concerning a broker's escrow account, the disbursement of escrowed funds must not be delayed due to any dispute over the personal or brokerage funds that may be present in the account.)

The broker must avoid conversion. **Conversion** occurs if the broker unlawfully takes funds belonging to others for his/her own personal use. For example, a broker using such funds to pay for a personal trip is considered conversion.

Escrow funds must be deposited in one of the following ways:

- in a savings bank, commercial bank, or credit union
- in a Florida title company that has trust powers
- with an attorney admitted into the Florida Bar (if specified in the contract)

The broker may have as many escrow accounts as needed provided that the following requirements are met:

- The broker is a signatory (the responsible party for the account) on any and all accounts.
- The broker makes available to the Department of Business and Professional Regulation (DBPR) any records associated with the escrow accounts for examination and audit by the DBPR.
- The records are kept for a minimum of five years from conclusion of activity on any transaction. However, if the records of the broker were the subject of any lawsuit, the broker must retain the records for an additional period of two years subsequent to the conclusion of the lawsuit but in no event less than five years. This may ultimately mean that the broker retain these records for as much as seven years.

In the event that there is an error in an escrow account, the broker is given a reasonable amount of time to correct the error if there is no shortage of funds and the error poses no significant threat of economic harm to the public.

Interest-Bearing Accounts

A broker's escrow account may be an interest-bearing or noninterest-bearing account. Before placing funds in an interest-bearing escrow account, all parties must agree in writing, and the written agreement must specify who will be paid the interest and when that party inures the benefit of same. When the broker, by agreement, is the recipient of the interest, the interest must be transferred to the broker's operating account monthly. Accumulating interest that is not removed monthly can cause an overage and as such can also create commingling of funds for the broker.

It should be noted that provided that it is the broker's initial offense, a notice of noncompliance will be issued to the broker for failure to stop interest from accruing, which if not cured within 15 days will result in a citation. Furthermore, failure to obtain permission from all interested parties to escrow funds being placed in an interest-bearing account will also result in a citation issued to the broker.

MANAGEMENT OF ESCROW ACCOUNTS: ESCROW DISPUTE AND DISPOSITION OF FUNDS

It is not uncommon for a dispute to arise concerning how funds that are held by a broker are distributed. That is, **conflicting demands** may be made upon the escrowed funds when two parties (such as a buyer and a seller) do not agree as to how the funds should be disbursed. In this unfortunate event, the licensee must immediately notify the broker of the conflicting demands. The broker must follow strict rules, regardless of the demands made by the parties. These rules are described next.

First, the broker is required to notify the FREC in writing within 15 business days of the last demand made by either party for a distribution. Within the notification, the broker may request that the FREC issue an **escrow disbursement order (EDO)** instructing the licensee to distribute the funds to one party or the other. The FREC may or may not issue an EDO. Whether or not the broker receives the FREC EDO, the broker always has three disposition options (which must be initiated within 30 days following the last request by either party for funds held in escrow):

1. mediation
2. arbitration
3. litigation
    a. interpleader—a motion made to the courts to take possession of the funds held by the escrow agent/broker
    b. declaratory judgment—a legal decision made in resolution of uncertainty between two disputing parties

Let's look at an example of how the timing works when conflicting demands occur and the broker requests an EDO from the Commission.

1. A broker receives conflicting demands for escrowed funds on February 1.
2. The broker immediately notifies the Commission and requests they issue an EDO.
3. The broker continues to try to resolve the dispute and 10 business days have passed since the broker received the conflicting demands for the disposition of the escrow funds.

At this time, the broker has not received an EDO from the Commission. The broker now has 20 business days remaining of the 30 business days prescribed by law to institute any of the other lawful means of resolving the dispute. Regardless of whether or not the FREC issues an EDO, the broker must take the required steps toward the resolution and disposition of the disputed escrowed funds. In the event that the EDO is issued after the broker has already either resolved the dispute by settlement or the matter goes before the courts, the broker is required to notify the FREC within ten (10) business days that same has occurred.

It should be noted that if the Commission was to issue an EDO prior to other alternative dispute resolution remedies being instituted, the broker is cautioned to obey the order. Failure to do so may leave the broker exposed to civil liability as well as possible disciplinary action taken against the licensee. In addition, if the broker is sued and a judgment is recorded against them, they will not be eligible to have funds dispersed on their behalf from the state Real Estate Recovery fund. In the event that the broker follows the instructions contained in the EDO and is subsequently sued and loses, the FREC is authorized to pay the broker's judgment, court costs, and reasonable attorney fees.

> ## Coaching Tips
>
> Within 15 business days, the broker must send notification to the FREC and within 30 business days must institute one of the three settlement procedures following a good-faith doubt as to how to disburse disputed escrow funds. While good faith can be defined as *a willing party's desire to transact business*, good-faith doubt is when the broker questions or doubts the party's willingness and desire to transact business. When this occurs, law requires the licensee to institute one of the settlement procedures mentioned above. Please note that this must be accomplished within the time requirements established by the FREC. For example, a broker notifies the FREC in writing 9 days following the receipt of a dispute. In this case the broker has only 21 days to initiate a settlement procedure.

Good-Faith Doubt

We just looked at the steps a broker may take when conflicting demands are placed on funds held in the broker's escrow account. These same procedures may also be followed if the broker has a good-faith doubt as to who is entitled to receive the funds. **Good-faith doubt** means the broker doubts the parties' intention to conduct business honestly and to perform their duties under the contract. The situations that may cause a broker to have good-faith doubt are listed below.

Good-faith doubt may exist in the following situations:

- The closing date of the transaction has passed, and the broker has not received instructions (either conflicting or identical) from all parties concerning disbursement of the funds.
- The closing date of the transaction has not passed, but one party has expressed an intention not to go through with the transaction, and the broker has not received instructions (either conflicting or identical) from all parties concerning disbursement of the funds.

- In a transaction that fails to close, when one of the parties to the transaction fails to respond to any of the broker inquiries concerning escrow disbursements, then the broker must send a (certified) letter to the party that does not respond to the broker's inquiries that demand has been made for the escrowed funds. The notice should also state that failure to respond by a certain date will result in the funds being dispersed to the other requesting party.

If the broker has a good-faith doubt as to who is entitled to receive the funds, the broker must notify the FREC in writing within 15 business days and must initiate one of the following procedures within 30 business days:

1. request that the FREC issue an EDO instructing the licensee to distribute the funds to one party or the other
2. submit the matter to mediation
3. submit the matter to arbitration
4. submit the matter to a court of law (interpleader motion)

Next, let's look at the three disposition options, their differences, and their requirements.

Mediation

Other than arbitration and litigation (discussed next), mediation is a form of alternative dispute resolution. **Mediation** occurs when parties who are unable to agree among themselves seek the assistance of a third party (a mediator) for the purpose of providing a recommended nonbinding solution. In essence, the parties arrive at their own decision or conclusion through the recommended solutions provided by the mediator. FREC rules require this process to be completed within 90 days following the last request by either party for funds held in escrow, or the licensee must then institute one of the other disposition options.

Arbitration

Arbitration occurs when parties who are unable to agree among themselves seek the assistance of a third party (one or more arbitrators) who formulates a decision that is binding on all the parties involved. Prior to arbitration, each party must submit to the arbitrator or arbitration panel, as the case may be, that they will be bound by the decision. As a general note concerning this type of proceeding, arbitrator decisions are usually upheld in court and are very difficult to overturn through appeal. However, as a last resort, the broker may submit a dispute to litigation.

Litigation

Litigation means that the parties are entering into a lawsuit and are petitioning the courts to decide the outcome of the dispute. Litigation may also involve an **interplead** motion, in which the broker deposits the funds with the courts and petitions the courts to decide on the disbursement. If the petition is accepted, the courts decide on the outcome of disbursement and which party receives the funds. This process ultimately relieves the broker of any further responsibility regarding the disputed funds.

Use the mnemonic LAME to remember the procedures for the disposition of escrowed funds when there are conflicting demands:

- *Litigation*
- *Arbitration*
- *Mediation*
- *Escrow disbursement order*

RENTAL LISTS OR RENTAL COMPANIES

As there is no Florida law that would require a consumer from having to hire the services of a real estate licensee, some consumers seeking rental property have turned to the purchase of rental information from individuals or companies selling same. As a result, some real estate licensees are involved in selling rental information to prospective tenants. Anyone who furnishes rental information or rental lists for a fee is subject to rules concerning such lists. When a fee is involved, the individual or company must provide the purchaser of the list (the prospective tenant) with an agreement or receipt. The agreement must state that if the party is unable to successfully achieve a rental from that list, upon the demand of the party purchasing the list, the licensee must return at least 75% of the amount paid for the rental information list within 30 days.

Below is the required notice that must appear in the agreement in at least 10-point print:

> **Notice Pursuant to Florida Law**
> If the rental information provided under this contract is not current or accurate in any material aspect, you may demand within 30 days of this contract date a return of your full fee paid. If you do not obtain a rental you are entitled to receive a return of 75% of the fee paid, if you make demand within 30 days of this contract date.

Inaccurate Rental Lists

If a rental list is found to be outdated or inaccurate, the purchaser of the list would be entitled to a full refund. In addition, if the list is found to be intentionally outdated or inaccurate, a license infraction has occurred, and the licensee will be disciplined. This would be considered a first-degree misdemeanor.

This would subject the licensee to:

- license suspension or revocation
- a fine of at least $1,000 and/or the potential of imprisonment for up to one year

BROKER/SALES ASSOCIATE: AN EXPERT IN CERTAIN AREAS OF PROPERTY TRANSFER

When real estate licensees receive their license, they are considered under the law as experts in certain areas of the field. A licensee must always remember the limitations of providing advice that can otherwise be construed as the unauthorized practice of law. It is unlawful to practice law unless the individual has received entry to the Florida Bar. A licensee will be disciplined by the FREC for this unlawful practice. The penalty can result in suspension or revocation of the license. A real estate licensee should avoid offering opinions on subjects such as the condition of title. Opinions such as this if acted or relied upon can expose the licensee to liability and/or disciplinary action by the licensing authorities.

In addition, in the normal course of business a licensee may provide opinions of value. These opinions of value must be accurate as exaggeration of same can be viewed as a form of misrepresentation and will subject the licensee to civil liability as well as disciplinary action from the licensing authorities.

For example, it would be illegal for a licensee to overstate the value of a property to a prospective seller in order to get a listing. It is considered to be fraud, breach of contract, or breach of trust.

FIXING OF COMMISSIONS OR FEES

It is an illegal practice to fix or attempt to fix commission rates or fees on an industry basis. This practice falls under the federal Anti-Trust Act and is termed price fixing. However, it is not illegal for licensees to contact another brokerage to inquire what compensation is offered on a specific listing that they wish to cooperate with.

Sales associates may not contract directly with any principal. Sales associates must always operate for and in the name of the sponsoring broker that they are registered with. This also includes any and all compensation derived from real estate activities. Compensation is always arrived at by negotiation between the principal and the broker or brokerage. The sales associate's compensation is arrived at by agreement between the parties.

You previously learned that a real estate broker acts as the agent to the principal, and all sales associates employed by the broker act as agents of the broker but are subagents of the principal. Such is the case when talking about licensees within the employ of the broker that is acting as an agent for a principal. It is for this and other reasons that a real estate licensee cannot sue a principal directly for compensation. There is no direct relationship other than through the broker.

Remember, a real estate licensee is one who assists a broker in the disposition of the broker's business. The business is never that of the sales associate.

Kickbacks

Kickbacks are illegal. They are considered to be undisclosed secret profit. However, when compensation or something of value is first disclosed to all interested parties and the licensee receives informed consent from each and every interested party that would otherwise be affected by the payment of compensation, it is commonly referred to as a referral fee. As long as it is not prohibited by other law, this practice is legal. The sales associate must remember to never accept compensation directly from anyone other than the sponsoring broker. This includes referral fees or other valuable consideration.

> **Example** A real estate agent in New York City (NYC) refers a buying customer to a Florida broker who agrees to pay a portion of the Florida commission to the NYC broker or brokerage. This practice is common and legal. As long as the agent from NYC never crosses state lines to conduct this transaction, a Florida broker may legally pay that broker or brokerage a referral fee. This starts with the party being referred requesting the referral. Referral fees can be considered kickbacks when undisclosed and informed consent has not been given.
>
> In Florida, it is unlawful for any person to share or pay an unlicensed individual a commission or other compensation derived from real estate activities. There are two exceptions to the aforementioned. A licensee may share compensation with either a buyer or a seller of a property transaction.
>
> It is unlawful for any licensee to compensate any person for performing any unlicensed activity. Unlicensed activity in Florida is a very serious offense. It is treated as a third-degree felony.

BROKER'S POLICY MANUAL

In the normal course of running a business, a real estate broker may create and administer policy manuals. This is important for a number of reasons. In particular, it will help brokers to direct all licensees and employees (as the case may be) as to what the brokers or brokerage seek to achieve and how they go about achieving their goal. It will further help to underwrite risk. When the brokerage has employees as well as independent contractors, the broker is advised to create two separate manuals to address the legal and taxation needs of all parties. In addition, the policy manual should clearly address how the sales associate will be compensated by the broker or brokerage. Please note that due to the fact that a broker is responsible for the activities of all licensees within his/her registration, the broker's policy and procedures manual can be the only mitigating factor that holds the broker harmless when a licensee performs a rogue act.

CHANGE OF EMPLOYER: NOTICE OF CHANGE/ DUPLICATION OF RECORDS

When a sales associate changes employing brokers, the DRE must be notified of the change in broker within ten (10) days on a prescribed form. As licenses are not transferable, the sales associate's license ceases to be in force until the DRE receives such notification. When a sales associate transfers from one employing broker to another, the sales associate is *not* permitted to remove or copy any transaction records from the previous employer. The records belong to the employing broker, not the sales associate, even if the sales associate was involved in the transaction. The removal of the broker's records would constitute theft.

The aforementioned does not preclude the sales associate from receiving earned monies (paid in the future) from a previous employing broker. This may be as a result of monies due from a pending transaction that closed after the licensee has reassociated with another broker. Well-thought-out termination agreements are required to protect either party's interests.

Sales Associate Obligation to a Principal Following Termination of Employment

Termination of employment can occur in a number of ways. Two common ways might be:

1. completion of the terms of the agreement
2. expiration of the employment agreement (listing agreement) term

Sales or broker associates are required to maintain the confidentiality of their principal. This is regardless of a successful or unsuccessful conclusion to a transaction. Any information that the licensee has learned about the principal must remain within the licensee's confidence. Failure to keep confidential sensitive information can lead to both civil liability and/or a licensing violation.

Unauthorized Use of Names and Insignias of Real Estate Organizations

Under FREC rules, it is unlawful to display (after one's name) the name or insignia of a real estate organization or **professional association (PA)** that requires membership if one is not a member. Where use of the name or insignia represents that person is a member, unauthorized use violates trademarks and is a violation of FREC rules.

CHANGE OF ADDRESS: PROCEDURE AND PENALTY FOR FAILURE TO NOTIFY THE FREC

If a broker's or real estate school's business address changes, the DRE must be notified of the address change in writing within ten (10) days of the change.

(A license ceases to be in force until the DRE receives this notification.)

The broker or school must file a notice of the change of address, along with the names of any sales associates or instructors who are no longer employed by the brokerage or the school. The notice of the change of address also acts to change the address of each sales associate or instructor. In essence, the broker or school is notifying the DRE of any agents or instructors who will not be moving to the new address with the broker or the school. The licenses of those who choose not to go with the broker or the school revert to involuntary inactive. They remain involuntary inactive until they reassociate with another broker or school.

Similarly, if a licensee changes his current residential address, the DRE must be notified of the change in writing within ten (10) days. Failure to do so can and most probably will result in disciplinary action that includes fines and/or license suspension. In addition, any Florida resident who becomes a nonresident must also notify the DRE and subsequently comply with all nonresident requirements within 60 days.

LICENSE VERSUS REGISTRATION

It is important to understand that real estate licenses are *only* issued to qualified *individuals* and not to *business entities*. Thus, an individual receives a *license,* while a business entity receives a *registration*. The qualifications for a real estate *license* in Florida were covered in Chapter 2. We mentioned then that in order for an individual to receive a real estate license in Florida, an applicant must do the following three things:

1. successfully complete prelicense education
2. submit a fully completed application along with the necessary license fee
3. successfully sit for and pass the Florida state examination

As you can see from these licensing requirements, no one other than an individual person can accomplish items 1 and 3 above. Business entities cannot sit for prelicense courses or take exams. It is for this reason that those entities are required to register with the FREC.

As a good memory device, think of the aforementioned as you would a driver's license and registration. Only individuals are granted licenses to operate a motor vehicle, while the vehicle simply receives a registration allowing the vehicle to be driven by someone possessing a valid driver's license in accordance with state law.

Types of Business Entities: Permitted Registrations

The following types of business entities are permitted to register with the DBPR *as legally registered brokerage entities*:

- sole proprietorships
- partnerships
    - general partnerships
    - limited partnerships

- corporations
  - C corp
  - S corp
- limited liability companies
- limited liability partnerships

The formation and composition of each type of business entity will be discussed in the following sections.

Sole Proprietorships

A **sole proprietorship** is a business where the sole owner is the individual licensee. A sole proprietor may do one of the following:

- do business under his/her own name
- do business under a d/b/a (doing business as) name, *but not an incorporated name*, as long as the d/b/a is registered with the FREC

A sole proprietorship bears unlimited liability. That is, the sole proprietor is personally responsible for *all* the debts of the business that exceed the assets. If a lawsuit results from a real estate transaction, not only are the company assets at risk, but the owner's real and personal property are at risk as well. In addition, sole proprietors are responsible for any and all other licensees within their employ. This includes routine daily supervision of all sales staff directly employed by the sole proprietor/broker. A sole proprietor does not pay taxes as a business. Rather, a sole proprietor pays individual income taxes on any income earned in any given tax year. The proprietor's income is reported to the IRS by submission of a K-1. Furthermore, since sole proprietors will operate in their own name, they do not have to comply with the Florida Fictitious Name Act.

Partnerships

The next type of business entity that may register as a real estate broker is the partnership. There are two types of partnerships:

1. general partnerships
2. limited partnerships

General Partnerships

A **general partnership** is formed when two or more partners wishing to do business with each other comprise the business entity. The partnership is created by an express or implied agreement (contract) between all partners. Each partner bears joint and several liability for the other partners and for the partnership. Joint and several liability means each member of a group may be held individually liable for the acts of the entire group. This includes monetary obligations of the partnership and/or partners. Each partner bears unlimited liability for the debts of the partnership. Each partner may bind and obligate the other. For example, if one partner incurs expenses on behalf of the partnership, all other partners may be liable for those expenses, even if they were unaware of them.

If the partnership performs any real estate act as defined under Florida law, at least one of the partners in a general partnership is required to have an active broker's license. Any other partner who will perform a real estate act for compensation must also hold an active broker's license. Sales associates and broker associates may never be registered as partners in a general partnership.

The partnership name must receive a registration from the FREC. Registering the general partnership with the Florida Department of State is voluntary. Any change in the registration (such as resignation, termination, or death of a registered partner) must be reported to the FREC. All partners who will engage in real estate activities with the public must be licensed as brokers. In the event that the only active broker/partner resigns, dies, or is terminated, in order to maintain the registration of the partnership, the broker must be replaced within 14 calendar (not business) days or the partnership's registration will be canceled. In the event there is more than one active broker within the partnership and one of the active brokers resigns, dies, or is terminated, the broker may be replaced by another active broker. At that point, no change in the registration occurs. However, irrespective of any of these circumstances, the FREC must be notified of the substitution. It should be noted that sales associates and broker associates may never be general partners in a real estate brokerage partnership.

We just looked at the features of a general partnership. Another type of partnership is the limited partnership.

Limited Partnerships

A **limited partnership** can be created with one or more *general partners* and one or more *limited partners*. *General partners* make decisions and actively participate in the day-to-day operation of the business. *Limited partners* are not permitted to make decisions or otherwise participate in the management and operation of the business. Limited partners may not perform an active managerial role in the day-to-day operation of the partnership; they are strictly *passive* investors. In effect, limited partners are silent partners.

A limited partnership is formed by a written agreement that must be filed with the Florida Department of State. Each general partner bears *unlimited* liability. Each limited partner bears *limited* liability—up to the amount the partner has invested. If the partnership performs any real estate act as defined under Florida law, at least one of the general partners is required to have an active broker's license. Any other general partner who will perform a real estate act for compensation and/or deal with the general public must also hold an active broker's license. Sales associates and broker associates may not be general partners in a limited partnership; however, they may be limited partners. The partnership name must receive a registration from the FREC.

Any change in the registration (such as resignation, termination, or death of a general partner) must be reported to the FREC. In the event that the only active broker/general partner resigns, dies, or is terminated, in order to maintain the registration of the partnership, the broker must be replaced within 14 calendar (not business) days or face cancelation of the partnership's registration. In the event there is more than one active broker/general partner and one of the active brokers resigns, dies, or is terminated, the broker may be replaced by another active broker. At that point, no change in the registration occurs. However, irrespective of any of these circumstances, the FREC must be notified of the substitution. Limited partners are not required to register with the FREC.

Ostensible Partnerships

Another type of partnership is the **ostensible partnership**, which is an entity that appears to be a partnership but is not a real partnership. That is, the parties act like a partnership exists when in fact one does not. Because ostensible partnerships are deceitful, such entities are prohibited. When brokers who operate separate entities share space (which is common), their business should be separate from that of the other. This will avoid the perception of an ostensible partnership. Each party's identity should be separate and distinct from that of the other. Failure to do so will subject the licensee(s) to be disciplined.

Corporations

A **corporation** is defined as a legal person/entity organized under the laws of Florida or another state. A corporation may include one or more people. Individuals become part owners (shareholders or stockholders) by purchasing stock in the corporation. The shareholders elect a board of directors who manage the corporation while looking out for the shareholders' best interest. Officers are elected or appointed by the board of directors. Officers run and manage the day-to-day operations of the corporation. Corporations offer individual asset protection to their officers and shareholders. This means that the corporation is responsible for its obligations.

For example, if a creditor sues a corporation for money, the corporation itself has to pay if it loses the lawsuit. However, if the corporation does *not* have enough money to pay the creditor, the creditor may not look to the officers or shareholders of the corporation to pay what the corporation could not.

Corporations, unlike the previously discussed entities (partnerships), are subject to double taxation. When a corporation earns money, it can make a profit. These profits must be reported to the IRS and corporate taxes paid. When the corporation pays out dividends from its profits to its shareholders, the payments are considered income to the shareholders and also must be reported to the IRS and individual taxes paid. The net effect is double taxation—the money is taxed once on the profits of the corporation and once on the dividends paid to its shareholders. As a further note, the IRS has determined that a corporation can only pay or distribute a dividend after having made a profit. A corporation is deemed to be a legal person that stands on its own as a separate entity from its shareholders—therein lies the reasoning behind double taxation.

Corporations are formed as C corporations under a document called *articles of incorporation*. The articles of incorporation address the purpose and rules of operation of the corporation. A corporation can be either a domestic or a foreign corporation.

A *domestic* corporation is formed in and under the laws associated with the state of formation (e.g., a corporation formed under Florida laws in Florida would be a domestic corporation).

A *foreign* corporation is formed in and under the laws associated with another state (e.g., a corporation doing business in Florida but that was formed under the laws of another state).

A corporation may also be for profit or not for profit. If the corporation will operate as a real estate brokerage entity, the corporation must be registered with the FREC. The corporation must provide the FREC with necessary proof showing a legal corporate formation exists. If the corporation will operate as a real estate brokerage entity, at least one of the officers or directors must hold an active real estate broker's license (the qualifying or principal broker). Any other officers or directors who engage in brokerage activities must hold active broker's licenses. Sales associates and broker associates *may never be officers or directors of the corporation*. In addition, this means a sales associate or broker associate may not be designated a title (after his/her name) that would normally indicate that he/she is an officer of a corporation.

If there is only one active broker in a corporation, any change in the status of the active broker (resignation, termination of employment, or death) must be reported to the FREC, and a replacement broker must be registered within 14 calendar (not business) days. Failure to do so can result in cancelation of the corporation's registration. Cancelation of a registration of any legal entity renders the licenses held under that registration involuntarily inactive. If the corporation has more than one active broker, the corporation's registration would not be affected by the resignation, termination, or death of one of the active brokers. Regardless, the substitution must be reported to the DRE.

Limited Liability Companies

The last type of business entity that may register as a broker is the limited liability company, which was created recently as an allowed organizational form of legal entity. The characteristics of this type of business entity are summarized next.

Limited liability companies are basically hybrids of corporations and partnerships. A limited liability company has full liability protection to the same degree as a corporation. However, unlike corporations that have shareholders and profit that is subject to double taxation, a limited liability company has *members* and has profit that is not subject to double taxation. Rather, like partnerships, limited liability companies enjoy profit that is taxed once. Money comes into the company. The company pays no taxes on the income. The limited liability company then pays distributions out to its members, who must then report the income to the IRS and pay income tax on it. Thus, the entity does not pay taxes; only its members do. Each member's income is reported to the IRS utilizing the K-1 form.

Remember the following:

- A limited liability company does not have shareholders; it has members.
- A limited liability company does not have officers, such as a president, vice president, etc. It has titles, such as a managing member.
- The entity name must include either the words "Registered Limited Liability Company" or "LLC" at the end of the entity name.

Limited Liability Partnerships

Another type of business entity that may register as a broker is a limited liability partnership. It's important to distinguish limited liability partnerships from partnerships. A **limited liability partnership** is like a regular limited partnership but with one big difference—it does not have unlimited personal liability. Under a limited liability partnership, a partner is not liable for negligent acts committed by another partner. A partner is, however, liable for his/her own negligent acts. A limited liability partnership must file with the Florida secretary of state. The entity name must include either the words "Registered Limited Liability Partnership" or "LLP" at the end of the entity name. It is important to note that this type of business entity allows persons previously restricted from incorporating some personal asset protection. Examples of persons previously unable to incorporate include but are not limited to professionals such as attorneys, doctors, engineers, architects, and any other person described as a professional individual.

Entities That May Not Register as a Brokerage

We just looked at the types of business entities that are permitted to register as real estate brokers. There are also some legal entities that are *not* permitted to register as real estate brokerage entities:

- corporation sole
- joint ventures
- trusts
- associations and unincorporated associations

Corporation Sole

A corporation sole is typically a religious organization like a church. It is a not-for-profit entity. Therefore, it will never act as a for-profit brokerage.

Joint Ventures

A joint venture is not a legal entity; it is more of an arrangement that is usually designed for one specific project. The combining of two or more parties in a joint venture does not constitute a formation of a new legal person/entity. It is an arrangement that usually terminates at the end of that project. This does not prohibit the parties from working together in another arrangement, and it sometimes can lead to new future partnerships. Let's look at an example of how this arrangement can come about.

Example

Developer Max and developer Ian attend an auction. Both have the intention of purchasing the same property. Rather than competing and bidding against each other (resulting in overpayment for the property), they decide to joint venture the project and purchase the property together.

There are times whereby two separate real estate brokers are working as coagents to the same principal. This may be by choice of the brokers to combine their efforts and expertise to vie for an assignment that the other could not necessarily obtain alone. Then again, the principal may have two favored real estate brokers that work in different offices and cannot decide whether to grant the assignment to one or the other. The principal asks the two separate brokers to work together. In that situation, both brokers work as one agent to the principal.

Trusts

A trust engages in transactions that involve its own property. Acquisition and disposition of real property are on behalf of the trust and its beneficiaries. This is the primary reason why a trust may not register as a real estate brokerage.

Associations and Unincorporated Associations

Associations usually own or are responsible for operating property of some type or nature. Common examples include but are not limited to:

- a cooperative
- a condominium

Associations are normally created for that single purpose and not for engaging in the business of brokerage or other third-party relationships. This also includes unincorporated associations. An unincorporated association occurs when two or more persons perform activities and acts (such as in a private gated community) without legally forming or filing paperwork that would otherwise create an incorporated association.

What happens, legally speaking, when a group of people get together and decide to perform some task without filing any legal paperwork or establishing any formal legal structure? Whether they know it or not, they have formed an unincorporated association. "Unincorporated association" means an unincorporated group of two or more persons joined by mutual consent for a common lawful purpose, whether organized for profit or not.

OFFICERS AND DIRECTORS OF REAL ESTATE FIRMS

Under license law in Florida (as well as in most states in the union), a sales associate is prohibited from holding an officer or director position in a real estate brokerage corporation. Officer/director positions may only be held by someone holding a broker's license.

The same holds true for a general or limited partnership. In either arrangement, a sales associate may never be a general partner. The rationale is that it is a position of management that by law requires the general partner to hold broker status. This prevents anyone other than a licensed broker from operating a real estate brokerage.

TRADE NAMES

Previously in this chapter we defined a trade name as any name that is not the name of the licensee. When the name is a fictitious name, it must also conform and comply with the Florida Fictitious Name Act. It is important to note that sales associates may not utilize a trade name or register for a license in any name other than their true name.

Summary

Licensees, unless they are real estate brokers, must work under the license and supervision of a broker or developer. Real estate brokers are required to have a stationary office and register that office with the DBPR. Blind advertising is illegal. This includes any advertisement that does not mention or indicate that the advertiser is a real estate broker or brokerage. Escrow laws were created to protect the owner of the funds that are being held by another. In Florida, a broker may act as an escrow agent and is governed by strict rules concerning escrow accounts.

A broker must decide how to organize his/her business. A broker may do so through a variety of legal entity formation options. An understanding of each of these options becomes essential when choosing the right form and vehicle in operating a broker's business. It is recommended that the individual consult with his/her attorney and accountant prior to forming a business entity. Individuals receive licenses while legal business entities receive registrations. In each entity situation, if there is only one active broker, any change in the status of the active broker (resignation, termination of employment, or death) must be reported to the FREC, and a replacement broker must be registered within 14 calendar (not business) days or face cancelation of the registration. Trade names must be registered with the DRE.

Review Questions

1. A buyer gave a binder deposit to a sales associate on Friday. This money must be turned over to his/her broker by the end of:
   a. Friday
   b. Monday
   c. Tuesday
   d. Wednesday

2. The buyer and seller are quarreling over repairs for termite damage as required in the contract, and each has demanded the escrow deposit because of breach. The broker must:
   a. notify the FREC before 15 business days pass
   b. follow the seller's written instructions
   c. advise the parties to consult attorneys
   d. ask the DRE to issue an escrow disbursement order

3. Sylvia Black works for Acme Realty, and she is sending out calendars to neighborhoods where she would like to obtain listings. These calendars must contain:
   a. Sylvia's work address and phone numbers
   b. the name of Sylvia's broker
   c. Sylvia's business card, which indicates she is a broker associate
   d. the words "Acme Realty"

4. Jane has personalized the yard signs for her listings by placing toppers that state "Call Jane!"
   a. This is not legal unless Jane is the broker.
   b. This is a legal and common practice.
   c. This is OK if Jane's last name is on the sign.
   d. This is OK if the firm's name is on the sign.

5. The buyer gives an associate a binder deposit on Thursday. The money must be in the broker's escrow account no later than before the end of:
   a. Monday
   b. Tuesday
   c. Wednesday
   d. Thursday

6. The buyer came to the office on Monday and gave the binder deposit directly to the broker. The money must be placed in the broker's escrow account no later than the end of:
   a. Monday
   b. Tuesday
   c. Wednesday
   d. Thursday

7. Louise places an ad for Acme Realty in the local newspaper. The ad describes the property, gives the price, and states "For more information, call 555-2111."
   a. Louise cannot place ads for her broker.
   b. This is an example of institutional advertising.
   c. This ad constitutes a blind advertisement.
   d. There is nothing illegal about the situation.

8. Both the buyer and the seller have demanded the escrow deposit. The broker notified the FREC in writing seven days later. How many days does the broker have to institute a settlement procedure?
   a. 30 days
   b. 23 days
   c. 15 days
   d. 13 days

9. Which statement is true about an office sign?
   a. No sign is required if the firm operates out of a private home.
   b. The office address is a sign requirement.
   c. The names of all partners in a real estate partnership must be on the sign.
   d. "Licensed Real Estate Broker" must be on the sign.

10. Which entity CANNOT be registered as a real estate broker?
    a. corporation sole
    b. a for-profit corporation
    c. general partnership
    d. limited partnership

11. Two brokers own and operate separate real estate businesses. They are going to join together to oversee the rehabbing of an apartment building into condos, at which time they are going to market the condos. This:
    a. is a partnership and must be registered with the FREC
    b. joint venture, a temporary arrangement, is not registered with the FREC
    c. requires a written agreement that is filed with the Department of State
    d. is an ostensible partnership with shared liability

12. General Realty stores its office records in a storage facility at another location.
    a. All records must be kept on the premises for a period of five years.
    b. This is legal if the records are not destroyed.
    c. As long as the records are available, they can be in another place.
    d. The records must be available to auditors for at least seven years.

13. The seller refuses to pay the broker's $5,000 commission. The broker is holding $5,000 in escrow for this transaction. The broker:
    a. can take the $5,000 in lieu of the commission
    b. can hold up closing until the seller agrees to pay
    c. is allowed to place a $5,000 lien on the property
    d. can sue the seller in a court of law

14. Which of these statements about a limited partnership is FALSE?
    a. The limited partnership agreement must be filed with the Florida Department of State.
    b. The limited partnership must be registered with the FREC.
    c. The limited partners can be associates.
    d. Associates can be registered as licensed general partners.

15. When forming a general partnership as a real estate business:
    a. the general partnership agreement must be filed with the Florida Department of State
    b. the general partners must hold real estate licenses
    c. one general partner must be licensed as a broker
    d. all general partners must be licensed as brokers

16. Which statement is true concerning real estate brokerage trust funds?
    a. The broker may not place personal funds into an escrow account.
    b. The broker must dispense the interest if the funds are in an interest-bearing account.
    c. Interest-bearing accounts are not legal for trust accounts.
    d. A Florida attorney can hold the escrowed funds.

17. If only one partner in a general partnership has a broker's license and the license is suspended:
    a. the partnership is dissolved and must be reformed
    b. a new active licensed broker must be substituted for the previous one prior to the passing of 14 days
    c. the loss must be reported to the FREC
    d. all partners in a real estate partnership must be licensed as brokers

18. Super Sales Realty has agreed to market a builder's homes. Sales associates are assigned to the model homes, and potential buyers arrive at a designated location in response to the ads. The agents are using one of the model homes as a central place to meet the buyers and hand out sales brochures. When a buyer wants to make an offer, the agents take the buyer to the company's principal office to complete the paperwork.
    a. The model home is considered to be a branch office because buyers know to arrive at the location.
    b. This is a branch office because agents are assigned to the location.
    c. This is not a branch office because contracts and negotiations are signed and held elsewhere.
    d. An office sign must be placed on or about the entrance.

19. The escrow records of Surefire Sales were audited. Records showed that in June, the escrow account held $1,003 of the broker's personal funds.
    a. The broker is guilty of commingling.
    b. The broker has committed fraud.
    c. There is no illegality; the amount was less than $5,000.
    d. This is OK because the records are accurate and complete.

20. Jim works for Broker Smith, and Jim receives 50% of the money he generates for the company. After a closing, Broker Smith calls Jim and apologizes for spending Jim's share of the commission to pay the office rent.
    a. Smith is guilty of fraud.
    b. This is legal if Smith pays Jim later.
    c. Jim can charge Smith with conversion.
    d. All money belongs to the broker. Jim is out of luck.

21. Which of the following is the only first-degree misdemeanor in the practice of real estate?
    a. practicing without a license
    b. failing to follow laws regarding rental lists
    c. violating the Time Share Act
    d. violating the laws regarding advance fees

VIOLATIONS OF LICENSE LAW, PENALTIES, AND PROCEDURES

6

KEY TERMS

breach of trust
citation
complaint
concealment
conversion
culpable negligence
formal or administrative complaint
fraud
legally sufficient

mediation
misrepresentation
moral turpitude
notice of noncompliance
probable cause
recommended order
stipulation
subpoena
summary/emergency suspension order

LEARNING OBJECTIVES

After completing this lesson, you will be able to:

- explain the procedures involved in the reporting of violations, the investigation of complaints, and the conduct of hearings
- define the elements of a valid complaint
- discuss the composition of the probable cause panel
- recognize events that would cause a license application to be denied
- distinguish actions that would cause a license to be subject to suspension or revocation
- identify the procedure to seek reimbursement from the Real Estate Recovery Fund and individuals who would be eligible for it
- identify individuals who are not qualified to make a claim from the Real Estate Recovery Fund
- describe the monetary limits imposed by law on the Real Estate Recovery Fund
- explain the penalties for a first- and second-degree misdemeanors and what real estate activities are first-degree misdemeanors
- provide examples of the unlicensed practice of law
- illustrate presumptions for a party performing real estate services

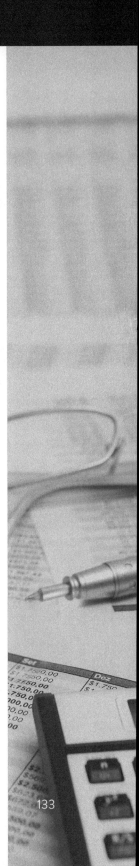

PROCEDURES FOR DISCIPLINING LICENSEES

In Florida, the disciplinary procedure begins with various aspects and parts of state law. Any licensees who bear the misfortune of disciplinary action taken against their license will be subject to state laws that cover each of the following:

- the investigative process
- the hearing process

These laws include but are not limited to:

- Chapter 120, F.S. (Administrative Procedure Act)
- Chapter 455, F.S. (Business and Professional Regulation: General Provisions)
- Chapter 475, F.S. (Real Estate Brokers, Sales Associates, Schools, and Appraisers)
- Chapter 61J2 (Florida Administrative Code)

The Complaint

The Division of Real Estate (DRE) acts on broad powers. These powers are given to the Department of Business and Professional Regulation (DBPR) by the Florida legislature. The aforementioned powers include but are not limited to investigation of any legally sufficient complaint that has been filed with the Department against any Florida licensee (person) or registrant (business) that has violated any state:

- rule
- regulation
- statute

The allegation does not have to involve real estate or occur in Florida. The term **legally sufficient** means that if the allegation is true, a rule, regulation, or statute has been violated. Therefore, the DRE is charged with the responsibility to investigate:

- all applicants for licensure by:
  - verifying information contained on the application
  - performing background checks
- all complaints that are received against a licensee
- any licensee who is believed to have broken any state or license laws in the absence of a complaint from the general public

For the first-time offender of a minor offense or infraction, it would not be uncommon for the licensee to receive a notice of noncompliance. A **notice of noncompliance** if not cured within the statutory allowed time (within 15 days) will result in the issuance of a citation. Think of it in the same manner as a notice of default that if not cured results in some legal action. If the notice of non compliance is corrected or cured within the 15 days, the licensee is back in compliance, and no further action is taken or required. However, when a citation is issued, this involves a disciplinary action taken against a licensee.

For example, the lender of a home mortgage informs the borrower that he/she is in default for nonpayment of a monthly mortgage installment. The lender then gives you a grace period to cure the default by making payment and bringing the account back to performing.

Minor offenses are those that generally do not affect the general public. For example, a minor offense where a notice of noncompliance would be issued might include but not be limited to:

- signage that does not conform to or comply with FREC rules

This investigative procedure and process is necessary for the FREC to carry out its role as a prosecuting unit. Let's take a look at the complaint process and the respective role that each unit of state government takes within this process.

THE COMPLAINT PROCESS, PROCEDURES, AND APPEAL

Complaint and Investigation

Because the license law was enacted to protect the health and welfare of the general public from losses resulting from those acting on behalf of others, the DBPR and the FREC respond very seriously to any complaint made by the general public against a licensee. A **complaint** can be defined as an allegation to a violation of a rule or law.

The first step in the complaint process is the filing of a complaint. It is then reviewed to determine that the complaint contains facts that are legally sufficient to warrant further investigation. Any written complaint that is legally sufficient and filed with the DBPR will be investigated (investigation is the second step). This is true even if the complaint was filed anonymously. In Florida, there is a statute of limitations for filing a complaint against a licensee. The complaint must be filed within:

- five years after the act (the alleged violation), or
- five years after the act was discovered or should have been discovered.

In all cases, a copy of the complaint must be sent to the licensee. There is one exception when the subject to a complaint would not receive a copy of the complaint. This would occur if the violation in question was criminal. If a complaint is made and later the complainant withdraws the complaint, the DBPR may continue with the investigation. As previously mentioned, if the DBPR believes that a licensee has violated the license law or any other state law and there is no complaint from the general public, the DBPR (on its own initiative) may conduct its own investigation into the matter. Once a licensee is brought up on allegations of license law infractions or other complaints against that licensee, the infraction review process begins. Let's examine this process.

When a complaint against any one or more licensees has been duly made and appropriately filed with the DBPR, the complaint itself will be examined to verify its validity. To establish the validity of a complaint, the DBPR must establish whether or not there is any indication that state laws have been broken or if any rules of either the DBPR or FREC have been violated.

> ### Coaching Tips
>
> If a violation is minor and is the licensee's first offense, the DBPR has the authority to issue a notice of noncompliance. The notice identifies the violation and describes steps the licensee must take to comply with the law. If the licensee fails to comply, disciplinary procedures may proceed. An example of a minor violation is failing to maintain the proper office sign.

In the event the DBPR establishes that a complaint is valid, the DBPR is required to investigate the matter. (Investigation is Step 2 in the complaint process.) During the investigation, depositions may be taken and **subpoenas** (an order requiring someone to appear in court or an order for the producing of records) may be issued for the attendance of witnesses and/or the production of relevant documents. In all cases, an investigative report is prepared and submitted by the legal division to the probable cause panel. We will examine the purpose and composition of the panel next.

Probable Cause Panel

Step 3 in the complaint process is the probable cause panel. Pursuant to the aforementioned, at the end of the investigation, the DBPR creates a report that is submitted to a probable cause panel. The panel consists of two appointed members of FREC who are appointed by the Commission chair. In the event that a panel cannot be formed in a timely manner by the Commission chair, a panel is appointed by the DBPR. The appointed panel then arrives at a decision as to whether probable cause exists. As prescribed under Chapter 455, F.S., former FREC members can serve on a probable cause panel.

Unlike Commission meetings, probable cause meetings are not open to the public. In fact, Commission members who do not serve on the panel are restricted from the panel meeting. This ensures a licensee will receive fair treatment under the laws that govern the disciplinary procedure.

At this point, the panel must decide within 30 days from receiving the investigation report whether or not **probable cause** exists (in this case, defined as reasonable grounds for prosecution of a licensee). This will be based upon the facts of the report submitted by the DBPR. This becomes the sole objective for the panel. Generally, a decision is reached within 30 days; there may be instances whereby the panel can ask for more time or for more information in order to render a decision.

If the panel determines that there is no probable cause, one of the following occurs:

- The case is dismissed via a letter of guidance (a letter that suggests action or actions to be taken concerning the subject).
- The DBPR elects to pursue the matter further on its own. If this occurs:
  - the matter is immediately referred to the FREC, and
  - the FREC will determine whether or not the matter requires further investigation.

    Within this process the FREC may involve and retain one or both of the following:
    - outside legal assistance
    - private investigators

If the panel determines that probable cause does exist, the disciplinary process continues.

Coaching Tips

Complaints do not become public until:

- 10 days after probable cause is determined, or
- 10 days after the licensee waives her confidentiality privilege.

Formal Complaint

Step 4 in the complaint process is the filing of a formal complaint. The DBPR is required to file a formal complaint against the respondent licensee. The **formal or administrative complaint** lists the charges set forth against the respondent licensee. The licensee then has a prescribed period of time to either accept or reject the charges set forth within the complaint (within 21 days from receipt of the administrative complaint). A licensee who responds to a formal complaint (in a timely manner) has three choices (an election of rights form):

1. The licensee can meet with a DRE attorney and request a **stipulation** (settlement of penalty). The stipulation must be approved by the FREC. The licensee may appear with or without legal representation.
2. The licensee can choose to not dispute the charges and elect to have an informal hearing held at an open Commission meeting. In this choice, the probable cause panel will not participate. Some agreement can be reached, at which point the matter will draw to an end.
3. The licensee can dispute the allegations set forth and request a formal hearing. In the event that any material fact (a fact that would be germane for one to come to a decision) of the allegation(s) is disputed by the licensee, a formal hearing is mandatory.

The Florida Division of Administrative Hearings (DOAH) will appoint an administrative law judge (ALJ) to preside over the formal hearing. The ALJ must be a member of the Florida Bar for at least the previous five years. In addition, the ALJ may not be a judge in the traditional sense. In order to give this procedure more weight, the current title of *administrative law judge* was changed from the previous title of *hearing officer*. At the conclusion of the formal hearing, the ALJ will issue a recommended order to the FREC. The **recommended order** includes:

- case findings
- a conclusion
- the recommended penalty

Should the licensee fail to respond to the formal complaint within the statutory allowed period of time, a final order (default judgment) will be entered against a licensee. When this occurs, the penalty usually will result in license revocation. This is a permanent removal from the practice itself.

If the charges contained are accepted, this ultimately results in a final order (judgment) setting forth the action to be taken against the respondent licensee. If the charges contained are not accepted, a hearing is then scheduled.

Formal or Informal Hearing

Step 5 in the complaint process is a formal or informal hearing. The hearing may entail informal or formal proceedings. During an informal hearing, the licensee presents his/her case, typically at a Commission meeting (probable cause panel members are excused). Following the hearing, the parties may resolve the issue. However, if the parties cannot agree as to how to settle the matter, a formal hearing is held.

A formal hearing takes place before a full-time Florida ALJ. The Division of Administrative Hearings (DOAH) employs the ALJ. The respondent licensee will be given a chance to present evidence, testimony, and defense against the allegations contained within the complaint. The process is similar to how a case is tried in either civil or criminal court, wherein each party presents facts and witnesses. The ALJ hears the case and concludes same by preparing a written recommended order. The recommended order is submitted to the FREC. The order includes the ALJ's case conclusions and recommended penalty(s). The penalty(s) is/are based upon what is permitted under FREC rules. This process is conducted within the rules of the courtrooms and not within the rules of the DBPR, DRE, or FREC.

At the conclusion of the hearing process, the presiding judge will draft an order recommending any applicable restitution and penalty to be assessed against the respondent licensee. The presiding judge will forward the conclusive order to the DBPR for further action and enforcement.

Final Order

Step 6 in the complaint process is the issuance of a final order. The FREC considers the judge's recommended order and issues a final order (a judgment). Issuance of the final order concludes the case against the licensee. In addition to the final order, the FREC can ask the secretary of the DBPR to issue a summary (emergency) suspension. Summary suspensions are requested when it is discovered a licensee has violated escrow laws and rules. This includes theft or conversion of funds belonging to others. The FREC may accept, modify, or reject the recommended order. Thus, although the DBPR investigates complaints, the FREC issues the final order. The final order:

- must be in written form
- must detail the charge(s)
- must be inclusive of determination of facts found through the case hearing
- must list the action taken against the licensee
- must advise the licensee that the final order may be appealed
- takes effect 30 days from entry

The FREC must promptly report to the proper prosecuting authority any criminal violation of any statute relating to the practice of a real estate professional regulated by the FREC.

Coaching Tips

If a violation poses an immediate danger to public health or safety, a hearing for **summary emergency suspension order** (emergency suspension of a license) may be held. In this situation, the final order must be issued by the DBPR secretary or legal representative. If a summary suspension is ordered, the order must be followed with a formal suspension or revocation hearing. In addition, a licensee may continue to practice up to the day the final order takes effect.

Appeal Process

The final step in the complaint process is the appeal process. If a respondent licensee disagrees with the final order issued by FREC, the licensee has the right under the Florida Statutes to appeal the order by requesting a judicial (court) review. It is this appeal step that allows the respondent licensee to challenge the findings of regulatory agencies such as the DBPR. In the event of any miscarriage of justice resulting from the disciplinary process, this final appeal process gives a respondent licensee a chance to overturn the decision. If the decision is in fact overturned, the licensee's privilege and ability to practice real estate are restored.

> **The Steps of the Complaint Process**
> 1. The complaint is submitted to the DBPR.
> 2. Investigation of the complaint commences, and the licensee is notified of the investigation.
> 3. A probable cause panel reviews the case to determine the existence of probable cause.
> 4. Drafting of a formal complaint commences if probable cause exists.
> 5. Formal or informal hearings commence.
> 6. Final order (judgment) is achieved, bringing the case to a close.
> 7. The appeal process (via the courts) begins.

Stay of Enforcement

We just learned that when a final order is issued by a regulatory body, the individual does have a right of appeal. This enables the individual to challenge the findings of the prosecuting tribunal. In order to protect the rights of individuals during the appeal process, a stay of enforcement is used by courts to stop execution of the judgment.

Writ of Supersedes

A writ is an order. It is an order issued by a court of higher authority such as an appeals court. It is a Latin word that means "to desist." A writ issued by a court instructs that something be done or authorizes a specific act to be accomplished. In the appeal process and until the final outcome of the appeal, a higher court can instruct a lower trial court to not allow enforcement of a final order or judgment. It is also referred to as a stay of proceeding. In the case of real estate licensing, an individual not subject to an emergency suspension order would be able to continue to practice.

LICENSE LAW VIOLATIONS AND PENALTIES

Under the powers granted to the FREC, it has the authority to:

- deny a license application for a variety of reasons including but not limited to:
  - the application is incomplete
  - the individual possesses a criminal record (misdemeanor or felony)
  - the individual lied on an application
- refuse to renew a license for various reasons; the most common for:
  - not completing the required postlicense education for either:
    - sales associate; or
    - broker
  - not completing the required continuing education

License law infractions will result in disciplinary action against a licensee. The following list of actions identifies just a few of the violations that result in immediate disciplinary action such as denial, revocation, and/or suspension of a real estate license by the FREC:

- obtaining a license through material misstatements on a license application
- engaging in **fraud** (performing an act intended to deceive), dishonesty, or **misrepresentation** (a false act or statement) in a business transaction
- being found guilty of, or pleading nolo contendere to, a crime involving **moral turpitude** (conduct that is contradictory to society resulting in a crime) and failing to disclose same
- failing to maintain principal office or branch office entrance signs as required
- failing on the part of the broker to register any branch office
- failing on the part of the broker to properly register a trade or fictitious name
- failing to supervise either of the following:
  - a broker associate
  - a sales associate registered with that broker/brokerage
- advertising in a false and/or misleading manner
- placing a blind advertisement
- failing to account for or to deliver to a person escrowed property as required by law
- being found guilty of **conversion** (legal term for stealing)
- being found guilty of commingling (mixing of funds belonging to others entrusted in the broker's possession with the broker's operation funds)
- failing to make a timely deposit of monies belonging to others requiring deposit into the broker's escrow/trust account
- failing to review trust account procedures to ensure accurate compliance with the law
- failing to provide necessary disclosure forms concerning:
  - single agent relationships
  - consent for transitioning from a single agent relationship to another relationship
- failing to include a definite date of expiration, description of the property, price and terms, fee or commission, and signature of the principal in a written listing agreement or failing to give a copy to the principal
- entering into any listing agreement that contains an automatic renewal clause
- paying a fee or commission for a real estate activity to an unlicensed person, even if only for a referral (Paying a commission to a broker licensed in another state is acceptable.)
- in the case of a sales associate, accepting a commission or compensation from anyone other than the employing broker
- in the case of a broker, employing a sales associate who is not properly licensed

Revocation/Suspension of Broker's License

The most serious type of (administrative) penalty issued by the FREC is revocation of one's license to practice real estate. Revocation of one's license represents a permanent removal from real estate practice, while suspension results in a temporary penalty. The FREC can suspend a license for up to 10 years. Under Florida law, if a broker's license is revoked and/or suspended, the licenses of all licensees registered under that broker automatically become involuntarily inactive. However, those affected licensees may reassociate and apply for a license with another broker willing to sponsor the individual. In order to do so, the new broker will need to submit DBPR form RE-11.

> **Example** Broker Betty's license is suspended. Sales Associate Sam was employed by Broker Betty. Sales Associate Sam may re-associate and apply for a license with another broker willing to sponsor him. Sales Associate Sam cannot open his own real estate business. Also, Sales Associate Sam is not required to retake the state exam.

Coaching Tips

A license is considered ineffective when it has been suspended or canceled or when it is inactive. A license is considered void when it has expired or has been revoked.

Exceptions to Permanent Revocation

There are exceptions to receiving permanent revocation of a license. These exceptions would include:

- filing an application to renew one's license without first completing the required continuing education
- filing an application for a real estate license that contains false or fraudulent information

Should either act occur, the individual is not able to reapply for a real estate sales associate's license for five years. However, the FREC may specify a lesser suspension period in their final order. This would normally occur when there are mitigating circumstances presented by the licensee at the hearing. When suspension or revocation is imposed on a licensee, the minimum fine in addition to the suspension or revocation of the license is $1,000.

Revoke a License without Prejudice (475.25[2], F.S.)

When a real estate license is issued by the Commission in error, the license may be cancelled or revoked by the FREC. Should this occur as a result of the aforementioned, that applicant will not be treated with any prejudice resulting from the error of the Commission.

Violations and Penalties

There are three types of penalties for license law violations:

1. administrative penalties, which are imposed by the FREC
2. criminal penalties, which are imposed by a court of law
3. civil penalties, which are also imposed by a court of law

Let's take a closer look at these types of penalties.

Administrative Penalties

The FREC is authorized to:

- deny a license
- suspend a license for no more than 10 years
- revoke a license
- place a licensee on probation
- impose a fine not to exceed:
    - $5,000 for each violation of Chapter 475 of the Florida Statutes (475, F.S.)—real estate brokers, sales associates, and schools
    - $5,000 for each violation of Chapter 455 of the Florida Statutes (455, F.S.)—business and professional regulation
- issue a citation
- place the licensee on probation

Citations

On a daily basis, DBPR investigators are out in the field and may randomly inspect and audit:

- real estate licensees
- real estate brokerage businesses
- real estate schools

While conducting a routine inspection, a DBPR investigator has the authority (for certain minor violations) to issue either a notice of non compliance or a citation to a licensee. A citation will subject a licensee to disciplinary action by the Commission. The **citation** identifies the violation and the penalty (e.g., fine, order to complete educational courses, etc.). Common offenses that could be cited include:

- blind advertising (advertising without clearly identifying that the advertiser is a real estate broker/licensee)
- inappropriate handling of escrow accounts such as:
    - not signing reconciliation statements
    - not dating the statements

When a citation has been issued, the licensee has 30 days to respond to the allegations contained within the citation. Failure to respond within the 30 days will result in the citation becoming a default final order. The licensee may choose to accept the citation in lieu of going through the hearing process described earlier. Should this occur, the citation results in a final order. A final order is the equivalent of a judgment rendered by a court. At that point, the matter concludes. However, should the licensee decide to dispute the allegations contained within the citation, the licensee must reply in writing within the 30-day period. Assume that a citation was issued to a licensee in error. In this situation, it is imperative that the licensee respond in writing within 30 days by contesting the allegations contained in the citation. When the citation is responded to within the appropriate time frame, a formal or informal hearing may be held.

In addition to the citation, other administrative penalties include:

- issuing a notice of noncompliance—we previously learned that a notice of noncompliance is a form of a default notice that is normally issued for minor license law violations that do not directly affect a member of the general public (i.e., improper signage)
- placing a licensee on probation
- depending on the infraction, requiring a licensee to sit for education course(s) in addition to a monetary penalty

Mediation

Mediation is a form of alternative dispute resolution and a recommended solution provided by a third person to the opposing parties. In this process, the disputing parties come to their own resolution through the recommended solutions provided by the mediator.

Violations and Recommended Penalties

61J2-24.001 Disciplinary Guidelines

The FREC provides a range of disciplinary guidelines. These guidelines set forth the disciplinary penalties that will be imposed upon licensees found guilty of violating Chapter 455 or 475, F.S. The purpose of these guidelines, is to inform licensees with the range of penalties that would be imposed for each violation. The following are the penalties that range from minor to severe:

- reprimand
- fine
- probation
- suspension
- revocation or denial

Pursuant to Section 475.25(1), F.S., combinations of these penalties are permissible by law. Nothing in this rule shall preclude any discipline imposed upon a licensee pursuant to a stipulation or settlement agreement, nor shall the range of penalties set forth in this rule preclude the probable cause panel from issuing a letter of guidance.

In addition to other penalties, the Commission may also place a licensee on probation (475.25[1], F.S.). Probationary conditions can include, but are not limited to, requiring a licensee to:

- attend appropriate courses
- submit to and successfully complete the state-administered examination
- be subject to periodic inspections and interviews by a DBPR investigator

A licensee who is a broker may be required to:

- place the licensee on a broker associate status
- file escrow account status reports with either the Commission or a DBPR investigator

The recommended penalties for acts that violate the statute are listed in the following table:

Violation	Penalties	
(a) Section 475.22, F.S. Broker fails to maintain office or sign at entrance of office	(a) Reprimand to $500 administrative fine	(a) 90-day suspension and $1,000 administrative fine
(b) Section 475.24, F.S. Failure to register a branch office	(b) Reprimand to $500 administrative fine	(b) 90-day suspension and $1,000 administrative fine
(c) Section 475.25(1)(b), F.S. Fraud, misrepresentation, and dishonest dealing	(c) $1,000 to $2,500 administrative fine and 30-day suspension to revocation	(c) $2,500 to $5,000 administrative fine and 6-month suspension to revocation
Concealment (*to hide from being discovered*), false promises, false pretenses by trick, scheme, or device	$1,000 to $2,500 administrative fine and 30-day suspension to revocation	$2,500 to $5,000 administrative fine and 6-month suspension to revocation
Culpable negligence or **breach of trust** (*failure to carryout fiduciary duties*)	$1,000 to $2,500 administrative fine and 30-day suspension to revocation	$2,500 to $5,000 administrative fine and 6-month suspension to revocation
Violating a duty imposed by law or by the terms of a listing agreement; aided, assisted, or conspired with another; or formed an intent, design, or scheme to engage in such misconduct and committed an overt act in furtherance of such intent, design, or scheme	$1,000 to $2,500 administrative fine and 30-day suspension to revocation	$2,500 to $5,000 administrative fine and 6-month suspension to revocation $2,500 to $5,000 administrative fine and 6-month suspension to revocation
(d) Section 475.25(1)(c), F.S. False, deceptive, or misleading advertising	(d) $250 to $1,000 administrative fine and 30- to 90-day suspension	(d) $1,000 to $5,000 administrative fine and 90-day suspension to revocation
(e) Section 475.25(1)(d), F.S. Failed to account or deliver to any person as required by agreement or law, escrowed property	(e) $250 to $1,000 administrative fine and suspension to revocation	(e) $1,000 to $5,000 administrative fine and suspension to revocation

(f)	Section 475.25(1)(e), F.S. Violated any rule or order or provision under Chapters 475 and 455, F.S.	(f) $250 to $1,000 administrative fine and suspension to revocation	(f) $1,000 to $5,000 administrative fine and suspension to revocation
(g)	Section 475.25(1)(f), F.S. Convicted or found guilty of a crime related to real estate or involving moral turpitude or fraudulent or dishonest dealing	(g) $250 to $1,000 administrative fine and 30-day suspension to revocation	(g) $1,000 to $5,000 administrative fine and suspension to revocation
(h)	Section 475.25(1)(g), F.S. Has license disciplined or acted against or an application denied by another jurisdiction	(h) $250 to $1,000 administrative fine and 30-day suspension to revocation	(h) $1,000 to $5,000 administrative fine and suspension to revocation
(i)	Section 475.25(1)(h), F.S. Has shared a commission with or paid a fee to a person not properly licensed under Chapter 475, F.S.	(i) $250 to $1,000 administrative fine and 30-day suspension to revocation	(i) $1,000 to $5,000 administrative fine and suspension to revocation
(j)	Section 475.25(1)(i), F.S. Impairment by drunkenness, or use of drugs or temporary mental derangement	(j) Suspension for the period of incapacity	(j) Suspension for the period of incapacity
(k)	Section 475.25(1)(j), F.S. Rendered an opinion that the title to property sold is good or merchantable when not based on opinion of a licensed attorney or has failed to advise prospective buyer to consult an attorney on the merchantability of title or to obtain title insurance	(k) $250 to $1,000 administrative fine and 30-day suspension to revocation	(k) $1,000 to $5,000 administrative fine and suspension to revocation
(l)	Section 475.25(1)(k), F.S. Has failed, if a broker, to deposit any money in an escrow account immediately upon receipt until disbursement is properly authorized. Has failed, if a sales associate, to place any money to be escrowed with the registered employer	(l) $250 to $1,000 administrative fine and 30-day suspension to revocation	(l) $1,000 to $5,000 administrative fine and suspension to revocation
(m)	Section 475.25(1)(l), F.S. Has made or filed a report or record which the licensee knows to be false or willfully failed to file a report or record or willfully impeded such filing as required by State or Federal Law	(m) $250 to $1,000 administrative fine and 30-day suspension to revocation	(m) $1,000 to $5,000 administrative fine and suspension to revocation
(n)	Section 475.25(1)(m), F.S. Obtained a license by fraud, misrepresentation, or concealment	(n) $250 to $1,000 administrative fine and 30-day suspension to revocation	(n) $1,000 to $5,000 administrative fine and suspension to revocation
(o)	Section 475.25(1)(n), F.S. Confined in jail, prison, or mental institution; or through mental disease can no longer practice with skill and safety	(o) $250 to $1,000 administrative fine and suspension to revocation	(o) $1,000 to $5,000 administrative fine and suspension to revocation
(p)	Section 475.25(1)(o), F.S. Guilty for the second time of misconduct in the practice of real estate that demonstrates incompetent, dishonest, or negligent dealings with investors	(p) $1,000 to $5,000 administrative fine and a 1-year suspension to revocation	
(q)	Section 475.25(1)(p), F.S. Failed to give Commission 30-day written notice after a guilty or nolo contendere plea or convicted of any felony	(q) $500 to $1,000 administrative fine and suspension to revocation	(q) $1,000 to $5,000 administrative fine and suspension to revocation

(r) Section 475.25(1)(r), F.S. Failed to follow the requirements of a written listing agreement	(r) $250 to $1,000 administrative fine and suspension to revocation	(r) $1,000 to $5,000 administrative fine and suspension to revocation
(s) Section 475.25(1)(s), F.S. Has had a registration suspended, revoked, or otherwise acted against in any jurisdiction	(s) $250 to $1,000 administrative fine and 60-day suspension to revocation	(s) $1,000 to $5,000 administrative fine and suspension to revocation
(t) Section 475.25(1)(t), F.S. Violated the Uniform Standards of Professional Appraisal Practice as defined in Section 475.611, F.S.	(t) $250 to $1,000 administrative fine and 30-day suspension to revocation	(t) $1,000 to $5,000 administrative fine and suspension to revocation
(u) Section 475.25(1)(u), F.S. Has failed, if a broker, to direct, control, or manage a broker associate or sales associate employed by such broker	(u) $250 to $1,000 administrative fine and suspension to revocation	(u) $1,000 to $5,000 administrative fine and suspension to revocation
(v) Section 475.25(1)(v), F.S. Has failed, if a broker, to review the brokerage's trust accounting procedures in order to ensure compliance with this chapter	(v) $250 to $2,500 administrative fine and suspension to revocation	(v) $1,000 to $5,000 administrative fine and suspension to revocation
(w) Section 475.42(1)(a), F.S. Practice without a valid and current license	(w) $250 to $2,500 administrative fine and suspension to revocation	(w) $1,000 to $5,000 administrative fine and suspension to revocation
(x) Section 475.42(1)(b), F.S. Practicing beyond scope as a sales associate	(x) $250 to $1,000 administrative fine and suspension to revocation	(x) $1,000 to $5,000 administrative fine and suspension to revocation
(y) Section 475.42(1)(c), F.S. Broker employs a sales associate who is not the holder of a valid and current license	(y) $250 to $1,000 administrative fine and suspension to revocation	(y) $1,000 to $5,000 administrative fine and suspension to revocation
(z) Section 475.42(1)(d), F.S. A sales associate shall not collect any money in connection with any real estate brokerage transaction except in the name of the employer	(z) $250 to $1,000 administrative fine and suspension to revocation	(z) $1,000 to $5,000 administrative fine and suspension to revocation
(aa) Section 475.42(1)(f), F.S. Makes false affidavit or affirmation or false testimony before the Commission	(aa) $250 to $1,000 administrative fine and suspension to revocation	(aa) $1,000 to $5,000 administrative fine and suspension to revocation
(bb) Section 475.42(1)(g), F.S. Fails to comply with subpoena	(bb) $250 to $1,000 administrative fine and suspension to revocation	(bb) $1,000 to $5,000 administrative fine and suspension to revocation
(cc) Section 475.42(1)(h), F.S. Obstructs or hinders the enforcement of Chapter 475, F.S.	(cc) $250 to $1,000 administrative fine and suspension to revocation	(cc) $1,000 to $5,000 administrative fine and suspension to revocation
(dd) Section 475.42(1)(i), F.S. No broker or sales associate shall place upon the public records any false, void, or unauthorized information that affects the title or encumbers any real property	(dd) $250 to $2,500 administrative fine and suspension to revocation	(dd) $1,000 to $5,000 administrative fine and suspension to revocation
(ee) Section 475.42(1)(j), F.S. Failed to register trade name with the Commission	(ee) $250 to $1,000 administrative fine	(ee) $1,000 to $5,000 administrative fine and suspension to revocation

(ff) Section 475.42(1)(k), F.S. No person shall knowingly conceal information relating to violations of Chapter 475, F.S.	(ff) $250 to $1,000 administrative fine and suspension	(ff) $1,000 to $5,000 administrative fine and suspension to revocation
(gg) Section 475.42(1)(l), F.S. Fails to have a current license as a broker or sales associate while listing or selling one or more timeshare periods per year	(gg) $250 to $1,000 administrative fine and suspension	(gg) $1,000 to $5,000 administrative fine and suspension to revocation
(hh) Section 475.42(1)(m), F.S. Licensee fails to disclose all material aspects of the resale of timeshare period or timeshare plan and the rights and obligations of both buyer or seller	(hh) $250 to $1,000 administrative fine and suspension	(hh) $1,000 to $5,000 administrative fine and suspension to revocation
(ii) Section 475.42(1)(n), F.S. Publication of false or misleading information; promotion of sales, leases, and rentals	(ii) $250 to $1,000 administrative fine and suspension to revocation	(ii) $1,000 to $5,000 administrative fine and suspension to revocation
(jj) Section 475.451, F.S. School teaching real estate practice fails to obtain a permit from the department and does not abide by regulations of Chapter 475, F.S., and rules adopted by the Commission	(jj) $250 to $1,000 administrative fine and suspension	(jj) $1,000 to $5,000 administrative fine and suspension to revocation
(kk) Section 475.453, F.S. Broker or sales associate participates in any rental information transaction that fails to follow the guidelines adopted by the Commission and Chapter 475, F.S.	(kk) $250 to $1,000 administrative fine and suspension	(kk) $1,000 to $5,000 administrative fine and 90-day suspension to revocation
(ll) Section 475.5015, F.S. Failure to keep and make available to the department such books, accounts, and records as will enable the department to determine whether the broker is in compliance with the provisions of Chapter 475, F.S.	(ll) $250 to $1,000 administrative fine and suspension to revocation	(ll) $1,000 to $5,000 administrative fine and 90-day suspension to revocation
(mm) Section 455.227(1)(s), F.S. Failing to comply with the educational course requirements for domestic violence	(mm) $250 to $1,000 administrative fine and suspension to revocation	(mm) $1,000 to $5,000 administrative fine and suspension to revocation
(nn) Section 455.227(1)(t), F.S. Failing to report in writing to the Commission within 30 days after the licensee is convicted or found guilty of, or entered a plea of nolo contendere or guilty to, regardless of adjudication, a crime in any jurisdiction.	(nn) $250 to $1,000 administrative fine and suspension to revocation	(nn) $1,000 to $5,000 administrative fine and suspension to revocation
(oo) Section 455.227(1)(u), F.S. Termination from a treatment program for impaired practitioners as described in Section 456.076 for failure to comply, without good cause, with the terms of the monitoring or treatment contract entered into by the licensee or failing to successfully complete a drug or alcohol treatment program	(oo) $250 to $1,000 administrative fine and suspension to revocation	(oo) $1,000 to $5,000 administrative fine and suspension to revocation

Source: © 2021 Mbition LLC

Criminal Penalties

In addition to administrative penalties imposed by the FREC, a licensee may be subject to criminal penalties imposed by the courts. Most violations of Chapter 475 of the Florida Statutes are considered second-degree misdemeanors, and penalties include one or both of the following:

- a fine of up to $500
- imprisonment for up to 60 days

It is important to note that legal entities such as corporations cannot be jailed and therefore may suffer extreme fines as a result of a crime. All fines are determined in a court of law. The FREC is not empowered to impose fines for criminal activities; however, any such activity must be reported to the appropriate authorities responsible for investigating crimes.

Penalties for first-degree misdemeanors include one or both of the following:

- a fine of up to $5,000
- imprisonment for up to one year

A first-degree misdemeanor is the violation for failure to provide accurate and current rental information when charging a fee. Also, there is one violation that is considered a third-degree felony—operating as any of the following without holding a valid and active license:

- a broker
- a broker associate
- a sales associate

Penalties for nonlicensed activity consist of:

- $5,000 fine per offense and/or up to five years in jail
- A cease and desist order issued by the DBPR against the violator as well as imposed fines of up to $5,000 per count
- Commencement of a criminal case (in criminal court) against the offender by the state district attorney

In addition to the aforementioned third-degree felony, the falsifying of an application also falls under this category.

Civil Penalties

Civil penalties may be imposed by the courts if an individual performs real estate services without a license. In this case, the courts may deny the individual the right to receive compensation for the service.

The Real Estate Recovery Fund

The Real Estate Recovery Fund has been established to reimburse members of the public for monetary losses suffered when real estate licensees violate the license law. If a person is adversely affected by the actions of a real estate licensee in a real estate transaction, the aggrieved person (under 475, F.S., and a violation of any part of same) may go to court to obtain a judgment against the licensee and ask for damages. If the judgment is issued and damages awarded, that person must first file a writ of execution to recover damages by liquidating the assets of the offending licensee. If this does not recover of all damages awarded, as a last resort, the injured person may seek to recover the remaining damages out of the Real Estate Recovery Fund. An action for recovery of damages must be brought within two years of the violation or discovery of the violation.

When payment is made out of the Real Estate Recovery Fund to satisfy a judgment against a licensee, the license of the person against whom the claim is made is automatically suspended. The licensee may also be subject to other disciplinary action. In order to restore the license to its previous status, the licensee must repay the full amount paid from the fund plus interest.

There are, however, exceptions to the previously stated penalties. Let's look at one potential scenario.

Example An escrow dispute arises between a buyer and a seller concerning the disbursement of escrowed funds. In this transaction, the funds are held by the broker in an escrow fund. Upon first notice of conflicting demands for the escrowed funds, the broker acts appropriately and follows the necessary procedures dictated by license law.

To resolve the matter, the licensee is required to do the following:

- Notify the FREC within 15 days from the last conflicting demand for escrowed funds.
- Request that the FREC issue an escrow disbursement order (EDO), which, if issued by the FREC, should be complied with by the licensee.
- Institute any of the escrow disbursement dispute processes within 30 days from the last request of conflicting demands for escrow funds.

An EDO is issued by the FREC and directs the licensee to disburse the escrowed funds to a particular party within the transaction. The broker complies with the EDO and is later sued in civil court by the opposing party to the transaction. A judgment is awarded in civil court and is issued against the licensee. At a later point, payment from the Real Estate Recovery Fund is made on behalf of the licensee. In this case, no action is taken against the licensee. A licensee who is directed by the FREC to act in accordance with an EDO, and does so, will:

- not be required to repay the fund
- not have his/her license suspended or revoked

The limit of payment from the fund for multiple judgments or settlements against a single licensee cannot exceed $150,000. The limit of payment for damages for a single transaction cannot exceed $50,000, regardless of the number of claimants.

The minimum balance for the fund has been established at $500,000. If the balance in the fund drops below $500,000, each licensee will be charged a special Recovery Fund fee when applying for initial licensure and when renewing a license. If the balance exceeds $1,000,000, the special fee will be discontinued until the balance falls below $500,000.

None of the following would be eligible to petition the fund:

- a person who is licensed attempting to recover for damages resulting from a transaction in which the person acted as a licensee
- a spouse of an offending licensee
- an individual who at the time of offence and sustained loss was operating without a valid real estate license
- a licensee who committed acts while on inactive status
- a corporation, branch office, or partnership, except through its individual licensees

Summary

The DBPR investigates complaints in order to determine whether or not a complaint is deemed legally sufficient to proceed in a case against any licensee. If a complaint is found to contain investigative grounds for charging a licensee, the matter is turned over to the FREC. A probable cause panel, which consists of two appointed members, is created next. Should the panel find that probable cause exists, a hearing is scheduled, which may be formal or informal. An administrative law judge presides over the hearing and issues a recommended order. The FREC issues the final order specifying the action to be taken against the licensee. The DBPR would issue a final order only in the case of a summary suspension. At this point the case is closed. The licensee may appeal the final order through the courts.

The Real Estate Recovery Fund acts as a last resort to recover damages suffered via the actions of licensees. The fund may only be petitioned after first obtaining a judgment in civil court. Only certain people are eligible to petition the fund. The limit of payment from the fund for damages for multiple judgments or settlements against a single licensee is $150,000. The limit of payment for damages for a single transaction is $50,000, regardless of the number of claimants. The minimum balance for the fund is $500,000. If the balance of the Real Estate Recovery Fund exceeds $1,000,000, any special recovery fund fees charged to licensees will be discontinued.

Review Questions

1. A complaint against a licensee was filed and investigated. The next step in the complaint process will be:
   a. the formal complaint
   b. an informal hearing
   c. a stipulation
   d. a probable cause determination

2. Punishment for a first-degree misdemeanor is a:
   a. fine of up to $500 and/or up to 60 days in jail
   b. fine of up to $1,000 and/or up to one year in jail
   c. fine of up to $5,000 and/or up to three years in jail
   d. fine of up to $5,000 and/or up to five years in jail

3. The Florida Real Estate Commission authorized payment of $7,000 from the Real Estate Recovery Fund because of wrong-doing by a licensee. Which of the following actions would result against the licensee's license?
   a. notice of noncompliance
   b. summary suspension
   c. automatic suspension
   d. probation

4. A broker followed the Florida Real Estate Commission's (FREC's) escrow disbursement order but was successfully sued by the other party. The broker must pay $40,000 in damages, plus $5,000 in court costs and $7,000 in attorney fees. The FREC will authorize payment from the Real Estate Recovery Fund of:
   a. nothing
   b. $40,000
   c. $50,000
   d. $52,000

5. Mary holds a sales license in Florida. Mary purchased some land and the property was misrepresented. Mary successfully sued the buyer's agent and was awarded a judgment for $30,000 plus $20,000 in punitive damages. The agent then declared bankruptcy, and a court-ordered asset search confirmed there are no assets to pay the judgment. Mary:
   a. cannot collect from the Real Estate Recovery Fund because she has a license
   b. cannot collect from the Real Estate Recovery Fund because the agent declared bankruptcy
   c. can collect $30,000 from the Real Estate Recovery Fund because she was the buyer
   d. can collect the entire $50,000 from the Real Estate Recovery Fund

6. The DBPR is authorized in the field to immediately issue:
   a. citations
   b. emergency suspensions
   c. administrative penalties
   d. fines of up to $1,000

7. Joan is an associate for True Sales Brokerage who was issued a citation by mistake. As a result, Joan:
   a. must pay the fine and file a protest
   b. can only sue in a civil court
   c. can petition the DRE for a formal hearing
   d. can file a written dispute of the citation within 30 days

8. The brokerage sign was not placed near the entrance, and an investigator issued a notice of noncompliance. How long will the firm have to take corrective action?
   a. 10 days
   b. 15 days
   c. 30 days
   d. 45 days

9. A broker who concealed a leaky roof was found guilty of misrepresentation and fraud in a brokerage transaction. The broker could be subject to:
   a. administrative punishment
   b. civil penalties
   c. imprisonment by a court of law
   d. administrative, civil, and criminal action

10. The most the Florida Real Estate Commission will authorize as payment from the Real Estate Recovery Fund for one licensee is:
    a. $25,000
    b. $50,000
    c. $75,000
    d. $150,000

11. What is the source of the money in the Real Estate Recovery Fund?
    a. the Foundation Trust Fund
    b. administrative fines
    c. the state general fund
    d. licensing fees

12. The DBPR is authorized to initiate an investigation of a complaint if:
    a. the act happened in Florida
    b. the complaint is signed
    c. the complaint is found to be legally sufficient
    d. the complaint involved real estate activity

13. A licensee received a formal complaint and does not dispute the charges. She decides her best course of action is to hire an attorney and meet with a DBPR attorney to negotiate any possible punishment. If an agreement is reached that is satisfactory to both parties, the agreement is termed a:
    a. stipulation
    b. final order
    c. recommended order
    d. citation

14. In the complaint process, a recommended order is issued by the:
    a. Florida Real Estate Commission
    b. secretary of the DBPR
    c. ALJ
    d. director of the DRE

15. The Florida Real Estate Commission decides on the appropriate punishment in each disciplinary case. This is a final order and would NOT include:
    a. placing the respondent on probation
    b. assigning fines and imprisonment
    c. suspending the license for up to 10 years
    d. permanent revocation of a license

16. Julia set up a business to sell apartment seekers lists of possible units available to rent in the surrounding area. Julia does not have a license. Julia can be found guilty of a:
    a. felony of the first degree
    b. felony of the second degree
    c. felony of the third degree
    d. misdemeanor of the first degree

17. When payment is made out of the Real Estate Recovery Fund to satisfy a judgment against a real estate licensee, which of the following is correct?
    a. No further action is taken on a civil basis.
    b. No action is taken by the Florida Real Estate Commission.
    c. The payment from the Recovery Fund is the licensee's insurance policy.
    d. The licensee against whom the claim is made is automatically suspended.

18. An audit of the firm's escrow records revealed that in May of last year, the broker failed to sign the monthly reconciliation. As a result:
    a. no action will be taken. This was an honest mistake.
    b. the broker will receive a citation
    c. the firm will receive a notice of noncompliance
    d. the auditor will issue a formal complaint

19. Broker Jones devised a land investment scam and enticed ten doctors to participate. When the scheme fell apart, each doctor individually sued the broker and received a $1,000,000 judgment against the broker, amounting to a total of $10,000,000. The broker declared bankruptcy, and the court confirmed the judgments could not be collected. The doctors asked to be compensated from the Real Estate Recovery Fund. The Florida Real Estate Commission will authorize the payment of:
    a. $50,000 to each doctor
    b. $75,000 to each doctor
    c. $150,000 to each doctor
    d. $50,000 split by the ten doctors

CHAPTER 7
FEDERAL AND STATE LAWS PERTAINING TO REAL ESTATE

KEY TERMS

blockbusting
familial status
handicapped status
property report

public accommodation
redlining
steering

LEARNING OBJECTIVES

After completing this lesson, you will be able to:

- explain the significance of the *Jones vs. Mayer* court case
- list the real estate included under the different fair housing acts
- recognize the groups protected under the 1968 Fair Housing Act
- list the property exempt from the Fair Housing Act of 1968
- understand the provisions of the 1988 Fair Housing Amendment
- describe the types of discriminatory acts that are prohibited under the 1968 Fair Housing Act
- describe the HUD process for handling a complaint under the 1968 Fair Housing Act
- describe the objectives and major provisions of the Americans with Disabilities Act
- describe the major provisions of the Florida Residential Landlord and Tenant Act
- describe the major provisions of the Interstate Land Sales Disclosure Act

INTRODUCTION TO FAIR HOUSING

There are two primary federal laws relating to fair housing:

1. the Civil Rights Act of 1866
2. the Civil Rights Act of 1968 (also known as the Fair Housing Act of 1968)

Let's look at the provisions of each of these laws.

155

The Civil Rights Act of 1866

The Civil Rights Act of 1866 prohibits all discrimination on the basis of race (with no exceptions) in the purchase, sale, lease, or other conveyance of real or personal property. In addition, the Civil Rights Act of 1866 does the following:

- defines a citizen as any person born in the United States
- mandates rights of property ownership to include:
    - buying
    - selling
    - leasing of real and personal property
    - rights to all citizens are extended without regard to previous servitude

The Civil Rights Act of 1968 covers housing only with some exceptions, while the Civil Rights Act of 1866 covers race only with no exceptions.

Precedent Setting Court Rulings: Jones v. Mayer

Aside from the passing of the Civil Rights Act of 1968, which dealt with discrimination and fair housing, the second most significant fair housing development of 1968 was the Supreme Court decision in the case *of Jones v. Alfred H. Mayer Company*. In its ruling, the court held that the Civil Rights Act of 1866 "prohibits all racial discrimination, private or public, in the sale and rental of property." This decision is important because although the 1968 federal law exempts individual homeowners and certain groups, the 1866 law prohibits all racial discrimination without exception. So despite any exemptions in the 1968 law, an offended person may seek a remedy for racial discrimination under the 1866 law against any homeowner, regardless of whether the owner employed a real estate broker and/or advertised the property. Where race or color is involved, no exceptions apply.

Coaching Tips

In 1987, U.S. Supreme Court decisions implied that the 1866 law, to which there are no exceptions, extended to ethnic and/or religious groups as well.

The Civil Rights Act of 1964

The Civil Rights Act of 1964 created laws that made discrimination based on race, color, religion, sex, or national origin unlawful. It also changed and ended:

- racial segregation in schools
- in the workplace
- **public accommodations** (any facility that serves the general public)
- unequal application of voter registration requirements

The Act by itself lacked the teeth for enforcement. In subsequent years, the Act was updated to include the provisions necessary for proper enforcement. On July 2, 1964, the Act was signed into law by President Lyndon B. Johnson.

The Civil Rights Act of 1968

The second law is the Civil Rights Act of 1968, also known as the Fair Housing Act of 1968. This act also makes it illegal to discriminate in the purchase, sale, lease, or other conveyance of real property. The Fair Housing Act later was amended in 1974 and again in 1988. Please note that the 1974 and 1988 addition of protected classes were amendments to the Federal Fair Housing Act of 1968.

This act differs from the Civil Rights Act of 1866 in two ways:

1. It extends the criteria on which discrimination is prohibited to the following:

    - race (Fair Housing Act of 1968)
    - color (Fair Housing Act of 1968)
    - religion (Fair Housing Act of 1968)
    - national origin (Fair Housing Act of 1968)
    - sex or gender (1974 amendment added this protected class)
    - **familial status**—families with children under the age of 18 and pregnant women (1988 amendment added this protected class)
    - **handicapped status**/individuals—persons with either a physical and/or mental disability (1988 amendment added this protected class)

    It should be noted that the 1988 amendment to the Federal Fair Housing Act of 1968 became the blueprint for creation of the 1992 Americans With Disabilities Act (ADA).

2. It covers discrimination related only to housing.

Groups Not Covered

Unlike other states that have specific laws that supplement the federal housing laws, Florida will generally adhere to the federal laws. Therefore, certain groups will not be covered under the Federal Fair Housing Act. Some of the groups that are not covered include but are not limited to:

- marital status
- age
- lawful occupation
- sexual orientation
- military status
- citizenship/alienage

Properties Covered

The Fair Housing Act of 1968 applies to the sale, lease, or other conveyance of the following types of housing:

- any single-family home owned by a private individual when:
  - a real estate broker is used
  - discriminatory advertising is used
  - single-family housing not owned by individuals
- single-family housing owned by an individual who:
  - owns more than three houses
  - sells more than one house in 24 months (other than his/her own)
- multiple-family dwellings of five units or more
- multiple-family dwellings of four or fewer units if the owner does not live in one of the units

Coaching Tips

While some categories of housing are not covered in the Fair Housing Act of 1968, they are still covered under the Civil Rights Act of 1866, which makes it illegal to discriminate on the basis of race under any circumstances. This is true as a result of *Jones v. Mayer*, a significant court case that upheld the Civil Rights Act of 1866.

Exemptions

We just looked at the properties covered by federal fair housing laws. Under the federal fair housing laws, certain exemptions are provided and exist under defined circumstances. The following are some of the exemptions:

- a dwelling containing 1- to 4-family housing where the property owner or a member of the property owner's family resides in one of the units. Please note that this exemption does not apply in either one or both of the following instances:
  - the services of a real estate licensee is used
  - discriminatory advertising has been used
- facilities reserved only for their respective membership of private organizations and not for use by or with the general public
- facilities where 100% of the occupants are 62 years of age or older or 80% of the occupied units are occupied by at least one person who is 55 or older
- facilities of or within a house of worship or other religious sector that are strictly for the benefit of their constituents and not used commercially

Prohibited Acts

The Fair Housing Act prohibits the following acts of discrimination when they are based on race, color, religion, sex, or national origin:

- refusing to sell, rent, negotiate, accept a purchase offer, or otherwise deal with any person

Example Broker Bill is negotiating a listing with Seller Sue. Sue informs Bill that she will not sell her property to anyone who is not a "God-fearing Christian." Because refusing to sell on the basis of religion is a forbidden practice, Bill should refuse to accept the listing.

- changing the terms or conditions for buying or selling

Example Sky Towers Apartments has a policy of collecting a $500 security deposit from its tenants. However, in the case of families with children, Sky Towers requires a security deposit of $1,000. This variation in the terms of the apartment leases on the basis of familial status is a violation of fair housing laws.

- changing the terms or conditions for financing the sale of property or repair a dwelling or otherwise denying such a loan as a means of discrimination

Example Citywide Mortgage Company has a policy of refusing to make loans for properties located in the Valley View neighborhood, claiming that borrowers from Valley View have historically been at higher risk of default. Because this policy does not consider the creditworthiness of individual borrowers from Valley View, it is more than likely intended to discriminate against such borrowers on the basis of some other characteristic, such as race or national origin. This is known as **redlining**.

- advertising that housing is available to only some buyers or otherwise excluding some buyers

Example Jones Realty advertises its listings in the classified section of the local newspaper. The ads include the slogan "Jones Realty—specializing in homes for Asian immigrants." The ad's implication that certain housing is more suitable to persons of a particular race, color, or national origin is a clear violation of fair housing requirements. This is known as **steering**.

- claiming that housing is not available for inspection, rent, or sale when it actually is available

Example When George applies to rent an apartment, the manager takes his application but informs him that there are no units currently available. While it is true that all the units are currently occupied, one of the tenants is due to move out in three days. The manager simply prefers to rent the unit to a woman because he/she believes they make better tenants. This is a case of unlawful housing discrimination on the basis of sex.

- making a profit by inducing owners of housing to sell or rent because of the prospective entry into the neighborhood of persons of a particular race, color, religion, national origin, handicap, or familial status

Example Acme Real Estate Company is running a direct mail campaign attempting to solicit listings from the predominantly white Alderbrook neighborhood. Included in the direct mail package are the results of a demographic study that projects that the population of Alderbrook will become increasingly nonwhite in the next few years. Use of such "scare tactics" to generate profit through increased listings puts Acme in violation of fair housing laws. This is known as **blockbusting**.

- excluding access to real estate services, such as multiple listing services or brokers' associations, thereby denying people membership or limiting their participation in any multiple listing service, real estate brokers' organization, or other facility related to the sale or rental of dwellings as a means of discrimination

Example A multiple listing service cannot lawfully exclude brokers from participation on the basis of their race, color, sex, religion, age, national origin, familial status, or handicap.

Housing for Older Persons

The Fair Housing Act is intended to protect any legal resident from discrimination on the basis of:

- race
- color
- national origin
- religion
- sex
- handicap
- familial status, which includes in the definition:
    - families with children under the age of 18 living with parents or legal guardians
    - pregnant women and anyone attempting to get custody of children under 18

As a result of the 1988 amendment to the Fair Housing Act that prohibited discrimination on the basis of disability and familial status, a greater consideration of Congress was directly intended to the preservation and creation of housing specifically designed to meet the needs of our aging population (senior residents). Housing that conforms to the Act and falls under the description and definition of housing for "older persons," is exempt from compliance to familial status, under the following circumstances:

- It is occupied solely by persons who are 62 or older.
- It houses at least one person who is 55 or older in at least 80% of the occupied units, while demonstrating intent to house persons who are 55 or older.
- HUD has approved the dwelling as designed for occupancy by elderly persons under a federal, state, or local government program.

As a direct result of the aforementioned, housing that addresses and complies with the legal definition of senior housing or housing for older persons described above may legally exclude families with children.

In addition to the discriminatory acts just presented, there are two additional types of discriminatory acts that deserve special attention because they make up the majority of the complaints against licensees under the Fair Housing Act of 1968. These are:

1. steering
2. blockbusting

It is important to note to the reader that discrimination applies to all real property transactions. This includes commercial transactions as well. In fact, all real estate transactions are subject to fair housing and discrimination laws.

Steering

Steering refers to the practice of influencing potential buyers to buy only in certain areas or neighborhoods on the basis of race, color, religion, sex, or national origin. Steering includes:

- directing minority buyers away from certain areas
- directing minority buyers toward predominantly minority areas or areas of changing makeup

Steering accounts for most of the complaints filed under the provisions of the Fair Housing Act of 1968.

> **Example** A prospective buyer enters the office of a real estate brokerage and proceeds to say the following about their search: "I just arrived from Los Angeles and I'm looking for the Beverly Hills of east coast Florida. Where would that be?" The agent responds, "You want to live in Palm Beach County."

In the above example, the prospective buyer was a Tester (an enforcer of fair housing and human rights) the licensee is guilty of steering for responding to the question in that manner.

Blockbusting

Blockbusting, also referred to as *panic selling*, is the illegal practice of inducing owners to sell their properties by using information about changes or expected changes in the makeup of the neighborhood.

For example, a licensee might attempt to induce homeowners to sell their home by claiming that the racial makeup of the neighborhood is about to change and that this change would cause property values to fall, schools to deteriorate, or crime to increase. Any inducement such as this is blockbusting and is illegal under the Fair Housing Act of 1968.

Equal Housing Opportunity Poster

An equal housing opportunity poster can be obtained from the Department of Housing and Urban Development (HUD). Displayed in a broker's office, it informs the public about fair housing laws and shows the firm's intention to comply. Displaying the poster is not a legal requirement, but when HUD investigates a broker for discriminatory practices, it considers failure to display it as evidence of noncompliance.

Source: www.HUD.gov

Enforcement

Any individual who feels discriminated against may take action to enforce the fair housing laws. There are various ways, on a federal level, that someone can enforce the Fair Housing Act of 1968, such as:

- filing a written complaint with HUD in Washington, D.C.
- filing an action in court (U.S. District Court or a state or local court)
- filing a complaint with the U.S. attorney general

The Civil Rights Act of 1866 can only be enforced by filing a suit in federal court.

State Law

On a state level, Florida has its own fair housing law. In fact, certain provisions of state law are more restrictive in many ways than federal laws. In other ways, federal laws are more restrictive than state laws. Whenever there is a conflict between the state and federal laws, the rule to follow is: *The more restrictive provision will normally prevail over the other.*

INTRODUCTION TO FAIR HOUSING VIOLATIONS

Previously, you learned about the major provisions of fair housing laws. It is important to know what these laws provide to ensure fair housing opportunities for everyone. It is also very important for you to understand how to conduct your business in compliance with fair housing laws. Now you will learn about some of the practical situations in which the issue of fair housing can arise, as well as some general practices to follow to ensure that you comply with the law.

FAIR HOUSING VIOLATIONS: RESPONSIBILITY AND LIABILITY OF REAL ESTATE LICENSEES

A licensee has violated the law if equal service is denied to anyone on the basis of race, color, religion, ancestry, sex, national origin, familial status, or handicap. If a licensee violates the law in this manner, the licensee may be subject to severe penalties including:

- loss of license
- civil damages and penalties
- criminal prosecution, fines, and imprisonment

In order to ensure that you do not violate fair housing laws, you should do three things:

1. fully understand your responsibilities under fair housing laws
2. constantly monitor your own actions to ensure that they are in compliance with the law
3. attend fair housing seminars and workshops

As you evaluate your actions, it is important that you look both at the *effects* of your actions and at your *intent*. It is not sufficient that your intention is not to violate the law. It is possible that your actions may result in a violation, even if that is not your intent. There are several areas (some that we have covered) in which violations of the fair housing law are most common:

- blockbusting
- improper listings
- refusing to show property to minorities
- steering
- advertising
- less favorable treatment of minority buyers
- redlining

Note that the first two violations occur while working with a seller, while the last five occur while working with a buyer. Let's look at each of these in more detail.

Blockbusting

There are two situations in which a charge of blockbusting is most likely to be made:

1. when a sales associate attempts to get a listing by conveying information about a minority group in the neighborhood or coming into the neighborhood

2. when a sales associate uses an intensive solicitation campaign (e.g., phone calls, letters, door-to-door canvasing) in a neighborhood whose makeup is changing (in terms of one or more minority groups)

Let's look at a sales associate inducing a sale by conveying information about a minority group.

Putting It to Work

> **Example** A sales associate was trying to get a listing on the Smiths' house by convincing them to sell and move somewhere else. The sales associate stated to the Smiths that a Hispanic family had bought a house down the street from them.

This is a violation of the law because the sales associate stated that a change was occurring in the racial makeup of the neighborhood in order to induce the Smiths to sell.

Improper Listings

There are two categories of improper listings you should guard against:

1. refusing to accept a listing because the owner is a minority
2. accepting a listing from a seller who attempts to place restrictions on selling to one or more minority groups

Let's look at an example for each of these.

Putting It to Work

> **Example 1** An Asian owner called a sales associate and asked to have her home listed for sale. The home was located in the Chinese section of town. When the sales associate learned of the location of the home, he turned the listing down. He stated that he did not know much about that part of town but knew that buyers had often had difficulty getting loans for homes in that area.
>
> Was there a violation? Yes. The sales associate's refusal to list the home was found to be based on the owner's race and the racial makeup of the neighborhood. The fact that loans had been difficult to get was irrelevant and is using someone else's discrimination as an excuse. The effect is the same—racial discrimination. A sales associate must make the same effort to sell property owned by a minority as he would make to sell property owned by a nonminority.

Example 2 An owner wants to sell his home but only to an African American person. He contacts a sales associate who has several listings in the area and asks her to sell the home for him, but only to an African American.

Can the sales associate legally do this? No. The sales associate must comply with fair housing laws even if the seller does not. She should tell the owner that she may accept the listing only if he lifts the restrictions and that he may be violating the law.

Refusal to Show Property to Minorities

It is a violation of the law to refuse to show property to a person because that person is a member of a minority group. Let's look at an example.

Putting It to Work

Example A Hispanic sales associate was showing a young Caucasian divorced mother properties for sale. When the woman asked about a property in a predominantly Hispanic neighborhood, the sales associate refused to show the property and attempted to discourage her, by saying, "Don't you think you would enjoy living in another area better? I think it would be more suitable for your family situation."

Is there a violation? Yes. This is clearly a case of refusing to show property based on race.

Steering

Steering refers to the practice of influencing which neighborhood a buyer buys in, in either one of the following ways:

- directing a minority buyer toward minority or changing neighborhoods
- directing a nonminority buyer away from minority or changing neighborhoods

Let's look at an example.

Putting It to Work

Example A sales associate was showing a businessman several homes. The buyer was looking through the sales associate's multiple listing book when he spotted a home he particularly liked. When the sales associate saw which home he liked, she commented: "I don't think you will like that area. It is changing." The sales associate was aware that the neighborhood had recently become integrated.

Was there a violation? Yes. The sales associate's comment referred to a change in the racial makeup of the neighborhood. The sales associate was steering the buyer away from this neighborhood.

Advertising

Discrimination in advertising is prohibited by fair housing laws and must be avoided, even if the discrimination is not intentional.

Putting It to Work

Example

A sales associate placed the following ad:
"Asian families notice bargain-priced agent's home."

Was there a violation? Yes. Even though the agent claimed that the reference to "asian families" was done only to point out the oriental design, the advertisement referred to the racial makeup of potential buyers.

Less Favorable Treatment of Minority Buyers

A charge of less favorable treatment of a minority buyer usually occurs because a sales associate does one of the following:

- insults or ignores a minority buyer
- refers a minority buyer to a licensee of the same minority group
- does not use his/her best efforts to close a sale
- gives preference in submitting a nonminority buyer's offer over a minority buyer's offer
- treats minority buyers differently in terms of financial matters

Let's look at an example.

Putting It to Work

Example Just before closing, a listing broker found out that the buyers on a property were African American. He immediately called the company that was to provide a termite clearance letter and told the company to raise the cost of the letter from the previously stated price of $175 to $380. Because of the increased cost of the termite letter, the sale did not close.

Was there a violation in this situation? Yes. The listing broker discriminated against the buyers. He discouraged their purchase by artificially raising the price of the termite letter.

It is important to note that discriminatory violations arise and occur as a result of perception issues. It is not how a licensee may view the wrongdoing as much as it is the perception of the person affected by the act.

Redlining

Redlining is the practice of discriminating when making loans in a neighborhood because of the makeup of the neighborhood in terms of race, color, religion, national origin, or sex. Redlining refers to either refusing to make loans in such neighborhoods or making loans at less favorable terms. Redlining also applies to the issuance of insurance policies. For example, an insurance company refuses to issue a homeowner's policy because the property is located in a declining neighborhood.

Fair Housing Act—Enforcement

Fair housing laws are enforced on a federal level by:

1. HUD and
2. the Department of Justice

In addition, fair housing laws are administered and enforced by:

1. the state and
2. local fair housing units

Lawsuits that are initiated are adjudicated on a civil level in federal and state courts.

Complaints are filed with HUD, and the aggrieved party has one year from the date that the violation occurred to file the complaint. In the event a complaint is filed, HUD will investigate to determine if any violation has occurred. HUD's first step will be to initiate a gathering of the involved parties in order to reach a conciliation agreement (a resolution agreement arrived at and reached voluntarily by the respective parties).

HUD has also been known to refer certain complaints to state and local fair housing agencies for enforcement.

When a breach of a previous conciliation agreement occurs the Department of Justice is the enforcing prosecuting party for lawsuits brought to federal court. For first offenses, the maximum fine is $10,000. If the party is a repeat offender within the previous five years, the maximum penalty is $25,000.

> ## Coaching Tips
>
> ### Additional Regulations
>
> Earlier in this chapter, you learned about fair housing laws. You should also be aware of some additional regulations that are related to fair housing, such as:
>
> 1. Civil Rights Act of 1964—This act prohibits discrimination in housing programs that receive federal funding.
> 2. Equal Credit Opportunity Act—This act prohibits discrimination in the credit application process based on race, color, religion, sex, national origin, marital status, or age or because the individual receives income from a public assistance program. This act requires a lender to originate a loan merely on creditworthiness.
> 3. Americans with Disabilities Act—Title III of this act prohibits discrimination based on disability by places of public accommodation and commercial facilities. (Places of public accommodation are privately owned businesses and nonprofit organizations open to the public.) This act applies to:
>   - properties available to the public that were built after 1990
>   - properties available to the public that were rehabbed after 1990
>   - multifamily housing built after 1990 whereby a certain percentage of units must be wheelchair accessible
> 4. State and local laws—Some state and local laws prohibit discrimination based on additional classes or categories of individuals.
>
> In addition, the Code of Ethics of the National Association of REALTORS® (NAR) prohibits discrimination. According to the NAR Code of Ethics, when providing real estate services, a Realtor is prohibited from discriminating against individuals because of their race, color, religion, sex, handicap, familial status, or national origin. An individual who believes he/she has been discriminated against by a Realtor may file a complaint with the local Board of Realtors. The Board of Realtors is authorized to take disciplinary action against a Realtor if the board determines that a violation has occurred.

Americans with Disabilities Act of 1990 (ADA)

The 1988 amendment to the Community Development Act of 1974 added two additional classes:

1. persons with physical disabilities
2. persons with mental disabilities

As a direct result of the 1988 Amendment of the Federal Fair Housing Act and passed by the U.S. Congress in 1990, the ADA prohibits discrimination based on disability. The ADA also requires:

- that employers provide reasonable accommodations to employees with disabilities
- certain accessibility requirements on public accommodations, including commercial facilities

Under the ADA, disabilities include both mental and physical conditions. The following are only some examples of conditions that could easily qualify under the Act as disabilities:

- deafness
- blindness
- intellectual disability

In addition, new construction built after the enactment of the ADA had the following requirements:

- Light switches must be installed at a height accessible by a person in a wheelchair.
- Interior passages must be wide enough to accommodate a wheelchair; while a building (if multifamily) must have:
  - ramps where access elevations exist
  - elevators that could accommodate a wheelchair

The aforementioned would apply to any new construction and/or renovation of a public facility, an area dedicated to the public and commercial facilities. The federal law applies to all construction built after 1992.

Interstate Land Sales Full Disclosure Act

The Interstate Land Sales Full Disclosure Act (ILSA) is a federal consumer protection law designed to prevent fraudulent practices and schemes in the sale of **subdivided lands** (large parcel divided into smaller legal parcels) offered for sale and purchased sight-unseen by consumers. The Act requires full disclosure of the property's condition to all prospective purchasers. The disclosures made must always be honest and accurate. A developer can be liable in the amount of $1,000 for each violation of ILSA. In addition, if found guilty of making untrue statements to purchasers regarding the subject property, a violator can be punished with fines of up to $10,000 and/or imprisonment for up to five years.

Subdivisions of 100 units or less are exempt from ILSA but must be registered with Consumer Financial Protection Bureau before lots for sale can be offered by either mail or telephone.

Under ILSA, any developer of 25 lots or more must make necessary disclosures to purchasers when selling residential property. The disclosure is presented in the form of a **property report**. The property report must contain all pertinent information on the form of disclosure. Florida law provides the purchaser of subdivided land with a seven-day right of rescission from point of contract signing. The right of rescission is valid when the property report has been presented prior to the purchaser signing the contract. In the event the property report has not been given to the buyer prior to contract signing, the purchaser has up to two years from the date of contract signing to rescind the transaction.

FLORIDA HOUSING LAWS

Previously in this chapter, we looked at the federal fair housing laws. Now we will go over state laws related to housing.

The Florida Fair Housing Act

The purpose of the Florida Fair Housing Act is to promote the availability of housing for all residents regardless of race, color, religion, national origin, gender, handicap, or familial status. Concerning members of the aforementioned protected classes, it is unlawful to:

- refuse housing
- refuse financing or the inclusion of different and onerous terms than those offered to persons of an unprotected class
- refuse a disabled individual from making reasonable modifications to a dwelling to accommodate the disability
- take retaliatory actions because an individual exercises any rights under fair housing laws

Complaints under the Act are enforced by the Florida Commission of Human Rights in tandem with HUD. Complaints will normally be filed with both agencies.

The Florida Residential Landlord and Tenant Act

The Florida Residential Landlord and Tenant Act was originally designed to define the relationship between a landlord and a tenant.

Specifically, the Act was designed to define that relationship as it would apply only to a residential property containing dwelling units. The following terms are specifically defined under the Act:

- landlord—the property owner/lessor
- tenant—the legal occupant/lessee under a mutually executed lease agreement within a rental property
- dwelling—any property where one or more persons legally reside

In order to have a valid enforceable contract, the agreement must contain all the essential elements necessary to make that contract enforceable. An enforceable contract is one that will stand up in court. (Contracts are discussed in much greater detail in Chapter 11.) One of those essential elements of an enforceable contract is a competent party. A lease is considered a contract. In Florida, no persons under the age of 18 years old are considered to be competent parties. Therefore, in order to have an enforceable lease agreement, the lessee must be 18 years of age or older.

Leases Covering Residential Dwelling Units

When a lease covering a residential dwelling unit (as defined under the Florida Statutes) is entered into between a landlord and tenant, each party to the lease has performance obligations to the other party. Let's take a look at these obligations, beginning with the landlord's obligations.

Landlord's Requirements Under a Lease

The landlord's requirements under a lease include:

- maintaining the demised premises (*Demised premises* refers to the property that has been leased.)
- properly handling security deposits and rent paid in advance

Let's go over each of these responsibilities.

Maintaining the Demised Premises

A landlord has duties with regard to the day-to-day maintenance of the rental property. A landlord is required to:

- provide a unit for rental that meets all codes relating to rental property in Florida
- provide the following simple yet necessary services in operating the property:
    - properly functioning systems for heat and hot water
    - trash removal (from the property itself)
    - extermination
    - maintenance of the structure and its grounds at least within minimum standards required for habitation

Handling Security Deposits and Rent Paid in Advance

Chapter 83.49, F.S., deals with the appropriate measures concerning the handling and disposition of deposits and advance rents. Deposits are not limited to only security deposits but also include items such as:

- pet deposits
- any contractual deposits that were agreed to in advance by the landlord and tenant

- damage deposits
- advance rents

Generally, upon execution of a residential lease, the tenant will deposit with the landlord:

- the first and last month's rent
- a security deposit in the amount of one or more months' rent

The security deposit is designed to protect the owner against a number of possible tenant-related losses resulting from the tenant's occupancy. Possible losses include nonpayment/underpayment of rent or damage to the dwelling unit by the tenant or the tenant's visitors. Under the Florida Residential Landlord and Tenant Act, the landlord is required to place deposits received from the tenant within a separate bank account. The account:

- must be held and maintained within a Florida institution
- may be an interest-bearing or noninterest-bearing account
  - If the account is held as an interest-bearing account, the tenant is required to receive either 75% of that annual interest amount or an annual simple interest rate of 5%.
- must be held separate from the landlord's operating account
  - The landlord may not use the account's funds, pledge the funds as collateral, or commingle the funds. Commingling refers to mixing funds belonging to others with personal funds.

In lieu of holding funds in a separate account, the landlord may post a bond in the amount of $50,000 or the amount of the security deposits/advance rents, whichever is less. In this situation, the landlord is required to pay the tenant interest at an annual simple interest rate of 5%. No later than 30 days after the landlord receives any security deposit and/or advance rents, the landlord must:

- notify the tenant as to how these funds are being held on deposit
- provide the tenant with the name and address of the institution holding these funds

At the end of a lease, the landlord has certain obligations regarding the handling of security deposits that have been placed in his/her possession. When the lease term expires, the landlord is required to:

- notify the tenant in writing within 15 days that the landlord intends to retain part or all of the deposit currently in the landlord's possession
- indicate the reason for retention of the funds
- send this notice via certified mail for proper delivery
- allow the tenant 15 days thereafter to either agree or disagree with the contents of the claim

If the tenant challenges the landlord's claim to the deposit, the outcome of the challenge will be decided in court. At such time, the losing party will be responsible for paying the other's costs and expenses associated with either bringing the action or defending the claim.

In the event that the landlord has not imposed any claims on the deposits, the landlord must deliver these funds to the tenant within 15 days from termination of the lease. In addition, through a doctrine of laches (meaning, "assert your rights or lose them"), if the landlord has remained silent on any claim or imposition on the deposit for longer than 30 days, he/she loses the right to any further claim on the deposit.

We have been looking at the obligations of the landlord under a lease. Now, let's go over the obligations of the tenant.

Coaching Tips

Security Deposits

- Landlord must notify tenant within 30 days of intention to retain part or all of the security deposit.
- If landlord remains silent on any claim or imposition on the deposit for longer than 30 days, he/she loses the right to any further claim on the deposit.
- Landlord must indicate the reason for retention of the funds.
- Landlord must send the notice via certified mail for proper delivery.
- Landlord must allow 15 days for tentant to agree or disagree with the contents of the claim.
- If landlord doesn't impose a claim on the deposit, he/she must deliver same to tenant within 15 days from termination of the lease.

Tenant's Requirements Under a Lease

The Florida Residential Landlord and Tenant Act requires tenants to continuously use their best efforts toward maintaining the demised unit in accordance with any and all relevant housing codes. This includes, but is not limited to:

- complying with sanitary codes as they apply to dwelling units
- maintaining the interior unit plumbing fixtures
- maintaining the interior unit air conditioning
- maintaining the interior unit appliances
- following any other rules and regulations contained within the lease or dwelling complex
- providing the landlord with any reasonable access allowed under state laws or necessary for the performance of the landlord's responsibilities under the lease

Terminating a Lease

A lease can be terminated by the tenant or by the landlord. A member of the U.S. Armed Forces may terminate a lease under the following circumstances:

- when the member of the U.S. Armed Forces is stationed 35 miles or more from the rental property (as a direct result of orders)
- when the member of the U.S. Armed Forces is involuntarily or prematurely discharged or released from active duty

Terminating the lease would entail the following process:

- Provide the landlord a written notice of the intent to terminate the tenancy at least 30 days prior to desired termination date. The lease expires 30 days after the landlord's receipt of the 30-day notice. A letter should be included with the notice to terminate from the commanding officer as proof of written verification of the tenant's military service orders.
- At termination, the tenant would be liable for the pro rata portion of rent due up to the date of termination.

Landlord's Access to Premises

As long as a tenant is not in default, the landlord may not disturb the tenancy. However, it would not be considered unreasonable for the landlord to require access to the premises from time to time in order to inspect and to effectuate maintenance or repairs. As the existing tenant nears lease expiration, the landlord may require access to show the premises to a prospective tenant.

Under Florida state law and based on the aforementioned, with reasonable notice, the tenant would be required to provide access. In the event of emergency and in order to preserve and protect the demised premises and the life safety of other residents, state law permits the landlord to enter the premises.

Vacating Premises

When a lease expires on a residential unit, the landlord is required to follow laws governing end of term and security deposits.

For example, when the landlord is not asserting a claim to security funds on deposit, the landlord must return to the tenant the full amount (with any accrued interest) within 15 days. Should the landlord wish to assert a claim for funds on deposit, he/she has 30 days to notify the tenant. The notification must be written and sent by certified mail to the tenant's current address. Should this occur, the tenant then has 15 days to lodge any objection to the landlord's claim.

Unlike what actions other escrow funds held require, under Florida state law, brokers who are holding deposits and/or any advance rents are not required to report any conflicting demands and disputes to the FREC. They are free to disperse the funds without following the escrow disbursement dispute process.

Termination by Tenant

Landlords are required to provide a tenant with a habitable unit or living complex. That is, the property must meet certain minimum standards. From time to time, the landlord and tenant will disagree as to what is considered to be minimum standards. Constructive eviction occurs when the landlord causes or permits a situation to occur that makes it impossible for the tenant to enjoy the premises under the terms of the lease. However, because a valid and enforceable lease exists between the landlord and tenant, the tenant must first:

- notify the landlord in writing as to the defect/default item to the property
- allow the landlord the ability to correct said defect/default within seven days *prior to* constructive eviction

Termination by Landlord

Conversely, a landlord may find him/herself with a nonperforming tenant. This usually results from nonpayment of rent but can result from other types of tenant defaults (e.g., disturbing other tenants by creating too much noise). When rent is involved, the landlord may terminate the lease by providing a three-day notice to the tenant, which will demand either the rent in question or that the tenant deliver physical and legal possession of the demised premises to the landlord. If the tenant willfully vacates, the landlord is still required to do one of the following:

- refund the security deposit in its entirety within 15 days of the vacating of the premises
- properly notify the tenant if any security deposit will be retained by the landlord

If the tenant fails to vacate the premises, the landlord's only option is to seek actual eviction. Actual eviction refers to the legal removal of the tenant from the leased property because the tenant violates some provision of the lease.

A landlord may not simply evict a tenant without going through a specific eviction process. The eviction process requires judicial intervention. This means that the landlord must obtain a judgment from the courts prior to removing the tenant and/or the tenant's belongings from the unit. The following steps must be taken during the eviction process:

- The tenant must receive notice of the demand for possession of the property in writing.

- The landlord must file an eviction complaint with the appropriate county court.
- If the complaint is not answered by the tenant in a timely manner, a default judgment is entered in favor of the landlord.
- If the complaint is contested by the tenant, the case will be heard before the court to determine a judgment on the matter.
- If the judgment is awarded to the landlord, a writ of possession is executed by the sheriff.
- It is only at this point that the landlord (with the sheriff's assistance) may physically and legally remove any remaining tenant possessions from the unit.

Summary

Federal and state housing laws affect sellers, buyers, landlords, and tenants. These laws also affect how a licensee must service and deal with the general public. The services that are offered by a real estate brokerage should not differ from one person/party to another. Testers are members of programs that enforce the rights of home seekers. Their mission is to determine whether the information or services that come out of a licensee's office is influenced by race. Therefore, licensees should avoid any practice that can be perceived as a violation of state or federal housing laws. In addition, the licensee is urged to attend Fair Housing seminars and courses that cover this material.

Review Questions

1. Broker Bill is a business broker and has a contract to sell a candy store. The owner instructed Bill to refrain from showing the business to racial minorities. What is true about this situation?
   a. Bill represents the owner and must honor the owner's request.
   b. The owner can do this, but Bill cannot.
   c. This violates the Civil Rights Act of 1866.
   d. This violates the Civil Rights Act of 1968.

2. A couple of Asian descent asks you to show them properties only in Asian neighborhoods. You:
   a. may honor this request
   b. would be guilty of blockbusting
   c. would be guilty of redlining
   d. would be guilty of steering

3. All of the following steps must be taken during the eviction process EXCEPT:
   a. The tenant must receive notice of the demand for possession of the property in writing.
   b. The landlord must file an eviction complaint with the appropriate county court.
   c. The landlord is entitled to 200% rent damages.
   d. If the complaint is not answered by the tenant in a timely manner, a default judgment is entered in favor of the landlord.

4. How long does a landlord in Florida have to notify the tenant of the location of advance fees collected and held by the landlord?
   a. All tenants must be informed about the money before 15 days pass.
   b. The tenant must be notified in writing; no time limit exists.
   c. If the money leaves Florida, the landlord has 60 days.
   d. Tenants must be informed in writing within 30 days of paying the fees.

5. If the tenant willfully vacates, the landlord is:
   a. required to refund the security deposit in its entirety within 15 days of the vacating of the premises
   b. not required to notify the tenant if any security deposit will be retained by the landlord
   c. must refund the deposit in 30 days
   d. both b and c

6. Sure Fire Insurance refuses to write insurance policies for homes in Palm Shores because minorities live there. This is an example of:
   a. redlining
   b. steering
   c. blockbusting
   d. channeling

7. A private club has maintained a clubhouse and rental rooms on the beach for more than 70 years. Only club members can rent the club's rooms. The club's rental restrictions:
   a. predate fair housing laws and are grandfathered in
   b. violate fair housing laws in the Civil Rights Act of 1968
   c. are legal because private clubs are exempted
   d. are legal if the club accepts minorities as members

8. Fran owns a vacant rental unit in a Spanish-speaking neighborhood in Tampa. She decides to advertise the vacancy in a Spanish-language newspaper in Tampa.
   a. The choice is Fran's to make.
   b. Fran is guilty of steering.
   c. The neighborhood is Spanish-speaking; this is an example of redlining.
   d. This is legal as long as the ad isn't discriminatory, and the services of a real estate licensee is not used.

9. Joseph has a new listing in a neighborhood in St. Petersburg. One of the features of the neighborhood is a beautiful Catholic church. The church building is a local landmark and is often featured on postcards and pictures in the papers. Joseph places an ad in the paper that states the home for sale is "near St. Mary's." This is an example of:
   a. a common practice in real estate ads
   b. discrimination prohibited as redlining
   c. landmarks and can be referred to in ads
   d. steering

10. In a large apartment complex, it is policy to place married couples in one building and singles in another on the theory that the singles party and create noise. This policy:
    a. is an example of steering
    b. is not steering but does violate fair housing laws
    c. does not violate any laws
    d. is discrimination based on familial status

11. The security deposit is designed to protect the owner against a number of possible tenant-related losses resulting from the tenant's occupancy. Possible losses include all of the following EXCEPT:
    a. nonpayment of rent
    b. inability to pay the mortgage
    c. damage to the dwelling unit by the tenant
    d. damage to the dwelling unit by the tenant's pets

12. Security deposits must be:
    a. placed in the landlord's operating account
    b. placed in any U.S. bank in or outside of Florida
    c. always noninterest-bearing accounts
    d. held and maintained within a Florida institution

13. Any property where one or more persons legally reside is referred to as:
    a. a primary residence
    b. a vacation home
    c. a dwelling
    d. all of these

14. It is the policy of management of an apartment complex to place families with children in the building near the playground equipment.
    a. Management has violated fair housing laws
    b. This is legal if the parents are informed
    c. The policy is legal if the parents agree with the placement
    d. Marital status is not protected in housing. This policy is legal

15. Steve is 85 years old and has an above-average income and an excellent credit rating. Steve applied for a 30-year loan to buy a vacation condo, but the lender said a 15-year loan was the only loan Steve could qualify for.
    a. At his age, Steve is glad for any loan at all.
    b. The lender has no legal obligation to lend money.
    c. Age is NOT a protected status in lending decisions.
    d. Fair housing laws protect age in residential property.

16. A Presbyterian church sponsors a retirement home for retired Presbyterian ministers and their spouses. No other persons can lease the units.
    a. This is discrimination in housing based on religion.
    b. The Church can do this under a special exemption in fair housing requirements.
    c. Churches can be granted fair housing exemptions on a state-by-state basis.
    d. Religious discrimination is not addressed in fair housing laws.

17. The landlord's requirements under a valid lease include all of the following EXCEPT:
    a. maintaining the premises
    b. properly handling security deposits
    c. making decorative repairs to the tenant's unit
    d. properly handling any rent paid in advance

18. An African American couple called the realty firm and asked to inspect a house the firm just listed. The listed home is located in an African American neighborhood.
    a. This is an example of steering.
    b. Showing the couple the listing is redlining.
    c. You must show the couple all the listings in this price range.
    d. The act of showing the couple the house is legal.

19. The Florida Residential Landlord and Tenant Act was originally designed to:
    a. define the relationship between a landlord and a tenant
    b. protect landlords who lease residential units
    c. protect tenants who lease commercial units
    d. none of these

20. Eviction is a judicial process in Florida and must be carried out by the courts. The first step in a legal eviction is notification of the tenant. This could be accomplished by any of the following EXCEPT:
    a. mailing the notice to the tenant
    b. posting the notice on the door
    c. knocking on the door and hand the notice to the tenant
    d. paying the sheriff's department to notify the tenant

21. In Florida, the Florida Landlord and Tenant Act states that the landlord must:
    a. make the required repairs in seven days or face prosecution
    b. make the required repairs in 15 days or face prosecution
    c. make the required repairs in 30 days or face prosecution
    d. provide a unit for rental that meets all codes relating to rental property in Florida

CHAPTER 8

PROPERTY RIGHTS
ESTATES AND TENANCIES: CONDOMINIUMS, COOPERATIVES, COMMUNITY DEVELOPMENT DISTRICS, HOMEOWNERS ASSOCIATIONS, AND TIME-SHARING

KEY TERMS

community development districts (CDDs)	leasehold estate
condominium	life estate
cond-op	personal property
cooperative	proprietary lease
declaration of condominium	prospectus
estate for years	real estate
estate in land	real property
exempt property	remainderman
fee simple estate	right of survivorship
fixture	separate property
freehold estate	tenancy at sufferance
homeowners association	tenancy at will
homestead	tenancy by the entireties
joint tenancy	tenancy in common
land	time-share

LEARNING OBJECTIVES

After completing this lesson, you will be able to:

- define real property based on the definition in Chapter 475, F.S.
- list and explain the physical components of real property
- explain the four tests courts use to determine if an item is a fixture
- distinguish between real property and personal property
- describe the bundle of rights associated with real property ownership
- list the principal types of estates (tenancies) and describe their characteristics
- describe the features associated with the Florida Homestead Law
- distinguish among cooperatives, condominiums, community development districts, homeowners associations, and time-shares and describe the four main documents associated with condominiums

INTRODUCTION AND HISTORIC PERSPECTIVE OF PROPERTY OWNERSHIP

Most of our real estate terminology is derived from the old English feudal system of property ownership. The feudal system dates as far back as the Renaissance period. In simple terms, this system of property ownership meant that land ownership was a vested interest held only by the Crown. To this day, the United Kingdom, as well as worldwide British mandates and territories, still subscribe to this system of property ownership. Therefore, if the Crown was the only party with land ownership rights and interests, noblemen or lords (as they were called) received a grant/gift of land from the Crown. In essence, this grant was the Crown's reward to the nobility for loyalty and service.

This system of property ownership later evolved to what is known today as the allodial system. The difference between the two systems is simple:

- Feudal system—Land (the ground and all permanent attachments) ownership vests only with the Crown. The Crown acts as the grantor by granting only possession of the property to the nobleman who in turn becomes the grantee. The nobleman only has a possessory right in the property but not ownership in the land. This directly resembles leased property as we know it today. In essence, the estates were reversionary and defeasible. This meant that at any point, the Crown, who was the sole owner of the land, would be able to recapture the granted property. Therefore:
    - land is owned by the Crown and not by the individual(s)
    - individuals possessed rights of possession for their lifetime only (resembles today's allodial system version of a life estate)
    - individuals did not possess an inheritable estate

Coaching Tips

It is important to point out that property ownership is comprised of two components:

1. the *fee*, which represents the direct ownership within the land
2. the *leasehold*, which represents the possessory right to the land and improvement(s)

Based on this, it was possible then, as it is now, that one party could have ownership/vested rights within the land or the fee, while another party received a leasehold interest in the property.

- Allodial system—The feudal system evolved into the allodial system. Under the allodial system, the purchaser received more than just a possessory right to the property. This system provided vesting/ownership rights to the land

and any improvements to the property. These rights are greatly limited by the rights of government. However, under this system:
  - land vests with the individual owner(s) of the property
  - the owners possess an inheritable estate

REAL PROPERTY COMPOSITION: LAND REAL ESTATE AND REAL PROPERTY

There are two categories of interests held in land:

1. interests held by government
2. interests held by individuals

Interests held by individuals are referred to as estates in land. An **estate in land** is the degree, quantity, nature, and extent of one's interest in the land. The term estate in land refers to an individual's interest in the land and not to the land itself or the physical properties of the land. Therefore, an estate in land is the interest held in land (**real property** or **real estate**).

The term *property* refers to the rights of ownership. The term *estate* means ownership in property. What type of property or estate one holds can be defined by either one of two types of property. Let's explore the first type (real property) in detail.

1. Real property or real estate (Chapter 475.01, F.S.) is any interest or estate (ownership) in land. The definition under state law also includes:
   a. any interest in business enterprises
   b. business opportunities, including:
      i. any assignment
      ii. leasehold
      iii. subleasehold
      iv. mineral right

The definition of real property or real estate does not include any of the following:

- any cemetery lot or right of burial in any cemetery
- the renting of a mobile home lot
- recreational vehicle lot in a mobile home park or travel park

Furthermore, real property is land and all things attached to and affixed to it. This would include ownership in the:

- fee (land)
- leasehold (improvements)

The permanence of any attached item (i.e., house, wood deck, etc.) to the land makes that item real property. Although at its inception, an improvement made to real property may have been personal property, the manner by which the improvement was attached to the land categorizes it as real property. In the same manner, real property can be severed from its attachment to real property. When this occurs, the severed real property now becomes personal property.

Physical Components of Real Property

There are three basic physical rights that are attributable to real property ownership:

1. Surface rights. Included in surface rights are water rights, which consist of:

    - Littoral rights—Those rights that occur when land adjoins a stationary body of water such as oceans, lakes, or seas. They are generally navigable bodies of water.
    - Riparian rights—Those rights that occur when land adjoins rivers, streams, or other flowing bodies of water. They are usually nonnavigable bodies of water.

    When land joins a flowing body of water, the owner has the right to limited, nonexclusive use of the water out of the watercourse (i.e., river or stream). The owner does not own the water itself but may use it for reasonable purposes.

    The boundary of the property carrying riparian rights depends on whether the river or stream is navigable or not. If it is navigable (meaning boats can travel on it), the land owner's property ends at the high water mark. If it is not navigable, the land owner's property ends at the middle of the watercourse (i.e., river or stream).

2. Subsurface rights. Subsurface rights are those rights to everything contained below the surface of the land in question. They extend to the center of the earth's core. Included within these rights are:

    - oil
    - gas
    - mineral rights

3. Air rights. Air rights are defined as the total legal bulk of an improvement made to land to include any used or unused development rights. The total size of the improvement is regulated by local zoning ordinances.

It is important to note that some properties are not built (within the existing improvement) to the full extent that zoning permits, and, as such, unused development rights remain. In certain cases, this may permit the owner of these unused development rights to further enlarge the improvement or allow by means of transfer (under certain conditions prescribed by local zoning ordinances) of those same rights to another neighboring or adjacent property. Historic/landmark property is a typical example of an unused air rights candidate. Where historic/landmark districts within a municipality may impede further development of that property, the unused building rights (subject to zoning laws and ordinances) become an asset that can be sold and transferred.

Given the rights discussed above, it would not be unimaginable for a property owner (whose sole interest was in the surface rights) to sell his subsurface and air rights to two separate parties. This scenario creates three separate ownerships within the property rights of one parcel of land.

Doctrine of Prior Appropriation: Accretion, Erosion, Alluvion, and Reliction

The riparian rights of an owner in some states are limited by the doctrine of appropriation. This doctrine states that the first owner to divert water for his/her own use may continue to do so, even if it is not fair to other owners along the watercourse.

A littoral right is the right of landowners to use the water in a lake, ocean, or sea that adjoins their property. Landowners may use or enjoy the water touching their land provided they do not alter the water's position by artificial means.

Surface rights extend from border to border of any property. Other terms and factors that affect land ownership bearing littoral or riparian rights include:

- accretion—the gradual build-up to a shoreline or bank of a waterway
- alluvion—the build-up of land by accretion
- erosion—the loss of land resulting from the elements
- reliction—the increase of land resulting from the permanent receding of a body of water

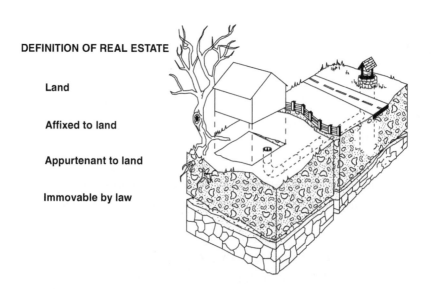

FIGURE 8.1
Source: © 2021 Mbition LLC

> ### Coaching Tips
>
> Chapter 475.01, F.S., defines real property in the following manner: "Real property" or "real estate" means any interest or estate in land and any interest in business enterprises or business opportunities, including any assignment, leasehold, subleasehold, or mineral right; however, the term does not include any cemetery lot or right of burial in any cemetery; nor does the term include the renting of a mobile home lot or recreational vehicle lot in a mobile home park or travel park. (See Figure 8.1.)

Real Versus Personal Property

While we learned earlier that real property is considered immovable in nature and includes land and all improvements affixed thereto, personal property includes all other property that is not real property. **Personal property** is also known as chattel or personalty. As a helpful guide, if it is moveable, it is personal property.

There are two categories of chattel:

1. chattel personal
2. chattel real

An item of chattel personal is an item of personal property that is moveable and is not attached to or associated with the real property. This includes items such as:

- automobiles
- tools
- furniture
- boats
- clothing
- money

An item of chattel real is an item of personal property that is not moveable or is attached to or associated with the real property. It may consist of tangible property or an intangible interest. Examples of chattel real that are considered to be tangible property include:

- trade fixtures
- emblements (crops)
- mortgage
- leases
- options
- easements

> ### Coaching Tips
>
> Real Property vs. Personal Property
> - Anything that is movable is personal property.
> - Anything that is non-movable is real property (includes fixtures).

FIXTURES

Fixtures are special categories of real property. They can be items that were initially real property or personal property. When permanently attached to the real property, a **fixture** becomes a part of the real property via utility and permanence of the object to the property.

> **Example** A tree is severed into wood and subsequently used to build a wood deck attached to a home. The original tree is categorized as real property via its roots. Once severed, it becomes personal property. When that same wood is attached to a home as a deck, it reverts back to real property.

In any real property transaction, buyers and sellers can often confuse the difference of what is a fixture versus what is personal property. The classic example would be the heirloom chandelier. Illumination receptacles are commonly referred to as light fixtures. Although they can be easily removed (with little or no damage to the property), the manner of their attachment and adaptation to the property have made light fixtures the subject of lawsuits within a purchase and sale contract. In order to avoid these problems, the sales associate may wish to review with the seller a punch list of items that would not be included in the sale of the property.

Plants, Trees, and Crops

In addition to the aforementioned, plants, trees, and crops growing on real property represent a special category of property. They can be either real or personal property under certain conditions. Their classification will depend on whether they are considered to be one of the following:

- fructus naturales
- fructus industriales

Fructus naturales are plants that are considered to be part of land, including:

- trees
- cultivated perennial plants (such as orange or apple trees)
- uncultivated vegetation of any kind (such as naturally growing shrubs, bushes, etc.)

Fructus industriales are plants that are cultivated annually. They are considered to be personal property. They are also referred to as emblements. They include cultivated crops such as corn, wheat, or vegetables.

Coaching Tips

Fructus naturales are plants that grow naturally without help from humans. They are considered real property.

> **Coaching Tips**
>
> Fructus industriales are plants that are cultivated by humans and depend on humans for their existence and growth. They are considered personal property. They are also referred to as emblements.

Legal Determination of a Fixture

Courts apply the following three tests when faced with determining whether or not an item is considered a fixture:

1. method of attachment
2. adaptability of the improvement to the property
3. intent or agreement of the parties

> **Coaching Tips**
>
> In some cases, the courts may even use a fourth test to make a determination as to whether an item is a fixture. The "relationship between the parties" becomes another method of dispute resolution.

Method of Attachment

Observance of how an improvement is made and ultimately attached aids in determining whether or not an item is classified as a fixture. If the removal of the item will result in damage to the property, it is usually classified as a fixture and a permanent part of the real property.

Adaptability of the Improvement to the Property

A close examination of how an item adapts to the real property can also determine whether or not an item is considered a fixture. Sometimes it is difficult to determine whether an item is permanently attached or not.

> **Example** A room-sized air conditioner may or may not be permanently attached. In cases such as these, it is necessary to look at whether the item has been adapted to the building. If the air conditioning unit is window mounted, it would not be considered a fixture. Conversely, if the unit is wall mounted (wall unit cut out), it would probably be considered a fixture.
>
> As another example, if storm windows are a standard size that could be used on other standard windows, the storm windows probably would not be considered a fixture. However, if the storm windows are custom fit to the windows, they

would probably be considered a fixture. The custom-fit window directly adapts to conform to the house.

Kitchen cabinets are deemed to be fixtures. Aside from the fact that they are an essential item within any kitchen (their adaptability to the room), removal would cause considerable damage. They also represent a design feature necessary to the room.

Intent or Agreement of the Parties

It is obvious that "good agreements make for good friends." When an agreement is made in advance, determining whether an item is deemed a fixture or personal property is simplified. Defining ownership of improvements that are made by a tenant in a lease will certainly avoid a landlord/tenant dispute at lease expiration. Listing items to be removed within a contract of sale will also avoid a dispute between buyer and seller.

Trade Fixtures

A special category of fixtures deals with fixtures used in a trade or business. Trade fixtures are items that are installed and used in the conduct of one's business. Therefore, when items are attached to or installed in real property for business purposes, the item(s) are considered personal property and may be removed at the end of a lease (which is more commonly the case) or at time of sale. They are deemed to be personal property items of the enterprise. For this to occur, two conditions are met:

1. The items must be removed *prior* to lease expiration.
2. The property is returned or restored to its original condition upon removal of the items.

> **Example** Department stores utilize wall units and shelving to display their inventory for sale. Their method of attachment to the property is generally permanent in nature. Whereby we define a fixture as any item that when removed will result in damage to the property, the wall units and shelves were initially installed with the intent that the interested party would have the right to remove them at time of sale or lease expiration.

The issue of whether an item is real property (fixture) or personal property is important in a number of situations:

- When property is sold:
    - A fixture, because it is real property, is sold as part of the property being sold.
    - Personal property is not sold as part of the real property and thereby remains the property of the selling party.

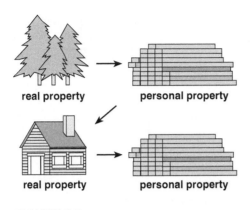

FIGURE 8.2
Source: © 2021 Mbition LLC

- When property taxes are assessed:
  - A fixture contributes to the value of the property in the form of an improvement. Generally speaking, when an improvement extends the life of the property or adds value through its utility, the item of improvement will cause higher property assessments. To the property owner, this translates into property tax increases.
- When property is appraised:
  - A fixture adds to the value of the property.
  - Personal property does not add to the value of the property.
- When insurance is issued on real property:
  - Fixtures are covered under the real property coverage.
  - Personal property is not covered or covered separately.

See Figure 8.2 for an illustration of real property and personal property.

Tests for fixtures can be remembered with the mnemonic device, MAI:

*M*ethod of attachment

*A*daptability of the improvement

*I*ntent or agreement between the parties

Basic Property Rights: Bundle of Rights

Aside from the title aspect to ownership in real property, ownership comes with other legal rights. These legal rights are termed as the bundle of rights. (See Figure 8.3.) The bundle of rights includes rights of:

- use/enjoyment—This right includes the ownership's right to use the property in any lawful manner prescribed by law.
- possession—The inception of this right commences on the day that title passes to the rightful owner. It includes the right of ingress (entry) and

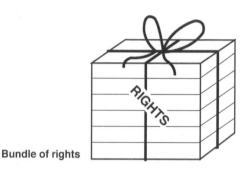

FIGURE 8.3
Source: © 2021 Mbition LLC

egress (exit) of one's property. It further includes the property owner's right to benefit from any income attributable to the property derived from rent.

- control—This right allows the property owner to improve the property through the addition of constructing improvements to the land. This right is regulated by local zoning and building codes.
- exclusion—This right allows the property owner to control who may enter the property. It also allows the property owner to enforce rights against any unlawful trespass by another.
- disposition—This right allows the property owner to sell, lease, mortgage, license, or gift all or a portion of the property to another.

TYPES OF ESTATES

There are two types of estates within the property system:

1. freehold estates (ownership of the property)
2. nonfreehold estates or estates less than freehold (leaseholds/leased property usually for a fixed term)

Freehold Estate

Before we can examine freehold estates, first, let's define the meaning of an estate. An estate refers to the degree, quantity, nature, and extent of interest (ownership rights) a person can have in real property. In simple terms, an estate signifies ownership in either real or personal property. There are various types of estates. The first type of estate in land is called a freehold estate. A **freehold estate** corresponds to what is commonly known as ownership interest in land (the fee). It is:

- an interest in land that may be held for an indefinite period of time. This includes property that is held for a lifetime (**life estate**) or longer.

- an entitlement to the holder to both the rights of:
    - ownership
    - possession

As a memory device, the term *freehold* represents the owner's ability to "freely hold a parcel of property" for as long as deemed appropriate by that owner.

There are several types of freehold estates:

- fee simple estates, including:
    - fee simple absolute
    - fee simple defeasible
- life estates

Some of the estates listed bear limitations and thereby create "variations to the theme." Let's examine the composition of these different variations.

Fee Simple Estate

As written earlier, property can be broken down into two parts:

1. fee—represented as ownership in the land and all rights contained therewith
2. leasehold—offers ownership (of a limited duration) and comes in the form of rights of possession within the improvement(s) to the fee (The giver of the leasehold is known as the lessor and has a reversionary right within the property upon expiration of the lease [the leasehold]).

A **fee simple estate** is the most comprehensive and simplest form of property ownership; it is ownership in land itself. Historically, before improvements were made to a property, the ownership process began with unimproved land. Therefore, the simplest and highest form of ownership came in this form. The importance of this type of estate is shown in the text regarding Rockefeller Center in New York City that directly follows.

Today, it is not uncommon to see property broken down with two separate parties involved:

1. the land owner (fee owner)
2. the developer/investor (holding a leasehold interest to the land)

We can conclude that not all land owners are developers and not all developers are land owners. With this thought in mind, major developments exist today that began as leasehold development.

Example In the early twentieth century, a 16-million-square-foot commercial space development was created in New York City in what is known today as Rockefeller Center. This development included Radio City Music Hall.

At its inception, the Rockefeller family donated the land under Rockefeller Center to Columbia University. While the land (or fee simple) was donated to Columbia University, the Rockefeller family reserved a long-term leasehold (in excess of 50 years) that enabled them to construct numerous office and entertainment structures. As a result of restructuring in the mid-1990s, today, both fee and leasehold are owned by the various owners who have purchased these properties.

The primary characteristics of a fee simple estate are as follows:

- They can be held for a lifetime or longer.
- Fee simple property ownership (in severalty or as a tenant in common with others) includes the right of inheritability (can be willed to heirs).
- Fee simple absolute is the most preferred, common, and desirable form of ownership. Fee simple absolute is the most complete form of ownership and the type that most property owners possess. It is not a defeasible estate. A fee simple absolute has three primary characteristics:
    1. It is the least restricted form of property ownership.
    2. It is limited only by government's rights of eminent domain, taxation, police power, and escheat.
    3. It is a nondefeasible estate. This means that it cannot be defeated (overcome) by another individual against the owner's will under any circumstances.
- Fee simple defeasible is lesser in its desirability insofar as ownership of real property is concerned. This type of ownership bears conditions or is conditional on whether or not certain or specific events occur. Property is transferred to another with certain conditions. In the event that these conditions are violated, the property owner's rights of ownership can be defeated with a right of reentry by the previous party. This type of estate can be determined by examination of the title being conveyed. Words that reference "but if" are usually followed by the conditions of title being conveyed.

Example Mrs. Black gave her property to a charity organization "for as long as it is used for elderly housing." The estate owned by the charity is a fee simple defeasible. In the event that the property is used for anything other than the stated conditions, title to the property reverts to Mrs. Black or her heirs.

Life Estates

The primary characteristics of life estates are as follows:

- They are held for a lifetime (but not longer).
- They are not inheritable and therefore may not be willed to heirs. There is one exception to the rule that life estates are not inheritable A life estate pur

autre vie is the exception, and it is based on the lifetime of a third party. Therefore, it is inheritable only if the life tenant dies prior to the named third party whose life the life estate was predicated on. For example, "A" gives a life estate pur autre vie to "B" for the life of "C." Later, "B" dies and wills the life estate pur autre vie to "D." As long as "C" is alive, "D" will be able to benefit from the inherited life estate. That life estate would continue until the death of the third party occurred. It is for this reason that a life estate pur autre vie is the exception.

- They are always reversionary estates or interests. This simply means that the original grantor receives ownership and all rights associated therein upon the death of the life tenant who is the grantee. The grantor is the giver of the grant while the grantee is the recipient of the grant. In other words, the death of the life tenant/grantee automatically terminates the life estate and all possessor rights associated therein.

It should be noted that in Florida, a life tenant (estate) can qualify for the homestead tax exemption. Currently in Florida, a full homestead tax exemption is $50,000 of assessed property value.

Voluntary Life Estates

Voluntary life estates are created by a voluntary act of the grantor. All of the life estates presented so far are voluntary in nature. There are three types of voluntary life estates:

1. Life estate in remainder, in which ownership of the fee simple estate reverts to a third party upon the death of the life tenant. The third party named to receive the fee simple estate is called the **remainderman** (see Figure 8.4a).
2. Life estate in reversion, in which ownership of the fee simple estate reverts to the grantor or heirs upon the death of the life tenant (see Figure 8.4b).
3. Life estate by reservation, in which ownership is transferred to another, and the selling party reserves or keeps a life estate for the rest of the selling party's life. Upon death of the selling life estate party, possession and use reverts to the buyer (see Figure 8.4c).

Statutory Life Estates

It is important to point out that in some states, some life estates are created not by voluntary action, but by law. These type of life estates are called statutory life estates. There are three types of statutory estates:

1. dower—a wife's right to receive, upon the death of her husband, a share of all property held or owned by the husband during the marriage
2. curtesy—a husband's interest in the property owned by his wife at the time of her death

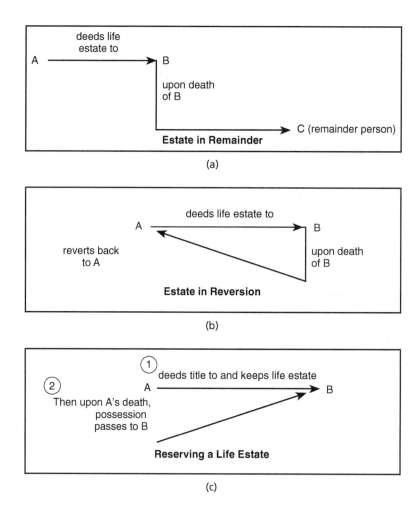

FIGURE 8.4
Source: © 2021 Mbition LLC

3. homestead protection—provides a life estate to a widow or widower (It should be noted that this is not the same thing as a homestead tax exemption. It is important to note that while a homestead creates a legal life estate and the homeowner is protected from certain creditors, it will not protect the homeowner from unpaid real property taxes or from a mortgage for purchase and cost of improvements.)

Nonfreehold Estates or Estates Less Than Freehold

Before we discuss nonfreehold estates or estates less than freehold, let's first review the differences between freehold estates and nonfreehold estates or estates less than freehold. The easiest way to remember the difference is as follows:

- Freehold estate means *ownership*.
- Nonfreehold estates or estates less than freehold means *rental or leased property*.

Nonfreehold estates or estates less than freehold are also called **leasehold estates**. These are interests in property for a definitive period of time. This applies to any property that is leased by a tenant. Where freehold estates are considered real property, nonfreehold estates or estates less than freehold are considered personal property.

Some basic terminology related to nonfreehold estates or estates less than freehold includes:

- The holder of nonfreehold estates or estates less than freehold is called the *tenant* or *lessee*.
- The property owner granting this estate is called the *landlord* or *lessor*.

The rights of the parties to the lease include the following:

- The tenant or lessee may occupy and use the property exclusively as long as tenant has a valid lease, abides by the terms and conditions provided within the lease, pays rent on time, and is not in default of any of the terms or provisions therein.
- The landlord or lessor cannot occupy or use the property until the lease has expired and the landlord/lessor has obtained legal possession of the property.
- During the lease term, the landlord/lessor is said to possess a reversionary interest in the property leased. This provides for the right to reclaim and regain legal possession of the property at the end of the lease term.

Types of Nonfreehold Estates or Estates Less Than Freehold

There are three categories of leasehold estates:

1. estate for years
2. estate at will
3. estate at sufferance

Estate for Years

An **estate for years** is a lease that has a specified starting and ending date. In spite of its name, it does not necessarily have to be for more than one year. In fact, it can be for any duration—as little as one day to many years. However, this would be predicated upon the specified duration stipulated within the lease.

Estate at Will

An estate at will is also referred to as a tenancy at will or, in Florida, a tenancy without a specified term. Simply put, it may be terminated by either lessor or lessee at any time (at will). Otherwise, it is a normal landlord-tenant relationship.

> ## Coaching Tips
>
> Some states place limitations on estates at will. Generally, these limitations tend to deal with notice requirements to terminate, requiring minimum notice periods from either party. For example, in order to terminate a month-to-month tenancy at will, Florida law requires that either party to the lease provide the other with notice of the intent to cancel the lease not less than 15 days prior to the end of that monthly period.

Estate at Sufferance or Tenancy at Sufferance

An estate at sufferance or **tenancy at sufferance** occurs when a tenant remains in possession beyond legal tenancy without the consent of the landlord/lessor. In this situation, the tenant/lessee is referred to as a holdover tenant or a tenant at sufferance. In this situation and if done in a timely manner, a tenant at sufferance or holdover tenancy can be evicted. However, if a tenant has the landlord's permission to remain in possession of the leased property after the initial term expires, this is a **tenancy at will** rather than a tenancy at sufferance. (See Figure 8.5.)

FORMS OF OWNERSHIP

There are two basic forms of property ownership:

1. sole ownership
2. concurrent ownership

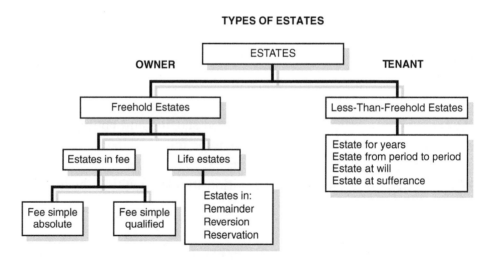

FIGURE 8.5
Source: © 2021 Mbition LLC

Sole Ownership: Ownership in Severalty

Sole ownership or ownership in property by one person is called an estate in severalty. The word *severalty* sounds like it should mean ownership by several people, but that is not the case. In fact, the root word of severalty is *sever*. A means of remembering this would be to think of severed ownership. Any freehold estate can be held in severalty.

Concurrent Ownership or Co-ownership

Any ownership held by two or more persons in property is called concurrent ownership. There are four types of concurrent estates/ownership:

1. joint tenancy (with rights of survivorship)
2. tenancy in common
3. tenancy by the entireties
4. community property

In each of these types of concurrent ownership, each co-owner holds an undivided interest in the property as a whole versus separate parts of the property.

Coaching Tips

Forms of Ownership at a Glance

- Ownership in severalty—Sole ownership or ownership in property by one person is called an estate in severalty. It is an estate that can be willed to heirs.
- Concurrent ownership—Ownership held by two or more persons in property is called concurrent ownership. There are four types of concurrent estates/ownership:
  1. joint tenancy (with rights of survivorship)—not inheritable, cannot be left by will
  2. tenancy in common—the only ownership vesting option that is willable
  3. tenancy by the entireties—reserved for married couples only; resembles joint tenancy for nonmarried individuals
  4. community property—equal division of marital property and debts; exist in some states, but most states, including Florida, require equitable or fair division

Joint Tenancy

In order to create this type of ownership, more than one party to the transaction is required. Therefore, any two or more persons may hold title as joint tenants. The primary distinguishing characteristic of **joint tenancy** is the fact that it carries the rights of survivorship. Survivorship means that when a joint tenant dies, his/her share or interest within the property automatically goes to any surviving joint tenant or tenants. The share or interest does not go to any heirs of the deceased joint tenant. The reason for this is the survivorship provision within the title to this vesting. Due to the survivorship provision, a joint tenancy is not willable or inheritable. Survivorship rights supersede and have full priority over any dower or curtesy rights. During the life of a joint tenant, the joint tenant may sell to whomever is willing to buy that interest within the property. However, upon the death of the joint tenant and in the absence of a sale during his/her life, the deceased tenant's share will always equally inure to the benefit of any remaining joint tenants.

Creation of a joint tenancy with rights of survivorship requires the presence of four unities:

1. Unity of time—All joint tenant owners must acquire the property at the same time.
2. Unity of interest—All joint tenant owners must hold equal degrees (shares) of interest (i.e., four parties each having a 25% interest in the property at time of purchase).
3. Unity of title—All joint tenant owners must acquire title in the same way. This must be in the form of one single title to the whole property (undivided interest).
4. Unity of possession—All joint tenant owners must hold an undivided interest in the possession of the whole property.

Coaching Tips

A helpful tool and mnemonic device is PITTS:

- *Possession* (unity of)
- *Interest* (unity of)
- *Time* (unity of)
- *Title* (unity of)
- *Survivorship* (rights of)

There are two important remaining points to discuss concerning joint tenancy:

1. As previously mentioned, joint tenants may sell to anyone they choose to during their life. This may be done without the consent of the other joint

tenant owners. However, any new owner who is outside of the initial acquisition becomes a tenant in common with the remaining living original joint tenants/co-owners.

2. Corporations may never hold ownership as joint tenants with rights of survivorship. Corporations have what is referred to as perpetual life. Therefore, it is safe to assume that a corporation will always outlive the joint tenant. It is for this primary reason that corporations may not hold title to property in this fashion. Corporations may hold property either in severalty or as tenants in common with others.

Tenancy in Common

Any two or more persons may hold title to property as tenants in common. Where the unity of possession is required, unlike joint tenancy, each tenant holds a separate title to his/her undivided interest within that subject property. Co-owners may sell their shares within the property at any time and to anyone with or without the other's consent. Rights of survivorship do not exist within this type of title holding. Therefore, **tenancy in common** bear the rights of inheritability. In addition, co-owners may hold equal or unequal shares within the property ownership. Unlike joint tenants, the unity of interest is not required.

Coaching Tips

In most states, when there are two or more owners of a property and no specific form of concurrent ownership is suggested or indicated, the owners by default are presumed (by law) to be tenants in common. Specifically, such is the case within Florida.

Joint Tenancy		Tenancy in Common
YES	Possession (Unity of)	YES
YES	Interest (Unity of)	NO
YES	Time (Unity of)	NO
YES	Title (Unity of)	NO
YES	Survivorship	NO

Tenancy by the Entireties

Tenancy by the entireties can be compared with joint tenancy. It is a special form of joint tenancy. The primary difference lies with the relationship of the parties.

Tenancy by the entireties is solely reserved for husband and wife relationships. It requires the following:

- The four unities of joint tenancy, namely:
    - possession
    - interest
    - time
    - title
- A fifth unity is called the unity of person. It is limited to ownership held jointly by husband and wife who are considered to be one person. As such, each spouse owns an undivided interest in 100% of the property. This tends to protect either spouse from a forced sale resulting from judgments against one but not the other.

Tenancy by the entireties normally carries the inherent right of survivorship. The **right of survivorship** can be defined as the right of a surviving party to the property of a deceased party. The right of survivorship:

- is an inherent characteristic of joint tenancy relationships and tenancy by the entireties
- is only recognized in about half of the states in the United States, including Florida

Under this holding of title, neither spouse may encumber the property or sell the property without the consent of the other. However, tenancy by the entireties may be terminated by any of the following:

- joint action of husband and wife
- divorce
- death of either spouse

Community Property

Community property is based on the concept that each spouse has an equal interest in any property acquired during marriage. Property acquired before the marriage or received after the marriage through a will or gift does not qualify as community property. Florida is not a community property state.

Partitioning of Ownership

Holders of concurrent estates/ownership have an undivided interest in the property. In some cases, this interest can be separated by partition. Partition is the dividing of common interests into separate interests owned in severalty. Joint tenancy and tenancy in common can be partitioned; however, tenancy by the entireties cannot. Partitioning can occur by two methods:

1. Partition in kind—The property itself can be subdivided and split among the owners.
2. Partition at law—The property can also be sold and the proceeds divided among the owners.

In addition, portioning can be brought about in either one of two ways:

1. The co-owners can agree voluntarily to the partition.
2. One or more co-owners can ask the courts to partition the property if the owners cannot agree among themselves.

Special Ownership Interests

There are also some special ownership interests in Florida, including:

- elective share
- exempt properties
- homestead

Elective Share

Elective share deals with the rights of a surviving spouse who has been excluded from the deceased spouse's will. In this situation, by law, the surviving spouse is entitled to a share of the decedent's estate. At present time, the elective share in Florida is 30% of the net estate. This does, however, bear some exclusions.

A spouse who was included in a will may also have rights if the share provided for under the will is less than the spouse stood to receive under state law. In this case, the spouse may be entitled to an elective share. For this to happen, the elective share must be greater than the share provided for within the decedent's will.

Exempt Properties

Another property right is referred to in Florida as exempt property. **Exempt property** refers to personal property that a spouse is automatically entitled to when the other spouse dies. In Florida, exempt property includes household items such as furniture and appliances with value of up to $10,000 plus automobiles. Such property may not be seized or sold by a creditor to satisfy a debt.

Homestead

Florida state law provides for an owner-occupant of a home to be eligible to receive homestead status. To be eligible, the homeowner must reside in the home and have legal title to the property as of January 1 of any given year. The homeowner must also file for the homestead exemption. It is the declaration of one's residence as a homestead that entitles the property owner to certain protections as well as benefits.

The purpose behind the **homestead** is to ensure that families with unsecured debts cannot be removed from their homestead as a result of a forced sale of the property. The creation of a homestead will protect and relieve the property owner from all debts that may result in a forced sale of the property except debts resulting from:

- unpaid real property taxes
- any unpaid special assessments
- recorded mortgages
- vendor liens, wherein the seller holds a lien on property when the sale involves a purchase money mortgage
- construction liens, such as mechanics and materialman's liens, wherein a supplier of labor or materials places a lien on the property if the labor materials are not paid for

It is important to note that the rise in assessed value for homestead property is capped at 3% per year or the Consumer Price Index (CPI)—whichever is less.

Liens are claims on the property of another. This subject will be discussed in greater detail in Chapter 9.

Homestead Exemption

Florida homestead law currently allows the owner of a property that qualifies as a homestead to receive an annual property tax exemption. With few exceptions, this does not mean that a qualified homestead will pay zero property tax. It simply provides for a credit against the property tax bill up to the amount of the exemption. At the present time, the maximum exemption is $50,000. The amount of the maximum homestead was increased from $25,000 to $50,000 in 2006. This was as a direct result of amendment #6 to the Florida Increased Homestead Exemption. This amendment took effect January 1, 2007.

The application of the exemption is then used to calculate one's annual property tax bill. The tax bill is calculated by deducting the homestead exemption amount (be it a partial or full homestead) from the assessed valuation applied to the property by the municipality assessor. Assuming no further exemptions are available to the property owner, the difference between the gross assessment and the homestead deduction acts as the net assessment. The net assessed value is then multiplied by the appropriate tax rate (or mil rate) for the area. Let's look at an example of this application:

Example

$100,000 Assessed Value of Property (prior to homestead deduction)
−50,000 Maximum Homestead Exemption
$50,000 Assessed Value Subject to Property Tax

COMMUNITY ASSOCIATIONS

So far, we have covered various forms of ownership of individual parcels of real property. Next we will examine ownerships in situations where communities of property are involved. (This is different from the concurrent ownership category called *community property*.)

Other than detached housing, there are four types of property ownership vehicles that one can purchase in a community:

1. condominiums
2. cooperatives
3. planned-unit developments
4. resort time-sharing developments

In community ownership, individual owners surrender some of their property rights in exchange for certain benefits of community living. In each form of community ownership, it is helpful to think of the community as a "city within a city" that has all the requirements for:

- some form of self-government of the citizens
- assessments or common area maintenance (CAM) to fund the operation of the community
- the provision of services

Condominiums

The first form of community ownership is called a condominium. A **condominium** is a form of individual fee ownership of a unit within a multifamily development property. The distinguishing features of a condominium are:

- ownership of separate property
- common property

The individual unit owner holds two types of interest in a condominium:

1. a fee simple title to the individual unit (Ownership of a condominium unit on the tenth floor of a high-rise tower [air lot] is no different than that of single-family home ownership [land lot]. Just like the owner of a single home property, the condominium unit owner receives a deed for the property.

    - These individual units are called **separate property**.

Coaching Tips

As each condominium unit represents an individual tax air lot, think of a high-rise condominium development as a vertical subdivision in the sky. Rather than selling the consumer a land lot (as in a land lot subdivision), a developer or individual reseller sells to the consumer an individual air lot.

2. an undivided interest (shared ownership) in the remaining elements in the development as tenants in common
    - These remaining areas are better known as common areas or common elements.

Separate property consists of the individual dwelling units. Technically, a dwelling unit consists of only the four walls. This includes space between the walls, floor, and ceiling of the unit.

Common property is everything else, including:

- land
- interior and exterior walls
- any other improvements such as pools and tennis courts
- hallways and stairs
- recreation areas and landscaping
- parking lots

In Florida, a condominium may be created by either one of the following ways:

1. new construction
2. conversion of a rental property to condominium ownership

Generally speaking, condominiums, by design, are more likely to be new construction as opposed to a conversion of rental property. Any type of private development can be organized as a condominium. How the property will be used has no effect on whether it can be organized in condominium form. The following are a few examples of properties that may be organized as condominiums:

- high-rise buildings
- garden apartments
- townhouse developments
- warehouses
- office buildings
- detached single-family dwellings

In order for a condominium development to exist, enabling legislation must be passed by the state. This type of legislation bears different names in different states, including:

- Horizontal Property Act
- Strata Title Act
- Condominium Act

In each of the aforementioned cases, legislature provides for horizontal subdivision of the air space above the land into cubicles called air lots. Each unit (within the development) occupies one air lot.

In Florida, both the sales and the day-to-day operations of condominiums must comply with the Florida Condominium Act. Compliance is set forth within Chapter 718 of the Florida Statutes, or 718, F.S.

As previously stated, title to a condominium comes in the form of a deed. The deed that covers the entire property is called the master deed. By splitting the fee (land) title to the air space above the land, each separate unit owner is able to receive a deed to the unit. Remember, real property is always transferred from one person to another by deed. This is the instrument used for transferring real property from one party to another. Once recorded, these deeds give their owners:

- fee simple title to their unit
- an undivided interest in the land and other common areas of the property, held as tenants in common with others

Condominium ownership rights are as desirable as those of private home ownership. These ownership rights give the owner the right (with reasonable restrictions that may apply) to:

- sell without association approval
- sublease without association approval (However, some associations do require a right of first refusal on any subleasing or sale. If this association right is exercised, it must be on the identical terms as those offered to a tenant or buyer. Some associations have restrictions and/or limitations on subleasing.)
- gift (with no occupancy restrictions or constraints)
- will to heirs (with no occupancy restrictions or constraints)

This type of ownership and community living arrangement requires some form of governing authority within the development. This is achieved through the creation of an owners or condominium association. As ownership in each individual unit vests with the unit owner, each unit owner automatically becomes a member of the association. The association is normally organized as a not-for-profit corporation. An owners association has the duty to control, regulate, and maintain all of the common areas.

The association may elect a board of managers and/or a third-party property management company to run the day-to-day activities of the condominium (common in properties with 25 units or more). Condominium fees (called *common charges*) are assessed to provide money and liquidity to pay for such things as:

- maintenance of common areas
- insurance
- management and legal fees
- property tax on common areas
- reserves for future capital expenditure

These common charges are based, predicated, and derived on proportionate share of total expenses in running the association's operations. The proportionate share of each owner's obligation to fund common charges is determined and established by dividing the living unit's square footage by the square footage of the entire condominium property. In formula form this is represented as follows:

$$\text{Unit square footage} \div \text{Total condominium square footage}$$

Similar to rental income-producing property, common charges are paid monthly. Each unit owner receives a separate property tax bill from the municipality. Each unit owner is charged with the responsibility of paying the tax bill directly to the governing municipality. As in single-family housing, property taxes form a lien on the property until the taxes are paid. Failure to pay the taxes will ultimately result in a rem proceeding (foreclosure proceeding for unpaid property tax).

Financing for each unit is exclusively arranged by the individual unit owner. There is no joint liability between owners for loans on the individual units. Any mortgage resulting from a borrowing (specifically) for the common areas are achieved by the owners association (who acts as the mortgagor).

Maintenance of the condominium areas are handled as follows:

- Common area maintenance and repairs are the responsibility of the owners association.
- Individual unit owners bear the responsibility for maintenance and repairs to each respective unit (unless the repairs are inside the walls).

Condominium Creation

In order to create a condominium, the Florida Condominium Act (718, F.S.) provides for the creation and/or submission of certain documents such as:

- **declaration of condominium**—the instrument used to create the condominium
- bylaws—dictate how the owners association may run the facility
- plat map—provides the legal description required for each unit as well as its location within the development
- conveyance document—used for deeding title to the condominium

In addition, on a primary sale, the developer is required to provide a disclosure statement to each buyer. When a consumer initially purchases a unit from the sponsor/developer, the disclosure document is commonly referred to as a **prospectus**. Due to the nature of the public offering of the units and laws governing same, the disclosure document is initially termed a *prospectus*. With regard to all subsequent resales, the same document is referred to as the offering plan. This is intended to advise the buyer of the right to rescind any contract to purchase within the later of 15 days of signing the contract or of receiving all condominium documents. In the event of a resale from a previous owner (outside of the developer of the project) of an existing condominium unit, the buyer only receives a three-day right of rescission from the time of signing the contract and receiving all required condominium documents.

In the resale case above, any real estate licensee holding a deposit from a prospective purchaser of a condominium unit who acts on the right of rescission within the allotted lawful time period is required to promptly refund in full to the purchaser all deposits previously held by the licensee.

Cooperatives

Another form of community ownership is a cooperative. In a **cooperative**, title to the land, building, and all other improvements to the property are held by the cooperative corporation. The cooperative is organized as a not-for-profit corporation. Anyone who purchases within a cooperative is only purchasing shares of stock in the corporation. Where the cooperative corporation holds fee simple ownership to the land and improvements made to the land, the stockholder is only given shares of stock and an occupancy agreement that conveys rights of occupancy to the respective unit. This agreement is called a **proprietary lease**. Only shareholders are permitted by the cooperative to occupy the unit. Although the issuance of a proprietary lease may resemble a lease for rental property, the monthly payment by the shareholder(s) is not made in the form of rent; it is made and referred to as monthly maintenance. The cooperative corporation is responsible for payment of:

- any payments required by a lender for the underlying mortgage (if any)
- property tax for the entire property (shareholders do not receive individual tax bills and they do not pay property tax directly to the charging municipality)
- repairs and maintenance
- management expenses

Each unit shareholder pays a proportionate share in one fixed monthly fee termed *maintenance*. The unit proportion toward maintenance is generally calculated on a per share basis. Shares are allocated to each unit. Allocation of how many shares are issued to each unit is derived by:

- square foot size of the unit versus the overall property bulk (size)
- location of the respective unit in the property
- exposure (certain facing exposures are more desirable than others)
- floor height within the property (i.e., second floor versus twentieth floor)
- views and outdoor space (terraces or balconies)

As a short informational note, *terraces* are defined (in most areas) as the outdoor space built above another unit's living space. A *balcony* is defined as an extension protruding out over airspace. Balconies do not have a living area below the floor of the balcony. In addition, cooperative living and ownership resembles a landlord/tenant relationship. The shareholder owns shares of stock in a corporation but does not own the unit.

The cooperative occupants are composed of all shareholders to the cooperative. The shareholders elect a board of directors who are charged with running the day-to-day activities of the cooperative. In almost all cases, rights associated with a shareholder in a cooperative will bear a *more restrictive* living arrangement than that of a condominium.

Cooperative boards, at their sole discretion, may do the following:

- screen new shareholder purchases
- reject any sale that a shareholder may propose
- grant their approval and consent to the transfer of shares and issuance of a new proprietary lease
- deny or consent to any subleasing
- charge a flip tax to the selling shareholder at the time of sale (This is usually an income-generating device for the cooperative to build their financial property reserves. In many cases, this may amount to approximately 2% of the selling price.)

In Florida, activities concerning formation and disclosure issues are governed by the Cooperative Act (719, F.S.). The act requires disclosure of the following related to cooperatives:

- a legal description of the property
- description of the common areas associated with the property
- title held
- liens
- easements
- outstanding or pending lawsuits as they relate to the cooperative
- judgments related to the cooperative
- manager of the property
- date of completion (if not substantially completed)
- operating statements and budgets
- sale and resale procedures

Coaching Tips

As a further note, cooperatives and condominiums are organized as not-for-profit entities. As a result, previously, the IRS restricted cooperatives and condominiums from receiving more than 20% of their annual operating budget from passive-income activities. This is more commonly referred to as the 80/20 rule. Active income (80%) is defined as the maintenance, while passive income (no more than 20%) is derived from investment income-producing activities such as:

- collection of rents on cooperative owned, such as:
    - retail space(s)
    - garage rents
    - cellular antennae(s)
    - satellite dish
    - vending machine income
    - any other income-producing vehicle attributable to the property outside of maintenance

Due to the 80/20 rule, in other states, a hybrid of condominiums and cooperatives has emerged. This hybrid is called a **cond-op**. A cond-op begins as condominium property when the land is owned. A developer seeks to solve the 80/20 issue by retaining ownership in the commercial portion of the property. The developer sells the residential units to individuals while reserving and retaining the commercial parts of the property for future income-producing purposes. This income benefits only the developer and indirectly solves the 80/20 issue for the property. The end result becomes:

- condominium ownership in the land by the condominium owners association (representative of the residential units)
- condominium ownership in the land by the developer for the commercial spaces such as:
    - retail spaces
    - garage facility

The residences are structured as a cooperative setup with condominium bylaws. This allows the cooperative shareholder condominium flexibility concerning sales and subleasing. From an income tax point of view, a cooperative offers higher tax benefits with respect to maintenance than that of a condominium. The extra benefit usually is a result of a per share deduction of the interest attributable to the underlying mortgage that generally exists in a cooperative and not in a condominium. Tax deductibility creates a marketing tool for the developer concerning sales of residential units. The 80/20 issue has been eliminated. Today, the term *cond-op* is more closely and commonly associated with new development constructed on leased land (long-term leasehold).

Planned-Unit Development (PUD)

A planned-unit development (PUD) will normally consist of individually owned homes within a community ownership of common areas. The common areas are often developed as recreational areas. The ownership of common areas in a PUD differs from that of a condominium.

In a condominium:

- The individual unit owners own the common areas as tenants in common.
- The owners association is responsible for maintenance of the common area only.

In a PUD:

- The community association owns the common areas, and the unit owners own a share of the association.

PUDs are created by local zoning laws rather than state laws. There is usually a trade-off involved in the development of the property:

- The developer is allowed to build on smaller lots, thus increasing the density of the homes.
- In exchange, the developer is required to create and develop the common areas (often as recreational areas, other uses, and a greater amount of open air space).

In a condominium, each unit owner in a PUD owns the land, the air above the land, and the unit itself. Because the unit owner owns the air above the land, vertical stacking is not possible. As a result, the most common forms of buildings are single-family detached dwellings or attached townhouses.

Resort Developments: Time-Share

Time-share is a method of dividing up and selling a living unit for a specified period each year. Time-shares are almost exclusively resort-type properties, such as hotels, condominiums, townhouses, villas, recreational vehicles parks, and campgrounds. The primary advantage to time-sharing resort property is that it becomes possible to afford a vacation retreat that could not otherwise be afforded.

Time-share developments may be organized in three ways:

1. The right-to-use format gives the buyer the right to occupy a unit within the development for a specified time (usually one week) each year for a specified number of years (usually up to 40 years, after which the interest in the property reverts back to the developer).
2. The interval ownership format gives the buyer the right to fee simple ownership of a unit along with other buyers and the use of the property for one

week each year. Unlike the right-to-use format, the purchaser receives a deed at closing.
3. The club plan gives the buyer a membership in a club that owns the property and the right to use the property for one week each year.

Like condominiums and cooperatives, the Florida Time-Share Act (721, F.S.) is designed to protect the general public from suffering economic loss from lack of seller/developer disclosures.

The Florida Time-Share Act requires that:

- any sales associate selling time-shares hold a current and valid real estate license
- the seller/developer disclose that the buyer has a right to rescind any contract to purchase a time-share at the later of within 10 days of signing a contract or receiving the public offering statement. The public offering statement contains certain required disclosures as well as a permit authorizing the developer to sell time-shares.

Time-shares that are registered with the Securities and Exchange Commission (SEC) are exempt from the Florida Time-Share Act.

Homeowners Associations

In Florida, domestic corporations formed and charged with the responsibilities for the operation of a community is referred to as a **homeowners association** or simply, **association**. The definition is expanded to include a mobile home subdivision whereby the voting membership is made up of parcel owners where membership is a mandatory condition of parcel ownership and which is authorized to impose assessments that, if unpaid, will result in a lien on the parcel.

Disclosures Required Under the Florida Homeowners Association Act (Chapter 720.401, F.S.)

Under Chapter 720, F.S., prospective purchasers who will be subject to payments and membership in a homeowners association are entitled to receive necessary disclosures prior to executing a contract for purchase and sale. The disclosures should include but may not be limited to the following:

- Name of community
- The buyer will be obligated to be a member of a homeowners association.
- There have or will be recorded restrictive covenants governing the use and occupancy of properties in this community.

- The buyer will be subject to pay assessments to the association.
  - Assessments may be subject to periodic change.
- Buyer will additionally be obligated to pay special assessments to the respective municipality, county, or special district. All assessments are subject to periodic change.
- Buyer's failure to pay special assessments or assessments levied by a homeowners association could result in a lien on the property.
- Buyer may also have an obligation to pay rent or land use fees for recreational or other commonly used facilities as an obligation of membership in the homeowners association.
- The developer may have the right to amend the restrictive covenants without the approval of the association membership or the approval of the parcel owners.
- The statements contained in this disclosure form are only summary in nature, and, as a prospective purchaser, you should refer to the covenants and the association governing documents before purchasing property.
- The documents are either of public record and can be obtained from the record office in the county where the property is located or are not recorded and can be obtained from the developer.

The disclosure must be supplied by the developer or by the parcel owner if the sale is by an owner who is not the developer. In addition, any contract for sale must include, in prominent language, a statement that the potential buyer should not execute the contract or agreement until he/she has received and read the disclosure summary required by this section.

Furthermore, each contract for the sale of property governed by disclosure must contain in conspicuous type a clause that states:

"If the disclosure summary required by section 720.401, Florida Statutes, has not been provided to the prospective purchaser before executing this contract for sale, this contract is voidable by buyer by delivering to seller or seller's agent or representative written notice of the buyer's intention to cancel within 3 days after receipt of the disclosure summary or prior to closing, whichever occurs first. Any purported waiver of this voidability right has no effect. Buyer's right to void this contract shall terminate at closing."

When the disclosure summary is not provided to a prospective purchaser in a timely manner, the purchaser may legally void the contract. In order to do so, the purchaser can accomplish same by delivering to the seller or the seller's agent written notice canceling the contract within three days after receipt of the disclosure summary or prior to closing, whichever occurs first.

Community Development Districts (CDDs)

Under Chapter 190, F.S., a **community development district (CDD)** is defined as an alternative means to municipal creation, management, and financing of infrastructure necessary to the creation and use of supporting community development. Under Chapter 190.048, F.S. (sale of real estate within a district; required disclosure to purchaser), each contract for the purchase and sale of either:

- a parcel of real property, and/or
- the initial sale of a residential unit in the CDD shall include the disclosure statement below in boldfaced and conspicuous type:

> "THE (Name of District) COMMUNITY DEVELOPMENT DISTRICT MAY IMPOSE AND LEVY TAXES OR ASSESSMENTS, OR BOTH TAXES AND ASSESSMENTS, ON THIS PROPERTY. THESE TAXES AND ASSESSMENTS PAY THE CONSTRUCTION, OPERATION, AND MAINTENANCE COSTS OF CERTAIN PUBLIC FACILITIES AND SERVICES OF THE DISTRICT AND ARE SET ANNUALLY BY THE GOVERNING BOARD OF THE DISTRICT. THESE TAXES AND ASSESSMENTS ARE IN ADDITION TO COUNTY AND OTHER LOCAL GOVERNMENTAL TAXES AND ASSESSMENTS AND ALL OTHER TAXES AND ASSESSMENTS PROVIDED FOR BY LAW."

Summary

Real property or real estate is land and all improvements permanently attached to the land. Real property can be held by individuals and operating business enterprises. There are two types of estates: freehold (owned) or nonfreehold (leased). Title may be held in several ways. There is sole ownership and ownership held in conjunction with others. Sole ownership is held in severalty, while ownership held with others or concurrent owners has various vesting options available to the owning party. There are various other vehicles of ownership other than single-family detached housing. These would include condominiums, cooperatives, PUDs, and time-shares. Licensees must have a clear understanding as to differences concerning the variety of ownership vehicles.

Review Questions

1. Margo owns a one-third interest in a property, and she received a deed for her interest. One of Margo's cousins owns a one-sixth interest. Margo can sell her one-third, give it away, or leave it in a will. Margo's interest is a:
   a. tenancy by the entireties
   b. leasehold estate
   c. tenancy in common
   d. joint tenancy

2. Which of the following items would most likely be declared by the seller as being personal property?
   a. chandelier
   b. doorbell
   c. ceiling fan
   d. refrigerator

3. One of the advantages of declaring a homestead in Florida is protection from forced sale for:
   a. mortgage liens
   b. tax liens
   c. credit card debts
   d. IRS liens

4. Purchasers of condominiums in Florida must be given required disclosures before or at the time of signing a purchase contract. The documents include:
   a. the Public Offering Statement
   b. a declaration
   c. management fees
   d. proprietary lease

5. Jose gave a house to his stepmother for as long as she lives. After Jose's stepmother dies, Jose's sons will own it. The stepmother's interest is a:
   a. reversionary estate
   b. remainder estate
   c. life estate
   d. fee simple estate

6. Florida law that states "a form of ownership of real property wherein legal title is vested in a corporation or other legal entity" and "beneficial use is evidenced by an ownership in the association and a lease" best describes:
   a. cooperatives
   b. time-sharing
   c. condominiums
   d. estates in severalty

7. Suzie and Jack are married and own a home in both their names. They have children who are their legal heirs. Suzie dies.
   a. Jack owns the home outright.
   b. Jack owns a half-interest in the home; the children own their mother's half.
   c. Ownership would depend on Suzie's will.
   d. Jack has a life estate in the home, and the children are vested remaindermen.

8. Rebecca has complete and absolute ownership of two vacant lots in a nearby subdivision. Rebecca is married to Brad. Rebecca's interest is a(n):
   a. joint tenancy
   b. estate by entireties
   c. fee simple estate, ownership in severalty
   d. remainder estate

9. In order to calculate the real property tax that contains a homestead exemption, the homestead exemption is:
   a. subtracted from the assessed value
   b. a limit of what the property taxes can be
   c. exempted from property taxes on certain homes
   d. available for all homeowners

10. Alice agreed that her tenant could live in the unit through April of next year. The tenant's estate is a(n):
    a. tenancy by entireties
    b. estate for years
    c. tenancy at will
    d. tenancy at sufferance

11. The tenants' lease expired, and the tenants are still living in the unit. This is a(n):
    a. tenancy by entireties
    b. estate for years
    c. tenancy at will
    d. tenancy at sufferance

12. The list of property rights that constitute title in Florida would NOT include:
    a. exclusion
    b. possession
    c. severalty
    d. disposition

13. Which of the following estates features survivorship?
    a. by the entireties
    b. tenancy in common
    c. estate in severalty
    d. estate for years

14. Which of these statements about a planned-unit development (PUD) is FALSE?
    a. PUDs allow for commercial use like grocery and drug stores.
    b. Doctors' offices are a permissible use within the development.
    c. Homes are clustered within large green spaces.
    d. Industrial parks are an allowed PUD idea.

15. Which of the following would be a way to determine whether or not an item is a fixture?
    a. The item is too large to move.
    b. The manner by which the item is movable.
    c. The item is used as part of a business.
    d. The item provides a necessary function, such as a stove.

16. Joe's lot is on the beach. When there is a storm, waves deposit more sand, so Joe's lot is getting bigger. This process is called:
    a. reliction
    b. erosion
    c. buildup
    d. accretion

17. Fern purchased a farm and later discovered an oil company has a right to sink wells on a part of the farm's pastures. Fern cannot exclude the equipment. Fern's purchase did not include the:
    a. surface rights
    b. air rights
    c. subsurface rights
    d. surface and subsurface rights

18. Cathy's interest in an orange grove is an estate in severalty. This means Cathy:
    a. is not the only owner
    b. must have a tenancy in common
    c. may be a joint tenant
    d. does not share the ownership

CHAPTER 9
TITLE DEEDS AND OWNERSHIP RESTRICTIONS

KEY TERMS

abstract of title
acknowledgment
actual notice
adverse possession
alienation
assignment
chain of title
condemnation
constructive notice
deed
deed restrictions
easement
eminent domain
encroachment
escheat
further assistance
general warranty deed

graduated lease/variable lease
grantee
granting clause
grantor
gross lease
ground lease
habendum clause
lien
net lease
percentage leases
quiet enjoyment
quitclaim deed
seisin
sublease
testate
title
warranty forever

LEARNING OBJECTIVES

After completing this lesson, you will be able to:

- differentiate between voluntary and involuntary alienation
- explain the various methods of acquiring title to real property and describe the conditions necessary to acquire real property by adverse possession
- distinguish between actual notice and constructive notice
- distinguish between an abstract of title and a chain of title
- explain the different types of title insurance
- describe the parts of a deed and the requirements of a valid deed
- list and describe the four types of statutory deeds and the legal requirements for deeds
- list and describe the types of governmental and private restrictions on ownership of real property
- distinguish among the various types of leases

CONCEPT OF TITLE: OWNERSHIP IN A BUNDLE OF RIGHTS

Title to property (whether real or personal property), represents ownership to the holder of same. Aside from the title aspect of ownership in real property, property ownership comes with other legal rights. These legal rights are called the bundle of rights. (See Figure 8.3 on page 189.) The following are included in the bundle of rights:

- Use/Enjoyment—This includes the ownership's right to use and enjoy the property in any manner prescribed by law.
- Possession—The inception of this right commences on the day that title passes to the rightful owner. It includes the right of ingress (entry) and egress (exit) of one's property. It further includes the property owner's right to benefit from any income attributable to the property derived from rent.
- Control—This right allows the property owner to improve the property through the addition of constructing improvements to the land. This right is regulated by local zoning and building codes.
- Exclusion—This right allows the property owner to control who may enter the property. It also allows the property owner to enforce his/her rights against any unlawful trespass by another.
- Disposition—This right allows the property owner to sell, lease, mortgage, license, or gift all or a portion of the property to another.

Equitable Title

Equitable title is the legal benefit obtained by a buyer making installment payments (under a land contract, contract for deed or an installment sales contract) with a financial or equitable interest in that subject covered property. For example, during the installment payment contract period, an equitable titleholder derives indirect benefits from a property's potential appreciation in value that may naturally occur over time.

It is important to note that there is a direct difference that exists between legal title and equitable title. Under the law, legal title affords a property owner the ability to enforce ownership rights when they are infringed upon. However, there is a direct separation from equitable rights particularly in an installment sales contract (a.k.a. contract for deed or land contract). In this type of transaction, a seller transfers equitable title rights to a buyer. This is done in exchange for a contract that requires the purchaser (vendee) to make scheduled timely installment payments to the seller (vendor). In addition, the vendee/purchaser may also be required to perform certain other duties that may be called for under the contract. Upon full satisfaction of all installment payments (and other terms of the contract) the buyer/vendee receives legal title conveyed by the seller/vendor. Prior to receipt by the seller/vendor of all payments called for under the contract, the deed is held by the seller/vendor as collateral for performance of all of the terms and conditions contained in the contract. As a further note and by operation of law, equitable title is transferred voluntarily or involuntarily.

Coaching Tips

Think of an installment sales contract the way you would a layaway plan for an item. Until all installments under the layaway plan have been paid, the retailer will hold the item as collateral. Once the terms under the layaway plan have been met, title is transferred.

Transfer by Voluntary Alienation

In real estate, the **title** is the sum of all facts or evidence of ownership. When title is transferred between parties, the process is referred to as **alienation**. In simple terms, alienation means a transfer. Alienation can be either voluntary or involuntary.

Voluntary alienation is the willful transfer of the property with the consent and control of the owner:

- During life this is accomplished via a deed. The deed is the instrument used to transfer real property from one person to another.
- At death, this is accomplished via a valid will (passing **testate**).
    - The parties to the will consist of the following:
        - If the maker of the will is a male, he is called the testator.
        - If the maker of the will is female, she is called the testatrix.
        - The recipient of real property is called the devisee.
        - The recipient of personal property is called the beneficiary.
    - Property conveyed by will is referred to as:
        - devise, if it is real property
        - bequest, if it is personal property

Coaching Tips

It is imperative to understand that possessing a deed does not necessarily constitute legal ownership in the real property. A deed (which is only an instrument of paper) reflects legal ownership only when the deed has been accepted for recording by the county clerk's office. The county clerk only accepts valid deeds for recording.

Involuntary alienation is the unwillful transfer of the property against the wishes and control of the owner.

- During life, this is accomplished as follows (see Figure 9.1):
  - court judgment
  - foreclosure action
  - bankruptcy
  - **eminent domain** (a public taking of private property through the process known as condemnation)
  - **adverse possession** (a lawful taking of another's property based on specific conditions and requirements; usually a private taking). In Florida, a person who attempts this form of acquiring property must fulfill the following conditions:
    - open and notorious occupation of the property belonging to another in the color of title
    - must be continuous occupation for seven or more years
    - while possessing the property of another, the adverse possessing party has paid the property taxes for same
- At death, this is accomplished through **escheat** (due to no existence of a valid will or remaining heirs to accept the property, the property goes to the state).

FIGURE 9.1
Source: © 2021 Mbition LLC

It is important to note that upon the death of an individual, escheat is the only form of involuntary alienation that can occur.

TRANSFER BY DESCENT

When a person dies intestate (without a valid enforceable will) and has heirs who can be identified, the Florida laws of descent will apply. In order to distribute the decedent's estate appropriately, one of the first steps is determining which partie(s) are rightful heirs. Examples of rightful heirs would include but are not limited to the following parties:

- a surviving spouse
- children
- other direct or indirect family members (i.e., grandparents and cousins)

It would not be unusual to find that when a decedent passes intestate, the surviving spouse and children would receive greater overall attention and consideration.

One of the next steps may be determining the eligibility of real and personal property that comprises the estate. This process will be decided by the respective courts. When homestead real property is included in the decedent's estate, the tendency of the courts suggests the order of distribution would be first to the surviving spouse and any minor children and then to adult children and any other eligible family member.

Before any estate distribution (by descent) can occur, all expenses, governmental and otherwise, must be paid. This includes but is not limited to unpaid taxes.

There are several ways that title to real property can be transferred:

- deed—when real property is gifted or sold
- will—inheritance
- adverse possession
- acts of nature

We just looked at public restrictions that may be placed and affect real property ownership. Now let's examine private restrictions on real property that would include:

- **deed restrictions** (restrictions on the ownership of private property that are contained in deeds)
- liens
- easements
- leases

Deeds are the most common method used to convey title while the holder of the title is alive. Inheritance is the process of conveying title after the holder of the title has died. (This will be covered later in this chapter.)

DEEDS

A **deed** is an instrument that is used to convey and transfer the ownership interest in real property from one or more parties to another. A deed is used to convey any fee estate, any life estate, or certain easements. A deed is also used to transfer real property gifted or willed to another.

Florida requires that all deeds be in written form. In addition, the Statute of Frauds requires that all deeds:

- be in writing
- be signed by the grantor in order to transfer title

In order to record the deed in the public records, acknowledgment is usually required. **Acknowledgment** means that the grantor (seller) must acknowledge the signature to the grantee (buyer). This is achieved by the grantor signing the deed before a notary public. The notary acts as a legal witness for hire. The notary's role is to witness the signature of the grantor (only after presentation of appropriate ID). This witnessing is a determination and testament to the grantee that the grantor is who he/she is claiming to be (the rightful owner of the property). In order to record the deed, the document must be acknowledged. Otherwise, it will not be accepted by the county clerk. Only the *grantor* acknowledges a deed.

> ## Coaching Tips
>
> Some deeds contain deed restrictions. This can be deemed as the most common form of private restriction on ownership of real property. These restrictions are found in deeds. Once these restrictions are in place and recorded, enforcement becomes critical on the part of property owners or these restrictions may be vacated via the doctrine of laches (the use and enforcement of one's rights or loss of same resulting from lack of enforcement and assertion of those rights). Therefore it is up to the subdivision, unit owners, or any other party benefiting from the restriction to enforce same. In particular, a purchaser of property should pay close attention to restrictions contained within a deed. Some of the most common urban easements include but are not limited to air and light. Suburban restrictions may have minimum size home requirements.

Examples of common deed restrictions would be:

- a minimum set-back requirement from an adjacent neighbor's property line
- a minimum square footage required to construct living space

As you just learned, when real property is sold or otherwise conveyed, the ownership is transferred through the use of a document called a deed. When personal property is sold or otherwise conveyed, this is done through the use of a document called a bill of sale. When a home is sold, for example, the ownership of the land and its improvements (real property) are transferred with a deed. If any personal property is sold at the same time, such as furniture, tools, etc., it must be transferred in a separate bill of sale. The actual act of conveying ownership of real property is called a grant. There are two parties to a deed:

1. **grantor**—the party who transfers title (the seller)
2. **grantee**—the party to whom the title is transferred (the buyer)

Requirements of a Valid Deed

As noted previously, deeds *must always be written*. In addition, to be considered valid and enforceable, they *must* include the following seven elements:

1. **Competent grantor**—The grantor must be legally competent. In most states, this means that the grantor must be of:
   - legal age (18 in Florida)
   - sound mind

   In many states, the grantee:
   - must also be of sound mind, but
   - need not be of legal age (a minor can be the grantee)

In Florida, the grantee does not have to be of sound mind. A mentally incompetent person can be the grantee; however, due to a lack of legal capacity as a competent party, the grantee may be unable to convey title as a grantor to another without assistance from some form of guardian.

Name of grantor and grantee—Both names must be stated on a deed for purposes of chain of title. The chain of title is similar to a bicycle chain containing links. Each link represents a previous or current owner. This allows interested parties to research the public records for the purposes of identifying the correct owner of record. (If the deed is to be recorded, the addresses of the grantor and grantee must be provided along with their names.) A fictitious name may be used by the grantee. If a fictitious name is used, the deed is still valid, but the same name must be used when the property is later transferred to another person to preserve the chain of title.

2. Consideration—The deed must state that consideration was given by the grantee to the grantor. The consideration can be either one of the following:

    - valuable consideration—money or its equivalent
    - good consideration—one not expressed in monetary terms, such as love and affection

In Florida, the actual amount of consideration does not need to be stated. Often, a nominal amount is stated, such as, "One dollar and other good and valuable consideration."

3. Words of conveyance—These words indicate the intent of the grantor to transfer title. The words *grant* and *convey*, either alone or in combination, are commonly used in the conveyance. Another name for the words of conveyance is the **granting clause**.

Coaching Tips

The granting clause is just one derivative of the feudal system of the medieval/Renaissance period in English history. In this period and time, the Crown owned all the lands, the peasants were tenants and occupants of the land, and title to land and property were granted by the Crown to the king and queen's noblemen.

4. Property description—The deed must adequately describe the property being conveyed. Any legally recognized method of description can be used (government survey method, metes and bounds, lot and block). A street address is not acceptable as it does not identify the property boundaries and is subject to change.

5. Habendum clause—This is the clause in a deed that describes the nature and type of interest being conveyed. The clause will normally begin with the words "to have and to hold."

6. Grantor's signature—A deed must be signed by the grantor in order to be valid. The signature of the grantee is not required. Some states require that the grantor's signature be witnessed. In Florida, the grantor's signature must be witnessed by two people.

7. Voluntary delivery and acceptance—To be valid, a deed must be delivered by the grantor to the grantee and accepted by the grantee. Delivery does not have to be a physical act of handing over the deed. If the grantor indicates by his/her actions that he/she intends for the grantee to own the property, then delivery has occurred. Delivery of a deed is presumed to have occurred if one of the following takes place:

    - The deed is found in the possession of the grantee.
    - The deed is recorded.

    Acceptance is presumed to have occurred if the grantee:

    - retains the deed
    - records the deed
    - encumbers the title
    - performs any other act of ownership

To be valid, a deed must be delivered during the grantor's lifetime.

Exceptions and reservations—This is a clause contained in a deed where the grantor retains or creates an exception for a right(s) or interest(s) in the property being sold. An example would be a right of way (easement).

Appurtenances—When a property is sold, appurtenances are items or rights that are attached to and form a part of a property. These can include but are not limited to easements.

Coaching Tips

The Seven Essential Elements of a Deed

1. Competent grantor (and names of grantor and grantee)
2. Consideration
3. Words of conveyance
4. Property (legal) description
5. Habendum clause
6. Grantor's signature
7. Voluntary delivery and acceptance

Additionally, in Florida, a valid deed must be in writing.

Nonessential Element

One element found in most deeds, but not required, is the habendum clause. If the habendum clause is included, it contains the type of estate being granted. The **habendum clause** tells the extent of interest transferred.

TYPES OF STATUTORY DEEDS

We have just discussed the essential elements needed to constitute a valid and enforceable deed. Now let's examine the types of deeds that may be used to convey real property.

There are several types of deeds:

- general warranty deed (full covenant and warranty deed)
- special warranty deed
- bargain and sale deed
- quitclaim deed

These types of deeds are all commonly used and are accepted instruments of conveyance in Florida. These deeds differ primarily in the guarantees (warranties) provided about the title being conveyed. Guarantees are provided through covenants included in the deed. The covenants (which are promises) are the means by which the grantor agrees to defend the title against the claims of all other persons.

General Warranty Deed

The **general warranty deed**, also called the full covenant and warranty deed, is the most common form of deed. A general warranty deed provides the greatest guarantee about the title being conveyed.

> **Coaching Tips**
>
> A covenant against encumbrances does not state that there are no encumbrances on the property, only that all encumbrances that exist are stated in the deed.

> **Coaching Tips**
>
> **Quiet enjoyment** is often confused and should not be mistaken for peace and quiet. This clause in a deed or in a lease deals only with the issue of title and/or rights associated with the estate.

Special Warranty Deed

The special warranty deed is used when the grantor is unable or unwilling to include all the covenants just discussed. It includes only one covenant, the covenant against encumbrances. In effect, the grantor warrants against his/her own acts. The grantor warrants that he/she has not encumbered the property beyond those encumbrances stated in the deed. The grantor does not warrant that someone else had not encumbered the property prior to his/her assuming ownership.

> ### Coaching Tips
>
> In some states, like New York, the special warranty deed is called the bargain and sale deed with covenant.
>
> The special warranty deed is often used when the grantor is acting as an agent, or fiduciary, for a principal, such as a trustee or executor of a will. The agent is willing to warrant that he/she has not encumbered the property but is not willing or able to provide any other warranties.

Bargain and Sale Deed

A bargain and sale deed conveys the grantor's interest in the property but contains no warranties about the state of the title. It *implies* that the grantor has a claim to, or an interest in, the property but does not provide this warranty.

Quitclaim Deed

The **quitclaim deed** contains *no warranties* to title, either expressed or implied. In simple terms, it can be defined to be an instrument of release and/or transfer (as it may apply to any claim). The quitclaim deed simply conveys whatever interest the grantor held at the time of conveyance. The grantee has no recourse to the grantor if the title proves to be defective. The quitclaim deed is not inferior to any other deed in terms of its ability to transfer title. It is different only in that it provides no warranties about the status of the title.

The quitclaim deed may be used to transfer any type of estate, including fee simple and life estates. Normally, however, it is used to convey or release minor interests in real estate for the purpose of clearing title defects or clouds on a title. For example, it may be used by anyone who held a lien that had since been satisfied, in order to release the owner from the lien. It is also an instrument commonly used to convey real property from one family member to another.

Special purpose deeds are real property transfer instruments commonly used in applicable transactions that include but are not limited to:

1. Personal representative deed—the legal instrument used to transfer the real property of a deceased person to an heir or beneficiary. The personal representative is called the executor when the deceased dies testate or the court-appointed administrator when the deceased dies intestate.
2. Guardian's deed—the legal instrument used to transfer real property to a grantee (buyer) when the grantor (seller) is a minor or any other person who is legally considered unable or incapable of making his/her own decisions. Guardians are court-appointed parties who are charged with the advancement and oversight of the incompetent party. This includes decisions on the sale of real property.
3. Committee's deed—the legal instrument used between two or more parties to an agreement when the parties to the agreement owe performance of obligations to each other. An example is committees appointed by a court in a bankruptcy or foreclosure proceeding.
4. Tax deed—the legal instrument used to transfer ownership of real property from private ownership to government. This occurs when the property owner is delinquent in the payment of property taxes. In order to collect the unpaid taxes, the tax deed grants government the authority to transfer the property to a purchaser.

Coaching Tips

The different types of deeds that have just been covered provide different types of guarantees (in the form of warranties) about the title being conveyed. They do not convey different "amounts" of title or different "degrees" of title. The "amount" or "degree" of title conveyed is determined by the type of estate being conveyed, such as a fee simple estate, a life estate, etc.

Deed Clauses

Deeds contain the following covenants:

- covenant of seisin
- covenant against encumbrances
- covenant of quiet enjoyment
- covenant of further assistance
- covenant of warranty forever

Let's examine each one.

Covenant of Seisin

In the covenant of **seisin**, the grantor warrants that he/she is the owner of the property and that he/she has the right to convey the property.

Covenant against Encumbrances

In the covenant against encumbrances, the grantor warrants that there are no encumbrances on the property that are not mentioned in the deed.

Covenant of Quiet Enjoyment

In a covenant of quiet enjoyment, the grantor warrants that the grantee will enjoy the property free of claims by anyone else.

Covenant of Further Assistance

This obligates the grantor to perform any acts necessary to protect the title being conveyed to the grantee. The covenant of **further assistance** is also called the covenant of further assurance.

Covenant of Warranty of Title

A covenant of warranty of title (covenant of **warranty forever**) ensures that the grantor will bear the expense of defending the title against the claims of others. There is no time limit on a covenant of warranty of title.

Preparation of Deeds

State law determines who may prepare a deed. In some states, attorneys must prepare a deed while other states allow the property owner to prepare the deed. Some states allow the real estate broker who acted as the agent for the sale to prepare the deed.

It is important to note that the unauthorized practice of law by any real estate licensee is a licensing offense and will subject the licensee to disciplinary action. The licensee is therefore cautioned to limit his/her activities to just filling in blanks within preprinted forms previously prepared and approved by an attorney admitted to the state bar or by the agent's principal.

Acknowledgment of Deeds

In order to be admissible for public records, a deed must be acknowledged in most states. Acknowledgment is a formal declaration of the following:

- The person signing the document is the person named in the document.
- The signing of the deed is a free and voluntary act.

Acknowledgment is done before an authorized official, usually a notary public, who is responsible for ensuring that the person signing the deed is the grantor named in the deed.

> ### Coaching Tips
>
> The acknowledgment is the declaration made by the grantor, not the certification by the notary public. The deed must be signed by the grantor. Acknowledgment is the grantor's statement of ability to convey, not the certification of the notary public.

TITLES

In real estate, the title is the sum of all facts on which ownership is founded.

An **abstract of title** includes:

- a full summary of all instruments affecting the title to a property, such as deeds, wills, grants, etc.
- a statement of all liens and encumbrances affecting the property and their present status

No single document proves title to property. Title to a property is based on an evaluation of the abstract and other instruments indicated by the abstract.

Marketable title is one that is free of reasonable doubt as to ownership.

Chain of title is the record of ownership transactions that connects the present owners to the original source of title.

One method of determining marketable title is through a title opinion. Title opinions are made and given by attorneys. In essence, the attorney scrutinizes in a careful manner the abstract of title. The opinion letter or certificate of title opinion, as it is more commonly known, will indicate any encumbrances, liens, or easements that affect the property. Although the certificate of title is an acceptable instrument for determining marketable title, one should be cautioned that the certificate is merely an opinion of the title based on a review of the abstract and is not in any way a guarantee.

Public Records

Before the enactment of the Statute of Frauds in England in 1677, ownership of a parcel of land was largely determined by who was in physical possession of the land. Possession gave notice of ownership. After 1677, written deeds were required to show transfer of ownership from one owner to another. Public records were instituted to record deeds so that no disputes would arise about who held the most current deed. It also provided a means of search and research of the public records by interested parties concerning any recorded parcel of property. Public records can be examined by anyone at any time as desired.

Constructive Notice

Since 1677, two ways to give notice of a claim or right to land (ownership) have evolved:

1. by recording documents in the public records that give written notice to that effect
2. by physically occupying the property

According to law, if an interested party wants to determine ownership, the party must do the following:

- examine the public records
- look at the property itself to see who occupies it

Constructive notice combines these two ideas:

1. People give notice by public recording and occupancy.
2. It is presumed that anyone interested in the property has inspected both the records and the property itself to determine ownership.

Acknowledgment is the act of a party to a legal document that:

- authenticates the document's legal validity, and
- certifies that the party signing the document is in fact that person. (This certification is accomplished by the services of a notary public. A notary is hired to certify the signatures on the respective transaction document[s]. The county clerk will not accept a deed for recording that has not been acknowledged. This process will prevent recording of fraudulent documents.)

REMEMBER: The party signing the document(s) is the one who acknowledges while the notary acts as the legal witness.

Lis pendens is the formal legal notice of a pending action or lawsuit. In real estate transactions, it is filed against the property in question. It is constructive notice of a grievance to an agreement and is filed to prevent any transfer until that grievance is resolved.

For example, a seller accepts an offer and signs a purchase and sale contract for $100,000 from buyer 1. Buyer 2 subsequently offers the seller $125,000 and the seller accepts buyer 2's offer and moves to terminate the contract with buyer 1. Buyer 1 rejects the seller's attempts to terminate the contract and files a lis pendens to assure the maintaining and asserting of buyer 1's rights to solely purchase that property.

Actual Notice

Constructive notice is based on a *presumption* that the records and property have been inspected. **Actual notice** is specific knowledge based on what you have *actually* seen, heard, read, or observed.

Recording

Instruments affecting title (such as deeds) are recorded in the jurisdiction in which the land is situated. They are usually recorded at the county level, sometimes at the city level, but never at the state level. Recordation is a privilege allowed by the law and is not required by law. Recordation allows owners to give public notice of their claim to ownership.

Torrens Land Titles

Torrens land titles is a system of registered land titles. Very few states use this system. In states that do, the Torrens system:

- verifies ownership of property using a single document
- establishes the status of the title including any existing encumbrances other than tax liens

The Torrens system does not require an additional title search to determine ownership, since title verification is based on a single document. In order for the Torrens system to be used in a state, it requires enabling legislation known as a Torrens Title Act. Theses are the steps taken to establish a Torrens land title:

1. A quiet title action is filed in court. This asks the court to ascertain the true condition of the title.
2. The court determines the condition of the title.
3. The court orders the registrar of titles to issue a Torrens title certificate to the property.

The Torrens title certificate identifies the:

- exact boundaries of the property
- name of the title holder
- encumbrances on the title

Once a title is registered, any subsequent liens or encumbrances must be entered on the registrar's copy of the certificate of title in order to give constructive notice. When registered land is conveyed, the grantor gives the grantee a deed. The grantee presents the deed to the registrar of title who destroys the old certificate and issues a new one naming the grantee as owner. The Torrens system exists in several states, but its use is extremely rare. It is the principal or only system used in about ten states.

Title Insurance

Title insurance is an insurance policy that protects the insured against a loss that might be sustained by a defective title or any liens or encumbrances. In general, title insurance protects against such defects in title as:

- forged documents
- undisclosed heirs
- documents filed incorrectly
- mistakes in legal interpretation of wills
- gaps in the chain of title

The two most common types of title insurance are:

1. owner's title insurance
2. lender's policy or mortgagee's title insurance

Contrary to popular belief, the vast majority of title insurance policies issued are for the mortgagee's title insurance. These policies cover losses suffered by the mortgage company, not the buyer.

Owner's Title Insurance

Owner's title insurance names the owner as the insured. It is issued in an amount equal to the acquisition cost of the property. Some policies include an inflation clause that increases the amount of coverage as the property appreciates in value. Owner's title insurance remains in force for as long as the owner or the owner's heirs retain an interest in the property. Owner's title insurance is terminated only when the owner or the owner's heirs no longer have any interest in the property. The title insurance process is shown in Figure 9.2.

Mortgagee's Title Insurance

A mortgagee's title insurance policy is issued in an amount equal to the original balance on the mortgage loan. The coverage decreases as the loan is amortized (paid off) and terminates when the loan is fully paid.

Both owner's and mortgagee's title insurance are single-premium policies. The mortgagee's title insurance policy premium is paid only once—when the policy is issued. Because the amount of coverage provided by the mortgagee's policy is lower, it costs slightly less. This is due to the fact that the amount being financed is less than the total purchase price (which includes the property owner's down payment).

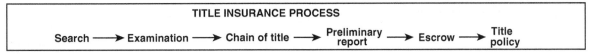

FIGURE 9.2
Source: © 2021 Mbition LLC

EASEMENTS

So far you have learned about three general types of interests in real property:

1. government interest
2. individual interest—freehold and nonfreehold estates
3. business interest

There are three remaining categories of interests in land:

1. easements
2. encroachments
3. liens

An **easement** is the right to use or occupy the property of another in a limited way. The right to cross another's property (easement) can also be termed as a right of way. The holder of an easement does not have any ownership in the property, or even possession of the property, only the use of the property for a specific purpose. An easement is not an estate in land.

Easements can be categorized into three types:

1. easement appurtenant
2. easement in gross
3. party wall easement

EASEMENT APPURTENANT

An easement appurtenant requires two or more properties, usually adjacent to each other, called:

1. a dominant estate (or dominant tenement)
2. a servient estate (or servient tenement)

The easement is the right of the owner of the dominant estate to use the property of the servient estate. The owner of the servient estate grants the easement. An easement appurtenant runs with the land, which means the easement becomes a part of the land itself (the dominant estate).

If the owner of the dominant estate dies or sells the property, the easement remains with the dominant estate. If the owner of the servient estate dies or sells the servient estate, the easement remains with the dominant estate. (See Figure 9.3.)

Easement in Gross

An easement in gross involves only one property, the servient estate. There is no dominant estate. The holder of the easement in gross has the right to use part of the servient estate for a specific purpose (see Figure 9.4). Some examples of easements in gross include easements for telephone lines, sewer lines, gas lines,

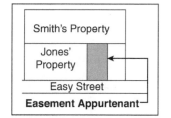

FIGURE 9.3
Source: © 2021 Mbition LLC

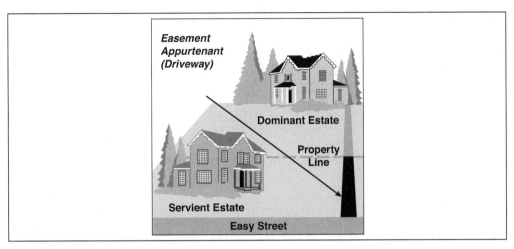

FIGURE 9.4
Source: © 2021 Mbition LLC

power lines, and ditch easements for storm runoff. All of these are examples of easements held by a business or the government and are called commercial easements. Commercial easements belong to the government or business and are not attached to a parcel of land (like an easement appurtenant), so there is no dominant estate. The servient estate is the land on which the business or government has a right of use. All future owners of the servient estate are bound by the easement. Commercial easements are assignable (transferable). For example, one telephone company may sell or transfer its easement for phone lines to another telephone company.

A second type of easement in gross is a personal easement in gross. This type of easement is similar to a commercial easement in gross, except for the following:

- The holder is a person, not a business or government.
- A personal easement in gross terminates with the death of the holder.
- The holder cannot transfer the easement.

Example

John grants Bill an easement to cross his property to get to his favorite fishing spot on a lake.

Party Wall Easement

A party wall easement exists when a single wall that forms part of two buildings is located on a lot line. In this case, each owner owns the half of the wall on her property plus an easement in the other half of the wall on the adjacent property. An example would be a wall between two adjacent units in a fee simple townhouse development.

Licenses

A license is a personal privilege to use another's land in a limited manner. A license is *not* a right or interest in land, but it is covered here because it is similar to and often confused with a personal easement in gross.

The following are the primary differences between a license and a personal easement in gross:

- A license must be terminable at the will of the person who granted it (licensor).
- A personal easement in gross cannot be revoked.

The following are the ways a license is like a personal easement in gross:

- A license cannot be assigned (transferred to another).
- A license terminates on the death of either party or the sale of the property owned by the person granting the license or upon the expiration of the license that was granted for a prescribed period of time.

A very common example of a personal license is a license to hunt on another's property. Easements appurtenant and commercial easements in gross are transferable. Personal easements in gross and licenses are not transferable.

Creation of Easements

Easements can be created in five different ways:

1. private grant—a written agreement between the landowner and the easement holder (This is the most common method of creation.)
2. prescription—the acquisition of an easement by continuous, hostile, uninterrupted possession for a period set by law (In Florida, it is 20 years.) The process of achieving an easement by prescription bears a direct resemblance to the process of achieving adverse possession. In each case, a taking or use of another's property occurs without remuneration. The difference is that in easement by prescription, you acquire an easement. In adverse possession, you acquire ownership of the property itself. (Adverse possession was described earlier in this chapter.)
3. **condemnation**—the acquisition of an easement by the government under the power of eminent domain
4. reservation—occurs when a landowner reserves, or retains for him/herself, the easement in a deed that conveys title to the land to another party
5. necessity—prevents a landowner from becoming landlocked, which means having no way to reach a street or road (This arises when an owner sells a parcel of land that has no access to a road but owns adjacent property that does have road frontage. Necessity requires the creation of an easement on that property to reach the property without frontage. The seller cannot sell the property and refuse to grant the easement.)

Coaching Tips

Use the mnemonic POPCORN to remember the five different ways easements can be created:

- *Private grant*
- *O*
- *Prescription*
- *Condemnation*
- *O*
- *Reservation*
- *Necessity*

Coaching Tips

- Deed restrictions limit the use of property.
- Prescription involves the adverse use of property.
- Reservation refers to reserving or retaining an easement in a deed.
- Condemnation is the process used by the government to acquire easements under eminent domain.
- Adverse possession is used to acquire title to property. It is not a method of creating an easement.

Note that it is *not necessary* for an easement to be in writing to be created. For example, an easement may be created by prescription by simply using the servient estate for a period of time prescribed by law.

Termination of Easements

Easements can also be terminated in five different ways:

1. release—the party holding the easement gives a written release to the owner of the servient estate, usually in the form of a quitclaim deed
2. abandonment—the party holding the easement fails to use it for a sufficient period to raise the presumption of release
3. vacation—this is termination by court order when the need for the easement no longer exists
4. merger—this occurs when the dominant and servient estates are combined or come under one ownership
5. expiration—expiration occurs if the easement was created for a specified period of time

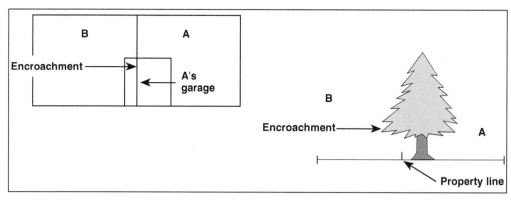

FIGURE 9.5
Source: © 2021 Mbition LLC

ENCROACHMENTS

An **encroachment** is an unauthorized intrusion of a building, fixture, or other improvement on the land of another. (See Figure 9.5.) An encroachment can constitute either one of the following:

- a trespass if it encroaches on the land
- a nuisance if it violates the neighbor's airspace

For example, a fence built by Smith is located 2 feet onto Jones's property. This constitutes a trespass. The limbs of a tree on Jones's property extend 15 feet over Smith's property. This constitutes a nuisance.

Encroachments can be discovered in two ways:

1. Survey—A survey will definitely disclose the existence of an encroachment, even if it cannot be detected by casual observation.
2. Observation—Some encroachments are obvious and can be detected by simply looking at the property.

Encroachment disputes that cannot be resolved between the owners involved may be settled by the court, which may order the removal of the encroachment.

Coaching Tips

In Florida, if a property owner builds a fence or other structure that encroaches onto the land belonging to a neighbor, and this condition lasts for seven or more years, an implied easement is created.

LEASES

In Chapter 8, we looked at three types of estates in land created by leases:

1. Estate for years:

- An estate for years is a lease that has a defined, prescribed, and fixed lease term. It contains a predetermined commencement and expiration date.
- Upon expiration of the fixed term, the lease will either terminate and the tenant will relocate or the lease may be renewed/extended through a new agreement at either the same rent or at a newly negotiated rent.
- This lease type is not terminable upon either the sale of the property or the death of either party to the transaction.

2. Estate at will:

- An estate at will has no definite term.
- Vulnerability exists on the part of both parties regarding rent increase or decrease.
- Either party to the transaction has the chance to change the terms of the deal.
- An estate at will can be terminated by notifying the other party as to the intent to cancel.
- In order to terminate this type of estate in Florida, proper notice must be given. For example, in order to terminate a month-to-month tenancy at will, Florida law requires that either party provide the other with notice of the intent to cancel the lease not less than 15 days prior to the end of that monthly period.

3. Tenancy at sufferance:

- Tenancy at sufferance occurs when a previous leasehold estate is terminated and the tenant/lessee refuses to return possession of the demised premises (leased property) to the landlord/lessor.
- A tenant at sufferance is most commonly referred to as a holdover tenant. The tenant is not considered a trespasser.
- A tenant is considered to be at sufferance usually because of the landlord's failure to issue the existing tenant a renewal/lease extension.

Basic Principles of Leases

A lease is a contract by which one person is given the right to occupy or use the property of another. A lease:

- can be either written or oral to be valid and enforceable
- requires the payment of rent by the tenant to the landlord
- can be for a definite or indefinite period of time

The Statute of Frauds requires that:

- leases for more than one year must be written to be enforceable
- leases for one year or less that are oral are enforceable

Parties to a lease consist of the following two parties:

1. The landlord is called the lessor. The landlord is usually the owner, but this is not always the case. For example, a landowner (or the owner of the fee) leases land to another. The party who leases the land under a long-term ground lease later develops the land with a building (office or residential units). The developer then has the right to lease out the offices or residential units to others. However, the developer may only do so up to the term the developer has leased the land from the landowner.
2. The tenant is called the lessee.

Real property is broken down into two components:

1. the land, also referred to as the fee
2. the improvement affixed to the fee, referred to as the leasehold

A leasehold is the interest or estate in land that a tenant acquires by virtue of a lease. Real estate law treats a leasehold as personal property (as you learned earlier in Chapter 8). However, in most states, the *licensing law* treats a leasehold as real property. This treatment allows licensing law to regulate the activities of those involved in the leasing of property as a business.

Types of Leases

There are several different types of leases that are commonly used in residential and commercial transactions. These specific types of leases can be associated with any of the three leasehold estates just reviewed. The different types of leases will be covered next.

As the application of a lease is required within a particular transaction, a variety of different lease types are available to the landlord for use, such as the following:

- gross lease
- net lease
- percentage lease
- ground lease
- graduated lease/variable lease
- sublease or sandwich lease
- index lease

> ## Coaching Tips
>
> While an index lease may at times be tied into an inflationary index such as the consumer price index (CPI), it is really a modified gross lease that allows the landlord to increase rents resulting from increases of operating expenses and property taxes. The increased expenses become operational and property tax pass-throughs that increase the rent that the tenant pays to the landlord. The base rent is paid as written in the gross lease with "additional rent" provisions within the lease covering the landlord's increased cost of operation.

Gross Lease

The following is true in a **gross lease**:

- The tenant pays a fixed monthly rent only.
- In residential leases, the landlord pays all expenses of ownership, operation, and maintenance, including such things as taxes, insurance, utilities, etc., whereas in commercial lease transactions, the landlord provides within the lease for the pass-through of increased property expenses over a base amount. This is usually expressed within the lease as a base year. The landlord (via lease clause) has the right to pass through to the tenant the increased cost of operations and property taxes that occur over the base year amount. The tenant pays these costs in the form of additional rent. This is still considered a gross lease by commercial property terms.
- In Florida, all leases involving residential multifamily properties are gross leases. However, it is not uncommon for tenants to pay their own unit-related utility costs.

Net Lease

The following is true in a **net lease**:

- The tenant pays a fixed monthly rent, *plus some or all* of the expenses associated with the property, such as taxes, insurance, utilities, etc.
- The landlord pays only those expenses not paid by the tenant.

If the property is not a single-tenant property, the portion of the expense that the tenant or tenants would be responsible for is based and predicated on the tenant's ratio of occupied space in relation to the total building area. This is commonly referred to as the tenant's proportionate share.

For example, a tenant occupies 10,000 square feet of space in a building that totals 100,000 square feet. In this case, the tenant would occupy 10% of the property and would therefore be responsible for 10% of the expenses.

> ## Coaching Tips
>
> To help remember which lease is a gross lease and which lease is a net lease, remember that the lease is being described from the landlord's point of view:
>
> - A gross lease to the landlord means that expenses have to be deducted from the payment the landlord receives.
> - A net lease to the landlord means that expenses do not have to be deducted from the payment received from the tenant. The money received is *net* to the landlord.
>
> In addition, terms such as *triple net* and *double net* are slang expressions used to communicate that a certain item or all items are net of rents. This slang terminology comes up within *net lease* transactions and is not really the textbook terminology. The correct expression is simply *net* of some or all of the expenses. However, students should be familiar with the slang terminology as well.

Percentage Lease

Percentage leases are commonly used for retail establishments in shopping malls. The landlord receives a percentage of the gross sales of the business as part or all of the rent. When a shopping mall is successful, it is common for the retailer to pay a higher minimum base rent plus a higher percentage of sales. The percentage of gross sales can be from either one of the following:

- the first dollar representing sales, or
- when the retailer exceeds an agreed-upon gross sales dollar amount. The gross sales dollar amount threshold is usually representative of the retailer's breakeven on store operational costs. In some markets, the term is commonly referred to as the natural break or the *natural breakeven*.

The percentage lease is most common with publicly listed stock exchange companies versus mom-and-pop operations. It is easier to audit a public company for gross sales than a privately owned mom-and-pop enterprise.

Example

A retail tenant will pay $5,000 per month representing the minimum base rent being charged. This will be paid whether or not the retailer sells its product. In addition, the retailer will pay to the landlord an amount of 5% of all sales over the natural breakeven. The natural breakeven would be calculated as follows:

- Step one:
  - Annualize the monthly rent: $5,000 × 12 = $60,000 per annum.

- Step two:
  - Divide the annual rental by the percentage of sales: $60,000 ÷ 0.05.
  - The result is $1,200,000 of sales equals the natural breakeven.
  - Therefore 5% of any sale over that amount goes to the landlord as additional rent over and above the $5,000 minimum monthly base rent.

Ground Lease

A **ground lease** is a long-term lease of land. Certain landowners (or fee owners) prefer to avoid becoming developers of property. In some cases, this is due to:

- lack of knowledge or expertise required to develop the property
- lack of funds to develop the property
- capital, market, or construction risks
- the desire to collect ground rent (as an annuity) from those seeking to take on the aforementioned risks

Generally speaking, ground leases typically require that the lessee construct a building or an improvement on the land. This type of lease (although it is categorized as a ground lease) takes the form of a net lease. This will require the lessee/developer to pay for property taxes, insurance, and any other expenses associated with the land and ultimate improvements to the land. However, bear in mind that if improvements result in an income-producing property, the lessee/tenant will keep the rent proceeds achieved from the improvement.

Graduated Lease/Variable lease

In a **graduated lease**, (or **variable lease**) the tenant pays a fixed rent for an initial period, but the rent increases at specific intervals thereafter. A graduated lease can be used in a variety of situations:

- for long-term leases:
  - to cover an increased general cost of living
  - merely to protect the owner's ability to capitalize on improved market conditions that result in higher rents
- for a retail store in a shopping center or mall where a clientele has not yet been established

To attract a tenant in slow market conditions, the landlord will start the tenant's lease at a cheaper rental rate at lease inception. However, the rental rate will increase incrementally over the term of the lease so the tenant will pay a higher rate at the tail end of the lease. Psychologically, because the tenant will pay the higher rental rate, it becomes easier for the landlord to renew the tenant at an even higher rent then the previous rental rate.

Coaching Tips

You should be aware that commercial leases bear longer terms than those of residential leases. Therefore, landlords may be faced with good or bad market conditions at any time. Therefore, a landlord may prefer starting a tenant at a lower rent that will graduate even higher over the term of the lease. At the end of the initial lease term, the landlord will generally experience easier lease renewal negotiations to maintain the higher rent (or even receive a rent increase). The landlord's reasoning is that psychologically the tenant (exclusive of market conditions) is accustomed to paying the higher amount.

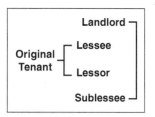

FIGURE 9.6
Source: © 2021 Mbition LLC

Sublease or Sandwich Lease

A sublease or sandwich lease occurs when a leased property is subleased. When property is **subleased**, the original lessee (the tenant) becomes the lessor to the new tenant (the sublessee). The original lessee (the sublessor) is sandwiched between the landlord and the new tenant, the sublessee. (See Figure 9.6 for a visual of this relationship.) An easier way to view this arrangement would be to identify the parties in other terms. Assume the following party names:

- The property owner/landlord is the overlandlord.
- The original primary tenant is the overtenant.
- The new tenant/sublessee is the undertenant.

Example

The overlandlord prime leases to the overtenant who in turn subleases to the undertenant. The overtenant is sandwiched between the overlandlord and the undertenant. It should be noted that this directly resembles what we term a *sublease*.

Index Lease (Modified Gross Lease)

An index lease, also known as a modified gross lease, contains a provision for future rent increases based on increased operating costs to the landlord (for taxes, insurance, utilities, janitorial services, etc.). It contains an escalator clause that provides for the rent increase based on some economic indicator called an index. There is usually a cap on the allowable annual rent increase. This type of lease is usually used for long-term commercial leases.

Contract versus Economic Rent

Contract Rent

Contract rent is the amount of rent the tenant must pay the landlord under the terms of the lease contract.

Economic Rent

Economic rent is the amount of rent the property could be rented for on the open market at a given time if it were available for rent. At the time the lease contract is signed, the economic rent and the contract rent are the same. As the lease matures, the economic rent will often exceed the contract rent.

Security Deposits

Generally, upon execution of a residential lease, the tenant will give a security deposit to the landlord. The security deposit is designed to protect the owner against a number of possible tenant-related losses resulting from the tenant's occupancy. Possible losses include nonpayment of rent or damage to the dwelling unit by the tenant or the tenant's visitors. (The provisions of the Florida Residential Landlord and Tenant Act dictating how security deposits are to be handled was discussed in Chapter 7.)

Essentials of a Valid Lease

For a lease to be considered a valid and enforceable lease, it must contain the following essential elements:

- competent parties—the lessor and lessee (In Florida, a person must have reached the age of 18 to be considered a competent party.)
- an adequate legal description of the property (A formal legal description is not required, so a street address is acceptable.)
- an agreement to convey possession rights by the lessor to be accepted by the lessee (the demising clause)
- signatures—of both parties

In addition, a lease should include the following:

- provision for payment of rent (the consideration)
- the term of the lease to include
  - the starting date and ending date, along with the total duration of the lease
  - the exact lease term indicated in years, months, and days

In addition, the rent should always be expressed in annual amounts payable in equal monthly installments. Failure to do so may result in a month-to-month tenancy versus that of a multiyear lease.

Example

Jones (lessor) enters into a one-year lease with Smith (lessee) on January 1 for a monthly rental of $500. In late May of the same year, Smith notifies Jones of his intent to vacate at the end of the following month (June 30 of that year). Smith vacates and Jones seeks unpaid rent from July through December, only to find out that Smith had a month-to-month lease and no additional rent was due.

In order for Jones to have collected the remaining July through December rent, Jones needed to properly state in the lease that it was a one-year lease "at an annual rental of $6,000 to be paid in equal monthly installments of $500 in advance at the first of each monthly period."

Termination of a Lease

A lease can be terminated in the following ways:

- Expiration—If the original term of the lease expires, the lease is terminated.
- Mutual agreement—Both landlord and tenant can agree to terminate a lease.
- Destruction or condemnation of the property—If property is destroyed, damaged, or condemned to the point that it cannot be used, the lease is terminated.
- Breach of contract—If either party violates the terms of the lease, the lease may be terminated at the discretion of the other party; however, it is always best to allow the courts to decide the appropriate course of action. Take these, for example:
  - If a tenant uses the property for a purpose that violates the lease, the landlord may elect to terminate the lease and evict the tenant.
  - If the landlord for a commercial property violates a noncompetition clause in the lease by leasing another storefront in the same shopping center to a competitor of the tenant, the tenant may elect to terminate the lease.

A breach of the terms of a contract may also result in eviction of the tenant. There are two types of evictions:

1. Actual eviction—This is the legal removal of the tenant from the leased property because the tenant violates some provision of the lease.
2. Constructive eviction—This occurs when the landlord causes or permits a situation to occur that makes it impossible for the tenant to enjoy the premises under the terms of the lease. For example, if a landlord allows the water in an apartment to be shut off, leaving the tenant without water, the landlord has caused constructive eviction.

There are some significant situations under which a lease is *not* terminated. A lease for years is not terminated by:

- the death of either party—should either party die during the lease period, the deceased party's estate is bound by the terms of the lease.
- the sale of the property—if the property is sold during the lease period, the new owner becomes the lessor and is bound by the lease contract.

> **Coaching Tips**
>
> Both a tenancy at will and tenancy at sufferance are terminated by the death of either party or the sale of the property.

Assignment and Subletting

A tenant may assign or sublet leased property unless otherwise prohibited in the lease. **Assignment** is the transfer of *all* rights that the tenant (assignor) holds in the property to another (assignee). The new tenant, the assignee, once approved by the landlord, becomes primarily liable for performance (payment of rent) under the lease contract. Unless a novation (substitution) of obligation occurs or the original tenant receives a release from the obligation, the original tenant (the assignor) remains secondarily (ultimately) liable.

A sublessor is the original tenant who sublets to a new tenant when property is subleased. Subletting is the transfer of *some but not all* of the rights and interests in the leased property held by the original master tenant or overtenant. The original tenant (the sublessor) retains some reversionary rights, the right to retake possession of the property after the new tenant (the sublessee or undertenant) vacates. Unlike the assignment, regardless of the overlandlord consenting to the sublease, the original tenant (or overtenant) remains solely liable to the landlord for performance under the lease contract (payment of rent). The sublessee is liable only to the original lessee, not to the landlord. The subtenant is also not a direct tenant of the landlord and, as such, has no parity with the property owner. (See Figure 9.7.).

When a property is sold whose current operation is as rental property, in Florida, the buyer is bound to the terms of all existing leases. This is called *sale subject to lease*. At closing, security deposits are transferred from the seller to the buyer. The same is the case for any change in rental or managing agent(s) entrusted with deposits or advance rents. The aforementioned are required under the Florida Residential Landlord and Tenant Act.

LIENS

Previously, you learned about several types of interests in real property and encumbrances to property ownership. Now you will learn about the last type of encumbrance, called a lien.

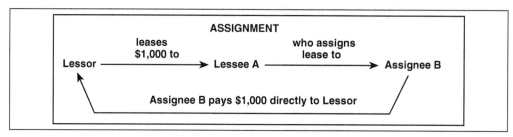

FIGURE 9.7
Source: © 2021 Mbition LLC

A **lien** is a legal hold or claim for the repayment of debt/owing that:

- one person has upon the property of another
- is used as security for a debt

There are two parties to a lien. The lienor is a person who has a right of lien upon the property of another. The lienee is a person whose property is subject to a lien.

There are several types of liens that you should know about:

- mortgage liens
- tax liens
- mechanic's liens
- judgment liens
- deficiency judgment liens

Mortgage Liens

A mortgage lien is created when a property owner borrows money using the property as collateral. Under the mortgage document, the property is pledged and used as security by the lender for the repayment of the loan. The lien is the instrument through which the lender's interest in the property is secured. In essence, until the loan is repaid to the lender, the borrower continues to own the property while the lender maintains and holds a lien on the property.

Coaching Tips

The process of pledging the property as collateral is also known as hypothecation.

Tax Liens

There are five major types of tax liens:

1. ad valorem property tax liens
2. special district assessment (improvement tax)/property tax liens

3. federal income tax liens (issued and placed by the Internal Revenue Service)
4. estate/inheritance tax liens
5. corporate tax liens

Ad Valorem Tax Liens

Ad valorem taxes are normally referred to as property taxes that are assessed according to the value of the property. An ad valorem tax lien is levied and attached on a property at the beginning of each tax year. That same lien is removed only when payment for that tax period has been received and credited. When someone fails to pay the ad valorem taxes that have been assessed on a property, collection procedures are instituted by either one of the following:

- the municipality
- in some cases, individuals or entities that purchase municipal tax liens

In most municipalities, the tax liens are sold to investors. This saves municipalities the wasteful use of public funds to pay for legal fees, court costs, and the time required for judicial tax foreclosure and sale of the property. Furthermore, by selling the tax lien to a private person or entity, the property remains a performing, tax-paying property.

Either a municipality or an investor initiates a procedure to collect on the lien via a foreclosure sale of the property. This procedure is the collection process for any outstanding amounts plus interest and penalties.

Special District Assessment/Tax Liens

Special assessment taxes are assessed on certain properties only in order to pay for improvements for those properties affected. An example would be a special assessment tax to pay for street lights in a neighborhood at the owners' request. When special assessment taxes are assessed, a tax lien is placed on the property. When the taxes are paid, the lien is removed.

Federal Income Tax Liens

Federal income tax liens arise when federal income taxes are not paid.

Estate/Inheritance Tax Liens

Upon the death of an individual or entity, taxes are levied on all personal property and real property in the form of a tax lien.

Corporate Tax Liens

The Internal Revenue Service (IRS) requires that all corporations pay corporate taxes on all annual profits derived by that corporation through its operations.

> **Coaching Tips**
>
> Income tax liens, estate/inheritance tax liens, and corporate tax liens all fall into the category of general liens. That is, these liens apply to all property, both real and personal, of the lienee. General liens will be described in more detail later in this chapter.

Mechanic's Liens

A mechanic's lien protects those people who supply labor or materials in the construction or improvement of buildings. If the labor or materials are not paid for, the person supplying them has the right to place a lien against the property for which the labor or materials were supplied. In Florida, a mechanic's lien must be filed and recorded with the circuit court clerk within 90 days after the completion of the work or the furnishing of the last materials in order for the lien to have priority over any mortgage liens established after the labor or materials were initially supplied. To enforce a claim against a mechanic's lien, a lienor must file a lawsuit in court within one year. In order to give notice of the claim and to protect the lien from expiration while the suit is pending, the lienor may file a notice of lis pendens in the public records.

Judgment Liens

When a person wins a lawsuit against another person in court to receive monetary damages, the person winning the suit is awarded a judgment. When the judgment is recorded in the public records, it becomes a judgment lien against all the property, both real and personal, of the defendant (the loser of the lawsuit). Thus, judgment liens are considered to fall within the category of general liens. If the lienee (the loser of the suit) does not voluntarily pay the amount of the damages awarded by the court, the court will issue a writ of execution that directs the sheriff to sell enough of the lienee's property to pay the damages and the cost of the sale.

It should be noted that judgment liens are general liens and attach to all real and personal property of the lienee.

Deficiency Judgment Liens

A deficiency judgment arises when a property is foreclosed on and sold to satisfy a debt. If the proceeds from the sale of the property are not sufficient to satisfy the outstanding balance on the debt, the mortgagee may obtain a deficiency judgment. This judgment serves as a lien on all of the mortgagor's assets. The right to recover the deficiency results from mortgage loans that are recourse. This occurs when the borrower has given their personal guaranty for any shortfall. If the mortgagor fails to pay the remaining balance on the property, the lien is enforced like any other judgment lien. The mortgagor's property, both real and personal, can be sold to pay off the remaining balance. Mortgage liens are voluntary liens. This means that the borrower/property owner is willingly allowing the lien to be placed on his/her property in exchange for the money loaned by the lender. This will be discussed later in this chapter.

It is important to note that not all mortgages give the lender the right to a deficiency judgment. Mortgage loans that are recourse loans (those where the borrower personally guarantees the repayment of the borrowed amount) versus those mortgage loans that are nonrecourse (those where the borrower does not personally guarantee the repayment of the borrowed amount). For the loan to be nonrecourse, it will usually have an exculpation clause. This clause basically says that the bank will only look to the collateral property for repayment of the debt. Deficiency judgment liens are general liens and attach to all real and personal property of the lienee.

Categories of Liens

Deficiency judgment liens can be categorized in two ways:

1. Voluntary versus involuntary
2. General versus specific

Voluntary liens are liens created by an agreement of the parties. An example would be a mortgage lien.

Involuntary liens are created by the operation of law. Examples would include:

- a tax lien from failure to pay property
- taxes
- a mechanic's lien for failure to pay for work done
- a judgment lien or a deficiency judgment lien

Involuntary liens are also called statutory liens. (See Figure 9.8.)

A general lien is one that attaches to all property owned by the lienee. Examples of general liens include:

- federal income tax lien—a statutory lien that can occur when federal income taxes are not paid

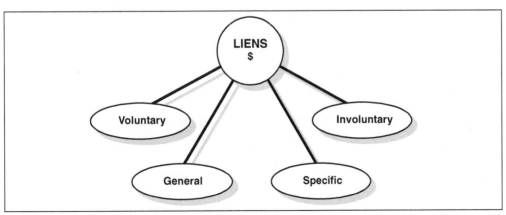

FIGURE 9.8
Source: © 2021 Mbition LLC

- judgment lien—a statutory lien that results from court action brought against the lienee
- deficiency judgment lien—a statutory lien that results when the proceeds from a foreclosure sale are insufficient to satisfy the outstanding indebtedness

A specific lien attaches only to a specific property identified in the lien. Examples of specific liens include a:

- property tax lien when taxes are not paid
- mortgage lien when a mortgage is used in financing
- mechanic's lien when work done is not paid for

Coaching Tips

General lien versus specific lien:

- General liens attach to all property owned.
- Specific liens attach only to a specific property.
- Specific liens are also called special liens.

Voluntary lien versus involuntary lien:

- Voluntary liens are created by an agreement between parties.
- Involuntary liens are created by an act of law.
- Not all general liens are involuntary liens.
- Statutory liens are created by the operation of law.

Priority of Liens

When two or more liens exist (first mortgage lien or superior lien and a second lien or junior lien), it becomes important to determine the priority of liens. In most states, priority is determined by race statutes. In general, race statutes give priority on the basis of the date of recordation of a lien in the public records. The first to be recorded has priority. There are two exceptions to this rule:

1. Real property tax liens take priority over all other liens on a given property, regardless of when they were recorded. Both ad valorem tax liens and special assessment tax liens have priority over all other types of liens.

Coaching Tips

Federal income tax liens do not have any special priority. They take priority on the date of their recordation just like any other lien other than a property tax lien.

2. A mechanic's lien takes priority on the basis of one of the following:
   - when the work began
   - when the materials were delivered, not the date the mechanic's lien was recorded

Transfer of Encumbered Title

A lien is an encumbrance on the title to the real property to which it attaches. To transfer the title, one of the following must occur:

- The lien is satisfied.
- The lien is assumed by the person to whom the title is being transferred (the grantee).

Summary

Real property like other personal property can be transferred from one person to another. Real property is transferred by deed while personal property is transferred by bill of sale. There are various deed instruments that are accepted as transfer instruments. The ownership in real property may come with private (deed restrictions) or public restrictions (such as zoning). Whereas an estate (ownership in real property) is conveyed to another by deed, possession rights to property are transferred by lease. There are a variety of leases that are used (as applicable). Liens are claims on the property of another for repayment of an indebtedness. Liens are either voluntary or involuntary. They also fall into two categories of liens; general or specific. Title searches help to identify liens that exist on property.

Review Questions

1. A deed that has been transferred is one that has been:
   a. signed by a competent grantee
   b. acknowledged
   c. signed by a competent grantor
   d. signed by the grantor and grantee

2. A deed that would carry the least buyer protection is a:
   a. special warranty deed
   b. general warranty deed
   c. quitclaim deed
   d. bargain and sale deed

3. Anna paid cash for her orange grove. She took her deed and immediately recorded it at the county clerk. If the deed is accepted for recording by the county clerk, which of the following is true?
   a. It is not considered legal notice.
   b. It is called constructive notice.
   c. It provides actual notice by recording the deed.
   d. It is called recorded notice.

4. Which of the following best describes the covenant of seisin clause contained in a deed?
   a. promises the grantor is the legal owner
   b. warrants the title is clear
   c. guarantees the grantor has not ruined the title
   d. states the price that was paid for the property

5. The clause in a deed that promises the grantor will defend the grantee's right to own the property is the:
   a. covenant of no encumbrances
   b. covenant of warranty forever
   c. covenant of quiet enjoyment
   d. covenant of further assurance

6. The clause in a deed that assures that the seller is the true owner of the property is:
   a. seisin
   b. no encumbrances
   c. quiet enjoyment
   d. warranty forever

7. If the sale contract is silent regarding the deed the seller will provide the buyer at closing, in Florida the seller must provide the buyer with a:
   a. quitclaim deed
   b. bargain and sale deed
   c. special warranty deed
   d. general warranty deed

8. A valid deed in Florida must be:
   a. executed with two witnesses
   b. acknowledged
   c. signed by a grantee
   d. recorded

9. A list of everyone who has ever owned a property from the time the property was first conveyed to the present owner is:
   a. an opinion of title
   b. a chain of title
   c. title insurance
   d. a lis pendens

10. An opinion of title in Florida can be issued by:
    a. an attorney
    b. a broker
    c. a title company
    d. anyone

11. Local townspeople have been crossing a farmer's field to get to a good fishing spot on the river for more than 20 years. This access to the farmer's land is:
    a. illegal trespass
    b. an encroachment
    c. an implied easement
    d. an easement by prescription

12. Susan came home and discovered that workers from the power company had entered her gated backyard in order to access the power poles behind her fence. Under these circumstances, this entry is:
    a. an encroachment on her property
    b. an easement in gross
    c. illegal entry; Susan can sue
    d. an easement by prescription

13. An owner's title insurance policy:
    a. is issued for an amount no greater than the debt and is transferable
    b. is issued for an amount no greater than the purchase price and is not transferable
    c. is a legal requirement in Florida when purchasing real property
    d. is issued to protect the lender

14. Jane's aunt Mary died. While helping her mother clear out her aunt's home, Jane discovered a deed for the house signed by her aunt with two witnesses deeding the house to the Red Cross. Mary died without a will and has a son, John. Who owns Mary's house?
    a. The Red Cross owns the house.
    b. By escheat, the state owns Mary's house.
    c. Mary's son, John, owns his mother's house.
    d. Jane's mother, Mary's sister, owns the house.

15. The deed to Solomon's lot and house states the house must be painted sage green as long as the building stands. This is an example of a:
    a. deed restriction
    b. requirement Solomon can waive
    c. whim by a former owner that is not legal
    d. subdivision covenant

16. Jerry pays $1,000 per month to live at an apartment. Jerry's apartment developed a leak in the roof. Jerry called the owner to come fix the roof right away. Jerry's lease is a:
    a. gross lease
    b. net lease
    c. percentage lease
    d. ground lease

17. The storefront merchant in a successful mall must pay a fixed amount of money for occupying the space. In addition, the merchant must pay a share of the mall owner's taxes, insurance, and other operating expenses for the property. The merchant's lease is:
    a. unconscionable and can be rescinded
    b. a percentage lease
    c. a net lease
    d. a gross lease

18. The right of a government to take private property when needed for a public purpose is called:
    a. escheat to the state
    b. condemnation
    c. eminent domain
    d. a public grant

19. The East to West Railroad Company is planning a new route through George's farm. George strongly objects to this action and the price he is being paid for the eminent domain and condemnation action taken against his property. Which of the following statements is true?
    a. George can commence an action in court to dispute the amount of compensation he is being paid for his farm.
    b. A court can give George an injunction to stop the railroad.
    c. George can sue the railroad for damages.
    d. George can simply refuse to sell.

20. Which of the following liens will be paid first?
    a. a property tax lien filed on January 1, 2015
    b. a mechanic's lien filed on December 1, 2014
    c. a special assessment lien filed on February 12, 2014
    d. a mortgage lien filed on March 26, 2015

10

LEGAL DESCRIPTION

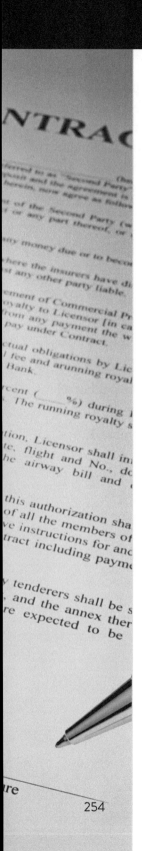

KEY TERMS

base line
benchmarks
check
datum
government survey system
legal description
lot and block
metes and bounds
monument

point of beginning (POB)
principal meridian
range
section
survey
terminus
township
township line (tier)

LEARNING OBJECTIVES

After completing this lesson, you will be able to:

- describe the purpose for legal descriptions
- understand the licensee's role and responsibilities as they pertain to legal descriptions
- explain and distinguish among the three types of legal descriptions
- describe the process of creating a legal description using the metes and bounds method
- locate a township by township line and range
- locate a particular section within a township
- understand how to subdivide a section
- calculate the number of acres in a parcel based on the legal description, and convert to square feet
- explain the use of an assessor's parcel numbers
- apply the measurements associated with checks, townships, and sections

PURPOSE OF LEGAL DESCRIPTIONS

There is a direct purpose and need for why legal descriptions exist. Through the use of legal descriptions, courts are able to uphold the rights of a property owner.

The method or concept for use will aid in identifing and describing a specific parcel or parcels of real property. This process is accepted by our legal court system. By utilizing any of the acceptable methods of legally describing property, boundary lines are established between neighboring properties.

TYPES OF DESCRIPTIONS

There are four methods of describing property:

1. metes and bounds
2. government rectangular survey
3. recorded subdivision plat maps
4. informal reference, such as street address or locally recognized name

For the purpose of transferring title, only the first three are legally acceptable. These three are called **legal descriptions**.

The fourth method, informal reference, is not accurate enough for title transfer; however, it can be used in a listing because no transfer of title is involved (but it is best to use a legal description).

Only the three legal description methods can be used for deeds and any other contracts involving title transfer. Let's examine each of the three methods.

Metes and Bounds

The first method of legal property description is called **metes and bounds**. *Metes* means the distance that is always measured in feet, and *bounds* always refers to and means direction. The metes and bounds method is the oldest method of legal description. A **datum** refers to a position from which a distance or distances can be measured, while datum lines are horizontal lines that aid in measuring heights and depths. The best way to understand a metes and bounds description is to think of it as a set of instructions you would give someone on how to walk around the outside boundaries of the property. It is important to note that a metes and bounds description will always begin with a **point of beginning (POB)**. It will always end at the POB as well (at the terminus).

For example, you might tell someone, "Start at the well and go north for 100 feet to the creek. Then turn right and go east for 150 feet to a large oak tree. Then turn right and go south for 100 feet to a large rock. Then turn right and go 150 feet back to the well." This is an example of a simple metes and bounds description using natural monuments. The natural monuments used were the well, the creek, the large oak tree, and the rock. As you saw in the example, a monument is an object that is used to define a corner of a parcel of property. (A corner is any place where you change direction while walking around the property.)

A **monument** may be:

- a natural monument—a natural object such as a tree or rock, like the ones used in the example
- a permanent monument—a man-made object such as an iron pin driven into the ground or a concrete marker placed by a surveyor

The metes and bounds method using natural monuments was used primarily in the past when surveyors were not generally available or when land was plentiful and inexpensive. The metes and bounds method using permanent monuments is commonly referred to today as a survey of property and is used as the primary method of description in many states. Metes and bounds descriptions are very useful in describing parcels of property that are irregular in shape, because they can describe *any* property by using directions of travel such as compass bearings that are used to describe the direction of the boundary lines (see Figure 10.1), distance of travel, and monuments. The advantage of permanent monuments is that permanent monuments last longer and are not as likely to be moved. However, even permanent man-made monuments may be occasionally moved or destroyed. To protect against this possibility, metes and bounds descriptions are tied to what are called permanent reference markers (discussed later in this chapter).

A metes and bounds description *must always* begin at a POB. It ends at the terminus, which is always at the POB.

The POB is:

- identified as the POB on the plat
- usually marked by an iron pin placed by the surveyor

The POB must be precisely identified. If the location of the POB is vague or unclear, the resulting legal description is invalid, which means that the contract or deed based on the description may be void. From the POB, the boundaries of the parcel are described using the direction and distance of travel from a permanent monument or the location and distance between natural monuments. The description must always return to the POB. Any description that does not return to the POB is defective (invalid), which means that the contract or deed based on the description may be void.

With the metes and bounds method, direction is typically measured using compass directions. Compass directions are expressed in degrees, minutes, and seconds. There are 360 degrees in a circle, 60 minutes in a degree, and 60 seconds in a minute. Compass directions also involve the directions north, south, east, and west. A direction begins by indicating whether the primary direction is north or south and then rotating the appropriate number of degrees, minutes, and seconds to either the west or the east. The maximum number of degrees is 90. (See Figure 10.1.)

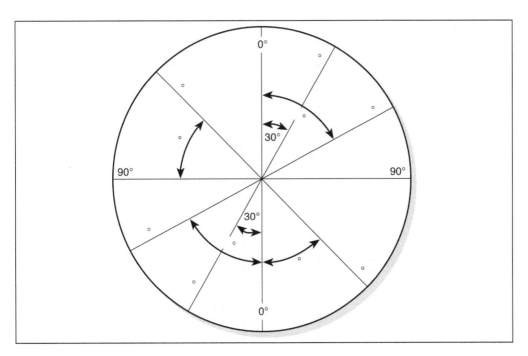

FIGURE 10.1
Source: © 2021 Mbition LLC

Example

- South 45 degrees west indicates a direction that is halfway between due south and due west.
- North 89 degrees east indicates a direction facing almost due east (90 degrees east would be due east).

When a metes and bounds description is used, errors are possible and the actual distance between monuments may be different from the distance given in the metes and bounds description. When this happens, the actual distance takes precedence over the distance stated in the metes and bounds description.

Government Survey System

The second method of legal property description is called the **government survey system**, which was established by Congress in the mid- to late 1780s. It has been applied in most states since that date with few exceptions. The states where the government survey system is used are primarily in the West and Midwest and a few states in the South, such as Florida. It has not been applied to those states that were formed prior to the mid-1780s, including the original 13 states and a few others. The basis of the system stems from the logic that you can identify any point on a plane by reference to two axes.

Each **principal meridian** (north and south running lines) is intersected by only one **base line** (east and west running lines). Throughout the United States, there are 36 different intersecting principal meridians and base lines. In Florida, the principal meridian and base line intersect in Tallahassee. As a result, it is named the Tallahassee Principal Meridian and Base Line. The overall size of each system varies from system to system. The outermost boundaries of a system are irregular in shape and often conform to the border between states.

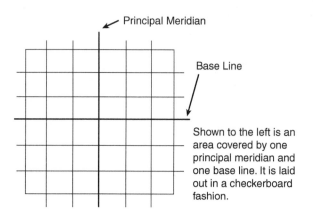

Shown to the left is an area covered by one principal meridian and one base line. It is laid out in a checkerboard fashion.

Guide Meridians

Due to the earth's spherical shape, the north/south meridian lines respectively meet at the north or south poles. As a result, the parallel north/south lines that meet at the respective poles require a solution. Therefore, guide meridians (north and south lines) are drawn every 24 miles to the east and west of the principal meridian. These lines end every 24 miles from the principal meridian and provide the offset necessary (approximately 50 feet away) to correct for the spherical shape of the earth.

Correction Lines

Correction lines are made up of east/west lines situated every 24 miles to the north and south of the base line. A **check** is the 24-mile square that is achieved through the intersecting guide meridians.

Ranges and Tiers

Here is the best way to remember the difference between a range and a tier:

- A range runs north and south. All three words—*range*, *north*, and *south*—have five letters.
- A tier runs east and west. All three words—*tier*, *east*, and *west*—have four letters.

The term **township** is defined by the intersection of a **tier** and range and also refers to both of the following:

1. a square parcel of land formed by the intersection of range lines and township lines (**township lines** are drawn every 6 miles north and south of a base line, thereby forming east and west parcels of land.)
2. a row of townships running east to west

As a helpful tool, think of the following:

- West is to the left of the principal meridian.
- East is to the right of the principal meridian.
  - Tiers run east to west (tier, east, and west all have four letters).
- North is above the base line.
- South is below the base line.
  - **Ranges** run north to south (range, north, and south all have five letters).

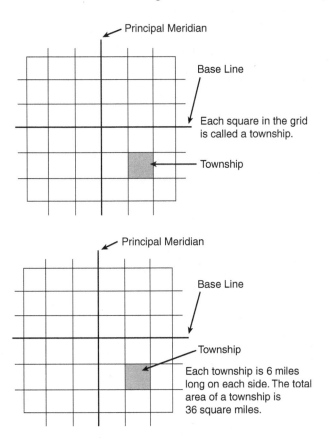

There is one special situation that results in sections that have slightly different measurements from the normal measurements just presented. Because of the curvature of the earth's surface, the dimensions of some townships must be corrected (usually the townships contained along the northwest perimeter of the drawn guide meridians). Because of this correction, some of the sections along the northwest borders of a township are smaller than the rest. These sections are about 50 feet narrower than the other sections. This occurs as a result of correction lines that are drawn every 24 miles to the west and east of the principal meridian. This correction accounts for the curvature of the Earth, particularly at the north and south poles where meridian lines meet.

Sections

Each township contains 36 sections. Each **section** measures 1 mile square. Each section within a township is represented by a number from 1 to 36. Section 1 is always found in the northeast corner of a township. The numeric progression is westward of Section 1 until Section 6. Section 7 is found directly to the south (below) of Section 6 and continues eastward until Section 12. Section 13 is found directly to the south of Section 12 and continues westward until Section 18. This numeric progression of sections continues in the exact same manner as just described until Section 36 is reached. Section 36 is always found in the southeast corner of a township.

HINT: If you draw a horizontal line that follows the numeric progression, the line would resemble an "S."

When writing or identifying a legal description of a section:

- the appropriate section number appears first
- the tier, referenced by its number and direction, appears second
- the range number and direction appear last

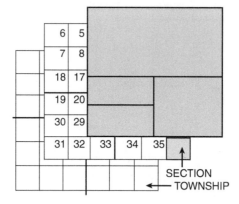

Example Section 14, Tier 14 South (T14S), Range 4 West (R4W), of the Tallahassee Principal Meridian and Base Line.

BASIC FACTS

Introduction

Throughout this chapter, you will be presented with a summary of some basic math relationships that are involved in the government survey system. The presentation of these facts will consist simply of a set of statements of equivalent values.

Example

1 section = 640 acres

Before we begin working with the basic facts for the government survey system, we need to cover one general math concept.

Let's begin with the figure below. Let's assume that the figure represents a square parcel of land that measures 4 miles on each side.

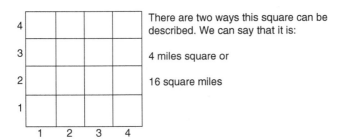

There are two ways this square can be described. We can say that it is:

4 miles square or

16 square miles

Let's look at the difference in these two descriptions.

Notice that each side of the square is 4 miles long. One way it can be described is to say that it is 4 miles square.

If the square measured 3 miles on each side, it would be described as 3 miles square.

A square that measured 10 miles on each side would be described as 10 miles square. The other way to describe the parcel shown below is 16 square miles. This description simply states the area of the square.

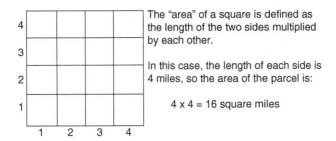

The "area" of a square is defined as the length of the two sides multiplied by each other.

In this case, the length of each side is 4 miles, so the area of the parcel is:

4 x 4 = 16 square miles

A square parcel that has sides measuring 3 miles would have an area equal to 3 miles × 3 miles, which is called 9 square miles.

A square parcel that has sides measuring 10 miles would have an area equal to 10 miles × 10 miles, which is called 100 square miles.

In the remainder of this lesson, we will practice working with two sets of basic math facts relating to the government survey system. Before we begin with the first set, let's review the major units of measurement in the government survey system.

The checkerboard layout that is formed around the intersection of a baseline and a principal meridian is illustrated next.

The checkerboard is divided into units called townships, as shown in the figure below:

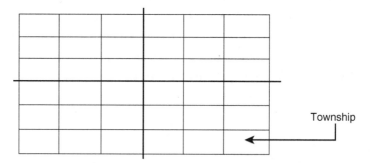

Now, let's look at the first set of basic math facts relating to the government survey system:

$$1 \text{ township} = 6 \text{ miles by } 6 \text{ miles}$$
$$1 \text{ township} = 6 \text{ miles square}$$
$$1 \text{ township} = 36 \text{ square miles}$$
$$1 \text{ section} = 1 \text{ mile square}$$
$$1 \text{ section} = 1 \text{ square mile}$$
$$1 \text{ section} = 640 \text{ acres}$$
$$1 \text{ township} = 36 \text{ sections}$$

The size of a section is important when trying to determine the number of acres in a tract of land (see Figure 10.2). As mentioned previously, each section represents 1 square mile and contains 640 acres. Sections can be broken down into smaller parcels.

For example, a section can be broken down into quarter sections. Each quarter section contains 160 acres:

$$640 \text{ acres} \div 4 = 160 \text{ acres}$$

Each quarter section can then be broken down further. One quarter of one quarter of a section contains 40 acres:

$$640 \text{ acres} \div 4 = 160 \text{ acres}$$
$$160 \text{ acres} \div 4 = 40 \text{ acres}$$

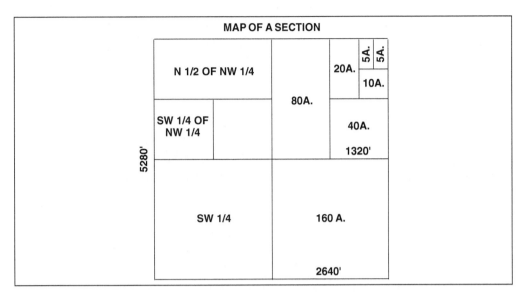

FIGURE 10.2
Source: © 2021 Mbition LLC

Similarly, if the section is broken down further, one quarter of one quarter of one quarter of a section contains 10 acres:

$$640 \text{ acres} \div 4 = 160 \text{ acres}$$
$$160 \text{ acres} \div 4 = 40 \text{ acres}$$
$$40 \text{ acres} \div 4 = 10 \text{ acres}$$

Assume that you want to determine the size of a tract of land. If you know the tract of land consists of the northeast quarter of Section 6, you would calculate the size as follows:

$$640 \text{ acres} \div 4 = 160 \text{ acres}$$

Let's look at another example.

A tract of land consists of the southwest quarter of the northeast quarter of Section 6. In this situation, the size of the tract is calculated as follows:

$$640 \text{ acres} \div 4 = 160 \text{ acres}$$
$$160 \text{ acres} \div 4 = 40 \text{ acres}$$

The tract contains 40 acres:

$$640 \text{ acres} \div 4 = 160 \text{ acres}$$
$$160 \text{ acres} \div 4 = 40 \text{ acres}$$

Now, let's look at another set of basic math facts relating to the government survey system:

$$1 \text{ acre} = 209 \text{ feet by } 209 \text{ feet}$$
$$1 \text{ acre} = 209 \text{ feet square}$$
$$1 \text{ acre} = 43{,}560 \text{ square feet}$$

1 mile = 5,280 feet
1 mile = 320 rods
1 rod = 16.5 feet

> ## Coaching Tips
>
> One acre is not exactly 209 feet square (209 feet by 209 feet). It is actually 208.71 feet square, but for convenience we will round this measurement off to 209.

Lot and Block Survey Method (Recorded Plat Method)

The third method of legal property description is called recorded plats. A plat is simply a map of a subdivision. Plats are usually created by a developer or subdivider when a parcel of raw land is subdivided into building lots. As a helpful tool, think of subdividing as "buying by the acre while selling by the lot." Plats are recorded in the public land records when the subdivision is created. It can or will contain a list of any restrictive covenants that will apply to the subdivision. After a plat is recorded, any property located in the subdivision can be identified by reference to the recorded plat.

The plat (map) of a subdivision of land is a rendering of a plot of land that is broken down into units called **lots and blocks**. A lot is a sections of land that a house is built on. A block is the largest unit within a subdivision, and it is made up of various lots. The plat also shows the boundaries of all streets and easements in the subdivision and any other relevant details of the subdivision.

"And" in Legal Description

From time to time, you will need to determine the acreage in a legal description that contains the word "and." The method used to calculate the aforementioned is this:

Step 1. Calculate the acreage applicable to the description to the left of the word.

Step 2. Calculate the acreage applicable to the description to the right of the word.

Step 3. Add the sum of Step 1 and Step 2 together to arrive at the total number of acres.

Assessor's Parcel Number

In the recording process, parcel numbers are issued to property. These numbers are issued by tax assessors. Parcel numbers are issued as an aid in the assessment of the property. They are used for tax collection purposes. Tax maps are based upon recorded plat maps of subdivisions. As previously stated, every parcel in a particular county is listed by or with a parcel number. The minimum information shown includes but may not be limited to:

- the parcel owner's name
- the address of record shown on the assessment roll
- the assessed value of both land and structure

Preparation and Use of Surveys

When purchasing a parcel of real property, it would not be uncommon for the purchaser to request a survey of the subject property be prepared. The survey acts as a form of due diligence (doing your homework) on the part of the buyer. The **survey** will show and uncover the boundaries of the property as well as uncover any encroachments in adjoining properties by others.

Benchmarks

A permanent reference marker (PRM) is a precisely identified location that is identified by reference to latitude and longitude. Permanent reference markers are also referred to as **benchmarks**.

Summary

In order for a parcel of improved or unimproved land to be conveyed from one party to another, a formal legal description of that parcel must be referenced. This legal description provides the boundaries of any parcel in question. The postal address of a property is not a legal description. There are various acceptable methods for the legal description of land. This includes the government rectangular survey system, metes and bounds, and recorded plats.

Review Questions

1. What method of legal description is only used in subdivisions?
   a. government survey system
   b. lot and block method
   c. metes and bounds
   d. tax ID method

2. What section is due south of Section 2?
   a. Section 12
   b. Section 11
   c. Section 3
   d. Section 8

3. Where is Section 31 located in every township?
   a. the northeast corner
   b. the northwest corner
   c. the southeast corner
   d. the southwest corner

4. Which of these legal descriptions contains 2.5 acres?
   a. the SW ¼ of the SE ¼ of the NE ¼, Section 11, T1S, R1E
   b. the SW ½ of the SE ¼ of the NE ¼ of the NE ¼, Section 11, T1S, R1W
   c. the SW ¼ of the SE ¼ and the NE ¼ of the NW ¼
   d. the S ½ of the SW ¼

5. Calculate the number of acres in the NW ¼ of the SE ¼ and the SE ¼ of section 16.
   a. 10 acres
   b. 80 acres
   c. 100 acres
   d. 120 acres

6. Which legal description has been in use the longest?
   a. metes and bounds
   b. lot and block
   c. government survey system
   d. natural monument system

7. What is the most critical feature of the metes and bounds legal description?
   a. use of natural monuments
   b. presence of permanent monuments in the landscape
   c. an accurate POB
   d. guide meridians

8. What compass direction is directly opposite of N 40°E?
   a. N 40°W
   b. S 40°E
   c. S 40°W
   d. N 80°E

9. How many sections are in a township?
   a. 16
   b. 10
   c. 72
   d. 36

10. Which method of legal description is the least accurate?
    a. metes and bounds
    b. lot and block
    c. government survey system
    d. informal reference

11. The south boundary of section 12, T2N, R3W is:
    a. 8 miles north of the baseline
    b. 6 miles north of the baseline
    c. 10 miles north of the principal meridian
    d. 10 miles north of the baseline

12. How many acres are in a section of land?
    a. 640 acres
    b. 320 acres
    c. 160 acres
    d. 40 acres

13. Which of the statements is FALSE?
    a. A section is one mile square.
    b. A section covers one square mile.
    c. There are 36 sections in a township.
    d. A section contains 36 acres.

14. Deanna purchased one half of a section and gave one quarter of that section to her son, Charles. How many acres did Charles receive?
    a. 320 acres
    b. 160 acres
    c. 80 acres
    d. 40 acres

15. Guide meridians and correction lines are placed every:
    a. 1 mile
    b. 6 miles
    c. 12 miles
    d. 24 miles

16. How many square feet are in 1 acre?
    a. 640
    b. 26,780
    c. 43,560
    d. 87,120

17. In Florida, where do the principal meridian and base line intersect?
    a. Orlando
    b. Tallahassee
    c. Jacksonville
    d. Green Swamp

18. A vertical strip of land, 6 miles wide and parallel to the principal meridian, is a:
    a. range
    b. township tier
    c. section
    d. check

19. In the government survey system, a fragmented piece of land that is not entirely square that was on the gulf, for example, is called a:
    a. check
    b. plot
    c. government lot
    d. benchmark

20. The requirement for a legal description is that:
    a. it must be sufficient that a surveyor could find it
    b. the street address must accompany the description
    c. enough for the local county standards
    d. an official street address will do

11
REAL ESTATE CONTRACTS

KEY TERMS

assignment
attorney-in-fact
bilateral contract
competent
contract
culpable negligence
exclusive agency listing
exclusive right to sell listing
fraud
liquidated damages
meeting of the minds

net listing
novation
open listing
option contract
Statute of Frauds
Statute of Limitations
unenforceable
unilateral contract
valid contract
void contract
voidable contract

LEARNING OBJECTIVES

After completing this lesson, you will be able to:

- list and describe the essentials of a contract
- distinguish among:
    - formal
    - parol
    - bilateral
    - unilateral
    - implied
    - expressed
    - executory
    - executed contracts
- describe the various ways in which an offer is terminated
- describe the various methods of terminating a contract
- explain the remedies for a breach of contract
- describe the effect of the Statute of Frauds and the Statute of Limitations
- describe the elements of an option
- differentiate among the various types of listings
- explain and describe the various disclosures required in a real estate contract
- recognize what constitutes fraud
- recognize what constitutes culpable negligence

DEFINITIONS

A **contract** is an agreement between two parties. It can be an agreement to do something or to refrain from doing something. If it is an agreement to refrain from doing something, it is called a contract for forbearance.

In general, contracts can be written or oral. Although the validity of an oral contract without proper witnesses is difficult to prove, oral contracts in Florida are enforceable. However, the Statute of Frauds dictates and requires that all contracts involving either the purchase of or sale of any parcel of real property *must* be in writing to be enforceable. An oral contract is called a **parol** contract.

THE STATUTE OF FRAUDS

In 1677, the English crown enacted law to eliminate fraudulent transfers at the expense of innocent landowners. As a result of this old English law, the Statute of Frauds was created and adopted by the states of the union.

The **Statute of Frauds** is a law that states, among other things, that some real estate contracts must be in writing to be enforceable. According to the Statute of Frauds in Florida, the following types of valid real estate contracts must be written to be legally enforceable:

- deeds
- real estate purchase and sales contracts
- options
- leases for more than one year
- listings for more than one year

According to the Statute of Frauds in Florida, the following types of valid real estate contracts are enforceable if they are oral:

- leases for a period of one year or less
- listings for a period of one year or less

Status of Oral Contracts	VALID	ENFORCEABLE
Open Listings	YES	YES
Leases—one year or less	YES	YES
Sales Contracts	YES	NO
Leases—over one year	YES	NO
Exclusive Listings	NO	NO
Options	NO	NO
Debt Instruments (Mortgages)	NO	NO
Deeds	NO	NO

There are two exceptions to the statute of frauds:

1. Partial performance—the statute of frauds will not apply under the following two conditions:

> a. Either full payment or partial payment has been made.
> b. The buyer has made improvements to the subject property or has physically taken possession of the property.
>
> 2. Executed contracts—demonstrates that an agreement existed when any type of performance would have suggested same preparation of contracts.

In most states, contract preparation is accomplished by using an attorney who has been trained to deal with such matters. In Florida and in noncomplex owner-occupant residential transactions, real estate licensees will sometimes be the party preparing the contract for purchase and sale (discussed in greater detail later in this chapter). In any event, the party preparing the contract must always insure that the contract clearly spells out the terms of the transaction as well as the responsibilities of the respective parties. Real estate licensees engaging in the preparation of contracts must exercise caution to avoid the unauthorized practice of law.

STATUTE OF LIMITATIONS

In Florida (as well as other states), the **Statute of Limitations** means that there is a deadline to file a legal complaint against another. If one misses that deadline, he/she is prohibited by the statute of limitations from proceeding with the complaint. This applies to civil as well as criminal complaints.

Below are just a few examples of the statute of limitations for various types of complaints:

- Contracts—5 years (written Chapter 95.11.2b); 4 years (oral Chapter 95.11.3k) 1 year for specific performance (Chapter 95.11.5a)
- Fraud—4 years (Chapter 95.11-3j)
- Personal injury—4 years (Chapter 95.11-3o)
- Collection of rents—5 years (Chapter 95.11-2b)
- Domestic judgments—20 years (Chapter 95.11-1)
- Slander/Libel—2 years (Chapter 95.11-4g)

VALID VERSUS VOID AND VOIDABLE

From a legal standpoint, there are three types of contracts:

1. valid
2. void
3. voidable

Valid Contract

A **valid contract** is one that is legally sufficient and meets all the essential requirements of the law to create a contract between two or more persons.

A valid contract can be either enforceable or unenforceable:

- enforceable—a valid contract that can be enforced in a court of law
- **unenforceable**—a contract that cannot be enforced in a court of law. An unenforceable contract is valid until challenged in court

An unenforceable contract is usually one that is valid but is not written and therefore cannot be enforced in court. Such is the case concerning the transfer of real property from one party to another. In real estate, some contracts must be written to be enforceable, while others do not need to be written, such as an open listing agreement.

As required by the Statute of Frauds and with no exceptions, all contracts for the purchase or sale (in part or in whole) of any parcel of real property must be in written form to be considered valid and enforceable. This issue will be covered in more detail later in this chapter.

Void Contract

A **void contract** is one that is not recognized legally and has no legal effect. From its inception, the agreement lacks one or more of the necessary essential requirements for the creation of a valid and enforceable contract. For example, a contract to perform any unlawful or illegal act is void from inception. It lacks the requirement of a legal objective. (The requirements for a valid contract, including legal objective, will be described in detail later in this chapter.)

It is important to understand the following:

- A void contract is not binding on either party.
- Even though a void contract may seem to be a contract, it is not a contract at all.

Voidable Contract

A **voidable contract** is one that is capable of being voided by one of the parties to the contract. It is binding on one party to the contract only and is valid until action is taken by one party to make it void.

Although the contract seems to be valid on the surface, it may lack one or more necessary essential requirements for the creation of a valid and enforceable contract. For example, a contract for the purchase and sale of real property involving a minor as either the buyer or the seller is a voidable contract. Because the minor is not considered to be a competent party, only the minor may void the contract (see Figure 11.1.)

CONTRACT VALIDITY AND ENFORCEMENT REQUIREMENTS

There are four elements that are required for a contract to be valid. These four elements can be remembered by the mnemonic CALL. A valid contract CALLs for these four requirements:

LEGAL EFFECTS OF CONTRACTS

✓ VALID
  binding and enforceable

✓ VOIDABLE
  one party can cancel due to fraud, duress, or undue influence, but the other side cannot cancel

✓ UNENFORCEABLE
  appears valid but cannot be enforced in court

✓ VOID
  no legal effect, no contract

FIGURE 11.1
Source: © 2021 Mbition LLC

1. Consideration
2. Agreement
3. Legal objective
4. Legally competent parties

Consideration

The first requirement of a valid contract is consideration. Consideration is a promise that someone makes to give up something of value. In a typical home sale, the seller promises to give up the home, and the buyer promises to give the seller money (the purchase price).

Coaching Tips

In a real estate contract, consideration is not the earnest money but the exchange of the purchase price (or something else of value) for real property.

Example A painter signs a contract in which he/she promises to paint a house (a consideration) in exchange for money (a consideration).

There are two types of considerations:

1. Valuable consideration—Anything that has a monetary value such as money, services, merchandise, etc. (The promise of something that has monetary value is also considered valuable consideration, such as a buyer's promise to buy and pay the purchase price and a seller's promise to sell real property.)

2. Good consideration—Something of worth that does not have a monetary value such as love, affection, or goodwill.

   Good consideration is involved when a person gives real property as a gift. In this case valuable consideration (real property) is exchanged for good consideration (love and affection).

Agreement

The second requirement of a valid contract is mutual agreement or mutuality. This is sometimes called a **meeting of the minds** or offer and acceptance. This means that there must be a mutual agreement on the provisions of the contract.

> ### Coaching Tips
>
> You will encounter a variety of legal terms that end in the letters OR and EE. Here is a helpful tip in identifying and remembering the parties and their role within the situation:
>
> OR at the end of a word is the owner of, or giver of, whatever is owned and is given.
>
> An example of this is offeror. The offeror is the owner of or giver of the offer or counteroffer. As you will learn later in this chapter, the offeror can be either the buyer or the seller.
>
> EE at the end of a word is the receiver of, or recipient of whatever has been given. An example of this is offeree. The offeree is the receiver or recipient of the offer or counteroffer. The offeree can be either the buyer or the seller.
>
> There are generally no exceptions to this rule; however, there is one spelling exception, which is employer. The ER ending is treated as if it had an OR ending, therefore, providing the same definition as the OR. The employer is still the owner/giver of the employment.

Legal Objective

The third requirement for a valid contract is that it must have a legal purpose. A contract cannot call for or contain any action that violates the law. A contract whose objective is illegal is void and cannot be enforced in court.

Legally Competent Parties

The fourth requirement for a valid contract is that the parties to the contract must be legally **competent**. A competent party can be defined as a person or legal person with the ability and capacity to enter into a binding and enforceable contract.

There are three primary categories of people who are *not* legally competent:

1. minors
2. intoxicated persons
3. insane persons

The first group of individuals who are not legally competent are minors. A minor is a person who has not reached the legal age requirement (age of majority). In Florida, the legal age (the age of majority) is 18. Most contracts with minors are voidable, as long as the minor elects to void the contract while still a minor or within a reasonable period after reaching the age of majority. (The definition of a *reasonable period* is determined by the courts.)

The second group of individuals who are not legally competent are intoxicated persons. A contract made by an intoxicated person is typically voidable.

The third group of individuals who are not legally competent are insane persons. An insane person is an individual of unsound mind who has been declared incompetent by the court and has been appointed a guardian. Such individuals cannot enter into contracts. Any contract signed by an insane person is void. If a person who has no guardian signs a contract and is *later* judged to be incompetent *at the time of the signing*, the contract is voidable.

Most individuals who do *not* fall into one of the three categories just covered are considered competent to enter into contracts on their own behalf. In addition, two other categories of entities enter into valid contracts:

1. attorneys-in-fact
2. corporations

An **attorney-in-fact** is someone who has been granted power of attorney limited to a specific transaction named in a document. A contract entered into by an attorney-in-fact is valid when the power of attorney has been properly granted.

Corporations are considered to be artificial, or legal, persons and may enter into valid contracts. However, the contract must be executed and carried out in a manner that is consistent with the corporation's prescribed methods. The law is designed in such a manner that a corporation is treated as a legal person and/or entity in itself. Like an individual, a corporation has its own separate identity. Its identity stands separate and apart from that of its shareholders who bear no corporate responsibilities on a personal level. A corporation is issued a separate tax identification number, which is not unlike that of an individual social security number. See Figure 11.2 for valid real estate contracts.

Authority of Real Estate Licensees to Prepare Contracts

In Florida and in the normal course of business, it would not be unlikely for a real estate licensee to prepare a simple contract for the purchase and sale of a residential property or unimproved land intended for owner-occupant residential

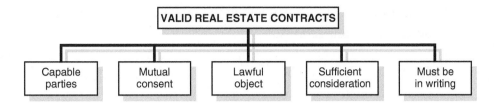

FIGURE 11.2
Source: © 2021 Mbition LLC

purposes. In these types of simple transactions, a licensee would most probably utilize a printed form of contract. The most widely used form of contract for these types of transactions in Florida would be a Florida Realtors/Florida Bar Residential Contract for Sale or Purchase. This type of contract requires caution on the part of the licensee when preparing same. A real estate licensee may fill in the blanks of contracts preapproved by the owner and/or his/her attorney.

This contract should not be used for transactions considered complex, such as:

- installment sales contract (contract for deed or land contract)
- construction of improvements contract
- option agreements
- exchange contracts
- purchase and sale of a business

The licensee must always be cautious to avoid the unauthorized practice of law. If preparation appears complicated, the licensee should refer the matter to an attorney.

CLASSIFICATIONS OF CONTRACTS

Contracts can be categorized in the following ways:

1. expressed versus implied
2. bilateral versus unilateral
3. executed versus executory

Expressed versus Implied

An expressed contract is one in which the intent of the parties is stated (expressed) in the contract itself. An expressed contract can be either written or oral.

> **Example** (1) A contract to sell real estate is an expressed contract because the intent of the seller to sell and the buyer to buy is stated in the contract; (2) a verbal lease on an apartment for three months is an expressed contract because the parties verbally state their intent.

An implied contract is one in which the intent of the parties is not stated but is indicated by their actions.

Example If you order food in a restaurant, your actions (ordering the food) imply a contract on your part to pay. The acceptance of the order by the waiter implies that the restaurant will deliver food in return for your paying the check.

Bilateral versus Unilateral

The second way of categorizing contracts is in terms of the nature of the commitments made by the parties to the contract. Contracts are said to be either bilateral or unilateral.

A **bilateral contract** is one in which both parties promise to give up something or to perform in such a manner as required by the agreement. A promise is exchanged for a promise (see Figure 11.2).

Example A real estate sales contract is a bilateral contract. Both parties promise to give up something. The seller promises to give his/her home to the buyer. In return, the buyer promises to give money to the seller.

Coaching Tips

A bilateral contract is like a two-way street. This means that it is not an agreement whereby only one party is required to act in accordance with the promises contained in the contract (an option to purchase where a seller must sell but the buyer is not required to purchase). A bilateral contract requires that both parties act on the promises contained in the contract, ultimately to the benefit of both parties (a buyer's promise to buy and a seller's promise to sell).

A **unilateral contract** is one in which only *one* party promises to give up something. A promise is exchanged for some act or performance by the other party (see Figure 11.3).

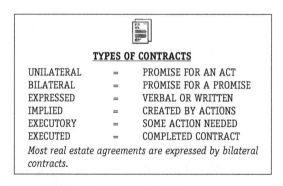

FIGURE 11.3
Source: © 2021 Mbition LLC

Example A sales bonus offered to a salesperson is a unilateral contract. The company promises to pay a bonus if sales targets are met, but the salesperson does not promise to meet those goals.

> ### Coaching Tips
>
> A unilateral contract is like a one-way street. It is an agreement that benefits only one party to the transaction.

One of the best examples of a unilateral contract in real estate is the option contract. An option is a contract that gives someone the right but not the obligation to buy a property. Under an option contract, the property owner gives a potential buyer the right to buy the property at a prescribed price for a prescribed time period (the option period). To ensure that the option received is considered valid and enforceable, the potential buyer gives the property owner valuable and substantial consideration for the option period. During the option period, the buyer may purchase the property if he/she chooses to, whereby the owner would have to comply and sell at the agreed-upon price. However, the property owner cannot force the buyer to purchase the property.

Another common example of a unilateral contract in real estate would be an open listing (for sale by owner). The licensee can, but is not obligated to, participate in the transaction. However, the seller would be required to pay the licensee if he/she delivered an acceptable sales transaction. In this unilateral agreement, the seller would be the only party required to perform.

The option creates a "one-way street," or a one-party promise—the owner promises to sell (if the buyer chooses to buy), but the buyer does not promise to buy.

Executed versus Executory

The third way of categorizing contracts is in terms of whether or not they have been completed. Contracts are said to be either executed or executory.

An executed contract is one in which all requirements of the contract have been fulfilled and the parties have done what they agreed to do in the contract. In essence, all interested parties to the transaction have fully performed (see Figure 11.3).

Example When a real estate sales contract is closed or settled, it is executed.

> ### Coaching Tips
>
> Don't confuse an executed contract with executing a document. Executing a document simply refers to the process of signing the document.

An executory contract is a contract where some act still needs to be performed for the contract to be executed. It is one in which some or all requirements have not yet been completed (see Figure 11.3).

Example A real estate contract that has been signed by both parties but has not closed is an executory contract because all the requirements of the contract have not been completed (e.g., transfer of title, payment of purchase price, etc.).

Formal and Informal Contracts

The difference between a formal and informal contract is whether it is in writing or if it is oral. Informal contracts are oral, while formal contracts are always in writing.

> **Coaching Tips**
>
> In order for a contract involving the transfer of any interests in real property to be enforceable in Florida, the Statutes of Frauds requires that the contract be an agreement in written form.

> **Coaching Tips**
>
> To avoid any unpleasant experiences concerning misstatements, it is always good practice to remember the following: If you tell the truth, you don't need a good memory.

CONTRACT NEGOTIATION

In order for a contract to be created, we've learned that certain elements and conditions must exist. There must always be an offer and an acceptance. This creates the condition of mutual agreement. In order for mutual agreement to be achieved, three general conditions must be met:

1. One party (the offeror) must make an offer to the other party (the offeree).
2. The offeree must accept the offer.
3. The offeree must communicate the acceptance to the offeror.

If the offeree chooses not to accept the original offer of the offeror, he/she may make a counteroffer, which is a new offer substituted for the original offer. The counteroffer extinguishes the original offer. A counteroffer automatically terminates the original offer and constitutes a totally new offer, even if only one minor item is changed in the counteroffer.

It is important to understand that an offer can be withdrawn, even if was accepted, if it is not communicated or delivered. An offer can't be withdrawn after acceptance is communicated or delivered. Only the person who made the offer can withdraw it.

Another condition for accomplishing a mutual agreement is that none of the following may occur:

- intentional misrepresentation
- innocent misrepresentation
- mistake

Coaching Tips

An offer can be terminated in any of the following ways:

1. counteroffer
2. rejection
3. withdrawal by offeror
4. expiration of an offer based on a time limit for acceptance (lapse of time)
5. death or insanity of either party
6. destruction of the property that is the subject of the offer

Intentional Misrepresentation

Intentional misrepresentation is an act intended to deceive someone in order to get that person to give up something of value. It can result from intentionally giving false information or withholding relevant information.

Intentional misrepresentation results in fraud. Examples of fraud include:

- A seller tells a buyer that the property he is selling is zoned commercial when he knows that it is zoned residential.
- A seller is aware that the roof of her house leaks but conceals this fact from the buyer.
- When fraud occurs, the injured party has the option to rescind (cancel) the contract or to leave it in effect.

Innocent (Unintentional) Misrepresentation

Innocent misrepresentation is the giving of incorrect information by one party without the intent to deceive.

Example A prospective home buyer asks the seller if the city bus stops near the house, and the seller says "yes" without realizing that this service had been discontinued the week before.

In the case of innocent misrepresentation, although it may not be intentional on the part of the injuring party, the injured party has the option to rescind (cancel) the contract if it is done in a timely manner. In the event the innocent misrepresentation occurs due to the act or acts of a licensee, the licensee may be exposed to very serious civil liabilities. Furthermore, and perhaps even more important, the licensee will be the subject of disciplinary action by the Florida Real Estate Commission (FREC). When an individual receives a license, he/she is considered (in the eyes of the regulatory agency) as being an expert. The general public views licensees in the same light. Therefore, when proceeding with a real property transaction, it is important to realize that any misstatement(s), particularly a misstatement that results in a financial or other loss by a customer, subjects the licensee to severe disciplinary action by the FREC.

Mistake

A mistake is an error in the facts of a transaction that occurs:

- mutually by both parties
- unintentionally
- without negligence

Example A buyer is given directions to look at a property for sale, and the buyer goes to see the property alone. The buyer mistakenly looks at the wrong vacant property and writes a contract to buy. After closing, the seller and the buyer discover the error. In this case, the buyer thinks he is buying one property, and the seller thinks she is selling another. In the case of a mutual mistake such as this, the contract is void because there is no mutual agreement.

The last condition that must be met to achieve mutual agreement is that the offer and acceptance must be genuine and freely given. There can be no duress or undue influence used to obtain agreement. Duress is forcing someone to do something against his/her will. Undue influence is taking unfair advantage of someone.

If a contract is obtained under either of these conditions, the injured party has the option to rescind (cancel) the contract or leave it in effect. Thus, it is voidable.

Coaching Tips

Parties who are not legally competent are not precluded from receiving personal property from a legally competent party. If a person not legally competent desires to sell personal property, that person would be required to do one of the following:

- reach the age of majority (if a minor)
- not be intoxicated at the time of entry to a contract for the purchase and sale of real or personal property
- have a court-appointed guardian perform the transaction on behalf of that person

TERMINATION OF CONTRACTS

Methods of Terminating Contracts

Most contracts are discharged by performance of the contract requirements (i.e., they are executed). This is always the preferred way. However, aside from performance of the object, some alternatives exist, such as the following:

- assignment
- novation
- termination

Assignment

Assignment is the transfer of one's entire interest in an executory contract to another person. Executory contracts can be assigned unless prohibited in the contract. Executed contracts cannot be assigned because they have already been fully performed.

> **Example** Deeds are executed contracts and cannot be assigned.

Novation

Novation involves substituting a new contract for an old contract or substituting a new party for an old party under an existing contract. Novation is also a means of general release from previous contractual obligations. Examples of novation would include:

- Assumption of an existing mortgage whereby the lender officially releases the original borrower for the substitution of the new borrower/home buyer.
- An assignment of a master lease by the master tenant whereby the over landlord/property owner officially releases the original master tenant for the substitution of the new assigned master tenant.

The following items are facts about the assignment of contracts:

- The person who assigns his/her interest is the assignor.
- The person to whom the interest is assigned is the assignee.
- Once the assignment is made, the assignee becomes primarily liable for fulfillment of the contract.

However, unless there is a novation agreement relieving the assignor of liability, the assignor remains ultimately liable (contingent liability) if the assignee fails to perform as required.

The following is an example of contingent liability in a transaction:

- The landlord leases space (the overlease) to the tenant who in turn, subsequently, subleases the demised space or unit to the subtenant.

- Although the subtenant accepts responsibility to make all the rental payments to the sublandlord who in turn pays the landlord, the sublandlord still retains liability for total performance under the overlease to the landlord.
- A mortgage assumption by a new buyer without a novation/release agreement would also constitute a contingent liability to the seller/original borrower. In the event that the new buyer defaulted on the loan, the seller/original borrower would be secondarily responsible to the lender for repayment of the loan.

Coaching Tips

A sublease is also known as a sandwich lease. The tenant is sandwiched between the subtenant and the landlord (discussed in Chapter 9).

As previously discussed, novation is the substitution of a new contract between two parties that terminates and replaces an old contract or the substitution of new parties for an existing contract. However, the difference between assignment and novation is related to the withdrawing party's liability. With assignment, the assignor is still ultimately liable for performance. With novation, the withdrawing party is released from liability.

Example When a buyer assumes an existing loan from a seller, novation occurs if the original borrower is released and a new party is substituted in the mortgage note contract.

Termination

Termination can occur in a variety of ways, such as the following:

- mutual agreement of the parties
- expiration of time
- rescission of avoidable contract
- operation of law

Mutual Agreement of the Parties

Simply put, the interested parties to a contract unanimously decide that the contract should be terminated, possibly because of a number of unforeseen events that arise in any transaction. It may be simply that the parties don't care for each other or some other reason that leads them to a mutual termination of the relationship.

Expiration of Time

Many contracts have time limitations or restrictions. If a time limitation or restriction expires, the rights associated with the contract terms expire.

> **Example** Landlord Ian leases an apartment to Tenant Max for a period of one year. At the end of that lease term, all rights of possession to the apartment by Tenant Max terminate (if not renewed), and possession reverts back to Landlord Ian.

> **Example** Buyer Max is granted a three-month option to purchase Seller Ian's home. Seller Ian agrees to sell to Buyer Max for $500,000. Buyer Max agrees to pay Seller Ian $5,000 for the three-month option, and Seller Ian agrees. The three-month anniversary of the option comes, and Buyer Max fails to buy the home. Buyer Max's $5,000 option fee to Seller Ian is forfeited, and the option is terminated via the expiration of time.

Coaching Tips

Remember that an option is used for the purposes of buying time.

Rescission of a Voidable Contract

Rescission of a contract can be defined as voiding or canceling the contract, whereby the parties to the contract are placed back in their original positions prior to the creation of the contract.

Operation of Law

Operation of law can be defined as the voiding of a contract resulting from the inability of the parties to perform under the contract because of:

- discovery or the existence of fraud
- expiration of the Statute of Limitations concerning the nature of the contract

Other causes of operation of law include the following:

- destruction of the property
- bankruptcy of either party
- death of one of the parties

If one of the parties to a contract dies, the contract is terminated only if it requires an act that only the deceased person could perform. In the absence of a provision to the contrary, real estate sales contracts are not terminated by the death of one of the parties. The contract is binding on the deceased person's estate, regardless of whether it is the buyer or seller who dies.

The Uniform Vendor and Purchaser Risk Act covers cases where real property involved in a sales contract is destroyed. If the property is destroyed before either possession of the property or title to the property has passed to the buyer (while the contract is executory), the seller is at risk. This means that if the property is destroyed while the contract is executory, the buyer is not obligated to go through with the sale and is entitled to his/her money back.

BREACH OF CONTRACTS

A breach of contract occurs when one party fails to live up to his/her contractual obligations for no legal reason(s). When this occurs, the other party (either buyer or seller) is referred to as the innocent party. The innocent party under a breach of contract has certain rights that can be used to remedy the breach of contract. A breach of contract does not relieve either party of his/her obligations under the contract and does not terminate the contract. A breach of contract will generally involve litigation between the aggrieved parties. Let's take a look at some remedies that are available to the parties.

Remedies for Breach

Whenever a breach of contract occurs, the aggrieved party has certain rights. In order to remedy a breach, the innocent party has the right to do the following:

- Partial performance—The innocent party may accept partial completion of the contract as satisfactory.
- Rescission—The innocent party may rescind (cancel) the contract unilaterally, or the parties may mutually agree to rescind. Rescission is the opposite of specific performance, whereby the parties are placed back into their original position as if the contract never existed.
- Sue for specific performance—The innocent party may sue the other party in court to carry out the requirements of the contract as written.
- Sue for damages—The innocent party may go to court to pursue a judgment for monetary damages. The amount is determined by the courts and would be based upon the facts concerning the case.
- **Liquidated damages**—The parties may determine in advance a sum to be paid to the innocent party in the event of a breach. Normally in residential and commercial sales transactions, the deposit tendered by a buyer serves as the liquidated damages resulting from a default by the buyer.

Liquidated Damages

A sales contract may include a statement that if the buyer breaches the contract, the seller may demand forfeiture of the earnest money deposit as liquidated damages. However, this may prevent the seller from suing for additional monetary damages. The innocent party must take action to remedy the breach of contract within a specific time period set by the Statute of Limitations. This is an example of the doctrine of laches. Laches are rights that one has inherent in any situation; however, if those rights are not asserted or exercised in a timely manner, one will lose those rights. In essence, use them (assertion of rights) or lose them.

"Time Is of the Essence"

As you work with contracts, you may encounter the phrase "time is of the essence." This phrase means that the contract must be performed on or before the date specified in the contract. A party who fails to meet the deadline is guilty of a breach of contract.

Coaching Tips

In general, when a suit for specific performance is sought as a remedy for a breach of contract:

- A buyer can usually win a suit for specific performance under a valid contract.

- A seller may have more difficulty in winning a suit for specific performance because normally the seller can be adequately compensated by monetary damages.

CONTRACTS IMPORTANT TO REAL ESTATE

Employment Contracts (Listing Contracts/Agreements)

Listing contracts/agreements can be best categorized as employment agreements. To avoid misunderstandings from arising, conditions requisite to the employment are generally clearly stated. With regard to listing agreements, the same holds true. As in any employment contract, compensation should always be stated clearly. The same holds true for listing agreements. Therefore, it is not unlikely for a real estate licensee to enter into preclusionary agreements.

For example, a real estate broker agrees to only be entitled to receive compensation if and when the transaction closes and all funds have been transferred by the buyer to the seller. In some states and in Florida, failure to include preclusionary language in a listing agreement might expose the paying party (in this case, the seller) to compensate the licensee even if the transaction does not close.

> ## Coaching Tips
>
> It is important to note the importance of the term *employment*. In any real estate transaction, in order to be legally entitled to receive compensation, there are generally three basic transactional events a licensee should be aware of and ready to prove at a minimum:
>
> 1. The individual or entity is licensed throughout the transaction and receipt of compensation.
> 2. The individual or entity has been employed/authorized to transact on behalf of another in a transaction.
> 3. The individual or entity is the procuring cause (the person(s) or entity(s) that as a result of their efforts brought about the transaction).
>
> Note that being employed/authorized (see #2 above) can be a requirement of grave importance. For example, if a person is not employed/authorized to transact on another's behalf, that person most probably will not be able to prove that he/she was the procuring cause of the transaction.

In Florida, there are four types of legally authorized listing agreements that are commonly used. The four types include:

1. **Exclusive right to sell listing**—Of the four listing agreement types, for the broker, this listing agreement is the most desirable arrangement. In this type of agreement, the seller appoints one agent to transact business on his/her behalf with the intent of achieving a successful conclusion (the sale of the property). During the term of this type of agreement, regardless of which party succeeds in the sale of that property, the broker will be compensated. This would include a sale that is effectuated by others such as:

    a. any other broker
    b. the seller
    c. a family member
    d. any other person or entity

2. **Exclusive agency listing**—In this type of agreement and as in the case above, the seller still appoints one agent to transact business on the seller's behalf with the intent of achieving a successful conclusion (the sale of the property). However, this listing agreement provides the seller with a reservation

to sell the property on his/her own. Should that occur, the exclusive agency broker is not compensated. In the event any other cooperating party effectuates a sale, the exclusive agency broker is compensated under the agreement.

3. **Open listing**—In essence, open listings are properties that are for sale by owner (FSBO). The owner may attempt the sale of the property without the use of a real estate licensee or may engage one or more agents to effect a sale. In either case, in this type of listing agreement, the property owner will only compensate the party who is the procuring cause within the transaction. This arrangement is the least desirable for the broker.

4. **Net listing**—A net listing is where a seller is seeking a stated amount as the final purchase price. The purchase price does not include the broker's compensation for a successful conclusion to that transaction. Therefore, the broker markets the property at an agreed upon listing price that is greater than the net amount the seller wishes to receive. The licensee is cautioned that any amount retained by the licensee as net compensation should reflect a customary amount commensurate with the services provided. Otherwise, the licensee's compensation may be viewed as "unjust enrichment."

Example A seller enters into a net listing with a broker. The net amount that the seller wants is $100,000. This amount does not include a provision for the broker to be paid, and therefore, the seller and the broker agree to list the property at $130,000. The property sells for $125,000. Under these conditions the licensee is entitled to a brokerage fee of $25,000. However, the seller may find this amount to be excessive in relationship to transactions of similar type.

In most states, net listing agreements are unlawful. In Florida, net listings are legal. Due to fraud and potential deception that may arise out of these relationships, regulators would discourage a licensee from accepting and entering into this type of relationship.

Buyer Broker Agreements

A growing area of real property brokerage has evolved over time. Today it is very common for a buyer to seek representation within a more formal type of arrangement. The same aforementioned agreements (exclusive agency or exclusive right to procure) that apply to a seller of property can be used to provide representation to a buyer. We refer to these agreements as buyer-broker agreements.

Sales Contracts

A contract of sale is a written agreement wherein a seller agrees to sell and a buyer agrees to buy real estate on the terms and conditions set by the contract. In order to arrive at the final terms of a purchase and sales contract, both buyer and seller posture themselves through a process referred to as negotiation. A contract of sale is commonly called a sales contract. It is the contract that is signed when a buyer offers to buy a house from a seller. As previously mentioned, offer and acceptance are required elements toward creation of a binding enforceable contract. When both seller and buyer sign a sales contract (that may or may not include a buyer's earnest money deposit), a binding agreement on the sale has been reached, but the actual transfer of the property does not occur at that point. The actual transfer of ownership of the property occurs at a later date after a process called a closing or settlement. During this period of time and until closing of title, the buyer is said to have equitable title. For example, after the contract is signed by both parties, the buyer may require the seller to obtain the buyer's consent concerning changes to the property. The reasons for having a sales contract followed by a closing at a later date include the following:

- The buyer needs time before a transaction is completed to determine whether the seller has good title and the legal right to convey title.
- The buyer needs time to arrange financing.
- The contract determines the duties and obligations of the parties to the sale at closing.

Each real estate sales contract must contain certain information, such as:

- names of the parties to the contract
- description of the property being sold
- date, time, and location of closing
- purchase price and financing terms
- amount of earnest money or binder deposit being held and by whom
- type of deed
- any personal property that will be included in the sale
- broker(s) associated with the transaction (if applicable)
- all required disclosures

Earnest Money

Earnest money is paid by the buyer at the time the sales contract is signed. Although there are no state or federal laws that require a deposit under the purchase and sale contract, it is a good business practice. The following are reasons why deposits are part of customary practice within these transactions:

- An earnest money deposit shows good faith on the part of the buyer and increases the likelihood that the buyer will perform his/her obligations under the contract.
- In the event of a buyer's default under the terms of the contract, earnest money usually acts as the liquidated damages to the seller.

> **Coaching Tips**
>
> Earnest money is not the consideration in the contract. (The consideration is the promise to pay the purchase price for the property.)

If earnest money is held by a broker, the broker is required to place the money into an escrow (trust) account immediately. As we learned in Chapter 5, *immediately* is defined as:

- for the broker—no later than the close of banking business on the third business day following receipt of the earnest money deposit (weekends and holidays not included).
- for the sales associate and broker associate—any deposit entrusted to a sales associate or broker associate must be delivered to the broker no later than the end of business of the next day from receipt of the money.

Equitable Title

Equitable title or an equitable interest provides titleholders with any potential appreciation in value that occurs from contract signing to closing. During the post contract signing and closing stage, the buyer cannot sell the property to reap the benefits of value increase; however, he/she can do so after closing.

It should be noted that there is also legal title. Legal title is defined as the ownership (in part or in whole) interest in property, and it is enforceable by law.

Information Included in the Sales Contract

It is important to understand and be familiar with the contents of a sales contract. Not all sales contracts are the same, nor is there any statutorily prescribed form of contract of purchase and sale. However, as no two deals are identical, the topic of information included in the sales contract will likely be the same.

Let's examine some of the information that is likely to be contained in the contract:

- Date, time, and place of closing—can be on any agreed to date, time, and location
- Purchase price–an amount that is usually expressed in U.S. currency
- Terms of financing (if any)—this section will express:
  - if financing will be used
  - the amount of loan that will be sought
  - if there is a contingency for failure to obtain a loan commitment under the stipulated terms
- Quality of title that is being conveyed—a determination that the title is marketable
- Type of deed—with or without warranties and covenants

- Items of personal property to remain or remove—usually an area of litigation resulting from unspecified and unclear intentions to remove certain items of property
- Type of evidence of title to be provided—usually arrived at through a title search
- Items of proration—property costs and other items as they stand on the day of closing (Determination of who owes whom is accomplished through the closing statement.)
- Required disclosures (next topic of discussion)
- Radon gas disclosure
- Energy-efficiency disclosure
- Lead-based paint disclosure
- Homeowner association disclosure
- Flood insurance disclosure
- Condominium and cooperative disclosures
- Transaction processing fees and other brokerage charges
- Property tax disclosure
- Building code violation disclosure
- Seller's disclosure to accompany listing agreement
- Florida Realtors/Florida Bar Residential Contract for Sale or Purchase contract forms—a printed form of contract used in residential sales (but not for complicated transactions) created by the Florida Realtors in conjunction with the Florida Bar. It is commonly used in Florida by real estate licensees.

Disclosure of Defects That Materially Affect the Value of Residential Property

Johnson v. Davis/Property Defect

Johnson v. Davis was a precedent-setting case in Florida regarding residential transactions. This case held sellers of residential property accountable and responsible for disclosure of material defects (that are known to the seller) affecting the value of the property. Prior to *Johnson v. Davis*, the theory of caveat emptor (let the buyer beware) was a standard practice in residential transactions. Now, sellers must disclose all material defects to the property. In addition, *Rayner v. Wise Realty Co. of Tallahassee* required that sellers disclose to licensees the condition of the property.

"As Is" provision

Normally, the term *as is* means a seller will not effectuate any specified repair to the property prior to closing. Although this may appear to simplify the process of required disclosure, it is important to note that merely stating the term *as is* in a contract may not relieve the seller or licensee of future liability for failure to disclose a known material defect that would otherwise affect the value of the property if it were known to the buyer. The Florida Realtors/Florida Bar Residential Contract has a version for an *as is* sale.

Duty of Disclosure by Licensees

Through training, real estate licensees are held at a higher level than that of a consumer. With the issuance of a license comes great responsibility to the general public. License law compels the licensee to provide the consumer with a variety of disclosures. As a direct result of the aforementioned, it is the duty of any real estate licensee to disclose any known defect(s) that would otherwise affect the value of the property. Failure to do so will normally result in a disciplinary action and/or a civil suit.

State and federal laws require that prior to or at the time of signing a real estate sales contract, the buyer must be provided with following disclosures:

- radon gas disclosure
- lead-based paint disclosure
- energy-efficiency disclosure
- condominium or cooperative disclosure
- homeowner association disclosure
- property tax disclosure
- *Johnson v. Davis* property defect
- building code violation disclosure

Radon Gas Disclosure

Radon is a colorless, odorless toxic gas that is the by-product of the natural decay of uranium. Radon gas enters a building from the ground through openings around plumbing or through cracks in the foundation.

Radon gas is hazardous because it can cause damage to the lungs; it is also a known carcinogen. Florida state law Section 404.056 requires that all contracts for purchase and sale of real property contain a disclosure statement explaining what radon is, and the disclosure must be provided to a buyer prior to or at the time of signing a sales contract.

Lead-Based Paint Disclosure

Lead-based paints were used in most homes built before 1978. Exposure to lead can cause serious health problems, especially in children and pregnant women. Federal law requires the disclosure of known information on lead-based paint before the sale of most housing built before 1978. Sellers must also provide buyers with a federally approved pamphlet titled Protect Your Family from Lead in Your Home. Sellers must also allow the buyer a 10-day period to test for lead-based paint. Sellers, however, are not required to pay for this testing. It should be noted that the Environmental Protection Agency (EPA) frequently audits the offices of real estate brokers to check that lead-based paint disclosures are attached to all sales transactions. Failure to attach the disclosure results in an EPA fine of $11,000 per violation.

Energy-Efficiency Disclosure

According to the Florida Building Energy-Efficiency Rating Act, a potential buyer must be provided with a brochure explaining that the buyer has the option to obtain an energy-efficiency rating on the building and that the energy-efficiency rating may qualify the buyer for an energy-efficient mortgage. This brochure must be provided to the buyer prior to or at the time of signing a sales contract.

Condominium or Cooperative Disclosure

If the property being sold is a condominium or cooperative, any disclosures required under the Florida Condominium Act or the Florida Cooperative Act must be provided. Failure to provide all required disclosures provides the buyer with the right to cancel the contract.

Homeowner Association Disclosure

The purpose of a homeowner association is often to maintain and improve local properties and property values. Such associations may enforce restrictive covenants, which are agreements that may limit the use and physical features of property. If a property is subject to a mandatory homeowner association, the buyer must be provided with a disclosure statement concerning the association, any restrictive covenants, and any assessments (fees). Licensees have a responsibility to provide or make available to a purchaser all information concerning this matter.

Property Tax Disclosure

Florida law requires that a seller provide a prospective buyer with a disclosure of the tax levied on the subject property. The disclosure must be made to the buyer prior to the execution of a contract for purchase and sale. The purpose of the disclosure is to inform the buyer of the current tax levied on the property in the year of sale and to note that this tax is not a representation of the future tax following the year of sale. A municipality will normally reassess the taxes of a property that has recently sold. Reassessment is based upon the market value of the sale. Reassessment can result in an upward or downward move in property taxes.

Building Code Violation Disclosure

Any property owner who has existing building violations or faces enforcement of violations must disclose in writing to the buyer the existence of:

1. the violation,
2. information regarding any proceedings of enforcement (including but not limited to any notices or other applicable documents), and
3. disclosing to the buyer that he/she will be responsible for all remediation costs necessary to bring the property up to current code.

The aforementioned event and cost should be addressed in the purchase contract. In addition, within five days following closing of title, the seller must provide the appropriate code enforcement agency with:

1. the purchaser's name,
2. the purchaser's address, and
3. copies of all written disclosures given the buyer.

Failure to submit the any of these can subject the seller to substantial civil liability.

Time Limits

When a contract is offered, it usually includes a specific time period in which a response must be made by the offeree. If the offer is not accepted in that time, the offer terminates. If no stated period for a response is included, the offer terminates after a reasonable time. (The courts ultimately determine what is a *reasonable time*.)

Acceptance

The contract offer must be accepted *exactly* as it is written. Any change in the offer, no matter how minor, automatically *terminates* the original offer and constitutes a counteroffer.

Back-up Contract

A back-up contract is a contract of sale accepted by the seller with the stated understanding that the seller has already accepted a prior offer.

Binder

A binder is a short purchase contract used in some states to secure a real estate transaction until a more formal contract can be prepared by an attorney. Binders may or may not be enforceable.

OPTION CONTRACTS

As explained earlier, an option is a contract that gives the right to buy a property but does not require the receiver of the option to buy the optioned property. For this reason, an **option contract** falls under the category of a unilateral contract. As previously learned in this chapter, a unilateral contract is where only one party is required to perform.

Example

Mr. Green owns a parcel of undeveloped property. Mrs. White is considering the possibility of building a shopping center on that property but is also looking at other sites. In order to give herself some time to make up her mind and to ensure that Mr. Green's property will not be bought by someone else in the meantime, Mrs. White might decide to purchase an option to buy Mr. Green's property. If she does, the option contract that she signs will allow her to purchase the property during the option period if she so chooses. Mr. Green, the owner of the property, cannot force Mrs. White to purchase the property, but he must sell to her if she chooses.

In this example, Mr. Green, the owner, is the optionor because he gives Mrs. White the option to buy his property. Mrs. White, the potential buyer, is the optionee because she receives the option (the right to buy the property).

In general, the optionor is the owner of the property, the one who gives an option to someone. The optionee is the person who receives an option to buy someone else's property.

An option contract gives an exclusive right to buy. This means that no one other than the person holding the option (the optionee) can buy the property during the option period. In effect, an option is a way of protecting your right to buy a property for a certain period of time while preventing anyone else from buying it. The period the option is in effect must be specified in the option contract. The option contract must include a specific ending date. The option contract must also specify the sales price of the property when it is signed. It is not acceptable to wait until the optionee decides to buy the property (exercise the option) to set a sales price. During the period the option is in effect, the optionee (the potential buyer) has the right to exercise the option. Exercising the option means the optionee chooses to buy the property as provided for in the option contract. Only the optionee can exercise the option because the optionee is the one who holds the right to buy. When the optionee exercises the option to buy, the option contract automatically becomes a sales contract for the sale of the property.

When an option is signed the optionee must pay a valuable consideration (money or its equivalent) to the optionor. In Florida, in order for an option to be valid and enforceable, there must be adequate (substantial) consideration exchanged. An option contract with only token or nominal consideration is considered unenforceable. In effect, the optionee is buying the right to purchase the property under the terms of the option. Usually, if the option is exercised and the property is purchased, the money paid by the optionee for the option right is applied to the purchase price, but this is subject to negotiation before the option is signed. If the option to buy is not exercised, the money paid to obtain the option is forfeited.

Miscellaneous Characteristics of Options

An option contract must contain all the essential elements of a valid contract. As a result, when the option is exercised it automatically becomes a binding sales contract. The listing broker on an optioned property is not entitled to a commission until the option is exercised. Options are assignable unless prohibited in the option contract.

Let's examine what interest exists in the property encumbered by an option contract:

- During the option period, the optionor retains title and all rights to the property.
- The optionee has no legal rights in the property under the option contract.
- Once the option is exercised, the buyer has equitable title.

Let's also examine the categorizing of option contracts:

- Until an option is exercised, it is an executory contract. Once exercised, it is an executed contract.
- Because only one party is obligated under an option contract, it is a unilateral contract.

An option differs from a right of first refusal in that a right of first refusal:

- is a right to have the first opportunity to buy the property if and when it becomes for sale.
- has no predetermined price for buying the property.
- has no fixed time to purchase the property.

However, with an option contract:

- the optionee has an exclusive right to buy the property.
- there must be a predetermined price for the property.
- the option must be in effect for a fixed period of time.

When an optionee holds an option to buy a property, the optionor (the owner) may sell the property during the option period. However, the option remains in effect and must be honored by the new owner. The optionee can compel the new owner to sell the property under the terms agreed to by the previous owner.

Installment Sales Contract

An installment sales contract may also be referred to as a:

- land contract
- contract for deed
- contract for title

An installment contract is a contract of sale under which:

- the seller retains title and holds the deed.
- the purchaser takes possession while installment payments are being made.

An installment contract is often used when the seller provides financing for the sale but is not sure of the buyer's ability to pay. The seller retains title, thus eliminating the need for foreclosure in the case of default. If the buyer defaults, he/she forfeits all payments and can be evicted like a rental tenant. In some states, an installment contract is used most commonly for resort-type property. *Legally*, the seller is the property owner:

- The seller holds legal title.
- The buyer holds equitable title until the property is paid for.

Practically, the buyer is the owner of the property. The buyer:

- pays property taxes.
- deducts interest payments for tax purposes.
- claims any depreciation if the property is income producing.

Types of Contracts

Contract of Sale	Deed
Back-up Contract	Deed of Trust
Binder	Lease
Installment Contract	Listing Contract
	Mortgage

Coaching Tips

To remember how installment sales contracts work, view this kind of transaction as identical to a layaway plan for the purchase of real property. In a layaway plan of personal property:

1. Installment payments are made for the full cost of the item in question.
2. The retailer retains possession of the item as collateral for the full payment of the purchase price.
3. When all installment payments have been made, the retailer will transfer the ownership of the item by issuing a bill of sale. Of course, in a real estate transaction the deed is received as the transfer of ownership instrument.

MISCELLANEOUS REAL ESTATE CONTRACT CONSIDERATIONS

Procuring Cause

It is not uncommon for a seller of property to compensate a real estate broker or brokerage a commission for the sale of the property. By doing so, the paying party seeks assurances that the party receiving payment was the procuring cause to the transaction. This means that if not for the efforts of that party, the sale of the property would not have been brought about. The statement as to who is to be compensated as the procuring broker is normally found in the section captioned "Broker." In this section of the contract, the parties are agreeing on which broker or brokers brought about the transaction. Although no one can prevent lawsuits from happening, this may prevent someone unrelated to the transaction from winning a claim to compensation.

Telephone Solicitation Laws

Under Section 501.059, F.S., the Department of Agriculture and Consumer Services maintains a no sales solicitation list. Any person who has placed his/her name on this list may not be contacted for the purposes of solicitation. A licensee may contact a person on the list if that person places a yard sign stating the property is available for sale or lease. Furthermore, a licensee may also contact an individual or party for which the licensee has done business with previously. Failure to adhere to the Florida telephone solicitation laws will subject the licensee to fines.

Under federal law, the licensee can contact business relations within 18 months and customer inquiries within the Past three months. Furthermore, under federal law, contact with a seller who is selling his/her property without the use of a real estate licensee may occur only if the licensee making contact has an actual buyer.

Multiple Listing Service (MLS)

MLS is a service provided by local real estate boards. Their purpose is to provide the agent with the ability to quickly identify properties available for sale or lease. It is also intended to promote and foster clearer communication and cooperation between listing and selling agents. Membership is normally by subscription.

Ethical Practices

In order to receive a real estate license in Florida, a license applicant must be honest and trustworthy. This includes the duty to disclose defects that affect the value of the property if known by the interested party. When there is any doubt as to what course of action to take on this subject, the best action is to always disclose what one knows. Failure to do so may result in **fraud** (intentionally or unintentionally attempting to deceive another for personal profit) or culpable negligence on the part of the individual responsible for same. **Culpable negligence** can be defined as acting recklessly without thinking about the risk of one's actions to others.

Summary

Contracts are legal documents. Preparing a legal document is considered practicing law, and only attorneys are permitted to draft these documents. Because most real estate licensees are not attorneys, most licensees cannot prepare legal documents such as deeds and mortgages. Doing so would be considered unauthorized practice of law and subject the licensee to both civil liability and disciplinary action by the FREC. This includes the addition of riders to a contract. However, there are certain types of contracts that licensees are permitted to prepare, including sales contracts on simple transactions and listing contracts. Licensees are not permitted to draft an option contract. However, licensees are allowed to fill in the blanks in a preprinted, "form" option contract that has been prepared by an attorney.

Review Questions

1. Which of the following best describes the Statute of Frauds?
    a. It sets standards for fraudulent behavior.
    b. It states contracts must have termination dates.
    c. It requires competent parties for contracts.
    d. All transfers of real estate in part or in whole must be in writing to be enforceable.

2. Which of these contracts is an exception to the Statute of Frauds?
    a. a lease agreement for six months
    b. a 13-month listing agreement
    c. a statutory deed
    d. any unilateral contract

3. Broker Andrew agreed to sell his neighbor's house within the next four months at a 3% commission, and Andrew and the neighbor shook hands on the deal. Andrew sold the house three months later for $320,000, but the neighbor refused to pay the fee. According to the Statute of Frauds, Andrew:
    a. should have had his neighbor sign a listing agreement
    b. can sue but should have no expectation of prevailing in court
    c. can expect Florida courts to force his neighbor to pay
    d. can sue his neighbor for fraud

4. Which of these contracts is NOT an exception to the Statute of Frauds?
   a. a 12-month lease agreement
   b. an oral sale contract where the buyer has moved into the home
   c. a 6-month lease agreement
   d. a 13-month listing agreement

5. The Statute of Limitations for a parol contract is:
   a. one year
   b. three years
   c. four years
   d. five years

6. The broker for ABC Realty posted a notice on the office bulletin board that stated the first agent to sell three houses in the next calendar quarter will receive a $3,000 bonus. This is an example of a(n):
   a. bilateral contract
   b. unilateral contract
   c. parol contract
   d. illegal compensation

7. Harmon had a buyer in his car and knocked on the door of a for-sale-by-owner. Harmon identified himself as a real estate licensee and asked if the seller would show them the house. Harmon brought an offer from the buyer that the seller accepted, but the seller refused to pay Harmon a commission. If Harmon sues, he:
   a. cannot expect to collect any money
   b. could possibly lose his license
   c. should find another line of work
   d. can expect to be successful in recovering just compensation

8. The sales contract is expected to close on the 30th of the month. On the 29th, the contract is considered to be a(n):
   a. executory contract
   b. voidable contract
   c. unilateral contract
   d. exclusive right of sale contract

9. Which of the following is NOT a remedy for a breach of contract?
   a. a suit for specific performance
   b. collection of liquidated damages
   c. a suit to rescind on the breach
   d. operation of law

10. An adult signed a written contract with a minor. This means:
    a. the contract is illegal
    b. the adult can walk away
    c. the contract is void
    d. the contract is voidable

11. Which of these is NOT an essential element of a valid and enforceable contract?
    a. competent parties
    b. signed and witnessed
    c. consideration
    d. legality of object

12. A seller says she wants your real estate company to sell her home. However, she is also talking to her cousin about buying the home. If she sells to her cousin, she doesn't want to pay the commission. This describes a(n):
    a. exclusive agency listing
    b. open listing
    c. net listing
    d. exclusive right of sale listing

13. The seller has signed a listing stating the seller will accept any offer that provides the seller with a stated minimum amount. This listing is a(n):
    a. exclusive agency listing
    b. open listing
    c. net listing
    d. exclusive right of sale listing

14. One real estate company is given a listing. No matter who sells the property, the listing broker will be paid. This is a(n):
    a. exclusive agency listing
    b. open listing
    c. net listing
    d. exclusive right of sale listing

15. Millie and Gary are thinking of leasing a home that was built in 1972. Before they can sign the lease agreement:
    a. they must be provided with and sign the lead-based paint disclosure
    b. they must have the home inspected for lead-based paint
    c. the seller must pay for a lead-based paint inspection
    d. all lead-based paint must be contained or removed

16. A meeting of the minds (an essential element of a contract) comes about:
    a. when the offer is made in writing
    b. when the contract is signed by the offeror
    c. when the offeree signs the contract
    d. when the acceptance is communicated

17. Bernie signed a contract to purchase a house and was scheduled to close the sale on the 30th of the month. Bernie's friend, Celia, begged Bernie to let her buy the house instead, so Bernie assigned the contract to Celia. One week before closing, Celia changed her mind about buying. In this circumstance:
    a. Celia will have to buy the house
    b. the contract is void
    c. Bernie will have to buy the house
    d. the seller doesn't have to sell

18. Which of these actions will terminate a contract?
    a. The seller dies.
    b. The contract is assigned without a novation.
    c. There is no binder deposit.
    d. The contract is not in writing.

19. In Florida, only an attorney can prepare legal documents. However, in which of these contracts can a real estate licensee carefully fill in the blanks?
    a. deeds
    b. notes
    c. leases
    d. options

20. Which of the following laws states that there is a deadline to file a legal complaint against another?
    a. the statute of frauds
    b. the statute of limitations
    c. the operation of law
    d. the legal contract standards law

21. Which statement is true regarding the radon gas disclosure?
    a. The disclosure must be a separate document.
    b. If radon gas is found, the seller must fix it.
    c. All property must be inspected for radon gas.
    d. The buyer can choose to ignore the warning.

RESIDENTIAL MORTGAGES

12

KEY TERMS

acceleration clause	mortgage
assumption	mortgagee
blanket mortgage	mortgagor
buy-down	note
contract for deed (land contract)	novation
deed in lieu of foreclosure	partial release clause
defeasance clause	PITI
discount point	prepayment clause
due on sale clause	prepayment penalty
equity	promissory note
escrow	receivership clause
estoppel certificate	right to reinstate
hypothecation	satisfaction of mortgage
interest	short sale
land development loan	statutory equity of redemption
lien theory	subject to the mortgage
lis pendens	subordination agreement
loan origination fee	takeout commitment
loan servicing	title theory
loan-to-value ratio	

LEARNING OBJECTIVES

After completing this lesson, you will be able to:

- distinguish between title theory and lien theory
- describe the essential elements of the mortgage instrument and the note
- describe the various features of a mortgage including down payment, loan-to-value ratio, equity, interest, loan servicing escrow account, PITI, discount points, and loan origination fee
- explain assignment of a mortgage and the purpose of an estoppel certificate

- explain the foreclosure process and distinguish between judicial and nonjudicial foreclosure
- describe the mortgagee's and the mortgagor's rights in a foreclosure
- calculate loan-to-value ratio
- explain the use of discount points and calculate approximate yield on a loan
- distinguish among the various methods of purchasing mortgaged property

MORTGAGE CONCEPTS: MORTGAGE LAW

A **mortgage** provides security for a note through a process called hypothecation. **Hypothecation** means that the real property is pledged as security for repayment of a loan *without* surrendering possession or giving up ownership of the property. In essence, mortgage is a securitization instrument that places the property (by the borrower) as *collateral* for securing the repayment of the loan. Therefore, it would be safe to remember that a mortgage is collateral.

Coaching Tips

You can also think of a mortgage in the same manner as one would utilize a security deposit for the rental of a living unit. The security deposit protects (in this example) the property owner (to a limited degree) against a tenant not paying the rent or against property damage at the end of the tenancy.

As just stated, whenever a property is hypothecated as security for a loan, the following occurs:

- the owner retains possession and ownership of the property, while
- by holding the mortgage on the property, the lender holds a lien on the property as security for repayment of the loan.

It is interesting to note that the Spanish word *hypoteca* is the word describing a mortgage. It is also the same or similar in other languages such as French or German.

There are two different legal theories concerning the manner in which real property is hypothecated. These theories determine the legal practice used in different states for dealing with real property hypothecation. The two theories are:

1. title theory
2. lien theory

TITLE THEORY

The mortgage is commonly used to secure notes on real property in more than half of the United States, including Florida. It should be noted that there are two types of notes:

1. secured notes (those with collateral)
2. unsecured notes (those with no collateral)

In most of the remaining states, the instrument that is used to secure real property notes is called the deed of trust or trust deed.

In a **title theory** state, there are three parties to a loan secured by real property:

1. trustor (property owner/borrower)
2. trustee (neutral third party appointed by the lender to hold the naked title)
3. beneficiary (lender)

Under the title theory approach, there is no such instrument known as a mortgage. The instrument that is used in place of a mortgage (which is used in a lien theory state) is called a trust deed or deed of trust. In this type of loan, the trustor (borrower) actually conveys/transfers legal title to the property to the beneficiary (lender). The conveyance/transfer is referred to as holding naked title.

It is forbidden for the beneficiary/lender to hold the naked title. Therefore, the beneficiary and trustor give the naked title to an appointed trustee whose sole responsibility within the transaction is to hold the naked title in trust for one party or the other until one of the following events occurs:

1. Upon full satisfaction of the repaid loan, title is reconveyed to the trustor.
2. In the event of a default under the terms of the note and the lapse of any statutory redemption period, title is transferred to the beneficiary.
3. Should the borrower decide to sell the property secured by a trust deed, the lender may require that the note be paid in full at closing. The Trustee, upon satisfaction, would reconvey the trust deed through a reconveyance deed to the Trustor.

A trust deed provides security for a note. Trust deeds are the instruments used in place of a mortgage. This type of instrument is applicable in states that subscribe to the title theory for financing of real property.

In a trust deed, there are two clauses that create the primary difference between the trust deed and a mortgage:

1. the reconveyance clause
2. the power-of-sale clause

The reconveyance clause requires the trustee to reconvey the title to the trustor (the borrower) when the loan has been paid in full. This reconveyance is done with either one of the following:

1. a release deed (a type of quitclaim deed)
2. a marginal release

The marginal release is a notation of satisfaction written in the margin of the trust deed in the public records (see Figure 12.1).

The power-of-sale clause provides for nonjudicial foreclosure. It allows the property to be sold at public auction in the event of default by the borrower without going to court. The sale is called a trustee's sale. The power-of-sale clause (and its resulting nonjudicial foreclosure) is the primary difference between lien theory and title theory.

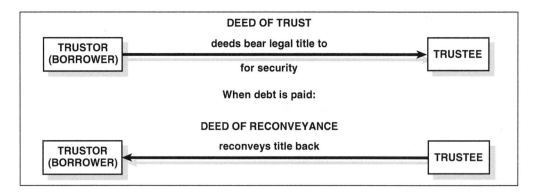

FIGURE 12.1
Source: © 2021 Mbition LLC

Coaching Tips

The title given to and held by the trustee is referred to as *naked title*. The naked title is held by the trustee as security for the beneficiary until the debt is paid. During the borrowing period and as long as the trustor/borrower is not in default under the terms and conditions of the trust deed, the beneficiary is not permitted to hold or possess the naked title. That is the primary reason for the neutral third party in this transaction—namely, the trustee. This is termed naked title because the trustor/borrower has literally signed the deed to the property in favor of the beneficiary. When the debt is paid in full, the trust deed becomes null and void and the trustee is then required, through the use of a reconveyance deed, to transfer the property back to the trustor unencumbered. This is the equivalent of a satisfaction of repayment of the debt. During the borrowing period, the borrower holds equitable title in the property while the trust deed is in effect.

Coaching Tips

In title theory states the following holds true:

- There is no mortgage—a trust deed is used.
- The borrower is called the trustor.
- The lender is called the beneficiary.
- The neutral third party is called the trustee.
- The trustee is appointed by the lender and not by the borrower.
- The trustee holds the naked title to the property while the note is in effect.
- The trustee reconveys the property back to the trustor upon satisfaction of the terms associated with the note and trust deed.
- Transactions are closed in escrow and not on contract as in lien theory states.

LIEN THEORY

In a **lien theory** state, a transaction consists of:

1. two parties
2. two instruments used within the transaction

Under the lien theory approach to mortgage hypothecation, it is important to understand the following:

1. The legal title remains in the possession of the borrower.
2. The mortgage held by the lender creates a lien on the title in favor of the lender.

Coaching Tips

As is the case with the majority of the states in the union, Florida is a lien theory state.

Loan Instruments: Lien Theory

When real property is sold utilizing any type of financing, two primary documents are always involved in the financing process:

1. the promissory note or bond
2. the mortgage

Coaching Tips

A **note** that is secured by a mortgage is known as a secured note, while a note that is not secured by a mortgage is known as an unsecured note.

Promissory Note (Essential Elements)

A **promissory note** is the instrument whereby the borrower promises to repay money borrowed from the lender. In Florida, a note (signed by an individual) or bond (signed/issued by business entities) must accompany all mortgages. The note acts as the following:

- Prima facie (on face value) evidence of the borrowing. This simply means that the note by itself is evidence of the borrower's debt to the lender.
- It states the terms under which the borrower agrees to repay the loan, such as:
  - the annual interest rate
  - the term of the loan
  - the type of loan (e.g., interest only, fully amortized, partially amortized)
- It is also deemed a negotiable instrument.

A negotiable instrument means that the ownership of the instrument can be transferred to another person, either by sale or gift. A mortgage provides a legally enforceable pledge of property of equal or greater value as security to the lender for repayment on a note by the borrower. It acts as the collateral. As previously stated, it secures the note with the collateralized property.

> ### Coaching Tips
>
> Think of it this way—unless a lender is comfortable with the collateralization of the loan, the lender will not be willing to arrange financing on the purchase of the real property.

A promissory note, note, or bond (the name used for a note with business entity borrowing) will contain specific terms agreed to by the borrower and lender. The note will always contain two primary clauses:

1. a prepayment clause
2. an acceleration clause

Mortgage Instrument

We've just spoken about promissory notes. Now let's examine the second instrument (mortgage) used in lending transactions in lien theory states and the parties thereto.

Parties to the Mortgage

There are two parties to the mortgage:

1. The borrower—The borrower is called the **mortgagor** because the borrower gives/conveys the mortgage (collateral or security) to the lender.
2. The lender—The lender is called the **mortgagee** because the lender is the one to whom the mortgage (collateral or security) is given/conveyed.

> ### Coaching Tips
>
> A good way to remember which party is which in a mortgage is to remember the OR and EE rule. Words that end in OR are the owners or givers of whatever is owned or being given. Words that end in EE are the receivers of whatever is owned or being given.

As previously mentioned in the section entitled lien theory, whenever borrowing on real property occurs, the property owner/borrower, in addition to signing a promissory note evidencing the debt, will also execute a separate instrument called a mortgage. The mortgage acts as the security/collateral agreement necessary to create a note that is now secured by real property (a secured note). When the borrower signs the mortgage instrument, it legally allows the lender to record a lien against the property. The lien constitutes the legal security device the lender requires in exchange for issuing the loan. Remember:

- A note without a mortgage means the note is unsecured (i.e., credit card debt).
- A mortgage without a note is meaningless because a mortgage is simply security for a note.

Satisfaction of Mortgage

Upon full repayment of the terms of the loan and mortgage, the borrower receives a document that reflects same. This document is called a **satisfaction of mortgage**. The satisfaction of mortgage acts as the instrument or vehicle that allows for the removal of the lender's previous lien.

First Mortgages versus Junior Mortgages

When reference is made to a first mortgage or a junior mortgage, these financing terms are generally used to describe and/or to determine the priority of a loan(s) relationship to any other recorded lien on the property.

For example, think of the first recorded mortgage (by date of recording) as being the senior loan, while any subsequent loan such as a second mortgage would be described as a junior mortgage. These financing terms set forth the priority of who will receive compensation and in what order same is received. In the event of a default by the borrower, the priority of recorded liens (particularly to a recorded lien holder) becomes a very important consideration. The first lien would be paid first while all subsequent liens (if any) receive consideration in the order of their recording. This means that a second lien may or may not be paid some, all or any, of the amounts owed them. It is no secret that all institutional financing seeks a first position and very rarely will accept any position other than a first position.

Coaching Tips

Think of the aforementioned in the same manner as you would when addressing a father and a son, both bearing the same names. Whereas the father is referred to as the senior, the son is referred to as the junior. One is deemed to be older by the suffix granted after the name. The aforementioned subject is exactly the same except that rather than referencing people and their age, we are referencing loans, their age, and the relationship to each other concerning priority.

Subordination Agreements

A **subordination agreement** is a legal document used to make the claim of one party junior to (or inferior to) a claim in favor of another. It is generally used to grant first lien status to a lienholder who would otherwise be secondary to another party, with the approval of the party that would otherwise have first lien. Typically subordination arises when there are two existing mortgages, a first mortgage and a second mortgage, and the mortgagor intends to refinance the first mortgage. If the holder of the second mortgage does not subordinate the lien of its mortgage to the new mortgage, the new lender will not refinance the first mortgage. However, the second mortgage holder does not want to release its mortgage and refile, due to additional costs and priority problems, so it will subordinate its lien to the lien of the replacement mortgage.

Loans usually take priority based on the date on which they are recorded in the public records. Take these, for example:

- What is commonly referred to as a *first mortgage* is the one that was recorded first for a particular property. We just learned earlier that another name for a first mortgage is a *senior mortgage*.
- What is commonly referred to as a *second mortgage* is the one that was recorded second for a particular property. We also just learned earlier that another name for any mortgage recorded after a senior mortgage is a *junior mortgage*.
- The exception to this rule would be a clause that waives the right to priority. This clause is called a subordination clause.

For example, in a lease this is the clause that states that the rights of the leasehold interest are secondary to that of a previous or subsequent lien or interest in the real property. A subordination clause is a major requirement by all lenders on income-producing, leased property. Institutional lenders do not take second or subsequent lien positions when originating loans. A property containing leases without a subordination clause may render the property unfinanceable.

Another example of a subordination agreement would be when a long-term ground lease is in place on unimproved land and the lessee/tenant seeks a construction loan to build an improvement. Due to the landowner's first interest in the property, by virtue of land ownership, the lender will require the lessor/landowner to subordinate their first position to a second junior position. In the development world, this is a common occurrence.

ESSENTIAL ELEMENTS OF THE MORTGAGE

Important mortgage provisions include the promise to repay the loan, taxes, insurance, and the covenant of good repair; these are a variety of promises that a borrower must make to a lender. These promises or covenants are contained in both the note and the mortgage.

In addition to and supplementing the aforementioned, a mortgage may also contain the following:

- one or more covenants, which are promises made by the mortgagor to the mortgagee
- a due on sale clause (also known as an alienation clause)

There are several other covenants that may be included in a mortgage, such as:

- Covenant to pay taxes—As previously discussed, the borrower promises to keep all taxes paid as the taxes come due. In most if not all loans secured by a mortgage, the lender will usually impound an amount necessary to cover the property tax payment (usually 1/12 of the amount required with each payment). This impounded amount is over and above the monthly payment for principal and interest. The portion of the additional payment is placed into an interest-bearing escrow account benefiting the borrower. The lender pays the property tax for the borrower from that account. This event does not occur when a borrower can demonstrate 100 percent prepayment of the taxes. The lender is concerned that the property tax is always current. As previously learned, property tax liens come before all others. This could defeat the lien perfected by the lender.
- Covenant of insurance—As previously discussed, the borrower promises to keep the property adequately insured during the life of the mortgage. As in property taxes, the lender will usually impound an amount necessary to cover the property insurance payment (usually 1/12 of the amount required with each payment). This impounded amount is over and above the monthly payment for principal and interest and property taxes. As in the case of the taxes, the portion of the additional payment is placed into an interest-bearing escrow account benefiting the borrower.
- The lender pays the property insurance premium for the borrower from this account.
- This event does not occur when a borrower can demonstrate 100 percent prepayment of the annual property insurance premium. The lender is concerned that the property insurance is always current. This will protect the lender's lien in the event of fire/casualty issues to the property. The total of the principle, interest, taxes, and insurance is referred to as PITI.
- Covenant against removal—The borrower promises not to remove any of the improvements to the property, which would reduce its value as collateral. Any removal or addition to the property will generally require the lender's prior written consent.
- Covenant of good repair—The borrower promises to maintain all improvements in good repair and not to permit them to deteriorate. This is also a concern for the lender. A lender is more concerned with the retention of the property's value than anything else. In the event of a borrower default on the terms of the mortgage, the property's value will be the lender's only form of outstanding balance recovery.

- Covenant of reentry—The borrower promises to allow the lender to enter the premises at reasonable hours to ascertain that all other covenants are being adhered to. The lender rarely exercises this right.

Should the mortgagor (borrower) fail to adhere to these covenants, the mortgagee (the lender) may declare the note to be due and payable by involving the acceleration clause and demanding full and immediate payment.

Essential Elements

There are a number of elements that may appear in a mortgage instrument, but the following will always appear:

- the parties to the mortgage
- a granting clause in a mortgage, which:
    - is similar to the granting clause contained within a deed
    - transfers legal title from the borrower, in title theory states
    - creates a title lien, in lien theory states
- a defeasance clause (which gives the borrower the right to defeat the lien by paying off the loan in accordance with the terms and conditions of the promissory note)

Other Mortgage Provisions

Prepayment Clause

The **prepayment clause** contained within the mortgage will provide the borrower with the ability to prepay the outstanding principal balance (in part or in whole), either with or without a penalty. However, there are four possible scenarios that can arise concerning the prepayment clause within a mortgage:

1. The note may not be prepaid at all.
2. The note may not be prepaid for a fixed period (lock-in clause); however, subsequent to the lock-in period, it may be prepaid.
3. The note may be prepaid with *no* penalty at any time.
4. The note may be prepaid, but a penalty must be paid for doing so.

In this case, the penalty is called a **prepayment penalty**. Whereas a prepayment *clause* is required in a mortgage, the penalty becomes optional on the part of the lender. Some commercial loans are issued subject to the lender receiving *yield maintenance*. This means that the borrower may prepay the outstanding balance in part or in whole at any time; however, the penalty for prepaying would equal the total amount of interest that the lender would have received had that loan lived to its maturity.

Acceleration Clause

The **acceleration clause** allows the lender to demand full and immediate payment (accelerate the payment) if the borrower fails to meet all terms of the note. The acceleration clause also allows the lender to couple other clauses contained within the mortgage document. For example, by invoking the alienation clause (or due on sale clause, described shortly), when a property secured by a nonassumable mortgage is sold, the acceleration clause will also come into play. The lender accelerates the remaining principal balance of the loan upon the closing of title. When the acceleration clause is invoked, the lender is said to *call* in the note.

Although the promissory note is evidence of the existence of the loan, it is essentially only a promise to repay a loan. It does not provide any collateral as security that the loan will be repaid. Because of this, the lender will require that a mortgage be executed to provide this security. For the collateral to specifically apply to a loan, the mortgage will always reference the promissory note.

Right to Reinstate

Pursuant to Florida law and prior to a lender exercising the right to accelerate the maturity of the note, a mortgagor/borrower has the **right to reinstate** the mortgage by paying all the past due amounts on the mortgage. This would include but may not be limited to:

- principal
- interest
- late fees
- possible lender costs for collection

Alienation Clause (Due on Sale Clause)

The word *alienate* means "to transfer," such as transferring property from one to another. The alienation clause permits the mortgagee to call in the note if the mortgagor transfers the property either through sale or gift. This clause is commonly referred to as the **due on sale clause**. It is used to prohibit the assumption of the mortgage loan by a buyer or the use of a wraparound mortgage.

As a memory device, think of the alienation clause as *alienating* the rest of the world from the benefits of the loan, thereby making the loan unassumable by any other person outside of the original borrower.

It is important to note that in a blanket mortgage that contains a partial release clause, the due on sale clause does not operate in the same fashion. First, a **blanket mortgage** is any mortgage that covers more than one parcel of property. Blanket mortgages usually contain partial release clauses. A **partial release clause** allows the owner to:

- sell off lots or units in a condominium
- have the lender remove the lien for each sold parcel

This type of loan and clause is common in a subdivision without the due on sale clause calling in the entire outstanding amount.

Defeasance Clause

The **defeasance clause** in a mortgage:

- is the right of the mortgagor (borrower) to defeat the lien held by the mortgagee/lender by fulfilling all the terms and conditions of the loan (In essence, the defeasance clause in the mortgage provides the borrower with the right to defeat the lien by paying off the loan.)
- makes the mortgage null and void when paid in full

Common Mortgage Features

You have learned that a mortgage is an instrument that provides collateral as the security for a loan. It is used in conjunction with a promissory note, which is evidence of borrowing. Let's now examine some of the common features and/or requirements contained in mortgages.

Down Payment

In each loan transaction structured as a mortgage on real property, there are generally two components that make up the entire amount of the loan:

1. lender loan amount (debt financing)
2. borrower's down payment (equity or initial investment)

The amount of down payment will be established by the terms of the loan and will represent the amount of **equity** or borrower discretionary funds necessary for the borrower to bring on the day of closing. The amount of down payment will always be affected by two general components:

1. loan amount
2. percentage of down payment required

The aforementioned is arrived at through loan-to-value ratios (discussed next).

Loan-to-Value Ratio versus Borrower Equity

Loan-to-value ratio (LTV) is the amount of loan (in percentage terms) that a lender would be willing to loan to a borrower on real property. In formula form:

LTV = loan amount ÷ the lesser of the appraised value or purchase price of the property (whichever is less)

It is important to understand that the LTV by a lender is always calculated at the lesser of:

1. the contract purchase price of the property to the buyer/borrower; or
2. the appraised value of the property

Generally, and the majority of the time, lenders look to the appraised value for LTV determination and loan underwriting. However, when values are rising in a changing market environment, lenders will utilize the contract purchase price as their benchmark for originating the loan amount. This event occurs when the appraised value is greater than the contract sale price.

It should also be noted that by law, banks may not originate greater than loan-to-value ratios of 80/20 without charging a premium for mortgage insurance. This premium applies to any amount that exceeds the 80 percent borrowed amount ratio. For example, a buyer requires 90 percent financing with a 10 percent down payment (or initial investment, as it is sometimes called). Whereby a lender quotes an interest rate of 7 percent on the 80 percent loan portion, the borrower will pay a higher interest rate amount for the overage amount. That interest premium disappears when the LTV reaches 78 percent or below. The added premium is called private mortgage insurance (PMI).

In commercial transactions, when a borrower lacks funds necessary for a down payment, equity financing is available. These loans are commonly referred to as mezzanine financing.

Interest

When one borrows money from a lender, there are two general considerations and components that constitute the borrower's repayment to the lender:

- principal
- interest

While principal represents the original dollar amount borrowed, interest is the amount of rent that the borrower pays the lender for use of their funds. This is representative of the time value of money. **Interest** represents the time value of money due the lender for the outstanding principal balance. In simple terms, think of an interest payment in the same manner as you would the payment of rent. A tenant will pay a property owner rent for use of the owner's property. The borrower is paying a prescribed percentage rate to the lender as rent for the use of the lender's funds. This interest or rent payment continues until the borrower reaches a zero balance for principal funds originated by the lender.

Loan servicing is a business that mirrors that of property management services. Loan servicing occurs when a lender or other servicing organization manages the collections of principal, interest, and impounds or escrowed amounts that may be used to pay for property taxes or insurance. These collections from a given borrower are normally for the benefit of others. This can occur when the originating lender sells the loan in the secondary market to investors such as Fannie Mae, Ginnie Mae, or Freddie Mac. The loan seller normally retains the right to service the loan and to collect a fee for same. Once payments are collected by the loan servicing party, the funds are then distributed to the respective party(s) that have purchased same.

Escrow (Impound) Account/Principal, Interest, Taxes, and Insurance

When loans on real property are originated, in addition to principal and interest payments, the borrower is responsible to pay for both property tax and property insurance. Generally, these items become lender **escrow** amounts (impound) that are over and above the cost of principal and interest payments. When this occurs, the monthly payment now takes the form of **PITI**:

- Principal
- Interest
- Taxes
- Insurance

In order to best protect the lender's lien, most lenders (if not all) will require the borrower to deposit monies into an escrow account primarily to compensate for the cost of property tax and property insurance. It should be noted that at all times, property tax liens trump and supersede all other liens. This may even include an IRS tax lien that would be secondary to that of the property tax lien. Therefore, as a result of the aforementioned, any unpaid tax on a property exposes both the property owner and lender to losing that property to the municipality in a tax foreclosure or a tax lien sale. The same can be said for a property that does not have an insurance policy on the structure. In the event of a property catastrophe such as fire, the lender's lien is greatly affected by the lack of insurance and proceeds to rebuild the structure.

Earlier in this chapter, we learned that the borrower covenants to continuously keep the property in good repair. In fact, most mortgages will require the borrower to obtain the lender's consent prior to making any improvements to the mortgaged property. Where this may sound unreasonable to a property owner/borrower, remember that the lender will usually be the party that stands the most risk to lose in these transactions. In most lending transactions, the borrower has less at risk monetarily than the lending party. This is based upon the amount of the loan as it relates to the borrower's initial investment or equity (loan to value ratio).

Discount Points

When loans are originated by either institutional lenders or mortgage bankers, it is not unusual for the borrower to be charged an amount(s) that appears in the form of discount points. A **discount point** represents 1 percent of the borrowed amount that is paid up front as a fee by the borrower to the lender. It is considered as pre-paid interest. As a general rule of thumb on a 25-to 30-year loan, one discount point may equal up to 0.125%, or 1/8 percent on the yield realized by the lender. Simply put, lenders charge discount points in order to enhance the return they receive on loans they originate. Payment of discount points can also be a way that lenders can offer below market interest rates to borrowers in need of same.

For example, assume market interest rates for financing are at 5%. Assume further that a borrower can only make an investment work if he/she obtained a loan at 4.5%. By using the above rule concerning the payment of discount points, by paying the lender approximately four discount points at closing of the loan, the lender most likely would originate the loan at 4.5% as opposed to the market rate of 5 percent. This rate reduction practice is commonly referred to as a **buy-down**. Given the aforementioned rule of thumb, the four discount points paid at closing of the loan would equate to an additional 4/8 or 1/2%. Therefore, using this rule of thumb concerning the payment of discount points, a 4.5% interest rate with four discount points is really the same loan as 5 percent with no points.

Loan Origination Fee

Previously, we learned that discount points act as a tool for the borrower to buy down the rate of interest as needed. For the lender, we learned that from a yield standpoint, payment of points increases the lender's ultimate return.

In addition to the payment of discount points, a borrower may be faced with the payment of a loan origination fee at closing of a loan. The **loan origination fee** is commonly associated as being a processing or servicing fee for arranging the financing over and above the cost of discount points. The amount of the fee is normally quoted to the borrower by the lender or mortgage broker (as the case may be) at the point an application for a loan is submitted.

It is noteworthy to mention that prior to implementation of TILA-RESPA (Truth in Lending Act and Real Estate Settlement Procedures Act), discount points and origination fees appeared as charges from a lender on a HUD-1 Settlement Closing Statement. As of October 2015, this is no longer the case. Under the new TILA-RESPA, the HUD-1 and Good Faith Estimate are replaced with two new forms:

1. the Closing Disclosure
2. the Loan Estimate

In addition, under the Truth-In-Lending Simplification Act (TILA or TILSRA), the lender is also required to make certain disclosures to a borrower who fills out an application for:

- a loan
- an application for the extension of credit

In either of the events above, the required disclosures under TILA/TILSRA would include and may not be limited to:

- the dollar amount that the cost of credit will cost the borrower (finance charge)
- interest or finance charge must be expressed in the form of Annual Percentage Rate (APR)
- the amount of credit that will extended to the borrower
- the total amount the borrower will have paid after all scheduled payments are made

The aforementioned must be provided to the borrower within three days from receipt of the application by the lender.

Take-out Commitment

Construction loans are used to construct an improvement on real property. In certain circumstances, a **land development loan** can be viewed as:

- another form of construction financing
- acquisition financing

Furthermore, these loans provide high risk to lenders and are always short-term loans.

A **takeout commitment** is a long-term loan arranged in the manner of a mortgage on real property. It is used to arrange the permanent financing mostly on new construction. It is the takeout (loan) commitment that provides the developer with the long-term financing necessary to fund or pay off the original construction loan. It is not unusual for the lender of the construction loan to also be the originator of the takeout commitment. With that in mind, prior to commencing with construction of a new improvement or major rehabbing of an existing project, both loans are normally arranged for simultaneously.

Assignment of the Mortgage

When a lender originates a loan he/she intends to sell, the assignment of the mortgage is the lender's right to transfer the mortgage to a third party. In most cases when mortgages are sold the new mortgage holder will notify the borrower that he/she has purchased the loan and all future payments be directed to him/her.

Estoppel Certificate

The **estoppel certificate** is a document that is completed by a *borrower* to acknowledge the full amount of the debt that the borrower owes. It is usually used when a lender is about to sell the mortgage note and the purchaser wants to verify the amount and terms of the note as well as the borrower's acknowledgment of the debt. Estoppel certificates are also used by owners of income-producing property to certify the rent roll for the buyer. Most will leases require that the tenant periodically execute estoppel certificates in the favor of the landlord. These certificates are used in two primary instances:

1. when the owner is selling the property
2. when the owner is placing debt on the property

In the first instance above, the buyer would normally require the seller to certify the rent roll or the income proceeds received from the rentals. Investors purchase income, not the brick and mortar. The improvement is merely the vehicle that houses the income. Therefore, the only instrument that allows the seller to oblige the buyer is the estoppel certificate. This certificate is ultimately executed by each tenant.

In the second instance above, the lender requires the certificate for the same reason as in the first instance, except that the lender is not purchasing the property. The lender is originating a loan predicated upon the income stream to that property.

> ### Coaching Tips
>
> In a lease, an estoppel certificate is the document a tenant provides to the landlord to certify the following:
>
> - The lease is in full force and effect.
> - The amount of rent currently being paid is in fact the rent being paid.
> - The amount and form of security deposit currently being held by the landlord is acknowledged as correct.
> - The tenant has no offsets, credit, or defenses to the payment of rent.

Methods of Purchasing Mortgaged Property

Before the 1960s, few mortgages included an alienation (due on sale) clause. Because of the rapid rise of interest rates since that time, alienation clauses have become common. Today, virtually all conventional (nongovernment) loans include an alienation clause that enables the lender to require the loan be paid in full upon the alienation (transfer) of the ownership. Alternatively, the lender may choose to increase the interest rate on the assumed loan to the current market rate. Before 1986, Federal Housing Administration (FHA) loans were freely assumable and did not require the new borrower to qualify for the loan. Before 1988, Department of Veterans Affairs (VA) loans were freely assumable and did not require the new borrower to qualify. In 1986 for FHA loans and 1988 for VA loans, changes were made that placed some restrictions on the assumption of these loans. Now both FHA and VA loans may require the buyer to qualify to assume the loan.

Subject to the Mortgage

Subject to the mortgage is the direct opposite of assumption. In a subject to the mortgage transaction, the buyer is not assuming the loan but merely making the payments associated with that loan. In order for this arrangement to occur, the existing loan must not contain a due on sale clause. In this arrangement, the seller (as the original borrower):

- will give up possession of the property to the buyer
- transfers the deed for the property to the buyer
- remains contingently liable for performance on the loan

The buyer merely makes the payment for the loan. In the event of a default by the buyer, the seller is responsible to the bank. The buyer has no relationship whatsoever with the bank.

On closing of the deal and on the closing disclosure statement, niether documentary stamps on the note nor the intangible taxes are computed (closing disclosure statements will be discussed in Chapter 14).

This arrangement should not be confused with a contingency on receiving financing on a purchase and sale contract.

Changing Loan Balance: Assumed Mortgages

Often, the most troublesome part of dealing with a loan **assumption** (which is the transaction when a new borrower assumes repayment responsibilities for the original borrower) is the fact that the loan balance on the assumed loan changes between the time a sales contract is signed and the closing of the sale. This problem occurs when the purchaser agrees to buy the property at a fixed price by assuming a loan. The difference in the selling price and the remaining balance is the amount of cash that the buyer must pay the seller. The problem arises when the buyer doesn't realize that the amount of cash that he/she will have to pay may increase if the loan does not close right away. Let's look at why this happens.

Example The buyer agrees to buy a property for $100,000 by assuming the seller's loan. At the time the contract is signed, the situation looks like this:

Sales price	$100,000
Remaining balance	−80,000
Cash required	$ 20,000

By the time the sale is closed, the situation may look like this:

Sales price	$100,000
Remaining balance	−79,000
Cash required	$ 21,000

The difference in the cash required at closing, which the buyer did not expect, results because the payments made on the loan between the signing of the sales contract and the closing date reduced the remaining principal. (The amount of reduction used in this example is larger than normal in order to illustrate the point.)

Because of this situation, there are two ways a loan assumption can be handled:

1. a loan assumption with price to control
2. a loan assumption with cash to control

The situation described above is an example of a loan assumption with price to control. In other words, *price to control* means that the selling price will be set, and the selling price (along with the changing loan balance) will *control* the amount of cash to be paid by the buyer. In a loan assumption with cash to control, the buyer and seller do not agree on a fixed sales price. Instead, they agree that the buyer will pay the seller a fixed amount of cash and assume the remaining loan balance as of the date of closing.

The situation as of the date of the contract and closing would look like this:

	Date of Contract		Date of Closing
Remaining balance	$80,000	Remaining balance	$79,000
Cash to be paid	$20,000	Cash to be paid	$20,000
Sales price	$100,000	Sales price	$99,000

The contract calls for a fixed amount of cash to be paid, which remains at $20,000. The loan balance decreases by the time the closing occurs. The result is that the actual selling price remains the same. However, the amount the buyer needs on the date of closing increases by the amount the seller reduces the mortgage by payments applied to the principal.

The contract calls for a fixed amount of cash to be paid, which remains at $20,000. The loan balance decreases by the time the closing occurs. The result is the actual selling price at closing is less than the amount it would have been if the sale had closed the day the contract was signed. In this situation, the amount of cash paid is set at a specific amount that does not change. The remaining loan balance and the actual sales price do change between the time of the signing of the sales contract and the closing date. As a result, the amount of cash paid controls the selling price, and this situation is referred to as cash to control.

Effects of the Due on Sale Clause

You learned earlier in this chapter that the alienation clause or due on sale clause permits the mortgagee to call in the note if the mortgagor transfers the property either through sale or gift. It is used to prohibit the assumption of the mortgage loan by a buyer or the use of a wraparound mortgage.

Novation

The term **novation** represents a substitution of a new agreement for an old agreement. It can also be a substitution of a new party for an old party. If novation is granted, it provides a release from a previous obligation. Examples of novation include but are not limited to:

- Loans—Buyer A wishes to assume Seller B's existing mortgage. Seller B is willing to allow the assumption with the condition that Seller B receives novation (release) from the lender. Without novation from the lender, Seller B would remain contingently liable for any default by the assuming party (Buyer A).

- Leases—Tenant A wishes to assign his/her lease to Tenant B. The landlord is willing to approve the assignment from A to B. In order to avoid remaining on the hook to the landlord after the assignment commences, Tenant A would require novation (release) from the landlord.

Contract for Deed (Land Contract or Installment Sales Contract)

It is not uncommon for a lender to refuse a loan for the acquisition of unimproved land. Real estate sales of unimproved or improved land can be made under a contract for deed (a.k.a. a land contract or installment sales contract). Unlike regular contracts of purchase and sale where the full purchase price is paid on the day of closing and the deed is transferred to the buyer, a contract for deed operates in a different fashion. In a **contract for deed**:

- Upon contract signing and payment of the down payment, the buyer (vendee) receives possession of the property as well as equitable title.
- The buyer continues to pay installments over the term of the contract until all payments have been made.
- The seller (vendor) retains possession of the deed as collateral until all sums have been paid and other contract terms have been met.

A contract for deed can be viewed as a financing instrument as the seller acts as the lender. Furthermore, a contract for deed bears resemblance to a "layaway plan" arranged with a retailer. For example:

- In a layaway plan, the selling retailer will retain ownership/possession of the article until all installments called for under the plan have been paid. Once all payments are made, the article and bill of sale are transferred to the buyer/vendee.
- Under a contract for deed:
    - the seller grants possession of the property
    - the buyer has equitable title
    - the seller retains the deed as collateral until all payments are received under the terms of the contract

Advantages of utilizing a contract for deed include but are not limited to:

- The seller is only responsible for capital gains taxes on the amounts received in the year received.
- The buyer receives financing from the seller rather than a conventional lender or mortgage banker.
- Closing costs to the buyer are minimized using seller financing as opposed to conventional lending practices.

Disadvantages of utilizing a contract for deed include but are not limited to the following:

- Buyer only receives possession and not the deed to the property until all payments have been made.
- The seller, unless the contract is recorded or restricts the seller, can pledge the property covered by the contract for deed to a lender for unrelated financing. Should the seller subsequently default under the other financing arrangement, this event may place the buyer in jeopardy of his/her priority of rights to the property.

DEFAULT: CONSEQUENCES OF DEFAULT

Foreclosure

Foreclosure is a legal procedure that is implemented when a borrower defaults on a loan secured by real property. Once the foreclosure has occurred, the property is sold in order to satisfy the debt. There are two types of foreclosures:

1. judicial foreclosure
2. nonjudicial foreclosure

Judicial Foreclosure

Judicial foreclosure is the most common form of foreclosure. It requires that the lender go to court to foreclose. The foreclosure proceeding serves two purposes:

1. The lender obtains possession of the property.
2. The equity of the owner/borrower is liquidated.

In order to conduct a foreclosure sale, liquidation of the owner/borrower's equity of the property becomes as important as obtaining possession. The foreclosure proceeding provides the vehicle for the lender to subsequently conduct a foreclosure sale. The proceeds from the foreclosure sale will go toward satisfying (in part or in whole) the unpaid note amount. The foreclosure process includes the following ten steps:

1. The mortgagee/lender invokes the acceleration clause, thereby making the entire balance due.
2. A title search on the property is conducted.
3. A notice of lis pendens is filed that informs the public that there is an action pending.
4. A receiver may also be appointed to remove the owner from daily management of the property. This is done to:
   a. preserve any income attributable to the property
   b. preserve the property's condition during the foreclosure process (This right falls under the **receivership clause** of the mortgage.)

5. A lawsuit is filed.
6. If the court rules in favor of the lender, a public auction is held to sell the property. A public notice advertises the sale of the property by public auction.
7. Once the sale is completed, the court clerk is then required to file the certificate of sale with the court. Assuming all has proceeded in accordance with the laws governing the foreclosure sale and the highest possible price has been obtained, the court will approve the sale.
8. The lender is paid from the proceeds of the sale.
9. The buyer receives the title.
10. Any monies that are left over from the foreclosure sale after satisfying all outstanding liens against the property are then given to the mortgagor/borrower.

In most states, the sale of foreclosed property is usually conducted by the county sheriff and is often called a sheriff's sale. At the sheriff's sale, the lender will usually bid the principal amount remaining on the loan because of the following reasons:

- A lower bid by anyone else would not satisfy the outstanding balance of the loan.
- The lender would be paying itself for the loan.
- All bidders other than the lender must pay cash.

Deficiency Judgment

Loans secured by mortgages are originated in one of two forms:

1. recourse loans
2. nonrecourse loans

When a recourse loan is originated, the borrower is personally guaranteeing full performance in the repayment of the note. This type of loan contains a clause within the mortgage called the deficiency clause. This clause allows the lender to recover from the defaulting borrower the difference between the proceeds from the foreclosure sale versus the outstanding note balance.

If a foreclosure sale recovers less than the outstanding balance amount, the lender would seek a deficiency judgment from the courts to enforce a deficiency clause. If a deficiency judgment is obtained, the lender may seek recovery of the differential from the original borrower. The amount of the deficiency judgment is limited to the amount of the outstanding debt that is not recovered.

Nonrecourse loans contain a clause commonly referred to as an exculpation clause. This clause removes any personal guarantee and performance on the part of the borrower. Therefore, the lender may only look to the property for recovery of the unpaid principal balance and not to the borrower for any proceeds resulting from the borrower's default on the loan.

> ## Coaching Tips
>
> A deficiency judgment clause would only appear in a recourse loan.
>
> A nonrecourse loan would contain an exculpatory clause, which means that the lender may only look to proceeds of the property (if any) as repayment for any unpaid debt resulting from foreclosure on the borrower.

Excess from Sale

If the property sells for more than the debt, the excess amount goes to the satisfaction of any other secured and recorded liens. If there are no other outstanding recorded unpaid liens on the property, the remaining money is given to the mortgagor (the owner who defaulted).

Statutory Equity of Redemption

Some states give a borrower a period of time after foreclosure to repay the debt and take back ownership of the property. This is called **statutory equity of redemption**. As in most lien theory states, Florida law provides for redemption rights only up to the time of the foreclosure sale.

Deed in Lieu of Foreclosure (Non-Judicial Foreclosure)

In some cases, the borrower may avoid foreclosure by signing the property over to the lender. This is done using a document called a **deed in lieu of foreclosure**. (A deed in lieu of foreclosure is also commonly referred to as a *friendly foreclosure*.) The instrument conveys all rights, title, and interest held by the borrower to the lender. This action must be approved by the lender in advance before the borrower may use this approach.

Lis Pendens

Lis pendens is a recorded notice of pending legal action or litigation that specifically pertains to a parcel of real property. The notice warns that if anyone acquires the property after the date of recording of the lis pendens, that purchasing party may be bound by the outcome of litigation with the previous selling party. Lis pendens is used to preserve rights while litigation is pending.

Short Sales

A **short sale** is defined as any sale where the note loan balance is greater than the property value at time of sale or at the time of a foreclosure sale. As a direct result of the financial crisis that occurred in 2007, many homeowners found themselves trapped in highly leveraged properties with mortgage balances that exceeded the value of the property. When this occurs, the property or mortgage is said to be "upside down." As just stated, this means that the loan balance is greater than the value of the property. Due to this dilemma, any homeowners wishing to sell their property would find themselves trapped.

Given the aforementioned events, a seller of property that was upside down needed the permission of the lender to conclude a sale at less than the outstanding balance of the mortgage. If the lender approved, the sale could proceed. This, is commonly referred to as a short sale.

Summary

Whether one purchases a home or invests in income-producing property, financing usually is involved. The lending documents and their contents become critical aspects for both the success of the homeowner and the investor. Remember that Florida is a lien theory state that encompasses a two-party, two-instrument transaction. The two parties are the mortgagor/borrower and the mortgagee/lender. The two instruments are the promissory note acting as evidence of the borrowing, and the mortgage acting as the collateral/security pledged by the mortgagor/borrower to repay the loan. There are many loan options to fit the needs of the borrower. Prior to a lender originating a loan, the borrower must pass certain qualifying lender requirements. These requirements must meet loan underwriting standards.

Review Questions

1. In a title theory state:
   a. The borrower holds the title.
   b. The mortgagor holds the title.
   c. The trustee holds the title.
   d. The title company holds the title.

2. Which of the following is true in a lien theory state, such as Florida?
   a. The lender holds the property until the note is paid.
   b. The buyer owns the property, while the lender has a lien.
   c. The borrower gets a mortgage to buy the property.
   d. The buyer owns the mortgage and the lender owns the note.

3. Mortgages, like stocks and bonds, are negotiable instruments. When mortgages are sold in the secondary market, the selling of the mortgage is accomplished via:
   a. assignment of mortgage
   b. hypothecation
   c. the subordination agreement
   d. a letter of estoppel

4. The clause contained in a mortgage that can effect whether or not a loan may be paid off prior to its maturity date is best described as:
   a. an exculpatory clause
   b. the prepayment clause
   c. the due on sale clause
   d. a prepayment penalty clause

5. The clause in a mortgage that requires a new buyer to find her own financing is the:
   a. subordination clause
   b. exculpatory clause
   c. alienation/due on sale clause
   d. prepayment penalty clause

6. The defeasance clause in a mortgage requires the lender to:
   a. pay the debt in full when the property is sold
   b. record a satisfaction of mortgage when the note is paid off in full
   c. pay the entire balance in case of default
   d. precollect taxes and insurance

7. When Tudor Investment purchased a mortgage from Jack's Finance, the company ordered a letter of estoppel. This document:
   a. legally transfers the ownership of the mortgage
   b. legally establishes the remaining balance of the loan
   c. notifies the buyer of the new owner of the mortgage
   d. allows the investor to change the interest rate

8. A buyer is in default on the note. This allows the lender to:
   a. commence with a foreclosure proceeding
   b. sell the property to someone else
   c. sue for all of the back payments that are owed
   d. seize the property in lieu of the debt

9. Foreclosure is a judicial process and is lengthy and expensive to the lender. Once the foreclosure has begun, the buyer has a right to stop the foreclosure by paying all back payments, the interest on the money that is owed, and the expenses the lender has paid in the foreclosure process. This right to stop foreclosure and regain the ownership of the property is known as:
   a. the right to reinstate
   b. the acceleration clause
   c. the receivership clause
   d. the equity right of redemption

10. A monthly payment for real property that includes payments for insurance and taxes as well as scheduled repayment of the debt is known as:
    a. PITI
    b. wraparound payment
    c. taxes and insurance
    d. PMI

11. A property sale in which the seller holds the title until the buyer has completed the stated requirements in the contract is known as a:
    a. wraparound mortgage
    b. lease with an option to buy
    c. contract for deed
    d. reverse annuity mortgage

12. When Jackson defaulted on the note he signed in order to purchase a resort hotel, the lender had the property sold through a foreclosure proceeding. The sale didn't bring enough money to satisfy the note. The lender had no further recourse and absorbed the loss because of a clause in the mortgage known as the:
    a. subordination clause
    b. acceleration clause
    c. exculpatory clause
    d. satisfaction of mortgage

13. In the purchase of real property, the instrument that acts as evidence of the borrowing and obligates the mortgagor for the debt is the:
    a. mortgage
    b. note
    c. letter of estoppel
    d. alienation clause

14. A deficiency judgment occurs:
    a. in a non-recourse loan
    b. in the defeasance clause
    c. in a recourse loan
    d. none of these

15. When borrowing money, which of the following represents the borrower's initial investment?
    a. the down-payment
    b. the loan
    c. the earnest deposit
    d. none of these

16. The amount of loan (in percentage terms) that a lender would be willing to loan to a borrower on real property is determined by which of the following?
    a. sale amount
    b. loan to value ratio
    c. appraisal
    d. the greater of a or c

17. Which of the following represents a substitution of a new agreement for an old agreement or a new party for an old party?
    a. assumption agreement
    b. novation
    c. due on sale
    d. alienation

18. Which of the following is the most common form of foreclosure
    a. non-judicial
    b. friendly
    c. mutual
    d. judicial

19. Steele wants to sell a lot in his new subdivision to Jones. Steele will need his lender to remove their lien on the lot to Jones. Which of the following loans provides the release?
    a. blanket mortgage loan
    b. wraparound loan
    c. package loan
    d. buy-down loan

20. Which of the following describes a loan that covers more than one parcel of property?
    a. purchase money loan
    b. reverse annuity loan
    c. wraparound loan
    d. blanket mortgage loan

MORTGAGE MARKET OPERATIONS

13

KEY TERMS

adjustable rate mortgage (ARM)
amortized mortgage
balloon payment
biweekly mortgage
conforming loan
disintermediation
home equity loan
index
intermediation
level payment plan mortgage
lifetime cap
margin
mortgage broker

mortgage fraud
mortgage loan originator
mortgage insurance premium (MIP)
negative amortization
package mortgage
partially amortized/balloon mortgage
payment cap
periodic cap
purchase money mortgage (PMM)
reverse annuity loan
teaser rate
up-front mortgage insurance premium (UFMIP)

LEARNING OBJECTIVES

After completing this lesson, you will be able to:

- describe the mechanics of an adjustable rate mortgage and the components of an ARM
- describe the features of an amortized mortgage and amortize a level-payment plan mortgage when given the principal amount, the interest rate, and the monthly payment amount
- distinguish among the various types of mortgages
- describe the characteristics of FHA mortgages and common FHA loan programs
- identify the guarantee feature of VA mortgage loans and the characteristics of VA loan programs
- explain the process of qualifying for a loan and how to calculate qualifying ratios
- distinguish among the primary sources of home financing
- describe the role of the secondary mortgage market and know the features of the major agencies active in the secondary market

- describe the major provisions of the federal laws regarding fair credit and lending procedures
- recognize and avoid mortgage fraud

FEDERAL RESERVE SYSTEM

The Federal Reserve System (the Fed) is the central banker of the United States. The Fed is responsible for the ebb and flow of the country's money supply. The Fed is composed of 12 privately owned regional Federal Reserve banks and a vast number of member commercial banks. The Fed sets reserve requirements for its member commercial banks. The reserve requirements set forth the amount of funds that the member banks must maintain on deposit at any one time. The Fed uses reserve requirements to control the country's money supply. That is, the Fed can decrease the money supply by increasing the reserve requirement (which reduces the amount of money in circulation). Conversely, the Fed can increase the supply of money by decreasing the reserve requirement (thereby increasing the amount in circulation). Reserve requirements also affect the amount of leverage that banks may use at any time to generate funds for loans. The greater the reserve requirement, the less funds available for loans. Due to the scarcity of money in these times, this directly affects interest rates.

Another method to control the money supply that the Fed can institute is open-market operations. This is where the Fed buys and sells securities. A tightening of the money supply occurs through the sale of securities by the Fed. (Funds from the sales are held by the Fed, reducing the money supply.) Conversely, an increase in the money supply occurs when the Fed buys securities.

Another means for the Fed to tighten or loosen the money supply is by raising or lowering the discount rate, which is the interest rate the Fed charges to its member banks for borrowing funds. The higher the rate the Fed charges its member banks, the greater the cost of those funds to individual borrowers. As a result, the number of borrowers is greatly reduced.

FEDERAL HOME LOAN BANK SYSTEM

Whereas the Fed governs commercial banks, the Federal Home Loan Bank System (FHLB) is the regulatory body that governs savings associations (also known as savings and loan associations [S&Ls]). Like the Fed, the FHLB has 12 district member savings associations. The FHLB acts as a provider of reserve credit for the member savings associations, thereby ensuring mortgage fund availability. Member savings associations are chartered through and regulated by the Office of Thrift Supervision.

FEDERAL DEPOSIT INSURANCE CORPORATION

The Federal Deposit Insurance Corporation (FDIC) insures individual accounts up to $250,000 per account that are held within its member institutions.

The FDIC is run by a board of governors. Its powers are derived through the Deposit Insurance Fund and two of its subsidiaries, Savings Association Insurance Fund and the Bank Insurance Fund.

INTERMEDIATION

Intermediation occurs when thrift institutions (commercial banks and savings associations) receive inflows of money into savings accounts. The purpose on the part of the depositor is to achieve high-yielding returns on the investment. These savings in turn are used to invest in larger investment projects. Intermediation results in funds being available for mortgages.

DISINTERMEDIATION

Disintermediation occurs when those same thrift institutions experience the opposite effect of intermediation. Disintermediation occurs when depositors withdraw their savings to achieve higher yielding returns on invested capital through other alternative investment vehicles. Disintermediation results in a scarcity of money available for mortgages.

Coaching Tips

When thrift institutions (commercial banks and savings associations) receive inflows of money into savings accounts, it is called intermediation.

Disintermediation occurs when depositors withdraw their savings in order to achieve higher yielding returns on invested capital within alternative investment vehicles.

PRIMARY AND SECONDARY MORTGAGE MARKETS

There are two major components to the financial markets that provide the source of funds for real estate financing:

1. the primary mortgage market
2. the secondary mortgage market

Primary Mortgage Market

The primary mortgage market is where lenders originate loans. These lenders include:

- savings and loan associations
- commercial banks

- insurance companies
- mortgage companies
- mortgage brokers
- mutual savings banks
- municipal bonds
- credit unions
- pension, endowment, and trust funds

There are five major sources of loans for residential real estate in the primary mortgage market:

1. savings and loan associations
2. mortgage companies
3. mortgage brokers
4. commercial banks
5. private lenders (including sellers)
6. credit unions

Savings and Loan Associations

Savings and loan associations (S&Ls) make loans primarily on residential property. Historically, S&Ls have made the majority of all residential real estate loans; however, in the 1990s, mortgage companies became the primary supplier of such loans. The funds for the loans they make come from their depositors.

Mortgage Companies

It is important to understand that a mortgage acts as collateral for securing a promissory note (secured note). A **mortgage loan originator** is anyone who works with a borrower to obtain a mortgage loan. Normally, this is the mortgage banker or anyone who originates mortgage funds to willing borrowers. A mortgage company (mortgage banker) makes loans, using its own money, and then sells the loans to long-term investors. Once the loans have been sold, the mortgage company often retains the servicing of the loan (collects payments, keeps records, etc.) in return for a fee, such as 0.25 of 1% of the outstanding loan balance. Because mortgage companies sell their loans in the secondary mortgage market, they primarily make government-backed mortgages (such as Veterans Affairs [VA] and Federal Housing Administration [FHA] loans). These loans can be easily sold in the secondary mortgage market. However, mortgage companies have also become active in conventional loans. Since the early 1990s, mortgage companies have become the largest originators of residential real estate loans.

Mortgage Brokers

Mortgage brokers are often confused with mortgage bankers. Mortgage bankers are defined as a company or an individual who originates loans to others with his/her own funds and with the intent of selling those loans to investors. Mortgage brokers do not typically loan their own money, and they usually do not service the loans themselves.

Mortgage brokers bring together borrowers and lenders for a fee, usually based on a percentage of the loan. The lender then makes the loan directly to the borrower, and the mortgage broker has no further role.

Commercial Banks

Like S&Ls, commercial banks also obtain funds from depositors to make loans. Commercial banks primarily make short-term loans, such as business loans and real estate construction loans. These loans are usually higher risk loans and carry higher interest rates.

Historically, commercial banks have been the primary source for short-term residential real estate loans, such as construction loans, interim loans, or second mortgage loans. Interim loans, often called *swing* or *bridge* loans, are made to buyers who are buying a new home but haven't sold their existing home. The interim loan replaces the equity that they will eventually receive from the sale of their existing home. Historically, commercial banks rarely made long-term residential loans. However, this trend is changing, and commercial banks have become a significant source of residential loans.

Private Lenders

Private lenders are individual citizens who make loans and include two major categories:

1. individuals who are in the business of making first or second mortgage loans
2. sellers who assist in financing the sale of their own property

Of these, the most common private lender is a seller who is selling his/her own property. Sellers are also the source most preferred by buyers. Seller financing is particularly attractive to a buyer if the seller has a large equity in the property being sold or new financing is not available or desired by the buyer. Seller financing is commonly referred to as a **purchase money mortgage (PMM)**.

The five sources of residential financing just described will meet your buyer's needs for residential financing in most situations. However, there may be other sources that may be appropriate in some cases. You should consult your broker for information on these other sources or if those listed earlier do not meet your needs in a particular situation.

Credit Unions

Credit unions are organized as not-for-profit organizations. Their purpose and existence are to serve their members. Like other financial institutions, a credit union will accept member deposits.

In addition, when compared with other lending institutions, it would not be uncommon to find that credit unions originate loans at reasonable interest rates.

> ## Coaching Tips
>
> 1. Prior to the 1990s, S&Ls were the largest source of residential real estate loans. Since that time, mortgage companies have become the largest source of such loans.
> 2. Mortgage brokers don't make loans. They bring borrowers and lenders together for a fee.
> 3. S&Ls are primary lenders but not private lenders.

The lenders just covered are the major sources of residential real estate loans. In addition to these lenders, there are two additional sources of loans in the primary mortgage market that provide loans for nonresidential real estate:

1. insurance companies
2. municipal bonds

Insurance Companies

Insurance companies invest premiums paid by their policyholders. They usually specialize in large-scale projects, such as commercial and industrial properties. Insurance companies rarely make loans on owner-occupied residential properties.

Municipal Bonds

Municipalities can issue bonds for real estate purposes. The interest paid to investors to obtain the funds is tax exempt. The bonds usually carry interest rates 1 to 2% below market rates. These instruments are generally used to promote affordable housing projects that benefit the general public. However, municipal bonds are also used for large commercial projects that create jobs and provide other economies to the public. Banks and S&Ls use their deposits to make loans. Origination fees cover operational expenses and profit.

As previously discussed, there are two major components to the market that provides the source of funds for real estate financing: the primary mortgage market and the secondary mortgage market.

You have already learned about the primary mortgage market where loans are originated (see Figure 13.1). At this point, you will learn about the secondary mortgage market.

Secondary Mortgage Market

The secondary market should not be confused with where the general public seeks a second mortgage. The secondary mortgage market provides an outlet where those who originate loans may sell their loans in order to secure capital to make more loans.

- The primary mortgage market is where loans are originated.
- The secondary market is where these same loans are sold in lots.
- Commercial banks prefer to make short-term loans such as commercial and construction loans.
- S&Ls and mortgage companies primarily make long-term residential loans.
- Mortgage companies originate loans and sell the loans in the secondary market.
- Mortgage brokers don't make loans. They bring borrowers and lenders together for a fee.
- Higher risk carries higher interest rates.

FIGURE 13.1 Primary Mortgage Market at a Glance
Source: © 2021 Mbition LLC

The purpose of the secondary market is to provide liquidity for the primary market (see Figure 13.2). It is the ultimate source of a large percentage of the money used for real estate loans. There are several major institutions in this market, including:

- Fannie Mae (Federal National Mortgage Association [FNMA])
- Ginnie Mae (Government National Mortgage Association [GNMA])
- Freddie Mac (Federal Home Loan Mortgage Corporation [FHLMC])

Fannie Mae

The Federal National Mortgage Association (FNMA) is commonly referred to as Fannie Mae. It is the oldest and largest institution in the secondary market. It was started as a government-owned enterprise in the, became a private for-profit corporation in 1968, and is now (as of 2008) a government-sponsored enterprise again. The privatization of FNMA led to the creation of the Government National Mortgage Association (GNMA). We'll discuss this subject next.

Fannie Mae sells bonds to obtain money to buy loans. It buys and sells FHA, VA, and conventional loans to and from sources in the primary market. It buys more mortgages than any other entity.

Ginnie Mae

The Government National Mortgage Association (GNMA) is commonly referred to as Ginnie Mae. It was created by the government when Fannie Mae became

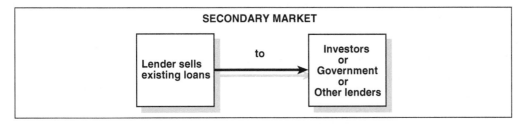

FIGURE 13.2
Source: © 2021 Mbition LLC

private. It is a federal agency in the Department of Housing and Urban Development (HUD). It provides funds primarily by guaranteeing the payment of securities sold to the public and backed by mortgages. The mortgages are insured by the FHA or guaranteed by the VA.

Freddie Mac

The Federal Home Loan Mortgage Corporation (FHLMC) is commonly known as Freddie Mac. It was created by Congress in 1970 as a private corporation but was placed into federal conservatorship in 2008. Its primary purpose is to increase the supply of residential financing by purchasing loans. It now deals primarily in conventional mortgages and, to a lesser extent, FHA and VA mortgages. Its funds come from packaging the mortgages it buys into securities and selling those securities to private investors in the general public.

Conforming Loans

In order for Fannie Mae and Freddie Mac to purchase a loan in the secondary market, the loan must be conforming to the guidelines of Fannie and Freddie. A **conforming loan** is a loan that conforms to the lending guidelines published by Freddie Mac. If the loan does not conform to the guidelines, Freddie Mac will not purchase it. This would be referred to as a nonconforming loan.

Portfolio Lender

Portfolio lenders are lenders who make money from fees obtained by originating loans. They also profit from the margins or spreads obtained on loans. Figure 13.3 summarizes the major institutions of the secondary market.

- Fannie Mae (FNMA) is the Federal National Mortgage Association.
  - Fannie Mae is a federally chartered private corporation.
- Ginnie Mae (GNMA) is the Government National Mortgage Association.
  - Ginnie Mae guarantees securities issued by others.
  - Ginnie Mae is a part of HUD.
  - Ginnie Mae was formed when Fannie Mae became a private organization.
- Freddie Mac (FHLMC) is the Federal Home Loan Mortgage Corporation.
  - Freddie Mac was the third government-chartered organization.
  - Freddie Mac issues its own securities.
- HUD is a federal agency.
- FHA and VA are branches of federal agencies.
- The FHA insures FHA loans made by qualified lenders.
- The VA guarantees VA loans.
- The VA guarantees loans made by lenders.

FIGURE 13.3 Secondary Market at a Glance
Source: © 2021 Mbition LLC

Now that you have learned something about the major institutions in the secondary mortgage market, let's take a look at how the secondary market functions. Let's begin with a brief history of loans in real estate.

THE HISTORY OF LOANS

Amortized Loans

One major development in real estate finance after the Depression was the introduction of amortized loans. As a result of the National Housing Act of 1934 and the creation of HUD, amortized loans offered a number of advantages over straight loans, such as the following:

- They were typically made for a longer term (15–20 years), which lowered the total annual payment.
- They allowed payments to be made monthly, not annually like straight loans, making it easier to budget for and make payments.
- Each monthly payment covered not only the interest due but also included an amount applied toward the repayment of the principal. This meant that the borrower would have completely paid for the property at the end of the loan rather than having to come up with the full principal payment as in the case of a straight loan. Lenders embraced this type of payment plan. Previously, loans had been structured as interest-only loans. The lender received only the annual interest and no principal payment or reduction (balloon loan). The creation of amortized loans gives the lender a greater return of periodic funds and also provides a greater level of lender liquidity.

Because of these more liberal repayment terms, amortized loans increased the demand for loans by making home ownership possible for more people and also helped reduce the number of foreclosures on financed property. Because of this, amortized loans were very popular with lenders as well as buyers.

The following are some of the primary characteristics of a fully amortized loan:

- Monthly payments are constant throughout the term of the mortgage. This method results in a zero balance of principal and interest when held to maturity and paid in accordance with the terms of the note and mortgage.
- On a 30-year term mortgage, approximately the first seven years of the loan term, the payment will be apportioned in the following manner:

    - 95% applied to interest
    - 5% applied to principal

    After the seventh year the reduction trend reverses:

    - 95% applied to principal
    - 5% applied to interest

30- and 15-Year Terms

Although loan terms vary and are negotiated between the borrower and the lender, there are two popular types of loan terms:

1. 15 year—the payments are higher
2. 30 year—the payments are lower

Amortizing a Level Payment Plan Mortgage

For example, a **level payment plan** mortgage is an **amortized mortgage**. An amortized mortgage is when each installment payment is constant over the life of the loan. As you just learned, in the early years, the majority of the payment goes toward paying the interest with some principle reduction. In later years, the majority of the payment is applied against the principle loan balance. When amortizing a level payment plan mortgage, you must perform a three-step process. In formula form:

1. solving for the first month's payment:

    Principal borrowed amount × Annual interest rate ÷ 12 = First month's interest payment

2. solving for the amount apportioned toward principal reduction:

    Monthly mortgage payment − Interest attributable to the first month's payment = Payment applied to principal

3. solving for the remaining principal balance:

    Original principal borrowed amount − Payment applied to principal = Remaining principal balance

For example, assume the interest rate on a 30-year mortgage loan is 10% on a principal amount of $120,000 and a monthly payment of $1053.09.

Step 1: Solving for the first month's interest payment

$120,000 × .10 = 12,000 (annual interest) ÷ 12 = $1,000 (first month's interest)

Step 2: Solving for the amount apportioned toward principal reduction

$1053.09 − 1,000 = $53.09 (amount apportioned toward principal reduction from the monthly payment)

Step 3: Solving for the remaining principal balance

$120,000 − 53.09 = $119,946.91

By repeating the aforementioned steps, one can solve for a later period principal balance.

Federal Agencies

Another major development in real estate finance after the Depression was the creation of two new agencies by the federal government:

1. the Federal Housing Administration (FHA)
2. the Federal National Mortgage Association (FNMA, or Fannie Mae)

Because of the importance of a strong housing market to the economic recovery needed after the Depression, the federal government created these agencies to increase the money supply available for residential loans. Let's briefly look at these agencies.

Federal Housing Administration

The first agency created by the federal government to assist in the financing of real estate was the Federal Housing Administration (FHA). The purpose of the FHA is to insure loans made by private lending institutions, such as S&Ls and mortgage companies. By providing insurance that protects the lender against losses when a borrower defaults, the FHA reduces the lender's risk. This encourages lenders to make loans on real estate that they might not make otherwise, thus increasing the supply of money available for real estate loans. The FHA has several different loan programs that are designed for different types of properties and different categories of borrowers. The FHA's most popular loan program is the FHA 203(b) loan. This is the basic FHA loan program for residential property for one to four families. The FHA 234(c) loan is the popular program used for condominium housing.

Fannie Mae

After the Depression, the federal government also created the Federal National Mortgage Association (FNMA), commonly referred to as Fannie Mae. Its original purpose was to purchase loans made by lenders that were insured by the FHA. The creation of Fannie Mae helped solve one of the biggest problems that limited the availability of funds after the advent of amortized loans. With amortized loans, the lender was not able to recoup money as fast as with straight loans because amortized loans were made for much longer terms. Consequently, lenders had less money to loan to borrowers. The federal government addressed this problem by creating Fannie Mae, whose purpose was to purchase FHA-insured loans from lenders who originated the loans. When these loans were purchased from the lender, the lenders in effect received their money back from Fannie Mae and were able to loan the money again to another borrower. This had a dramatic effect on the availability of funds for real estate loans. The creation of Fannie Mae was the first step in the development of what has come to be called the secondary mortgage market, whose primary purpose is to purchase loans from lenders who originate them. The lenders who originate the loans sold to the secondary mortgage market collectively make up what is referred to as the primary mortgage market. Fannie Mae is still the world's largest agency engaged in the purchase of loans from lenders in the primary mortgage market.

LOAN DISCOUNTING

The term discounting refers to selling a loan for less than the face value. Let's look at how this process works and why it is important.

The owners of a property may be faced with taking a second mortgage (purchase money mortgage [PMM]) in order to sell their property. If they need cash, they might induce an investor to purchase the note by offering the note at less than value.

> **Example** A seller takes back a $10,000 PMM in the sale of his home. To convert this note to cash, he could attempt to sell this asset to an investor. To induce the investor to buy, the seller may offer the note for $9,000. The investor would receive interest on $10,000 and will ultimately be paid back $10,000 on only a $9,000 investment. The process of discounting ultimately increases the yield (return on investment) for the purchaser of the loan. The same basic process occurs when a primary lender sells a loan to the secondary market. If a lender anticipates it will have to discount a loan to sell it to the secondary market, the lender will charge discount points to the borrower to make up the difference. This process will, hopefully, keep the lender in business so people can continue to borrow money to purchase things.

Discount points are used as prepaid interest paid at closing. As you have just seen, by charging a loan discount that is paid in the form of discount points, the lender is able to increase its yield (or earnings) on the loan, while still being able to sell the loan in the secondary market at a discount. A lender is said to discount the loan when it charges discount points. Each discount point is equal to 1% of the loan amount.

For example, if a lender charges two discount points, the fee is 2% of the loan amount. Four discount points would be 4% of the loan amount. The loan discount is the actual dollar amount by which the loan is discounted.

For example, if three discount points are charged on a $50,000 loan, the loan is said to be discounted by $1,500, which is $50,000 multiplied by 3% (0.03). One discount point is equivalent in yield to the lender as 1/8 of one percentage point in interest. As you learned earlier, when a lender charges discount points, the additional fee increases the lender's yield on the loan. As a general rule, each discount point paid at closing increases the lender's yield by approximately the same amount as increasing the interest rate on the loan by 1/8 of 1%.

For example, if a lender charges two discount points, this is roughly equivalent to raising the interest rate on the loan by 1/4 of 1% (0.0025). This means that a loan at 10% with two discount points is equivalent (in terms of the lender's yield) to a loan at 10.25% with no discount points.

Let's apply this rule to a VA loan made by a lender. If the interest rate on a VA loan is 9% and the prevailing market rate on conventional loans is 9.75%, the difference in the interest rates is 0.75%. (This difference of 0.75% expressed in eighths of a percent is 6/8%.) Because one discount point is equivalent to 1/8%, the lender would have to charge six discount points on the VA loan to earn a comparable yield on a VA loan and a conventional loan (or to be able to sell the loan in the secondary market).

The interest rates on two loans differ by 0.5%. How many points would the lender need to charge on the one with the lower interest rate to get an equivalent yield on the two loans? As you have just seen, discount points affect the yield the lender receives on a loan and the lender's ability to sell it in the secondary market.

Because of this, discount points may be charged or not charged on a loan, depending on a number of factors, including:

- what the lender can make on other investments
- the amount a secondary lender is willing to pay for the loan at a given interest rate

Factors such as these make up the forces of supply and demand for loan funds. These forces of supply and demand determine whether discount points will be charged and if so, the number of points charged.

When loan money is plentiful in the secondary market (secondary lenders are more willing to buy loans) and borrowers are scarce, discount points tend to decrease or disappear. When loan money is limited and there are many borrowers, points tend to reappear or go up.

In general, the number of discount points charged by lenders on real estate loans is a good reflection of market conditions for financing in the community. When discount points are charged, the supply is low and the demand is high. When discount points are not charged (or are low), the supply of money is high and the demand is low.

Because of supply and demand, which affects the availability of loan money as well as the interest rates and discount points charged by lenders, it is important for you as a licensee to constantly monitor the market for loan funds. You should check with the lenders you work with at least weekly so that you will have current information at all times.

LOAN-TO-VALUE RATIO

The loan-to-value ratio (LTV) is used to set a limit on how much money can be loaned on a particular property. It is expressed as a percentage and is computed in the lesser of either of two ways:

1. the amount of the loan is divided by the sales price, or
2. the amount of the loan is divided by the appraised value of the property, whichever is smaller.

> **Example** The sales price of a property is $100,000. The property is appraised at $105,000. In this example, the loan amount is divided by the sales price ($100,000) because the sales price is less than the appraised value ($105,000). The maximum LTV allowed by lenders varies for different types of loans.

CONVENTIONAL LOANS

A conventional loan is one that is not issued, insured, or guaranteed by a government agency. Interest rates on conventional loans are negotiated with the lender. Closing costs and discount points charged on conventional loans may be paid by either the buyer or seller. Conventional loans are divided into different types based on their LTV. The LTV is simply the amount of the loan divided by the sales price or the appraised value, whichever is smaller. While loans of varying ratios may be available, for the purposes of this course, conventional loans will have LTVs of 80%, 90%, or 95%, unless otherwise stated. The LTV allowed is usually no more than 80% unless private mortgage insurance is obtained. Typically, if private mortgage insurance is obtained, conventional loans can be made up to an LTV of 95%. Loans with private mortgage insurance are called insured conventional loans. Private mortgage insurance (PMI) acts just like FHA insurance, except that the insurance is provided by a private insurance company, not a government agency. PMI protects the lender against losses if the borrower defaults on the loan. PMI is usually required by a lender if the LTV exceeds 80%. The borrower pays an insurance premium for PMI, usually 1% or less at the origination of the loan, and less than 1% annually. Once the LTV is reduced below 80%, the PMI can usually be dropped.

Coaching Tips

1. The LTV is usually limited to 80% unless mortgage insurance is obtained.
2. The LTV allowed can be higher than 80% if PMI is obtained to cover the amount over 80% of the value.
3. With PMI, the LTV may be as high as 90 or 95%.

Previously, you learned some of the characteristics of conventional loans. Now you will learn more about the following aspects of conventional loans:

- different types of conventional loans
- down payments and how they are calculated
- PMI payments

Types of Conventional Loans

Conventional loans have different features based on their LTV. The most common categories of conventional loans are 80%, 90%, and 95% LTV loans. This does not mean that a loan must be made that is exactly 80%, 90%, or 95% of the sales price. It only means that the conventional loan will have different characteristics depending on whether the loan is considered to be an 80%, 90%, or 95% loan. When a conventional loan is made for an amount that is not exactly 80%, 90%, or 95% of the sales price, the following guidelines apply:

- A loan for which the loan amount is less than 80% is considered an 80% loan.
- A loan for which the loan amount is more than 80% but less than 90% is considered a 90% loan.
- A loan for which the loan amount is more than 90% but less than 95% is considered a 95% loan.

For example, a property is sold for $82,000, and the buyer makes a down payment of $6,000. What type of conventional loan would the buyer obtain?

Step 1: Determine the loan amount:

$$\$82{,}000 - \$6{,}000 = \$76{,}000$$

Step 2: Divide the loan amount by the sales price:

$$\$76{,}000 \div \$82{,}000 = 92.7\%$$

Because the loan amount is greater than 90%, it is considered to be a 95% loan. Let's look at another example.

A property is sold for $70,000, and the buyer makes a down payment of $16,000. What type of conventional loan would the buyer obtain?

Step 1: Determine the loan amount:

$$\$70{,}000 - \$16{,}000 = \$54{,}000$$

Step 2: Divide by the sales price:

$$\$54{,}000 \div \$70{,}000 = 77.1\%$$

Because the loan amount is less than 80%, the loan is considered to be an 80% loan. Let's look at a third example.

A property is sold for $120,000, and the buyer makes a down payment of $17,000. What type of conventional loan would the buyer obtain?

Step 1: Determine the loan amount:

$$\$120{,}000 - \$17{,}000 = \$103{,}000$$

Step 2: Divide by the sales price:

$$\$103{,}000 \div \$120{,}000 = 85.8\%$$

The loan amount is 85.8%, which is greater than 80% but less than 90%, so the loan is considered to be a 90% loan.

Interest Rate

The interest rate on a conventional loan is set by the agreement between the borrower and the lender. It is usually a market rate.

There are two types of conventional loans:

1. loans that the lender originates (and holds to maturity) with its own funds
2. loans that the lender originates with federal funds and intends to sell in the secondary market

The interest rate on the aforementioned is usually the same but can vary.

Assumption

Conventional loans are generally not assumable. They will contain a due on sale or alienation clause. However, even loans that are not assumable can be transferred and assumed if the lender consents to the transfer and assumption of same.

Under certain circumstances, a conventional lender might consider permitting the assumption. This could occur if the loan was originated with the lender's own funds. It would be extremely difficult to achieve this with a loan that was sold to another investor in the secondary market.

Prepayment

Most conventional fixed rate residential loans provide for the prepayment of principle without the borrower paying a penalty. A prepayment penalty is generally found as a component of a commercial loan.

Adjustable Rate Mortgage

An **adjustable rate mortgage (ARM)** is any loan that, over the term of the loan, periodically allows the lender (under prescribed terms) to raise or lower the interest rate. The rate of an ARM loan is determined by two items:

1. **index**—either Treasury notes (usually the 10-year note is the benchmark for mortgages) or London Interbank Offer Rate (LIBOR)
2. **margin** or spread—percentage above the margin representing the lender's profit for originating the loan.

The total of #1 and #2 above represents the interest rate the borrower will have to pay on the borrowed funds.

Adjustments

Based on what is stated in the loan documents, ARM loans will adjust periodically. The period of adjustment can vary from loan to loan. Common adjustment periods are annual; although it would not be unusual to see other periods.

Interest Rate Caps

There are at least two common types of caps inherent in ARM loans:

1. **periodic caps**—the limitation on the amount that the interest rate can increase during any adjustment period
2. **lifetime caps**—the maximum, not to exceed rate of the loan over the life of same

Payment Cap

During the adjustment period, a **payment cap** limits the amount the monthly payment can increase. This is to protect a homeowner from runaway rising interest rates. This arrangement can result in **negative amortization** (when the balance owed increases with every payment). This occurs when the capped payment is less than the adjustment payment (from daily increases to the index) now requires. The difference is subsequently added on to the borrowed principle.

Teaser Rate

The **teaser rate** is the rate used to attract borrowers by offering a below-market initial interest rate. The rate is locked in for a prescribed period of time (that varies), after which the rate is subject to periodic adjustment.

Partially Amortized Loans

A **partially amortized loan** is any loan whose entire borrowed principal loan balance cannot be retired at time of maturity by the monthly payments of principal and interest. This means that there is a remaining balance. This remaining balance is referred to as a balloon or the final **balloon payment**.

For example, assume a borrower cannot afford a 15-year loan payment but can afford a 25-year term payment that is significantly lower. The lender is only willing to extend a 15-year loan maturity; however, the lender offers the borrower the ability to make a payment based upon a 25-year loan term. It is not possible to pay off a loan that matures in 15 years by making a payment that is based on a 25-year loan term. Therefore, the remaining balance is the balloon payment. Another form of balloon payment loan would be any type or form of an interest-only loan. At maturity, the balloon payment becomes the entire borrowed amount. This is due to only making interest payments with no principal deduction.

Biweekly Mortgage

A **biweekly mortgage** differs from any other type of mortgage in the following way:
- the borrower makes payments every two weeks as opposed to every month
- the payment is 50% of the monthly amount and the result is 26 biweekly payments that accrue to the equivalent of 13 months of 100% monthly payments. This will shorten the borrower's payback period while saving the borrower substantial interest payments with no principle reduction.

Package Mortgage

A **package mortgage** is any loan that includes both real and personal property as the lender's held collateral.

For example, when the real property loan amount falls short of the borrower's/purchaser's expectations, the borrower then proposes to pledge both the real property and a Tiffany chandelier (personal property item) to bridge the gap. The lender agrees to accept both real and personal property as collateral for originating the package mortgage.

Down Payments

Many times a borrower makes the minimum down payment and chooses to obtain the largest loan he/she can qualify for. When this is the case, the category of loan selected (80%, 90%, or 95%) determines the loan amount. From the loan amount, it is then necessary to calculate the amount of the down payment. The procedure for calculating the down payment in this situation requires two steps.

Step 1: Determine the dollar amount of the loan.
Step 2: Subtract the loan amount from the sales price to get the down payment.

Different lenders have different policies on how to determine the exact amount of a loan as a percentage of the sales price. Let's look at an example to see how this is handled.

A buyer is applying for an 80% loan on a property that is selling for $76,400. Eighty percent of $76,400 is $61,120. Some lenders would make the loan for exactly that amount. Other lenders would round the amount off to the next lowest $100 and make the loan for $61,100. In addition, the FHA approves loans in increments of $50. Many lenders that make FHA loans, however, make loans only in increments of $100.

Step 1: Determine the dollar amount of the loan.

Because of these differences, it is best to adopt a policy of always rounding the loan amount down to the next lowest $100. This ensures that the contract you write will be acceptable to any lender. Let's look at an example.

A property is being sold for $110,500 with a 90% conventional loan. What is the loan amount?

First multiply $110,500 by 90%:

$$\$110{,}500 \times 0.90 = \$99{,}450$$

Next, round down to the next lowest $100:

$$\$99{,}450 = \$99{,}400$$

The loan amount is $99,400.

Step 2: Calculate the down payment.

Once the loan amount is determined, subtract the loan amount from the sales price to get the down payment. Let's look at an example.

A property is being sold for $87,500 with a 95% conventional loan. What is the down payment?

First, calculate the loan amount:

$$\$87{,}500 \times 0.95 = \$83{,}125$$

Round down to the next lowest $100:

$$\$83{,}125 = \$83{,}100$$

The loan amount is $83,100.

Last, subtract the loan amount from the selling price:

$$\$87{,}500 - \$83{,}100 = \$4{,}400$$

The down payment is $4,400.

Home Equity Loan

Home equity loans consider only the equity portion a property owner has in a property. Equity is defined as the amount left over after deducting all outstanding loan balances from the market value. The formula for calculating the equity in a home is:

Appraised Value × Loan-to-value ratio (LTV) − Outstanding loan balance(s) = Equity

In the past, home equity loans have been used to fund home improvement and/or credit debt consolidation.

Home Equity Conversion Mortgage (HECM) or Reverse Mortgage

As we age, there are two considerations that are difficult to prepare and plan for:

1. predicting life expectancy; and
2. the total funds that will be required to support a retirement lifestyle

It would not be uncommon to find that those reaching retirement have underestimated their future needs and cost of living. As a result of this underestimation, the person is forced to look to other sources for income. Selling their home and moving elsewhere may seem to be their only solution; however, another option is available: an HECM or reverse mortgage.

Although the aforementioned is a most unfortunate dilemma to be faced with, the reverse mortgage or HECM allows homeowners to remain in their home while receiving funds in a lump sum, periodically, or in the form of a line of credit. In essence, the homeowners are utilizing the equity built up in their home to fund their retirement.

As it applies to these types of loans, the only loan insured by the federal government is the HECM. This loan can only be obtained through an FHA-approved lender.

Homeowners who reach the age of 62 are eligible for an HECM or a reverse mortgage. Eligibility requires that homeowners have a sizable equity position in their home.

Private Mortgage Insurance Payments

As you learned earlier, conventional loans of 90% and 95% usually require that the borrower obtain PMI. Some lenders may require PMI on 80% conventional loans in some cases as well. PMI protects the lender against default by the buyer on a conventional loan. It requires the payment of a premium, which is usually calculated as a percentage of the loan amount. PMI is charged to the borrower when a new loan is originated, but the payment of the PMI premium is negotiable, and it may be paid by either the buyer or seller. When the seller pays the PMI, it must be paid in cash at closing. When the buyer pays the PMI, it may be paid in one of the following three ways:

1. It may be paid in cash at closing.
2. It may be financed along with the mortgage payment.
3. It may be paid partially in cash at closing with the rest financed along with the mortgage payment.

The method used to calculate the amount of the PMI payment depends on whether it is paid in cash or financed. Let's look first at the case where the PMI is paid in cash at closing. The calculation is the same regardless of whether the buyer or the seller makes the payment. The exact amount of the PMI premium varies from lender to lender.

For purposes of illustration, we will use the following values for PMI:

$$90\% \text{ loans}—2\%$$
$$95\% \text{ loans}—2.5\%$$

The amount of the PMI when paid in cash is determined by multiplying these percentages by the amount of the loan. For example, a 90% loan is obtained by a buyer on a property selling for $88,500. What is the amount of the PMI premium?

Step 1: Determine the amount of the loan:

$$\$88,500 \times 0.90 = \$79,650$$

Step 2: Round down to the next lowest $100:

$$\$79,650 = \$79,600$$

This is the final loan amount.

Step 3: Multiply the loan amount by 2% because this is a 90% loan:

$$\$79,600 \times 0.02 = \$1,592$$

The amount of the PMI premium is $1,592.

Here's another example. A $60,000 home is financed with a 95% conventional loan. Using the rates for PMI given earlier, what is the amount of the PMI premium?

Step 1: Determine the amount of the loan:

$$\$60,000 \times 0.95 = \$57,000$$

Step 2: Calculate the PMI amount using a 2.5% rate:

$$\$57,000 \times 0.025 = \$1,425$$

You learned earlier that a buyer may pay part of the PMI in cash at closing, with the rest financed along with the monthly mortgage payment. In this situation, the amount of the monthly payment is calculated using a standard factor. The exact factor used varies from lender to lender, but for study purposes in this course, we will use a value of 1/4%. Note that the factor used is 1/4% (or 0.0025). Do not confuse this amount with 2.5% (or 0.025), which is used to determine the PMI on a 95% loan when the PMI is paid in full at closing.

This factor (1/4%, or 0.0025) is used to determine the annual amount of premium to be paid. The amount of the monthly payment is calculated from the annual amount. Let's look at an example.

A 90% conventional loan is used to purchase a home for $80,000. The buyer will pay part of the PMI at closing and finance the rest. What is the amount of the monthly PMI payment?

Step 1: Determine the loan amount:

$$\$80,000 \times 0.90 = \$72,000$$

Step 2: Determine the amount of the annual premium, using the factor mentioned above:

$$\$72,000 \times 0.0025 = \$180$$

Step 3: Divide the annual premium by 12 to get the monthly premium:

$$\$180 \div 12 = \$15$$

The monthly payment for PMI is $15.00.

Let's look at another example.

A new home is purchased for $66,900 using a 95% conventional loan. The buyer will pay part of the PMI at closing and finance the rest. What is the monthly PMI payment?

Step 1: Determine the loan amount:

$$\$66,900 \times 0.95 = \$63,555$$

Step 2: Round down to the next lowest $100:

$$\$63,555 = \$63,500$$

Step 3: Determine the annual premium:

$$\$63{,}500 \times 0.0025 = \$158.75$$

Step 4: Determine the monthly premium:

$$\$158.75 \div 12 = \$13.23$$

FHA LOANS (NONCONVENTIONAL)

The second major category of loans you should be familiar with is FHA loans. The FHA loan programs are administered through the Federal Housing Administration. Since 1965, the FHA has been an agency within HUD. The three main purposes of the FHA are to:

1. promote improved housing standards
2. assist in the stabilization of the mortgage market
3. provide mortgage loan insurance

Note that the FHA does not make loans itself or provide housing. FHA insures loans originated by qualified lenders.

Loan Insurance Programs

The most familiar function of the FHA is to provide loan insurance programs. The FHA insures loans made by private lenders that meet certain guidelines and standards. The FHA mortgage insurance protects the lender against losses resulting from default by the borrower. The money that provides the FHA insurance protection to lenders comes from the insurance premiums that are paid on each loan insured by the FHA. The premium charged by the FHA is called the **mortgage insurance premium (MIP)**. In addition, any borrower that takes out an FHA loan is required to pay the **up-front mortgage insurance premium (UFMIP)**. We will look at the MIP in more detail later in this chapter.

The FHA has several different loan programs that are designed for different types of properties and different categories of borrowers. These programs include the following:

- Section 203(b)—standard loan program
- Special terms for veterans
- Section 245—graduated payment loan program

Section 203(b)—Standard Loan Program

The Section 203(b) program is the basic FHA loan insurance program for residential property for one to four families. Most FHA loans are limited to owner-occupied properties. The characteristics of the Section 203(b) loan program will be covered later in this chapter. However, before looking at this program in detail, let's look briefly at two other FHA loan programs.

Special Terms for Veterans

The FHA program for veterans is similar in purpose to VA loans but is administered by the FHA, not the VA. The FHA program provides lower down payment loans for veterans.

There is a maximum loan amount that is different for high-cost and low-cost areas. These loan limits may change frequently, so you should check with a lender for the current limits. The veteran must pay a down payment that is calculated in the following way:

0% on the first $25,000 of the sales price
5% on the amount between $25,000 and $125,000
10% of everything over $125,000

Section 245—Graduated Payment Loan Program

The Section 245 program is designed to assist first-time buyers who might otherwise be unable to buy because of rising prices. Its main feature is that the monthly payments on the loan are lower in the first year of the loan and increase over a period of years until the final payment level. The Section 245 graduated payment loan (GPM) program is limited to single-family, owner-occupied houses. The maximum loan term is 30 years. There is a maximum loan amount that is different for high-cost and low-cost areas. These loan limits may change frequently, so you should check with a lender for the current limits. The Section 245 GPM program currently has several different plans that provide different schedules for increasing the loan payment. Each plan differs in terms of the amount of the increase each year and the number of years to reach the maximum payment amount:

	% Yearly Increase	Years to Reach Maximum Payment
Plan I	2.5%	5
Plan II	5%	5
Plan III	7.5%	5
Plan IV	2%	10
Plan V	3%	10

Of these plans, Plan III is the most common.

203(B)—STANDARD LOAN PROGRAM

Now that we have looked briefly at the types of loan programs available through the FHA, let's look at the characteristics of the basic loan insurance program, the Section 203(b) loan program.

Loan Insurance

The 203(b) loan program promotes home ownership by providing insurance for loans on residential real estate. The FHA does not loan money. It insures loans made by primary lenders against losses due to default. Here's how the FHA loan insurance program works:

- The borrower holding an FHA-insured loan defaults on the loan.
- The lender forecloses.
- The property is sold.
- If the proceeds of the sale are less than the outstanding balance on the loan, the FHA pays the lender the difference.

To pay for losses such as these, the FHA charges all borrowers an MIP on FHA-insured loans. MIPs protect the lender against default of the borrower. It insures the top portion of the loan over 80% LTV. The bottom 80% is usually underwritten by the lesser of the sales price or the appraisal. In 1991, the FHA began requiring borrowers to pay an up-front payment at closing and monthly payments over a period of years to cover the MIP (**UFMIP**). However, the regulations governing the payment of the MIP have been subject to frequent change over the past few years. Therefore, you may want to contact your lender to keep up-to-date on the MIP and its payment. The up-front and monthly MIP payments depend on the LTV and the term of the loan.

For example:

LTV	30-Year Loans ($625,500 or less)	15-Year Loans ($625,500 or less)
Below 90%	0.80% up front	0.70% up front
90%–95%	0.80% up front	0.45% up front
Over 95%	0.85% up front	0.45% up front

Cash Investment

All FHA-insured loans require a cash investment, which includes the down payment. The minimum down payment required on an FHA-insured loan is typically less than that required for a conventional loan, which is one of the major advantages of an FHA-insured loan for the buyer. Depending on the situation, the borrower may be allowed to purchase a home with a total-cash investment as low as 3.5% of the sales price or appraised value, whichever is less.

Qualifying Ratios

In qualifying a borrower for an FHA loan, monthly gross income is used to calculate qualifying ratios. There are two qualifying ratios used for FHA loans:

1. total monthly housing expense ratio—used to calculate the percentage of monthly income that is consumed by housing expenses. This ratio takes into account principal, interest, property tax, and insurance (PITI) payments in relation to monthly income. The FHA will originate the loan when the housing expense ratio is 31% or less. The formula for calculating the total monthly housing expense ratio is:

    Monthly housing expenses divided by monthly income =
    Housing expense ratio

2. total monthly expense ratio—used to calculate the percentage of monthly income that is consumed by the total monthly recurring expenses. The FHA will originate the loan when the total monthly expense ratio is 43% or less. The formula for calculating the total monthly housing expense ratio is:

    Total monthly expenses ÷ Monthly gross income =
    Total monthly expense ratio

Loan Amount

The maximum loan amount on an FHA-insured loan is set by the FHA. The maximum amount differs for high-cost and low-cost areas and varies from county to county. The loan limits may vary frequently, so you should contact a lender for assistance when dealing with FHA-insured loan amounts.

Another distinguishing feature of FHA-insured loans is that the FHA allows the loan amount to be based on the appraised value (or sales price) plus a percentage of the estimated closing costs. This allows the buyer to finance part of the closing costs and pay the costs over the life of the loan rather than having to pay cash for those costs at closing. The formula that the FHA uses for determining the loan amount when the buyer finances all or part of the closing costs has been changed several times in recent years and currently involves a fairly complex set of calculations. However, you should remember that the minimum cash investment the borrower can make is 3.5% of the sales price or appraised value, whichever is less.

The LTV for an FHA-insured loan varies depending on the amount of the loan and whether the property is located in a high-cost area or a low-cost area. The LTV is typically greater than 95%. The formula for determining the LTV for a specific situation has changed in recent years and currently involves a fairly complex set of calculations. If you would like additional information about FHA-insured loans, you should contact a lender.

Interest Rate

Prior to December 1983, HUD set the maximum allowable interest rate on FHA-insured loans. The interest rate on FHA-insured loans is now determined by negotiation between each individual borrower and lender, and the rates are affected by market conditions, just as conventional rates are.

Discount Points

Loan discount points may be charged on FHA-insured loans. When discount points are charged on an FHA-insured loan, the points may be paid by either the buyer or the seller, or they may be split between the buyer and seller. Historically, the interest rate on FHA-insured loans has been lower than on comparable conventional loans. Because of this, lenders usually charge a loan discount to increase their yield on the loan to be comparable to a conventional loan with a higher interest rate. The loan discount is charged in the form of discount points, with one point equal to 1% of the loan amount.

Maximum Term

The maximum loan term for an FHA-insured loan is 30 years. However, FHA has other programs designed to help a first time home buyer.

Closing Costs

The closing costs on FHA-insured loans generally include the same items as conventional loans. The closing costs are often paid by the seller. However, closing costs may also be paid by the buyer.

Escrow Accounts

All FHA-insured loans require that escrow accounts be established and that monthly payments for taxes and insurance (PITI) be made into the escrow accounts. As with conventional loans, these escrow accounts are established at closing through the payment of escrow items.

Loan Processing

The time required for processing an FHA-insured loan varies from lender to lender and with market conditions. It usually takes longer to process an FHA-insured loan than a conventional loan.

Appraisal

The property that is financed with an FHA-insured loan must meet certain standards that are specified in the FHA minimum property requirements (MPRs). Whether the property meets these standards is determined by an appraisal of the property. Appraisals for property on FHA-insured loans are conducted by fee appraisers, which are FHA-approved independent appraisers who conduct appraisals for a fee. An appraisal made for an FHA-insured loan serves two purposes:

1. It establishes the value of the property for loan purposes.
2. It serves as a conditional commitment to the borrower.

The conditional commitment means that the FHA is making a commitment to the borrower to insure a loan on the property as long as the borrower qualifies for the loan under the lender's qualifying requirements. The first purpose of the appraisal is to determine the reasonable value for the property. The appraisal for an FHA-insured loan is ordered by the lender who will make the loan, not the borrower. The FHA charges an appraisal fee, which must be paid in advance when the appraisal is ordered. The fee must be paid in cash. No form of credit is allowed by either the buyer or seller. Once the value of the property is determined and the conditional commitment is issued, the maximum amount that can be insured by the FHA on that property is set. The conditional commitment will also specify any repairs that must be made to the property before a loan will be insured by the FHA. The repairs must be sufficient to bring the property in compliance with the minimum property requirements.

When an FHA appraisal is ordered, the results of the appraisal will be given only to the lender, not the borrower. The appraisal is good for a specific period of time as follows:

- Existing properties—The appraisal is valid for 120 days.
- Proposed construction—The appraisal is valid for 120 days.

When a buyer seeks to obtain financing that is insured by the FHA, the sales contract is usually contingent on an FHA appraisal greater than or equal to the sales price. If such a contingency exists but the appraised value is less than the sales price in the signed contract, the buyer has four options:

1. Void the contract and request a return of the earnest money.
2. Pay the difference in the appraised value and the sales price in cash.
3. Renegotiate the sales price with the seller so that it does not exceed the appraised value.
4. Request a reconsideration of the FHA appraisal.

Let's look at some of these in more detail.

The borrower may pay more for a property than the FHA appraisal, but the total amount of the price above the allowable loan amount must be paid in cash.

(Second mortgages are rarely approved by the FHA.) For example, a house is appraised for $60,000 and the allowable loan amount is $57,500. If the buyer pays $60,000 for the house, the down payment is $2,500. If the buyer pays $65,000 for the house, the down payment must be at least $7,500 ($65,000 − $57,500). While this is a possible solution, it is not used often, because few people are willing to pay more than the appraised value. The borrower may also request that the appraisal be reconsidered. If this is done, the borrower must have a basis for a claim that the appraisal is too low, in the form of information on comparable properties in the same area. The information on these comparables must include several specific items that are beyond the scope of this course. Consult the FHA when dealing with a case such as this.

Restrictions

There are certain restrictions that apply to FHA-insured loans. First, the buyer generally must have cash for the entire down payment; however, in rare cases, the FHA may allow a second mortgage at the time the loan is made, but this is possible only with the knowledge and consent of the FHA. After the loan is made, second mortgages may be added by the owner or by a later buyer who assumes the loan. Periodically, there may even be a program available allowing the seller, or some other party, to make the down payment.

The second type of restriction is in the clauses allowed in the loan:

- Prepayment penalties are prohibited by law.
- The loan may contain a prepayment clause, but the clause must not contain a penalty for prepayment.
- Due on sale clauses are also prohibited.

Because due on sale clauses are not allowed in FHA-insured loans, this means these loans are assumable. However, changes have placed limits on the assumption of FHA-insured loans. Let's look at these changes next.

In the past, anyone could assume an FHA-insured loan without qualifying. However, changes in the regulations now require that the buyer qualify for the loan under certain conditions:

- For loans made prior to December 15, 1989, a buyer is not required to qualify to assume the loan.
- For loans made after December 15, 1989, a buyer is required to qualify to assume the loan.

Condominium Units

Aside from the popular FHA 203(b) loan programs, the FHA also originate loans on condominium units. The FHA also has loan programs for mobile homes and manufactured housing. For first-time home buyers the FHA offers special discounts for teachers, firefighters, and police officers buying HUD-foreclosed homes that are located in revitalization areas.

Qualifications

Although the maximum loan amount will vary by county for traditional forward FHA loans, the current base FHA loan limit in most of Florida counties for a single-family home is set at $275,665.00. Currently, a tri-merged credit report with a middle score of at least 620 is required. Under certain circumstances, middle scores as low as 580 can also qualify. However, regardless of individual credit scores, the FHA will review credit history to determine findings that meet FHA-approval guidelines.

Eligibility

In order to be eligible for an FHA loan, the property must be any of the following types:

- one-to four-family housing
- planned unit development (PUD), either attached or detached
- condominium
- mixed-use property that is used for housing and where the commercial portion does not exceed 25% of the gross living area

Loan Origination Fee

FHA-approved lenders may charge the borrower a loan origination fee at closing. This fee is reflected as payment of a discount point(s) from the borrower to the lender. Each discount point represents 1% of the borrowed amount.

Prepayment

Unlike conventional loans, FHA loans do not require penalties for prepayment of principal.

VA LOANS (NONCONVENTIONAL)

Qualifications

For an individual to qualify for a Veterans Administration (VA) loan, that individual must fit one of the following descriptions:

- has served at least 90 days of active duty and continue to be on active duty,
- served at least 181 days of active duty,

- served six years in the state reserves or National Guard, or
- is a surviving spouse of a deceased service member who died while in service.

The individual will also need to produce a certificate of eligibility. (This subject will be discussed in greater detail later in this chapter.)

The Department of Veterans Affairs (VA), formerly known as the Veterans Administration, is also a U.S. government agency that provides assistance in the financing of housing. It was established by the federal government as an independent agency by the Serviceman's Readjustment Act of 1944, also called the GI Bill of Rights and commonly referred to as the GI Bill. It was enacted to provide assistance to veterans who served in World War II and their surviving spouses.

Eligibility

As it pertains to a veterans loan, eligibility means that the veteran must meet the basic criteria regarding:

- character of the veterans service, and
- the required and appropriate length of service.

The entitlement becomes the amount that a veteran could have as the VA guarantee toward a mortgage loan. To qualify for the loan, an individual who is eligible for a VA loan must meet income and credit criteria. A lender must confirm that the individual applicant is an eligible veteran. The confirmation must occur prior to processing and closing of a loan. The lender can confirm a veteran's eligibility by requiring the veteran to produce a certificate of eligibility. Once the lender receives the certificate of eligibility, no further updating of same is required before closing.

The VA promotes home ownership for eligible veterans of military service by providing loan guarantees to lenders. The guarantee is different from an insurance program such as the FHA in that losses are funded directly out of federal tax funds. Because guarantee funds come directly from tax funds, no insurance premium is paid by anyone.

VA loans are guaranteed, not insured. Here's how the guarantee works:

- The veteran borrower defaults on the VA loan.
- The lender forecloses.
- The property is sold.
- If the proceeds from the sale are less than the outstanding balance on the loan, the VA pays the difference, up to certain limits, which are covered next.

> ### Coaching Tips
>
> The VA also has the option to buy the property from the lender and market the property itself.
>
> The limits on the amount of VA guarantee are as follows:
>
> - Loan amount of $45,000 or less: 50% of the loan amount is guaranteed.
> - Loan amount greater than $45,000 up to $144,000: 40% of the loan amount is guaranteed, or $36,000, whichever is less, but not less than $22,500.
> - Loan amount greater than $144,000: 25% of the loan amount is guaranteed up to the current maximum guarantee of $106,025.

The guarantee covers losses not recovered by foreclosure sale. The loan can be for any amount. A veteran's entitlement is the amount of guarantee he/she is eligible to receive on a guaranteed loan. The maximum entitlement is $104,250 (the maximum guarantee). The veteran may use all, or only part, of the entitlement in a given transaction. If he/she uses only part of the entitlement and sells the home by assumption without paying off the original loan, he/she may use the remaining entitlement on another home (the amount of veteran's full entitlement less the amount already used). If the veteran sells the home and pays off the original VA loan, the full entitlement is restored and may be used to buy another home.

Maximum Loan Amount

There is no maximum amount for a VA loan set by law. In general, however, lenders will not loan more than four times the guaranteed amount, or $424,100 (4 × $106,025). The veteran may buy a home for more than $417,000 with a VA loan, but the lender will require a down payment, usually 25% of the amount above $417,000.

Down Payment

One of the most distinguishing characteristics of a VA loan is that no down payment is required. (The LTV is equal to 100%.) Note, however, that a veteran may pay a down payment if he/she chooses to do so. The veteran must also qualify for the payments on a VA loan as on any other loan.

Term and Interest Rate

The maximum term for a VA loan is 30 years. The VA used to set a maximum allowable interest rate for VA loans. However, the VA no longer sets a maximum rate. The interest rate on a VA loan is now a matter of negotiation between the veteran and the lender, just as it is for FHA loans.

Discount Points

Historically, the interest rate on VA loans has been below the prevailing market rate for conventional loans, and VA loans have required the payment of what is called a loan discount. A loan discount is actually prepaid interest that raises the yield on the loan to the lender. The amount of the loan discount is expressed as discount points, or simply points. One discount point is equal to 1% of the loan amount. Historically, to protect the veteran's interest, the VA would not allow the veteran to pay the discount points on a VA loan, except in cases of refinancing. However, this has changed, and the veteran is now allowed to pay the discount points. With a VA loan, discount points may be paid by the veteran, or they may be paid by others such as the seller or a builder as well.

Closing Costs

The closing costs on a VA loan generally include the same items as a conventional loan. The closing costs may be paid by either the buyer or seller, and quite often they are paid by the seller.

Funding Fee

VA-guaranteed loans usually require the payment of a funding fee when the loan is originated. The funding fee is paid into a guarantee and indemnity fund, which is used to offset claims under the guarantee program. The amount of the funding fee depends on the amount of down payment made by the veteran as follows:

Down Payment	Funding Fee
No down payment	2.00% of loan amount
5% down payment	1.50% of loan amount
10% down payment	1.25% of loan amount

These amounts are for first-time users. Subsequent loans have a higher funding fee requirement. These funding fee amounts are for regular veterans; amounts are higher for individuals who have served in the military reserves. The funding fee can be paid by either the buyer or seller. The amount of the funding fee can be included in the loan amount and paid from the loan proceeds. The funding fee may be waived if the veteran has a service-connected disability. Like discount points or closing costs, the funding fee on a VA loan may be paid by either the buyer or seller.

Escrow Account

The monthly payments on a VA loan must include an amount that is paid into an escrow account to cover the annual property taxes and homeowner's insurance. The escrow account is established at closing when the borrower is required to pay several monthly escrow payments in advance. The amount of payment required varies with the time of year the closing occurs. After closing, the borrower must pay an amount into the escrow account each month, along with the principal and interest on the mortgage payment. The amount of the monthly escrow payment for taxes and insurance is equal to 1/12 of the total annual property tax and insurance bills. When these escrow payments are included in the monthly mortgage payment, the loan payments are referred to as PITI payments; PITI stands for principal, interest, taxes, and insurance. This is also known as a budget mortgage or budget payment.

Veteran's Liability

If a veteran defaults on a VA loan, he/she is liable to the VA for any losses the VA must pay as a result of the default. If another buyer assumes a VA loan, the veteran remains liable for any losses (unless he/she is released by the VA). If another veteran assumes a VA loan, it is possible to transfer the VA entitlement and the liability for VA losses to the new buyer, thus freeing up the original veteran's entitlement. This can be done only with VA approval. As on FHA loans, there are certain restrictions on VA loans.

VA loans may not include a prepayment penalty. Additionally, VA loans may not contain an alienation (due on sale) clause, so they can be assumed with no increase in the interest rate. Most VA loans made prior to March 1, 1988, can be assumed by any buyer without qualifying. However, for VA loans made on or after March 1, 1988, the VA requires that buyers qualify when assuming the loans.

Appraisal

A property that is financed with a VA loan must meet certain standards set by the VA. An appraisal of the property determines whether or not those standards are met. The appraisal must be conducted by a VA-approved fee appraiser. The VA appraisal report is called a certificate of reasonable value (CRV). An appraisal made for property on a VA loan serves three purposes:

1. It determines the acceptability of the property for a VA loan.
2. It establishes the value of the property for loan purposes.
3. It identifies any repairs that might be needed to qualify for a VA loan.

The value established by the appraisal is the maximum loan amount that can be loaned on a 100% VA-guaranteed loan. The loan amount cannot be greater than the appraised value in the CRV. To obtain a VA appraisal, the veteran requests the appraisal through the lender who will make the loan. The lender then requests the appraisal in writing from the VA. The VA charges an appraisal fee, which must be paid in advance when the appraisal is ordered. The fee must be paid in cash. No form of credit is allowed by either the buyer or seller. A VA appraisal is good for a specific period of time as follows:

- Existing properties—The appraisal is valid for 6 months.
- Proposed construction—The appraisal is valid for 6 months.

When a buyer seeks to obtain VA financing, the sales contract is usually contingent on a VA appraisal greater than or equal to the sales price. When such a contingency exists and the appraised value is less than the sales price in the signed contract, the buyer has four options:

1. Void the contract and request a return of the earnest money.
2. Pay the difference in the appraised value and the sales price in cash.
3. Renegotiate the sales price with the seller so that it does not exceed the appraised value.
4. Request a reconsideration of the VA appraisal.

Let's look at some of these in more detail.

The borrower may pay more for a property than the VA appraisal, but the total amount of the price above the appraised value must be paid in cash. (Second mortgages are not allowed if the sales price exceeds the appraised value.) For example, a house is appraised for $104,250, which is the maximum loan amount on a 100% loan. If the price of the house is $109,250, the veteran must make a down payment of at least $5,000 ($109,250 − $104,250). While this is a possible solution, it is not often used because few people are willing to pay more than the appraised value. The borrower may also request that the appraisal be reconsidered. If this is done, the borrower must have a basis for a claim that the appraisal is too low, in the form of information on three comparable properties in the same area. The information on these comparables must include several specific items that are beyond the scope of this course. Consult the lender when dealing with a case such as this.

Eligible Properties

VA-guaranteed loans may be used to finance loans on residential property for one to four families that will be occupied by the veteran. They may not be used by investors to finance rental property. In general, the LTV can be 100% for a VA loan, which means that the veteran is not required to make a down payment. However, in some situations, a lower LTV is required (meaning the veteran must make a down payment).

The VA does not permit loans to exceed the appraised value of the home. If the sales price exceeds the appraised value, the difference must be paid in cash. The VA does not set a maximum loan amount. However, in general, lenders will not loan more than four times the amount of the VA guarantee available to the veteran. (The amount of the veteran's guarantee is also called the veteran's entitlement.) Thus, if the veteran's entitlement is $104,250, the maximum loan on which the lender will allow an LTV of 100% is $417,000 (4 × $104,250). The amount of entitlement varies with the loan amount and has been increased by the VA over the years. To obtain current guarantee amounts, contact the VA or a lender who provides VA loans.

ASSUMPTION METHODS

In order to finance a property that is being purchased, a buyer can assume the seller's existing loan. In this situation, the buyer usually pays the seller a down payment equal to the seller's equity in the property and agrees to take over the seller's mortgage loan. There are actually two slightly different legal methods of doing this. The difference in the methods is small but very important. These two methods are called:

1. assuming and agreeing to pay a loan
2. taking (the property) subject to an existing loan

Assuming and Agreeing to Pay a Loan

This is the most common method of assuming a loan. In this method, the purchaser becomes ultimately liable for the payment of the loan after it is assumed. If the purchaser defaults, the lender will foreclose on the seller. If there is a deficiency after the property is sold (the property sells for less than the balance owed), the seller can then obtain a judgment against the purchaser for the amount of the deficiency. In some cases, the seller may sign a loan modification agreement with the lender that makes the purchaser personally liable for the payment of the debt, even without a judgment by the seller.

Taking Subject to an Existing Loan

In taking subject to an existing loan, the purchaser does not become liable for the payment of the debt as he/she does under an assumption and agreement to pay.

If the purchaser states that he/she wants to purchase by taking subject to the existing loan, you should do the following:

- Inform the seller that the purchaser will not be liable for repayment of the loan.
- Seek competent legal advice to obtain additional information about the legal problems involved in this situation.

There are other potential problems you should be aware of when a purchaser wants to purchase property by assuming a loan, such as limitations imposed by other clauses in the loan and a changing loan balance.

Limitations from Other Clauses

In many situations, other clauses in the seller's loan may affect the ability to assume the loan or the conditions required to assume it. For example, an alienation (due on sale) clause may specify the following:

- The loan may not be assumed and must be paid in full if transferred to someone else.
- The loan may be assumed, but the interest rate increases.
- The loan may be assumed, but the purchaser must qualify (meet the lender's financial requirements) to assume the loan.

Changing Loan Balance

A loan assumption is often troublesome because the loan balance on the assumed loan changes between the signing of a sales contract and the closing of the sale. One problem occurs when the purchaser agrees to buy the property at a fixed price by assuming a loan. The difference in the selling price and the remaining balance is the amount of cash that the buyer must pay the seller. The buyer often doesn't realize that the amount of cash that he/she will have to pay may increase if the loan does not close right away. Let's look at why this happens.

A buyer agrees to buy a property for $100,000 by assuming the seller's loan. At the time the contract is signed, the situation looks like this:

Sales price	$100,000
Remaining balance	– 80,000
Cash required	$20,000

By the time the sale is closed, the situation may look like this:

Sales price	$100,000
Remaining balance	– 79,000
Cash required	$21,000

The difference in the cash required at closing, which the buyer did not expect, results from the fact that the payments made on the loan between the signing of the sales contract and the closing date reduced the remaining principal. (The amount of reduction used in this example is larger than normal to illustrate the point.) Because of this situation, there are two ways a loan assumption can be handled:

1. a loan assumption with price to control
2. a loan assumption with cash to control

The situation described above is an example of a loan assumption with price to control. In other words, price to control means that the selling price will be set, and the selling price (along with the changing loan balance) will control the amount of cash to be paid by the buyer.

In a loan assumption with cash to control, the buyer and seller do not agree on a fixed sales price. Instead, they agree that the buyer will pay the seller a fixed amount of cash and assume the remaining loan balance as of the date of closing.

There is no right or wrong way to structure a loan assumption. Either one of these two methods can be used. The method to use in any particular situation can be negotiated between the seller and buyer. If you have a buyer who wants to purchase property using a loan assumption, be sure to explain to both the buyer and seller the impact of each of these methods so no one is surprised at closing.

In many cases, when a buyer assumes a seller's loan, the seller's equity is greater than the amount the buyer has available for a down payment. In this situation, a seller may accept a note (a promissory note) as part of the payment for the seller's equity. This type of purchase is referred to as a seller taking a second mortgage. The loan (note) is referred to as a purchase money mortgage. This kind of financing arrangement can be used in either one of the two types of loan assumptions discussed above.

Coaching Tips

If the first mortgage note on the property being sold is an uninsured conventional mortgage, the lender may not allow the seller to take a second mortgage when the loan is assumed if the remaining loan balance is more than 80% of the current appraised value.

When to Use an Assumption

When considering the use of a loan assumption as a method of financing, it is important to consider if a loan assumption is appropriate. The first step when considering an assumption is to always determine from the lender whether the loan can be assumed. For most conventional loans made in the past several years, a loan may be assumed as long as the buyer qualifies for the loan just as he/she would on a new loan. However, never assume that this is the case. You should obtain information from the lender about the assumption of the loan when you obtain a listing on the property.

For loans that can be assumed, the most important factor that affects the ability to sell a home with a loan assumption is the LTV for the outstanding balance on the loan. The higher the ratio, the lower the down payment, and therefore the buyer will likely want to assume the loan. Properties that have assumable loans with low seller's equity in the property (low down payment required) should be relatively easy to sell. As the LTV decreases, and the required down payment increases, the marketability of the home using a loan assumption decreases. Some of the conditions under which a buyer is more likely to consider purchasing a home using a loan assumption include the following:

- The seller will finance part of the selling price.
- Mortgage money is not available.
- The buyer is unable to get a new loan.
- The property has declined in value.
- There is a difference in interest rate.

Let's look at each of these conditions briefly.

One factor that can substantially impact the likelihood of selling a property with a loan assumption is the owner's willingness to finance part of the purchase. This is particularly true if the LTV is low, thus requiring a large down payment. The larger the down payment required, the more difficult it is to sell with a loan assumption. However, if the seller is willing to finance part of the down payment, the loan assumption becomes a much more attractive financing alternative.

Loan assumptions also become very attractive financing alternatives during conditions of tight money supply. When new loan money is not readily available, buyers have fewer options for financing, and loan assumptions can offer an opportunity to obtain a loan that could not be obtained otherwise.

In some cases, a borrower may be in a position to afford a loan but for some reason cannot qualify for a new loan. For example, the borrower may be recently self-employed and not have adequate income verification to qualify. In this situation, a loan assumption may be the borrower's only opportunity to obtain a loan.

In some special cases, a loan assumption may be the best financing alternative because the value of the property has declined, and a new loan could not be obtained for an amount greater than the existing loan balance.

Finally, loan assumptions are often an attractive financing alternative when they have an interest rate that is substantially below the current market rate for new loans. However, most conventional loans are no longer assumable at the rate at which they were initially made. Most conventional loans now include an alienation clause that permits the lender to raise the interest rate if the loan is assumed.

Closing Requirements

The closing process for a loan assumption is faster and cheaper than the closing process for a new loan. On a loan assumption, the lender will typically require the following items:

- A loan transfer fee—This fee is substantially below the cost of obtaining a new loan.
- Warranty deed—A copy of the warranty deed conveying the property to the buyer must usually be supplied to the lender at closing.
- Insurance—A fire insurance policy in the buyer's name must also be supplied to the lender at closing.
- Escrow account—The buyer and seller must agree for the seller to "sell" the escrow account to the buyer or transfer it to the buyer in lieu of prorating the escrow funds.

Advantages and Disadvantages

There are a number of potential advantages available to both the buyer and seller with a loan assumption. The advantages to the seller include the following:

- The costs of closing the loan are substantially lower, so the seller might be able to sell the home for less than with a new loan and still realize the same profit.
- The lender might agree to release the seller from liability under the loan under some conditions.
- If both the seller and buyer are veterans, the seller might be able to transfer the entitlement on the property to the buyer, thus freeing up his/her own eligibility for another VA loan. This requires VA approval.

The advantages of a loan assumption to a buyer include the following:

- The possibility of a lower interest rate, with savings in interest expense, if the interest rate on the assumed loan is below the current market rate.
- Substantially lower closing costs than on a new loan.
- Less time to close because of the reduced requirements for loan documents and processing.
- Less personal liability in some cases. If the borrower takes the loan subject to the existing loan, as discussed earlier in this chapter, the buyer has no personal liability for the repayment of the loan.

Conversely, there are certain disadvantages of a loan assumption to both buyer and seller:

- Buyer disadvantages—A loan assumption might require a large down payment. Also, the buyer may not be able to offer a loan assumption when the

property is sold to a future buyer. The longer the loan is held after assumption, the lower the loan-to-value ratio becomes, increasing the size of the required down payment. If the property increases in value, this problem becomes even greater.
- Seller disadvantages—Unless the seller is released from liability when the loan is assumed, the seller remains ultimately liable for the loan until it is paid off. If the new owner defaults, the lender may sue the original owner as well as the owner in default. In addition, a seller may have difficulty obtaining a new loan if he/she is still liable for a loan that has been assumed.

QUALIFYING THE BUYER

Underwriting

Underwriting is a term you will hear often when working with buyers who are trying to obtain a loan. Underwriting is the process of evaluating two things:

1. the value of the property as collateral for a loan
2. the buyer's ability to make the down payment and repay the loan

The purpose of evaluating these two items is to determine whether the lender is willing to make a loan to the buyer, and if so, the amount of the loan the lender is willing to make. Before we look at the process of underwriting, let's look at how the standards for underwriting are determined.

There are three primary sets of guidelines you will encounter:

1. the FHLMC, or Freddie Mac, guidelines
2. the FHA guidelines
3. the VA guidelines

Let's look at each set of guidelines in more detail.

Freddie Mac Guidelines

You will most likely encounter the guidelines developed by Freddie Mac. The Freddie Mac guidelines were developed for use with any loans purchased by Freddie Mac from a lender in the primary mortgage market. Because Freddie Mac is the largest purchaser of conventional loans in the secondary mortgage market, these guidelines are often used lenders when making conventional loans. It is important to understand that when a lender in the primary mortgage market originates a conventional loan, the lender is free to use any underwriting guidelines it chooses. However, if a lender desires to sell a mortgage in the secondary mortgage market, the lender must make the loan under the guidelines required by the secondary market. For loans sold to Fannie Mae or Freddie Mac, the guidelines developed by Freddie Mac must be used in making a conventional loan.

These guidelines are often called the FNMA/FHLMC guidelines, because they are used by Fannie Mae as well. Any loan approved under these guidelines is called a **conforming loan**. Because of the requirement of using the FNMA/FHLMC guidelines for loans to be sold in the secondary market, most lenders have adopted those guidelines for all their conventional loans.

There are four major factors used to qualify a buyer under the FNMA/FHLMC guidelines:

1. the borrower's income
2. the borrower's net worth and available assets
3. the credit history of the borrower
4. documentation of relevant information

The last two factors, the credit history of the borrower and the documentation of information, are generally the same to qualify for all loans. The first two factors, the borrower's income and the borrower's net worth and available assets, will be covered next.

Coaching Tips

It is important to understand that when a lender in the primary mortgage market originates a conventional loan, the lender is free to use any underwriting guidelines it chooses. However, if a lender desires to sell a mortgage in the secondary mortgage market, the lender must make the loan under the guidelines required by the secondary market.

Borrower's Income

The borrower's income is a major factor in evaluating a loan application because that income largely determines the borrower's ability to repay the loan. In evaluating the borrower's income, the lender will determine the amount of the borrower's stable monthly income. This amount is the borrower's base monthly income (for both husband and wife), plus any acceptable secondary sources of income, such as bonuses, commissions paid in addition to regular income, overtime pay, part-time employment, social security payments, interest earned on savings and/or investments, and alimony or child support. In order to determine whether secondary sources of financing will be accepted in evaluating the borrower's ability to repay a loan, the lender will evaluate the reliability of the income as well as the extent to which it will likely continue on an ongoing basis. When properly documented, secondary sources of income, such as bonuses, overtime pay, commissions paid on a regular basis, and part-time employment, are usually acceptable as part of the borrower's qualifying income. Other secondary income, such as alimony and child support payments, may or may not be acceptable, depending on the reliability of the payments, the qualifications of the person making the payments, and the time period over which they will be paid. Some sources of secondary income, such as unemployment or welfare payments, are almost never allowed as part of the borrower's stable monthly income because they are considered to be temporary income and therefore not reliable over time. The borrower's employment record is also used to evaluate the borrower's income.

Generally, the longer a borrower has been continuously employed by the same employer, the more favorable the record. Frequent changes in employment are generally perceived as a negative factor, unless they demonstrate a pattern of improvement in employment. The anticipated stability of continued employment is also a factor, so the identity and stability of the employer may also be considered. The final element in evaluating the borrower's income is the use of financial ratios to directly evaluate the borrower's ability to repay a loan. Under the FNMA/FHLMC guidelines (and the FHA and VA guidelines), there are two ratios used for evaluation purposes:

1. The ratio of the mortgage payment to stable monthly income (which is also known as the ratio to monthly housing obligations. The monthly housing obligations is the ratio of monthly income and PITI costs).
2. The ratio of all installment debts to stable monthly income (which is also known as the ratio to monthly total obligations. The monthly total obligations ratio measures the total monthly recurring expenses in relation to monthly income).

The first ratio is that of the monthly mortgage payment to the stable monthly income. Under FNMA/FHLMC guidelines, the amount of the mortgage payment should not exceed 28% of the borrower's stable monthly income. For example, if the borrower's stable monthly income is $2,000, the mortgage payment should not exceed $560, which is 28% of $2,000. If the mortgage payment exceeds 28% of the stable monthly income, the borrower's income is not considered adequate for the repayment of the loan.

The second ratio is that of the borrower's total monthly installment debt payments to the stable monthly income. Under FNMA/FHLMC guidelines, the amount of the total monthly debt payments should not exceed 36% of the stable monthly income. For example, if the borrower's stable monthly income is $2,000, the total debt payments should not exceed $720, which is 36% of $2,000. If the total debt payments exceed 36% of the stable monthly income, the borrower's income is not considered adequate to meet all debt requirements and repay the loan. This second ratio between total monthly installment debt payments and the stable monthly income is often referred to as the total debt service ratio. The above ratios are representative of conventional loans. Nonconventional loans (FHA/VA) have higher ratios.

Net Worth and Assets

The second major factor considered in qualifying the buyer is the buyer's net worth and the assets available to make the down payment and to provide adequate reserves.

The buyer's net worth is the difference between total assets and total liabilities. It is a value that provides a good indicator of the borrower's overall financial strength. If a borrower has a high net worth, it can offset some weakness in one or both of the ratios just covered. The borrower must have enough cash among assets to pay the down payment required on a loan. The most common type of conventional loan requires a down payment of 20% of the purchase price, or the appraised value, whichever is less. Conventional loans may also be made that require only a 10% or 5% down payment in some cases. These loans require the payment of private mortgage insurance. When a substantial part of the borrower's net worth is in the form of liquid assets, such as savings, money market certificates, etc., it provides additional strength to the borrower's ability to repay a loan because these assets are readily available to meet financial demands in emergencies. Under FNMA/FHLMC guidelines, the borrower is required to have available a minimum amount of highly liquid assets (cash or its equivalent) equal to mortgage payments for two months. This amount must be available over and above the amount needed for the down payment and any costs of closing the loan.

FHA Guidelines

Income Ratios

On April 13, 2005, HUD increased the allowable debt ratio for manually underwritten loans from 29/31 to 31/43. For an FHA loan, the ratio of the monthly mortgage payment to the stable monthly income should not exceed 31%. The ratio of the total monthly installment debts to the stable monthly income should not exceed 43%.

The debt ratios represent the relationship between an individual's income and expenses. These ratios are generally seen as two numbers like 31 over 43, or 31/43. The first number, 31, represents the relationship between the borrower's income and his/her new housing expense of rent and/or PITI (and/or any homeowner dues).

The second number, 43, represents the total monthly payment obligations, including housing expenses and all other debt such as credit cards, loans, and child support.

Down Payment

The amount of the down payment on an FHA loan is equal to the sales price less the loan amount. The formula that the FHA uses to determine the loan amount has changed several times in recent years and currently involves a complex set of calculations. Because of this, we will not cover the calculations in this course. However, you should remember that the minimum cash investment the borrower can make is 3% of the sales price or appraised value, whichever is less.

VA Guidelines

Underwriting

The guidelines to qualify for a VA loan are considerably different from the qualification guidelines for FNMA/FHLMC and FHA loans. For example, the VA considers what is called the residual income available after taxes are deducted. The specifics of qualifying for VA loans will not be covered in this course. You should consult your broker or a lender when qualifying a buyer for a VA loan. In addition to the financial ratios used to qualify a buyer for a VA loan, it is important to determine whether a buyer is eligible for a VA loan. Generally, a buyer who is eligible for a VA loan is a veteran who has served one of the following:

1. a minimum of 90 days' extended active duty in wartime, including World War II, Korea, and Vietnam
2. 181 days in peacetime prior to September 8, 1980
3. two years in peacetime after September 7, 1980

There is a list of specific dates from September 16, 1940, through the present and the number of days of service required during those times in order to qualify for a VA loan. You are not required to know this list of dates and the amount of service required. However, you should be aware that the days of service differ for different periods. You should consult your broker or a lender designated by your broker for a determination of eligibility.

There are two remaining factors important in the underwriting process, the credit history of the borrower and the documentation of the information supplied to the lender. The requirements for each of these are the same for all qualification guidelines.

Credit History

The borrower's credit history is an important factor in determining whether the borrower qualifies for a loan. A buyer who has consistently met his credit obligations on a timely basis is considered a good risk for a loan. The borrower must show all current debts on the loan application. If a borrower attempts to hide a debt by failing to list it on the loan application, the loan may be denied. The lender will also obtain the borrower's credit report from a credit reporting agency and occasionally will contact the borrower's creditors.

Documentation

The last factor in the underwriting process is documenting the information provided to the lender. There are two categories of documentation that may be required, depending on the nature and amount of the loan:

1. Regular documentation
2. Alternative documentation

Regular Documentation

Regular documentation refers to the level of documentation usually required on loans with a loan-to-value ratio of 80% or higher. Under regular documentation requirements, the lender will require at least three sources of documentation. The first is a verification of employment (VOE) form filled out by the borrower's employer that verifies the borrower's salary and length of employment. The second is a verification of deposit (VOD) form filled out by all financial institutions where the borrower has an account. The purpose of this form is to verify the availability of the cash needed to close the loan. The third is a credit report, which the lender will request from a credit reporting agency. Both the verification of employment and verification of deposit forms must be mailed by the employer or bank to the lender. These verifications may not be hand delivered or mailed by the borrower or a real estate agent.

Alternative Documentation

Alternative documentation is often available on loans of up to 90% of the sales price. Under alternative documentation, the verification of employment may be replaced by two current pay stubs and the borrower's W-2 tax form for the previous year. These are supplied to the lender by the borrower. The verification of deposit may be replaced by the borrower's three most recent bank statements, which are supplied to the lender by the borrower. With alternative documentation, the lender also requires a full credit report, just as with regular documentation.

Appraisal

There is one final documentation requirement for all loans. All loans require that the lender have a current appraisal of the property so the lender can establish the property's value. Regardless of the loan type, mortgage loans tend to be originated based on the amount that is the lesser of the purchase price or the appraised value.

Maximum Loan Amount

Another underwriting topic we need to cover is how the maximum loan amount for which a borrower can qualify is determined. Often, it is important for a buyer to know the maximum size loan he/she can obtain. This is determined by the following factors:

- the maximum amount of cash available for the down payment (and any other closing costs required)
- the maximum monthly loan payment for which the borrower can qualify

These factors may limit the amount of the loan that a buyer might obtain. For example, a buyer might have $10,000 available as a down payment. The maximum loan amount he/she could obtain depends on the type of loan. On a conventional loan, the maximum loan amount would be determined by the loan-to-value ratio:

- 95% loan—the maximum loan amount would be $190,000
- 90% loan—the maximum loan amount would be $90,000
- 80% loan—the maximum loan amount would be $40,000

With any of these conventional loans, the maximum loan amount might be reduced by the buyer's ability to qualify for monthly payments. For example, if a buyer made a down payment on a 90% loan of $90,000 at an interest rate of 9.5% for 30 years, he/she would have to qualify for monthly payments of $756.77. If the buyer could not qualify for such a payment, the maximum loan amount would be reduced. The maximum amount a buyer can qualify for on a loan may be determined by:

- the cash available for a down payment
- the ability to qualify for the monthly payment

Reverse Annuity Loans

When social security or pension income is insufficient to meet living needs, there is a loan option called a reverse annuity loan. A **reverse annuity loan** is a loan available for retirees or the elderly in the form of a home mortgage. Under this loan program, an elderly homeowner is given a long-term loan where monthly payments go against the property owner's equity in the home (the collateral). The loan is eventually repaid to the lender when the home is sold.

Rural Housing Loan (Land Development Loans)

In rural areas undeveloped land can be financed through rural housing land development loans. The USDA ultimately determines what "rural" means. This meaning also varies widely by state. If eligible, one can qualify for lower monthly payments and perhaps 100% financing. Some of the options available with this type of loan include but are not limited to:

- 100% financing with no down payment required at closing
- no mortgage insurance (means lower monthly payments)
- the loan's income eligibility cap varies by community

LOAN CHARGES

Charges are incurred when a buyer takes out a loan for real property. The term closing costs includes a number of different loan charges that vary from lender to lender.

There are two types of closing costs: variable costs and fixed costs. Variable closing costs are those that vary with the amount of the loan. Typically, variable costs are assessed as a percentage of the loan amount. The following are included in variable costs:

- lender's title insurance
- origination fees

Fixed closing costs are those that are assessed as a fixed fee and do not vary with the amount of the loan, including:

- appraisal fee
- attorney's fees (could also be variable if charged on an hourly basis)
- credit report fee
- survey
- recording fees
- pictures
- amortization schedule

Let's take a look at some of the different items included in closing costs.

Variable Costs

Title insurance is a variable cost. The title insurance policy protects the lender against any loss that results from defects in the title. Title insurance that protects the lender is called lender's title insurance or mortgagee title insurance and is always required by the lender but is not required by law. The buyer may also elect to obtain a purchaser's or fee title insurance policy, which protects against losses due to defects in the title. Unless this type of policy is obtained independently by the buyer, there is no such coverage provided in a typical closing procedure. The fees for title insurance are typically assessed as a specified fee per $1,000 of the loan amount.

Another type of variable closing cost is the origination fee. The origination fee is charged by the lender for processing the loan. It covers primarily the administrative costs to do the paperwork on the loan such as filling out forms and reviewing credit reports and appraisals. Origination fees are usually a percentage of the loan amount. On FHA and VA loans, the origination fee is limited to 1% of the loan amount. The origination fee may be paid by the buyer or the seller on all loans, including FHA, VA, and conventional loans.

Fixed Costs

Fixed closing costs include the following:

- Appraisal fee—This fee covers the cost of having the property appraised by a qualified appraiser. The appraisal is conducted so the lender can determine if the property provides adequate security for the loan. The buyer or seller may also obtain an independent appraisal of the property if desired, but the fee for such an appraisal is not included in the closing costs.

- Attorney fees—Attorney fees pay for legal services provided to the lender in closing the loan. The services provided usually include checking the title, preparing the various documents for closing, and conducting the closing meeting itself. Usually the attorney who conducts the closing meeting represents the lender, and the fees for this service are included in the closing costs. The attorney fees are usually a fixed amount ($400 and up).
- Credit report fee—This fee covers the cost of the credit report that the lender uses to evaluate the credit risk posed by the borrower. The seller may also insist on a credit report if an existing loan is assumed or if the seller extends credit to the buyer in the form of a purchase money mortgage.
- Survey—A survey may also be required by a lender; if it is, the fee for the survey is a fixed closing cost. Different lenders have different policies on when they require a survey. Some always require them; some only require a survey when there is a potential problem or for certain types of properties. Always check with a specific lender to determine its policy on surveys. The cost of the survey is determined by the surveyor and varies with the type of survey, size of property, and type of property.
- Recording fee—This is a fee charged by the county for recording documents in the public records. These fees are often in the range of $15 to $50.
- Pictures—Some lenders require pictures of the property being financed.
- Amortization schedule—Some lenders provide a printout or chart of the payment schedule, which shows such things as a month-by-month breakdown of interest and principal paid. The cost is usually about $10.

The payment of loan costs is normally the responsibility of the buyer because these costs are associated with obtaining a loan. However, the payment of these costs is negotiable between the buyer and seller, and either or both may pay closing costs. Also, local custom may determine who pays for specific items. Any sales contract should clearly specify who is to pay any or all of the closing costs.

Discount Points

Another fee often paid at closing is discount points. Earlier in this chapter, you learned the definition of discount points and what role they have in the financing process. On conventional, FHA, and VA loans, either the buyer or the seller may pay the discount points. Prior to 1993, the VA required that someone other than the buyer pay the discount points on new VA loans except in cases of refinancing by the veteran. Now, however, the veteran (the buyer) is allowed to pay the discount points on any VA loan. All loan costs may be paid by the buyer or seller on all loans.

There is one additional charge on VA loans—the VA funding fee. This fee is used to fund the expenses of operating the VA. The amount of the fee varies with the amount of the down payment and the military status of the veteran (e.g., active status, veteran, reservist). It may be paid by the buyer or seller. If the veteran is disabled, the funding fee may be waived.

Seller Financing

In addition to all forms of institutional and private financing available to a purchaser, a seller with substantial equity in the property can use that equity to provide financing to a qualified buyer/borrower. When the seller acts as the lender, the loan is called a purchase money mortgage (PMM). It is not uncommon for the seller to originate seller financing on a transaction involving a contract for deed (installment sales contract). Nothing in the aforementioned precludes the seller from also structuring the loan as an amortized mortgage.

Mortgage Bond Financing

Mortgage bond financing is defined as a bond that is likely secured by a mortgage or pool of mortgages. As a result, the bond or bonds are generally backed and secured by real property. In the event of a borrower default, the property pledged as security can be foreclosed on and sold to pay off the unpaid portion of the note/bond to the bondholders.

Mortgage Fraud

As a result of the subprime crisis and financial debacle of 2007, a greater need for mortgage fraud awareness was required. **Mortgage fraud** is when a prospective borrower lies on his/her loan application to improve the odds of securing a loan. Schemes such as money back at closing (through seller concessions) and the use of a straw buyer require the licensee's attention. Straw buyers are people who have no intention of ever living on the property. In fact, they are being paid a fee for the use of their credit information. In other cases, straw buyers can also result in or lead to the potential of identity theft. The reason for using a straw buyer is that the real applicant could not qualify for a loan on his/her own.

No Document Loans

Prior to the financial and subprime lending crisis, these loans were considered common. Where underwriting of loans required credit scores, employment verification, and other income information, these loans were originated with little or no supporting borrower documents. This practice most probably occurred because of low interest rates and an "easy money" marketplace. Aside from subprime and ARM loans contributing to the financial crisis, these loans also contributed to the financial problems the United States faced in 2007.

Equal Credit Opportunity Act

The Equal Credit Opportunity Act (ECOA) was passed in order to prohibit discrimination in loan underwriting on the basis of:

- sex
- marital status
- race
- religion
- age
- national origin

The ECOA also prohibits a lender from requiring an applicant's spouse to join in (sign) the loan application. In addition, the ECOA also prohibits discriminatory treatment of income from any of the following sources:

- alimony
- public assistance
- child support
- part-time employment

The ECOA further prohibits a lender from inquiring about child-bearing plans or the potential of family creation.

Consumer Credit Protection Act/Truth-in-Lending Act

The Truth-in-Lending Act (TILA) falls under Title 1 of the Consumer Credit Protection Act. The purpose of TILA is to help the consumer understand the full costs associated with borrowing. This allows the consumer to shop for better rates and terms.

The Federal Reserve Regulation Z

The Federal Reserve Regulation Z and TILA go hand in hand. Regulation Z specifically governs the advertising of credit terms. Advertisements of credit terms sometimes include terminology that triggers the need for further disclosures on the part of the lender/advertiser. These are referred to as triggering terms. When a triggering term is used, the following disclosures are required:

- the borrowed amount—is the principal-only portion of the borrowed amount
- total cost of finance charges—represents in a dollar amount the total finance charges the borrower could expect
- total payments over the life of the loan—includes both principal and interest payments that will be paid by maturity

Triggering terms include but are not limited to:

- a reference to monthly payments

- a reference to a dollar amount of the finance charge
- numeric or percentage reference to down payments (only 10% down or only $5,000 down)
- a reference to the term of a loan

An example of terminology that would not trigger further disclosure would be "low down payment."

Annual Percentage Rate (APR)

Under Regulation Z, when a triggering term is used (requiring further disclosure), one of the important disclosures is that the total cost of finance charges must be expressed in the form of annual percentage rate (APR). The APR includes all other loan costs and is the annual rate charged against the borrowed amount.

On certain lending transactions, TILA also provides a borrower with further protections. This includes a 3-day right of rescission on a refinanced loan, line of credit, and second mortgage financing but not on an acquisition or construction loan.

REAL ESTATE SETTLEMENT AND PROCEDURES ACT

The Real Estate Settlement and Procedures Act (RESPA) requires a lender to inform a buyer or seller as to the total cost of all advance fees that will be charged to the borrower at closing. This may include but not be limited to:

- appraisal cost
- survey
- lender's attorney
- environmental study
- lien search

In each of the services above, the lender must charge the borrower at the lender's cost. RESPA forbids kickbacks. RESPA generally applies to any closing involving a standard home mortgage as well as federally related transactions for one- to four-family properties. Currently, there are two disclosures that have been combined and integrated into the TILA/RESPA Disclosure Rule. This disclosure rule was legislated under the Dodd-Frank Act. The disclosure was placed in service as of October 2015. It is intended to protect consumers in all real property transactions where acquisition financing is originated. The two disclosures are:

1. The loan estimate—this document must be delivered or mailed by the lender to the borrower no later than the third business day following an application for credit. The loan estimate lists all costs of credit and transaction costs for the borrower. The form will separately list each closing cost that the borrower can expect.

2. The closing disclosure—this document must be given by the lender to the borrower no later than the three business days prior to closing on the loan. This form acts as the closing statement for the transaction. The form has five pages: Page 1 will contain the names of the parties and other transactional information. Page 2 will contain a list of the closing costs for each respective party to the transaction. Page 3 lists the amount of funds required by the buyer on the date of the closing. Page 3 also lists the amount that the seller will receive on the date of the closing. Page 4 contains detailed information on the borrower's loan. This includes all detail of the loan. Page 5 includes additional loan information about the borrower's loan. This includes actual details of the loan such as:

1. total number of payments
2. total interest to be paid on the life of the loan
3. the total amount to be paid over the life of the loan
4. the annual percentage rate

In addition to the aforementioned, Page 5 will also include:

1. the name(s) of the closing agent
2. the name of the lender
3. the name of the real estate broker or brokerage

Figure 13.4 summarizes the real estate financing process.

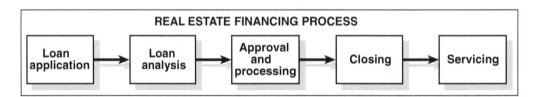

FIGURE 13.4
Source: © 2021 Mbition LLC

Summary

Loans are originated in the primary mortgage market; these same loans are bought and sold by others in the secondary market. As previously mentioned, the secondary market operations should not be confused with secondary financing on a property.

There are two types of loan options available to qualified borrowers. These options are either conventional mortgages or nonconventional mortgages. While nonconventional mortgages are government guaranteed, conventional mortgages are not. Nonconventional mortgages would include FHA and VA loans.

Points are charged to enhance the yield to the lender. One point represents 1% of the loan amount and is considered as prepaid interest.

Review Questions

1. The majority of the commercial banks in the United States:
   a. are regulated by the Office of Thrift Supervision
   b. are members of the Federal Reserve System (the Fed)
   c. belong to the Federal Home Loan Bank System
   d. are privately owned and are largely unregulated

2. Which of the following best describes what a discount point is?
   a. It is the prime rate given to a bank's best borrowers
   b. One point represents 1% of the borrowed amount
   c. It is the general interest rate the Fed sets for primary lenders
   d. It is the interest primary lenders charge borrowers to increase the lenders' profits

3. All of the following are correct about a conventional loan EXCEPT:
   a. it is not a government guaranteed loan
   b. it is an FHA loan
   c. it is guaranteed by a government agency
   d. it is a VA loan program

4. A lender makes profits from the margins or the spreads. The margin or spread is the difference between:
   a. cost of funds from FHA and the rate paid by the borrower
   b. cost of funds from the Fed and the rate paid by the borrower
   c. cost of funds from the VA and the rate paid by the borrower
   d. none of these

5. Fifth Federal Savings and Loan advertises itself as a "Member of the FDIC." This means:
   a. deposits are insured up to $100,000 per branch location
   b. deposits are insured up to $250,000 per account on deposit
   c. deposits are insured up to $100,000 per member institution
   d. the federal government will replace all deposits if the banking institution fails

6. The news from the stock market is unusually good, and depositors are withdrawing their money from banks and savings associations in order to buy stocks. This action by depositors has resulted in:
   a. disintermediation
   b. a decrease in interest rates
   c. intermediation
   d. more money available for mortgages

7. The primary mortgage market:
   a. is regulated by the Federal Home Loan Bank System
   b. is regulated by the Fed
   c. originates loans with qualified borrowers
   d. buys mortgages from lenders

8. The largest originators of residential real property loans are:
   a. mortgage bankers
   b. mortgage brokers
   c. mortgage companies
   d. commercial banks

9. The oldest participant in the secondary market is:
   a. the Federal National Mortgage Association
   b. the Government National Mortgage Association
   c. the Federal Home Loan Mortgage Corporation
   d. the Federal Home Loan Bank System

10. Which institution acts as a guarantor for mortgage-backed securities that are sold to the general public?
    a. The Federal National Mortgage Association
    b. The Government National Mortgage Association
    c. The Federal Home Loan Mortgage Corporation
    d. The Federal Home Loan Bank System

11. The institution created by Congress for the primary purpose of buying conventional loans from savings associations is:
    a. the Federal National Mortgage Association
    b. the Government National Mortgage Association
    c. the Federal Home Loan Mortgage Corporation
    d. the Federal Housing Administration

12. A lender charged 6% interest for a loan plus two discount points. The approximate yield to the lender is:
    a. 5¾%
    b. 6¼%
    c. 6½%
    d. 7%

13. Ramon has qualified to purchase a new home for $300,000. The loan is a 90% conventional loan and the lender is charging 2½ points. What will the points cost Ramon on this loan?
    a. $5,000
    b. $6,000
    c. $6,750
    d. $7,500

14. Which of the following statements is FALSE regarding the FHA 203(b) loan?
    a. The FHA guarantees the loan and sets the interest rates for borrowers.
    b. The FHA insures the loan and the borrower pays for the insurance.
    c. Limits are set by law and depend on the location.
    d. The FHA requires the borrower to make 3% minimum cash investment.

15. Which of the following statements is FALSE regarding the VA loan?
    a. The VA guarantees the loan.
    b. The VA loan is so secure to the lender that generally no down payment is required.
    c. The VA can make loans directly to active duty personnel, veterans, and spouses.
    d. The VA regulations state the veteran cannot be charged points on the loan.

16. If a veteran defaults on a VA loan, the maximum guarantee to the lender is:
    a. one-fourth of the value of the home up to $60,000
    b. one-half of the value of the home up to $60,000
    c. one-fourth of the value of the home up to $89,912
    d. one-fourth of the value of the home up to $106,025

17. The VA loan:
    a. always contains a due on sale clause
    b. eligibility is established by the Department of Veterans Affairs
    c. cannot be used for refinancing, construction, or repairs
    d. cannot be used for improvements to existing homes

18. The FHA government agency:
    a. requires the borrower to pay a one-time upfront mortgage insurance premium
    b. will process loans to build houses
    c. will automatically cancel the mortgage insurance premium on a condo after loan-to-value reaches 78%
    d. will not authorize adjustable rate mortgages

14 REAL ESTATE–RELATED COMPUTATIONS AND CLOSING OF TRANSACTIONS

KEY TERMS

arrears
credit
debit
level payment plan

preclosing inspection
principle
profit
prorate

LEARNING OBJECTIVES

After completing this lesson, you will be able to:

- compute the sales commission
- calculate the percent of profit or loss, given the original cost of the investment, the sales price, and the dollar amount of profit and loss
- define title closing
- list the preliminary steps to a closing
- prorate the buyers' and sellers' expenses
- calculate the dollar amount of transfer taxes on deeds, mortgages, and notes
- allocate taxes and fees to the proper parties and compute individual costs
- explain the rule of thumb for closing statement entries
- explain the major sections of the Uniform Settlement Statement (HUD 1)
- demonstrate ability to read and check the Uniform Settlement Statement (HUD 1) for errors

BASIC REAL ESTATE COMPUTATIONS

Review of fractions, decimals, percentages, and ratios:

- When utilizing fractions, decimals, percentages, and ratios, calculations are representative of a portion of a whole number. These are usually items that are less than the number 1.
- A fraction is part of a whole number.
- A decimal is a fraction that has been converted to the decimal equivalent within the decimal system.

- A percentage is a part of a whole, written in either decimal or percentage form.
- A ratio is a portion of a **principal** (original amount of investment or borrowed amount) amount that is expressed in either percentage or decimal form. It can be used to determine the **profit** (amount realized on an investment over and above the original invested amount).

For further illustrations of the aforementioned, please see the Math Busters section.

SALES COMMISSIONS

Sales commissions are calculated using the following formula:

$$\text{Sales Commission} = \text{Sales Price} \times \text{Percentage of Commission}$$

Calculating Selling Price, Cost, and Profit

When a seller is pricing a property for sale in the marketplace, they will include all transaction costs derived from the sale of the property. These costs will be added in over and above the price they seek as a net sales price. For example, a seller wishes to net at the point of sale $100,000. This is after paying a real estate broker a commission of 6%. Based on this information and in order for the seller to walk away with the net desired amount of $100,000, the minimum sales price would be as illustrated below:

Step 1: Establish who gets what.

The following is the breakdown on every dollar received in conjunction with this type of calculation:

- $0.94 to the seller
- $0.06 to the broker

Step 2: Divide the net sales price ($100,000) by the reciprocal amount ($0.94). The reciprocal of 6%, or 0.06, is 0.94. Remember there are only 100 pieces to a whole number or a dollar (as the case may be).

- $100,000 ÷ 0.94 = $106,382.98 (minimum sales price)

Calculating Price and Commissions

The price or value of a property may be determined by the following equations:

$$\text{Price} = \frac{\text{Annual Net Income}}{\text{Capitalization Rate}}$$

$$\text{Price} = \frac{\text{Income}}{\text{Rate}}$$

$$\frac{\text{Income}}{\text{Rate}} = \text{Price} \quad \text{So in this case} \quad \frac{\$42,000}{0.10} = \$420,000$$

In order to better understand these equations, let's cover two basic types of math problems:

1. those involving commissions on sales
2. those involving investments and return on investments

Then we will cover two additional problem types:

1. those involving estimates of value based on rates of return (capitalization problems)
2. those involving loans

Before learning how to solve the following problems, you will first learn a name for each type of problem. A big part of learning how to solve these problems is learning how to recognize and name the type of problem you are solving. Once you are able to do this, the process of completing the necessary calculations is much simpler.

Commission Problems

Let's begin with the first type of problem—those involving commissions paid on the sale of real estate. We will call this type of problem a commission problem. While solving commission problems, you will be organizing information in a way that will be used in the first four types of problems. We will refer to this method of organization as the T-bar.

Before working on the first commission problem, let's define some basic terms:

- commission (C)—the amount a broker receives for selling a property
- sales price (P)—the amount the property sells for
- rate of commission (R)—the commission expressed as a percentage of the sales price

Problem: A property sells for $120,000. The listing broker will receive a commission of 6% for selling the property. How much is the commission?

We can express the relationship between these three numbers using the T-bar as follows:

$$\frac{\text{Commission}}{\text{Sales Price} \mid \text{Rate of Commission}} \quad \text{OR} \quad \frac{C}{P \mid R}$$

The best way to remember this formula is to remember CPR. This will be the code for commission problems. The T-bar is a simple way to remember the arithmetic steps needed to solve a problem like the one above. Let's stop and take a look at how it works before we come back to our commission problem. The position of the numbers in the T-bar is important because the position determines whether a number is to be multiplied or divided by another number.

For example, the T-bar for commission problem is shown to the left (a). The first thing you should note is how the letters are placed in the T-bar. Whenever you learn a T-bar, you will be given a three-letter code to remember its contents. In this case, it is CPR. The first letter of the code always goes on top of the T-bar. The second letter always goes on the bottom left. The third letter always goes on the bottom right, as shown.

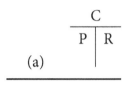

Now, let's look at how we use the T-bar to help solve problems. The first step to solve a problem is to block out one of the letters in the T-bar. Always block out the letter that is an unknown. The unknown is the number we are trying to find by solving the problem.

When we block out any one of the letters, we are left with two letters with a line between them. The direction of the line tells us whether to multiply or divide the numbers represented by the letters.

For example, if we block out the top letter as shown in (b), we are left with the P and R and a vertical line between them. (P and R are side-by-side.) The vertical line means that we multiply the two numbers.

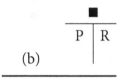

If we block out the P as shown in (c), we are left with the C and R and a horizontal line between them. (C is above R.) The horizontal line means that we divide the top number by the bottom number.

If we block out the R as shown in (d), we are left with the C and P and a horizontal line between them. (C is above P.) The horizontal line means that we divide the top number by the bottom number.

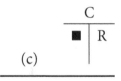

Let's go back and see how to use this T-bar to solve our commission problem.

Problem: A property sells for $120,000. The listing broker will receive a commission of 6% for selling the property. How much is the commission?

In this problem, we know the following:

Sales Price (P) = $120,000
Rate of Commission (R) = 6%

The one thing we don't know is the commission (C). But we can determine the commission by entering what we know into our T-bar, as shown next.

```
              C
    ─────────────────────
    $120,000 (P) │ 6% (R)
           ↑         ↑
Sales Price ─┘       └─ Rate of Commission
```

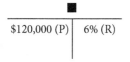

When we block out the unknown (C) as shown on the right, we are left with P and R separated by a vertical line. This means that we multiply $120,000 by 6% to get the value for C, as shown next:

$$\begin{array}{r} \$120{,}000 \\ \underline{0.06} \\ \$7{,}200 \end{array}$$

This tells us that C (Commission) is $7,200, which is the listing broker's commission.

Once you know the commission T-bar (CPR), you can work any problem of this type by substituting the two known values from the problem into the formula. Let's look at a similar commission problem.

Problem: A salesperson will receive 45% of a 6% commission for selling a property listed by her broker. If she sells a property for $150,000, how much will she earn?

The only thing different about this problem is that the salesperson doesn't get the entire commission. First, let's use the commission T-bar to determine the amount of the broker's total commission.

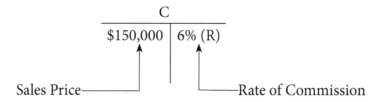

The broker's commission is $9,000:

$$\$150{,}000 \times 0.06 = \$9{,}000$$

The salesperson's commission is 45% of the total commission ($9,000), so the salesperson's commission is:

$$\$9{,}000 \times 0.45 = \$4{,}050$$

The salesperson will earn $4,050 for selling the property.

Now, let's look at how we can use the same T-bar to solve a problem that looks more difficult (but really isn't).

Problem: A broker lists and sells a property. As compensation, he receives a 5% commission that amounts to $7,800. What was the selling price of the property?

To solve the problem, enter the two things we know into the T-bar to find out what to multiply or divide.

$$\frac{\$7{,}800}{P \mid 0.05} \quad \begin{array}{l} \leftarrow \text{C = Commission Amount} \\ \leftarrow \text{R = Rate of Commission} \end{array}$$

When we block out the unknown (P), we are left with $7,800 over 0.05, which means to divide:

$$\$7{,}800 \div 0.05 = \$156{,}000$$

The house sold for $156,000.

Investment Problems

Now, let's look at investment problems. These problems can be worked using a T-bar similar to the one you just used. The T-bar is as follows:

$$\frac{\text{Profit}}{\text{Amount} \mid \text{Rate of}} \quad \text{OR} \quad \frac{P}{A \mid R}$$
$$\text{Invested} \mid \text{Return}$$

Note that the code for investment problems is PAR.

First, let's look at the elements in the investment T-bar:

- Profit—The amount of money made on an investment. It may also be called yield, income, or return.

> **Coaching Tips**
>
> Profit does not include and should not be confused with the original amount of money or the principal investment that the investor invested and got back. It is only the additional money earned above what the investor originally invested. Profit is usually the remaining income after the property's operational expenses have been paid.

- Amount Invested—The amount of money the investor spent initially in order to acquire the property (the selling price, not the down payment).
- Rate of Return—The percentage (rate) that the investor makes (or wants to make) on an investment. This amount ultimately equates the dollar profit amount found in the P of the T-bar. The rate of return is the percentage of the original investment needed as profit for parking one's money within an

investment. The receipt of interest given by a bank on deposits is another form of rate of return.

Now, let's look at a problem using the investment T-bar.

Problem: An investor purchased two lots for $30,000 each. She later divided the land into three lots and sold them for $25,000 each. What was her rate of return?

Let's look at what we know and don't know:

- Amount Invested—The investor paid $30,000 for each of two lots, for a total investment of $60,000.
- Profit—The investor sold three lots for $25,000 each, for a total price of $75,000.
- The price ($75,000) less the cost ($60,000) gives the profit, which in this case is $15,000.
- Rate of Return—This is what we want to find.

Now, let's take what we know and enter it into the T-bar:

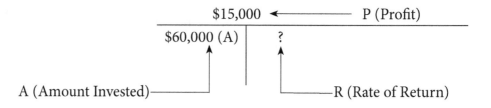

The investor's rate of return is 25%:

$$\$15,000 \div \$60,000 = 0.25$$

Now, let's look at a different type of problem using the same T-bar.

Problem: An investor wants to earn a return of $250 per month on an investment that has a rate of return of 8%. How much will the investor need to invest to do this?

Again, let's start with what we know and don't know:

- Profit—The amount that the investor wants to earn is $250 per month. For 12 months, this would be $250 × 12 = $3,000.
- Rate of Return—The investment yields a rate of return of 8%.
- Amount Invested—This is what we want to determine.

Now, let's take what we know and enter it in the T-bar.

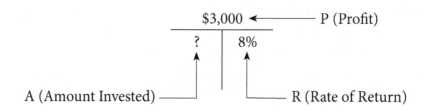

When we block out the unknown (A), we are left with $3,000 over 8%, which means to divide:

$$\$3{,}000 \div 0.08 = \$37{,}500$$

The investor must invest $37,500 to obtain the desired profit of $250 per month. Now, let's look at an investment problem that looks very different from those you just worked but is easy to work using the same T-bar.

Problem: A borrower borrows $6,000 and signs a note for it that must be paid off in 12 months, with interest at 10%. The lender then immediately sells the note to an investor for $5,000. What is the investor's rate of return?

First, let's look at what we know and don't know:

- Rate of Return—This is what we want to find. (It is not 10%.)
- Amount Invested—This is $5,000, the amount paid for the note.
- Profit—We must calculate the profit, as shown next.

At the end of the year, the note will have earned 10% of its face value of $6,000, or $600. When the note is paid off, the investor will have received a total of $6,600 (the original $6,000 principal plus $600 in interest).

The investor's profit is the total amount received less the amount he paid for the note:

$$\$6{,}600 - \$5{,}000 = \$1{,}600$$

Now, let's take what we know and enter it in the T-bar.

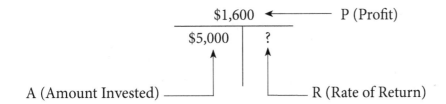

When we block out the unknown (R), we are left with $1,600 over $5,000, which means to divide:

$$\$1{,}600 \div \$5{,}000 = 0.32$$

The investor's rate of return is 32%.

Value Problems

Now, let's look at value problems. These problems can be solved using a T-bar similar to the ones you have just used:

$$\frac{\text{Income}}{\text{Rate of Capitalization} \mid \text{Value of Property}} \quad \text{OR} \quad \frac{I}{R \mid V}$$

Note that the code for value problems is IRV. The value T-bar is used to work problems based on the income method for appraising income-producing property. The income method uses the process of capitalization. Capitalization is the process of determining the value of a property from how much net income it produces. The capitalization rate is the percentage used for the rate of return that an investor obtains or desires to obtain by buying and owning the income-producing property.

First, let's look at the elements in the value T-bar (IRV):

- Income—The annual net operating income (NOI) that an income property produces. Note two important elements:
  - If the income is expressed as monthly or quarterly income, it must first be converted to annual income before using the T-bar.
  - If gross income is given, it must be converted to net income before using the T-bar.
- Rate of Capitalization—The rate of return that the investor receives or wants to receive.
- Value—The market value of the income-producing property.

Now, let's look at a problem using the value T-bar.

Problem: An investor is evaluating an income-producing property for possible purchase. The property produces a monthly net income of $3,200. If the investor wants to earn a 12% return, how much can she afford to pay for the property?

Again, let's start with what we know and don't know.

- Income—The monthly net income is $3,200. Multiply this by 12 to get the annual net income, which is $38,400.
- Rate of Capitalization—The investor wants to earn 12%, which is the rate of capitalization.
- Value—The value of the property is what we want to determine.

Now, let's take what we know and enter it in the T-bar.

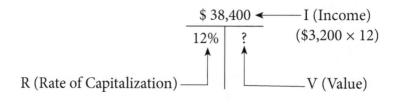

When we block out the unknown (V), we are left with $38,400 over 12%, which means we divide:

$$\$38,400 \div 0.12 = \$320,000$$

The value of the property is $320,000, which means the investor can pay $320,000 for the property and obtain a 12% return.

Now, let's look at a different kind of problem using the value T-bar.

Problem: An investor is considering an income-producing property that is valued at $560,000 using a capitalization rate of 8%. How much could the investor afford to pay for the property if a capitalization rate of 10% were used?

Before starting the problem, we need to look at our strategy. There are really two problems here:

1. the value of the property with an 8% rate.
2. the value of the property with a 10% rate.

The value we are interested in is the value with a 10% rate, but there is a problem. If we try to work the problem using a 10% capitalization rate, we'll find that there are two things we don't know (income and value) and only one thing we do know (the 10% capitalization rate). Because only one of the three items is known, we can't work the problem. The solution is to work the problem first using the 8% capitalization rate. This will determine the net income. Once this is done, we will have two known items (income and capitalization rate), which will allow us to work the problem with the 10% rate. Working the problem with the 10% rate will solve the problem.

First, let's look at what we know and don't know to work the problem using an 8% capitalization rate:

- Income—We don't know this yet, but we can find out what it is by using an 8% capitalization rate to solve the problem.
- Rate of Capitalization—In this case, it is 8%.
- Value—This is $560,000 when an 8% capitalization rate is used.

Now, let's take what we know and enter it in the T-bar.

```
                              ? ←————— I (Income)
                         ─────────────────
    R (Rate of    ——→ 8%  │ $560,000 ←— V (Value)
    Capitalization)        │
```

When we block out the unknown (I), we are left with 8% and $560,000 with a vertical line between them, which means we multiply:

$$0.08 \times \$560,000 = \$44,800$$

The annual net income for the property is $44,800.

Now that we know the annual net income for the property ($44,800), we can work the problem using a 10% capitalization rate to find out how much the investor could pay for the property valued at that rate of return. Let's look at what we know and don't know.

- Income—$44,800 (from the problem we just completed)
- Rate of Capitalization—10%
- Value—This is what we want to determine.

Now, let's enter these values in the T-bar (IRV).

$$\begin{array}{c|c} & \$44,800 \leftarrow \text{I (Income)} \\ \text{R (Rate of Capitalization)} \rightarrow 10\% & ? \leftarrow \text{V (Value)} \end{array}$$

When we block out the unknown (V), we are left with $44,800 over 10%, so we divide:

$$\$44,800 \div 0.10 = \$448,000$$

The property's value is $448,000 at a 10% capitalization rate.

There is one remaining type of value problem we will cover.

Problem: An investor owns an apartment building that is near an airport. Because of the airport noise, the investor is losing $200 per month net income. Using a capitalization rate of 8%, how much has the property lost in value?

This is an interesting application of the value T-bar. In this case, we don't need to know the actual value of the property, just the amount of value that has been lost. Let's look at how this is done. First, let's look at what we know and don't know.

- Income—This is the key to this problem. We know the amount of net income lost each month. If we convert this to an annual loss, we can use this amount directly in the IRV T-bar to get the amount of value lost as well. (To convert to annual income loss, we multiply $200 × 12 to get $2,400, which we'll use in the T-bar.)
- Rate of Capitalization—8%
- Value—In this case, we don't know the value. What we want to know is the loss in value. We can find it by using the loss in net income in our T-bar, as noted above.

Now, let's enter our values in the T-bar.

```
                    $2,400  ←——— I (Income LOST)
                   ─────────
R (Rate of    ——→  8%  │  ?  ←—— V (Value LOST)
Capitalization)
```

When we block out the unknown (V), we are left with $2,400 over 8%, which means we divide:

$$\$2{,}400 \div 0.08 = \$30{,}000$$

The loss in value is $30,000.

Loan Problems

There is one last type of problem that uses a T-bar, called a loan problem. The T-bar for a loan problem is as follows:

```
            Interest                    I
   ─────────────────────────   OR   ─────────
   Rate of    │ Balance of           R  │  B
   Interest   │ Loan
```

Note that the code for loan problems is IRB. First, let's look at the elements in the loan T-bar.

- Interest—The money the borrower pays the lender for the use of the lender's money. When solving problems, the interest must be converted to interest earned in a year.
- Rate of Interest—The interest rate is the percentage of the loan paid as interest in a year.
- Balance—The amount owed on the loan at any point in time. It is also referred to as the principal on the loan.

Now, let's look at a problem using the loan T-bar.

Problem: A borrower obtained a straight note of $12,000 for 6 months. At the end of the term of the note, he made a payment for the entire principal and interest of $12,660. What was the interest rate on the note?

Let's first look at what we know and what we don't know.

- Interest—The interest for 6 months is the total amount paid less the principal, which is $12,660 less $12,000, or $660. To convert this to annual interest, multiply by 2 to get $1,320.
- Rate of Interest—This is what we want to determine.
- Balance on Loan—The balance on the loan for the entire period was $12,000 because no principal payments were made during the term of the loan.

Now, let's enter these values in the T-bar (IRB).

```
                          $1,320 ←——————— I (Interest)
R (Rate of    ——→  ?   |
 Interest)             |  $12,000 ←——— B (Balance on Loan)
```

When we block out the unknown (R), we are left with $1,320 over $12,000, which means to divide:

$$\$1{,}320 \div \$12{,}000 = 0.11$$

The interest rate on the loan is 11%.

Let's look at a different type of problem that uses the loan T-bar (IRB).

Problem: A borrower obtains an amortized loan for $140,000 to be paid back over 30 years at an interest rate of 10.5%, with monthly payments of $1,280.64 including principal and interest. How much of the first month's payment is applied to the principal?

The key to this problem is to find the amount of the first payment that is applied to interest. Then you can subtract that amount from the monthly payment to determine how much of the first payment goes to the principal. To find the amount of interest in the first payment, we must first find the amount of interest paid per year. To find the amount of interest paid per year, we use the loan T-bar.

First, let's look at what we know and don't know.

- Interest—This is what we want to find. Once we know this, we can use it to find the interest in the first payment, and then we can determine the principal in the first payment.
- Rate of Interest—10.5%
- Balance on Loan—Because we are dealing with a new loan, the interest in the first month is based on a balance of $140,000.

Now, let's enter these values in the T-bar (IRB).

```
                                ? ←——————— I (Interest)
R (Rate of Interest)  ——→ 10.5% |
                                | $140,000 ←——— B (Balance on Loan)
```

When we block out the unknown (I), we multiply 10.5% by $140,000. This gives us $14,700.

The interest for the first year of the loan is $14,700.

To get interest paid in the first month we divide by 12:

$$\$14{,}700 \div 12 = \$1{,}225$$

The first month's payment includes $1,225 for interest. Because we know from the problem that the monthly payment is $1,280.64, we can find the amount paid to principal by subtracting:

$$\$1{,}280.64 - \$1{,}225.00 = \$55.64$$

The first month's payment includes $55.64 paid to principal.

CALCULATING COST AND PRICE

Before learning how to solve the problems in this section, you will first learn a name for each type of problem. A big part of learning how to solve these problems is learning how to recognize and name the type of problem you are solving. Once you are able to do this, the process of completing the necessary calculations is much simpler.

The two types of problems presented in this section are very similar and are basically the reverse of each other. We will call these problems cost problems and price problems. Let's start with an example of a cost problem.

Cost Problems

Problem: The Adams family sold their home for $122,400. This price is a 20% increase over the price they paid for it when they bought it. What did they pay for the house originally?

First, this is called a cost problem because it asks you to determine the original cost of the house. Before working the problem, let's look at some general elements you will find in a cost problem:

- First, you will be given the price at which the property just sold.
- Second, you will be given a percentage by which the recent selling price exceeds the original price.
- Third, you will be asked to find the original price.

Now, let's look at how we solve this type of problem. The solution is very simple and involves only three steps:

- **Step 1:** Add the percent that the price has increased to 100%.
- **Step 2:** Convert this percent to a decimal.
- **Step 3:** Divide the recent sales price by the answer from Step 2.

Now, let's work the problem above using these three steps, and you will see how easy it is!

- **Step 1:** Add the percent that the price has increased to 100%:
$$100\% + 20\% = 120\%$$
- **Step 2:** Convert this percent to a decimal:
$$120\% \text{ becomes } 1.20$$
- **Step 3:** Divide the recent sales price by the answer from Step 2:
$$\$122{,}400 \div 1.20 = \$102{,}000$$

$102,000 is the original price of the home.

Price Problems

Now, let's look at a similar type of problem—the price problem. Let's start with an example.

Problem: A seller plans to sell her home and wants to receive $152,000 after the broker's 5% commission is deducted. What should the sales price be?

First, this is called a price problem because it asks you to determine the sales price of the house. This problem is similar to the cost problem you just solved. Before working the problem, let's look at some general elements you will find in a price problem:

- First, you will be given a net amount that will be received or has been received.
- Next, you will be given a percentage by which the selling price exceeds the net amount.
- Third, you will be asked to find the selling price.

Now, let's look at how we solve this type of problem. The solution to this type of problem is very simple and also involves only three steps:

- **Step 1:** Subtract the percent to be deducted from 100%.
- **Step 2:** Convert this percent to a decimal.
- **Step 3:** Divide the net to be received by the answer from Step 2.

Now, let's work the problem above using these three steps, and you will see how easy it is!

- **Step 1:** Subtract the percent to be deducted from 100%:
$$100\% - 5\% = 95\%$$
- **Step 2:** Convert this percent to a decimal:
$$95\% \text{ becomes } 0.95$$
- **Step 3:** Divide the net to be received by the answer from Step 2:
$$\$152{,}000 \div 0.95 = \$160{,}000$$

The sales price should be $160,000.

Before we continue, let's stop and compare the cost and price problems you just solved. The table below shows a condensed comparison of the steps in each problem.

Cost	Price
1. Add a percent to 100%.	1. Subtract a percent from 100%.
2. Convert to a decimal.	2. Convert to a decimal.
3. Divide the decimal into a number.	3. Divide the decimal into a number.

As you can see above, the only difference in the way you solve the problems is the first step. If you remember whether to add or subtract in the first step, the rest is easy.

Let's look at a simple way to remember the correct first step. The best way to remember whether to add or subtract a percent to 100% is remember the mnemonic CAPS:

- Cost problem
- Add a percent to 100%
- Price problem
- Subtract a percent from 100%

Now, let's continue with another variation of the price problem.

Problem: The Greens sold their home after paying off their mortgage. From the sales price paid by the buyer, the escrow company deducted expenses totaling $612 and the broker's 6% commission. The Greens received a check from the escrow company for $65,188. What was the sales price of the house?

The only difference between this problem and the previous price problem is the net amount is affected by two things—the expenses totaling $612 and the broker's 6% commission. The first step in this situation is to add the expenses of $612 to the amount of the check received from the escrow company. (Think of this as a preliminary step you take before solving the problem as you did in the previous price problem.) We can then follow the steps we just covered to work the problem:

- **Preliminary Step:** Add the deductions ($612) to the check amount ($65,188). This equals a value of $65,800, which we will use as the net received.
- **Step 1:** Subtract the broker's commission from 100%:
$$100\% - 6\% = 94\%$$
- **Step 2:** Convert this percent to a decimal:
$$94\% \text{ becomes } 0.94$$
- **Step 3:** Divide the net received amount by the answer from Step 2:
$$\$65,800 \div 0.94 = \$70,000$$

The sales price of the house was $70,000.

There is another variation of this problem that you may encounter.

Problem: An investor purchased a second mortgage at a 15% discount and paid $15,640 for the note. What was the original face value of the note?

The solution to this type of problem involves the three steps used in the first price problem:

- **Step 1:** Subtract the percent of discount from 100%.
- **Step 2:** Convert this percent to a decimal.
- **Step 3:** Divide the amount paid to the seller for the note by the answer from Step 2.

Now, let's work the problem above using these three steps, and again, you will see how easy it is!

- **Step 1:** Subtract the percent of discount from 100%:
$$100\% - 15\% = 85\%$$
- **Step 2:** Convert this percent to a decimal:
$$85\% \text{ becomes } 0.85$$
- **Step 3:** Divide the amount paid for the note by the answer from Step 2:
$$\$15,640 \div 0.85 = \$18,400$$

$18,400 is the original face value of the note.

Now, let's look at one final variation of a price problem.

Problem: Mr. Jones just bought a house for $136,500. How much would it have to increase in value for Mr. Jones to resell it and pay a 5% commission without taking a loss?

To solve this problem, we use the same three steps as in the previous price problems:

- **Step 1:** Subtract the 5% commission from 100%:
$$100\% - 5\% = 95\%$$
- **Step 2:** Convert this percent to a decimal:
$$95\% \text{ becomes } 0.95$$
- **Step 3:** Divide the amount paid for the property by the answer from Step 2:
$$\$136,500 \div 0.95 = \$143,684$$

At this point, we know that the house must sell for $143,684, but that's not what we are looking for. The problem asks how much the house must increase in value. The last step is to subtract the amount Mr. Jones paid for the house from $143,684:

$$\$143,684 - \$136,500 = \$7,184$$

The house must increase in value by $7,184 for Mr. Jones to avoid taking a loss.

PRELIMINARY STEPS TO A CLOSING

Sales Contract to Closing

When you are an agent involved in the sale of property, the signing of the sales contract does not end your responsibilities. Between the signing of the contract and the day the sale is closed, your specific duties are determined by your broker's policy and by your relationship to the parties to the transaction (i.e., single agent for buyer or seller, transaction broker, or no brokerage relationship). Depending on the situation, you may continue to work with the buyer, the seller, and/or the lender to ensure a successful closing.

In this section, we will look at some of the steps that take place from the signing of the sales contract to the day of the closing. We will also look at duties an agent has at each of these steps.

There are three major periods during the time between the signing of the sales contract and the day of closing:

1. the period immediately after the sales contract is signed
2. the loan application process
3. the preparation for closing

Sale Pending Sign and Sold Sign Rule

In Florida, a real estate licensee must follow rules concerning the placement of "Sold" or "Sale Pending" signs. Let's now discuss the provision of the law regarding "Sold" signs. Previously, the Florida Real Estate Commission ruled that placing a "Sold" sign on a property prior to closing, without first obtaining the seller's consent was false advertising. Obviously a sold sign may discourage prospective purchasers from even looking at the property. The same would hold true if the sign stated "contract pending" or "sale pending." This rule has been changed. Licensees now have their choice of placing either a "Sold" sign or a "Sale Pending" sign. This allows the licensee to present the current status of the listing to the general public.

Notice of "Under Contract" to MLS

Listing notifications to the MLS may be placed in "Under Contract" or "Active with Contract" status. The meaning of "Active with Contract" suggests that there is a contract that contains contingencies and the selling party will consider back-up offers. In any event, the licensee should obtain the seller's permission to place a sign on the property before actually doing so.

Immediately after the sales contract is signed by all parties, make sure that each party to the transaction receives a copy of the signed contract at the time of signing. The following parties should receive a copy of the signed contract:

- the seller
- the buyer
- your broker
- the cooperating broker, if there is one

If there is a contingency in the sales contract, it is also your responsibility to make sure that everything possible is done by each party to fulfill the conditions of the contingency. For example, if the contract is made contingent on the buyer's ability to obtain new financing, you should monitor the buyer's application process to ensure that it progresses in a timely manner. (During this process, you must make sure your actions comply with the requirements of the Florida Brokerage Relationship Disclosure Act, described earlier in Chapter 4.) While it is best to try to avoid having contingency clauses in a contract, in most marketplaces throughout the country, contingencies cannot be avoided.

In addition to the contingency relating to new financing, there are other situations in which a contingency clause is likely to be involved, including:

- loan assumptions or approvals
- title insurance
- inspections of the property
- repairs to the property
- appraisals of the property
- surveys of the property
- a termite inspection
- buyer hazard insurance
- flood insurance
- contingencies such as:
    - the sale of the buyer's present home
    - obtaining favorable financing

Earnest Money Deposited

Normally a buyer will deposit earnest money with the closing agent. The deposit represents:

- a sign of good faith toward the purchaser's performance.
- money that the buyer has placed at risk if they do not perform.
- a credit for the buyer toward the remaining balance of the purchase price.
- liquidated damages to the seller in the event a buyer defaults on his/her contractual obligations.

From time to time, certain transactions may require the buyer to post additional deposit amounts at different time intervals. This would likely be determined by the contractual agreement of the parties.

Loan Applications/Assumptions

Loan applications and/or loan assumptions often involve contingency clauses within the contract for purchase and sale. Many loans now require that the buyer fulfill greater qualifications than previously on a new loan. This includes further qualification for the loan in order to assume it. When you have a listing on a property where a loan can be assumed, determination should be made at the time the licensee takes the listing whether the lender will require an application from the buyer to assume the loan. This will allow the licensee to advise any buyer in advance that an application will be required. Note that the licensee should also advise the lender at the time the licensee takes the listing that the seller intends to offer the existing loan to a buyer on a loan assumption. In the case of a loan assumption on a Veterans Affairs (VA) loan in which the seller wants to be released from liability on the loan, the licensee should ensure that the buyer cooperates with the lender and the VA in completing the release process.

Inspections of the Property

A contract may be contingent on an inspection of the property (for example, by a spouse or a home inspector). If a home inspection or termite inspection (see below) is required, the licensee should make sure that the inspection takes place as soon as possible. Failure to do so can result in costly delays because the property is tied up until the contingency is resolved and cannot be sold to anyone else. In the event that the contingency is not satisfied successfully, valuable time in getting the property back on the market will be lost.

Repairs to the Property

In addition, the contract may be contingent on the seller making repairs based on the results of a home inspection. Your obligation in dealing with this situation is to ensure that any actions required by the seller are completed in a timely manner (at least by the closing date). This might require you to provide the names of individuals who can do the work, but you should not order the work done yourself. Always have the seller order the work. The licensee should continue to monitor the progress of these repairs.

Appraisals of the Property

Another very common situation is a contingency on the appraisal of the property for a certain value. In fact, with most loans, such a contingency is required. When an appraisal is required, it is your responsibility to ensure it is completed in a timely fashion. To that end, you should always fully cooperate with the appraiser, even if you are only asked to unlock the property for them. When you are asked to assist an appraiser, remember you should neither ask the appraiser what the appraisal value is nor attempt to influence the appraisal in any way. Remember, appraisals are required on any transaction that falls under the definition of a federally related transaction. A federally related transaction is any transaction involving a financial institution insured or regulated by the federal government.

Surveys of the Property

At the lender's or buyer's request, a contract may also require that a survey of the property take place before closing. Surveys are used to determine boundary lines as well as uncover encroachments by neighboring properties.

Termite Inspection

Assisting the parties in complying with the contract might also include ensuring that a wood infestation inspection is completed and that a report is submitted to the closing agent. An inspection, a clearance letter, or a termite bond might be required in different situations. Any of these items may be required by the buyer, the lender, or a government agency such as the Federal Housing Administration (FHA) or the VA.

You should be aware that different forms and procedures are required by different sources. For example, the forms required for a clearance letter are different for the VA and the FHA. A termite bond that can be transferred from the seller to the buyer might be acceptable to some (but not all) conventional lenders but is not allowed with VA and FHA loans.

Title Insurance

Whether or not financing is involved, the purchase of a standard or extended coverage title insurance policy will protect the buyer against prescribed events that could lead to financial loss. On transactions involving the use of borrowed funds, there will probably be two policies:

- a buyer's title insurance policy
- a lender's title insurance policy

Sale of the Buyer's Present Home

A contract may also be contingent upon the sale of the buyer's present home. In this situation, if you are an agent for the seller, it is your responsibility to obtain information about the sale of homes in the area where the buyer's home is located. In this manner, the seller can make an informed decision whether such a contingency is a good idea. If you are an agent for the buyer, you should do everything possible to assist the buyer in the sale of his/her home. This includes listing the property for sale. If the property is not already listed the licensee can assist by referring the buyer to another broker (entering into a listing with the buyer would conflict with the relationship with the seller).

Loan Processing/Approval

Once you have completed your responsibilities immediately after the contract is signed, the next step in the closing process begins—the processing of the buyer's loan. During this step of the closing process, you may be working with the seller, the buyer, and/or the lender who will provide the financing.

The processing of the buyer's loan involves the following elements:

- selection of a lender
- loan application
- homeowner's insurance

Selecting a Lender

The first step in obtaining financing is the selection of a lender. It is important to understand who has the right to make this selection. A broker does not have the right to select the lender. The determination of who has the right to select the lender depends on whether the selection is specified in the sales contract or made after the contract is completed. The seller has the right to stipulate in a sales contract that the buyer must use a particular lender. For example, the seller may be a builder who entered into a contract with a lender to provide permanent financing in exchange for providing the construction loan. The seller may stipulate in the contract that only this lender may be used by the buyer. If a seller includes a stipulation in the contract that a particular lender must be used and the buyer signs the contract, the buyer must use the stipulated lender. The other option is to decline to sign the contract if the buyer does not want to be bound to a particular lender.

In another situation, a seller might stipulate in a contract that the buyer use the lender who made the seller's existing loan on the property. This might occur when the lender agrees to waive a prepayment penalty on the seller's loan if the buyer obtains a new loan from that lender. If the buyer signs the contract, the buyer is bound to use the seller's lender. If the buyer does not want to use the seller's lender, the buyer can decline to sign the contract.

Once a contract is signed by both the seller and the buyer, and the contract does not specify a particular lender, the buyer can choose which lender to use. In this situation, the seller may only request that a particular lender be used.

Loan Application

The second step in obtaining financing is the loan application. If you are working with the seller, keep the seller informed of the progress on the application. For example, you should let the seller know whether the buyer has submitted an application for a loan. The contract may stipulate the time period in which this should be done. You should also inform the seller as to whether or not the buyer is making a good-faith effort to comply with the contract. Failure to submit forms to the lender in a timely manner may indicate that the buyer is not making such an effort. Finally, you should let the seller know the results of the buyer's loan application. If you are working with the buyer, you could ensure that all forms required of the buyer are submitted in a timely manner.

In addition, you have the obligation to assist in resolving any problems that might arise. For example:

- If the appraisal is completed, and the property does not appraise at the required value, the licensee should assist the seller and buyer in finding an alternative solution or in renegotiating the contract as necessary.
- If the buyer fails to qualify, the contract may need to be renegotiated. For instance, if the buyer fails to qualify for a 90% loan, the seller might want to consider providing a purchase money loan for 10% of the sales price. The buyer could then apply for an 80% loan.

Homeowner's (Hazard) Insurance

During loan processing, the buyer must obtain a homeowner's (hazard) insurance policy with the lender named as a coinsured party. Evidence of coverage is shown by issuance of a certificate of insurance (COI). It may take several days for the policy to be issued, so you should inform the buyer of this fact so he/she will have adequate time to obtain the policy prior to the closing date. In addition, you should follow up to ensure that the policy has been obtained prior to closing and to deliver same to the closing agent.

Flood Insurance

In addition to homeowner/hazard insurance, when financing is involved, buyers of properties located within flood zones will be required by the lender to obtain flood insurance.

Coaching Tips

When financing is provided by a lender, that lender will always require the borrower to obtain homeowner's insurance to secure the lender's lien. This will protect the lender (as well as the borrower) against any casualty issue such as:

- fire
- vandalism
- theft
- destruction
- mold
- storm damage

Preparing for Closing

The final step of the closing process is preparing for the closing itself. You have three primary responsibilities in this area:

1. providing information to the closing agent
2. coordinating the date and time of the closing
3. preparing the buyer and/or seller for closing

Providing Information to the Closing Agent

The closing agent must receive a true and current copy of the sales contract. In addition to having the buyer/seller contact information, the closing agent needs the sales contract in order to complete a title search and to prepare the closing statements. On the day of the closing the closing statement will show how much money the seller will receive and how much the buyer must bring with them.

In addition, the closing agent needs a copy of the buyer's hazard insurance policy. If the insurance policy will be paid at closing, the closing agent will need to know the amount of the premium that will be paid. The closing agent also needs a copy of any termite clearance letter or report, if required, and the cost if it is to be paid at closing.

Coordinate the Date and Time of Closing

To prepare for the closing, you also need to coordinate the date and time of the closing. The date may be set after the buyer's new loan or loan assumption has been approved by the lender. Before setting a date and time, you should consider both the provisions of the contract and the schedules of the closing official, the buyer, the seller, and any brokers involved.

Prepare the Buyer and Seller for Closing

Your last duty in preparation for closing is to prepare the buyer and/or seller for the closing. This includes three specific tasks:

1. Inform the parties of the date, time, and place of the closing as much in advance as possible to ensure that they can be there.
2. Inform the buyer and/or seller of what to expect at closing.
3. Perform a final walk through with the buyer to determine the condition of the property one day before the closing.

Perhaps the greatest obstacle to a successful closing is a surprise at the closing table. You should do everything possible to avoid any such surprises. One helpful way to eliminate surprises is to review blank copies of all forms used at closing with the buyer and/or seller. Another way is to discuss all forms that will require a signature. The most important task, however, is to complete the closing statement as accurately as possible, and review it with the buyer and/or seller.

You should also remember that the provisions of the Real Estate Settlement Procedures Act (RESPA) have changed (this subject is discussed next). The Truth-in-Lending Act (TILA-RESPA (as it is now called) requires that the lender show the buyer the Closing Disclosure for financed transactions prior to closing as follows:

- The Closing Disclosure must be made available no less than three business days before closing.
- It must include an itemized list of charges to the buyer.

This information is helpful because it shows the buyer an itemized listing of all charges, which determines the amount of money the buyer will be required to pay at closing.

New TILA-RESPA Requirements

Pursuant to the aforementioned, the purpose of RESPA is to ensure that at the time of closing, a buyer in a residential transaction is informed of all settlement costs. This includes all transactions financed by a federally related mortgage loan. A federally related mortgage loan is any loan originated by an institution that is regulated, governed, or insured by the federal government. For the past 30 years, federal law has required that consumers receive two types of disclosures (in one document) when applying for a mortgage:

1. a Closing Disclosure, and
2. a loan estimate of settlement costs (closing costs)

    a. The loan estimate includes but is not limited to:
        i. fees that can change
        ii. fees that cannot change more than 10%
        iii. fees that are not subject to increase

Due to previous confusion in the administration of the forms, under the Dodd-Frank Wall Street Reform and Consumer Protection Act, the Act now requires the integration of the mortgage loan disclosures under the TILA and RESPA. Under the Act, both the TILA disclosure and good-faith estimate have been combined into one form. Furthermore, the new HUD-1 and final disclosure forms have simplified the ability of the consumer to better understand all of the costs associated with the borrowing. This form must be provided to the borrower applicant in no less than three business days prior to closing the loan. Information contained on the form will include:

- loan amount
- interest rate

- monthly payments
- costs associated with originating/closing the loan

Another change in law is associated with closed end mortgages. It will not apply to the following types of loans:

- home equity
- reverse mortgages
- mortgages secured by a mobile home
- any dwelling not attached to real property/land

The TILA-RESPA rule took effect on August 1, 2015.

Preclosing Inspection

As a purchaser, it is advised to perform a **preclosing inspection** (a final walk-through inspection) just prior to the date of closing. In doing so, the buyer will ensure that upon closing of the transaction, the condition of the property will be as previously bargained for. In addition to the final walk-through, closing documents will be reviewed with both buyer and seller usually a day or more before the actual day of closing. At this time, the buyer is informed as to what funds will be required from him/her on the day of closing. In addition, the earnest money check is prepared for closing, and the closing appointment is usually confirmed or rescheduled (as the case may be).

Prorated Expenses and Title Closing

A title closing is the consummation of a real estate transaction, when the seller delivers title to the buyer in exchange for payment of the purchase price by the buyer.

Prorating

Prorating or to **prorate** is the concept that the buyer and seller should pay the expenses or receive the financial benefits of owning a property for the part of the current year that they owned the property. When a cost item is prorated, this means simply that part of the cost will be paid by the seller and part of the cost will be paid by the buyer. Prorating is the process of determining how much of the item will be paid by the buyer and how much will be paid by the seller. The cost charged to the respective party is based on how long each party will own or has owned the property.

Before we look at prorating in more detail, let's cover some basic points about the process. The *closing day* is when ownership is transferred from the seller to the buyer, as illustrated using the timeline shown here.

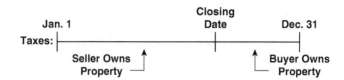

The seller owns the property before the day of closing. The buyer owns the property after the day of closing. But who owns the property on the day of closing? On the day of closing, the seller actually owns the property for part of the day (before all the paperwork is signed), and the buyer owns the property for part of the day (after the paperwork is signed). To avoid computing the costs for part of a day for the seller and part of the day for the buyer, the general rule for the purpose of prorating costs is the buyer owns the property on the day of closing for the entire day. This means that the buyer is responsible for all expenses of ownership on the day of closing. (In some cases, the seller is assumed to own the property for the entire day of closing.) This item becomes a function of negotiation.

Another concept related to prorating is the beginning and ending dates that a prorated item is in effect:

- Beginning date—The first date that a prorated item is in effect
- Ending date—The last date that a prorated item is in effect

For example, rent is always payable by the tenant to the property owner for the period in question in advance. If the closing is to take place at any point after the first of the month, the seller will owe the buyer the pro rata share or portion of the rent collected for that month.

Another example, property taxes are normally paid for the calendar year from January 1 through December 31. In this situation, January 1 is the beginning date for property taxes, and December 31 is the ending date.

From these facts, we can state that the period of ownership, with respect to any item to be prorated, is as follows:

- Seller's period of ownership—The time from the beginning date through the day before the closing date.
- Buyer's period of ownership—The time from the day of closing through the ending date.

Although there are many items of cost, the three major cost items that must be prorated on the date of closing are:

1. property taxes
2. homeowner's insurance
3. mortgage interest

For each of these items, the period over which they are prorated may differ:

1. *Property taxes* are prorated over the calendar year for which taxes are due.

2. *Homeowner's insurance* (only if the policy is assumed or transferred) is prorated over the actual period for which the policy was in effect (usually one year).
3. *Mortgage interest* is prorated over the month during which the closing occurs. This would apply to both new loans and assumed loans. In either case, the interest will be calculated accordingly and charged to the party bearing the responsibility to pay.

A typical situation for the proration of each of these items is illustrated next.

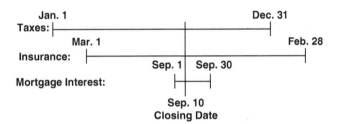

Note that each item is prorated over a different time period. The proration period corresponds to the period over which a particular item is paid.

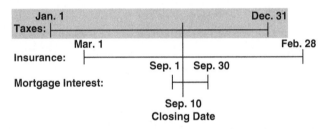

For example, taxes are paid and prorated over the calendar year from January 1 (beginning date) through December 31 (ending date).

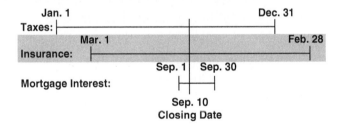

The homeowner's insurance is paid and prorated over a period of one year beginning on March 1 and ending on February 28 (the dates the policy is in effect).

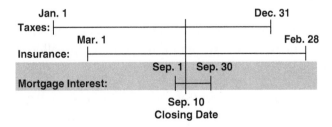

Mortgage interest is paid monthly and is prorated for the month of closing only. The beginning date for this proration is September 1, and the ending date is September 30.

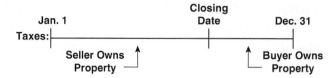

In each of these situations, the seller is responsible for the item's cost from the beginning date to the day before the closing date. The buyer is responsible for each item on the day of closing to the ending date.

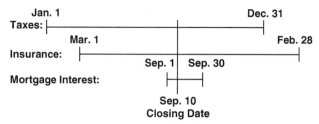

Prorating each of these items is based on different periods of time but involves the same process. Later in this chapter, we will cover the process of prorating taxes in detail. Right now, we will cover some general issues involved in the proration of property taxes.

Property Taxes

Property taxes are assessed for a 12-month tax year. Property taxes are based on a calendar tax year that runs from January 1 through December 31.

In Florida, although taxes are assessed on real property on the first day of any calendar year, these taxes are typically paid in **arrears**. This means taxes can be paid at the end of the tax year without penalty. Thus, in most situations, property taxes have not been paid by the seller prior to the date of closing. If the seller has not paid property taxes prior to closing, the seller must pay her prorated share of property taxes due on the date of closing, as illustrated next.

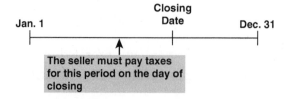

In order to determine the amount of taxes the seller must pay, we first prorate the seller's tax payment. In this situation, we prorate the seller's tax bill using the following three steps:

1. Determine how many days out of the year the seller will own the property.
2. Determine how much tax is due for each day (calculation of the daily rate).

3. Calculate the seller's tax payment from these two numbers (multiply the daily rate by the number of days that the seller owned the property).

Here is an example to illustrate how a seller's prorated share of the tax payment is calculated.

Assume that a seller has not paid annual property taxes of $877 prior to closing, and the closing date is March 13. Because the seller has not paid the taxes, the amount of tax payment the seller is responsible for must be calculated. This requires four steps.

Step 1: Calculate the number of days the seller was responsible for the tax bill prior to the month of closing. To do this, add up the total number of days in each month as follows:

January	31 days
February	+28 days
Total	59 days

Step 2: Add the number of days the seller is responsible for taxes in the month of closing. The number of days the seller is responsible for the taxes is always the same as the day before closing occurs. (The buyer is responsible for the day of closing.)

 59 days (from the first step)
+12 days (March 13 closing date)
 71 days = Total number of days the seller is responsible for paying the taxes

Step 3: Determine the amount of taxes for each day of the year as follows:

Annual tax bill ÷ 365 days

In this case, the annual tax bill is $877. The computation in this case is:

$877 ÷ 365 = $2.4027 per day

Coaching Tips

Once you determine the daily rate, *do not round it off*. Rounding the number at this point will cause the total to be in error. Remember, we are multiplying the number of days against an actual calculated daily rate. A rounding off of the daily rate will result in a proration that is either greater or less than the actual proration would normally be. For example: if the daily rate in Step 3 was rounded off to the nearest penny, we would multiply 71 days (as shown in Step 4) × $2.40. The product would equal a proration of $170.40 and not $170.59 as the correct proration is shown in the calculation in Step 4.

Step 4: Multiply the number of days the seller is responsible for the taxes by the amount of the tax per day, as follows:

71 days × $2.4027 = $170.59

In this case, the seller is responsible for a prorated amount of $170.59 for his/her share of the tax bill. Because he/she has not paid the taxes prior to closing, the seller must pay this amount at closing.

Coaching Tips

Proration rule—When taxes are not paid in advance, prorate seller's share to be paid to the buyer.

PRACTICE EXERCISES

Calculating the Number of Days Prior to the Month of Closing

Assume that taxes are paid on a calendar-year basis from January 1 through December 31.

1. A seller has not paid the property taxes before closing, which occurs on April 25. For how many days is the seller responsible for taxes prior to the month of closing?

   31 days in January
   28 days in February
   <u>31</u> days in March
   90 total days prior to the month of closing

2. A seller has not paid the property taxes before closing, which occurs on March 21. For how many days is the seller responsible for taxes prior to the month of closing?

   31 days in January
   <u>28</u> days in February
   59 total days prior to the month of closing

Calculating the Total Number of Days the Seller Is Responsible for Property Taxes

1. A seller has not paid the property taxes before closing, which occurs on April 17. For how many days is the seller responsible for taxes for the entire tax year?

   31 days in January
   28 days in February
   31 days in March
   <u>16</u> days in April (closing April 17)
   106 total days

2. A seller has not paid the property taxes before closing, which occurs on March 3. For how many days is the seller responsible for taxes for the entire tax year?

   31 days in January
   28 days in February
   _2 days in March (closing March 3)
   61 total days

3. A seller has not paid the property taxes before closing, which occurs on February 2. For how many days is the seller responsible for taxes for the entire tax year?

   31 days in January
   _1 day in February (closing February 2)
   32 total days

Calculating the Amount of Property Tax Due for Each Day of the Year

1. The annual property taxes on a property being sold are $1,026. What is the amount of tax due per day?

   $1,026 ÷ 365 = $2.8110

2. The annual property taxes on a property being sold are $652. What is the amount of tax due per day?

   $652 ÷ 365 = $1.7863

Calculating the Amount of the Seller's Tax Payment at Closing

1. A seller has not paid the property taxes of $738 before closing, which occurs on April 2. What is the amount of the seller's prorated tax payment at closing?

   Step 1: Calculate the appropriate number of days.

   31 days in January
   28 days in February
   31 days in March
   _1 day in April
   91 total days

   Step 2: Calculate the daily rate

   $738 ÷ 365 = $2.0219

   Step 3: Calculate the seller's prorated tax payment at closing.

   $2.0219 × 91 = $183.99

2. A seller has not paid the property taxes of $944 before closing, which occurs on March 20. What is the amount of the seller's prorated tax payment at closing?

   Step 1: Calculate the appropriate number of days.

   31 days in January
   28 days in February
   <u>19</u> days in March (closing March 20)
   78 total days

   Step 2: Calculate the daily rate.

   $944 ÷ 365 = $2.5863

   Step 3: Calculate the seller's prorated tax payment at closing.

   $2.5863 × 78 = $201.73

In the proration exercises, the 365-day method is applied, which uses the actual number of days in the proration period.

A second method of proration is called the 30-day-month method. This method assumes that there are 12 months in a year and each month has 30 days. Let's go over one of the previous examples, but this time the 30-day-month method will be applied.

3. The seller has not paid the taxes of $877 prior to closing, and the closing is on March 13. What is the total amount of the seller's prorated tax payment due at closing?

   Step 1: Determine the number of months the seller was responsible for the tax bill prior to the month of closing. In this case, the seller is responsible for 2 months prior to the month of closing (January and February).

   Step 2: Calculate the amount of taxes for each month of the year as follows:

   $877 ÷ 12 months = $73.0833 per month

   Step 3: Multiply the number of months the seller was responsible for the tax bill prior to closing (Step 1) by the amount of the tax per month (Step 2), as follows:

   $73.0833 taxes per month × 2 months = $146.1666

   This is the amount the seller owes for the period prior to the month of closing. We still need to calculate the amount the seller owes for the month of closing.

   Step 4: Determine the number of days the seller is responsible for taxes in the month of closing. In this example, the seller is responsible for 12 days in March. (The buyer is responsible for the day of closing.)

   Step 5: Calculate the amount of taxes for each day of the month. To do this, you divide the number of taxes per month (from Step 2) by 30 days, as follows:

   $73.0833 taxes per month ÷ 30 days = $2.4361 per day

Step 6: Multiply the number of days the seller was responsible for taxes in the month of closing by the amount of the tax per day, as follows:

$2.4361 taxes per day × 12 days = $29.2332

We now know the amount the seller owes for the month of closing. To arrive at the total amount the seller owes for taxes, we must add this value to the amount the seller owes for the months prior to closing (Step 3).

Step 7: Add Step 3 to Step 6 to calculate the total amount of the seller's prorated tax payment due at closing:

$146.1666 + $29.2332 = $175.3998

The seller is responsible for a prorated amount of $175.40 for his/her share of the tax bill.

In this chapter, two methods for prorating expenses at closing were discussed:

1. the 365-day method
2. the 30-day-month method

For the purposes of this course, you should always use the 365-day method, unless instructed otherwise (see Figure 14.1.)

Other Charges

Other charges are usually handled as individual expenses appropriate to the party that the expense applies to. These items are debits to the respective party. Examples include but are not limited to:

- commissions
- recording fees
- transfer taxes
- legal fees

Preparation of Document—Closing Statements

When preparing for closing, one of the most important facts to determine is how much money is exchanged between the buyer and seller. There are many items that must be accounted for. For example:

- The seller usually must pay off any existing loans.
- The amount of the property tax bill must be divided proportionately between the buyer and the seller.
- The property may be rented, and any prepaid rent or deposits must be accounted for.
- The buyer usually must make a down payment on new financing.
- The buyer or seller must also pay the costs of taking out the new loan.

TIME METHODS OF PRORATION

- **The 365-day method** uses the actual number of days in the proration period.
- **The 360/12/13 method** assumes that there are 12 months in the year and each month has 30 days.
  - There is no method called the 12-month method.
  - There is no method called the 30-month method.

CLOSING STATEMENT SECTIONS AND ENTRIES

There are three sections and parties in a closing statement:

1. **Seller**
2. **Buyer**
3. **Escrow/closing agent**

There are three sections for entries in a closing statement:

1. **Transactional entries**
2. **Proration entries**
3. **Expenses/closing costs**

ITEMS THAT REQUIRE SINGLE ENTRY ON THE CLOSING STATEMENT
ITEMS THAT ARE ALWAYS DEBITS AND NEVER CREDITS

Expenses:

- Legal fees—each party pays his/her own attorney
- Title insurance—usually paid by the buyer
- Broker commission(s)—customarily paid by the seller
- Miscellaneous items—paid by the benefiting party (as applicable)
- Recording fees
  - Deed—generally paid by the buying party
  - Mortgage—generally paid by the buying party
- Documentary stamps
  - Deed—generally paid by the selling party
  - Note—generally paid by the buying party
  - Intangible—generally paid by the buying party

ITEMS THAT REQUIRE DOUBLE ENTRY ON A CLOSING STATEMENT

Transactional information:

- **Sales price**
  - The buyer pays the sale price.
  - The seller receives money from the sales price; therefore, you must also credit the seller.
- **Deposit**
  - The buyer receives the deposit (credit).
  - The seller pays (returns) the deposit (debit).
- **Newly originated first mortgage (by a third-party lender)**
  - The buyer receives the loan from the lender as a credit.
  - The seller does not receive it; it is given to the escrow/closing agent.

FIGURE 14.1 Time Methods of Proration

- **Assumed first mortgage (by buyer from seller)**
  - The seller pays the loan (debit) by transferring her remaining balance to the buyer.
  - The buyer also receives the loan balance as a credit.
- **Second mortgage (originated as seller financing)**
  - The buyer receives the loan from the seller (who in this case acts as the lender) as a credit.
  - The seller issues the loan (from his/her equity) and receives a debit entry.

Prorations:
- **Property taxes (unpaid by seller)**
  - The seller pays, so it is a debit.
  - The buyer receives seller's portion of unpaid taxes, so it is a credit.
- **Property taxes (paid *in advance* by seller)**
  - The buyer pays his/her portion of the taxes following closing, so it is a debit.
  - The seller receives the buyer's portion of taxes, so it is a credit.
- **First mortgage interest (assumed) paid in advance of closing by seller**
  - Buyer pays (debit) buyer's portion of interest for month of closing.
  - Seller receives (credit) buyer's portion of interest for month of closing.
- **First mortgage interest (originated by third-party lender)**
  - Interest to lender is usually treated as a one-time expense (debit) to the buyer.
- **Second mortgage interest (normally seller financing)**
  - Buyer pays (debit) seller/lender the interest for month of closing.
  - Seller receives (credit) buyer's interest for month of closing.
- **Rent**
  - The seller pays (debit) prepaid rent due the buyer for month of closing.
  - The buyer receives the prepaid rent (credit) portion from the seller.
- **Insurance (assumption of seller's unused policy)**
  - Buyer pays (debit) seller the buyer's portion of remaining policy.
  - Seller receives (credit) buyer's portion of remaining policy.

FIGURE 14.1 (*Continued*)
Source: © 2021 Mbition LLC

In the remainder of this chapter, we will look at how these and other financial items are handled for the closing. For closing, the details of the financial elements of the transaction are summarized in documents called closing statements or settlement statements. Separate closing statements are usually prepared for the seller and the buyer. These documents list all the items to be paid and received by the buyer or seller and give the total amount that the buyer pays and the seller receives when the transaction is completed. On the next few pages you will find a condensed version of a closing statement. For the sake of explanation, both the buyer's and seller's closing statements are combined into one document.

CHAPTER 14 Real Estate–Related Computations and Closing of Transactions

Coaching Tips

The deposit must appear twice on the closing statement. The deposit is given to the selling agent at the time the offer is tendered. As a result, it is being held in trust by the seller's agent or the closing agent. Therefore, the second place that the deposit would appear would be in the broker's/closing agent section of the statement (not shown here).

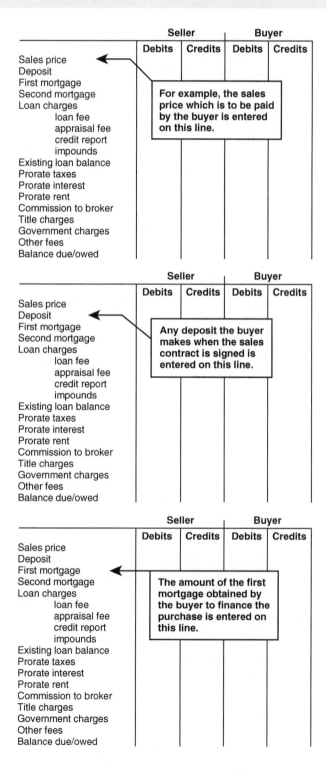

Coaching Tips

The mortgage must appear twice on the statement as well. When a newly originated loan is acquired through a lending institution, the loan amount is a credit for the buyer on the statement; however, the mortgage would also appear (as in the case of the deposit) in the broker's/closing agent section of the statement (not shown here).

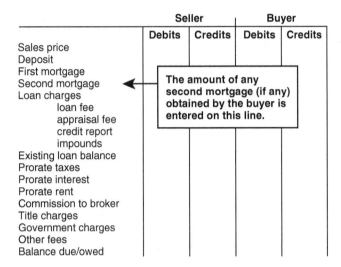

As you already know, the second mortgage is generally seller financing. As such, the seller receives a debit for the amount loaned to the buyer to complete the transaction. The buyer who receives the loan from the seller receives a credit entry.

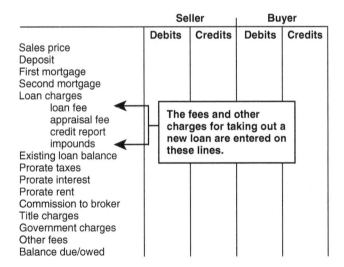

Loan charges are generally expense items that are charged to either the buyer or the seller. In the figure above, the expense items would probably be charged to the buyer because the benefiting party in relation to an item generally bears the responsibility of paying for that item.

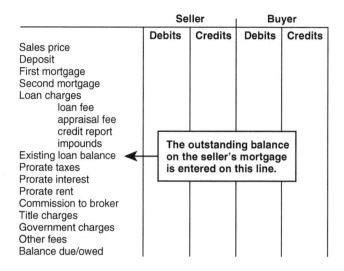

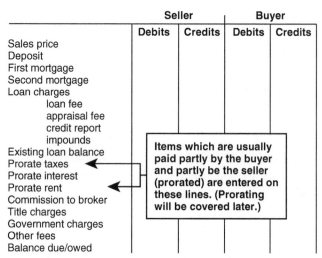

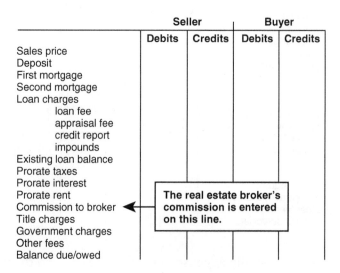

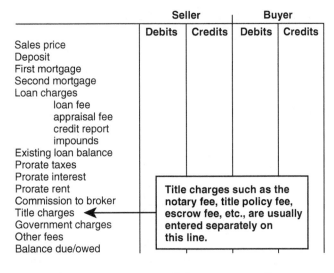

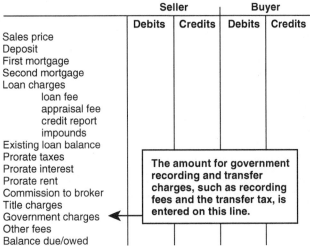

State Transfer Taxes

There are three types of state transfer taxes:

1. State documentary stamps (deed)

   - Customarily paid by the seller
   - The formula for calculating the tax is $0.70 per $100 (or any fraction thereof) of the full purchase price. It is important to note that in the event the property being sold is located in Dade County, the formula for calculating the tax is $0.60 per $100 (or any fraction thereof).

2. State documentary stamps (notes)

   - Customarily paid by the buyer
   - The formula for calculating the tax is $0.35 per $100 (or any fraction thereof) of all new and assumed mortgaged notes (does not apply to subject to mortgages).

3. Intangible tax (paid on recorded mortgages)

- Customarily paid by the buyer (paid only on new money that is introduced to the transaction; does not apply to assumed mortgages or subject to mortgages)
- The formula for calculating the tax is $0.002 (i.e., 2 mills) new mortgage amount(s)
- Converting mills to decimals

$$\frac{10}{1000} = \frac{1}{100}$$

	Seller		Buyer	
	Debits	Credits	Debits	Credits
Sales price				
Deposit				
First mortgage				
Second mortgage				
Loan charges				
loan fee				
appraisal fee				
credit report				
impounds				
Existing loan balance				
Prorate taxes				
Prorate interest				
Prorate rent				
Commission to broker				
Title charges				
Government charges				
Other fees				
Balance due/owed				

Other fees, such as survey and pest inspection fees, are entered on this line.

	Seller		Buyer	
	Debits	Credits	Debits	Credits
Sales price				
Deposit				
First mortgage				
Second mortgage				
Loan charges				
loan fee				
appraisal fee				
credit report				
impounds				
Existing loan balance				
Prorate taxes				
Prorate interest				
Prorate rent				
Commission to broker				
Title charges				
Government charges				
Other fees				
Balance due/owed				

The balance that the seller is due or the buyer owes is entered on this line.

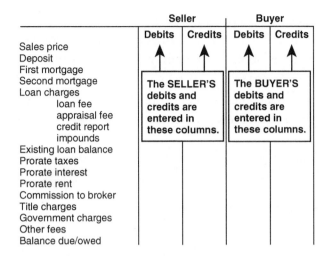

The purpose of completing the closing statements is to account for all details of financial elements of the transaction. There are many parties who have a financial interest in the closing of the transaction, including but not limited to:

- the buyer
- the seller
- the real estate broker(s) involved
- the lender on the seller's existing loan
- the lender on the buyer's new loan
- the escrow company
- the title insurance company

After completing the closing statements, all of these parties will have a clear accounting of the money they are due to receive or the money they must pay. For the buyer and seller, the amount due or owed is shown at the bottom of the statement under "Balance due" or "Balance owed." Let's now look at how the entries on the closing statements are made for each item.

When an item is entered on the closing statement for either the buyer or seller, we must first determine whether the item is a debit or a credit. Note below that both the buyer and seller have columns labeled "Debits" and "Credits" on their sides of the closing statement.

	Seller		Buyer	
	Debits	Credits	Debits	Credits
Sales price				
Deposit				
First mortgage				
Second mortgage				
Loan charges				
loan fee				
appraisal fee				
credit report				
impounds				
Existing loan balance				
Prorate taxes				
Prorate interest				
Prorate rent				
Commission to broker				
Title charges				
Government charges				
Other fees				
Balance due/owed				

A **debit** can best be thought of as a *payment* by someone to someone else. A **credit** is money that is *received* by someone from someone else. To determine who receives a credit or debit on an item, you must establish who owes or who is paying versus who is owed or who is receiving

The party who owes receives an entry in the "Debits" column, while the party who collects the payment receives an entry in the "Credits" column.

Coaching Tips

Think of debits and credits as you would your own personal checkbook. When you receive money (a deposit entry), the bank credits your account and your account balance increases. When you pay a bill and the check is presented to your bank for payment, your checkbook balance is debited or, in other words, results in a balance reduction.

Now, let's look at a typical real estate sales transaction to see which items are debits and which are credits to the buyer and the seller. First, we need to make an assumption that will help us in this situation. To determine the debits and credits on a closing statement, we will always assume that the first step in any transaction is the buyer paying the seller the full sales price in cash. This, of course, will not always be the case, but this assumption will make it much easier to understand debits and credits.

For example, a seller is selling her home to a buyer for $100,000. Remember, we assume that the buyer will pay the seller $100,000 in cash, regardless of how the buyer will actually pay for the home. The buyer's first payment of the sales price is entered as debit to the buyer. (Remember, a debit is a payment.)

Now, let's enter that debit to the buyer on a blank closing statement.

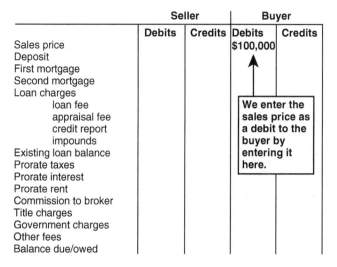

Because the buyer pays the sales price to the seller, we must also enter the sales price on the seller's half of the settlement statement. The seller receives the sales price as a payment; because the receipt of money is a credit, we enter the sales price as a credit to the seller.

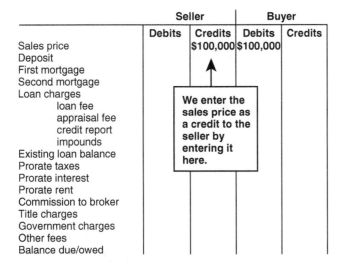

Once the seller receives the sales funds from the buyer, the seller will pay for various items, such as:

- The balance on an existing first mortgage
- The real estate broker's commission
- Escrow fees
- Title insurance
- Transfer taxes on the transference of the deed (based upon the total purchase price)

Because these are payments by the seller, these are entered as debits to the seller on the seller's half of the settlement statement, as shown next.

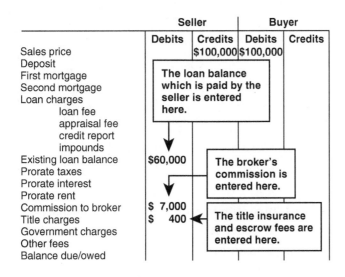

	Seller		Buyer	
	Debits	Credits	Debits	Credits
Sales price		$100,000	$100,000	
Deposit				
First mortgage				
Second mortgage				
Loan charges				
loan fee				
appraisal fee				
credit report				
impounds				
Existing loan balance	$60,000			
Prorate taxes				
Prorate interest				
Prorate rent				
Commission to broker	$ 7,000			
Title charges	$ 400			
Government charges				
Other fees				
Balance due/owed				

These three items just entered as debits to the seller are paid to someone other than the buyer. Therefore, they are not entered on the buyer's half of the settlement statement.

Now, let's look at two items that are paid by the seller to the buyer. The first of these is the earnest money deposit that the buyer made when the sales contract was signed. Because this was paid by the buyer to the seller prior to closing, the seller is still holding the buyer's deposit at the closing. Because the buyer will pay the entire sales price to the seller at closing, the seller must return the amount of the deposit to the buyer at closing. Because the buyer's deposit is paid by the seller back to the buyer, it is entered on both the seller's and the buyer's settlement statements. It is entered on the seller's statement as a debit because the seller pays the deposit back to the buyer. It is entered on the buyer's statement as a credit because the buyer receives the deposit back from the seller. These entries are shown on the next settlement statement. Regardless of who holds the earnest money deposit, and prior to closing, the holder of these funds must transfer the funds to the closing agent.

	Seller		Buyer	
	Debits	Credits	Debits	Credits
Sales price	$5,000	$100,000	$100,000	$5,000
Deposit				
First mortgage				
Second mortgage				
Loan charges				
loan fee				
appraisal fee				
credit report				
impounds				
Existing loan balance				
Prorate taxes				
Prorate interest				
Prorate rent				
Commission to broker	$7,000			
Title charges	$ 400			
Government charges				
Other fees				
Balance due/owed				

Debit the seller here since the seller PAYS the buyer.

Credit the buyer here since the buyer RECEIVES payment.

If the property is rented, the second item that the seller pays to the buyer is any prepaid rent that the seller has received. For example, let's suppose that a rental property is being sold and the tenant has prepaid the rent through the end of June. Closing will take place on the last day of May. In this situation, the seller has received a full month's rent that should go to the buyer because the buyer will own the property during the month of June. This situation is handled at closing as follows:

- The seller has received the June rent in advance and therefore must make a payment to the buyer for the amount of the rent.
- This payment is entered as a *debit* to the seller.
- The buyer receives the rent payment from the seller, so the amount of the rent is also entered as a *credit* to the buyer.

These entries are illustrated in the next settlement section.

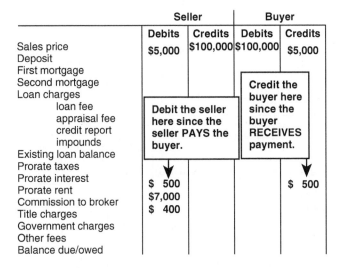

Coaching Tips

The amount of the prepaid rent must often be prorated. This means that each of the two parties will receive part of the prepaid rent. In the previous example, no proration is needed.

The last items we will cover are those that are paid by the buyer to someone other than the seller, including:

- loan origination fees
- structural pest control report
- escrow fees
- recording fees

The buyer might have to pay for many other expenses at closing, but all expenses would be handled on the settlement statement in the same manner. For simplicity, we will cover only loan origination fees and the structural pest control report.

Assume that a buyer/borrower arranges for a new level payment plan loan. A **level payment plan** or a level payment mortgage is a type of loan whose monthly payment amount remains the same throughout the loan. Such is the case for each month or payment period. Level payment plans afford borrowers the ability to know and understand exactly how much they will be obligated to pay for their loans on each pay period. Loan origination fees are charged to the borrower by the lender for making the new loan on the property. Let's assume that the amount of these fees is $3,500. These loan origination fees are paid by the buyer, so they are entered as a debit on the buyer's settlement statement. Because these fees are paid to the lender, not the seller, there is no corresponding entry on the seller's settlement statement. This entry is illustrated next.

	Seller		Buyer	
	Debits	Credits	Debits	Credits
Sales price		$100,000	$100,000	
Deposit	$ 5,000			$5,000
First mortgage				
Second mortgage			$ 3,500	
Loan charges				
loan fee				
appraisal fee				
credit report				
impounds				
Existing loan balance	$60,000			
Prorate taxes				
Prorate interest				
Prorate rent	$ 500			$ 500
Commission to broker	$ 7,000			
Title charges	$ 400			
Government charges				
Other fees				
Balance due/owed				

Debit the buyer here. Do not credit the seller.

If the cost of the structural pest control report is paid by the buyer, it is handled in the same way. The buyer pays this cost to the pest control company, so the amount is entered on the buyer's settlement statement as a debit. There is no corresponding entry on the seller's statement because the payment is not made to the seller. This entry is illustrated next.

	Seller		Buyer	
	Debits	Credits	Debits	Credits
Sales price		$100,000	$100,000	
Deposit	$ 5,000			$5,000
First mortgage				
Second mortgage			$ 3,500	
Loan charges				
loan fee				
appraisal fee				
credit report				
impounds				
Existing loan balance	$60,000			
Prorate taxes				
Prorate interest				
Prorate rent	$ 500			$ 500
Commission to broker	$ 7,000			
Title charges	$ 400			
Government charges			$ 150	
Other fees				
Balance due/owed				

Debit the buyer here. Do not credit the seller.

We need to look at one final situation—a loan assumption. Earlier, we covered the situation in which the seller pays off an existing loan when the loan is closed. In that situation, the existing loan amount is entered as a debit to the seller because the seller pays that amount at closing to the lender. When an existing loan is assumed by the buyer, the situation is different.

When a loan is assumed, the seller does not pay off the balance on the existing loan. Instead, the balance that is owed is transferred to the buyer, who assumes the obligation to repay the balance on the loan. In this case, the existing loan balance is still a debit to the seller because the loan balance must be satisfied (paid) in some way. In an assumption, the balance is paid by transferring the obligation to the buyer. Now the buyer has an entry for the loan balance on the buyer's settlement statement. The balance on the loan is entered as a credit to the buyer because the buyer actually receives an amount from the lender toward the purchase price that is equal to the balance on the existing loan.

Once all the relevant debits and credits have been entered on the seller's and buyer's settlement statements, how much each party must pay or will receive at closing can be determined. This is done by subtracting the total amount of all debits from the total amount of all credits for each party. Let's look at this computation for both parties, beginning with the seller. The next illustration shows a condensed summary of all the debits and credits for both the buyer and seller for the examples we have covered so far.

Total Seller Credits

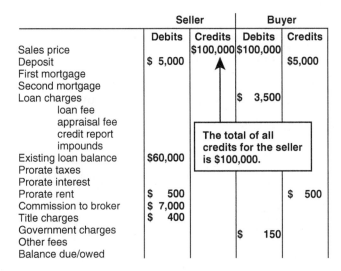

Total Seller Debits

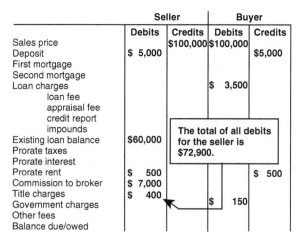

Check That Seller Will Receive at Closing

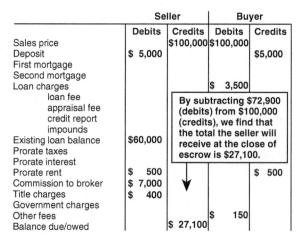

Now, let's look at the same computation for the buyer.

Total Buyer Credits

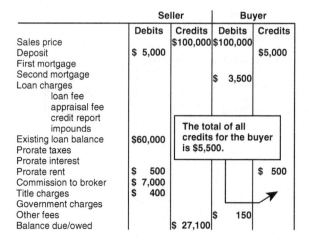

Total Buyer Debits

	Seller		Buyer	
	Debits	Credits	Debits	Credits
Sales price		$100,000	$100,000	
Deposit	$ 5,000			$5,000
First mortgage				
Second mortgage				
Loan charges			$ 3,500	
loan fee				
appraisal fee				
credit report				
impounds				
Existing loan balance	$60,000			
Prorate taxes				
Prorate interest				
Prorate rent	$ 500			$ 500
Commission to broker	$ 7,000			
Title charges	$ 400			
Government charges				
Other fees			$ 150	
Balance due/owed		$ 27,100		

The total of all debits for the buyer is $103,650.

Check Needed from Buyer at Closing

	Seller		Buyer	
	Debits	Credits	Debits	Credits
Sales price		$100,000	$100,000	
Deposit	$ 5,000			$5,000
First mortgage				
Second mortgage				
Loan charges				
loan fee				
appraisal fee				
credit report				
impounds				
Existing loan balance	$60,000			
Prorate taxes				
Prorate interest				
Prorate rent	$ 500			$ 500
Commission to broker	$ 7,000			
Title charges	$ 400			
Government charges				
Other fees			$ 150	
Balance due/owed		$ 27,100	$ 98,150	

Now when we substract the total debits ($103,650) from the total credits ($5,500), we get a negative number (−$98,150). Thus, the buyer will OWE this amount when escrow closes.

What is owed (debits) is subtracted from what is received (credits).

Summary

Customarily (with certain exceptions), a real estate broker's compensation is generally predicated on the closing and passing of title. In addition to the listing and selling process, in Florida and in many states, the broker may undertake the role of escrow and closing agent on the transaction. Even after a contract for purchase and sale has been signed, there remains much to do on the part of the licensee.

The broker or designated closing agent prepares the closing statement and delivers it to the interested parties to the sale. The declaration and responsibility to pay the required state transfer taxes are included in the statement. These taxes should not be confused with real property tax. There are three transfer taxes in Florida: (1) transfer tax on the deed (based on the full purchase price); (2) transfer tax on the notes (based upon new borrowed funds or assumed mortgages); and (3) intangible tax (solely based on new financing that is introduced to the transaction and that does not apply to assumed mortgages).

Review Questions

1. A buyer contracted to pay $50,000 for a small rental property. The buyer included $5,000 with the offer, which the broker is holding in escrow. The lender agreed to the assumption of an existing $35,000 mortgage and will lend another $10,000 as a new second mortgage. Calculate all of the transfer taxes due to the state for this transaction.
   a. $122.50
   b. $177.50
   c. $350.00
   d. $527.50

2. How will the earnest money deposit appear on the closing statement?
   a. credit to the buyer, debit to the seller
   b. credit to the seller, debit to the buyer
   c. credit to the buyer only
   d. credit to the seller only

3. How would prepaid property taxes appear on a closing statement?
   a. debit to the seller, credit to the buyer
   b. credit to the seller, debit to the buyer
   c. debit to the seller only
   d. debit to the buyer only

4. Mary purchased a lot in a subdivision for $50,030. Calculate the documentary stamps on the deed for which the seller will be charged.
   a. $350.70
   b. $350.21
   c. $175.10
   d. $100.00

5. How would prepaid rent appear on the closing statement?
   a. debit buyer, credit seller
   b. debit seller, credit buyer
   c. credit seller only
   d. credit buyer only

6. A buyer will obtain a new second mortgage for $73,000 as part of the price for a property. What are the documentary and intangible taxes to the state on the new loan?
   a. $912.50
   b. $511.00
   c. $401.50
   d. $225.50

7. How does the purchase price appear on a closing statement?
   a. credit to the seller, debit to the buyer
   b. debit to the seller, credit to the buyer
   c. credit to the seller only
   d. debit to the buyer only

8. A listing agreement specified the seller will pay the listing broker 6% of the sales price. A sales associate who works for the listing broker listed and sold the property for $200,000. What is the amount of the commission that will appear on the closing statement?
   a. $12,000
   b. $7,200
   c. $6,000
   d. $4,800

9. As a rule of thumb, how does the state documentary stamp tax on the deed appear on the closing statement?
   a. debit to the seller, credit to the buyer
   b. credit to the seller, debit to the buyer
   c. debit seller only
   d. debit buyer only

10. A property owner collected rent for June on June 1. The rent for the month was $900. The owner sells the property, and the day of closing is June 12. The day of closing is charged to the buyer. Calculate the proration.
    a. debit buyer $540, credit seller $540
    b. debit seller $530, credit buyer $540
    c. debit buyer $570, credit seller $570
    d. debit seller $570, credit buyer $570

11. When the transfer of a property closed, the state documentary stamp tax on the deed was $1,050; the state documentary stamp tax on the note was $420: and the intangible tax on the mortgage was $240. What was the purchase price of the property?
    a. $100,000
    b. $120,000
    c. $150,000
    d. $300,000

12. A buyer agreed to pay $125,000 for a property. The purchase includes financing at an LTV ratio of 80/20. In addition, the buyer must pay $3,000 in closing costs. The broker is holding $5,000 in escrow. How much additional cash must the buyer bring to closing?
    a. $15,000
    b. $20,000
    c. $23,000
    d. $25,000

13. Which of the following is the process of determining the value of a property from how much net income it produces?
    a. depreciation
    b. appreciation
    c. capitalization
    d. none of these

14. If a bank will make a 90% LTV loan on a house valued at $75,000 and $2,300 is paid as earnest money, how much additional cash must be brought along to the closing?
    a. $7,500
    b. $7,270
    c. $6,750
    d. $5,200

15. In Alachua County, a 27.5-acre parcel sold for $4,100 per acre. What is the documentary stamp tax on the deed?
    a. $225.50
    b. $394.25
    c. $789.25
    d. $789.60

CHAPTER 15
THE REAL ESTATE MARKETS AND ANALYSIS

KEY TERMS

buyer's market
demand
household
seller's market
situs
supply
transitioning market
vacancy rates

LEARNING OBJECTIVES

After completing this lesson, you will be able to:

- describe the physical characteristics of real estate
- describe the economic characteristics of real estate
- understand the factors that influence supply and demand
- distinguish among different ways of interpreting market conditions
- demonstrate understanding of the different market indicators

PHYSICAL CHARACTERISTICS OF REAL ESTATE

There are five primary characteristics of real estate:

1. Immobility and the importance of location—The location of property is fixed and not mobile. A property's location is what determines value to an owner or buyer.
2. Markets are slow to respond to change in supply and demand—When demand increases, the creation of new product is required to meet that demand. The problem, however, is creating the product. Once a residential single-family construction project begins, it can take as little as six months to as much as 12 months before construction is complete. The time period to construct multifamily housing is even longer—from 12 to 18 months. Therefore, supply of housing moves at a slow pace in response to a change in market conditions.

    Furthermore, a slowness to respond to changes in supply and demand will lead to other issues. For example, when the housing supply increases, this event will lead to an increase in the area **vacancy rate** (the availability of housing/commercial/manufacturing units compared with the total existing inventory expressed in percentage terms). In reverse, when supply decreases, this leads to a reduction in the area vacancy rate as well as higher pricing.

A buyer, seller, landlord, or tenant would need to exercise greater caution when transacting in changing environments. We have already learned that when consumer demand decreases while supply increases, the general result is downside pricing pressure. In the reverse, a failure to respond to changes in supply to meet increased demand results in upside pricing pressures. This was particularly evident during the financial banking crisis debacle of 2007. During the financial crisis of 2007, real estate housing foreclosures were in abundance. As a result of the crisis, it has taken many years for the existing inventory of properties for sale to be absorbed. Those times led to deep discounting on the purchase of:

- new homes
- existing homes
- foreclosed homes

These times have also led to stronger leasing markets throughout the country. Displaced individuals and families looked to the rental market for housing. The strength in rentals versus purchasing has continued into present day. The lack of available housing for lease has led to higher rent costs.

As a separate note, when the cost of renting catches up with the cost of owning a home, it is only logical to assume that the sales market will likely heat up again.

3. Indestructibility of land—Land cannot be made or destroyed. Physically, land is permanent. Therefore, improvements are ultimately added to the land. In some cases, added improvements are for owner/occupant purposes. In other cases, they are for income-producing purposes. In either case, the creation of these improvements is always governed by local laws. Ownership in real property is not considered to be a liquid investment. Therefore, anyone investing in real property is considered a long-term investor. This is due to the indestructibility of the land as well as the large initial investment required at the time the property is acquired. Additionally, real property is considered a long-term investment because of the property's ability to provide returns on invested capital. Furthermore, where improvements made to real property experience depreciation, land is not depreciable.

Coaching Tips

Only improvements made or added to the land are insurable; land is not.

4. **Highest and best use**—The principle of highest and best use (discussed in greater detail in Chapter 16) states that the greatest value of a parcel of land is determined by its highest and best use. Defined, this means the use that is the legal and most feasible use that would otherwise generate the highest possible value attributable to the land through the incorporation of that use. There are two types of highest and best use analyses:

   1. site as vacant
   2. site as improved

   In both types of analysis, the investor uses the information obtained by a study of other alternative legal site uses to determine the value to that investor. As a result of changes in zoning, there may be times where an existing improvement may yield a lower value than that of a different legal use. In this case, the investor adds in the cost of demolition or retrofitting to reposition the property appropriately.

5. **Nonstandardized; non-homogeneous (heterogeneous)**—No two parcels of property are the same. Therefore, each parcel is said to be heterogeneous or unique. Lots contained on the same street within a subdivision are different. A corner lot differs from the lot next to it merely by its location.

   Under our current tax laws, land is also non depreciable. Only an improvement suffers from depreciation caused by physical deterioration, functional obsolescence, and external/economic obsolescence. As a result of the aforementioned, the purchase of a property insurance policy will only cover the improvements and will not cover the land.

6. Governmental controls influence the market through:

   - zoning
   - building codes
   - taxes
   - other influences

   While the federal government controls our money supply, local laws such as zoning, building codes, and property/income taxes govern and influence development. Areas with low property taxation are more likely to experience growth than those with high property tax bases.

ECONOMIC CHARACTERISTICS OF REAL PROPERTY

There are various principles or elements that constitute a property's value. Timing is an essential element. Let's examine how the principles of demand and supply interact with market conditions.

Demand

Demand for property means that someone has a desire to own or use the property. If demand is to have an effect on the value of property, it must be accompanied by purchasing power. If someone desires a property but doesn't have the financial ability to act on that desire, there is no effective demand for the property. When someone has a desire for property and the purchasing power to act on that desire, the resulting demand for the property contributes to the property's value.

Price of Real Estate

When there is a high demand for property, prices rise. Conversely, when there is a greater availability of property, prices fall. Therefore, as a buyer, seller, or licensee, one must understand the scale of economies to succeed in the real estate marketplace.

For example, economic growth is stimulated when the marketplace sees the demand as exceeding the available supply. This is the reason supply is created. Supply is created to meet demand. The economic cycle of growth is always seen through the creation of supply that feeds the demand. Let's look at the stimulating factors that create demand.

Population and Households

When looking at population and household trends, it is easy to see that our overall population has grown considerably. A **household** is defined by the U.S. Census Bureau as a space designed for dwelling purposes occupied by one or more persons. Although each person in the population does not represent a household, one can make determinations as to the minimum amount of product required to meet the demand within a geographical area. A careful look at previous statistics concerning an area's inventory and sales output will help determine a market's absorption rate. One measure of absorption would be determining the average sales per month and compare the result to the available housing stock inventory.

In previous years, careful study has revealed that real estate markets, particularly those in the sunshine states like Arizona and New Mexico, have seen and experienced the greatest growth margins. This is certainly evident in the Florida housing market. The aforementioned growth is probably attributable to:

- colder winters in other parts of our nation
- job opportunities
- lower cost of housing and living
- population growth and
- possible lower state taxes

It is interesting to note that northeastern and midwestern states have lost a great deal of resident taxpayers to areas such as the sunshine states. The housing marketplace arena is the most active. Everyone needs a roof over his/her head.

This is the primary factor that drives the demand for housing. Population increase fuels the need for additional housing and other real property types, such as:

- schools designed to meet the needs of a growing community
- hospitals designed to meet the needs of the aging and sick
- office space
- government buildings
- recreational facilities
- parks
- playgrounds
- community facilities

Consumer Income

Income trends can make or break real estate markets. For example, high rates of unemployment could reduce the demand for purchased property. This event can lead to a decline in property values as well as diminish an area's desirability to a buyer. Population will gravitate to areas that offer the best employment opportunities. Lifestyles may become secondary to employment opportunities.

On the other hand, it is suggested by economists that lower property tax rates tend to increase one's disposable income This action is intended to result in increased demand. In addition, the retail service sector is solely reliant on the strength of the consumer for their retail businesses' success. A true sign of changing markets and economies can be seen with the tightness or oversupply of retail space. The availability of a large number of retail locations might indicate a softening of market conditions, while in the reverse, the unavailability of retail locations would indicate a tight or tightening market. However, today, changes in how the consumers shop has transformed retail centers and spaces. Partial credit for this transformation must go to the increased use of e-commerce. In particular, internet giant Amazon.com has disrupted the conventional brick and mortar retailers. This directly affects commercial retail property owners that are now faced with a transforming and re-engineering their retail holdings.

Availability of Mortgage Funds

Demand is dependent on the availability of borrowed funds at affordable rates. When interest rates are low, property values increase to reflect the availability of money within the credit system. However, when interest rates are high, property values drop. This is due to the increased cost for debt service, which occurs when the Federal Reserve tightens the available money supply. In recent years, interest rates have been at historic lows. The usual effect when interest rates increase is that prospective property buyers are faced with higher debt service payments and as a result, due to affordability, seek lower purchase prices.

With the aforementioned in mind, currently, mortgage rates are expected to steadily increase. At some point in the rate increase policy of the Fed, the higher costs end up pricing certain sections of the buying population out of the market. This is a contributing factor toward the cooling of the nationwide real estate/housing economy.

The following is an illustration of the significance of rising or falling interest rates to the consumer.

Example 1
Assume the following loan information:
- Loan amount: $500,000 fully amortized over maturity
- Interest rate: 10%
- Maturity/term of loan: 25 years
- Monthly payment: $4,543.50

Example 2
Assume the following loan information:
- Loan amount: $500,000 fully amortized over maturity
- Interest rate: 9%
- Maturity/term of loan: 25 years
- Monthly payment: $4,195.98

As you can see by Examples 1 and 2, a 1% (or 100 basis points) change in the rate equates to a monthly payment differential of $347.52. When annualized, the difference between a 9% loan versus a 10% loan is approximately $4,170.22 for each year of the loan. This can be a significant difference to a borrower.

Consumer Preferences

Consumers are also an important factor regarding demand. When shopping for housing, one consumer may seek new construction while another may seek older housing. Different consumer preferences at any given time and place will dictate demand. Examples of consumer preferences include:

- architectural styles:
    - Cape Cod
    - ranch
    - split-level
- single-family detached housing:
    - townhouse
    - cooperative high-rise
    - condominium high-rise

For example, the aging population may be considering downsizing from large homes to something smaller, such as apartments. In addition, the aging population would probably not want to climb stairs to their living area and, as such, would likely select a ranch-style home or an apartment in an elevator-equipped multi family complex.

To keep up with the demands of consumers, developers and property owners must recognize the needs of their constituency and keep up with changes that occur in housing preferences.

> ## Coaching Tips
>
> Demand factors at a glance:
> - price
> - population and households
> - consumer income
> - availability of mortgage funds
> - tastes or preferences

Supply

Supply (as it pertains to real property) can be defined as the amount of housing stock of properties available for sale or for lease. Let's examine some of the factors that make up and play an integral role in the supply of housing.

Availability of Skilled Labor

The creation of supply results from the work of craftspeople who practice various construction trades. In residential construction, this includes the following:

- electricians
- plumbers
- carpenters
- roofers
- masons

In commercial construction, many of these craftspeople will be utilized as well as:

- steel workers
- heating and air-conditioning contractors
- Sheetrock contractors

Any area of the country that experiences growth must also have available skilled labor. Growth is one of many economic cycles. The growth cycle occurs when the need to grow the supply side of the economy arises. As you will see, the growth cycle generally is sparked during times when inventories are low. It is important to note that a growth cycle is usually associated with a period where supply is created to feed the current demand. Furthermore, the creation of supply usually trails the demand needs by the amount of time required to create the demand product. This theory holds true for any product in demand by a consumer. Therefore, availability of skilled labor becomes imperative to the supplier.

Availability of Construction Loans and Financing

The construction industry is dependent on the availability of construction financing, including:

- short-term (interim) construction financing—Short-term loans are used to construct improvements. These loans are short-term in maturity (generally 12 to 18 months), and due to the nature of their risk, they usually bear higher rates of interest than those of other types of loans.
- long-term (takeout) loans—These loans pay for the construction loan and act as the property's permanent financing.

As interest rates on these types of loans rise, less supply is generated. When rates begin to fall or are steady, supply begins to increase.

Availability of Land

In many cities throughout the country, prime land availability has dwindled. Where there may appear to be abundant amount of land available, other factors may affect the desirability of that land to subdividers and developers. Zoning and local building codes can create major constraints within any development. This is particularly true when dealing with large tracts of land.

Cities with vast land availability will normally experience new speculative construction. However, due to the continuous availability of land in these areas, resale market values tend to be nonexistent because they cannot keep up with the value of newer construction.

Availability of Materials

As previously discussed, when we enter an economic growth economy, supply usually increases. In order to provide additional supply to the marketplace, the materials used in real property construction must be available. In the absence of construction material supply, the cost of constructing the improvement increases. From a project feasibility point of view, the increased cost will probably impede the development of the project.

INTERPRETING MARKET CONDITIONS

Whenever the economic climate changes, real estate markets are directly affected. The effect can be on a national or local level. There are generally three types of markets that buyers or sellers experience:

1. **seller's market**—This occurs when there are more buyers than there are sellers or available product
2. **buyer's market**—This occurs when there are more sellers than there are buyers.

3. **transitioning market**—This occurs at the end of a buyer's or seller's market. In this type of market, conditions tend to resemble a tug-of-war between the buyer and seller. At the end of a seller's market, a seller may not recognize the changing market conditions fast enough to capture a sale. Sellers who do not react to the shift away from a seller's market will lose out on opportunities to sell because they won't be flexible when pricing their homes.

    At the end of a buyer's market, a buyer may not grasp the need to pay more for a property. Therefore, a buyer may lose deals to other buyers who recognize the changing environment. Ultimately, that buyer will end up paying more for a property that he/she could have bought for less. Irrespective of market conditions, every day is a day to buy because prices usually go up.

Price Levels

Property price levels change frequently. There are various ways of recognizing when this happens:

- Issuance of new construction building permits indicates the amount of new housing supply.
- Increase or decrease in vacancies of rental property (However, vacancies can have the opposite effect and drive home sales prices down.).
    - When vacancies are on the rise, it is cheaper to buy than it is to lease.
    - When the supply of housing for sale increases beyond demand, it is cheaper to rent than it is to buy.
- Population increase within a community or region will always spur creation of new supply to meet the anticipated demand.

Coaching Tips

Previously, watching the retail sector was a wonderful indication of consumer trends. When retail stores experienced high vacancy rates, it was an indication that consumers were not spending as much money to support retail sales. The result became an increase in vacancies. Conversely, when the vacancy rate for retail stores in a marketplace was low, this was an indication that consumers had resumed spending trends, thereby increasing retail leasing of space. Such is not the case today. Currently, the internet has replaced conventional brick and mortar stores. Now, observing and monitoring online sales growth can be a stronger indication of the consumer's financial health.

Vacancy Rates

As previously discussed, vacancy rates are always an indication of market trends. Vacancy rates are generally quoted as percentages as opposed to numbers representing available product. Rising vacancy rates indicate a buyer's market while lower rates indicate a seller's market.

Sales Volume

The current market condition can be determined by examining the homes that have recently sold. Consumers today are in a much better position to gather information about pricing on previous sales because of the Internet. Today, there are various types of reports that are available and are published by real estate firms. This information is usually provided by real estate companies as a means of branding and marketing. Information contained within these reports may include:

- quarterly or semiannual sales information broken down by:
  - property type
    - single-family housing
    - cooperatives
    - condominiums
    - townhouses
  - neighborhood
  - percentage of increase or decrease in the sales pricing information from previously reported periods
- cost per square foot for the purchase of a property
- time on the market prior to a property's sale

Note that these reports are only as good or as accurate as the companies that compile them. Therefore, any information presented in these reports should be confirmed.

Area Preference—Situs

Situs is a Latin term used to describe a legal fixed location. Everyone has heard the expression "location, location, location." Situs, or area preference, is dictated by one's desire to be near certain amenities. For the view-minded person, this can be as simple as a location on or near waterfront property. For a business, this situs or area preference will be dictated by the business constituents and their ability to access the businesses' services.

Summary

Changes within the economic environment dictate whether or not to create supply or consolidate it. When conditions suggest an oversupply, new supply development comes to a halt. New construction will probably not resume until the existing inventory supply has gone through consolidation. Generally speaking, the amount of time that a market rises is probably the amount of time required to absorb any leftover product. The real estate housing market can sometimes seem immune and contrary to that of a deteriorating business climate. However, the financial economic and banking crisis of 2007 took no hostages. It decimated the housing market throughout the country. To date, the housing market is still in recovery mode. In order to capitalize on the times, buyers, sellers, and licensees must be able to recognize the cause for change in the real estate environment.

Review Questions

1. A factor that makes the real estate market different from other markets is:
   a. the real estate market is centralized
   b. information about individual real estate markets is readily available
   c. the real estate market is quick to respond to changes in supply and demand
   d. real property is not homogeneous

2. All of the following are true of land EXCEPT:
   a. it is indestructible
   b. it can be improved
   c. it can be depreciated
   d. it is imobile

3. Highest and best use of land:
   a. is unconditionally set by zoning
   b. is determined by examining any legally allowable alternative use
   c. will not change with time
   d. is not influenced by surrounding areas

4. Unlike the markets for stocks, bonds, commodities, and hard goods, the real estate market:
   a. is subject to government controls at all levels of government
   b. is independent of decisions by the Federal Reserve
   c. is only dependent on interest rates
   d. is quick to respond to changes in supply and demand

5. The U.S. Census Bureau has defined a person or group of persons who occupy a separate housing space as a:
   a. housing unit
   b. household
   c. home
   d. family unit

6. Which of the following statements does NOT describe the real estate market?
   a. Property is unique to its location.
   b. Land is indestructible.
   c. Real property construction has become standardized.
   d. Federal Reserve decisions influence the market.

7. Government controls are a large influence on the market for real property. An example of a direct control on the real estate market would be:
   a. monetary policy
   b. changes in the discount rate
   c. changes in the reserve requirement
   d. statewide and local building codes

8. All of the following are examples of state and local government on the real estate market EXCEPT
   a. building codes
   b. zoning ordinances
   c. building moratoriums
   d. open-market operations

9. Which of the following variables influences the demand for real property?
   a. Land is available.
   b. Skilled labor is readily available.
   c. Construction materials can be readily obtained.
   d. The price for rental housing is attractive.

10. Sales reports provide quarterly or semiannual sales information broken down by all of the following EXCEPT:
    a. property type
    b. brokerage that sold the property
    c. cost per square foot for the purchase of a property
    d. time on the market prior to a property's sale

11. When trying to predict the revival of a real estate market, people look to:
    a. the price of money
    b. decisions by the Federal Reserve
    c. the availability of skilled labor
    d. vacancy rates of existing properties

12. In recent years in the Florida housing market, buyers had to compete for desirable homes. This was an indication of:
    a. builder activity
    b. an increase in supply
    c. a seller's market
    d. a buyer's market

13. One of the leading indicators that the federal government looks to when predicting the economy is the construction industry. In terms of a local property market, an increase in the issuance of building permits and prices would indicate:
    a. a buyer's market
    b. a seller's market
    c. an influence on the prices for property
    d. a downturn in the market

14. While driving around your community, you notice a surprising number of "For Rent" signs. You might conclude that:
    a. the market is about to explode
    b. a seller's market is in effect
    c. rental signs may reflect a buyer's market
    d. more people have invested in property. An investor's market prevails.

15. One of the influences on the supply of property is:
    a. architectural tastes
    b. household composition
    c. consumer desires
    d. availability of construction loans

16. Which of the following statements does NOT describe the real estate market?
    a. An increase in price indicates a seller's market.
    b. Real estate is heterogeneous.
    c. Real estate is immobile.
    d. Demand rises as prices increase.

17. Which of the following has the greatest effect on the real estate market?
    a. actions by the Federal Reserve
    b. consumers
    c. large manufacturers and builders
    d. producers of goods

18. Highest and best use means:
    a. the use that is legal and most feasible that would otherwise generate the highest possible value attributable to the land through the incorporation of that use
    b. the use that is legal and most feasible that would otherwise generate the lowest possible value attributable to the improvement through the incorporation of that use
    c. the use that is legal and most feasible that would otherwise generate the highest possible value attributable to the improvement through the incorporation of that use
    d. both b and c

19. One indicator of the demand for housing in any particular housing market would be:
    a. a local increase in the occupancy rate that cannot be tied to reduced rents or other rental promotions
    b. the number of commercial building starts
    c. a projected increase in population numbers
    d. national housing trends

20. If the only change in the economy is a small increase in long-term interest rates:
    a. the real estate market will not be affected
    b. people will continue to buy homes
    c. the demand for homes may rise
    d. the demand for housing may fall

CHAPTER 16

REAL ESTATE APPRAISAL

KEY TERMS

appraisal
assemblage
automated valuation model (AVM)
comparative market analysis (CMA)
cost-depreciation approach
curable
depreciation
economic life
effective age
federally related transaction
gross rent multiplier (GRM)/gross rent income (GIM)
highest and best use
income capitalization approach
incurable
market value
overimprovement
plottage
principle of substitution
progression
reconciliation
regression
replacement cost
reproduction cost
sales comparison approach
situs
subject property
Uniform Standards of Professional Appraisal Practice (USPAP)
valuation

LEARNING OBJECTIVES

After completing this lesson, you will be able to:

- describe federal and state regulations pertaining to appraisal
- understand the appraiser's fiduciary relationship
- identify the economic and physical characteristics of real estate that affect market value
- explain what the Uniform Standards of Professional Appraisal Practice (USPAP) is and how it effects the valuation of real property
- distinguish among the various types of value
- define market value and describe its underlying assumptions
- distinguish among value, price, and cost
- describe the four characteristics of value
- distinguish among the principles of value
- differentiate among the three appraisal approaches to estimating the value of real property

- estimate the value of subject property using the comparable sales approach to value
- estimate the value of subject property using the cost approach
- estimate the value of subject property using the income approach
- reconcile the three approaches to establish the final value estimate
- calculate value using gross rent multiplier analysis
- explain how to prepare a CMA, comparing and contrasting with the sales comparison approach

REGULATION OF APPRAISING—FIRREA

The creation of Title XI of the Federal Institutions Reform, Recovery, and Enforcement Act of 1989 (FIRREA) was in response to the crisis created by the savings and loan institutions in the 1980s. Prior to its creation, it was not uncommon for lending institutions to experience submission of fraudulent appraisals performed by unqualified persons. These fraudulent appraisals resulted in financial loss for both borrowers and lenders.

As a result of these events, creation of FIRREA required that anyone performing an appraisal on a transaction that fell under the definition of a **federally related transaction** would have to be performed only by a state-licensed-certified, or general appraiser. A federally related transaction is any transaction-involving a financial institution either regulated or insured by the federal government. This would most likely include every form of institutional financing transaction.

It would not include:

- transactions where seller financing is involved
- transactions where private or personal funds are utilized

The purpose of FIRREA is primarily to protect the interests of those involved in real estate transactions. This would include:

- public policy interests
- financial institutions that are regulated or insured by the federal government

The law created required fraud protection in the valuation of real estate transactions. It required that those persons or entities involved in real estate appraisals that fell under the definition of a federally related transaction be:

- conducted by competently qualified licensed persons
- in accordance with uniform standards of practice
- subject to overall constant supervision of professional practice
- performed in writing

In order to address the problem and administer the law, the Appraisal Subcommittee (ASC) of the Federal Financial Institutions Examination Council (FFIEC) was created on August 9, 1989. The ASC was empowered to carry out its mission by:

1. monitoring certification and licensing of appraisers throughout the country
2. requiring and reviewing each individual state's compliance with the requirements of Title XI
3. issuing nonrecognition orders predicated on the results following a formal hearing. Such an order would disqualify anyone from a state that has been issued a nonrecognition order from the ability to participate in a valuation assignment by a regulated lending institution
4. creating and updating a national registry of state-certified and licensed appraisers who are approved and authorized to perform appraisals on a federally related transaction

APPRAISAL FOUNDATION

The Appraisal Foundation is an organization that incorporates both the:

1. Appraisal Standards Board
2. Appraisal Qualifications Board as part of the Foundation

It is a nonprofit organization and is considered the foremost authority for the valuation of real and personal property in America. The Foundation:

- creates qualifications and standards for the real property appraisal practice
- directs appraisers on methods and approaches to publicly recognized methods of valuation
- works in the advancement of the profession of valuation by requiring consistent and objective valuation procedures intended to ensure an independent valuation process

Appraisal Standards Board

An organization called the Appraisal Standards Board (ASB) is responsible for the development of Uniform Standards of Professional Appraisal Practice (USPAP). The ASB is part of the Appraisal Foundation.

Appraisal Qualifications Board (AQB)

An organization called the Appraisal Qualifications Board (AQB) is responsible for setting the qualifications for certified and licensed appraisers. The Appraisal Subcommittee is charged with enforcement of the qualifications set by the AQB.

STATE-LICENSED AND -CERTIFIED APPRAISERS

In Florida, there are three categories of appraisal licensing and designation:

1. certified general appraiser—permitted to provide appraisals on all types of real property transactions
2. certified residential appraiser—permitted to appraise all residential real property consisting of one to four units
3. registered trainee appraiser—must operate at all times under the direct supervision of either a certified or general appraiser

In each of these aforementioned categories, there are specific required courses that the appraiser must successfully complete and extensive experience requirements.

REQUIREMENTS FOR FEDERALLY RELATED TRANSACTIONS

Per Part 323 of the rules of the Federal Deposit Insurance Corporation (FDIC), transactions requiring a state-certified or -licensed appraiser include but are not limited to:

- All real estate-related financial transactions except those in which:
  - The transaction value is $250,000 or less.
  - A lien on real estate has been taken as collateral in an abundance of caution.
  - The transaction is not secured by real estate.
  - A lien on real estate has been taken for purposes other than the real estate's value.
  - The transaction is a business loan that:
    (i) Has a transaction value of $1 million or less.
    (ii) Is not dependent on the sale of, or rental income derived from, real estate as the primary source of repayment.
  - A lease of real estate is entered into, unless the lease is the economic equivalent of a purchase or sale of the leased real estate.
  - The transaction involves an existing extension of credit at the lending institution, provided that:
    (i) There has been no obvious and material change in market conditions or physical aspects of the property that threaten the adequacy of the institution's real estate collateral protection after the transaction, even with the advancement of new monies.
    (ii) There is no advancement of new monies, other than funds necessary to cover reasonable closing costs.
  - The transaction involves the purchase, sale, investment in, exchange of, or extension of credit secured by, a loan or interest in a loan, pooled loans, or interests in real property, including mortgage-backed securities, and

each loan or interest in a loan, pooled loan, or real property interest met FDIC regulatory requirements for appraisals at the time of origination.
- The transaction is wholly or partially insured or guaranteed by a U.S. government agency or U.S. government–sponsored agency.

Certified Appraisal Reports

At a minimum, all appraisals for federally related transactions must:

- comply and conform to generally accepted appraisal standards per **Uniform Standards of Professional Appraisal Practice (USPAP)** (USPAP constitutes the rules and code of ethics used in the preparation of appraisals.)
  - these standards are promulgated by the Appraisal Standards Board of the Appraisal Foundation
- be written and contain sufficient information to support an institution's decision to participate in the transaction
- be based upon the definition of market value
- be performed by state-licensed or -certified appraisers

APPRAISAL SERVICE OF REAL ESTATE

Before we discuss property pricing, you need to understand the distinction between the process of appraising a property and the process of pricing a property. An **appraisal** is a formal estimation or opinion of the value of real property as of a certain date (the as-of date). In most states, only a certified or licensed appraiser can make an appraisal of property.

In some situations, a real estate licensee may be called upon to help determine an appropriate price for a property. For example, a real estate licensee may be asked to assist a seller in determining a suitable price for a property or to assist a buyer in evaluating a price offered by a seller. In this course, we will refer to this pricing assistance as a **comparative market analysis (CMA)**. Another form of value opinion is called a broker price opinion (BPO). A CMA focuses on pricing and marketing, while the focus of an appraisal is always on the value of whatever is being appraised.

When a real estate licensee creates a CMA, the result is a recommended price for a property, not an appraisal. In fact, under Chapter 475 of Florida state law, a real estate licensee is prohibited from calling a CMA an appraisal, unless the licensee is a licensed or certified appraiser.

Chapter 475 is comprised of four parts:

- Part 1 affects real estate brokers, sales associates, and schools and appraisers (ss. 475.001–475.5018).
- Part 2 affects appraisers (ss. 475.610–475.631).
- Part 3 is known as the Commercial Real Estate Sales Commission Lien Act (ss. 475.700–475.719).
- Part 4 is known as the Commercial Real Estate Leasing Commission Lien Act (ss. 475.800–475.813).

Part 1, Chapter 475

As you previously learned, a federally related transaction is defined as involving any institution that is either governed, regulated, or insured by the federal government. As long as it is not considered a federally related transaction, licensees are permitted to perform real estate appraisals under the definition of Part 1 but cannot represent themselves as appraisers. Chapter 475.612(2) allows a Florida real estate licensee who is not a certified or licensed real estate appraiser to provide valuation services for compensation. Under this part, real estate licensees may continue to provide valuation services as long as they do not represent or hold themselves out as certified, licensed, or registered as appraisers. In doing so, there are certain rules and procedures to consider such as the following:

- The licensee should obtain a letter from the hiring party that the appraisal will not be used for a federally related transaction loan.
- If the licensee accepts an appraisal assignment as authorized under Chapter 475, the licensee must follow and not violate the USPAP.

Failure to follow the USPAP constitutes a violation of license law. A violation of USPAP results in one of the following:

- $5,000 fine
- license suspension
- license revocation

In order to perform an appraisal that falls under the definition of a federally related transaction, the individual preparing the report must be either a state-certified or licensed appraiser. Again it is important to note that a federally related transaction is any transaction that includes or involves a financial institution insured or regulated by the federal government.

Appraisal versus CMA

Appraisers must always conform to the USPAP. USPAP sets forth the procedures an appraiser must follow while performing appraisal services. Real estate licensees performing pricing duties (CMAs) are not required to conform to any of the provisions contained in USPAP. When an appraisal is conducted by a licensed/certified appraiser, the result is an estimate of the value of the property. The major difference between an appraisal and a CMA is that an appraisal will use definite and distinct principles of valuation applied by using the three approaches to value:

1. sales (market) comparison approach
2. cost (reproduction) approach
3. income approach

Furthermore, as previously stated, an appraisal will strictly focus on the value of the subject property, while a CMA will focus on the pricing of a property for marketing purposes. It is for this reason that lenders of money will loan only based on an appraisal and never on a CMA. In every appraisal that is conducted, the three approaches to valuation are applied. It is only within the reconciliation step of the appraisal process that one of the three approaches is given weight over the other two to determine the appraiser's final estimate of value. The most heavily weighted approach tends to be the approach most applicable to the property's category type and/or utility within the marketplace. It is also that approach that is said to clearly define the problem (the type of value being sought) to the appraisal.

A CMA, although similar in nature to that of the sales (market) comparison approach, only measures a property's value in an active marketplace where similar properties are currently being listed, have failed to sell within the prescribed listing period, or have already sold. It is primarily used for pricing purposes and not for valuation. In some cases, the approach used is based on the scope of the assignment. For example, a lender may not care about the application of the income approach used on a single-family home when the sole objective may be to protect and preserve the collateral held.

In any of the cases discussed, a CMA requires an active marketplace, while an appraisal conducted by a licensed or certified appraiser does not need an active marketplace to determine an estimate of value.

When a real estate licensee assists a customer in pricing a property, the result is a suitable price usually achieved by performing a CMA. As mentioned earlier, unless the licensee is either a certified or licensed state appraiser, a licensee may never call a CMA an appraisal. However, the same factors that affect the market value of a property also determine the appropriate price for a property. Because of this, it is important for real estate licensees to have considerable knowledge about the principles of valuation, which are covered in this chapter. Keep in mind, however, that these principles will be used only as a basis for pricing, not a formal appraisal process.

Broker Price Opinion (BPO)

A broker price opinion, or BPO, occurs when a property's value is estimated by a real estate broker or other qualified party and not a licensed appraiser. The BPO is normally predicated upon the subject property characteristics. As in a CMA, a BPO may never be referred to as an appraisal. Furthermore, a BPO is not used when lending is involved.

CONCEPT OF VALUE

Licensees are more involved in the valuation of real estate than they may realize. For this reason, the importance of valuation is stressed to the licensee. Licensees are often asked the question:

"What is my property worth?"

In order for a licensee to accurately, professionally, and properly respond to this question, the licensee must understand the concepts of valuation. If the valuation of a property is misjudged, the following may occur:

- The licensee may be disciplined by the Florida Real Estate Commission (FREC) for overestimating or underestimating the property's value while disposing of his/her responsibilities to a principal. The law of agency requires a licensee to exercise care as a professional and expert in real estate and to provide full disclosure as to a property's true value.
- Both the principal's and the licensee's time might be wasted trying to sell a property that has been overpriced for market conditions. This can also cause financial damage to the principal.

For the reasons just mentioned, it is important for licensees to understand the basic concepts of valuation. These concepts are described next.

Valuation is an impartial estimate or opinion of the value of a parcel of property. It is based on specific data that can be used to support and defend the estimate or opinion of value. It is usually required when real property is:

- sold or exchanged
- financed
- condemned
- taxed
- insured
- partitioned
- subject in a divorce

The *value* of a parcel of property is the present worth of all rights to current and future benefits of ownership. There are many types of value that can be appraised, including:

- market (most common value and will be discussed in the next topic)
- tax value (for income tax purposes)
- book (more commonly used in the valuation of businesses)
- insurable (value used to replace a loss)
- value in use (the value of a property that is not being used for its highest and best use)
- liquidation value (the value of a property in a forced or hurried sale)
- investment value (the value of a property based upon certain assumptions regarding capitalization rates and rates of return)
- assessed (value used for property tax determination)
- condemnation (value of property subject to taking by the government)
- salvage (value of damaged real or personal property)

Market Value

These different aforementioned types of value need not be the same because they are used for different purposes. By far, the estimate of value used most often in real estate transactions is the market value or fair market value. **Market value** is the price that an informed, willing seller would accept and that an informed, willing buyer would pay if:

- the buyer or seller is not under any pressure to buy or sell
- a reasonable amount of time is allowed for market exposure
- the transaction is an arm's length transaction, meaning that neither the buyer nor the seller bears relation to the other and that each party is dealing from equal bargaining positions

Market value is a theoretical value that can only be estimated. However, it is important to note to the reader that market value is required for a federally related transaction. The *market price* is the actual amount for which a property sells. Under ideal circumstances, the market price equals the market value, but this is not always the case.

VALUATION AT A GLANCE

Cost/Price/Value

There is a distinct difference between the terms *cost*, *price*, and *value*.

Cost is usually synonymous with:

- production
- the cost to produce an improvement

It is important to note that cost may or may not equal market price or market value. Either may be significantly less because of depreciation.

Elements of Value

In order to have value in the real estate market, the following four basic elements must exist:

1. demand
2. utility
3. scarcity
4. transferability

These basic elements of value can be remembered by the mnemonic DUST.

Demand

Demand for property means that someone has a desire to own or use the property. If demand is to have an effect on the value of property, it must be accompanied

> - Valuation determines a market value.
> - Valuation can determine an assessed value.
> - Valuation results in an estimated value.
> - The selling price may be different from the value.
> - The listing price may be different from the value.

FIGURE 16.1 Valuation at a Glance
Source: © 2021 Mbition LLC

by purchasing power. If someone desires a property but doesn't have the financial ability to act on that desire, there is no effective demand for the property. When someone has a desire for property and the purchasing power to act on that desire, the resulting demand for the property contributes to its value.

Utility

Utility means usefulness. If land has usefulness, it has utility. If land is useful, this usefulness contributes to its value. The most basic kinds of uses for real property include:

- providing shelter
- providing the opportunity for income, either as an investment or through business activities
- agricultural uses

The utility (usefulness) of property is affected by zoning ordinances and building restrictions because these limit the uses of property.

Scarcity

The scarcity of land also contributes to its value. If the supply of land were unlimited, it would have less value. The scarcity of land must be accompanied by some demand if the scarcity is to have an effect on the value of land. For example, if uninhabitable desert land was scarce, it would probably not go up much in value, because there is little demand for it. On the other hand, the scarcity of land in the downtown area of a major city contributes greatly to its value because there is a demand for it.

Transferability

The transferability of real property also affects its value. If the ownership of property cannot be transferred from one person to another, it does not have as much value. The degree of transferability of land can be affected by a number of factors, including liens, judgments against the owner, and clouds on the title. Legal problems such as these that affect the transferability of property can affect its value.

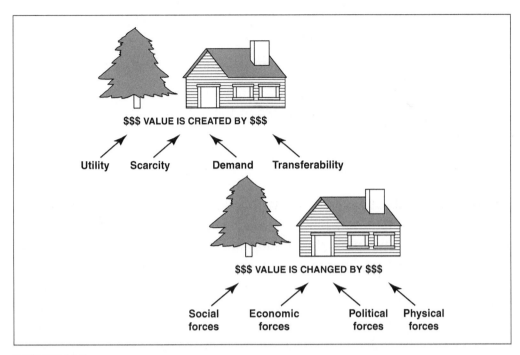

FIGURE 16.2
Source: © 2021 Mbition LLC

Utility, scarcity, demand, and transferability create value as shown in Figure 16.2.

PRINCIPLES (THEOREMS) OF VALUE

The value of property is a theoretical number that is affected by many factors. The major factors that affect value are summarized in the form of seven basic principles or theorems:

1. anticipation
2. substitution
3. highest and best use
4. competition
5. supply and demand
6. diminishing and increasing returns
7. conformity

Principle of Anticipation

The principle of anticipation is based on the concept that a buyer will buy property in anticipation of future benefits. No one enters an investment or purchase to lose money. An investor or buyer anticipates that the purchase will have greater value as time goes on. For example:

- An investor will buy in anticipation of future financial return on the investment.
- A homeowner will buy in anticipation of enjoying the shelter provided by a home as well as future financial gains.

This principle plays an integral role in the income approach (described in detail later in this chapter).

Principle of Substitution

The **principle of substitution** states that the maximum value of a property is determined by the cost to buy or build a similar property that is of equal utility and desirability because one property can substitute for another. In other words, smart investors would not pay more for a property with equal utility that they could purchase for less. For example, if two equally desirable homes are for sale in the same neighborhood and one is priced higher than the other, the lower priced one will generally sell first. Because the two homes are substitutable, the lower priced one represents the same value for a lower price and, therefore, will likely sell first.

The principle of substitution is also commonly practiced in everyday life. For example, you are shopping and see an article of clothing selling for $100 in a store. Later, while in a department store you find the same article selling for $75. It is only logical and reasonable to assume that any informed shopper would purchase the item from the department store selling it for $75 and not from the original store selling the same item for $100.

Principle of Highest and Best Use

This principle states that the greatest value of a parcel of land is determined by its highest and best use. The **highest and best use** is the legal and feasible use that generates the highest possible land value attributable to that use. There are two types of highest and best use analyses:

1. site as vacant (no structure or improvement exists)
2. site as improved (an improvement exists and may require demolition before a new improvement is developed)

In both types, the appraiser uses the knowledge obtained by a study of alternative site uses. The highest and best use of a site will be determined by the improvement placed or constructed onto that site that will yield the highest residual (left over) value to the site itself. In other words, when both the site and improvements are separated, what is left over is the site's value. For example, a 25-year-old home at the intersection of two major roads has value as a residence. However, due to recent changes in zoning, it probably has a higher value if it was used for commercial purposes, thereby creating its highest and best use. Real estate professionals should always be mindful of this principle of value and the fact that the current use of property may not be its highest and best use. However, in many urban environments, the current use of the site is usually its highest and best use.

> ### Coaching Tips
>
> It is important to understand the difference between the terms *land* and *site*. Land is what exists before any improvement entitlements to that parcel are in place, while site is when the owner has assembled all entitlements and the site is ready to be improved and developed.

Principle of Competition

The principle of competition says that when substantial profit is made, competition is encouraged. For example, if investors are making substantial profits by building rental property, more investors are likely to begin building similar properties to compete for the demand that exists for that type of housing.

Principle of Supply and Demand

This principle states that the value and price of property are affected by both supply (the availability of property to be purchased) and demand (the desire and ability of people to acquire property).

As supply increases relative to demand, prices tend to decrease. As supply decreases relative to demand, prices tend to increase. For example, it is generally true that when fewer homes are available for sale, the prices of homes go up.

Some of the factors that influence demand for real estate include:

- consumer income
- consumer preferences and taste
- population size and household composition (Household is defined by the U.S. Census Bureau as the people who occupy a separate housing unit.)
- availability of mortgage credit (Because most purchasers of residential property use borrowed money for the purchase, the availability of mortgage credit is important.)

Some of the factors that influence the supply of real estate include:

- availability of land
- availability of materials
- availability of skilled labor (e.g., plumbers, electricians, carpenters, etc.)
- availability of construction loans and financing

A buyer's market is one in which there are not enough buyers to buy all the property offered by sellers. This is called a buyer's market because supply and demand forces favor the buyer. A buyer's market can also be called a technical oversupply. A seller's market is one in which there are not enough sellers to meet the demand for property by buyers. This is called a seller's market because supply and demand forces favor the seller. To assess the market conditions, a real estate professional can review the following market indicators:

- the number of recent sales
- the recent sales prices
- the number of building permits issued for new construction
- vacancy rates for rental properties—The vacancy rate is the percentage of units that are unoccupied. A typical vacancy rate for rental units is 5%. If the vacancy rate decreases (as occupancy increases), rents are likely to increase, and renters often become motivated to buy homes

Principle of Diminishing and Increasing Returns

This principle refers to the fact that, at some point, the additional cost to upgrade a property does not produce a corresponding increase in overall value. For example, a home is located in an area near an airport that has just been constructed. It would probably not be prudent to remodel the house because the proximity to the new airport will likely limit the value of the house as a residence. That is, the cost to remodel may be $25,000, but the corresponding increase in value may be only $10,000. In this case, the remodeling is referred to as an **overimprovement**.

Principle of Conformity

This principle states that the maximum value of a property is attained when the property conforms to the usage and style of neighboring property. For example, a contemporary-style home that sells for $200,000 in a neighborhood of similar homes would likely sell for less than that in a neighborhood of traditional homes selling for $100,000. This principle is the basis for zoning regulations that require all property in a given zone to conform to the usage, size, and style prescribed for that zone.

OTHER VALUATION TERMINOLOGY

There are two remaining miscellaneous topics to be covered that relate to the appraisal of property:

1. assemblage versus plottage
2. regression versus progression

Assemblage versus Plottage

Assemblage refers to the process of combining two or more adjacent properties into one tract of land. For example, a developer might purchase several residential homes, remove the houses, combine the lots into one parcel, and build a shopping center on it. This would be assemblage. **Plottage** refers to any increase in value for a tract of land formed by combining two or more parcels. In essence, they are worth more combined than if they were sold individually. For example, the property bought by the developer just described is probably worth more when the lots are combined than when they are separate. This represents plottage.

> ### Coaching Tips
>
> **Situs** is a Latin term used to describe the location of a property. It is used in legal connotation.

Regression versus Progression

Regression means that neighboring properties lower the value of a given property. **Progression** means that neighboring properties raise the value of a given property.

Regression is a principle of appraisal that states that the value of a higher valued property is decreased if it is located among properties of lower value. For example, a house that costs $150,000 to build will have a lower value if it is in a neighborhood of $90,000 homes than if it were in a neighborhood of similar $150,000 homes.

Progression is just the opposite. It states that the value of a lower valued property is increased if it is located among properties of higher value. For example, a house that costs $85,000 to build will be worth more if it is in a neighborhood of $130,000 houses.

Figure 16.3 summarizes the differences between assemblage and plottage and regression and progression.

Assemblage versus Plottage
- Assemblage is the act of combining the properties.
- Plottage is the increase in value that occurs when properties are combined.

Regression versus Progression
- Regression means that neighboring properties lower the value of a given property.
- Progression means that neighboring properties raise the value of a given property.

FIGURE 16.3
Source: © 2021 Mbition LLC

Sales Comparison Approach

The **sales comparison approach** is based on a comparison of the **subject property** (the property being appraised) to similar properties that have recently sold. As with other approaches to appraisal, it assumes the basic principle of substitution (a smart investor will not pay more for something of equal utility that they can buy for less) in the purchase of real property. The sales comparison approach is also known as the market data approach. However, today, the sales comparison approach is the term that is more widely used. The sales comparison approach is also the most commonly used when valuing one- to four-unit residential property.

Example Using Market Approach

Assume that the subject property is a medium-quality, 25-year-old, three-bedroom home, with a two-car garage. The square footage for the home is 1,300 square feet. The appraiser locates three similar homes that have recently sold in the neighborhood at fair market prices. All have identical square footage and number of rooms.

Comparables

Data	Comparable A	Comparable B	Comparable C
Price paid	$223,900	$221,500	$216,000
Location	better than subject property	equal to subject property	equal to subject property
Lot size	equal to subject property	larger than subject property	smaller than subject property
Overall condition	better than subject property	equal to subject property	worse than subject property

Dollar Adjustment Factors per the Opinion of the Appraiser

Location difference	$1,000
Lot size difference	$1,500
Overall condition difference	$3,000

Adjustments

Data	Comparable A	Comparable B	Comparable C
Price paid	$223,900	$221,500	$216,000
Location	−1,000	0	0
Lot size	0	−1,500	+1,500
Overall condition	−3,000	0	+3,000
Price comparables would have sold for if they were like the subject home	$219,900	$220,000	$220,500

FIGURE 16.4
Source: © 2021 Mbition LLC

STEPS IN THE APPRAISAL PROCESS

There are seven basic steps that all appraisals will follow:

1. defining the problem
2. preliminary analysis, data selection, and collection
3. highest and best use analysis
4. estimation of land value
5. application of the three approaches (including the sales comparison approach)
6. reconciliation of value indication
7. providing the final estimate of value

Step 1: Define the Problem

The first step in all appraisals is to define the problem. This requires that the appraiser understand the type of value that is being sought by the appraisal. For example, if the appraisal will be used for purpose of real property tax reduction, the appraiser will need to determine the assessed value of the property. When the appraisal will be used for financing purposes, the appraiser will need to determine the property's market value. Once the appraiser has defined the value being sought, he/she will proceed to the next step in the sales comparison approach. It is also important to note that in all cases, the appraiser must have no interest or proprietary interest in the property being appraised.

Step 2: Data Selection and Collection

Locate and gather information on similar properties that have sold recently in the same neighborhood or area. These similar properties are called comparables (comps). The data compiled on comparables include:

- date of sale
- sale price
- location
- terms of sale
- physical characteristics
- amenities (extra features that add value)

Step 3: Determining the Highest and Best Use

Highest and best use is performed to determine which use will produce the greatest value attributable to the land. This step requires the appraiser to examine other alternative legal uses in comparison to the current use of the property. The purpose of this step is to determine whether the current use for the subject property is in fact the property's highest and best use. There are two types of highest and best use analysis:

1. Highest and best use as vacant—This approach is applied when land is unimproved. The appraiser will compare alternative legal uses for the property to determine which use provides the highest value from that use attributable to the land. For example, if a property is zoned for commercial use, the appraiser will probably compare all commercial uses (offices, retail, hotel/motel) to determine which of those uses produce the greatest land value.

2. Highest and best use as improved—As in the highest and best use analysis as vacant, this analysis views the current use of the property to determine if in fact that use is still the highest and best use as improved. Remember, in this case the land is not vacant. The land contains a previously built improvement. Therefore, the primary difference between the two highest and best use approaches is that this analysis requires the appraiser to consider demolition costs of the current improvement toward a determination of that property's highest and best use. This is the primary difference between each type of analysis.

Step 4: Estimate the Value of the Land

At this point the appraiser establishes the land value by comparing land values of other previously sold properties. Land comparables are always available. Regardless of the type of property sold, all sales include underlying land. Therefore, the appraiser evaluates previous sales to determine land value.

Step 5: Application of the Three Approaches and the Adjustment Process

All appraisals do not apply to all three approaches. The appraiser and client determine what approach should be used toward value determination. For example, Fannie Mae appraisals often do not include the income approach for residential property. Or commercial property with no comparables may use the Income Capitalization approach only. Comparables are to be adjusted in the following manner and sequence:

1. transactional adjustments, which include financing terms such as *seller financing* (which tends to be less expensive than conventional financing) and *sales conditions*
2. location adjustments, which include differences in the lot location such as a corner versus a rear lot
3. physical adjustments, which include differences in the comparables to the subject property such as a two-car garage versus a one-car port or a pool versus no pool

> ## Coaching Tips
>
> It is important to know that the appraiser never adjusts the subject property of the appraisal for differences. The appraiser always makes the adjustments to the comparables, thereby making them resemble (as closely as possible) that of the subject property. Comparables can be adjusted rather than the subject because the appraiser has already identified what the property has sold for.
>
> In addition, when adjustments are made to comparable properties, the following procedure and rule apply:
> - When the comparable property contains a compared feature that is superior or better than the subject property, the adjusted sales price of the comparable is reduced to reflect the the comparison.
> - In contrast, when the comparable property contains a compared feature that is inferior or less than the subject property, the adjusted sales price of the comparable is increased to reflect the comparison.

Step 6: The Reconciliation Process

Reconcile all the data from the comparables, and arrive at a price for the subject property. In this process, the appraiser reviews all value indications derived directly from the application of all three approaches. The appraiser then decides which approach should bear the most weight in the value determination. He/she will normally use the approach that best solves the problem of estimating value.

Step 7: Reporting the Value

The appraiser will then prepare the appraisal report, notating their indication of value. The sales comparison approach, shown in Figure 16.4, is the most widely used approach to pricing. It is given the most weight of the three approaches in determining a suitable price for residential property and vacant lots.

COST APPROACH (REPRODUCTION)

The sales comparison approach is widely used to determine a price for a property for which comparables are readily available. This requires an active marketplace. For some types of properties, the sales comparison approach is not useful because of the lack of comparables that have sold recently. For example, school buildings, fire stations, courthouses, and hospitals are not sold often enough to provide adequate data for a sales comparison approach to pricing. These properties are termed *special-use* or *single-purpose* properties. In these cases, the pricing approach often used is the cost approach. The **cost-depreciation approach** to pricing determines an appropriate price for property based on the current cost of reproduction or replacement of the improvements (as the case may be). In essence, the appraiser creates a comparable of the subject property by comparing it to a replica or not-exact replica of itself (as the case may be). We refer to this process as one of the following:

- reproduction cost
- replacement cost

Reproduction cost is the cost to produce an exact replica of the original subject property, using the same materials and construction techniques as the original.

Replacement cost is the cost to replace the improvements with another building that performs the same function and utility but is not an exact replica of the subject property. This process is also the basis for most insurers of real and personal property. Replacement refers to a building with the same function.

The steps in the cost approach to pricing are as follows:

- **Step 1:** Estimate the reproduction cost (new) of the improvement(s).
- **Step 2:** Estimate the accrued depreciation resulting from one or any of the following:
    - physical deterioration
    - functional obsolescence
    - economic/external obsolescence
- **Step 3:** Subtract the accrued depreciation (Step 2) from the reproduction cost (new) (Step 1)
    - Only the improvements are depreciated.
    - Land is never depreciated because it never wears out. The types of depreciation will be covered later in this chapter.
- **Step 4:** Estimate and add the value of the site.

The cost approach to pricing can be summarized in the following formula:

$$\begin{aligned} &\text{Reproduction cost (new)} \\ &- \text{Accrued depreciation} \\ &\underline{+ \text{Value of land}} \\ &= \text{Estimated price} \end{aligned}$$

Because people are reluctant to pay more for a given property than it would cost to build it new, the reproduction cost (new) is often used because it tends to set the uppermost limit to value.

The replacement cost approach to pricing requires an estimate be made of the cost to replace the improvements. This can be done in three ways:

1. the square foot method
2. the unit-in-place method
3. the quantity survey method

The Square Foot Method

The steps in this approach are as follows:

- **Step 1:** Obtain the construction cost of a similar building recently constructed.
- **Step 2:** Convert the cost of construction to cost per square foot.
- **Step 3:** Multiply the cost per square foot times the number of square feet in the improvement whose price is being determined.

A variation of this method is the cubic foot method, which uses cost per cubic foot rather than cost per square foot. The cubic foot method is used for buildings like warehouses that don't have standard ceiling heights.

The Unit-in-Place Method

The steps in this approach are as follows:

- **Step 1:** Estimate the installed cost of each major unit of the building that is being priced, such as the foundation, walls, roof, windows, doors, etc.
- **Step 2:** Add the cost of all the units that make up the building plus contractor profit and overhead.
- **Step 3:** The total estimated cost is the estimated price for the property.

The Quantity Survey Method

The steps in this approach are as follows:

- **Step 1:** Estimate the cost of all materials (by individual item price) and the cost of all labor.
- **Step 2:** Add the cost of all materials and labor.
- **Step 3:** Add the builder's profit or return on investment.
- **Step 4:** The total estimated cost is the estimated price for the property.

This method is very time consuming and is seldom used by appraisers. See Figure 16.5 for a summary of pricing methods.

Of these three aforementioned costing methods, the square foot method is used the most often but is the least accurate. The unit-in-place method is more

---

PRICING METHODS AT A GLANCE

- The quantity survey method uses the total cost of all labor and materials.
- The square foot method uses the size of a building to estimate its cost.
- The unit-in-place method is based on the total cost of all major elements.
- The quantity survey method is the most accurate but is used the least.
- The square foot method is used the most but is the least accurate.

FIGURE 16.5
Source: © 2021 Mbition LLC

accurate than the square foot method but also more difficult than the square foot method. The quantity survey method is the most accurate and the most difficult of the three but is used the least because of its difficulty.

In order to assist the appraiser in estimating unit costs, there are various material cost estimating manuals and publications available. These manuals and publications provide the appraiser with geographic per square foot unit cost.

DEPRECIATION

Depreciation is a loss of value attributable to one or more of three categories of loss. As you learned earlier in this chapter, in the cost approach to pricing, depreciation is subtracted from the estimated reproduction (or replacement) cost before determining the price for the property. (Because the cost approach involves the calculation of depreciation, this approach is also known as the cost-depreciation approach.) There are three different types of depreciation considered in the pricing process (see Figure 16.6):

1. physical deterioration
2. functional obsolescence
3. economic (external) obsolescence

Physical Deterioration

Physical deterioration is the wear and tear that results from normal use. For example, a frame house that needs a new coat of paint is suffering from physical deterioration.

DEPRECIATION AT A GLANCE

1. **Physical Deterioration**
   - Physical deterioration is wear and tear from age.
   - Physical deterioration arises from forces within the property.
   - Physical deterioration can be categorized as curable or incurable.
2. **Functional Obsolescence**
   - Functional obsolescence arises from forces within the property.
   - Functional obsolescence comes from outdated features.
   - Functional obsolescence can be categorized as curable or incurable.
     - Broken windows are typically classified as curable.
     - Removing support columns is considered incurable.
3. **Economic or External Obsolescence**
   - Economic obsolescence comes from factors outside the property.
   - Economic obsolescence is considered incurable.

FIGURE 16.6
Source: © 2021 Mbition LLC

Functional Obsolescence

Functional obsolescence is the reduction in value due to outdated features of the property, including:

- closets that are too small
- ceilings that are too high or low
- too few bathrooms
- inadequate wiring
- outdated design or architecture

Functional obsolescence also includes any loss in value due to an overimprovement to the property. An overimprovement is also referred to as super-adequacy.

Both physical deterioration and functional obsolescence can be categorized as curable or incurable. Both curable and incurable defects can be corrected, but the difference is whether it is economically feasible to correct the defects. A defect is considered **curable** if it is economically feasible to correct the problem. A defect is considered **incurable** if it is not economically feasible to correct the problem.

For example, if the cost of remediation exceeds the value added by remediating same, it is said to be incurable. In contrast, if the cost of remediation is less than the value added by remediating same it is said to be curable. Removal of a structural column is a good example of incurable functional obsolescence.

Economic (External) Obsolescence

The first two categories of depreciation were physical deterioration and functional obsolescence. Both of these types of depreciation arise from the characteristics of the property itself. In simple terms, these aforementioned issues are contained within the property line. The third category of depreciation is economic (external) obsolescence. It differs from the first two categories of depreciation in that it represents depreciation that arises from factors outside the property itself. Due to the fact that the value loss is attributable to external forces—outside the property line—economic (external) obsolescence is always said to be incurable.

Examples of economic obsolescence include:

- changes in the makeup of the surrounding area
- environmental impacts like noise pollution from an airport
- changes in highways that serve the property
- the closing of a major business nearby

Calculating Accrued Depreciation

Age-Life Method

The age-life method for calculating accrued depreciation tends to be the most common depreciation technique utilized by residential appraisers. It is not only easy to use, but it is also easy to explain to a client. It is also referred to as the straight-line method. Accrued depreciation is arrived at by using a two-step process:

- **Step 1:** obtaining the annual depreciation

  Reproduction cost (new) ÷ Economic life = Annual depreciation

- **Step 2:** obtaining the accrued depreciation

  Annual depreciation × Effective age = Accrued depreciation

The **effective age** of a property is based on the property's condition and use at the time of examination. The **economic life** of a property is the amount of time it is expected to be useful to its owner. In formula form:

$$\frac{\text{Effective Age} \times \text{Reproduction/Replacement Cost (new)}}{\text{Economic Life}} = \text{Accrued Depreciation}$$

The logic behind the use of this approach to the calculation of accrued depreciation is that deterioration occurs at a constant annual rate. Figure 16.7 illustrates the cost approach for determining the price of a property.

Income Approach to Pricing

Previously, you learned about the first two approaches to pricing—the sales comparison approach and the cost approach. Now, we will cover the third major approach to pricing—the income approach (see Figure 16.8).

The **income capitalization approach** is used primarily for income-producing properties such as:

- office buildings
- apartment buildings
- retail properties
- mixed-use properties

This approach is not normally suited to single-family dwellings, even those that are strictly rental properties. The approach eliminates the need to:

- identify comparables
- make any adjustments for differences in
  - transactional differences/costs
  - locational differences
  - physical differences

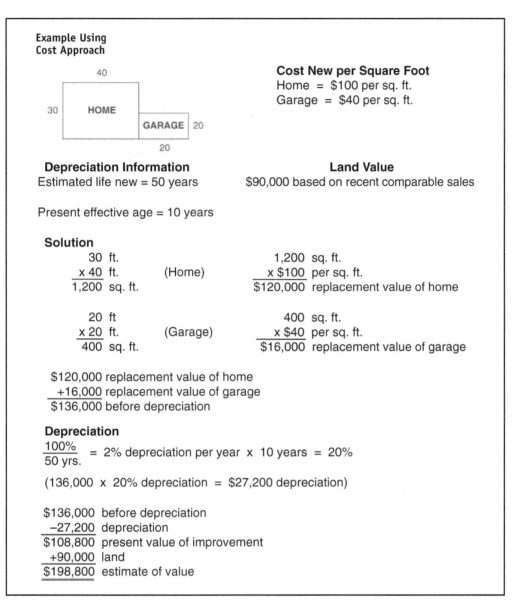

FIGURE 16.7
Source: © 2021 Mbition LLC

The income approach simply determines the annual income a property is expected to produce and converts that into a price for the property through a process known as capitalization.

Capitalization

Capitalization is the process for converting future income into current value. This is the process that is used to determine a price for a property. It can also be defined as the present worth of the property based upon the future income stream produced by that property. Any of the following formulas is used to determine value through the capitalization of income:

1. Rate × Value = **Income**
2. Income ÷ Value = **Rate**
3. Income ÷ Rate = **Value**

This formula is most commonly known as IRV.

In each of these formulas, *income* refers to *net operating income*, and *rate* refers to *the capitalization rate*. Capitalization rates are usually subjective prescribed rates of return that investors seek while being mindful of what the general market rate may command at time of analysis. In order for the process of overall capitalization to occur, net operating income (NOI) must be determined. The appraiser must reconstruct an annual income and expense operating statement for the subject property.

Example Using Income Approach

The property is a clean, but modest, 15-unit apartment with fair market rents of $700 per unit. The estimated factor for vacancies and collection loss is 5%.
Annual operating expenses include:

Property taxes	$9,450
Insurance	$1,000
Management and accounting	$10,000
Repairs and others	$12,000

The capitalization rate selected by the appraiser is 10%.

Solution

Potential gross income	$126,000	($700 × 15 units × 12 months)
Less vacancies and collection losses	−6,300	($126,000 × 5%)
Effective gross income	$119,700	
Less annual operating expenses	−32,450	($9,450 + 1,000 + 10,000 + 12,000)
Net operating income	$87,250	

$$\frac{\text{Net operating income}}{\text{Capitalization rate}} = \frac{\$87,250}{10\%} = \$872,500 \text{ Estimate of value}$$

If the capitalization rate selected had been 9%, the value would be:

$$\frac{\$87,250}{9\%} = \$969,444$$

If the capitalization rate were 11%, the value would be:

$$\frac{\$87,250}{11\%} = \$793,181$$

Observe this rule: *The higher the capitalization rate, the lower the value.* Therefore, you can see that the selection of the appropriate capitalization rate is critical!
The selection of an inappropriate capitalization rate can greatly distort value.

FIGURE 16.8
Source: © 2021 Mbition LLC

In order to construct an annual income and expense operating statement, licensees must understand the following formulas:

1. PGI − V&C + OI = EGI
2. EGI − OE = NOI

> **Terminology Legend**
> PGI—potential gross income
> V&C—vacancy and collection loss
> OI—other income
> EGI—effective gross income
> OE—operating expenses
> NOI—net operating income
> DS—debt service
> BTCF—before tax cash flow

We will look at the terms in these formulas, beginning with the first formula:

$$PGI - V\&C + OI = EGI$$

PGI stands for potential gross income. This is accomplished when the property in question is fully leased (existing property with operating history) or looked upon as fully leased (as in a new development). It estimates the property's income potential under the best of circumstances as if 100% rented.

V&C stands for vacancy and collection losses. There are times in any calendar or fiscal year when a vacancy arises or a tenant(s) does not pay the rent. Vacancy and collection losses are usually expressed in percentage terms of the PGI (e.g., 5%). It is safe to say that with very few exceptions, no property will be at 100% occupancy levels 100% of the time. It is for this reason at time of analysis that an investor will discount the PGI by a sensible V&C rate that reflects the market's conditions as it pertains to the specific site.

OI stands for other income that may be derived from the passive sources (of income-producing property) outside of the residence or office rents, such as:

- retail rents
- satellite/dish income
- parking revenue or rents
- vending machines, such as:
  - washer/dryer
  - beverage
  - candy

In commercial leases, OI can represent reimbursed increases in the cost of operating the property. This item is referred to in a commercial lease as additional rent and is normally the result of a lease escalation clause.

EGI stands for effective gross income. As you saw in the formula on the previous page, EGI is determined by subtracting from the PGI the V&C and adding in any OI.

Now, let's take a look at the second formula:

$$EGI - OE = NOI$$

EGI was calculated using the aforementioned first formula provided above.

In every income-producing property, there are costs associated with operating that property. These costs are broken down into three categories of operating expenses:

1. fixed expenses
2. variable expenses
3. reserves for replacements

Fixed Expenses

There are only two fixed property operating expenses. They include only the following:

1. real property taxes
2. property insurance

Due to the fact that fixed expenses do not fluctuate (in any given year) upward or downward resulting from leasing activities, they are considered fixed costs.

Variable Expenses

Variable expenses include items such as the following:

- maintenance
- repairs
- payroll
- garbage removal

Because variable expenses will fluctuate upward or downward (in any given year) as a result of leasing activities, they are considered to be variable and not fixed.

Reserves for Replacements

Every property will experience the need to make a major capital improvement over time. As all machinery and other major property components (exposed or not exposed to the exterior elements) experience obsolescence or other deterioration over time, the smart investor provides for a reserve fund. Reserves are cash on hand (should the need arise) to complete or make a major capital improvement that NOI cannot fund on its own. Reserve requirements will vary from property to property.

When financing is a consideration, minimum reserves are normally expressed in operating capital coverage needs versus cash earmarked for major capital improvements. In this case, lenders will seek the minimum reserve should consist of at least three months' operating capital.

At this point, the OE is then subtracted from the EGI; the result is the important NOI. As mentioned previously, the NOI is used in the capitalization process:

$$\text{Value} \div \text{Income Rate}$$

After calculating NOI, the desired capitalization rate must be determined. The capitalization rate is the rate of return on investment desired by the investor, expressed as a percentage. For example, if an investor wants a return of 10% on an investment, the capitalization rate would be 10%, or 0.10. Using the formula above, one can then capitalize the income in order to derive the property's value to that investor using that return rate of 10%. It is important once again to note that rates are subjectively arrived at by the investor.

Thus, the final step is to capitalize the net income by dividing it by the capitalization rate to get a price for the property. In simple terms, this concept lets the seller, buyer, and appraiser of income-producing real property determine the following:

- For a seller—How much to sell the property for
- For a buyer—How much to pay to purchase the property and its income
- For an appraiser—How much to value the property based on the purpose of the appraisal

Example Assume that an investor wants a return on an investment of 10%. A property under consideration generates an annual net income of $42,000. What price could the investor pay for the property according to the income approach at the capitalization rate of 10%?

Answer:

$$\text{Value} \div \text{Income Rate}$$

So in this case, $42,000 ÷ 0.10 = $420,000.

Based upon the above financial model and with a capitalization rate of 10%, the property generating an income of $42,000 would support a maximum sales/purchase price of $420,000. If the investor bought the property for $420,000, he/she would receive $42,000 in net income, which represents a return on investment of 10%—the desired return. The only remaining points you should remember are:

1. As the capitalization rate increases, the price of the property decreases.
2. As the capitalization rate decreases, the price of the property increases. (See bottom of Figure 16.8.)

GROSS RENT MULTIPLIER

We have just covered the three major approaches to pricing—the sales comparison, cost, and income approaches. These are all formal approaches to pricing. There is one remaining technique of property pricing—the **gross rent multiplier (GRM)/gross rent income (GIM)** technique. The GRM is *not* a formal approach to pricing. However, it can be another form of analysis within the income approach. It is used informally in selected applications involving income-producing property. Its primary use is for an investor who is evaluating several properties and wants a simple and quick way to eliminate some properties from consideration before doing formal price determinations. To use the GRM to get an informal estimate of price, complete the following steps:

- **Step 1:** Identify comparable properties that have been sold recently, and determine their gross monthly income.
- **Step 2:** Divide the price of each property by its gross monthly income. The answer is the GRM.
- **Step 3:** Average the GRMs for all the comparable properties.
- **Step 4:** Multiply the gross monthly rent for the subject property by the average GRM from Step 3. The answer is the estimate of price for the subject property.

The advantage of the GRM technique is that it is quick and easy. The disadvantage is that it uses the gross rent and doesn't take into consideration:

- any rent losses
- time to lease vacant units
- marketing costs
- actual property operating expenses

As a result, it is not a very precise or reliable estimate of price.

RECONCILIATION

All the approaches to pricing that can be applied to a property should be used to determine that property's price. This is not always possible, however. When more than one approach is used, the greatest weight is given to the approach that is best suited to that property. The process of arriving at a final estimate of value when more than one approach is used is called **reconciliation**. See Figure 16.9 for a summary of the three approaches to appraisal and Figure 16.10 a-c for a Uniform Residential Appraisal Report.

Depreciation is attributable to a loss of value of any kind resulting from any or all of the following three events:

1. functional obsolescence (outdated layout, lighting, columns, etc.)
2. physical deterioration (usually representative of poor maintenance and preventive maintenance programs)

> **THE THREE APPROACHES TO APPRAISAL AT A GLANCE**
> - The cost approach uses an estimate of the cost of construction as a basis for determining the price for a property.
>   - The cost approach is used when comparables are not available.
>   - A reproduction is an exact replica of a building.
>   - Depreciation is used in the cost approach.
>   - Current building costs are used in the cost approach.
>   - Land is never depreciated. Only improvements are depreciated.
> - The direct-sales comparison is another term for the market data approach.
>   - The market data approach is used for residential property.
>   - In order to derive value, the process compares recently sold properties known as comps to that of the subject property.
>   - Comparables are used in the market data approach.
>   - The market data approach is used most for residential property.
> - The income approach uses income generated as a basis for determining the price for a property.
>   - The income approach is used for income-producing property.
>   - Net income is used in the income approach to pricing.
>   - Net income is based on the future income after expenses attributable to the property or projected net income derived from a proforma statement.
>   - The income approach uses a process called capitalization.
>   - As the capitalization rate increases, the price of the property decreases.
>   - The gross rent multiplier (a monthly factor) approach is an informal means of comparing income properties.
>   - The gross income multiplier (an annual factor) is an informal means of comparing income properties.

FIGURE 16.9
Source: © 2021 Mbition LLC

3. economic/external obsolescence (declining neighborhoods, adverse zoning changes, high interest rates, etc.)

Both functional obsolescence and physical deterioration are losses in value and are conditions that exist within the property line. Economic/external obsolescence is a loss in value and is a condition that exists outside the property line.

PREPARING A COMPARATIVE MARKET ANALYSIS (CMA)

One of the most important tasks a licensee performs in servicing a listing is assisting a seller or buyer in determining an appropriate price for a property. This may be required when listing a house for sale, assisting the seller in setting a listing price, or assisting a buyer in determining the price for a contract offer. A market analysis is the technique that is used most often to determine a price for a property. A market analysis is a practical method of determining a reasonable estimate of a price at which a home will sell. This type of analysis is appropriate for marketing purposes and should not be confused with an appraisal.

Uniform Residential Appraisal Report

File #

The purpose of this summary appraisal report is to provide the lender/client with an accurate, and adequately supported, opinion of the market value of the subject property.

SUBJECT

Property Address | City | State | Zip Code

Borrower | Owner of Public Record | County

Legal Description

Assessor's Parcel # | Tax Year | R.E. Taxes $

Neighborhood Name | Map Reference | Census Tract

Occupant ☐ Owner ☐ Tenant ☐ Vacant | Special Assessments $ | ☐ PUD | HOA $ | ☐ per year ☐ per month

Property Rights Appraised ☐ Fee Simple ☐ Leasehold ☐ Other (describe)

Assignment Type ☐ Purchase Transaction ☐ Refinance Transaction ☐ Other (describe)

Lender/Client | Address

Is the subject property currently offered for sale or has it been offered for sale in the twelve months prior to the effective date of this appraisal? ☐ Yes ☐ No

Report data source(s) used, offering price(s), and date(s).

CONTRACT

I ☐ did ☐ did not analyze the contract for sale for the subject purchase transaction. Explain the results of the analysis of the contract for sale or why the analysis was not performed.

Contract Price $ | Date of Contract | Is the property seller the owner of public record? ☐Yes ☐No | Data Source(s)

Is there any financial assistance (loan charges, sale concessions, gift or downpayment assistance, etc.) to be paid by any party on behalf of the borrower? ☐ Yes ☐ No

If Yes, report the total dollar amount and describe the items to be paid.

NEIGHBORHOOD

Note: Race and the racial composition of the neighborhood are not appraisal factors.

Neighborhood Characteristics				One-Unit Housing Trends				One-Unit Housing		Present Land Use %	
Location	☐ Urban	☐ Suburban	☐ Rural	Property Values	☐ Increasing	☐ Stable	☐ Declining	PRICE	AGE	One-Unit	%
Built-Up	☐ Over 75%	☐ 25–75%	☐ Under 25%	Demand/Supply	☐ Shortage	☐ In Balance	☐ Over Supply	$ (000)	(yrs)	2-4 Unit	%
Growth	☐ Rapid	☐ Stable	☐ Slow	Marketing Time	☐ Under 3 mths	☐ 3–6 mths	☐ Over 6 mths	Low		Multi-Family	%
Neighborhood Boundaries								High		Commercial	%
								Pred.		Other	%

Neighborhood Description

Market Conditions (including support for the above conclusions)

SITE

Dimensions | Area | Shape | View

Specific Zoning Classification | Zoning Description

Zoning Compliance ☐ Legal ☐ Legal Nonconforming (Grandfathered Use) ☐ No Zoning ☐ Illegal (describe)

Is the highest and best use of the subject property as improved (or as proposed per plans and specifications) the present use? ☐ Yes ☐ No If No, describe

Utilities	Public	Other (describe)		Public	Other (describe)	Off-site Improvements—Type	Public	Private
Electricity	☐	☐	Water	☐	☐	Street	☐	☐
Gas	☐	☐	Sanitary Sewer	☐	☐	Alley	☐	☐

FEMA Special Flood Hazard Area ☐ Yes ☐ No | FEMA Flood Zone | FEMA Map # | FEMA Map Date

Are the utilities and off-site improvements typical for the market area? ☐ Yes ☐ No If No, describe

Are there any adverse site conditions or external factors (easements, encroachments, environmental conditions, land uses, etc.)? ☐ Yes ☐ No If Yes, describe

IMPROVEMENTS

General Description		Foundation		Exterior Description	materials/condition	Interior	materials/condition
Units ☐ One ☐ One with Accessory Unit		☐ Concrete Slab ☐ Crawl Space		Foundation Walls		Floors	
# of Stories		☐ Full Basement ☐ Partial Basement		Exterior Walls		Walls	
Type ☐ Det. ☐ Att. ☐ S-Det./End Unit		Basement Area	sq. ft.	Roof Surface		Trim/Finish	
☐ Existing ☐ Proposed ☐ Under Const.		Basement Finish	%	Gutters & Downspouts		Bath Floor	
Design (Style)		☐ Outside Entry/Exit ☐ Sump Pump		Window Type		Bath Wainscot	
Year Built		Evidence of ☐ Infestation		Storm Sash/Insulated		Car Storage ☐ None	
Effective Age (Yrs)		☐ Dampness ☐ Settlement		Screens		☐ Driveway # of Cars	
Attic	☐ None	Heating ☐ FWA ☐ HWBB ☐ Radiant		Amenities	☐ Woodstove(s) #	Driveway Surface	
☐ Drop Stair	☐ Stairs	☐ Other	Fuel	☐ Fireplace(s) #	☐ Fence	☐ Garage # of Cars	
☐ Floor	☐ Scuttle	Cooling ☐ Central Air Conditioning		☐ Patio/Deck	☐ Porch	☐ Carport # of Cars	
☐ Finished	☐ Heated	☐ Individual	☐ Other	☐ Pool	☐ Other	☐ Att. ☐ Det. ☐ Built-in	

Appliances ☐Refrigerator ☐Range/Oven ☐Dishwasher ☐Disposal ☐Microwave ☐Washer/Dryer ☐Other (describe)

Finished area **above** grade contains: | Rooms | Bedrooms | Bath(s) | Square Feet of Gross Living Area Above Grade

Additional features (special energy efficient items, etc.)

Describe the condition of the property (including needed repairs, deterioration, renovations, remodeling, etc.).

Are there any physical deficiencies or adverse conditions that affect the livability, soundness, or structural integrity of the property? ☐ Yes ☐ No If Yes, describe

Does the property generally conform to the neighborhood (functional utility, style, condition, use, construction, etc.)? ☐ Yes ☐ No If No, describe

Freddie Mac Form 70 March 2005 | Page 1 of 6 | Fannie Mae Form 1004 March 2005

FIGURE 16.10a Uniform Residential Appraisal Report
Source: www.fanniemae.com

Uniform Residential Appraisal Report

File #

There are	comparable properties currently offered for sale in the subject neighborhood ranging in price from $		to $	
There are	comparable sales in the subject neighborhood within the past twelve months ranging in sale price from $		to $	

FEATURE	SUBJECT	COMPARABLE SALE # 1		COMPARABLE SALE # 2		COMPARABLE SALE # 3	
Address							
Proximity to Subject							
Sale Price	$		$		$		$
Sale Price/Gross Liv. Area	$ sq. ft.	$ sq. ft.		$ sq. ft.		$ sq. ft.	
Data Source(s)							
Verification Source(s)							
VALUE ADJUSTMENTS	DESCRIPTION	DESCRIPTION	+(-) $ Adjustment	DESCRIPTION	+(-) $ Adjustment	DESCRIPTION	+(-) $ Adjustment
Sale or Financing Concessions							
Date of Sale/Time							
Location							
Leasehold/Fee Simple							
Site							
View							
Design (Style)							
Quality of Construction							
Actual Age							
Condition							
Above Grade Room Count	Total Bdrms. Baths	Total Bdrms. Baths		Total Bdrms. Baths		Total Bdrms. Baths	
Gross Living Area	sq. ft.	sq. ft.		sq. ft.		sq. ft.	
Basement & Finished Rooms Below Grade							
Functional Utility							
Heating/Cooling							
Energy Efficient Items							
Garage/Carport							
Porch/Patio/Deck							
Net Adjustment (Total)		□ + □ -	$	□ + □ -	$	□ + □ -	$
Adjusted Sale Price of Comparables		Net Adj. % Gross Adj. %	$	Net Adj. % Gross Adj. %	$	Net Adj. % Gross Adj. %	$

I □ did □ did not research the sale or transfer history of the subject property and comparable sales. If not, explain

My research □ did □ did not reveal any prior sales or transfers of the subject property for the three years prior to the effective date of this appraisal.
Data source(s)
My research □ did □ did not reveal any prior sales or transfers of the comparable sales for the year prior to the date of sale of the comparable sale.
Data source(s)
Report the results of the research and analysis of the prior sale or transfer history of the subject property and comparable sales (report additional prior sales on page 3).

ITEM	SUBJECT	COMPARABLE SALE # 1	COMPARABLE SALE # 2	COMPARABLE SALE # 3
Date of Prior Sale/Transfer				
Price of Prior Sale/Transfer				
Data Source(s)				
Effective Date of Data Source(s)				

Analysis of prior sale or transfer history of the subject property and comparable sales

Summary of Sales Comparison Approach

Indicated Value by Sales Comparison Approach $

Indicated Value by: Sales Comparison Approach $ Cost Approach (if developed) $ Income Approach (if developed) $

This appraisal is made □ "as is", □ subject to completion per plans and specifications on the basis of a hypothetical condition that the improvements have been completed, □ subject to the following repairs or alterations on the basis of a hypothetical condition that the repairs or alterations have been completed, or □ subject to the following required inspection based on the extraordinary assumption that the condition or deficiency does not require alteration or repair:

Based on a complete visual inspection of the interior and exterior areas of the subject property, defined scope of work, statement of assumptions and limiting conditions, and appraiser's certification, my (our) opinion of the market value, as defined, of the real property that is the subject of this report is $, as of   , which is the date of inspection and the effective date of this appraisal.

Freddie Mac Form 70   March 2005   Fannie Mae Form 1004   March 2005

FIGURE 16.10b (Continued)

Uniform Residential Appraisal Report

File #

ADDITIONAL COMMENTS

COST APPROACH TO VALUE (not required by Fannie Mae)

Provide adequate information for the lender/client to replicate the below cost figures and calculations.
Support for the opinion of site value (summary of comparable land sales or other methods for estimating site value)

ESTIMATED ☐ REPRODUCTION OR ☐ REPLACEMENT COST NEW	OPINION OF SITE VALUE .... = $
Source of cost data	Dwelling Sq. Ft. @ $ .... =$
Quality rating from cost service Effective date of cost data	Sq. Ft. @ $ .... =$
Comments on Cost Approach (gross living area calculations, depreciation, etc.)	Garage/Carport Sq. Ft. @ $ .... =$
	Total Estimate of Cost-New .... = $
	Less Physical Functional External
	Depreciation =$( )
	Depreciated Cost of Improvements............=$
	"As-is" Value of Site Improvements..........=$
Estimated Remaining Economic Life (HUD and VA only) Years	Indicated Value By Cost Approach ....=$

INCOME APPROACH TO VALUE (not required by Fannie Mae)

Estimated Monthly Market Rent $ X Gross Rent Multiplier   = $ Indicated Value by Income Approach
Summary of Income Approach (including support for market rent and GRM)

PROJECT INFORMATION FOR PUDs (if applicable)

Is the developer/builder in control of the Homeowners' Association (HOA)? ☐ Yes ☐ No Unit type(s) ☐ Detached ☐ Attached
Provide the following information for PUDs ONLY if the developer/builder is in control of the HOA and the subject property is an attached dwelling unit.
Legal name of project
Total number of phases   Total number of units   Total number of units sold
Total number of units rented Total number of units for sale Data source(s)
Was the project created by the conversion of an existing building(s) into a PUD? ☐ Yes ☐ No If Yes, date of conversion
Does the project contain any multi-dwelling units? ☐ Yes ☐ No Data source(s)
Are the units, common elements, and recreation facilities complete? ☐ Yes ☐ No If No, describe the status of completion.

Are the common elements leased to or by the Homeowners' Association? ☐ Yes ☐ No If Yes, describe the rental terms and options.

Describe common elements and recreational facilities

Freddie Mac Form 70 March 2005   Fannie Mae Form 1004 March 2005

FIGURE 16.10c (Continued)

Uniform Residential Appraisal Report File

This report form is designed to report an appraisal of a one-unit property or a one-unit property with an accessory unit; including a unit in a planned unit development (PUD). This report form is not designed to report an appraisal of a manufactured home or a unit in a condominium or cooperative project.

This appraisal report is subject to the following scope of work, intended use, intended user, definition of market value, statement of assumptions and limiting conditions, and certifications. Modifications, additions, or deletions to the intended use, intended user, definition of market value, or assumptions and limiting conditions are not permitted. The appraiser may expand the scope of work to include any additional research or analysis necessary based on the complexity of this appraisal assignment. Modifications or deletions to the certifications are also not permitted. However, additional certifications that do not constitute material alterations to this appraisal report, such as those required by law or those related to the appraiser's continuing education or membership in an appraisal organization, are permitted.

SCOPE OF WORK: The scope of work for this appraisal is defined by the complexity of this appraisal assignment and the reporting requirements of this appraisal report form, including the following definition of market value, statement of assumptions and limiting conditions, and certifications. The appraiser must, at a minimum: (1) perform a complete visual inspection of the interior and exterior areas of the subject property, (2) inspect the neighborhood, (3) inspect each of the comparable sales from at least the street, (4) research, verify, and analyze data from reliable public and/or private sources, and (5) report his or her analysis, opinions, and conclusions in this appraisal report.

INTENDED USE: The intended use of this appraisal report is for the lender/client to evaluate the property that is the subject of this appraisal for a mortgage finance transaction.

INTENDED USER: The intended user of this appraisal report is the lender/client.

DEFINITION OF MARKET VALUE: The most probable price which a property should bring in a competitive and open market under all conditions requisite to a fair sale, the buyer and seller, each acting prudently, knowledgeably and assuming the price is not affected by undue stimulus. Implicit in this definition is the consummation of a sale as of a specified date and the passing of title from seller to buyer under conditions whereby: (1) buyer and seller are typically motivated; (2) both parties are well informed or well advised, and each acting in what he or she considers his or her own best interest; (3) a reasonable time is allowed for exposure in the open market; (4) payment is made in terms of cash in U. S. dollars or in terms of financial arrangements comparable thereto; and (5) the price represents the normal consideration for the property sold unaffected by special or creative financing or sales concessions* granted by anyone associated with the sale.

*Adjustments to the comparables must be made for special or creative financing or sales concessions. No adjustments are necessary for those costs which are normally paid by sellers as a result of tradition or law in a market area; these costs are readily identifiable since the seller pays these costs in virtually all sales transactions. Special or creative financing adjustments can be made to the comparable property by comparisons to financing terms offered by a third party institutional lender that is not already involved in the property or transaction. Any adjustment should not be calculated on a mechanical dollar for dollar cost of the financing or concession but the dollar amount of any adjustment should approximate the market's reaction to the financing or concessions based on the appraiser's judgment.

STATEMENT OF ASSUMPTIONS AND LIMITING CONDITIONS: The appraiser's certification in this report is subject to the following assumptions and limiting conditions:

1. The appraiser will not be responsible for matters of a legal nature that affect either the property being appraised or the title to it, except for information that he or she became aware of during the research involved in performing this appraisal. The appraiser assumes that the title is good and marketable and will not render any opinions about the title.

2. The appraiser has provided a sketch in this appraisal report to show the approximate dimensions of the improvements. The sketch is included only to assist the reader in visualizing the property and understanding the appraiser's determination of its size.

3. The appraiser has examined the available flood maps that are provided by the Federal Emergency Management Agency (or other data sources) and has noted in this appraisal report whether any portion of the subject site is located in an identified Special Flood Hazard Area. Because the appraiser is not a surveyor, he or she makes no guarantees, express or implied, regarding this determination.

4. The appraiser will not give testimony or appear in court because he or she made an appraisal of the property in question, unless specific arrangements to do so have been made beforehand, or as otherwise required by law.

5. The appraiser has noted in this appraisal report any adverse conditions (such as needed repairs, deterioration, the presence of hazardous wastes, toxic substances, etc.) observed during the inspection of the subject property or that he or she became aware of during the research involved in performing this appraisal. Unless otherwise stated in this appraisal report, the appraiser has no knowledge of any hidden or unapparent physical deficiencies or adverse conditions of the property (such as, but not limited to, needed repairs, deterioration, the presence of hazardous wastes, toxic substances, adverse environmental conditions, etc.) that would make the property less valuable, and has assumed that there are no such conditions and makes no guarantees or warranties, express or implied. The appraiser will not be responsible for any such conditions that do exist or for any engineering or testing that might be required to discover whether such conditions exist. Because the appraiser is not an expert in the field of environmental hazards, this appraisal report must not be considered as an environmental assessment of the property.

6. The appraiser has based his or her appraisal report and valuation conclusion for an appraisal that is subject to satisfactory completion, repairs, or alterations on the assumption that the completion, repairs, or alterations of the subject property will be performed in a professional manner.

Freddie Mac Form 70 March 2005   Fannie Mae Form 1004 March 2005

FIGURE 16.10d (Continued)

Uniform Residential Appraisal Report

File #

APPRAISER'S CERTIFICATION: The Appraiser certifies and agrees that:

1. I have, at a minimum, developed and reported this appraisal in accordance with the scope of work requirements stated in this appraisal report.

2. I performed a complete visual inspection of the interior and exterior areas of the subject property. I reported the condition of the improvements in factual, specific terms. I identified and reported the physical deficiencies that could affect the livability, soundness, or structural integrity of the property.

3. I performed this appraisal in accordance with the requirements of the Uniform Standards of Professional Appraisal Practice that were adopted and promulgated by the Appraisal Standards Board of The Appraisal Foundation and that were in place at the time this appraisal report was prepared.

4. I developed my opinion of the market value of the real property that is the subject of this report based on the sales comparison approach to value. I have adequate comparable market data to develop a reliable sales comparison approach for this appraisal assignment. I further certify that I considered the cost and income approaches to value but did not develop them, unless otherwise indicated in this report.

5. I researched, verified, analyzed, and reported on any current agreement for sale for the subject property, any offering for sale of the subject property in the twelve months prior to the effective date of this appraisal, and the prior sales of the subject property for a minimum of three years prior to the effective date of this appraisal, unless otherwise indicated in this report.

6. I researched, verified, analyzed, and reported on the prior sales of the comparable sales for a minimum of one year prior to the date of sale of the comparable sale, unless otherwise indicated in this report.

7. I selected and used comparable sales that are locationally, physically, and functionally the most similar to the subject property.

8. I have not used comparable sales that were the result of combining a land sale with the contract purchase price of a home that has been built or will be built on the land.

9. I have reported adjustments to the comparable sales that reflect the market's reaction to the differences between the subject property and the comparable sales.

10. I verified, from a disinterested source, all information in this report that was provided by parties who have a financial interest in the sale or financing of the subject property.

11. I have knowledge and experience in appraising this type of property in this market area.

12. I am aware of, and have access to, the necessary and appropriate public and private data sources, such as multiple listing services, tax assessment records, public land records and other such data sources for the area in which the property is located.

13. I obtained the information, estimates, and opinions furnished by other parties and expressed in this appraisal report from reliable sources that I believe to be true and correct.

14. I have taken into consideration the factors that have an impact on value with respect to the subject neighborhood, subject property, and the proximity of the subject property to adverse influences in the development of my opinion of market value. I have noted in this appraisal report any adverse conditions (such as, but not limited to, needed repairs, deterioration, the presence of hazardous wastes, toxic substances, adverse environmental conditions, etc.) observed during the inspection of the subject property or that I became aware of during the research involved in performing this appraisal. I have considered these adverse conditions in my analysis of the property value, and have reported on the effect of the conditions on the value and marketability of the subject property.

15. I have not knowingly withheld any significant information from this appraisal report and, to the best of my knowledge, all statements and information in this appraisal report are true and correct.

16. I stated in this appraisal report my own personal, unbiased, and professional analysis, opinions, and conclusions, which are subject only to the assumptions and limiting conditions in this appraisal report.

17. I have no present or prospective interest in the property that is the subject of this report, and I have no present or prospective personal interest or bias with respect to the participants in the transaction. I did not base, either partially or completely, my analysis and/or opinion of market value in this appraisal report on the race, color, religion, sex, age, marital status, handicap, familial status, or national origin of either the prospective owners or occupants of the subject property or of the present owners or occupants of the properties in the vicinity of the subject property or on any other basis prohibited by law.

18. My employment and/or compensation for performing this appraisal or any future or anticipated appraisals was not conditioned on any agreement or understanding, written or otherwise, that I would report (or present analysis supporting) a predetermined specific value, a predetermined minimum value, a range or direction in value, a value that favors the cause of any party, or the attainment of a specific result or occurrence of a specific subsequent event (such as approval of a pending mortgage loan application).

19. I personally prepared all conclusions and opinions about the real estate that were set forth in this appraisal report. If I relied on significant real property appraisal assistance from any individual or individuals in the performance of this appraisal or the preparation of this appraisal report, I have named such individual(s) and disclosed the specific tasks performed in this appraisal report. I certify that any individual so named is qualified to perform the tasks. I have not authorized anyone to make a change to any item in this appraisal report; therefore, any change made to this appraisal is unauthorized and I will take no responsibility for it.

20. I identified the lender/client in this appraisal report who is the individual, organization, or agent for the organization that ordered and will receive this appraisal report.

Freddie Mac Form 70   March 2005   Page 5 of 6   Fannie Mae Form 1004   March 2005

FIGURE 16.10e (Continued)

Uniform Residential Appraisal Report   File

21. The lender/client may disclose or distribute this appraisal report to: the borrower; another lender at the request of the borrower; the mortgagee or its successors and assigns; mortgage insurers; government sponsored enterprises; other secondary market participants; data collection or reporting services; professional appraisal organizations; any department, agency, or instrumentality of the United States; and any state, the District of Columbia, or other jurisdictions; without having to obtain the appraiser's or supervisory appraiser's (if applicable) consent. Such consent must be obtained before this appraisal report may be disclosed or distributed to any other party (including, but not limited to, the public through advertising, public relations, news, sales, or other media).

22. I am aware that any disclosure or distribution of this appraisal report by me or the lender/client may be subject to certain laws and regulations. Further, I am also subject to the provisions of the Uniform Standards of Professional Appraisal Practice that pertain to disclosure or distribution by me.

23. The borrower, another lender at the request of the borrower, the mortgagee or its successors and assigns, mortgage insurers, government sponsored enterprises, and other secondary market participants may rely on this appraisal report as part of any mortgage finance transaction that involves any one or more of these parties.

24. If this appraisal report was transmitted as an "electronic record" containing my "electronic signature," as those terms are defined in applicable federal and/or state laws (excluding audio and video recordings), or a facsimile transmission of this appraisal report containing a copy or representation of my signature, the appraisal report shall be as effective, enforceable and valid as if a paper version of this appraisal report were delivered containing my original hand written signature.

25. Any intentional or negligent misrepresentation(s) contained in this appraisal report may result in civil liability and/or criminal penalties including, but not limited to, fine or imprisonment or both under the provisions of Title 18, United States Code, Section 1001, et seq., or similar state laws.

SUPERVISORY APPRAISER'S CERTIFICATION: The Supervisory Appraiser certifies and agrees that:

1. I directly supervised the appraiser for this appraisal assignment, have read the appraisal report, and agree with the appraiser's analysis, opinions, statements, conclusions, and the appraiser's certification.

2. I accept full responsibility for the contents of this appraisal report including, but not limited to, the appraiser's analysis, opinions, statements, conclusions, and the appraiser's certification.

3. The appraiser identified in this appraisal report is either a sub-contractor or an employee of the supervisory appraiser (or the appraisal firm), is qualified to perform this appraisal, and is acceptable to perform this appraisal under the applicable state law.

4. This appraisal report complies with the Uniform Standards of Professional Appraisal Practice that were adopted and promulgated by the Appraisal Standards Board of The Appraisal Foundation and that were in place at the time this appraisal report was prepared.

5. If this appraisal report was transmitted as an "electronic record" containing my "electronic signature," as those terms are defined in applicable federal and/or state laws (excluding audio and video recordings), or a facsimile transmission of this appraisal report containing a copy or representation of my signature, the appraisal report shall be as effective, enforceable and valid as if a paper version of this appraisal report were delivered containing my original hand written signature.

APPRAISER

Signature _____
Name _____
Company Name _____
Company Address _____

Telephone Number _____
Email Address _____
Date of Signature and Report _____
Effective Date of Appraisal _____
State Certification # _____
or State License # _____
or Other (describe) _____ State # _____
State _____
Expiration Date of Certification or License _____

ADDRESS OF PROPERTY APPRAISED
_____
_____

APPRAISED VALUE OF SUBJECT PROPERTY $ _____
LENDER/CLIENT
Name _____
Company Name _____
Company Address _____
_____
Email Address _____

SUPERVISORY APPRAISER (ONLY IF REQUIRED)

Signature _____
Name _____
Company Name _____
Company Address _____

Telephone Number _____
Email Address _____
Date of Signature _____
State Certification # _____
or State License # _____
State _____
Expiration Date of Certification or License _____

SUBJECT PROPERTY

☐ Did not inspect subject property
☐ Did inspect exterior of subject property from street
   Date of Inspection _____
☐ Did inspect interior and exterior of subject property
   Date of Inspection _____

COMPARABLE SALES

☐ Did not inspect exterior of comparable sales from street
☐ Did inspect exterior of comparable sales from street
   Date of Inspection _____

Freddie Mac Form 70   March 2005   Fannie Mae Form 1004   March 2005

FIGURE 16.10f (Continued)

As you learned earlier in this chapter, an appraisal will strictly focus on value. Furthermore, unless an individual is a licensed certified or general appraiser, it would be a violation of license law to call a CMA an appraisal.

When a licensee completes a market analysis to assist a customer in pricing a property, the result of the process is simply a determination of a suitable price, not an appraisal or an estimate of the value of the property. Often, when a real estate licensee determines a suitable price for a property on behalf of a customer, the licensee does so in a situation in which the property may also be appraised by a licensed appraiser. For example, when a seller lists a property for sale, a licensee may assist the seller in setting a price at which the property is offered for sale. When a buyer is found, the lender will require that an appraisal of the property be conducted before making a loan to the buyer.

The licensee's opinion of a suitable price may differ from a value that results from an appraisal for a number of reasons, including the following:

- Appraisals are usually made for a lender to determine the value of the property as security for a loan. The licensee's opinion is related to a sales price for the property. These are affected by different influences.
- An appraisal for loan purposes is based on the unencumbered value of the property, which means that the status of existing loans has no impact on the estimate of value. The licensee's opinion as to price should take financing issues into consideration because existing financing can affect the ability to sell a home as well as its price.

Principals should understand why the licensee's opinion as to price and an actual appraisal of the property may differ. In addition, before making use of a market analysis, or the information obtained in the process, licensees should check with their broker to determine the broker's policy on conducting a market analysis and to receive training the broker may provide in this area. Now, let's look at the process for completing a market analysis approach to pricing.

To complete a market analysis, you will be seeking to determine the fair market value for the property, which is defined as the price at which a willing seller will sell and a willing buyer will buy, when neither the seller nor the buyer is under abnormal pressure to act. For example, a home sold at a foreclosure sale would not meet these requirements for a fair market value because there were abnormal circumstances to the sale that would affect the price.

The fair market value for a property is determined by the actions of people. Earlier, you learned that the principle of substitution means that the appropriate price of a property is established largely by the price of similar properties that are substitutable for the property you are pricing. This is true because of people's actions. If a buyer can purchase a substitutable property for a lower price, he/she will normally do so. Therefore, a property will not normally sell for a higher price than that paid for similar, or substitutable, properties. These facts are the basis for the market analysis approach to pricing a property. A market analysis is simply a structured method to determine what people have been willing to pay for homes that are similar to, and substitutable for, the property you are pricing. The logic of the approach is that if homes in the same general neighborhood with similar features have sold for a certain price, then the property you are pricing should sell for approximately the same price. The most basic element of this approach, then, is to determine what similar properties in the same general neighborhood have sold for.

Before we look at the step-by-step process to complete a market analysis, let's take a look at sources of information that are available to determine what similar properties have sold for.

Gathering Appropriate Data

Sources of Information

There are several primary sources of information you should be familiar with, such as:

- multiple listing services
- professional reporting services
- company records, property appraiser offices, and clerks of court
- observation of the neighborhood
- list of homes currently on the market
- evaluation of effects of financing

Multiple Listing Services

Most multiple listing services (MLSs) provide their members with regular publications that contain information on properties currently for sale, as well as those that have recently sold and listings that expired without a sale. These publications can be extremely useful sources of information on the selling price of homes. Usually, these publications also contain not only the selling price of properties but also the method of financing and the length of time the property was on the market before it sold. Both of these are useful items in completing a market analysis.

Coaching Tips

MLSs may publish the price for which a property was first under contract. This may differ from the actual closing price. You should determine the policy of the MLS of which your firm is a member. When necessary, contact the listing broker to determine an actual closing price for a property you use in a market analysis.

Professional Reporting Services

There are also national and local firms that compile data on real estate properties that sell this information to brokerage firms. Their information usually comes from public records or from appraisers and appraisal firms who subscribe to their service. The type of information from services such as these can differ and may range from limited information, such as name, address, date of sale, and selling price, to more detailed information, such as square footage, number of rooms, age, type of construction, condition of the property, amenities, and type of financing.

Company Records

Another source of information is your brokerage firm's records. Many firms keep detailed records of transactions in which their company was involved. If your company is active in the area in which you are doing a market analysis, these records can be very helpful. Also, you may be able to obtain information from other companies' records in exchange for providing information from your company's records. This may also include an inspection of information from property appraiser offices and clerks of court.

Neighborhood Observation

Regardless of where you obtain your primary information for a market analysis, you should always ride through the neighborhood to get a first-hand look at the neighboring properties. This will give you valuable information about characteristics of relevant properties, such as architectural style, condition of the house, landscaping, and lot size. This information will help you determine which properties are most comparable to the property you are pricing.

List of Homes Currently on the Market

You should also consider the asking price for homes currently on the market. Because these homes have not yet sold, the prices are not as useful as the actual selling price. The primary use for such information is to assess the competition from other available homes.

Evaluation of Effects of Financing

When you complete a market analysis, you will have to consider the effect of different methods of financing on the price of property. The type of financing can significantly affect the price at which a property will sell. Financing that makes it easier to buy a property (or otherwise benefits the buyer) will usually increase the price of the property. For example, two similar houses are for sale. Owner A wants all cash and will not pay any closing costs or discount points. Owner B will finance part of the sale, requires only a small down payment, and will charge an interest rate that is two percentage points below the market rate. Of these two houses, Owner B's will almost surely sell for a higher price because of the more favorable financing available.

There are five general rules of thumb that will help you adjust the price of a property based on the type of financing:

1. An all-cash sale will result in the lowest price. (Cash is always in limited supply.)

2. The next lowest price will be on a loan assumption. (The cash down payment is usually larger than a down payment on a new loan.)
3. The next lowest price is on a conventional loan on which the buyer must pay all points and closing costs. (The price will likely increase if the seller pays some or all of these.)
4. The next to highest price will be a house that has a Federal Housing Administration (FHA) or Veterans Affairs (VA) loan on which the seller pays the discount points and especially if the seller pays the closing costs also.
5. The highest price will occur when financing is available on the best possible terms, as in the example given earlier.

The impact of the financing considerations can be illustrated in the following example.

Example You are pricing a property in a neighborhood where there were two recent comparable sales. House A sold for $53,000 with VA financing on which the seller paid six points. House B sold for $50,000 with a conventional loan on which no discount points were required. If your seller is not prepared to pay any of the closing costs and/or points for the buyer, the price of the property should be closer to $50,000 than $53,000. If the seller is willing to pay some of these costs, the price could be closer to $53,000 than $50,000 because the previous sale at $53,000 included the payment of such costs.

Because of the effects of factors such as financing on the price of property, it is always best to adhere to the following rule to the maximum extent possible: Always use the properties for a market analysis that have the fewest differences you can find from the subject property. This minimizes the need to make adjustments to the price of the comparable properties based on these differences. Let's now take a look at the step-by-step procedure to complete a market analysis.

Completing the Market Analysis

The market analysis process involves the following six steps:

1. Obtain information on the subject property.
2. Obtain information on comparable properties.
3. Fill in the worksheet.
4. Make adjustments for differences.
5. Attach "weights" to the adjusted prices.
6. Reconcile the values of adjusted prices to determine a range of pricing.

Subject Property Information

Prior to entering information in the worksheet you will use to complete a market analysis, the first step is to compile information about the subject property. The properties that you use to determine the price of your subject property are called comparable properties, or comps. When selecting your comparables, keep in mind the following:

- The more comparables you have, the better, but you need at least three to six comparables for a valid assessment.
- The more similar the comparables are to the subject property, the better.
- The more recent the sale, the better; use properties sold in the past six months, if available.
- Properties with prices significantly above or below other comparables should not be used because this usually means some abnormal factor was involved.

Obtain Information on Comparable Properties

After you obtain the information listed on your worksheet for your subject property, you should obtain the same information on your comparables, plus the following information:

- the listing price and terms
- the number of days the property was on the market before it sold
- the actual selling price and terms

One of the guidelines for selecting comparable properties is to use properties that are as similar as possible to the subject property. The definition of what is as similar as possible will depend on the situation.

Example You are pricing a 15-year-old brick ranch home with seven bedrooms, two baths, and a double carport. You find that five homes have sold in the neighborhood within the past six months. One of these is a two-story, one is a split-level, and three are ranch style. In this situation, you should use only the ranch-style houses in your analysis.

In this example, if you had found six ranch homes, your criteria for selection could have been even more specific. For example, if one ranch was frame construction, one was stucco, and four were brick, you would use only the four brick ranches because these are more similar to your subject property.

If you were even more fortunate and found that three of the brick ranch houses had the same number of rooms as your subject property, then you could have used only those three because of their similarity to the subject property.

In general, you should be as selective as you can in choosing the comparables and still have at least three to work with.

Fill in the Worksheet

Once you have selected your comparables and you have information on each one, begin to enter information on your worksheet. First, enter the basic information about each of the comparables you selected in the top section of the worksheet. Once you have done this, you are ready for the next step in the process—making adjustments.

Making Adjustments

The objective in making adjustments is to adjust the price of each comparable property so that the price of that comparable more accurately reflects the features of the subject property. When making adjustments, you always adjust the price of the comparable to bring it in line with the subject property. You never adjust the price of the subject property. (You determine the price of the subject property from the adjusted comparables, which will be covered in a later step.)

> **Example** You find that a comparable property is identical to your subject property except the comparable property has a fireplace and your subject property does not. In this case, the price of the comparable is slightly higher because it has a feature that the subject property does not. Another way of looking at this is that the subject property will probably not sell for quite as much as the comparable because it lacks a feature that the comparable property has. When this is the case, you must subtract an estimate of the value of the fireplace from the price of the comparable property. This makes it more comparable by taking out the value of the extra feature.

Let's look at the opposite situation.

> **Example** You find a comparable property that is identical to your subject property except that it does not have a fireplace and your subject property does. In this case, the price of the comparable property is slightly lower because it lacks a feature that your subject property has. Another way of looking at this is that your subject property will probably sell for a little more than the comparable because it has an extra feature not found in the comparable property. When this is the case, you must add an estimate of the value of the fireplace to the price of the comparable property. This makes it more comparable by adding the value of the extra feature to the price of the comparable. There is a rule that might help you remember how to adjust the price of the comparable in situations such as these: If the comparable is inferior to the subject property, you add to the price of the comparable. Remember this rule by the mnemonic CIA:

- *Comparable*
- *Inferior*
- *Add*

If you remember the CIA rule, then you also know that if the comparable is superior to the subject property, you subtract.

In order to make actual adjustments of the type we have just covered (transactional, locational, and physical), you will need to know an approximate value for each feature that differs in the subject and comparable properties. For example, if you need to subtract the value of a fireplace from the comparable property, you obviously need to know the fireplace's value.

This is an aspect of market analysis that requires some input from your broker. Because values for features such as these can vary depending on the location of the property as well as many other factors, you should ask your broker for guidance in selecting these values. In this course, these values will be given whenever you need them to complete a market analysis problem.

Assigning "Weights"

Once you have adjusted the price of each comparable, the next step is to assign a "weight" to each comparable. The purpose of the weight is to reflect your assessment of the similarity of each comparable to the subject property. A property that is more similar to the subject property should be given a higher weight than one that is less similar to the subject property. Weights are assigned using percentages.

REPLACEMENT COST PRICING

The sales comparison approach is the best and most convenient method for pricing property when data on the sale of comparable properties are readily available. For some types of properties, the market approach is not very useful because of the lack of comparables that have recently sold. For example, homes in rural areas, homes in neighborhoods where the market has been inactive, and specialty homes that are unique because of design or age are all difficult to price because of the lack of adequate comparables. In these cases, the pricing approach that is often used is the *cost approach*. The cost approach to pricing gives an estimated price for a property based on the current cost of replacing or reproducing the improvements.

Reproduction cost is the cost of precisely duplicating the original structure, using the same materials and construction techniques as the original. *Replacement cost* is the cost of replacing the improvements with another building that performs the same function but is not an exact replica of the subject property.

Of these two types of cost approaches, the replacement cost approach will be the most useful to you and the one that we will cover in the remainder of this lesson. The reproduction cost method is not as useful because changes in building techniques, styles, and designs over the years make it almost useless to consider reproducing a particular building exactly as it was built originally.

The replacement cost approach is based on providing a new structure that has the same utility as the property being evaluated but using building methods more appropriate to the time the appraisal is made. Reproduction is often difficult or impossible because of changing techniques and availability of materials.

The replacement cost approach is based on the following formula:

$$
\begin{aligned}
&\text{Value of land} \\
+\ &\text{Replacement cost} \\
-\ &\text{Depreciation based on improvements only} \\
\hline
=\ &\text{Estimated price}
\end{aligned}
$$

In order to understand how to use this approach to pricing, we need to look at each part of the formula separately. The process is very simple if we take it one step at a time. The four steps in the replacement cost approach to pricing are as follows:

- **Step 1:** Estimate the price of the land as if it were vacant.
- **Step 2:** Estimate the replacement cost of the improvements (i.e., buildings) on the land.
- **Step 3:** Add the price of the land and the cost to replace the building.
- **Step 4:** Make deductions for depreciation on the building (the land is not depreciated).

Step 1: Estimate Land Value

The first step of the replacement cost approach to pricing is to determine the price of the land as if it were vacant. There are two ways to do this. The first is to use the sales comparison approach that you learned about earlier in this chapter. This would require obtaining data on the sale of comparable vacant lots. If adequate data on comparables are not available, the next best approach to determine the price of the land is to ask one or more knowledgeable and reputable builders in the area to tell you what they would pay for the property as a building site if it were available. As an example, let's assume that you have talked with the appropriate knowledgeable builders and found that the land for a subject property has a value of $30,000.

Step 2: Estimate Replacement Cost

The second step in the process is to estimate the cost to replace the building. This can be done in three ways:

1. the square foot method
2. the unit-in-place method
3. the quantity survey method

Each of these approaches has been covered; here is a summary of the relative merits of each of these methods.

- The square foot method is the easiest to complete but the least accurate.
- The unit-in-place method is more accurate than the square foot method and also more difficult to complete than the square foot method.
- The quantity survey method is the most accurate and the most difficult of the three. It is used the least because of its difficulty.

Even though the square foot method is not as accurate as the other methods, it is the most useful approach because of its simplicity and ease of use. We will cover this method in the remainder of this chapter. However, you should always keep in mind that the results of this method are not generally as reliable as those for the market comparison method or for other types of replacement cost methods.

Now let's take a look at how to complete a replacement cost estimate of price using the square foot method. There are three steps involved in using the square foot method. Because these are all part of Step 2 in the overall process, we will label them as substeps.

Here are the substeps in the square foot method:

1. Determine cost factors that are the cost of construction per square foot for each major element of the house.
2. Determine the actual square footage in each major element of the house being priced.
3. Multiply the cost factors from Step 1 by the number of square feet in each major element from Step 2 to get an estimate of the cost to replace the building.

Determine Cost Factors

The first substep in the square foot method is to determine the cost factors that represent the cost of construction per square foot for the major elements of a house. This is the most important step in the entire pricing process because it has the biggest impact on the final price estimate. Because of this, it is important to obtain the best estimates possible for the cost of construction per square foot. The best method for determining the cost per square foot is to ask one or more reputable builders who have experience building properties of similar style and quality in the area of the subject property. An experienced builder will have fairly accurate estimates of the cost of construction per square foot readily available. If you do not know any builders with these qualifications, ask your broker to recommend one or more. If neither you nor your broker is able to identify an appropriate builder, another possible source is a cost estimate handbook that provides replacement cost factors. Ask your broker for help in finding one.

Let's assume that you have contacted three reputable builders with appropriate experience in the area and have found that the cost of construction appropriate for the different elements of a house are:

- First-floor heated area—$50 per square foot
- Second-floor heated area—$25 per square foot
- Garage—$30 per square foot
- Basement—$15 per square foot

The most expensive element of the house is the first-floor heated area because, by convention, the cost of the foundation and roof go with the first-floor construction. The second-floor heated area is less expensive because it does not require another roof, and the floor is less expensive than the foundation. The basement and garage are the least expensive areas because they require less interior finish work, plumbing, electrical work, etc.

Determine Actual Square Footage

The second substep in the square foot method is measuring the actual square footage of the major elements of the house. The square footage should be calculated by measuring the outside dimensions of the house. (It is a good idea to have a 100-foot metal tape measure for doing this.) In measuring these dimensions, it is also a good idea to make a sketch of the floor plan of the house to use in recording your measurements and calculating the square footage.

The easiest way to determine the square footage is from a sketch or floor plan. First, divide the floor plan into smaller segments so that each segment is a rectangle for which you can determine the length of each side. Once your sketch has been divided into rectangles, determine the square footage of each rectangle and add up the square footage for each one to get the total square footage.

Using the example below, to get the total square footage for the house, total the amounts for the different elements as follows:

480 sq. ft.	Garage
2,432 sq. ft.	First-floor heated area
+ 1,440 sq. ft.	Second-floor heated area
4,352 sq. ft.	Total square footage

Determine Replacement Cost

Once you know the actual square footage for the house, the final substep is to calculate the cost to replace it. To do this, we need our cost factors from Step 1 and the total square footage for each element of the house that we calculated in Step 2. Then multiply the square footage for each category by the cost per square foot for that category to determine the estimated replacement cost for each category. To get the total estimated replacement cost for the entire house, add up the numbers. The final estimate of the cost to replace the house is $172,000.

Step 3: Add Replacement Cost and Land

Once you have determined the value of the land and calculated the cost to replace the building, add these two values together. This gives the total estimated cost of the land and buildings before depreciation is deducted. In our example, this is done as follows:

Value of land	$ 30,000
Estimated replacement cost	$172,000
Total	$202,000

Step 4: Deduct Depreciation

The next step in the process is to deduct for the effects of depreciation. The value of almost any existing house will be less than the cost to replace it because of the effects of depreciation.

Previously, you learned that there are three major types of depreciation:

1. physical deterioration
2. functional obsolescence
3. economic (external) obsolescence

Let's review each of these types briefly.

Physical Deterioration

This is the wear and tear that results from normal use. For example, a frame house that needs a new coat of paint is suffering from physical deterioration.

Functional Obsolescence

Functional obsolescence is the reduction in value due to outdated features of the property, such as:

- closets that are too small
- ceilings that are too high or low
- too few bathrooms
- inadequate wiring
- outdated design or architecture

Economic (External) Obsolescence

This is the loss of value due to external conditions and might include such situations as:

- changes in the makeup of the surrounding area
- environmental impacts like noise pollution from an airport
- changes in highways that serve the property
- the closing of a major business nearby

Both physical deterioration and functional obsolescence arise from the characteristics of the property itself. Economic obsolescence represents depreciation that arises from factors outside the property. To estimate the depreciation for a given property, we must consider the effects of each of these types of depreciation.

The type of depreciation that is most common is physical deterioration, or the wear and tear from normal use. We can estimate the amount of such depreciation using a method called the cost to repair. The first step in this procedure is to make a careful inspection of the property, making note of any items that need repair or replacement. For example, you might find that a house needs a new coat of paint, a new roof, or new carpet. Once you have identified all such items, you can then determine the cost to repair by contacting local contractors and/or the appropriate building supply companies for estimates. The total of the estimates for all such repairs is the total estimate for depreciation using the cost to repair method.

The other types of depreciation—functional obsolescence and economic obsolescence—are more difficult to deal with. Functional obsolescence, also referred to as loss in value due to changing consumer demands, usually results from the way a property is designed and built. That is, functional obsolescence is not caused by repairs that are needed but results from changes in consumer preferences. Similarly, economic obsolescence is depreciation that cannot be solved through repairs because it arises from factors outside the property. A general decline in values in a neighborhood due to commercial construction nearby is difficult to quantify in the absence of sales comparison on the sale of comparable properties. Specific methods for dealing with these types of depreciation are beyond the scope of this course; you should consult with your broker for methods to deal with them when the need arises.

Once you have estimated the amount of depreciation for the house you are pricing, subtract this amount from the replacement cost estimate from Step 3. In the case of our example, let's assume that we inspected the property and found the need for repairs that totaled $16,000.

We would then calculate the final estimated price for the property as follows:

Replacement cost + land	$ 202,000
Less depreciation	$ 16,000
	$186,000

The final estimated price for the house is $186,000.

AUTOMATED VALUATION MODEL (AVM)

An **automated valuation model (AVM)** is a name given to a database service that provides real estate property valuations to the real estate industry. By analyzing values of comparable properties, these services are able to calculate a property's value. They can be generated in a short period of time. All of the following would utilize AVMs

- lending institutions
- appraisers
- investors

The AVM database is derived from:

- a review of the public record data available at the time of inspection
- computer programing that provides an estimate of selling price for a residential property

Information normally found in AVMs includes:

- property tax municipal values
- market values for many residential properties
- comparable sales of like properties
- recent sales history and subject property

There are other types of computer-generated CMA software. Many are offered through the local MLS. However, there are products available for purchase such as Cloud CMA.

Summary

Valuation is a critical part of real estate practice. It involves the three approaches to appraisal:

1. the sales comparison approach
2. the cost approach
3. the income approach

In addition, licensees perform comparative market analysis (CMA) to determine marketing pricing. This should never be called or confused with an appraisal. Appraisals strictly focus on value.

Various parties to a transaction are dependent on the valuation process. This includes

- buyers/tenants
- sellers/landlords
- lenders
- other interested parties to a transaction

For the aforementioned reasons only a licensed certified or general appraiser may be utilized on any transaction that falls under the definition of a federally related transaction. When a seller is considering listing property with a licensee, the seller is generally more concerned with the value of the property for marketing purposes. Therefore, it is important that the licensee know how to perform the CMA.

Review Questions

1. Which of the following describes the most probable price that a property should bring in an open market?
   a. median value
   b. sales price
   c. market value
   d. exchange value

2. A comparable property sold for $100,000. The comparable property is in better condition than the subject property (a value of $13,000). However, the comparable property has fewer square feet than the subject property ($10,000 for square feet). What is the adjusted value of the comparable property?
   a. $123,000
   b. $103,000
   c. $ 97,000
   d. $ 87,000

3. All of the following are steps included in the square foot method EXCEPT:
   a. obtain the construction cost of a similar building recently constructed
   b. convert the cost of construction to cost per square foot
   c. divide the cost of construction by the comparable sales price
   d. multiply the cost per square foot times the number of square feet in the improvement whose price is being determined

4. An appraiser made an adjustment because the home contains a poor traffic pattern. This is an example of:
   a. curable physical deterioration
   b. functional obsolescence
   c. incurable physical deterioration
   d. external obsolescence

5. Expenses on a property are $12,920. What is the monthly net income if the property is purchased for $209,000 with a rate of return of 12%?
   a. $38,000
   b. $25,080
   c. $3,167
   d. $2,090

6. In the income capitalization approach to value, which of these would NOT be an operating expense?
   a. mortgage payment
   b. hazard insurance
   c. electric bill
   d. reserves for replacement

7. An investment property produces $48,000 annual net operating income. The prospective investor wants a 12% return. Based on this information, what is the most this investor would be willing to pay for the property?
   a. $25,000
   b. $33,000
   c. $300,000
   d. $400,000

8. An investment property has a potential gross income of $60,000. There are no vacancies. Annual expenses are $30,000. With a return of 20%, what is the value of the property?
   a. $60,000
   b. $90,000
   c. $150,000
   d. $300,000

9. Effective gross income is a result of:
   a. net operating income divided by an appropriate capitalization rate
   b. potential gross income minus vacancy and collection losses
   c. net operating income divided by the price
   d. before-tax income minus the debt service

10. A building that is 5 years old has a reproduction cost of $100,000. The economic life of the property is 25 years. Using the cost depreciation approach, what is the building's estimated value?
    a. $20,000
    b. $80,000
    c. $100,000
    d. $120,000

11. All of the following are true regarding the age-life method for calculating accrued depreciation EXCEPT:
    a. the method tends to be the most common depreciation technique utilized by residential appraisers
    b. it is easy to use and explain to a client
    c. it is used as a residual technique
    d. it is also referred to as the straight-line method

12. An appraiser made an adjustment because the roof shingles are curling from exposure to the tropical sun. This is an example of:
    a. functional obsolescence
    b. curable external obsolescence
    c. incurable external obsolescence
    d. physical deterioration

13. In an appraisal, the appraiser would assign a greater mathematical weight to the sales comparison approach for:
    a. a community college
    b. the police station
    c. a vacant lot zoned for residential use
    d. an industrial property

14. In an appraisal, the basis of all three approaches to value is:
    a. the square foot approach
    b. depreciation of existing improvements
    c. the principle of substitution
    d. loss in value for any reason

15. A homeowner built a $60,000 pool in a neighborhood of homes that sell for $120,000. This is an example of:
    a. External obsolescence
    b. An overimprovement
    c. Functional obsolescence
    d. Progression

16. A contractor charged a homeowner $57,000 to remodel the home's kitchen. This is an example of:
    a. market value
    b. cost
    c. consumer price index
    d. assemblage

17. Which type of cost would be used to estimate the value of a church building?
    a. effective cost
    b. historical cost
    c. replacement cost
    d. estimated cost

18. In an appraisal, an adjustment was made to a home's value because the adjacent neighborhood is in disrepair. This is an example of:
    a. functional obsolescence that is curable
    b. physical deterioration that is curable
    c. incurable physical deterioration
    d. external obsolescence

19. Capitalization rates are usually:
    a. subjective prescribed rates of returns that investors seek
    b. the same rate for all investors
    c. are always a prescribed rate dictated by the lender
    d. both b and c

CHAPTER 17
REAL ESTATE INVESTMENTS AND BUSINESS OPPORTUNITY BROKERAGE

KEY TERMS

appreciation
asset
basis
capital gain or loss
cash flow
equity
going concern value

goodwill
leverage
liquidation analysis
liquidity
personal property
risk
tax shelter

LEARNING OBJECTIVES

After completing this lesson, you will be able to:

- distinguish among the different types of real estate investments
- identify the advantages and disadvantages of investing in real estate
- distinguish among the various types of risk
- explain the importance of an investment analysis
- describe the similarities and differences between business brokerage and real estate brokerage
- describe the type of expertise required in business brokerage
- distinguish among the methods of appraising businesses
- describe the steps in the sale of a business

INVESTMENT REAL ESTATE TERMINOLOGY

Introduction

An investor's goal is to seek out investments that ultimately meet the investor's three primary objectives:

1. an annual return on the invested capital (represents investor profit, return on investment)

2. preservation and/or return of the principal investment (represents return of investment)
3. appreciation derived during the property-holding period

However, when discussing the investment of capital funds, it is important to note that investors are not buying the "bricks and mortar." It is not the real property or the stocks, bonds, or purchase of a business that an investor seeks. Rather, it is primarily:

- the cash flow associated/generated with the investment
- desired yields associated with the cash flows to the investor

Investors primarily seek returns of and on their investments.

Cash Flow

Cash flow is what delivers returns (profits) to the investor. **Cash flow** also refers to receipts, less payments over a period of time. Therefore, real property, not unlike other investment types, is merely the investment vehicle that houses the cash flow that investors truly seek. In fact, regardless of the vehicle that houses the cash flow, the moment that vehicle does not produce the required returns, or other vehicles provide higher returns (profits) than the current investment vehicle, the investor will sell and move into a more aggressive alternative vehicle.

Many investors gravitate toward real property as their investment vehicle of choice. This is primarily because, historically, investment in real property not only yields profits during the holding period but also tends to retain its overall value over time.

Investments and vehicles always react in a cyclical manner. When times are good, they increase in value; when times are bad, they decrease in value. The investment property's value is a direct derivative of the income that is attributable to the property at any given time.

Leverage

Leverage refers to the use of borrowed funds with the anticipation of earning substantial profits not only on the investment but also on the borrowed funds. For example, an investor may purchase a property by making a down payment equal to 25% of the value of the property and borrow the remaining 75%. The property may immediately begin generating a return for the investor on the full value of the property even though his/her own capital investment was only 25% of the property's value.

Leveraging can be advantageous when planned appropriately. Planning starts with establishing the effects of the debt on the cash flow. The cost of the annual debt service (amount paid for principal and interest on the loan) must be subtracted from net operating income attributable to the property. The difference will determine if earnings are sufficient to cover the debt placed on the property. (A positive value indicates that earnings are sufficient to cover the debt. A negative value indicates that earnings are not sufficient.)

> ### Coaching Tips
>
> In order to always generate a positive cash flow, the capitalization rate (the rate of return used to derive how much a buyer/investor would be willing to pay to own the cash flow generated by a particular parcel of property) should always be greater than the loan constant (the periodic cost/payment of principle and interest based on a borrowed amount). For example, if the loan constant is based on a rate of 5%, positive cash flow would be achieved by utilizing any capitalization rate that is greater than 5%.

Capital gain or loss

Capital gain or loss is the difference between the property's cost basis and the sales price after deducting the cost of the sale and adding to the cost basis any capital improvements made to the property during the holding period. Under current tax laws, there are two types of gains:

1. short-term gain—any gain realized in a single tax year (12 months or less)
2. long-term gain—any gain realized in two or more tax years (12 months and one day or more)

The length of time an investment is held directly affects the taxpayer and tax liability. This subject will be discussed in greater detail in Chapter 18.

Basis

Basis is the amount attributable to the property (which is usually the purchase price or adjusted purchase price) by the Internal Revenue Service for the purpose of calculating:

- annual depreciation allowances (during holding)
- capital gain or loss (at point of sale)

Appreciation

Appreciation refers to any increase in the value of property. This can be realized through:

- inflation, or
- simply holding the asset for increased value.

Equity

Equity refers to the difference between the market value of a property and the unpaid balance of any loans or other liabilities on that property. At the point of acquisition of real property, the equity is represented by the purchaser's initial investment (down payment) amount on the property. In simplified terms, equity is the portion of value the investor owns in the property after deducting any outstanding loan balance or other property liabilities. In formula form:

Equity = Property value − Any outstanding debt or other liabilities

Liquidity

Liquidity refers to the ability to convert an **asset** (real or personal property that has value) into cash by selling it. An asset that can be readily sold and converted to cash is considered liquid. For example, stocks are considered liquid assets while real property would not be considered to be a liquid asset.

Risk

Real estate investors are exposed to risk. **Risk** refers to the chance of losing one's invested capital. When making a decision about investment property, an investor must analyze any outside influences that might comprise risk. Examples of risk include but are not limited to:

- investment risk—the probability or likelihood of the investment not yielding the expected return on any particular investment
- business risk—the possibility an investment will not deliver the anticipated profits and may in fact experience a loss
- capital risk—the risk that the investor may lose all or part of the principal dollar invested

Tax Shelter

Investing in real property provides legal tax advantages in the form of deductions that are taken against the property's earned income. An investment that results in legal tax advantages is sometimes referred to as a **tax shelter**.

THE LICENSEE REGARDED AS AN EXPERT

Investors often seek the guidance of a real estate licensee to locate a property for an investment opportunity. In addition, the real estate licensee will most likely provide assistance in the analysis of the investment. Therefore, a licensee must have a thorough knowledge and clear understanding of the investment-analysis process. However, keep in mind that, although their are no laws that govern the investment analysis, the unauthorized practice of law is a direct violation of licensee law. Strongly consider this before giving investment guidance and advice to an investor.

Types of Investments: Property Types and Subtypes

Before we look at real estate as an investment, we should review the common types of real property:

- residential
- commercial
- industrial
- agricultural
- mixed use

Residential Property

Under zoning definitions, residential property is any property intended for dwelling purposes. However, the term is expanded when discussing it in transactional terms. Within this context, transactional residential property is defined to include the following:

- improved property containing one to four units intended for dwelling purposes
- unimproved property that, when and if improved, will consist of one to four units intended for dwelling purposes
- farm/agricultural land of 10 or fewer acres

Residential property as a basic property group takes on many forms. Residential property subtypes consist of:

- single-family homes
- multifamily dwellings
- condominiums
- cooperatives
- condops (hybrid of condo/coop formation)
- rental units
- agricultural land of 10 or fewer acres (agricultural land with more than 10 acres is considered nonresidential, agricultural property)

Because housing is a necessity for all people, it is in greater demand than other types of real property. Due to this demand, the residential housing market is the most active market in the country of all the basic property group types.

All of the following are considered nonresidential property:

- improved or unimproved property with greater than four dwelling units
- all investment property, regardless of its use

In essence, all income-producing residential and nonresidential property falls under the category of investment property, while only residential properties containing greater than four units are also considered investment property. In fact, and particularly from a financing standpoint, there are two types of property transactions:

- residential transactions
- commercial transactions

Investment property is not for dwelling purposes by its owner(s). Investment property is used as a vehicle that generates cash flow that equates to income for the investor.

Commercial Property

Commercial property is any property that is used by business or operating enterprises. Commercial property includes:

- offices
- retail establishments
- hotels/motels

Offices

Office buildings house businesses. Depending on their proximity within given marketplaces, office buildings are constructed in a variety of sizes. They can be low-rise, mid-rise, or high-rise. The location and zoning of a particular parcel of real estate will dictate the size and height of a building. Office buildings may be either single- or multi-tenant properties. The bulk (total zoning-approved building size in square footage) of any development is always determined by zoning allowances.

Retail Establishments

Retail property takes many shapes and forms. The size of a retail facility dictates what category of retail the property takes. For example, urban retail can be the neighborhood store on your block; however, with careful planning, larger projects can be created. The retail facility's success depends on the needs of the community surrounding it. Some of the different forms of retail property include the following:

- regional shopping centers
- shopping malls
- strip centers

- neighborhood shopping centers
- factory outlet malls/centers

Hotels/Motels

Most people perceive hotel/motel properties as short-term and transient residences. However, a careful inspection of the public records concerning zoning categorization reveals that these properties are zoned as commercial (not residential).

In many cases, it would not be unusual for zoning to allow a "multi" use for hotels/motels. For example, a particular hotel may be a 400-room high-rise in a central urban location. It would not be unusual to split the property into two—in theory, a building inside another building. The lower portion may consist of short-term hotel accommodations, while the upper portion may consist of permanent housing such as cooperative or condominium housing. An example of this would be the world-renowned Plaza Hotel in New York City. That property has undergone a transformation that will mirror the concept of the "building within the building." Lower floors are being used for interim/transient short-term stays (hotel), while the upper floors—with their dramatic views of Central Park and the New York skyline—will be luxury condominiums. The Plaza Hotel will be considered a mixed-use property. Mixed-use properties will be covered in more detail later in this chapter.

Industrial Property

Industrial property consists of uses associated with manufacturing, including:

- heavy manufacturing—where raw materials are manufactured for use
- light manufacturing—assembly lines where raw materials made in the heavy manufacturing area are assembled and made into something (i.e., automobile assembly line)
- loft buildings—where finished products are stored and then distributed
  - warehousing
  - assembly and distribution

Heavy and light manufacturing are usually associated with the conversion of raw materials into a finished product. This would be substantially different from a warehousing use. While heavy and light manufacturing spaces are used to create the finished product, the warehouse is used to store the finished product prior to its distribution to the marketplace (e.g., the neighborhood store).

Agricultural Property

Agricultural property refers to various types of farm lands over 10 acres. In many cases, investors purchase agricultural property that is located in the path of future development with the idea that the value of the property will increase because of development or that the property will be rezoned in the future.

Mixed-Use Property

Since the mid-1980s, mixed-use property has been very popular. In some cases, municipal tax benefits are available on these types of properties. These tax benefits are offered when there is a need for housing and/or other property uses in an area. This property type can be a new development, or, more recently, conversion of a previous single-use property into a multiuse property. For example, developers have taken buildings that have experienced both functional and economic obsolescence problems and converted them into mixed-use property. These properties will incorporate two or more legal property use types. An example of this would be commercial uses on the lower portion of the property in question and residential uses on the upper portion. As previously discussed, commercial uses may vary from offices to retail establishments to hotels or motels.

Business Opportunities

Although the purchase and sale of a business generally falls under the category as a personal property transaction, contrary to this, in Florida, Chapter 475 includes business opportunities in the definition of real estate. Business opportunities include but are not limited to:

- the sale or lease of a business
- the sale of a business's assets (stocks, bonds)

A savvy investor will try to find hidden assets through the purchase of a business. For example, the purchase of a department store chain may be worth more as a real estate play than the business's actual activity. This would hold true when the business owns the real estate locations it occupies.

Coaching Tips

Property Descriptions at a Glance

- Residential property includes improved property containing one to four units intended for dwelling purposes or unimproved property that, when and if improved, will consist of one to four units intended for dwelling purposes.
- Commercial property includes offices, retail establishments, and hotels/motels.
- Industrial property includes manufacturing facilities and warehouses.
- Agricultural property refers to various types of farm lands over 10 acres.

GOALS OF INVESTMENTS

We just looked at the types of real properties that may be of interest to investors. As previously mentioned, some of the reasons for real property investment include:

- an annual return on the investor's invested capital (represents investor profit) (This is also known as the return on the investment [ROI].)
- preservation and/or return of the principal dollar investment (This is also known as the return of investment or capital recapture.)
- increased values derived during the property holding period (This is also known as appreciation.)

With these objectives in mind, let's look at the advantages and disadvantages of investing in real estate compared to other types or vehicles of investment.

Advantages of Investing in Real Estate

Due to the scarcity of unimproved land within active real estate markets, investors gravitate to long-term investment in real property. Some of the advantages of real property investment include:

- a good rate of return
- a hedge against inflation
- equity buildup
- the use of leveraging (borrowed funds) versus buyer's outlay of cash within one investment
- tax advantages

A Good Rate of Return

One of the objectives of investing is to achieve a good annual return on invested capital. In essence, the goal is to make a profit by putting money to use in an investment. Compared to other investment alternatives, generally, real estate typically provides a higher rate of return. Real estate investment, like any other vehicle, is cyclical in nature. However, the long-term investor will achieve large benefits by investing in and holding real property.

A Hedge Against Inflation

Because of the scarcity of strategically located property, over the years, real property investment has kept up with inflationary trends. Inflation refers to an increase in the supply of money in the economy without a corresponding increase in the production of goods and services. Inflation results in an increase in prices and a corresponding decrease in purchasing power (that is, a decrease in the value of a dollar). As the purchasing power of the dollar decreases, many investments lose value over time. However, this is not true with real estate because the value of real property typically increases faster than inflation. Inflation is generally considered a negative within the overall economy; however, inflation is embraced by the property owner. The result for the owner is an immediate increase in the overall value of the property. This equates to a value over and above the owner's initial investment cost. This increase in value occurs regardless of the income attributable to the property at that time. Appreciation normally would occur through the increase in rents attributable to that property. The unnatural increase in value due to inflation may result in the owner's ability to refinance the property at a higher property value than the rents would normally command for that property.

Leverage

As it applies to real property transactions and lending, leverage or leveraging is the use of borrowed funds. In residential transactions, it would not be unusual to see loan-to-value ratios of up to 80%. Because of the risks associated with investment property, lenders are reluctant to provide loan-to-value ratios greater than 75%. In many cases, lenders will not lend greater than 70% loan-to-value ratios. Higher leverage loan amounts are available, but they come at a greater expense than customary loan-to-value ratios.

Equity Buildup

When real property increases in value, the result is equity buildup. Equity refers to the difference between the market value of a property and the unpaid balance of any outstanding loans on that property. Equity increases (builds up) as any loan is paid down and as the property appreciates. Appreciation refers to any increase in the value of property.

Tax Advantages

Real estate investments have many tax advantages (although some of the advantages were limited or eliminated by the 1986 Tax Reform Act). Some of the advantages that still exist include tax deductions for interest payments, taxes, and depreciation on improvements. An investment that results in tax advantages is sometimes referred to as a tax shelter. Tax issues related to real property ownership are discussed in more detail in Chapter 18.

Disadvantages of Investing in Real Estate

Some of the disadvantages of real property investment include:
- illiquidity
- market conditions
- the need for property management
- risk

Illiquidity

Liquidity refers to the ability to convert an asset into cash by selling it. An asset that can be readily sold and converted to cash is considered liquid. For example, stocks are considered liquid assets. An asset that *cannot* be readily sold and converted to cash is considered illiquid. Real property is considered illiquid because quick sales are not easily achieved. Therefore, one of the disadvantages of investing in real estate is illiquidity of the investment.

Market Conditions/Market Is Local in Nature

A real estate investment may be adversely affected by the market. For example, a change or an erosion of market conditions can result in loss of property value. This would be a direct result of lower rents attributable to the property during these times. Because land cannot be moved, the market for real estate is a local one, and real estate investors often have preferences for certain geographic areas.

Management/Need for Expert Help

Another disadvantage of investing in real estate is management. Managing real property can be both time consuming and labor intensive. Depending on the property and the investor, the investor may choose to manage the property him/herself or be an absentee owner. If the investor chooses to be an absentee owner, a property manager would be hired. In addition to hiring a property manager, a real estate investor may also require the services of attorneys, financial consultants, and other professionals.

Risk

Real estate investors are exposed to risk. Risk refers to the chance of losing one's invested capital. When making a decision about investment property, an investor must analyze the risk.

There are various types of risk any investor must take into consideration prior to investing money. The following risks associated with general business conditions must be assessed:

- business risk
- financial risk
- purchasing-power risk
- interest-rate risk
- risks that affect return
- liquidity risk
- safety risk

Risks Associated with General Business Conditions

Business risk is related to any variation between predicted income and expenses and actual income and expenses.

Financial risk is related to the ability of the investment to pay operating expenses from the various sources of funds, including income from operations, equity, and borrowed funds.

Purchasing-power risk is associated with inflation, which reduces the value of any yield from an investment. (As mentioned previously, inflation results in an increase in prices and a corresponding decrease in purchasing power; that is, a decrease in the value of a dollar.)

Interest-rate risk is caused by a change in interest rates. For example, when there is a loan on a property, any increase in the interest rate by the lender can result in a decrease in the value of the property.

There are other risks that can affect the return on the investment as well as the return of the invested capital. These risks include the following:

- Liquidity risk—The risk associated with any loss that might result if the investment has to be sold quickly.
- Safety risk—The chance of losing one's invested capital (market risk) and/or expected earnings (risk of default).
- Market risk—The risk resulting from a decrease in the market value of the investment.
- Risk of default—The chance that the investor's actual earnings will be less than expected.

Coaching Tips

Risk at a Glance

- Risk related to any variation between predicted income and expenses and actual income and expenses is business risk.
- Purchasing-power risk refers to risk associated with inflation, which reduces the value of any yield from an investment.
- Liquidity risk refers to risk associated with any loss that might result if the investment has to be sold quickly.
- Market risk refers to risk resulting from a decrease in the market value of the investment.
- Interest-rate risk refers to risk caused by a change in interest rates.

PROPERTY INVESTMENT ANALYSIS

Before purchasing nonresidential property, a complicated investment review process occurs. This review process requires an understanding of the terms and conditions within any lease on a property, as well as effect of these terms and conditions on the property income bottom line. Therefore, a licensee assisting an investor is required to have a keen awareness of lease clauses and their financial impact on the investor when reviewing leases.

For example, commercial leases tend to be modified gross leases. This means that the tenant/lessee will pay an amount that is established as the base rent to the landlord/lessor. However, it is prevalent today that commercial leases contain provisions that cover the owner against increased costs in operations due to real property tax increases or increased costs in delivering the services expected by the tenant that are called for in the lease. These clauses, called escalation clauses, entitle the owner to bill the tenant for cost increases.

Most commercial leases break down rents into two types of payments:

1. Base rent—The amount that the landlord and tenant have initially agreed upon.
2. Additional rent—Any amounts paid to the landlord for one or all of the following items:
   - property tax increases
   - operating expense increases
   - utility costs paid by the landlord that are reimbursable by the tenant
   - any service within the property performed by the landlord on the tenant's behalf that requires a reimbursement from the tenant

The licensee is required to look at a broad number of factors that affect value in the analysis. Some of the factors that require careful review include:

- external economic influences
- locational considerations
- financial analyses
- risk analyses

External economic influences can exist on either a national or a local level. On a national level, upward or downward changes in interest rates affect the cost of borrowed funds to the investor. On a local level, zoning constraints affect a property's use or size in relation to investor requirements.

Because these influences are outside the property line, they are items and trends that are not in the control of the investor. However, the investor may be positively or negatively impacted by a change in national or local trends.

An investment analysis must also include an examination of locational considerations, which include:

- zoning
- site and environmental factors
- time-distance relationships to amenities (The relationship of a property to amenities or supporting facilities, measured in both distance and time, is referred to as linkage.)

Another component of the investment analysis is a financial analysis, which should include:

- an income versus expense analysis (cash flow analysis)
- an examination of current leases
- the need for any future capital improvements
- any present and future local law compliance issues
- present and future market conditions

The investment analysis also includes a risk analysis, which is an examination of the following:

- any potential changes in interest rates (Any change in rates will affect the way an investor looks at acquisition value. As mentioned earlier, the higher the rate is for borrowed funds, the greater the cost of servicing the annual debt, thereby creating lower value.)
- property income and its ability to cover:
    - operating expenses
    - debt service
    - a loss in property value

NATURE OF BUSINESS BROKERAGE

Previously, we looked at the issues involved in investing in real estate. Another area of investment is business brokerage, which is the buying, selling, or leasing of a business. Business brokerage presents many great opportunities for investors.

Comparison to Real Estate Brokerage

Business brokerage is similar to real estate brokerage because it almost always involves the sale of real property or the assignment of a lease. Also, under Chapter 475, Florida Statutes (F.S.), individuals engaged in the purchase or sale of a business for a fee must hold a Florida real estate license.

Differences from Real Estate Brokerage

You should be aware of some important differences between business brokerage and real estate brokerage. One difference is business brokerage may involve the transfer of assets other than real estate, such as personal property, corporate stock (of a corporation), and goodwill. Unlike real property that is unmovable, **personal property** is anything not categorized as real property, in that the item is movable. **Goodwill** refers to an intangible asset that usually reflects the following:

- the business's name recognition
- the business's customer base
- the business's employees

Additionally, the value of a business does not necessarily equal the value of the real estate. The value of a business as an operating entity is called the **going concern value**. This value is not just the value of the tangible property. Rather, it also includes intangible assets, such as goodwill, trademarks, patents, copyrights, etc.

Another difference is purchasers of businesses tend to consider a larger geographic area than the typical home buyer. Therefore, as a result of the aforementioned statement, it is safe to conclude that markets for business enterprises are typically wider in geographic scope and reach than markets for individual parcels of real estate.

Expertise

Because business brokerage differs from real estate brokerage, business brokerage requires special expertise in other areas. For example, a licensee engaged in business brokerage must have a clear understanding of the following:

- tax laws
- business accounting
- corporate finance (the ability to analyze financial statements)
- valuation of businesses to include use of:
  - comparable sales analysis (review of comparable sales of similar businesses if available)
  - cost approach (reproduction/replacement and depreciation analysis)
  - income capitalization analysis (income/capitalization analysis to calculate value)
  - **liquidation analysis** (analysis used to determine the value of a business under a forced or hurried sale)

The business broker or brokerage must also possess knowledge in business entity formation, including:

- corporations, whose value lies in stock value
- partnerships
- limited liability partnerships
- limited liability companies
- trusts

> ### Coaching Tips
>
> **Business Brokerage at a Glance**
>
> - Business brokerage is similar to real estate brokerage in that business brokerage almost always involves the sale of real property or the assignment of a lease.
> - Business brokerage may involve the transfer of assets other than real estate, such as personal property, corporate stock (of a corporation), and goodwill.
> - A Florida real estate license is required for both real estate brokerage and business brokerage.
> - The value of a business as an operating entity is called the going concern value.
> - Purchasers of businesses tend to consider a larger geographic area than the typical home buyer.

STEPS IN THE SALE OF A BUSINESS

The following are some of the steps that would take place during the sale of a business:

1. The business is listed.
2. The business assets are determined.
3. An estimated value for the business is determined. This is achieved by a review of the business financial statements.
4. The value of all liabilities is subtracted from the estimated value of the business.
5. If the business is a corporation, the value of the business is divided by the total number of shares of stock to determine the value per share. The value per share is multiplied by the number of shares to be sold.
6. Compliance with applicable laws must be verified.

7. The business is marketed.
8. A buyer is located.
9. Closing takes place.

Valuation of a Business

As just mentioned, one of the steps in the sale of a business is estimating the value of the business. The methods of appraising a business are similar to the methods of appraising real property. These methods are listed below:

- Comparable sales analysis—The process of comparing the business being appraised to similar businesses that have sold recently.
- Cost approach—The process of estimating value based on the current cost to reproduce or replace the improvements.
- Income capitalization analysis—The process of estimating the income a business can be expected to produce and converting that into an estimated value using a capitalization rate.
- Liquidation analysis—The process of estimating the assets, liabilities, and amount the business could be sold for in the event the business is terminated or goes bankrupt.

It is important to note that lenders are primarily interested in the liquidation value of a business than any other type of value analysis. Another acceptable term for liquidation value for businesses might be *book value*. A key element and ingredient in deriving valuation of a business is accomplished through a careful study of the business's financial statements.

Coaching Tips

Valuation Analysis at a Glance

- Comparable sales analysis involves comparing the business being appraised to similar businesses that have sold recently.
- The cost approach involves estimating value based on the current cost to reproduce or replace the improvements.
- Income capitalization analysis involves estimating the income a business can be expected to produce and converting that into an estimated value using a capitalization rate.
- Liquidation analysis involves estimating the assets, liabilities, and amount the business could be sold for in the event the business is terminated or goes bankrupt. It is also called book value.

Summary

Investors will park money in investments to achieve returns on those investments through their cash flows. Real property is a popular vehicle that houses investments. Prior to purchasing real property, investors are cautioned to analyze a variety of issues (risk) that directly affect the investment potential of the acquisition. Carelessness and complicity generally will lead to loss of invested capital. Licensees are advised to seek more education in this arena. A thorough understanding of cash flows becomes essential to successful investment.

Business brokerage creates opportunities for licensees to earn money. This field entails the purchase and sale of businesses and their respective assets. In Florida, anyone who engages in this practice for a fee must hold a real estate license. Knowledge is required in evaluating financial statements. This is required in order to derive the appropriate value of the business. Valuation of a business is derived in a similar manner to that of property valuation. The value is achieved through the application of the sales comparison approach, the cost approach, the income approach, or the liquidation approach to valuation. It will also involve the use of financial statements.

Review Questions

1. There are many reasons why investors choose to invest in real property. Which of the following would NOT be a correct statement?
   a. It provides a good rate of return.
   b. It acts as a hedge against inflation.
   c. The taxpayer receives tax deductions from interest and taxes paid.
   d. It is a liquid investment.

2. Risk is the possibility of losing some portion, or possibly all, of your investment. One type of risk associated with property investment is the possibility that the property will not generate enough money to cover the operating costs of the property. This type of risk is known as:
   a. business risk
   b. financial risk
   c. purchasing power risk
   d. safety risk

3. Investors may believe the greatest advantage of investing in property is leverage. Leverage is defined as:
   a. Your property pays all its own bills, such as the insurance, taxes, and all maintenance costs
   b. Your property is paying back the money you borrowed in order to make the purchase
   c. The tax advantages you gained allow you to shelter income from the property from tax payments
   d. The use of borrowed funds to purchase the property and to maximize returns

4. All of the following are steps in the sale of a business EXCEPT:
   a. the business sale is recorded with the county clerk
   b. the business assets are determined
   c. an estimated value for the business is determined
   d. the value of all liabilities is subtracted from the estimated value of the business

5. Which of the following makes real property investment unique?
   a. the influence of the national economy
   b. fluctuations in the cost of money
   c. changes in the tax codes that may reduce after tax cash flow
   d. the local nature of property markets

6. Which of the following would be considered the most active type of real property purchase?
   a. shopping centers
   b. office buildings
   c. residential property
   d. industrial property

7. Limiting the uses allowed for land in any community is governed by:
   a. federal land-use laws
   b. the rights of individual states
   c. municipal zoning requirements
   d. overall county ordinances

8. Christian borrowed the bulk of the money he used to purchase an apartment complex. He anticipates that income activities derived from the property will not only pay all the expenses associated with his ownership but will also yield additional funds to invest in another property. The additional funds he hopes to use can best be classified in business terms as:
   a. return on investment
   b. refinancing
   c. before-tax cash flow
   d. equity buildup

9. The amount attributable to the property (which is usually the purchase price or adjusted purchase price) by the Internal Revenue Service for the purpose of calculating annual depreciation allowances and the capital gain or loss is the:
   a. acquisition cost
   b. book value
   c. depreciable value
   d. basis

10. All of the following would be considered good will EXCEPT:
    a. the business's name recognition
    b. the business's customer base
    c. the business's employees
    d. the business's bank accounts

11. A financial analysis would include all of the following EXCEPT:
    a. an income versus expense analysis (cash flow analysis)
    b. an examination of current leases
    c. a regional market analysis
    d. any present and future local law compliance issues

12. An annual return on the investor's invested capital represents:
    a. the return on investment
    b. the return of the principal investment
    c. the equity dividend rate
    d. the cash break-even rate

13. Capital gain realized in a single tax year is subject to which of the following:
    a. long-term capital gains tax
    b. short-term capital gains tax
    c. recapture tax rate of 25%
    d. both a and c

14. Under Chapter 475, F.S., individuals engaged in the purchase or sale of a business for a fee:
    a. need not hold a Florida real estate license
    b. must hold a Florida real estate license
    c. must hold a Florida business broker license
    d. both a and c

15. knowledge of business entity formation would include all of the following EXCEPT:
    a. corporations whose value lies in stock value
    b. partnerships
    c. limited liability partnerships
    d. joint ventures

16. Liquidity refers to:
    a. the ability to convert an asset into cash by selling it
    b. the amount of borrowed funds
    c. the amount of equity in the property
    d. none of these

17. Industrial property includes all of the following uses EXCEPT:
    a. recreation
    b. heavy manufacturing
    c. light manufacturing
    d. loft buildings

18. All of the following are advantages of real property investment EXCEPT:
    a. a good rate of return
    b. it is a liquid investment
    c. a hedge against inflation
    d. equity buildup

19. When appraising real property, an appraiser must use all three approaches to appraisal. In addition to these three approaches, which of the following approaches to value would be used when performing a business appraisal?
    a. insurance valuation
    b. replacement cost
    c. liquidation analysis
    d. assessed valuation

20. All of the following are disadvantages of real property investment EXCEPT:
    a. illiquidity
    b. market conditions
    c. the need for property management
    d. it is a liquid investment

18 TAXES AFFECTING REAL ESTATE

KEY TERMS

ad valorem
assessment limitation (Save Our Homes benefit)
assessed value
capital gains
community development districts
debt service
exempt properties
installment sale
immune properties
just value
like-kind exchange
mill
special assessment
tax rates
taxable income
taxable value

LEARNING OBJECTIVES

After completing this lesson, you will be able to:

- distinguish among immune, exempt, and partially exempt property
- describe the various personal exemptions available to qualified owners of homestead property
- compute the property tax on a specific parcel, given the current tax rate, assessed value, eligible exemptions, and transfer of assessment limitation difference (Save Our Homes portability), if applicable
- list the steps involved in the tax appeal process
- describe the purpose of Florida's Green Belt law
- calculate the cost of a special assessment, given the conditions and amounts involved
- describe the advantages of home ownership
- explain how to determine taxable income of investment real estate
- distinguish between installment sales and like-kind exchange

REAL PROPERTY TAXATION—LOCAL IMPORTANCE

Real property taxation is a primary source of revenue for both state and local governments. The federal government does not have the authority to tax real property directly; however, it does have the authority to tax the sale of real property by charging a tax on all capital gains.

In addition, other state and local sources of revenue include but are not limited to:

- sales tax
- income tax
- public utility revenues—revenue sources received from public utilities. For example, in Hollywood, Florida, these sources include but are not limited to:
  - water supply
  - wastewater
  - system connection charges
  - large user sales
- user taxes—a tax due on use or consumption of taxable goods and/or services that is not paid but owed at time of sale or service

Determination of "Just Value"

There are two categories of taxes on real property:

1. Ad valorem taxes—the general tax that every property owner in Florida is assessed
2. Special assessment taxes—an improvement tax that is only assessed to the property owners in the tax district that benefits from an improvement

Ad Valorem Taxes

Ad valorem taxes are based on the value of land and the improvements to the land. **Ad valorem** is a Latin term that means "according to valuation." Ad valorem taxes are assessed on real property on a regular basis (usually annually) and are used by the government as a primary source of revenue to fund government operations.

The **assessed value** of property is the value for the purpose of determining property taxes. Florida law has established that assessed value is based on **just value**, or the fair market value of the property. It should be noted that assessed value may not always reflect the property's market value. In addition, there may be times where assessed value is greater than market value; however, for the most part, the market value is greater than the assessed value. In some other states, assessed value is a percentage of the market value. In Florida, assessed values are established annually. The county property appraiser is given the task of establishing the assessed value through an appraisal. For most parcels, this involves the following:

- a careful review of the property characteristics
- an analysis of highest and best use
- the application of the three approaches to value (sales comparison, cost, and income—see Chapter 16)

When the county property tax appraiser is reviewing an income-producing property, the income capitalization approach will most likely be used to determine the assessed value. In many states, the taxing authority relies on operating income and expense statements. In these states, property owners are required to submit operating statements to the assessor. This enables the assessor to appropriately capitalize the net operating income attributable to that property to arrive at a value conclusion.

Some of the information that would be included and reviewed to determine the assessed value of an income-producing property would be:

- occupancy
- vacancy information
- rents received
- leasing incentives (such as rent abatement)
- expenses being paid

Amendment I (Property Tax)

On January 29, 2008, Florida passed an amendment on the treatment of property tax. The amendment comes in four parts:

1. Homestead exemption was increased from $25,000 to $50,000. It does not apply to school taxes.
2. Portability provided property owners ability to transfer benefits derived by Save Our Homes (SOH). The limit of transfer is up to:
   a. $500,000 to a new homestead within two years of relinquishing the previous homestead.
   b. Entire cap value is permitted to be transferred even if the just value of the new homestead is greater than the relinquished one.
   c. When a new homestead's value is less than the new homestead, the percentage of benefits may be transferred to the new one.
   d. SOH benefits may be used toward a new homestead anywhere in Florida within two years of the former homestead as long as the new one is created by January 1.
      i. This provision applies to all taxes, including school taxes.

3. Personal property exemption:
   a. Each tangible personal property tax return receives a $25,000 exemption and this applies to all taxes.
   b. Eligibility begins with completion of individual annual Tangible Personal Property Return by April 1.
4. Non-homestead property assessment cap
   a. Annual limit of 10% assessment cap (resembles SOH)
   b. Does not apply to school taxes
   c. Cap is removed when a property changes ownership or changes use
   d. Expires after 10 years unless subsequently reapproved by voters

Save Our Homes

In Florida, assessed values are updated annually. The SOH amendment to the state constitution restricts the amount the assessed value of homestead property can increase (**assessment limitation**). The increase in assessed value of a homestead is limited to the lesser of:

- 3% over the preceding year's assessed value
- the percentage change in the Consumer Price Index

When the property is transferred, these limits are lifted and the property is assessed at its just value. Thus, in some cases, the assessed value may rise significantly when property is sold or otherwise transferred (if the property value had increased significantly during the seller's ownership). As of calendar year 2005, sellers of residential property (as defined by 475, F.S.) in Florida are required to provide a buyer with a property tax disclosure. This disclosure primarily is intended to inform the buyer of the following important information:

- The property tax amount at the time of sale may not be the same amount in the subsequent year following the sale.
- A reassessment may also be triggered as a result of the sale.

Grievance Process for Contesting Property

Tax Assessments

Most of any county's revenue is derived from property taxes. Therefore, as you have previously learned, the job of the county appraiser is to assess the value of property for the purpose of taxation. In Florida as in other states, property taxes are used to fund the operations of local and state government.

On occasion, the county property appraiser may establish an assessed value that the owner does not consider fair and accurate. Under the law, the property owner has the right to contest the assessment derived by the county property appraiser by taking the following steps:

- Step 1:

    In Florida, a property owner is given an opportunity to contest the findings of the county property appraiser within 25 days after the notice of assessment is mailed. The owner or his/her representative will go before the county property appraiser's office to obtain a reduction determination. The property owner is then given a chance to argue and present the facts as to why a property assessment reduction is appropriate. During this process, the property owner may appear on his/her own behalf or have a representative appear for him/her. Representatives may include, but are not limited to:

    - another appraiser hired by the property owner
    - a lawyer
    - a property tax reduction service representative

- Step 2:

    In the event that the county property appraiser's office rejects the request for reduction, the property owner has the right to appeal the findings of the county property appraiser's office by going before the Value Adjustment Board. The board itself is comprised of five elected members.

- Step 3:

    The board will determine whether or not the appeal should be granted or denied. If granted, the board has the power to adjust the assessment accordingly. If denied, the property owner is left with only one final alternative—litigation. An a certiorari proceeding occurs in court. This proceeding is a formal litigation appeal process and the final relief that is available to a taxpayer. The court will either uphold previous determinations or will order a reassessment of the property, which may or may not yield net tax relief to the taxpayer.

Coaching Tips

Property Tax Grievance Process at a Glance

There are three ways an owner can contest a property tax assessment:

1. Within 25 days after the notice of assessment is mailed, the owner or the owner's representative can go before the county property appraiser's office to obtain a reduction determination.
2. If the request for reduction is rejected, the owner can appeal the findings of the county property appraiser's office by going before the Value Adjustment Board.
3. If the appeal is rejected by the board, the owner has another alternative—litigation by way of an a certiorari proceeding.

Immune and Exempt Properties

Certain properties are immune (nontaxable) from taxation, including:

- government-owned buildings
- other property designated as immune includes properties such as municipal airports and military bases

Immune properties are not subject to taxation.

Other properties are exempt (or partially exempt) from taxation. **Exempt properties** are subject to taxation, but the owner is not obligated to pay all (or part) of the taxes. Examples of exempt properties include:

- property owned by churches and charitable organizations (as long as it is used for a religious or charitable purpose)
- homesteads
- property owned by widows or widowers, individuals who are blind, or individuals with other disabilities

Let's look at some of the types of exempt properties.

Homestead Exemption

An owner of real property in Florida is entitled to claim his/her primary residence as a homestead. A $50,000 real property tax exemption is available for anyone who qualifies for the exemption. This $50,000 exemption is applied only against the assessed valuation of the home. Although a property owner may own more than one home in Florida, only one property may be eligible for the homestead exemption.

To qualify, the property owner must have owned the property as of January 1 and must show proof of ownership to the county property appraiser's office no later than March 1. Let's look at how the homestead exemption works. Here is the formula for calculating property tax that includes a homestead:

$$\begin{aligned}
&\text{Assessed Property Value} \\
&-\text{ Granted Homestead Exemption} \\
&=\text{ Property Value Subject to Taxation} \\
&\times\text{ Mill Rate/Tax Rate} \\
\hline
&=\text{ Annual Tax}
\end{aligned}$$

Example Assume a property has an assessed value of $100,000, and the owner qualifies for the homestead exemption. The **taxable value** of the property is calculated by subtracting the exemption from the assessed value:

$$\begin{aligned}
&\$125{,}000 \text{ Assessed Value} \\
&\underline{\$\ 50{,}000 \text{ Homestead Exemption}} \\
&-\ \$\ 75{,}000 \text{ Taxable Value}
\end{aligned}$$

Thus, the amount of the property tax will be based on the taxable value, not the assessed value.

Blind Individuals Exemption

Persons who are legally blind are entitled to a $500 property tax exemption. This exemption is in addition to the $50,000 homestead exemption. Thus, if an individual is legally blind and qualifies for a homestead exemption, the total property tax exemption is $50,500.

Surviving Spouse Exemption

A spouse of a deceased individual is entitled to an additional $500 property tax exemption. However, the exemption ceases if that person remarries.

Disability Exemption

A person who is considered 10% or more disabled as a result of a disability incurred while in military service is entitled to an additional $5,000 property tax exemption. Persons who are totally and permanently disabled due to disabilities incurred in military service are entitled to a total exemption from property taxes. Certain totally and permanently disabled nonveterans may also qualify for total exemption from property taxes (such as a quadriplegic). Upon the death of the disabled veteran, this benefit may extend to the widow's or widower's spouse.

It should be noted that in 2001, the Florida legislature provided the right, but not the obligation, to grant additional exemptions on homestead taxes to persons 65 years of age or older who reside within a low-income household.

Coaching Tips

Property Tax at a Glance

- Immune properties are not subject to taxation.
- Exempt properties are subject to taxation, but the owner is not obligated to pay all (or part) of the taxes.
- The homestead exemption is available to Florida resident(s) on their primary residence.
    - The amount of a full homestead exemption is $50,000.
    - The exemption is $500 for individuals who are blind, widows, or widowers.

Individuals who are 10% or more disabled due to a service-related disability are entitled to an additional $5,000 property tax exemption.

Green Belt Law Exemption

Florida has a law known as the Green Belt law. This law provides favorable tax treatment for agricultural properties. Under this law, the assessed value must be based on the property's current agricultural use and not the highest and best use of the property. In some cases, agricultural land may be located in an area where the property would have a much higher value if it were converted to another use (such as commercial, current agricultural use aka value in use). Thus, the law provides benefits (but is not an exemption) for farmers by reducing their potential tax bills. Any change in how the property is classified must be filed prior to March 1 of any year. In the event the classification change is denied, the property owner may seek relief through the property tax grievance process.

A Greenbelt classification provides for:

- continuance of agricultural activities (provides farmers with the ability to grow agricultural products)
- environmental benefits including items such as:
    - clean water and air
    - open space
    - wildlife
    - recreational use

Provisions include:

- Filing form DR-482, Application and Return for Agricultural Classification of Lands, between January 1 and March 1, with the property appraiser in the county where the property is located.
- A Greenbelt Classification will not transfer automatically to the new owner.
- Statutory requirements are found in F.S. 193.461.
- The property must be used for agricultural purposes, defined as:
    - good-faith commercial agricultural use
    - length of time in agricultural use
    - continuity of use
    - size of property
    - leases
    - indicated efforts
    - other occasionally applicable factors
    - no minimum number required of:
        - acreage
        - livestock
        - pine trees
        - number of orchard trees

Overview of Establishing the Real Property Tax

State and local governments are funded by many sources of revenue, including sales tax, income tax, public utility revenues, and real property taxes. In most places throughout the country, real property taxes act as the largest revenue source to fund the government. In Florida, where there is no individual state income tax, property taxes become essential toward funding the government. The following districts rely on taxes for funding:

- county
- city
- special districts
- schools

Each of these districts submits its request for annual budgeting. Each taxing unit uses separate **tax rates** that relate to its financial operational needs. The sum total of all the budgets, once approved, becomes the annual fiscal budget. Revenues must be collected to fund the budget. Real property taxes come from the district's tax base, which is the total taxable value of all real property in the district. The end result of the aggregate of each taxing unit is the property tax bill.

The **mill** rate (or millage rate) is the rate of taxation on the taxable value. The mill rate is expressed as thousandths of a dollar. One mill equals 1/1,000 of one dollar. (One mill also equals 1/10 of one cent.)

To convert the mill rate to dollars, divide the number of mills by 1,000. For example, 40 mills equals 0.04 dollars:

$$40 \div 1,000 = 0.04$$

Conversely, to convert dollars to mills, multiply the dollars by 1,000. For example, 0.008 dollars equal 8 mills:

$$0.008 \times 1,000 = 8$$

The millage rate is set by the local government entity by dividing the amount of revenue needed from property taxes by the total taxable value of all real property in the district. The total amount of revenue needed from real property is equal to the annual fiscal budget less any nonproperty tax revenue. This is shown in the following formula:

$$\frac{\text{Annual Fiscal Budget} - \text{Nonproperty Tax Revenue}}{\text{Total Taxable Value}}$$

Let's look at an example.

Assume the annual budget for the county is $16,500,000, and revenues from sources other than real property taxes equal $500,000. If the taxable value of real property in the county equals $2,000,000,000, then the tax rate is calculated using the following formula:

$$\frac{\$16{,}500{,}000 - \$500{,}000}{\$2{,}000{,}000{,}000}$$

The tax rate in this case is 0.008 per dollar of taxable value, or 8 mills.

Once the property is assessed and the mill rate is set, taxes can be computed for a given property using the following formula:

$$\begin{aligned}
&\text{Assessed Value} \\
-\ &\underline{\text{Exemption, if any}} \\
=\ &\text{Taxable Value} \\
&\underline{\text{Mill Rate}} \\
=\ &\text{Taxes to Be Paid}
\end{aligned}$$

Let's look at an example.

Assume that the owner of a property qualifies for a homestead exemption and the assessed value is $100,000. If the mill rate is 8 mills, the taxes for the property are computed as follows:

$$\begin{aligned}
&\$100{,}000 && \text{Assessed Value} \\
-\ &\underline{\$\ \ 25{,}000} && \text{Exemption} \\
&\$\ \ 75{,}000 && \text{Taxable Value} \\
\times\ &\underline{0.008} && \text{Mill Rate (8 mills)} \\
&\$\ \ \ \ \ 600 && \text{Taxes to Be Paid}
\end{aligned}$$

The above mill rate (8 mills) is given as an example only. The actual rate may vary from area to area.

Truth-in-Millage (TRIM)

Tax laws require the county tax offices to mail the assessed value and the millage rates for the county, municipality, and school board prior to the actual rendering of the tax bills. This is done to give the property owner time to determine whether or not over-assessment has occurred as well as to file a grievance. This notice is referred to as the truth-in-millage (TRIM) notice.

Ad valorem taxes in Florida are levied on a calendar-year basis. The tax year begins on January 1 and ends on December 31. Ad valorem taxes are paid in arrears, which means they are paid at the end of the tax year. Thus, although taxes are levied on January 1 and a lien is placed on the property on that date, the taxes can be paid any time during the tax year without penalty or late fee. Ad valorem tax liens have priority over all other property tax liens.

Taxes can be paid in a variety of ways, such as in one payment or in four installments. If a taxpayer pays the taxes promptly, the municipality may make a discount available. Taxes are delinquent if they are not paid by April 1 of the following year. If property taxes are not paid when due, the property may be sold to pay for the taxes.

Special Assessment Taxes

Special assessment taxes are improvement taxes that are levied to fund a specific project that benefits only some of the citizens in a government jurisdiction known as **community development districts**. Examples of uses for special assessment taxes would include but not be limited to:

- street paving in a neighborhood
- water and sewer installation
- street lights for a street or neighborhood

The amount of the tax is based on the benefits received, not necessarily on the value of the property owned. Special assessment taxes are usually collected in a series of payments spread over a period of years and assessed on the basis of the front footage (on the mapped road/street) of the property.

When the assessments have been paid off, the special assessment district is dissolved and the tax is terminated. Special assessment tax liens take priority over all liens except ad valorem tax liens.

In some cities, special assessments take the form of Business Improvement Districts (BIDs). The intent is to create jobs while improving the health, safety, and welfare of the general public. Only the affected area where municipal improvement takes place is responsible for a special assessment.

As a helpful hint, think of a municipal special assessment in the same manner as a special assessment charged by a cooperative condominium or a homeowners association (HOA). Special assessments on the aforementioned examples will only occur when improvements to the property have been made. The special assessment in a condominium, cooperative or HOA represents a lien on the subject property until all special assessments are paid.

Coaching Tips

Property tax means both ad valorem and special assessment.

- Special assessment taxes are used for specific projects.
- Size and front footage are only two of the factors that affect value.
- Cost may or may not be related to current value.
- Improvements attached to land are also real property.
- The value established for the purpose of determining taxes is called assessed value.
- The county property appraiser is given the task of establishing the assessed value through an appraisal.

Nonpayment of Real Property Tax and Tax Certificates

On April 1 of any given year, real property taxes become delinquent in Florida. A late fee is assessed at a percentage of the delinquent amount. In May, tax delinquencies are advertised in the local newspapers at least once per week for three weeks. These advertising costs will also accrue on top of the delinquent tax amount. On June 1 the tax collector is compelled by law to hold a tax certificate sale/auction. A tax certificate is a lien on unpaid/delinquent property tax. It is not title to property. When sold, it represents a sum derived from:

1. amount of unpaid tax
2. late fee assessed by municipality
3. advertising costs
4. tax sale costs

To the purchaser of a tax certificate, interest accrues in the manner of simple interest monthly. Redemption of a tax certificate by a delinquent property owner requires the payment amount to include

- the cost of the certificate to the investor
- all interest accrued to date of redemption

FEDERAL INCOME TAX

The federal government has the authority to tax income. There are basically three categories of income that a taxpayer may earn during the course of a tax year:

1. active income
2. passive income
3. portfolio income

Exempt income is income that is not subject to taxation.

> ### Coaching Tips
>
> This chapter provides a brief overview of the federal tax issues related to real property. In many real situations, the necessary calculations will be much more complex than those covered in this chapter. In any situation, it is advisable that the taxpayer seek the advice of a professional tax advisor.

Active Income

Active income includes compensation derived directly from employment activities, such as:

- salary/wages
- commissions
- gratuities

Passive Income

Passive income encompasses income from a business activity or investment where the individual is passive and not actively in charge of the day-to-day management of that investment. All real and personal property investments fall into the category of passive unless the taxpayer is an active participant (meaning that it is their occupation). Examples include:

- limited partnerships
- income from income-producing real property investments where the individual receives profits but is not actively engaged in the real estate business
- profits from the sale of stocks
- any other investment where the taxpayer is not participating in an active role

Portfolio Income

Portfolio income represents income derived from passive investment holdings. The portfolio holdings can be either real or personal property and include such items as:

- stock dividends
- interest earned on deposits or loans
- royalties earned on intellectual property
- annuities

Coaching Tips

Categories of Federal Taxable Income at a Glance

- Active income refers to compensation derived from employment, such as wages/salary, commissions, and/or gratuities.
- Passive income is income from a business activity or investment where the individual is passive and not actively in charge of the day-to-day management of that activity or investment.
- Portfolio income is income derived from stock dividends, interest, royalties, and annuities.
- Exempt income refers to income not subject to taxation.

FEDERAL INCOME TAX AND REAL PROPERTY

There are two major issues involving federal income tax and real property:

1. whether or not certain items may be deducted when calculating income tax due
2. how income tax is calculated when real estate is sold

How these issues are handled depends on whether you are an individual who owns a home or a business or investor who owns property.

Deductions

Expenses related to real estate ownership may be deducted from income when calculating income taxes. The list of items that can be deducted depends on whether you are an owner/occupant of a home or the owner of a business or investment property (see Figure 18.1). Let's compare these by looking at a list of what is deductible in the two situations.

An individual who owns a home may deduct the following items from his/her income to determine the taxable income:

- property taxes
- mortgage interest, including:
  - origination fees to obtain a mortgage (i.e., points)

When loans require the borrower to pay upfront charges (origination fees), these charges are deductible in the year that they are incurred. These origination fees are paid to the lender and act as a form of pre-paid interest. These fees enhance the yield to the lender. However, this does not apply to refinanced loans. In this situation, the borrower is required to recover or amortize the same over the life of the loan. He/she may only deduct that portion as it relates to the term of the loan (i.e., 5-year loan, deduct 20% per year) In essence, the points are amortized over the remaining term or life of the loan. Interest on home equity mortgages up to $100,000. Interest on loans exceeding $100,000 is not eligible as a deduction.

It is important to note that real property acquisition closing costs are not deductible on residential owner-occupant and commercial transactions. In each case, closing costs must be added to the property purchase price and forms the property's adjusted tax basis.

For example, a property sells for $480,000, and the buyer spends $20,000 in closing costs for legal fees, accounting fees, appraisal fees, survey fee, title insurance, and other related costs. The adjusted sales price or tax basis would be $500,000.

IRA Withdrawal

Many taxpayers are unaware that anyone who falls under the definition of a first-time home buyer may withdraw from his/her IRA up to $10,000 without penalty

REAL ESTATE ASPECTS OF THE TAX REFORM ACT 1986, TAX REVENUE ACT 1987, TAXPAYER RELIEF ACT OF 1997, AND OTHER RECENT REVISIONS

Summary of Rules for Homeowners

1. Mortgage interest deductions are allowed for acquisition debt (purchase money loan) up to a maximum loan of $1 million on all combined mortgages on a first and second residence. If you borrow more than $1 million, the interest paid on the excess over $1 million is not deductible. No interest deduction is allowed for three or more personal-use homes.
2. For the refinance of an existing home, the remaining loan balance on acquisitions loan(s) plus $100,000 will be the maximum refinance loan allowed if the homeowner wishes to deduct all the interest as a qualified home loan. However, if a refinance loan exceeds the home's value, a portion of the interest paid is not deductible.
3. The $250,000 for singles and $500,000 for joint-filing married couples exemption noted on previous pages are still valid.
4. Installment sale treatment is still allowed for homeowners.

Summary of Rules for Income Property Owners

1. Depreciation (cost recovery) on buildings and improvements is 27½ years for residential rental and longer periods for nonresidential rental. The straight-line method must be used.
2. Rental property mortgage interest is fully deductible against rental income, with no dollar loan limits such as the $1 million cap placed on homeowners. However, any tax loss created by interest and depreciation deductions fall under the passive tax loss rules listed herein.
3. Real estate rentals are considered "passive" investments and produce either passive income or passive loss, depending on the property's cash flow. The general rule is that a passive real estate loss can only be used to offset other passive income, NOT active or portfolio income such as salaries, commissions, profits, interest, and dividends. Prior to tax law changes, real estate losses could be used to offset active or portfolio income.
4. Special $25,000 exception to the passive loss rules if a person meets the following test:
    a. Is an individual owner of 10 percent or more interest in rental real estate
    b. Is actively involved in the management (owner can use property managers but he or she must make the key decisions)
    c. Has a modified adjusted gross income of $100,000 or less
    If the owner of rental real estate meets this test, he or she can use up to $25,000 in passive losses from real estate to offset active or portfolio income, such as salaries and interest, after first offsetting passive income.
5. If the rental property owner's modified adjusted gross income exceeds $100,000, the $25,000 amount is reduced $1 for every $2 above the $100,000. Any unused passive losses from rental real estate can be carried forward to reduce future passive income and gain upon sale of the property. The passive loss rules do not eliminate the investor's right to use real estate losses. However, the law's changes will, in some cases, delay the right to use the loss until a later date, such as the date of resale.
6. The right for a real estate investor to do a 1031 tax-deferred exchange remains the same; recent tax law changes have not eliminated this technique.
7. Installment sales treatment for real estate investors is still allowed. Installment sale treatment for real estate dealers has been abolished.

There are many other tax law changes, but these are the items that have a major impact on real estate. The preceding is listed for information purposes and should not be considered tax advice. For tax advice, a person should seek competent tax advisers.

FIGURE 18.1
Source: © 2021 Mbition LLC

to apply toward a down payment for the purchase of real property. However, the individual would have to pay income taxes on the $10,000 withdrawn.

A business or investor who owns property may deduct the following:

- property taxes
- mortgage interest

Note also that there are three additional items that may be deducted by a business or investor who owns property:

1. expenses of operation
2. depreciation
3. operational losses

These items are deductible on business/investment property but not on a personal residence.

Deductions on Residential Property Interest on Mortgage

With residential property, the interest paid during a year on all mortgages on first and second homes is deductible from income. Delinquent or late payments that are accrued by December 31 of each year are not deductible for that year. Extensive prepayment of interest is not allowed. Only interest due and payable by the end of the year plus one month can be claimed as a current deduction.

In addition, discount points charged on mortgage loans are considered prepaid interest. Therefore, discount points are deductible in the year that they are paid.

Local Property Taxes

On residential and commercial property, taxes are deductible in the year they are paid.

Uninsured Casualty Losses

Casualty losses occur by fire, theft, weather, earthquakes, floods, and other natural causes. Casualty losses that are not covered by insurance may be deductible from income in the year that they occur. An uninsured casualty loss is only deductible if it exceeds a $100 IRS deductible plus 10% of the taxpayer's adjusted gross income. For example, if a chandelier is stolen and it is not covered by insurance, the loss would be deductible in that year if the uninsured amount exceeds $100 plus 10% of the owner's adjusted gross income.

INVESTMENT REAL ESTATE

Investment property, with very few exceptions, is income-producing property. As a result, let's examine the formula used to calculate both:

1. cash flows—the cash transaction world
2. income tax—the income tax world

Step one:

      PGI (potential gross income)
- V&C (vacancy & collection)
+ OI (other income)
= EGI (effective gross income)

Represents Income minus Expenses

Step two:

      EGI (effective gross income)
- OE (operating expenses)
= NOI (net operating income/cash flow)
- ADS (annual debt service/mortgage)
= BTCF (aka, cash throw off/flow and is used to calculate the cash on cash return)
- IT (income tax)
= ATCF (after tax cash flow)

The aforementioned formula is explained in greater detail below:

(PGI) Potential gross income—income derived from an income-producing property viewed under the best of conditions (as 100% leased)

(– V&C) Vacancy and collection—an arbitrary investor percentage rate used to reflect market conditions and expectations of either:

1. vacancies that may arise in any given year
2. collection issues due to bad credit tenancies

(+OI) Other income—passive income derived from non-active property sources such as:

- parking income
- vending machines
- satellite dish income
- reimbursed expenses
- submetering of electric

(= EGI) Effective gross income—is the income after making deductions for vacancy/collections and adding in any other income.

What we just learned represents the income side of the equation. Now let's examine the expense side of the equation.

Calculating the Net Operating Income (NOI)

In order to derive the net operating income (NOI), operating expenses are deducted from the effective gross income (EGI), but first let's define fixed versus variable expenses. Fixed expenses consist of two categories:

1. real property tax
2. real property insurance

These are considered fixed expenses as they are unaffected by leasing/occupancy/vacancy levels. However, all other property expense items are considered variable. These variable expenses include repairs, utilities, cleaning, and garbage removal. As leasing/occupancy/vacancy levels increase or decrease, variable expenses will move in the same direction.

We just learned that:

> (EGI) Effective gross income
> (– OE) Operating expenses
> (– RR) Reserves for replacements
> (= NOI) Net operating income (property cash flow)

Now we will calculate the before tax cash flow by subtracting any annual **debt service**/mortgage costs (periodic, usually monthly, interest and principal payments) from the NOI:

(NOI) Net operating income
(– ADS) Annual debt service
= (BTCF) Before-tax cash flow (cash throw-off/used to calculate the cash on cash return aka equity dividend rate)

Finally, to derive the after-tax cash flow, income taxes are subtracted from the BTCF:

> (BTCF) Before-tax cash flow
> (– IT) Income tax
> (= ATCF) After-tax cash flow

Determining Taxable Income

The first step toward determining **taxable income** starts with the NOI. Earlier when we deducted the operating expenses, this also included amounts set aside as reserves for replacements. A reserve is cash on hand intended to effectuate a major capital improvement or replacement program that NOI will not be able to fund. It is important to note that a reserve is not an operating expense and as such the calculation, when reserves have been deducted in the cash transaction world, begins with adding the reserve deducted back into the NOI. This will result in adjusted net operating income as shown below:

> (NOI) Net operating income
> (+ RR) Reserve for replacements
> (= ANOI) Adjusted net operating income

From here,

- mortgage interest (MI)
- annual depreciation (AD) (explained next) and
- any carryover/suspended losses are deducted from the ANOI (previous losses passive in nature that must be brought forward. Annual allowance is $3,000 in the absence of passive gains.)

(ANOI) Adjusted net operating income
(– MI) mortgage interest
(– AD) Annual depreciation
(– CSL) Carryover/suspended loss
(= TI) Taxable income

The final step to calculating the income tax is to multiply the taxable income against the income tax rate (ITR):

(TI) Taxable income
(× ITR) Income tax rate
(= IT) Income tax

Deductions on Business/Investment Property

With business or investment property, mortgage interest, local property taxes, and uninsured casualty losses are deductible in the year they are paid. The rules for some of these are different than for a personal residence, but the differences are beyond the scope of this course. There are also some items that can be deducted with business/investment property but not with personal residences. Let's look at two of these deductions:

1. expenses of operation
2. depreciation

Expenses of Operation

With business or investment property, certain expenses of operation are deductible in the year they are paid, including:

- repairs to the property
- maintenance costs, such as for repair of appliances
- insurance
- management fees
- utilities

Note that the list does not include vacancy losses, which are not deductible.

Depreciation

Depreciation is a deduction for business/investment property but not deducted for a personal residence. In the investment world, depreciation is also commonly referred to as cost recovery. Depreciation is a loss due to three events:

1. physical deterioration
2. functional obsolescence
3. external obsolescence

Depreciation is a tax deduction that is based on the concept that all property loses its value over time because the property ages and must be replaced. Consequently, the tax law allows a business or investor to deduct the cost of the property over a period of years. Remember, this deduction cannot be taken on a personal residence.

Note that depreciation is a tax issue and does not mean the property will actually lose its value or require replacement at the end of the depreciation period. In fact, the property will usually appreciate (increase in value) rather than depreciate (decrease in value) over the period the property is depreciated for tax purposes. Nevertheless, the owner is allowed to deduct an amount for depreciation when computing taxes. For tax purposes, depreciation can be thought of as the deduction of a certain percentage of the cost of any improvements to land over a period of years set by the tax law. (An example of an improvement is a building.)

Note that depreciation is based only on the cost of improvements to real estate, not the land itself. Land is never depreciated.

Depreciation is allowed on all improvements, including fruit and nut trees, as well as more familiar improvements, like buildings. Depreciation is not a choice for the taxpayer. The IRS requires the property owner depreciate the permanent improvement(s) made to property. Land is never depreciable. A good way to separate the value of improvements from the value of the land itself is by using the property tax assessment statement from the municipality as an example. The tax assessment is broken down into two categories—the value of the land itself and the value of any improvements to the land. When a property is assessed for tax purposes when it is sold, these values will reveal the original cost of the land and improvements. Now let's look at an example.

A residential rental property was purchased for $100,000. The value of the land included in this purchase price was $20,000.

In this situation, the land value is 20% of the total value of the property ($20,000 ÷ $100,000 = 0.20, or 20%). Thus, the value of the improvements amounts to 80% of the total value of the property.

In addition to the $100,000 purchase price, there are other costs associated with acquiring the property, including attorney fees, appraisals, surveys, etc.

Collectively, these costs are referred to as the cost of acquisition or closing costs. Assume the following cost of acquisition for our example:

$6,000 Commissions
$4,000 Legal Fees
$1,500 Appraisal
+$ 900 Survey
$12,400 Cost of Acquisition

The total cost to acquire the property is equal to the purchase price plus the cost of acquisition:

$100,000 Purchase Price
+$ 12,400 Cost of Acquisition
$112,400 Total Cost to Acquire Property

Because depreciation is based on the improvements only (and not the land), we must determine how much of this total cost is attributed to the improvements.

As mentioned earlier, the improvement portion of the property is 80%. Therefore:

$112,400 Total Cost to Acquire Property
× 0.80 80% Improvement Portion
$ 89,920 Total Cost Attributed To Improvements

This amount is used to calculate depreciation and is referred to as the depreciable basis.

For residential rental property, the law allows the improvements to be depreciated over a period of 27.5 years.

The amount to be depreciated, $89,920, divided by 27.5 years gives an annual depreciation amount of $3,270. This amount may be deducted each year for depreciation.

There are different mathematical formulas for computing the amount of depreciation. The previous example used the simplest formula, called the straight-line method of depreciation, in which the amount of depreciation is the same each year. The straight-line method using the 27.5-year recovery period is used for residential rental property put into use after December 31, 1986. The straight-line method of depreciation is also used for some nonresidential (commercial) real property. However, the 27.5-year recovery period used for residential rental property is not used for nonresidential real property. The recovery period used for nonresidential real property depends on when the property was put into use. For nonresidential property put into use after May 13, 1993, the recovery period is 39 years.

Another method of calculating depreciation, called the accelerated method, can be used on some real property put into use before December 31, 1986. The primary difference is that this method results in greater values for depreciation in the early years and less depreciation in later years.

In this chapter, we looked at a few of the methods used to calculate depreciation. The remaining methods of calculating depreciation are beyond the scope of this course. The method that must be used for a particular property depends on the type of property (nonresidential versus residential rental property) and the date when the property was put into use. To determine which method applies to a particular property, an owner may need to consult a professional tax advisor.

Tax on Sale of Property

We just looked at the different real estate related expenses that may be deducted from income for tax purposes. The second major issue relating to real estate and income taxes is the payment of taxes on any profits made when real estate is sold.

When real property is sold, the profits that are made are called *gains*. Generally, gains from the sale of real property are **capital gains**, which are taxed. These taxes are called capital gains taxes. Later, we will look at the tax rate for capital gains. However, let's look first at how the amount of capital gain is determined when real property is sold. The procedure is slightly different for residential and business or investment property, so we will begin with residential property.

Capital gain is the difference between the amount realized on the sale of the property and the adjusted basis of the property:

$$\begin{array}{r} \text{Amount Realized} \\ - \underline{\text{Adjust Basis}} \\ \text{Capital Gain} \end{array}$$

Let's look at each of the terms in the formula for calculating capital gains in more detail.

The sales price of the home is obviously the price at which the home was sold. For tax purposes, however, certain expenses of the sale may be deducted from the sales price for determining profit. The result of these deductions is the amount realized.

The amount realized is the actual selling price of the property *less* the costs of the sale, including:

- real estate commissions
- any closing costs or points paid by the seller
- attorney fees
- survey costs

By subtracting these items from the sales price, the amount of profit for tax purposes is reduced by the amount of these expenses, which lowers the amount of tax that must be paid.

> ### Coaching Tips
>
> The costs of a sale are not deductible from the seller's income in the year they are paid unless the costs are interest expenses. One deductible interest expense is an interest prepayment penalty charged by a lender when the seller's mortgage is paid off after the home is sold.

The second item in the formula is the adjusted basis. The basis is simply the original cost of the home, including the cost of acquisition such as attorney fees, appraisal reports, etc. For tax purposes, this basis is adjusted for certain other expenses.

The adjusted basis equals the basis (purchase price and cost of acquisition) plus the cost of any capital improvements to the property, such as the addition of a room, swimming pool, patio, etc., or remodeling of a kitchen or bathroom. By adding these items to the basis, the amount of profit for tax purposes is reduced by the amount of these expenses, which lowers the amount of tax that must be paid.

By treating major improvements to the property as capital improvements, the costs of these items are not deductible from income in the year they are paid. In addition, the costs of these items increase the amount that is subject to depreciation, so their cost is depreciated over the life of the ownership.

Earlier, we pointed out that the computation for capital gains from the sale of real property differs for residential and business or investment property. Let's take a look at how the tax calculation differs in these two situations.

As you just learned, the amount of profit on residential property that is subject to taxation is calculated by the following formula:

$$\begin{array}{r} \text{Amount Realized} \\ - \underline{\text{Adjust Basis}} \\ \text{Capital Gain} \end{array}$$

There is only one difference in this formula when business or investment property is sold—how the adjusted basis is calculated.

As you learned earlier, the owner of a business or investment property is allowed to deduct from income an amount for depreciation each year the property is owned. In order to avoid double benefits for depreciation (which is taking deductions during the holding period and maintaining the same adjusted basis at time of sale), the formula for the adjusted basis must be modified. This modification entails subtracting the total amount of depreciation deducted during the ownership of the property from the adjusted basis. The modified formula is shown next along with the formula for residential property.

Residential Property	Business/Investment Property
Purchase Price	Purchase Price
+ Cost of Acquisition	+ Cost of Acquisition
+ Capital Improvements	+ Capital Improvements
Adjusted Basis	− Accumulated Depreciation
	Adjusted Basis

There are four more situations we will cover regarding income taxes:

1. exclusion of capital gains from the sale of a home
2. capital gains tax rates
3. installment sales
4. real estate exchanges

Exclusion of Capital Gains

Under the current tax law, some homeowners can exclude from their taxable income some or all of the gain they earn when they sell a home. Homeowners can exclude gain up to a maximum of $250,000 (or $500,000 if married filing a joint return). Because home prices have risen substantially over the past three decades, the $250,000/$500,000 exclusion of gain is an important tax break for many homeowners. In the next section of this chapter, we will look at this exclusion in more detail.

Qualifying Rules

To qualify for this exclusion, a homeowner must meet an ownership test and a use test.

Ownership Test

A homeowner must have owned the home for at least two years during the previous five-year period ending on the date of sale.

Use Test

A homeowner must have lived in the home as his/her principal residence for a period totaling two of the previous five years ending on the date of sale. This two-year period may be continuous or interrupted and the homeowner does not have to occupy the property as a principal residence on the date of sale. Temporary absences for vacations, hospital confinements, etc., count as periods of use even though the home may be rented out or occupied by others during such absences.

Amount of Exclusion

If a homeowner sells a personal residence, the homeowner may be permitted to exclude gain on the sale up to one of the following:

- $250,000
- $500,000 if all of the following conditions are true:
  - The homeowner is married and files a joint tax return for the year of the sale.
  - Either spouse meets the ownership test.
  - Both spouses meet the use test. (However, if only one spouse meets the use test, that spouse can exclude up to $250,000 of gain on a separate or joint return.)
  - Neither spouse is excluding gain from the sale of another home during the year. (However, if each spouse sells a home during the same year, each can exclude up to $250,000 of gain.)

Exercising the Exclusion

Typically, homeowners are only allowed to take the $250,000/$500,000 exclusion of gain once every two years. That is, a homeowner cannot exclude gain on the sale of a home if during the previous two-year period the homeowner sold another home and excluded all or part of the gain from the previous sale. Gain from the recent sale must be included in the homeowner's taxable income. However, the homeowner may be allowed to claim a reduced exclusion if the home was sold because of a change in health or place of employment. To learn more about claiming a reduced exclusion, taxpayers should consult the relevant IRS publications or an experienced tax advisor.

Prior to the enactment of the Taxpayer Fairness Act of 1997, homeowners 55 years of age or older enjoyed a once-in-a-lifetime tax exclusion on gain from the sale of their residences of up to $125,000. Even if this privilege was exercised, exclusion of gain under the current law is available to these homeowners. The $250,000/$500,000 exclusion is not a once-in-a-lifetime exclusion. If certain conditions are met, a homeowner can exercise this exclusion each time he/she sells a home.

Capital Gains Tax Rates

If a homeowner sells a home and does not qualify for the exclusion, capital gain from the sale is taxable. The maximum tax rate in 2017 on a capital gain depends on the bracket of income the individual is claiming status under the tax laws. The maximum capital gains tax rate that applies to a specific transaction depends on two factors:

1. the type of property sold
2. how long the property was held before the sale. (For example, gains from the sale of property owned for more than one year are categorized as long-term gains and are taxed at a maximum rate of 20% for high income earners making over $400,000 (single) and $450,000 (married filing jointly and 15% for taxpayers earning up to $400,000 for single earners and $450,000 for married filing jointly). Gains from the sale of property owned one year or less are categorized as short-term gains and are taxed at the taxpayer's ordinary income tax rate.

Currently, federal regulators are working to overhaul the complicated U.S. income tax system. The intention is to simplify filing, reduce fees for reporting, and lower the tax rate for corporations and individuals.

This book will not cover how to determine the capital gains tax rate for specific situations.

Installment Sales

In an **installment sale**, the seller receives payment for the property over a period of years. In this situation, the seller can avoid paying the entire amount of taxes on any gain from the sale in the year the sale took place. Rather, the seller can postpone the payment of taxes to future years, when the installment payments are actually received. This arrangement resembles a layaway plan. The buyer receives possession while making the installments under the contract, however, in this transaction, the seller holds the deed as collateral for total payment under the installment contract.

Real Estate Exchanges

Real estate exchanges may defer taxes that would otherwise be due if a property were sold. Exchanges of real property are often referred to as tax-free exchanges, but they are not really tax free; the tax payments are postponed. The correct term for exchanges is *tax deferred*. The only properties eligible for tax-deferred exchanges include real property held for investment, income, trade, or business. Personal residences are not eligible. (Residential investment property, such as an apartment complex, is eligible because it is considered investment property.) If properties are exchanged on a tax-deferred basis, both properties must be one of these eligible types of properties. (This is referred to as a **like-kind exchange** because the two properties traded are both eligible.) Any eligible type of property may be traded for any other eligible type of property. For example, a vacant lot owned by an investor may be traded for a duplex or an office building because both properties would be eligible.

In order to effectuate an exchange, strict rules must be followed. This includes but is not limited to:

- identifying eligible properties that can be exchanged
- timelines/deadlines for closing the transaction

The timeline allows for the following:

1. to close on the replacement property (the earlier of six months or income tax return due date including all extensions)
2. to identify replacement candidate(s) (the first 45 days following the sale of the relinquished property). The 45 days are part of the requirements directly above in the first point.

There are two possible trade situations—a trade in which the values of two properties are the same and a trade in which they are different. When the values of two properties are the same, neither party is required to pay income tax resulting from the exchange. In this situation, the cost basis for tax purposes is the same for the two properties, and no tax is due because there is no gain or loss for either party. When the values of the two properties are not the same, the party trading the lower valued property usually gives the other party money or an item of value in addition to the real property exchanged. This money or item is called boot.

In this situation, the party who trades a lower valued property for a higher valued one (trades up) will not pay taxes resulting from the exchange. The party who trades a higher valued property for a lower valued one (trades down) will pay taxes resulting from the exchange. This occurs for one of the following reasons:

- the payment of boot
- the exchange of mortgages with different balances

Let's look at each of these.

When a boot is paid along with an exchange of real property, the person who receives the boot is liable for taxes on the amount (or monetary value) of the boot. A tax liability also occurs when two properties are exchanged that have two different mortgage balances, even if no boot is paid. If a taxpayer receives a smaller mortgage balance in exchange for a larger one, the difference in the balances is considered income to that taxpayer and is called mortgage relief. The amount of the mortgage relief (reduction in mortgage balance) is taxable. There is also a reverse exchange. This occurs when the replacement property is purchased and closed on before the sale of the relinquished property. It is also a more expensive proposition than its counterpart.

2018 TAX REFORM ACT

As of January 1, 2018, the new Tax Reform Act came into effect. Therefore, the following information has been added to this chapter to cover parts of the new Tax Reform Act.

Tax Cuts and Jobs Act of 2017

In December 2017, Congress passed the Tax Cuts and Jobs Act. This resulted in much needed corporate and personal tax reform.

Under the Act, there are areas that remain the same and others that have changed.

What has Changed and What Remains the Same

Long-term Capital Gains Tax

Under the new tax act, there is no change in the tax structure for capital gains tax. Capital gains tax is still assessed at either of the following levels:

- 20% for high income earners
    - single filers earning over $425,800,
    - married filing jointly over $479,000,
    - head of household over $452,400,
    - married filing separate over $239,500
- 15% for non high income earners
    - single filers earning $38,600 - $425,800,
    - married filing jointly $77,200 - $479,000,
    - head of household over $51,700 - $452,400,
    - married filing separate over $38,600 - $239,500
- 0% for income earnings in the two lowest income brackets
    - single filers earning $38,600
    - married filing jointly $77,200
    - head of household over $51,700
    - married filing separate over $38,600

Furthermore, the definition of short-term or long-term gain remains the same as under the Tax Reform Act of 1997. The ACA (Medicare) tax of 3.8% for high income earners has not been repealed and remains in effect.

A Snapshot of the Short-term Capital Gains Tax

Short-term capital gains tax remains the same, except that the gain is assessed at the new ordinary income tax rates as applicable to the tax payer.

The following is a snapshot of ordinary income tax rates and brackets for 2018:

- Single Filers
    - 10% - marzginal rate earners from $0 - $9,525
    - 12% - marginal rate earners from $9,525 - $38,700

- 22% - marginal rate earners from $38,700 - $82,500
- 24% - marginal rate earners from $82,500 - $157,500
- 32% - marginal rate earners from $157,500 - $200,000
- 35% - marginal rate earners from $200,000 - $500,000
- 37%z - marginal rate earners from over $500,000
- Married Filing Jointly
  - 10% - marginal rate earners from $0 - $19,050
  - 12% - marginal rate earners from $19,050 - $77,400
  - 22% - marginal rate earners from $77,400 - $165,000
  - 24% - marginal rate earners from $165,000 - $315,000
  - 32% - marginal rate earners from $315,000 - $400,000
  - 35% - marginal rate earners from $400,000 - $600,000
  - 37% - marginal rate earners from over $600,000
- Head of Household
  - 10% - marginal rate earners from $0 - $13,600
  - 12% - marginal rate earners from $13,600 - $51,800
  - 22% - marginal rate earners from $51,800 - $82,500
  - 24% - marginal rate earners from $82,500 - $157,500
  - 32% - marginal rate earners from $157,500 - $200,000
  - 35% - marginal rate earners from $200,000 - $500,000
  - 37% - marginal rate earners from over $500,000
- Married Filing Separately
  - 10% - marginal rate earners from $0 - $9,525
  - 12% - marginal rate earners from $9,525 - $38,700
  - 22% - marginal rate earners from $38,700 - $82,500
  - 24% - marginal rate earners from $82,500 - $157,500
  - 32% - marginal rate earners from $157,500 - $200,000
  - 35% - marginal rate earners from $200,000 - $500,000
  - 37% - marginal rate earners from over $500,000

Standard Deduction

The Standard Deduction has doubled to $24,000 for married couples that file taxes jointly (previously $13,000). Single filers are now given a $12,000 standard deduction (previously $6500). Head of household deduction is increased to $18,000 (previously $9,550). It is important to note that except for the standard deduction, the aforementioned individual tax rates are due to expire after 2025. Furthermore, in 2019, an inflation gauge will be applied to the standard deduction. This is likely to accelerate a bracket increase.

Personal Exemptions

Personal exemptions are suspended under the Act and are set at $4,150 for 2018–2025.

Healthcare

The Act eliminates the provision in the ACA/Obamacare that penalizes individuals for not having health insurance coverage. This will take effect in 2019. It should be noted that although the health insurance mandate remains in place, the penalty is reduced to $0 and the repeal of penalty is not reversed in or after 2025.

Inflation Gauge

Previously, the IRS utilized the All Urban Consumers version of the Consumer Price Index to measure inflationary trends for taxation indexing. Under the Act, the All Urban Consumers version of the Consumer Price Index will be replaced with the Chain Weighted COI-U. This index considers consumer spending habit changes when pricing of what the consumer purchases shifts upward or downward (as the case may be).

Deductions/Family Child Tax Credits

Under the Act, the child tax credit (CTC) is increased to $2,000. The CTC is not available to taxpayers with adjusted gross income greater than $400,000 for married filing joint couples. Changes to this area expire after 2025.

Head of Household

The Act continues to include the head of household filing status in place.

Itemized Deductions

Itemized deductions have been affected in the following ways:

1. Mortgage Interest Deduction – Previously, the mortgage interest deduction on the acquisition of real property was capped at $1,000,000 for any taxpayer filing married filing jointly. This amount is reduced to $750,000. This change in mortgage interest deduction will expire after 2025
2. State and Local (Property) Tax Deduction (SALT) – Previously, SALT was deductable from an individual's Federal tax return. Under the Act, SALT deduction is limited to a deduction of up to $10,000 through 2025.
3. Other Itemized Deductions – Under the Act, the charitable contributions deduction remains in place with some changes. Interest deductions for student loans remain unaffected. Taxpayers with uninsured medical expenses in excess of 7.5% of adjusted gross income can deduct same.

The following are some of the itemized deductions that are suspended through 2025:
- alimony payments (after 2019 and are permanent)
- home office expenses
- licensing and other regulatory fees
- bad business debts
- professional fees/dues
- moving expenses (except for active duty military personal

4. Alternative Minimum Tax (AMT) – The exemption amount is increased to $109,400 for married couples filing jointly. Phase out is increased to $1,000,000 and both amounts are set to expire in 2025. The AMT was originally designed to prevent high-income earners from paying no tax or minimal tax by using tax avoidance laws that were in place. It requires the taxpayer to calculate a tax liability twice. The tax then becomes the greater of the two calculations.

5. Retirement Plans – Contribution amounts remain unchanged. A 401K contribution is still limited to $18,000 for those under 50 years of age. For those over 50 years of age, the amount of contribution remains at $24,000. Individual Retirement Account (IRA) contribution amounts remain at $5,500 for those under 50 years of age and $6,500 for those 50 years or older.

6. Student Loans and Tuition – remains unchanged

7. Estate Tax – The estate tax exemption is increased to $11.2 million in 2018. In 2017, the exemption amount was $5.6 million.

A Breif Overview of Business Taxes Under the Act

Corporate Tax Rate

The Tax Reform Act was originally designed to lower corporate tax rates to help US corporations to compete with other multi-national foreign companies. As a result, the corporate tax rate has been reduced to a single rate of 21%. Previously, the corporate tax rate was approximately 35%. This rate was one of the highest rates paid by a major country. The 21% tax rate takes effect in 2018. Another change was the repeal of the Corporate Alternative Minimum Tax (CAMT).

Accelerated Depreciation or Immediate Expensing

Previously, the cost recovery schedules (i.e., depreciation schedules) required depreciation over straight-line periods (previously 5 years). Under the new

Act, shorter life capital expenditures or investments can be accelerated and written off immediately. The change will be phased out over a 5-year period by 20% per year.

Pass-through Income

Pass-through businesses consist of the following legal business entities:

- sole proprietorships
- S-corporations
- partnerships
  - limited partnerships
  - general partnerships
- limited liability corporations
- limited liability partnerships

Under the Act, a 20% deduction for pass-through income is in place. The 20% deduction is capped at 50% of income from wages or 25% of wage income plus approximately 2.5% of other qualifying type of property. This was designed to prevent high-income bracket tax payers from utilizing pass-through income as a means of tax avoidance. Previously, taxpayers in the top income brackets paid 39.6% on pass-through earnings.

Treatment of Interest

Under the Act, interest deduction is limited to 30% of total earnings before interest, taxes, depreciation and amortization (EBITDA). Previously there was no cap on interest deductibility for businesses.

Foreign Earnings

In an effort to improve our nation's infrastructure, the Act considers the total repatriation of cash and property held by US corporations abroad. In doing so, the ACT provides the following:

- taxing of overseas profits at 15.5% for cash and equivalents and
- 8% for reinvested earnings
- creation of a tax system for business that only taxes domestic earnings

There are many other aspects associated with the Act; however, the information covered herein briefly highlights tax issues that may affect real property acquisition, ownership/holding, and reversion (sale) of property.

Summary

Federal state and local taxation affects both individuals and businesses engaged in real property ownership. On state and local levels, property taxes are levied on real property. On a federal level, income derived from income-producing activities is taxed. Both individuals and businesses engaged in real property ownership need to familiarize themselves with the impact of taxation. Tax knowledge is essential when making buying or selling considerations and/or decisions. Licensees should familiarize themselves with the impact of taxation on real property purchases and sales. Although licensees are cautioned against giving any type of tax advice, licensees should have knowledge of this subject.

Review Questions

1. In Florida, taxes on real property are calculated:
   a. on a quarterly basis
   b. biannually
   c. on a fiscal year basis
   d. for each calendar year

2. Property taxes become a lien on real property in Florida:
   a. January 1
   b. April 1
   c. November 1
   d. December 1

3. In Florida, unpaid property taxes from the previous year become delinquent on:
   a. December 31 of the following year
   b. November 1 of the following year
   c. April 1 of the following year
   d. January 1 of the following year

4. John was shocked when he received his TRIM notice, and he wants the assessed value of his property lowered. What is the first thing John must do?
   a. File a suit against the taxing authority.
   b. Go to the county property appraiser's office to contest the assessed value.
   c. Contact the county tax collector or a representative.
   d. Make an appointment with the Value Adjustment Board.

5. The notice of John's assessed property value and the current millage rate for the county, school board, and city was mailed on August 5. John wants to file a protest regarding the assessed value. How long does he have to protest?
   a. John must file a protest on or before August 15.
   b. John has until August 30 to file a protest.
   c. John's protest must be filed by September 1.
   d. John must register his protest before October 15.

6. Horace went to the county property appraiser's office to protest the assessed value of his property but received no satisfaction. If John wants to continue his quest for a lower assessed value, what is the next step?
   a. John can go to the Value Adjustment Board.
   b. Contact the county tax collector or a representative.
   c. Register his protest in writing with the county appraiser.
   d. Litigate.

7. Governments do not pay property taxes to each other in Florida, so government-owned property is not assessed for property tax purposes. Thus, government-owned property is:
   a. partially exempt from taxation
   b. exempt from taxation
   c. immune from taxes
   d. disallowed from taxes

8. Harry was granted a $25,000 partial homestead tax exemption. His home has a market value of $275,000. The assessed value of the home is $213,000. What is the taxable value?
   a. $275,000
   b. $213,000
   c. $250,000
   d. $188,000

9. Harry's property is subject to a tax rate of 24 mills. Use the figures in Question 8 to calculate Harry's property taxes.
   a. $6,600
   b. $5,112
   c. $6,000
   d. $4,512

10. Gary was wounded in the Vietnam War and the VA has rated Gary's disability at 30%. Gary has declared a homestead on his residence in Florida and has been granted a full homestead exemption. Last year, Gary's wife died. What is Gary's homestead exemption?
    a. $31,000
    b. $55,500
    c. $26,000
    d. $25,500

11. Sue is a widow who lives in Plantation in Broward County. County taxes are 9.4 mills. City taxes are 9.6 mills. School board taxes are 6 mills. Sue is eligible for a 50% homestead exemption. How much will Sue save in taxes because of her exemption?
    a. $705.00
    b. $697.50
    c. $637.50
    d. $625.00

12. The tax rate for a particular local government is the result of:
    a. the Florida State Legislature
    b. registered voters of the state
    c. majority vote of voters in each tax district
    d. how much money each department of the local government needs

13. Charles is widowed and legally blind. He has qualified for a homestead 50% exemption. The market value of his home is $175,000, and the assessed value is $93,000. The city tax rate is 9.1 mills, the school board tax is 7.8 mills, and the county tax rate is 8.4 mills. Calculate the county taxes Charles must pay.
    a. $1,720.40
    b. $1,707.75
    c. $1,695.10
    d. $562.80

14. The law that caps the assessed value for homestead property is the:
    a. Value Adjustment law
    b. Save Our Homes
    c. the Seventh Amendment
    d. the Green Belt law

15. Florida's Green Belt law was passed:
    a. to provide green space within city development
    b. in order to protect the environment
    c. to provide clean air and drinking water for Floridians
    d. to protect farmers

16. When assessing the value of agricultural land, tax assessors:
    a. must use a constant value on all land used for farming.
    b. can never value farmland at its highest and best use.
    c. are not required to perform a full appraisal.
    d. must factor in the highest and best use of the land.

17. John and Mary are married and file taxes married filing jointly. They sold the home they lived in for five years and realized a profit of $617,000. What is the result?
    a. They will be exempt from taxes on the profit if one of them is over 55 years old.
    b. There will be no taxes due on the profit if they purchase a home of equal or greater value within 18 months of the sale.
    c. The profit over $500,000 will be taxed as a capital gain.
    d. There is no capital gains tax due.

18. An industrial property sold for $125,000. Land was 20% of the value. Calculate the annual depreciation. Round to the nearest dollar.
    a. $4,545
    b. $4,364
    c. $3,584
    d. $2,564

19. One advantage of home ownership is the:
    a. deduction of mortgage payments on a first and second residence
    b. deduction of taxes on a first home only
    c. deduction of taxes on a first and second residence
    d. deduction of mortgage payments on a first home only

20. When a lender charges points for a loan involving a principal residence:
    a. all points can be deducted for income tax purposes in the year they were paid
    b. points are deductible only when they are amortized out over the life of the loan
    c. points on loans are only deductible as an expense for income property
    d. points are not deductible in the year paid if the loan was a refinance

21. Homeowners would NOT be allowed to deduct which of the following expenses for IRS tax purposes?
    a. ad valorem taxes
    b. depreciation
    c. mortgage interest
    d. up to $500,000 profit when selling the home

22. Investment property owners would NOT be allowed to deduct which of the following expenses for IRS tax purposes?
    a. depreciation
    b. hazard insurance
    c. reserves for replacements
    d. ad valorem taxes

CHAPTER 19

PLANNING, ZONING, AND ENVIRONMENTAL HAZARDS

KEY TERMS

asbestos
buffer zone
building code
building inspection
building permit
certificates of occupancy
concurrency
environmental impact statement
health ordinance
nonconforming use
planned unit development (PUD)
R-value
special exception
Special Flood Hazard Area
variance
zoning ordinances

LEARNING OBJECTIVES

After completing this lesson, you will be able to:

- describe the composition and authority of the local planning agency
- explain the purpose of land use controls and the role of zoning ordinances
- identify the provisions of Florida's comprehensive plan and the Growth Management Act
- distinguish among the five zoning classifications
- distinguish among zoning ordinances, building codes, and health ordinances
- explain the purpose of a variance, special exception, and nonconforming use
- calculate the number of lots available for development, given the total number of acres contained in a parcel, the percentage of land reserved for streets, and other facilities and the minimum number of square feet per lot
- describe the characteristics of a planned unit development
- understand the basic provisions of the National Flood Insurance Program

THE HISTORY OF URBAN (CITY) PLANNING AND ZONING

Prior to the implementation of zoning regulations, restrictions were put into place by the early urban planners of our nation. These restrictions included prohibiting or limiting certain uses of property in areas when those uses were in conflict with the remainder of the community's land use. However, due to the industrial revolution and prior to the implementation of zoning regulations, most of the country was experiencing a laissez-faire (French for "let proceed") approach to land use regulations.

In addition, prior to the invention of the elevator and its implementation in high-rise construction, most properties were low rise in height. This ensured that all properties in some manner conformed to the surrounding properties. Therefore, each property was able to enjoy unlimited open air and light.

For example, in New York City, the use of the elevator in commercial construction gave birth to high-rise properties. In the early 1920s, the construction of the Equitable Building in lower Manhattan created problems for the neighboring properties. Properties neighboring the Equitable Building high-rise were now deprived of the air and light that they enjoyed before the Equitable Building was built. These properties experienced (as the day went on) loss of light directly resulting from the height of the property. The building's height cast a six-acre shadow over the neighboring properties, which infuriated the neighboring property owners. As a direct result of this event and the birth of high-rise construction, New York City's first zoning resolution was born. Many other municipalities probably experienced similar urban planning issues that required the creation and adaptation of zoning resolutions.

Certainly, the decisions that were made in those days affected the future of how land use would evolve. Urban planners were now charged with the municipality's future growth and land uses. Some of the areas of concern were:

- air and light
- creation of zoning districts with the intent of creating conformity within those zones
- height restrictions
- density issues
- health, safety, and welfare of the constituency

Note that the concerns were different from city to city. For example, in cities that were financial or business capitals, early development trended vertically. In less populated areas, development trended horizontally. Therefore, local planning agencies were created. Florida's Growth Management Act of 1985 mandated the creation of additional infrastructure to account for the expansion of development to satisfy the growth in population. Prior to the commencement of any new development, the act called for the creation of infrastructure to include consideration in areas such as:

- water and wastewater treatment facilities
- the creation of new sewer systems
- the building of roadways

As a result of the Growth Management Act of 1985, the Department of Community Affairs was given the responsibility under Chapter 163, Florida Statutes

(F.S.), to regulate city, county, and regional plans. This would also play the major role in the guiding and controlling of future growth throughout the state.

Some of the goals of local and regional plans were to create:

- savings of tax money by preventing sprawl (damaging development in rural places)
- providing adequate infrastructure in order to provide necessary municipal services
- providing for road rights of way
- requiring property improvement setbacks
- protecting municipalities from costly drainage, flooding, or other potential environmental problems
- reducing political and equity problems in siting landfills, prisons, and other land development improvements

MASTER PLAN

Zoning ordinances are usually tied to a long-range master or comprehensive plan for future growth in the community. Under the Florida Growth Management Act of 1985, all levels of government (city and county) are required to establish comprehensive plans for future growth. A comprehensive plan must contain certain elements that are coordinated with the comprehensive plans of surrounding areas. A comprehensive plan must address:

1. future land use
2. traffic circulation
3. sanitary sewer, solid waste, drainage, and water
4. conservation and protection of natural resources
5. recreation areas
6. housing
7. coastal area management and protection, if applicable
8. intergovernmental coordination

The Florida Growth Management Act of 1985 also has a concurrency provision. According to this provision, sufficient infrastructure (sewer, water, and transportation systems) must exist before new development is permitted.

THE PROCESS OF PLANNING

The process of planning includes reviewing various types of studies that indicate the following:

- past trends
- current trends
- projected trends

One primary area of study that is important to note is the business environment, which creates employment. There are two types of business industries to study:

1. Base industry—Local businesses that attract people and money from other parts of the nation such as resort and recreation industries.
2. Service industry—Services the local constituency through various trades such as convenience stores and local retailers.

Local Planning Agency

Each local government must establish a local planning agency (or local planning commission). The local planning agency is responsible for developing the comprehensive plan. The local planning agency must ensure that development in the community is consistent with the comprehensive plan. The local planning agency is responsible for:

- subdivision plat approval
- site plan approval
- sign control

Composition

The local planning agency is composed of members of the public who are typically appointed by the city or county commission. These members are typically volunteers, not paid employees. The members of the planning agency are not trained as city or county planners. Rather, they come from a variety of professions and make recommendations based on what they believe is in the best interest of the residents of the community. Members on planning boards are not elected; they are appointed. It is for this reason that members serving on a planning board are not compensated. Serving is voluntary. However, the planning agency does have a support staff made up of individuals who are paid employees and trained planners. The size of planning boards varies depending on a municipality's size and need for area coverage.

Subdivision Plat Approval

Before a subdivision can be developed, the developer must submit a subdivision plat to the local planning agency for approval. The subdivision plat is a visual map of the subdivided land. It is an architectural rendering of the subdivided parcels that will indicate:

- egress (exit) from the subdivision
- ingress (entry) into the subdivision
- sidewalks where applicable

Note that prior to the approval and recording of the plat map of subdivision by the necessary authorities, the subdivider may not sell and/or transfer subdivided lots to the public.

Site Plan Approval

For large developments (other than subdivisions), the developer must submit a site plan to the local planning agency for approval. The site plan is a detailed description of the project.

Signage Control

The local planning agency is also responsible for signage control. The purpose of signage control is to ensure that signs do not distract drivers or create dangerous conditions. It is also designed to control the use and installation of unsightly or unusual signage that may not conform to a neighborhood's standards.

FLORIDA'S COMPREHENSIVE PLAN

Every state ultimately requires the implementation of a comprehensive plan. The comprehensive plan ultimately provides the blueprint for the future growth and expansion of any municipality. Therefore, the importance of appropriate planning is critical. The plan itself will identify what the municipality residents desire as the future growth of their city, town, or village.

The state of Florida regulates the comprehensive plan (Chapter 163, F.S.) through the Local Government Comprehensive Planning and Land Development Regulation Act. The intent and purpose of Chapter 163, F.S., are frequently reviewed, updated, and modified to include future planning requirements. Some of the areas covered within the current plan include but are not limited to:

- the role of local and state government in planning
- protecting important state facilities and resources
- protecting the state economy in areas such as:
    1. agriculture
    2. tourism
    3. military presence
    4. economic diversification
    5. workforce development
    6. community planning

It is important to note that all new amendments to the state plan should always comply with existing state laws and requirements.

In addition to the aforementioned, the plan must contain certain elements that should be coordinated with the plans of surrounding areas to include but not be limited to:

- future land use
- traffic circulation
- water
- sanitary and storm sewers
- solid waste treatment resources
- conservation of natural resources
- recreation
- housing coastal zone protection (where relevant)
- intergovernmental coordination
- utilities

The aforementioned is always easier said than done. It is no easy task to foresee the future needs and requirements of a municipality without careful planning. Different people have different visions of what is necessary and what will benefit the needs of the many. In particular, any plan will require the need for sufficient land use control. This can be accomplished through the implementation of local and state ordinances regulating same. Furthermore, it will be necessary to plan required future major capital improvements through concurrency management requirements. **Concurrency** means requiring and insuring that the creation of public facilities and services by local government are available to support any local development. This is mandated by the Florida Growth Management Act. Simply put, new development must be located in close proximity to where services are available or will be available. Where services are proposed, there must be assurances that the plans and capital necessary to create these services exist.

Optional Elements

Optional elements of a comprehensive plan may also include but not be limited to controls for:

- landmark and historical preservation
- scenic preservation
- economic and public buildings

It is important to note that concurrency will allow for new development only after a minimum level of public infrastructure is in place on or around the development site.

ZONING LAND USE RESTRICTIONS AND BUILDING CODES

Public land use controls are enacted to ensure an orderly pattern of growth in a community and to preserve property values. These controls are established under a local government's police power, primarily at the county and city level, through enabling legislation. These powers are also designed to protect the public in areas such as:

- health issues through state and local health ordinances
- safety issues through state and local building codes

Zoning Ordinances

The principal mechanism of public land use control is through **zoning ordinances**. Within these ordinances, property is also classified by type. Through zoning ordinances, the government and local municipalities can regulate such things as:

- permitted uses for land
- type, size, and height of structures built on the land
- open-air requirements in relation to site improvement
- density factors that will dictate the project size and occupancy of the land
- location of structures on the land such as setback requirements, including:
    - rear yard
    - side yard
    - frontage setbacks, when necessary

There are several zoning classifications:

1. Residential (use for dwelling purposes)

    This type of zoning regulates:

    - lot size (the as of right minimum size required in acreage or square feet to constitute being a legal single and separate lot/buildable property)
    - set backs (distance between structures and the property line. Setbacks are generally set forth within municipal ordinances or zoning regulations). In urban communities where high-rise construction is prevalent, the most common subject of setback is to provide a neighboring property with:
        - air
        - light
        - density (which is the maximum number of homes allowed to be built per acre of land)

    Homes will usually have a setback of some type from the property's boundary. Setbacks can be used for the installation of public utilities.

lot coverage—lot coverage is defined as the percentage of the overall area of the site occupied by a legal improvement. The formula for calculating the percentage of coverage is:

Total buildable area (below the roof and at ground level) ÷ Total lot (land) area = Lot coverage percentage

For example, the owner of a lot/land measuring 100 ft × 100 ft intends on building an improvement with a total building area of 3,000 square feet. The formula above is applied in the following manner:

- Step 1: calculate the total square footage of the lot/land:
  100 × 100 (lot dimensions) = 10,000 square feet (total lot/land square footage)
- Step 2: 3,000 (proposed buildable square feet)
  ÷ 10,000 (total lot/land square footage) = 30% lot coverage

2. Commercial—use is normally for commerce and business purposes. It includes:
    - offices
    - retail space
    - hotels/motels
    - other business district uses

   This type of zoning regulates:
    - the intensity of use
    - parking requirements
    - height and size limitations

3. Industrial—a category of land uses that includes:
    - heavy industrial—where raw materials are converted to useful materials
    - light industrial/manufacturing—useful parts are assembled into a finished product
    - warehouse/loft space—the finished product is stored for transport and delivery

It is important to note that the purpose of this this type of zoning controls emissions, effluents, noise, odor, smoke, and chemicals.

4. Agricultural—property used for farmland
5. Special use—includes property owned by the government such as:
    - municipal government buildings
    - post offices
    - schools

Please note that other than the aforementioned five categories, another category exists: a mixed-use property is a hybrid of two allowed uses within one parcel of property. This may include but not be limited to:

- the upper floors of a building used as residential units
- the lower floors of the same building in commercial uses such as:
  - medical space
  - retail space
  - office space

Wherever two different zones border each other, zoning will usually require the creation of a buffer zone, which is a strip of land that varies in size from community to community and acts as a separator between two zones. Buffer zones are of importance wherever residential zones border and abut commercial or industrial zones.

BUILDING CODES

Building codes are often confused with zoning ordinances. **Building codes** set the allowable minimum standards for construction of improvements on real property. They are established under the government's police powers, but they are not part of the zoning process. Enforcement of the Florida Building Code is accomplished through the issuance of:

- **building permits**—grant permission to construct improvements and are issued by local government
- **building inspections**—inspections conducted by representatives of local building departments to establish construction conformance with filed plans and specifications on new construction as well as code compliance on existing construction
- **certificates of occupancy**—issued to a property owner by the local building department and state that the property conforms to all current building codes and may be occupied
- **R-value**—references the thickness of construction insulation material. The R-value measures the retention and resistance to cold and heat. The higher the R-value number, the greater the resistance to heat flows.

The police power of condemnation is used to accomplish the actual taking of private property for the public's benefit. Eminent domain is the government's right to take private property for the benefit of the general public in areas such as new public transportation, new highways, and various other public uses.

HEALTH ORDINANCES

Building codes exist to protect the public's health, safety, and welfare. Zoning ordinances control project bulk (size) while preserving the environment. **Health ordinances** are created to further protect the public's general health, safety, and welfare. In suburban development, it plays a significant role in the creation of land subdivision. The same holds true in urban and high-rise construction.

APPEALS AND EXEMPTIONS

Zoning Board of Adjustment

The Zoning Board of Adjustment is a body of government charged with listening to appeals made to zoning ordinances by private property owners. Appeals come in many forms. Three of the most common are:

1. variances
2. special exception
3. legally non conforming use

Variance

When a zoning ordinance is already in effect, any new structure or modifications to existing structures must conform to the ordinance. Permission for an exemption to some of the specific requirements within a zoning classification may sometimes be granted through a zoning **variance**. Variances can only be issued within a zoning classification and cannot be used to change the zoning classification for a given property. To obtain a variance, the property owner must demonstrate that a hardship exists or that complying with the zoning would create a hardship.

There are two types of variances:

1. area
2. use

Area Variance

Area variances grant the property owner permission to utilize land in a way that is in conflict with current zoning area requirements because the property owner cannot satisfy one of the following:

- physical requirements of zoning
- dimensional requirements of zoning

For example, a zoning ordinance may require that houses are built at least 30 feet back from the road. If the topography of a particular parcel of land does not allow a structure to be built that far back from the road (e.g., because of the slope of the land, or location of a body of water, etc.), the owner may be granted a variance allowing the house to be built closer to the road.

Use Variance

Use variances grant the property owner permission to utilize land in a way that is prohibited under the current zoning. In order to be eligible to obtain a use variance, a property owner will have to demonstrate some of the following criteria:

- The property owner is experiencing hardship.
- The property owner hardship is exclusive to that owner's property versus the entire neighborhood or area.
- As a result of the hardship, the property owner is unable to capture the economic benefits inherent to property ownership.
- If the variance is granted, the general character of the neighborhood will not be altered.
- The hardship is not self-created.

Note that variances are generally not granted without public hearings.

Special Exception

A property owner may also be granted a **special exception**, which allows a specific use for a specific property. Usually, a special exception is permitted when the use of the property would be in the public interest. For example, a property owner may be issued a special exception allowing a hospital to be built on land that is zoned for residential use if the local area is in need of a hospital.

A special exception is different from a variance. A variance is only issued when an owner is able to show that complying with the zoning would create a hardship. A special exception is issued when the public would be best served by a land use that differs from the existing zoning.

Legally Nonconforming Use

When zoning for a particular property is changed or implemented after a property is built, a **nonconforming use** results if the property does not conform to the new zoning ordinances. New or revised ordinances usually contain a grandfather clause that allows the nonconforming property already in existence to remain in use. However, the grandfather clause usually will not allow the property to be remodeled or expanded.

Developments of Regional Impact

Any development in Florida that will affect residents in more than one county is referred to as a development of regional impact. An **environmental impact statement** must be prepared to address the impact that the project may or will have on the environment and its neighboring communities. This may require the installation of additional utilities and street lamps, and traffic considerations.

Planned Unit Development

A **planned unit development (PUD)** is a type of development that incorporates a variety of different yet compatible land uses. For example, in exchange for creating a greater amount of open space, the developer is granted a greater density for constructing housing. This may include but not be limited to:

- housing
- recreational facilities
    - golf
    - tennis
    - health spas
- commercial facilities
    - restaurants
    - community services

Environmental Impact Study (EIS)

Throughout the nation, large development projects are constructed frequently. The nature of the development (residential, commercial, industrial, and mixed use) will be dictated by the area's need for the development and allowed zoning associated with that project. In Florida, when proposed development may have a long-term effect on the surrounding environment, before a permit is issued, the developer will be required to produce an Environmental Impact Study (EIS). The EIS studies the long-term effects the development can have on the area and environment.

For example, the new development will produce a daily minimum of 5,000 trips into and out of an area that has historically had only 500 daily trips. As a result, it may determine that five additional new traffic lights will need to be installed and egress and ingress lanes widened. The cost of these additions can be realized through municipal impact fees that may or may not be paid by the developing party.

Flood Zones

National Flood Insurance Program (NFIP)

As most homeowner insurance policies will not protect a homeowner from damage resulting directly from flooding, Congress created the National Flood Insurance Program (NFIP) in 1968. Its purpose was to provide a means of protection to property owners against damage to property due to flooding. The NFIP will provide flood insurance to a:

- homeowner
- renter
- business owner

In addition, communities that create required flood management and floodplain construction regulations are eligible to qualify for federally subsided flood insurance programs. Furthermore, any land that bears high risk for flooding falls into a category called **Special Flood Hazard Areas** (SFHAs). These areas are also commonly referred to as floodplains. These floodplains are found on Flood Insurance Rate Maps. They are listed as per NFIP criteria.

It is important to note that any developments within SFHAs have limitations on how construction may be performed. The purpose behind these limitations is to preserve and not obstruct the natural flows of water. For example, if a property is to be improved in an SFHA, the following would apply:

- residential structures must have the first floor constructed above the "Base Flood Elevation"
- nonresidential structures must be water tight or must meet the aforementioned residential requirement

It is interesting to note that approximately 40% of the purchasers of the national flood insurance are Florida property owners. It is also noteworthy that certain flood zones will require the purchase of flood insurance in financed real property transactions.

Coaching Tips

- Public land use controls regulate growth—not limit it.
- A grandfather clause allows a nonconforming use to remain.
- A grandfather clause is used when a new ordinance is passed.
- A nonconforming use occurs when a new ordinance is passed.
- A variance is an exemption from an existing or preexisting zoning ordinance.
- Variances never change the zoning classification.
- Variances are often granted for expansion.
- Variances are granted either for use or for area.
- A **buffer zone** is a strip of land that varies in size from community to community and acts as a separator between two zones.

INDOOR AND OUTDOOR ENVIRONMENTAL HAZARDS

Water Supply

Florida residents are fortunate to have a plentiful source of groundwater. These groundwaters are commonly referred to as aquifers. In Florida, the primary source of drinking water comes from these aquifers. Therefore, most of the groundwater is carefully protected and preserved to avoid contamination. However, chemicals like nitrates as well as bacteria and other microbes pose a great threat of contamination to this extremely important water source. These contaminants can enter the water source through the ground via:

- leaking storage tanks (oil, gas, etc.)
- application of pesticides and fertilizers
- landfill
- inappropriate waste disposal

As an owner of a home that contains a private well, you should always be aware of the potential risks to the groundwater and household water supply. Both well water and public water must meet the same standards and requirements to be considered potable (consumable).

Septic Tank

Septic tank systems are private wastewater treatment and disposal systems and are common in areas where municipal sewer systems are nonexistent. Approximately 30% of Florida's population utilizes septic tank systems for wastewater treatment and disposal. This process helps to preserve Florida's groundwater that provides almost 90% of the state's drinking water. In order to construct a septic tank system, one would require a permit as well as inspection of the system by the Environmental Health Section of the Florida Department of Health in each county.

Asbestos

Asbestos is a natural fiber material that has been previously used as a fire retardant material in modern construction. Consistent exposure and prolonged inhalation of asbestos fibers can cause serious and fatal illnesses. These illnesses include:

- mesothelioma
- asbestosis (a type of pneumoconiosis)
- malignant lung cancer

The use of this fire-retardant construction material was banned in the mid-1970s.

Radon

Radon is a colorless, odorless radioactive gas that occurs from the natural decay of uranium, radium, and thorium in rocks and soil. In areas without adequate ventilation, high radon levels can substantially increase the risk of lung cancer. The only way of detecting radon levels is by testing. It is the surrounding soil composition either under or around the property that can affect indoor radon levels. When this occurs, the gas enters the home through cracks in the foundation or through sump pumps. Radon gas is easily remediated. The EPA offers guides for radon remediation. Systems with vent pipe(s) and fan(s) are used to reduce radon levels. These systems will not require major changes to a home. In homes where only a crawl space exists, similar type systems can also be installed.

These systems will prevent high levels of radon gas from entering the home in the future. Chapter 404, F.S., requires that real estate contracts for purchase and sale or lease must contain a radon disclosure. The timing for the disclosure can be at or before contract signing. In addition, Chapter 404 does not require the buyer or the seller to perform the testing of radon levels prior to transacting a sale or lease.

Toxic Waste in Soil

Any individual or organization that generates waste in Florida is required by law to identify and evaluate their waste. The Resource Conservation and Recovery Act (RCRA), contained in Title 40 of the Code of Federal Regulations Part 261, contains lists that specify a variety of wastes that are regulated. The Act also includes characteristics for identifying nonlisted hazardous waste. Hazardous wastes that are not handled and disposed of adequately can cause groundwater pollution. As previously stated, approximately 90% of Florida's drinking water is derived from groundwater. As such, wastes become a serious public and private consideration for environmental protection.

There are assurances that hazardous wastes are handled appropriately as well as in accordance with federal and state rules and laws; this responsibility falls under the control of the Compliance and Enforcement subsection of the Department of Environmental Protection (DEP). This subsection provides compliance assistance to the public and the regulated community and to enforce the laws regulating the handling of hazardous waste.

Underground Storage Tanks

Underground storage tanks are used for (but not limited to) storing:

- oil
- gas
- chemicals

The concern about these tanks is that either future spillage or leakage will occur. These chemicals then can enter the ground and can easily pollute the soil or groundwater. Chapter 62-761, F.S., provides standards for the registration, construction, and maintenance of storage systems in Florida that are greater than 110 gallons in size.

Lead Paint

Many homes and condominiums built prior to 1978 contain lead based paint. When this paint peels or chips, the fear is that the lead dust created from if can be easily ingested. When ingested, lead dust in the home can pose serious health hazards to its occupants. Home buyers and renters have important rights to know whether lead may be present. Federal law requires that prior to signing contracts of sale or leases, the buyer or renter must be presented with a lead disclosure. This is mandated and enforced by the EPA. Failure to attach a lead disclosure form to a contract of sale or lease can result in a fine of $11,000 per offense. Today, it is not uncommon for the EPA to audit the offices of real estate brokers to check for compliance.

Mold

Due to the humid climate in Florida (as well as other parts of the country), mold has become a big contemporary issue. Unlike temperate zones with changing seasons, in Florida it is not uncommon to run air-conditioning all year around to avoid moisture build-up and the growth of mold from the humid conditions inherent in Florida. Molds are types of fungi. Various health problems can come from exposure to certain types of mold:

- infection
- certain toxic effects
- allergic reaction
- irritation

    Other symptoms consist of:

    - hay-fever–like symptoms
    - shortness of breath
    - infections from certain molds, viruses, and bacteria

Molds can also trigger asthma attacks.

Chemical Contamination

Chemical contamination is a major contemporary issue in Florida as well as throughout the nation. For example, it has been recently determined in Florida that pesticides used for strawberries are contaminating the groundwater in Florida. As you learned earlier, Florida's groundwater is responsible for 90% of the drinking water in that state. As a result, measures must be taken to avoid contamination of the groundwater from chemicals and other pesticides.

Structural Damage and Wood-Destroying Organisms

1. Termites are wood-eating flying insects that can cause considerable structural damage to a home or other improvement. In Florida, four types of termites can be found:

    - subterranean termites—these termites require a moist environment.

- dampwood termites—these termites require moisture and seek wood that is water saturated.
- drywood termites—these termites require very little moisture in the wood that they ultimately infest.
- conehead termites—these termites are generally found in isolated parts of south Florida. They require moist environments that are similar to those infested by the subterranean termite. They are known to forage and nest in a most unique manner.

2. Carpenter ants are not wood-eating organisms. Unlike termites, they remove wood rather than eat it as they create areas in the wood itself for nesting.
3. The decay of wood or other materials used in construction can occur through simple natural processes. This is similar to the natural decay of a plant.

Comprehensive Environmental Response, Compensation, and Liability Act (CERCLA)

The Comprehensive Environmental Response, Compensation, and Liability Act (CERCLA) was passed in 1980. The law is commonly known as Superfund.

- CERCLA enables the EPA to enforce responsibility for environmental cleanup.
- CERCLA allows the EPA to receive reimbursement for contamination cleanup and the Superfund to receive reimbursement for remediation costs incurred by EPA.
- The Superfund Amendments and Reauthorization Act (SARA) of 1986 provided the teeth for enforcement of CERCLA.
- It also identifies potentially responsible parties (PRPs) to run a coordinated cleanup of contaminated land.
- It set forth joint and several liability (that either one or more PRPs might be identified as responsible for the cost of cleanup) for past and present owners.

The Innocent Landowners Defense provides for the protection of an innocent landowner from cleanup responsibilities under CERCLA. In order to qualify under the Act, the landowner must have:

- acquired property after all hazardous substances were disposed of at the facility
- conducted all appropriate inquiries into the previous ownership and uses of the property
- been unaware at the time of purchase or had no reason to know of the existence of hazardous substance contamination
- exercised due care with respect to the hazardous substance concerned

Real estate licensees who are involved in these types of property transactions should proceed with extreme caution. The real estate licensee should be familiar with environmental laws such as CERCLA.

Summary

Decisions we make today affect how development will occur tomorrow. Social acceptance of development projects becomes essential to ensure success. Urban planning is instituted to regulate the progress of growth while preserving elements such as air and light. Building codes exist to protect the public's health, safety, and welfare. Zoning ordinances control project bulk (size) while preserving the environment. Zoning ordinances can be appealed when a property owner faces financial undue hardships as a result of zoning. Whenever a project affects the residents of more than one county in Florida, development of regional impact studies is performed. The intent of this study is environmental preservation.

Groundwater in Florida is serviced by groundwater aquifers and supplies approximately 90% of potable drinking water in Florida. The need to avoid contamination is of greater importance and requires curtailing the use of chemicals and fertilizers. In addition, natural minerals such as asbestos pose a health threat and have been banned in the use of modern-day construction and development. Radon gas also poses a health threat. The colorless, odorless radioactive gas is a threat through the natural decay on uranium and other naturals materials contained in our soils. Properties constructed prior to 1978 require lead paint disclosures be given to a buyer or renter. In Florida, mold is also a big issue and can cause health risks. Termites and other wood-destroying organisms also pose a threat to a structure. In 1980, CERCLA was created to establish a process for identifying persons responsible for the cost of cleanup. In 1986, SARA added the teeth for enforcing CERCLA.

Review Questions

1. During the Industrial Revolution and prior to the creation of zoning laws, the lack of emphasis on city planning was generally due to:
   a. the movement of disaffected persons to the West
   b. an increase in the number of family farms
   c. the philosophy of laissez-faire
   d. the movement from farms to the city

2. The requirement of Florida's Growth Management Act that electricity, drinking water, roads, parks, sewers, etc., must be present before new building permits can be issued is the:
   a. services provision
   b. concurrency provision
   c. infrastructure requirement
   d. environmental provision

3. Another requirement of the Growth Management Act is that all communities must have a plan of how the community will expand in the future and how this plan must be designed to curb urban sprawl. This plan is referred to in the law as the:
   a. comprehensive plan
   b. environmental impact statement
   c. services plan
   d. growth management plan

4. The requirement for all communities to have in place a comprehensive plan gave rise to local planning commissions. Local planning commission members are:
   a. elected by the local community
   b. appointed, unpaid members who advise city officials
   c. the final decision makers on city expansion
   d. are community board members

5. All of the following can be caused by mold EXCEPT:
   a. infection
   b. certain toxic effects
   c. allergic reaction
   d. if touched it acts as a poison

6. While local planning commissions usually act in an advisory capacity, they often have the final authority in several local matters. Final authority of planning commissions would NOT include:
   a. site plan approval
   b. subdivision approval
   c. zoning ordinances
   d. sign control

7. Florida's comprehensive requirements state that a city's comprehensive plan must:
   a. control lot size in subdivisions
   b. set building height and size limitations
   c. address traffic circulation
   d. control emissions and effluents

8. The comprehensive plan allows:
   a. control of density
   b. control of intensity of use
   c. issuance of building permits
   d. land use control ordinances

9. Zoning ordinances are:
   a. considered spot zoning
   b. federally regulated
   c. public voted policies
   d. is the principal mechanism of public land use control

10. Sarah wants permission to exceed the setback requirements on her lot. In order to do so, she:
    a. would appeal to the planning commission
    b. would apply for a variance
    c. go before the Value Adjustment Board
    d. must litigate

11. State building codes are:
    a. enforced by the state
    b. enforced by local governments
    c. is based on county regulations
    d. based on population density

12. Residential zoning is designed to regulate:
    a. density
    b. intensity
    c. traffic
    d. social services

13. Commercial zoning is designed to regulate:
    a. density
    b. intensity
    c. easements
    d. air quality

14. A strip of land that separates one land use from another is a(n):
    a. easement
    b. buffer zone
    c. green space
    d. variance

15. Arthur needs a variance in order to build a pool in his back yard. In order to have a variance granted, Arthur must prove:
    a. a hardship regarding the use of the land exists
    b. the lack of a pool will cause an economic hardship when he sells
    c. other homes in the neighborhood have pools like this
    d. he needs a pool to meet his wife's medical requirements for recovery

16. A mobile home park is zoned residential and is populated by persons over the age of 62. The city decided to allow doctors' offices on a nearby street, although that area is also zoned residential. This is an example of a:
    a. nonconforming use
    b. special exception
    c. change in zoning
    d. special use

17. Jack followed the zoning requirements when he built a small convenience store on his corner lot. Later, the city changed the zoning to multifamily use. In this situation:
    a. Jack's store is a legally nonconforming use
    b. Jack will have to close his business
    c. Jack must ask for a variance
    d. Jack must go to court

18. A local developer has acquired a parcel of land that is large enough to divide into 25 home sites after allowing for sidewalks, streets, and green space. Before the developer can develop the land, he must submit the subdivision plat to the:
    a. City Building Code Enforcement
    b. local planning commission
    c. Enforcement of Florida Building Codes
    d. Department of Housing and Urban Development

19. All of the following controls are optional elements of a municipality's comprehensive plan EXCEPT:
    a. landmark and historical preservation
    b. vetting controls on allowed business
    c. scenic preservation
    d. economic and public buildings

20. The broadest restrictions on the use of property from the private sector came from:
    a. police power
    b. eminent domain
    c. deed restrictions
    d. zoning ordinances

ADDENDUM: INTRODUCTION TO RESIDENTIAL PRODUCT KNOWLEDGE

KEY TERMS

asbestos
chemical contamination
corner lot
cul-de-sac lots
double-hung
flag lot
green building
insulation
interior lot
key lot

R value
shingles
single-hung
subdivision
T lot
toxic waste
underground storage tanks
urea-formaldehyde foam insulation
zero lot line

LEARNING OBJECTIVES

After completing this lesson, you will be able to:

- explain how building codes regulate building construction
- distinguish among the various types of lots
- distinguish among the various types of roof styles
- identify different foundation styles
- identify the various window styles
- understand situations that may require a real estate licensee to use a licensed contractor
- describe basic residential building components and materials
- explain the mechanical and electrical systems that go into a home
- identify the various types of insulation and minimum R values
- explain the various environmental hazards associated with real estate

INTRODUCTION

Your entry into the real estate industry will require more than general knowledge of law, terminology, and the day-to-day operational duties associated with the practice of real estate brokerage. It will require common sense and product knowledge. This addendum was written as additional material to familiarize you with basic construction terminology, building codes that regulate the construction industry, and some of the materials that are used in everyday construction of improvements.

Although this material is not required for achieving a real state license, it is included here as additional information for the student.

BUILDING CONSTRUCTION STANDARDS

Local Regulations

Local regulations consist of the following codes:

- building codes
- housing codes
- electrical codes
- fire codes
- plumbing and mechanical codes

LOT TYPES

A lot is defined as a portion of an approved subdivision. **Subdivisions** are larger parcels of real property that are divided into smaller parcels known as lots. Residences may be built on various types of lots. Some of the different types of lots include:

- corner lots
- interior lots
- T lots
- cul-de-sac lots
- key lots
- flag lots
- zero lot line

Corner Lots

A **corner lot** sits at the intersection of two streets. The lot has frontage along both streets. (Frontage refers to the length of the property that abuts the street.)

Coaching Tips

When dimensions of property are quoted, by practice, the first dimension is normally indicative of the frontage. For example, a lot with dimensions consisting of 50 × 100 would indicate a frontage of 50 feet and a depth of 100 feet.

Interior Lots

An **interior lot** is surrounded by other lots on three sides (left, right, and rear). The interior lot has frontage on just one street.

T Lots

A **T lot** is a type of interior lot that is located at the end of a T intersection.

Cul-de-sac Lots

Cul-de-sac lots are located at the end of a cul-de-sac (a dead-end street with a circular turn-around). They are part of a subdivision. Because of the curved turnaround, these lots are often irregular in shape—that is, they are tapered with a smaller frontage but larger backyards. These lots generally are the most desirable lot(s) in a subdivision. This is because they are at the furthest end of the subdivision where there is no vehicular traffic.

Key Lots

A **key lot** is surrounded by many other lots. Often, a key lot is an extremely deep lot. The side yard abuts the rear of many different properties that are located on a street that runs perpendicular to the street where the key lot is located.

Flag Lots

A **flag lot** is shaped like a flag on a flagpole. Often, a flag lot is located behind another lot. The flagpole portion of the lot is the access road or driveway that runs along the front lot to the street. The flag portion of the lot is the square or rectangular lot that is located behind the front lot.

Zero Lot Line

A **zero lot line** refers to residential lot construction where the improvement is constructed up to or very close to the property line. Residential construction may be built this way in order to capture more usable space. The following are some examples of this type:

- rowhouses
- garden homes
- patio homes
- townhomes

> ## Coaching Tips
>
> ### Lots at a Glance
>
> - A corner lot sits at the intersection of two streets.
> - An interior lot is surrounded by other lots on three sides (left, right, and rear).
> - A T lot is a type of interior lot that is located at the end of a T intersection.
> - A cul-de-sac lot is located at the end of a cul-de-sac.
> - A key lot is surrounded by many other lots (often a deep lot that abuts the rear of many different properties along its side yards).
> - A flag lot is shaped like a flag on a flagpole.
> - A zero lot line contains residential construction up to or very close to the property line.

PRODUCT KNOWLEDGE—BASIC RESIDENTIAL DESIGN, MATERIALS, AND SYSTEMS

We will now examine various components of residential construction starting with the roof.

Roofs

Roof Styles

There are five basic types of roofs you should be familiar with:

1. gable—a roof sloping on two sides
2. hip—a roof sloping on four sides
3. gambrel—a roof divided into two sections with different slopes for each section. Only two sides of the roof are sloped
4. mansard—a roof with two sections with different slopes (like the gambrel), but all four sides of the roof are sloped
5. shed roof—a roof that is considered one of the stabler of the different styles and designs. This is due to the roof sloping on all four sides of the building

All of the major roof styles are illustrated in Figure A.1.

Roof Construction

You should also be familiar with what is called the *pitch* of a roof. The pitch is the angle of the slope of the roof. The steeper the slope is, the greater the pitch. A roof with a steeper pitch will normally last longer than a roof with a lower pitch.

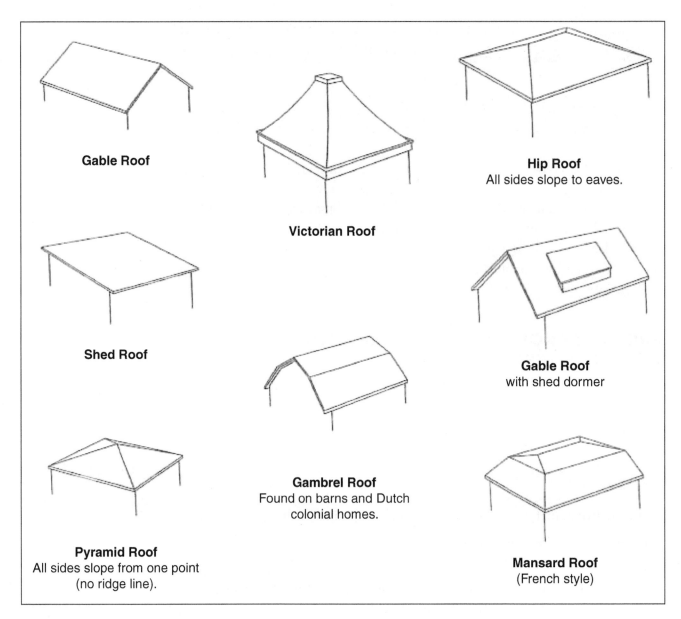

FIGURE A.1
Source: © 2021 Mbition LLC

The most common types of roof construction are:

- trusses
- joists and rafters
- joists alone
- post and beam

Trusses

Trusses are framing units that are assembled at a factory and usually consist of several triangle-shaped sections. The shape allows the trusses to support the weight of the roof across a long area. (Interior load-bearing walls may be unnecessary with trusses.) With trusses, hurricane clips are often used. Hurricane clips are metal strips that are nailed and secure the rafters to the top horizontal wall plate.

Rafters and Joists

Rafters are sloping parallel beams that support the roof while joists are horizontal parallel beams located below the rafters. The ceiling is attached to the joists.

Joists Alone

In some situations, the roof is supported directly by the joists, such as with a flat roof.

Post and Beam

With post-and-beam roofing, beams that support the roof rest on posts or columns. The roof is supported by the beams and posts rather than bearing walls or trusses. Once the framing for the roof has been constructed, the roof sheathing is attached. Common roof sheathing materials include boards, plywood, or pressed board. Roofing materials are attached to the sheathing. Most residential roofs consist of asphalt shingles. To construct an exterior wall, sheathing is attached to the studs. The sheathing is then covered with waterproof building paper. The exterior finish materials of the walls (siding) are applied on top of the building paper.

Type of Materials

Sheathing

Sheathing is the first layer of the exterior finish materials placed on the outside of the wall studs or roof rafters. Sheathing materials are usually boards, plywood, pressed board, or wallboard.

Coaching Tips

Solid sheathing means the boards forming the sheathing are butted next to each other so there are no gaps. The exterior finish materials of the walls and roof are applied on top of the sheathing.

Shingles

Shingles are exterior coverings that are generally overlapping individual units. These units are typically flat and rectangular shaped and installed in courses. Shingles are available in a variety of materials that include but are not limited to:

- wood
- composite material
- plastic
- metal

Fasteners

Fasteners are generally used to secure construction building materials.

Hurricane Anchors

Hurricane anchors are used in conjunction with shutters. Shutters are used to protect from wind and other flying debris damage. Depending on the type of shutter one has in mind, with research and good information about different types of fasteners and anchors, you can decide what shutter solutions are best suited for your home. Due to the damage that can result from a storm in Florida, hurricane shutters are installed by homeowners to protect against damage caused by wind and flying debris.

Walls: Bearing and Nonbearing

Bearing Wall

A bearing wall is a wall that bears the weight of the structure above the wall. It supports ceiling joists, an upper story, or the roof of the house. All exterior walls of a house are bearing walls, but only some walls within a house are bearing walls. If the wall serves only to divide the interior space into rooms and is not used to support the structure above it, the wall is *not* a bearing wall. If the wall supports the structure above it, it *is* a bearing wall. Bearing walls are particularly important when considering remodeling.

Nonbearing Wall

Nonbearing walls can usually be altered or removed without major effects on the overall structure. A bearing wall should not be altered or removed except by a qualified individual because changing or removing a bearing wall can result in severe damage to the structure. Because of their importance, bearing walls are often constructed with stronger materials and techniques than nonbearing walls. Bearing walls are often difficult to identify in an existing house because there are no obvious signs that indicate that a wall is a bearing wall. Bearing walls can be constructed at any angle to other walls, doorways, etc.

Exterior Wall Covering

To construct an exterior wall, sheathing is attached to the studs. Common sheathing materials include boards, plywood, pressed board, or wallboard. The sheathing is then covered with waterproof building paper. The exterior finish materials of the walls (siding) are applied on top of the building paper. A wide variety of exterior wall coverings exist, including:

- siding
- stucco
- masonry
- concrete block

Materials that would be used include:

- shingles
- sheathing
- building paper
- studs

Ceiling/Walls: Joist

A joist is a supporting beam in the floor or ceiling. All joists are parallel to each other and are usually spaced 16 inches apart.

Windows

There are various window styles available. Some of the most common styles of windows include:

- single-hung windows
- double-hung windows
- horizontal sliding windows
- casement windows
- jalousie windows
- fixed windows

Single-Hung Window

A **single-hung** window consists of two sashes, one of which can be raised or lowered to open or close the window. A sash is a frame made of wood, steel, aluminum, or vinyl that holds a pane of glass.

Double-Hung Window

A **double-hung** window consists of two sashes, both of which slide vertically, allowing the window to be opened at the top and bottom.

Horizontal Sliding Window

A horizontal sliding window consists of sashes that slide horizontally to open or close the window.

Casement Window

A casement window consists of a hinged sash that can be opened by swinging the sash outward.

Jalousie Window

This type of window consists of horizontal overlapping glass louvers that pivot to open or close (similar to window blinds).

Fixed Window

A fixed window consists of a sash that cannot be opened.

> ## Coaching Tips
>
> **Windows at a Glance**
>
> - A fixed window consists of a sash that cannot be opened but can be raised or lowered to open or close the window.
> - A single-hung window consists of two sashes, only one of which can be raised or lowered to open or close the window.
> - A double-hung window consists of two sashes, both of which slide vertically, allowing the window to be opened at the top and bottom.
> - A casement window consists of a hinged sash that can be opened by swinging the sash outward.
> - A jalousie window consists of horizontal overlapping glass louvers that pivot to open or close.
> - A fixed window consists of a sash that cannot be opened.

Windows also come in all different types of finishes and materials:

- aluminum
- wood
- steel
- vinyl

Insulation

Insulation is a construction material used to reduce the hot and cold air transfer in a property. Insulation is just as important in warm climates to keep the heat out of the home as it is in cold climates to keep the heat in the home. There are several types of insulation:

- loose-fill—insulating materials that can be put in place by hand
- blanket and batt—insulation, usually made of fiberglass, available in rolls (blankets) or sheets (batts)
- sprayed-on—insulating materials that are sprayed on surfaces
- foil—insulating sheets with aluminum foil backing that reflects heat

- rigid—rigid panels of insulation
- foam—insulating materials that are mixed with a foam and poured or sprayed into place

The standard method to rate the effectiveness of insulation materials is the **R value**. The R stands for resistance to heat flow. The higher the R value for a particular insulation material, the better the insulation effect. The Department of Energy has established insulation recommendations for homes. The recommended levels of insulation, expressed in R values, differs for different areas of the house (e.g., under the roof, inside exterior walls, etc.) and varies from one locale to another due to differences in climate.

MECHANICAL SYSTEMS AND EQUIPMENT

The following is a summary of the major mechanical systems described in this section:

- heating system
- cooling system
- plumbing system
- hot water system
- electrical system

Heating Systems

There are many types of heating systems, including systems that utilize:

- warm air
- water
- steam
- electricity

Warm Air

Warm (or hot) air heating systems typically utilize some type of blower to distribute heated air to rooms in a building through ducts. Heated air enters the rooms through registers. A space heater is another type of warm air heating system. A space heater is a small unit that typically uses a fan to blow warm air into a room.

Water

Another type of heating system uses water. Hot water is held in a boiler. Electric circulators are used to pump the heated water through pipes into radiators or into additional pipes embedded in the floors, walls, or ceilings, and the heat is transferred into rooms.

Steam

Steam heat is produced by a boiler with a firebox underneath it. When water boils, the pressure builds and forces the steam through pipes into radiators.

Electricity

Electricity can be either a fuel to heat air or water in a furnace or a direct source of heat itself. Resistance elements convert electricity into heat. These resistance elements are embedded in the floors, walls, and ceilings in the area being heated.

Coaching Tips

Heating Systems

- Warm (or hot) air heating systems:
  - utilize some type of blower to distribute heated air to the rooms of the building through ducts; and
  - distribute heated air into the rooms through registers.
- Hot water systems:
  - hold hot water in a boiler.
- Steam systems:
  - produce steam heat by a boiler.
- Electric systems:
  - use resistance elements, which convert electricity into heat. These resistance elements are embedded in the floors, walls, and ceilings.

Types of Fuel

There are several types of fuel, including coal, fuel oil, natural gas, electricity, and solar energy. In the past, coal was the most popular fuel source. Today, most coal systems are obsolete. Fuel oil is popular in certain areas of the United States, mainly the Northeast and Northwest. At one time, fuel oil was competitively priced, but recently it has become expensive. Fuel oil requires an on-site storage tank. Natural gas, which can be delivered by a pipeline, does not require any storage tanks. Natural gas has typically been the most economical fuel in most areas of the country.

Another fuel source is electricity. Because electric systems require no furnace or ducts, they are the least expensive to install. However, the electricity needed to run such systems can be expensive. Solar energy, which comes directly from the sun, is still the least developed source of heat. However, as the technology advances, and as other fuel sources are depleted, the use of solar energy will increase. Furthermore, with sustainability issues and green building becoming more and more popular, it is not unlikely that future new construction and rehabilitation projects will take solar energy into greater consideration.

Wherever natural gas service is available, multi-family properties that were previously using heating oil have converted to natural gas heat. Aside from the cost savings realized from the conversion, these properties now have a **dual heating system**. This means that the property can be heated by gas or oil. Should a breakdown of the gas heating plant occur, the oil furnace can substitute as an alternate heating plant until repairs or resupply of gas. resumes.

Cooling Systems

In the past, buildings were cooled with windows and/or fans. Now, most newly constructed buildings have a centralized air-conditioning system. Types of air-cooling systems include:

- window units
- central air-conditioning
- heat pumps
- fans
    - ceiling
    - attic

Window Air-Conditioning Units

To cool a single room or small area, a window air-conditioning unit can be installed easily and plugged into a regular outlet.

Central Air-Conditioning

Central air-conditioning systems may be custom-made or factory-assembled packages that are connected at the residence. The condenser unit is placed outside the house. The condenser transforms refrigerant gas into a cool liquid. A pipe runs from the condenser to the air-handling unit inside the house. The air-handling unit, which consists of an evaporator and a fan, is connected to ducts that distribute cool air throughout the house.

Heat Pumps

Heat pumps are actually used for both heating and cooling. A heat pump is basically a reversible air-conditioning unit. A heat pump takes heat from the outside air or ground and distributes it inside to warm the house in winter. Conversely, the system extracts warm air from inside the house to cool the house in summer. Heat pumps are most efficient in areas with mild winters, including Florida.

Ventilation by Fans

If moisture builds up in spaces that are not ventilated, rot and decay may occur. Ventilation is crucial to prevent water condensation. Air flow is needed in the attic, behind the wall covering, and through the basement or crawl space. This air flow may be obtained by providing holes of varying sizes, which are protected with screens to keep out insects and small animals. The ventilation system may also include attic, basement, kitchen, and bathroom fans.

Plumbing Systems

A plumbing system has two purposes:

1. to supply adequate clean water to the home
2. to remove waste from the home

The pipes carrying clean water must be strong enough to sustain the pressure necessary for water to flow through them. Pipes that remove waste typically do not use pressure and, therefore, must be angled downward so that waste travels into the sewer system.

Sewers and Septic Tanks

As mentioned earlier, in addition to supplying clean water to a home, a plumbing system must remove waste from the home. There are several types of systems for removing waste. The preferred method is a municipal sewer system. Another alternative is a septic system.

A septic system is a private system that includes a large concrete septic tank buried in the ground. Waste material enters one end of the tank through a drain line coming from the house. Inside the tank, the waste separates into three parts:

1. solid waste, which sinks to the bottom
2. grease, which rises to the top
3. the remaining waste, which is liquid

The septic tank contains bacteria, which decompose the solid wastes and grease. Relatively clear liquid flows out the opposite end of the tank into a distribution box that directs the liquid into a network of buried perforated pipes called a leaching field. The liquid flows into the ground and is absorbed.

Water Supply

There are various sources of water, including:

- municipal (public-supplied water)
- well water (private wells on a property)
- private company

In all cases, water must meet the standards provided by the U.S. Department of Health. According to the Federal Housing Administration (FHA), public water should be used when it's available.

Hot Water System

A hot water system is a necessity. The supply is usually generated in a separate hot water heater, which is powered by electricity, gas, or oil. Additionally, hot water may be supplied from furnace heat. Hot water heater tanks vary in size. The size needed depends on the number of residents and the recovery rate for the unit (the time it takes to heat water). Standard hot water tanks range from 30 to 80 gallons.

Electrical System

Electricity is carried by transmission lines from power plants to homes. Electricity enters a home at a service entrance, where the electricity flows through a meter to a distribution panel. The distribution panel distributes the electricity throughout the home. The distribution panel has a master switch that can be used to cut off all electric service in the house in the event of an emergency.

The panel also contains a master fuse or a master circuit breaker that will automatically shut off the entire system if there is a power overload. A fuse is a piece of wire or metal that will melt and stop the current when the flow of electricity exceeds the prescribed amount. A circuit breaker is a switch that automatically turns off when the flow of electricity exceeds the prescribed amount.

The distribution panel feeds the incoming electricity to separate branch circuits. Each individual circuit is also protected by a fuse or a circuit breaker. In the event of an overload, it automatically shuts off without tripping the main fuse or circuit breaker. A typical panel box has 12 to 16 fuses or circuit breakers.

Electricity is measured in terms of amperes (or amps) and volts. Amps represent the amount of electricity; volts represent the force. The electricity capacity of homes, in terms of volts and amps, is described next.

Volts

In the past, homes were wired for 110 or 220 volts. Currently, homes are being wired for 120 or 240 volts. This increase in voltage is substantially due to the added electrical drawing appliances that are included in existing and new home construction, such as:

- washers
- dryers
- dishwashers
- central air-conditioning

Amps

A home may be designed to bring in 30, 60, 100, 150, 200, 300, or 400 amps of electricity. The standard for homes that do not have electric heat or central air-conditioning is 100 amps. In homes with electric heat, central air-conditioning, or a large number of appliances, service of 150 to 400 amps is needed. In smaller and older homes, 30- or 60-amp service may still be found.

FRAMING AND CONSTRUCTION

Framing refers to the underlying structure of a building. Although steel framing is occasionally used, most residences are built with wood-frame construction. There are several types of framing, including:

- platform framing
- balloon framing
- post-and-beam framing

Platform Framing

With platform framing, each story of the building is built as a separate unit. Each story then serves as a platform for the next story. Platform-frame construction is the most common type of framing.

Balloon Framing

With balloon framing, each wall stud runs the entire height of the building, from the floor of the lowest story to the roof of the building. This is different from platform framing, where separate, shorter wall studs are used for each story—that is, a wall stud for the first story runs from the floor of the first story to the ceiling of that story. A wall stud for the second story runs from the floor of the second story to the ceiling of that story.

Post-and-Beam Framing

With post-and-beam framing, beams that support the building rest on posts or columns rather than bearing walls. Post-and-beam framing is used in contemporary-style homes. Often, the framing remains exposed for decorative purposes.

A real estate professional should make note of any problems with the framing. The following problems may indicate structural defects:

- bulging exterior walls
- windows that are not properly functioning (may be a clue to structural damage)
- irregular roof lines
- sticking doors and windows
- sloping floors
- large cracks developing on the foundation, walls, or ceiling

If defects are suspected, professional consultants may be called in to confirm this opinion.

> ## Coaching Tips
>
> ### Framing
>
> - Post-and-beam framing—Beams that support the building rest on posts or columns rather than bearing walls.
> - Balloon framing—Each wall stud runs the entire height of the building, from the floor of the lowest story to the roof of the building.
> - Platform framing—Each story of the building is built as a separate unit and serves as a platform for the next story.

Damage by Wood-Destroying Organisms

An owner of a wood frame home must constantly monitor the home for organisms that destroy wood. The following represents some of the most common homeowner concerns:

1. Termites—flying, wood-eating insects. While no license is required for testing, remediation of termiticide requires licensing from the Department of Environmental Conservation (DEC).
2. Carpenter ants—insects capable of damaging any wood where they nest. Infestation can become severe when left untreated. It would not be unusual that in some cases, a colony of carpenter ants can develop other new satellite nests.
3. Decay—wood decay (also known as wood rot) is decomposing wood. This can occur as the result of actions by certain species of fungi. Although carpenter ants, termites, and other wood-destroying insects do not cause wood decay, they are attracted to soft decaying wood.

INDOOR AND OUTDOOR ENVIRONMENTAL HAZARDS

In recent years, there has been an increased concern about environmental protection. This concern has had an effect on the real estate profession. It has also led to sustainability/green building. Sustainability or **green building** (construction that lowers the impact on the environment) has emerged with great importance. For example, a real estate licensee is liable if he/she fails to disclose defects in a property that could affect the health or safety of the occupants. Because environmental hazards affect health and safety, a licensee is obligated to disclose if such hazards exist on property involved in a real estate transaction. Some of the environmental hazards that affect real property include the following:

- radon
- urea-formaldehyde foam insulation (UFFI) and formaldehyde gas

- asbestos
- lead
- groundwater contamination
- hazardous waste dumps
- underground storage tanks
- chemical contamination
- mold

In the remainder of this chapter, we will look at each of these types of hazards and some guidelines to follow to avoid legal problems related to environmental hazards.

Radon

Radon is a colorless, odorless toxic gas that enters a building from the ground through openings around plumbing or through cracks in the foundation. It is derived from the natural decay of uranium. Because it enters a building from the ground, radon gas is not typically a problem in high-rise buildings or the upper floors of commercial facilities. However, it can be a problem in some homes and schools. Radon gas is hazardous because it can cause damage to the lungs.

To find out if a particular property may be affected by radon gas, you can:

- contact a local, state, or federal environmental agency
- ask the owners of nearby property if they know of any problems
- recommend that the seller have the property tested for radon

Currently, it is not uncommon for a buyer to request a radon test before making an offer. Radon tests are easy to obtain, and if a problem is found, it is usually easy and inexpensive to correct. If a radon test is conducted, the results of the test must be disclosed to the seller and all potential buyers. There are publications available from the U.S. Environmental Protection Agency (EPA) for homeowners interested in obtaining information about radon gas. You may want to obtain copies of these publications to give to prospective buyers. You should also be aware that Florida state law requires that all licensees attach radon disclosure statements on all contracts.

Formaldehyde Gas

Formaldehyde gas is emitted by materials contained in the following household items:

- furniture
- draperies
- carpet
- plywood

Formaldehyde gas is also emitted by a thermal insulation called **urea-formaldehyde foam insulation**, which was used in many older homes. Formaldehyde gas may cause irritation to the eyes, nose, and throat. In addition, it may cause more serious problems such as cancer. However, the level of formaldehyde that typically occurs in a home is not sufficient to produce serious problems. If you suspect that a home contains urea-formaldehyde foam insulation, you should recommend that the seller do the following:

- Have the air inside the home tested for formaldehyde gas.
- Consult a health authority.

If a problem with formaldehyde gas exists, the material emitting the gas must be removed.

Asbestos

In the past, **asbestos** was used as insulation in many buildings because of its fire-retardant qualities. Asbestos fibers can cause serious lung diseases, including cancer. Although asbestos is typically found in older buildings with public occupancy, it also can be found in the ceilings, floors, and pipes in older homes. Some of the indicators of the presence of asbestos include:

- ceilings or walls covered with a grainy plaster
- ceilings or walls sprayed with a fluffy, stringy material
- pipes or boilers wrapped with fibrous material or with a cement or felt-type insulation

A licensee handling older buildings should have these buildings inspected for asbestos or recommend that the owner contact an asbestos consultant.

In addition, the seller and potential buyers should be informed if the licensee knows or believes that a building contains asbestos. If asbestos is found, the removal is a complicated and expensive procedure.

Lead

Exposure to lead typically comes from lead plumbing and lead-based paints. Serious problems can occur if an individual:

- drinks water containing lead particles from lead plumbing
- ingests flakes of lead-based paint
- inhales lead particles

For example, if lead particles are inhaled or ingested by an adult with high blood pressure, this condition may worsen. Also, children exposed to lead may suffer from impaired physical and/or mental development. Young children and pregnant women are at greater risk.

As a real estate licensee, you should be aware of the following issues related to lead contamination:

- Department of Housing and Urban Development (HUD) housing must be in compliance with HUD regulations related to inspecting and testing for lead contamination.
- The use of lead plumbing in a system connected to a public water supply is prohibited by the EPA.
- If the level of lead in a residential plumbing system exceeds EPA standards, HUD and Veterans Affairs (VA) assistance is not available.
- Homes with peeling paint built in or before 1978 are those most likely to experience lead contamination.

In addition, to protect families from exposure to lead, Congress passed the Residential Lead-Based Paint Hazard Reduction Act of 1992 (also known as Title X). Section 1018 of this law requires the disclosure of known information on lead-based paint and lead-based paint hazards before the sale or lease of most housing built before 1978. The Residential Lead-Based Paint Hazard Reduction Act includes the following requirements:

- Sellers and lessors must disclose the presence of known lead-based paint and lead-based paint hazards and provide available reports to buyers or renters.
- Sellers and lessors must provide buyers and renters with a federally approved pamphlet titled *Protect Your Family from Lead in Your Home*.
- Sellers must give buyers a 10-day period to conduct a lead-based paint and lead-based hazard inspection (at the buyers' expense).
- Sales contracts and leases must include certain disclosures.
- Sellers, lessors, and real estate agents share the responsibility for ensuring compliance. Thus, as an agent, you are responsible for informing sellers or lessors of their obligations under the law and for ensuring that they make the required disclosures.

Coaching Tips

The Residential Lead-Based Paint Hazard Reduction Act does not require the testing or removal of lead-based paint by sellers or lessors nor does it require either sellers or lessors to pay for a buyer or tenant to conduct a lead-based paint test.

Groundwater Chemical Contamination

Groundwater **chemical contamination** occurs when a supply of drinking water is contaminated by any of the following:

- pesticides and fertilizers used in farming
- leaking **underground storage tanks**

- hazardous **toxic waste** dumps
- mining
- any other source of contamination

To determine if groundwater may be contaminated, a licensee may do any of the following:

- Contact the appropriate health authority for information about the quality of the water.
- Ask the owners of nearby property if they know of any problems with the water.
- Inspect the property for the presence of dumping, mining, or other sources of contamination.
- Keep up-to-date on reports of groundwater contamination that could affect property in the area.
- Inspect the property for patches of oil, areas where nothing will grow, and other signs of contamination.
- Determine how the property was used by previous owners.
- Inspect the property for signs of previous commercial use, such as the presence of asphalt and/or cement.
- Contact the appropriate agency to find out if any previous owners were cited for violating environmental protection laws.
- Ask the seller and/or the appropriate authority if there are any underground storage tanks on the property.
- Inspect the property for air vents sticking out of the ground, which may indicate the presence of an underground storage tank.
- Hire an expert to test the groundwater for contamination.

Most tests for common groundwater contaminants are relatively easy and inexpensive. These tests can be conducted by private laboratories. However, if the water needs to be tested for industrial contaminants, the procedures are more complex and expensive. When such tests are needed, you (or the seller) should contact the proper environmental authority. If you know or suspect that there is a problem with the groundwater, you should inform the seller and any prospective buyers. Also, if there is reason to believe that the source of contamination is a hazardous waste dump or an underground storage tank, you should strongly encourage the seller and buyer to contact the appropriate environmental protection agency and/or health authority.

For example, if you know that a property was previously used as a gas station or oil distributor, you should recommend that the seller and/or buyer consult the appropriate environmental agency.

Disclosure Statement

As explained previously, whenever you know or suspect that a property is affected by an environmental hazard, you must disclose this to the seller and any potential buyers. One way to make a disclosure to potential buyers is to have the seller complete an environmental disclosure statement. The environmental disclosure statement may be a checklist of environmental conditions. The seller would simply check off all of the conditions that apply to his/her property. The licensee would give a copy of the checklist to any prospective buyers. The licensee may also decide to give buyers copies of any relevant government publications related to certain environmental conditions. By using an environmental disclosure form, licensees may protect themselves and the sellers from liability related to disclosure of property defects.

Due Diligence Investigation

The Superfund Amendments and Reauthorization Act of 1986 permits a property owner to use an innocent landowner defense if environmental problems arise after the owner sells the property. In order to use the innocent landowner defense, the owner must prove that a due diligence investigation of the property was conducted before ownership was transferred. A due diligence investigation is a very thorough and time-consuming process. There is a set of minimum requirements for the investigation. The following information must be included in the investigation:

- a review of previous and current ownership and use of the property, including uses involving environmental hazards
- a review of all previous inspections, investigations, litigation, etc., involving environmental hazards
- an evaluation of adjacent properties and any associated hazards
- a review of the drainage, sewer, and septic systems

This list is not a complete list of the requirements. A property owner who wishes to use the innocent landowner defense needs to obtain a thorough list and complete each requirement.

THE CONSTRUCTION DICTIONARY

Backfill

Backfill is the soil placed around the walls of a foundation to replace soil removed in the process of construction. Backfill is used to brace the foundation walls.

Commercial Acre

A commercial acre is the area remaining after an acre of land has been deducted for the footage for streets, curbs, sidewalks, parks, etc. It is the area available for constructing any buildings on the property.

> ### Coaching Tips
>
> This term should not be confused with a builders acre. In many states, a builders acre is comprised of 40,000 square feet of area. You should know that for all arithmetic calculations, an acre consists of 43,560 square feet in area.

Conduit

A conduit is a metal pipe or covering used to protect electrical wiring in a building.

Deciduous

A deciduous tree loses its leaves in the fall or winter; the type of tree that does not lose its leaves is called an evergreen tree.

Drywall

Drywall is the wallboard used on interior walls. It is also called sheetrock. It is called drywall because it is dry when nailed to the wall studs. This is in contrast to another form of interior wall finish called lath and plaster, in which the plaster is applied in wet form to the lath.

Elevation Drawing

An elevation drawing shows the front and side views of the exterior of the house as it will appear when construction is completed. This drawing illustrates the exterior finish as well as the placement of windows, doors, vents, skylights, etc.

Energy Efficiency Ratio (EER)

The EER is a number (a ratio) used to represent the energy efficiency of appliances such as refrigerators, air conditioners, etc. The higher the EER is, the greater the energy efficiency is. (This means that as the EER goes up, the amount of energy used goes down.)

Flashing

Flashing is sheet metal used on the roof of a house to protect against water seeping through the roof. It is used in areas where the shingles do not completely cover or seal a junction between two elements of the roof. For example, it is used where the gables of a roof join the main roof and around chimneys and vent pipes.

Footing

A footing is a concrete base or support under a foundation wall. It is made by pouring the concrete into a trench dug into the ground. The trench is wider than the foundation wall so that the weight of the foundation is distributed over a larger area of ground. The foundation is then constructed on top of the footing. There are three types of foundations:

1. Slab-on-grade—Slabs are flat pieces of concrete that rest on the ground or on footings that provide support. Note: With very few exceptions, basements are not typical in Florida. This is because most of Florida is at or below sea level; therefore, the water table is high and prevents the installation of basements.
2. Basement—A basement floor is constructed similarly to a slab.
3. Crawl space—Crawl spaces are similar to basements except that the height from the floor to the joists is less. Crawl spaces provide protection from flooding and also access to heating ducts, plumbing pipes, and wires.

Figure A.2 summarizes the elements of construction.

Foundation

The foundation is the part of the building that supports the first floor of the building and is attached to the ground. A foundation is most often made of poured concrete but may also be made of a combination of poured concrete and concrete block. The entire foundation consists of several components and may include the footing, foundation walls, bearing posts, and/or piers, depending on the type of structure. The foundation plan is a drawing that shows each of these various elements as they are to be constructed.

Header

A header is a beam that runs across the top of a door or window opening in the frame of a house. A header is used because the door or window opening is wider than the distance between normal wall studs, and additional strength is needed across this width to support the roof above the door or window.

Percolation Test

A percolation test is conducted by an engineer to determine the extent to which the soil is able to absorb water. A percolation test should be completed before a septic tank is installed. As a means of remembering, think of a percolation test as you would of percolated coffee makers. In this type of coffee maker, water boils

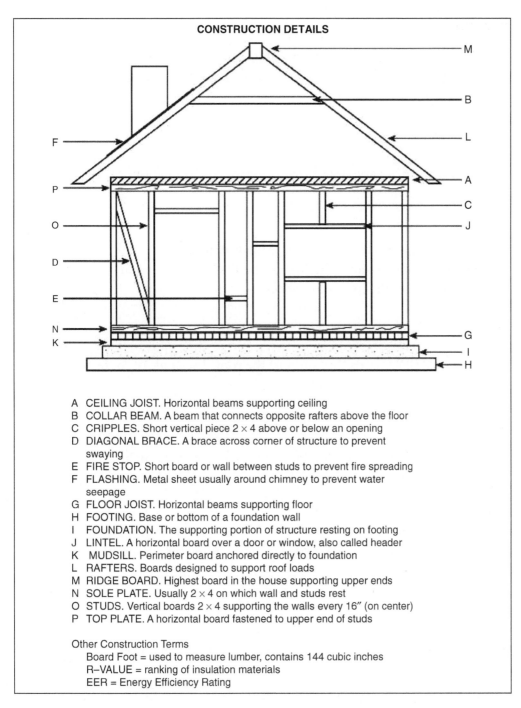

FIGURE A.2
Source: © 2021 Mbition LLC

and rises up the hollow tube through its top opening into the coffee grinds. The grinds are able to absorb the boiling water to its saturation point. Coarse grounds will absorb more water than will fine grounded coffee.

Plot Plan (Plot Map)

The plot plan is a map that shows the boundaries and dimensions of the property and the location of all improvements to the land, such as buildings, driveways, patios, walks, etc.

Potable Water

Potable water is drinkable water that is free of contamination.

R Value

The R value rates the effectiveness of insulation materials. The R stands for resistance to heat transmission. The higher the R value is for a particular insulation material, the better the insulation effect.

Rafter

Rafters are parallel boards that support the roof. The angle of these boards determines the steepness (or pitch) of the roof.

Ridgeboard

The ridgeboard runs across the length of the roof at its highest point. It is the highest structural point in a frame house or structure.

Sill

The sill is the lowest structural member of the frame of a house that rests on the foundation.

Soil Pipe

A soil pipe carries sewage waste from the house to the main sewer line.

Additional Dictionary of Construction Terms at a Glance

- Culvert: A drain that runs under a road.
- Flashing: Metal strips used to prevent water seepage.
- Footing: A concrete base or support under a foundation wall. It is made by pouring the concrete into a trench dug into the ground.
- Knob: A component in an outdated electrical system.

New England Colonial
A box-shaped two-story house with a center entrance, wood siding, and shutters.

Georgian Colonial
A brick two-story house with a center entrance and a hip roof.

Southern Colonial
A two-story house with pillars and shutters.

Dutch Colonial
A two-story house with a gambrel roof.

California Bungalow
A small, one-story house with a low-pitched roof.

California Ranch
A one-story house with a low-pitched roof and a sprawling floor plan.

Spanish
A house with a tile roof and arches.

Cape Cod
A house with a second story above the eaves, a high-pitched roof, wood siding and a large chimney.

French Provincial
A formal house with a high-pitched, slate hip roof, a stone or brick exterior, and shutters.

FIGURE A.3

Victorian
A house with ornate gables.

English Elizabethan
A house with a high-pitched, slate roof, rough half-timbers, and a plaster exterior.

Monterey
A two-story house with a front balcony.

French Norman
A house with a tower as the main entrance and a steep roof.

English Tudor
A house with a high-pitched, slate roof, a cathedral-like entrance, and a masonry exterior.

Mediterranean or Italian
A house with a tile roof, a stucco exterior, and rounded decorative work above the windows.

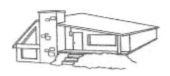
Contemporary
A house of modern design.

(b)

FIGURE A.3 (*Continued*)
Source: © 2021 Mbition LLC

- Sash: A frame that holds a pane of glass.
- Shake: Roofing material made of wood.
- Shell: The framework of a building.
- Shingles: Not considered sheathing. They make up one type of roof finishing material that is attached to the sheathing.
- Slabs: Flat pieces of concrete that rest on the ground or on footings that provide support.
- Slate: A type of hard rock.
- The R in R value: Stands for resistance to heat flow.
- Trusses: Framing units that are assembled at a factory and usually consist of several triangle-shaped sections.
- Sole plate: The sole plate is a horizontal member to which the wall studs are attached.
- Stud: Studs are vertical boards (usually a 2 × 4) that make up the supporting elements of a wall or partition. The maximum legal distance between studs is 16 inches.

Major architectural styles for residential homes are illustrated in Figures A.3a and A.3b.

Summary

Because most licensees will be dealing with both new and existing properties, product knowledge becomes essential. Licensees should familiarize themselves with common construction terminology. Housing in Florida is generally constructed with foundations consisting of slab on slab. This is primarily because the water table is high. Therefore, basements and crawl spaces are not common. Platform framing is the most common framing, and roof designs vary. Finishes would include improvements designed to protect against wind and other climate hazards. This would include storm screens and wind shading on windows and Florida rooms.

Review Questions

1. A type of framing that allows for open interiors without the interruption of many supporting walls would be:
   a. platform
   b. post and beam
   c. balloon
   d. joist

2. A double-hung window is a window that:
   a. features insulated glass
   b. opens from the bottom
   c. swings out to open
   d. opens from either the bottom or top

3. Air flow in a building:
   a. prevents water condensation
   b. provides more comfortable interiors
   c. promotes the flow of heat
   d. reduces accumulation of odors and gas

4. Insulation is rated by:
   a. depth of material
   b. the Department of Energy
   c. resistance to heat flow
   d. type of installation

5. Sarah plans to build an expensive two-story home with a stucco exterior. To reduce the possibility of cracks in the stucco finish, she might consider:
   a. platform framing
   b. balloon framing
   c. a pier foundation with a crawl space
   d. fixed windows

6. Today's homes have many electrical appliances that are used every day. Most homes are wired for:
   a. 110 and 220 volts
   b. 110 and 240 volts
   c. 120 and 220 volts
   d. 120 and 240 volts

7. A type of roof that features two planes with an overhang on two sides of the building is a:
   a. gable roof
   b. fip roof
   c. gambrel roof
   d. mansard roof

8. The pitch of a roof measures the roof's:
   a. height
   b. slope
   c. span
   d. run

9. A long skinny lot is known as a(n):
   a. key lot
   b. flag lot
   c. corner lot
   d. interior lot

10. Once the roof trusses are hoisted into place, the next step of roof construction is installing the:
    a. insulation
    b. shingles
    c. sheathing
    d. felt

11. Which type of window opens by swinging outward?
    a. jalousie
    b. fixed
    c. double-hung
    d. casement

12. Julian wants to add a second story to his ranch-style home. A major concern is whether:
    a. the foundation is deep enough
    b. a new roof system can be installed
    c. the bearing walls are adequate
    d. the design will be pleasing

13. The amount of the electrical flow along the transmission wires is measured in:
    a. wattage
    b. amps
    c. current
    d. volts

14. Brad is considering buying his neighbor's home that was built in the 1960s. The home is listed with ABC Realty. Before signing a contract for the house, ABC Realty:
    a. must give Brad an EPA pamphlet that describes the danger of lead-based paint
    b. can have Brad sign a waiver of the inspection requirements
    c. will provide a seller's statement that the seller will pay for a property inspection
    d. will give a statement that Brad must pay for a required inspection

15. All persons in Florida must be given a disclosure regarding the possibility of the presence of radon gas on the property at or before the time of entering into a sale and purchase or rental agreement. Which of these statements is true?
    a. Prospective buyers and lessees must sign the radon gas disclosure.
    b. All real property contracts must attach the radon gas disclosure.
    c. No inspection or remedy regarding radon is required.
    d. The radon disclosure cannot be included as a portion of the contract.

16. Asbestos was commonly used as insulation and a fire retardant in the 1970s. If asbestos is found in a property, which of the following would be correct:
    a. require the removal of asbestos material from buildings
    b. do not address the presence of asbestos in buildings. Federal laws prevail
    c. require that asbestos be encapsulated, a procedure safer than removal
    d. recommend that the owner contact an asbestos consultant to determine the best course of action

17. Which statement is FALSE regarding subdivisions?
    a. Winding streets in subdivisions are aesthetically pleasing.
    b. Four-way stops are safer in subdivision intersections.
    c. Conformity of the homes in the subdivision raises the value of all the homes.
    d. T-intersection lots are the most desirable lots and command a higher price.

18. A rectangular lot reached by a long access road is a(n):
    a. key lot
    b. interior lot
    c. cul-de-sac lot
    d. flag lot

19. In Florida, building codes are mandated by:
    a. the state of Florida
    b. local municipalities
    c. counties
    d. the type of zoning district

MATH BUSTERS GUIDE TO REAL ESTATE MATH

This appendix summarizes mathematical formulas commonly used by real estate professionals. By studying and memorizing these formulas, you will have a basic understanding of the key formulas needed to succeed in this course.

KEY FORMULAS

1. **Calculating Commissions:**

    Sales Price × Commission Rate = **Commission Amount**

2. **Calculating Commission Rate:**

    Net Sales Price (after Commissions but before Expenses) ÷ Commission Amount = **Commission Rate**

3. **Calculating Purchase Price:**

    Sales Price ÷ Commission Rate = **Purchase Price**

4. **Calculating Simple Interest:**

    Outstanding Loan Balance × Interest Rate = **Annual Interest**

5. **Calculating Total Interest:**

    Principal × Rate × Time = **Total Interest**

6. **Calculating Dollar Amount of Discount Points(s):**

    Loan Amount × Number of Points (in decimal form) = Dollar Amount of Points

7. **Calculating Area:**

   Triangle: Base × Height × 0.50 = Area of a Triangle
   Square: Side × Side = Area of a Square
   Rectangle: Length × Width = Area of a Rectangle

8. **Calculating Prorations (365/360 day method):**

   Monthly Prorations using a 365 day year

   Step 1:

   Amount ÷ Actual Number of Days in Month = Daily Rate

   Step 2:

   Daily Rate × Number of Days Attributable = Proration

   Monthly Prorations using a 360 day year

   Step 1:

   Amount ÷ 30 Days in Month = Daily Rate

   Step 2:

   Daily Rate × Number of Days Attributable = Proration

   Annual Prorations

   Step 1:

   Amount ÷ 360 Days or 365 Days (as case may be) = Daily Rate

   Step 2:

   Daily Rate × Number of Days Attributable = Proration

9. **Calculating State Transfer Taxes:**

   State Documentary Stamps on a Deed

   Step 1:

   Sale Price ÷ $100 (or any fraction thereof, round up) = Taxable Units of $100

Step 2:

Taxable Units of $100 × $0.70 (tax rate) = Deed Transfer Tax

Note: In Dade County, the tax rate on deeds is $0.60.

State Documentary Stamps on Notes

Step 1:

Note Amount ÷ $100 (or any fraction thereof, round up) = Taxable Units of $100

Step 2:

Taxable Units of $100 × $0.35 (tax rate) = Deed Transfer Tax

Note: This tax is applicable to new and assumed notes, but is not applied when the property is purchased subject to the mortgage.

Intangible Tax on Mortgage

New Mortgage Amount × 0. 002 (2 mills tax rate)¼ Intangible Tax

Note: This tax is only applied against new money introduced to the transaction and does not apply to assumed or to subject to the mortgage amounts.

10. **Calculating Real Property Taxes:**

    Step 1:

    Assessed Valuation – Homestead and/or Other Deduction = Adjusted Assessed Valuation

    Step 2:

    Adjusted Assessed Valuation × Tax or Mill Rate = Annual Property Tax

11. **Calculating Capitalization:**

    IRV

    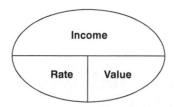

Income = Rate × Value
Rate = Income ÷ Value
Value = Income ÷ Rate

12. **Calculating Accrued Depreciation:**

   Lump-Sum Age-Life Method

   Effective Age
   ÷ Economic Life
   × Reproduction/Replacement Cost (new)
   = Accrued Depreciation

13. **Analysis of Cash Flow:**

   Cash World and Tax World

CASH WORLD	TAX WORLD
Potential Gross Income (PGI)	Net Operating Income (NOI)
− Vacancy & Collection Losses (V&C)	+ Reserve for Replacements (R&R)
+ Other Income (OI)	= Adjusted Net Operating Income (ANOI)
= Effective Gross Income (EGI)	− Mortgage Interest (MI)
− Operating Expenses (OE)	− Annual Depreciation Allowance (ADA)
= Net Operating Income (NOI)	− Suspended/Carryover Loss (SCL)
− Annual Debt Service (ADS)	= Taxable Income (TI)
= Before Tax Cash Flow	× Marginal Tax Rate (MTR)
− Income Tax (IT)	= Income Tax (IT)
= After Tax Cash Flow (ATCF)	

   Rent Per Square Foot

   Annual Dollars ÷ Number of Square Feet = Dollars per Square Foot

   Operating Expenses Per Square Foot

   Annual Operating Expenses ÷ Total Building Square Footage = Operating Expenses in Dollars per Square Foot

   Loan to Value Ratio (LVR)

   Represents the lender's investment in the property (loan) as compared with the lesser of the purchase price or appraised value (value).

   $$\text{LVR} = \frac{\text{Loan Amount}}{\text{Value}}$$

Example:

$$\text{LVR} = \frac{378{,}000}{472{,}500} = 0.80 \text{ or } 80\%$$

Debt Service Coverage Ratio (DSCR)

Represents the amount by which the NOI exceeds the annual debt service. Higher ratios are preferred as a hedge against:

- Loss of value
- Lower NOI
- Vacancies

$$\text{DSCR} = \frac{\text{NOI (Net Operating Income)}}{\text{ADS (Annual Debt Service)}}$$

Example:

If the net operating income is $75,600 and annual debt service is $56,100

$$\text{DSCR} = \frac{\$75{,}600}{\$56{,}100} \; 1.347, \text{ or rounded off to } 1.35$$

Operating Expense Ratio (OER)

Represents the amount of the effective gross income that will be used to pay operating expenses.

$$\text{OER} = \frac{\text{Operating Expenses}}{\text{Effective Gross Income}}$$

Example:

If annual operating expenses are $82,900 and Effective Gross Income is $158,500:

$$\frac{82{,}900}{158{,}500} = 0.523 \text{ or } 52.3\%$$

Cash Break-Even Ratio (CBR)

Represents the potential gross income that is absorbed by cash charges.

Formula:

$$\text{CBR} = \frac{\text{Operating Expenses} + \text{Debt Service} - \text{Reserves for Replacements}}{\text{Potential Gross Income}}$$

Example:
If reserves for replacements are $12,500 and potential gross income is $172,300:

$$\frac{\$82{,}900 + 56{,}100 - 12{,}500}{172{,}300} = 0.734 \text{ or } 73.4\%$$

Margin of Safety
Represents the difference between cash receipts/cash disbursements and is the difference between 1.00 and the cash break-even ratio.

$$\text{Margin of Safety} = 1.00 - 0.734 = 0.266 \text{ or } 26.6\%$$

Equity Dividend Rate (EDR)
Represents the rate of return to an investor on his equity from an income-producing property. It is computed by dividing before tax cash flow (BTCF) by the equity. EDR is referred to as cash-on-cash return.

$$\text{EDR} = \frac{\text{Before Tax Cash Flow}}{\text{Equity}}$$

Example:
If before tax cash flow is $15,000 and equity is $94,500:

$$\text{EDR} = \frac{15{,}000}{94{,}500} = 0.1587 \text{ or } 15.87\%$$

14. **Mortgage Loans: Conventional:**

Many lenders will use either or both of the following two ratios:

Monthly Housing Expense Ratio:

PITI = Principal, Interest, Taxes, and Insurance
PITI ÷ Monthly Gross Income = 28 percent or less

Total (Monthly) Fixed Obligations Ratio:

PITI + Total Monthly Obligations ÷ Monthly Gross Income = 36 percent or less

15. **Mortgage Loans: Nonconventional/FHA Insured:**

Buyer must meet the following two ratios

Monthly Housing Expense Ratio:

PITI ÷ Monthly Gross Income = 31 percent or less

Total (Monthly) Fixed Obligations Ratio:

PITI + Total Monthly Obligations ÷ Monthly Gross Income = 43 percent or less

16. Yield Calculation:

Loan Discount or Points:
The purpose is to increase the lender's yield on the money loaned through prepaid interest. Discount points may also be used to buydown the interest rate using the following rule of thumb: 1 point = 1/8 percent of loan amount on a 25- to 30-year loan.

17. Measures and Definitions:

Check:	A square parcel of land consisting of 24 miles on each side. It is used as a correction for the earth's curvature. A check contains 576 square miles that include:

- 16 townships
- 576 sections
- 368,640 acres

Township:	A square tract of land whose sides measure 6 miles each; it contains 36 sections of land, each being one square mile.
Section:	A square tract of land whose sides measure 1 mile each. Acres in a section: 640 acres of land Acres in a ¼ section: 160 acres of land Acres in a ¼ of a ¼ section: 40 acres of land Acres in a ¼ of a ¼ of a ¼ section: 10 acres of land Acres in a ¼ of a ¼ of a ¼ of a ¼ section: 2.5 acres of land
Acre:	43,560 square feet.
Mile:	5,280 linear feet.
Leverage:	Is the use of borrowed funds.

Loan Constant: Is the percentage of the initial loan that is repaid in equal monthly or annual installments. The two components that comprise the loan constant include:

1. Interest (discount rate)
2. Principal reduction (sinking fund factor)

The sinking fund factor provides the lender with a return of a portion of the principal amount originally loaned. Compound interest tables will contain a column entitled "Installment to Amortize $1.00." The numbers contained in this column are:

- Loan constants for different loan terms
- The sum of the discount rate and the sinking fund factor

Before Tax Cash Flow (BTCF): Is the cash return after making annual debt service. The BTCF is expressed in a dollar amount. It is also the cash throw-off or gross spendable income after deducting debt service but before making any income tax payment.

$$\text{Before Tax Cash Flow} = \text{Net Operating Income} - \text{Annual Debt Service}$$

Equity Dividend Rate (EDR): Is the ratio of the cash return (BTCF) divided by the investor equity. Equity dividend rate is also expressed in percentage terms.

ANSWERS TO CHAPTER REVIEW QUESTIONS

Chapter 1

1. C
2. D
3. D
4. A
5. C
6. D
7. B
8. A
9. C
10. B
11. C
12. D
13. A
14. D
15. A
16. C
17. D
18. B
19. B
20. D

Chapter 2

1. C
2. A
3. C
4. A
5. C
6. B
7. D
8. D
9. B
10. D
11. D
12. A
13. A
14. B
15. D
16. B
17. B
18. B
19. C
20. A

Chapter 3

1. A
2. C
3. A
4. D
5. B
6. C
7. D
8. B
9. A
10. C
11. C
12. A
13. A
14. C
15. D
16. A
17. B
18. A
19. C
20. A

Chapter 4

1. D
2. D
3. C
4. A
5. A
6. D
7. B
8. C
9. D
10. A
11. C
12. C
13. D
14. B
15. D
16. C
17. D
18. B
19. B
20. A

Chapter 5

1. B
2. A
3. B
4. A
5. B
6. D
7. C
8. B
9. D
10. A
11. B
12. C
13. D
14. D
15. C
16. B
17. B
18. C
19. A
20. C
21. D

Chapter 6

1. D
2. B
3. C
4. C
5. D
6. A
7. D
8. B
9. D
10. B
11. D
12. C
13. A
14. C
15. B
16. C
17. D
18. B
19. C

Chapter 7

1. C
2. D
3. C
4. D
5. A
6. A
7. C
8. D
9. D
10. A
11. B
12. D
13. A
14. A
15. D
16. B
17. C
18. D
19. A
20. D
21. D

Chapter 8

1. C
2. A
3. C
4. A
5. C
6. A
7. A
8. C
9. A
10. B
11. D
12. C
13. A
14. D
15. D
16. D
17. C
18. D

Chapter 9

1.	C	8.	B	15.	A
2.	C	9.	B	16.	A
3.	B	10.	A	17.	B
4.	A	11.	D	18.	C
5.	B	12.	B	19.	A
6.	A	13.	B	20.	C
7.	D	14.	C		

Chapter 10

1.	C	8.	A	15.	D
2.	B	9.	D	16.	C
3.	D	10.	D	17.	B
4.	C	11.	B	18.	B
5.	A	12.	A	19.	A
6.	C	13.	D	20.	A
7.	C	14.	C		

Chapter 11

1.	D	8.	A	15.	A
2.	A	9.	D	16.	D
3.	C	10.	D	17.	C
4.	D	11.	B	18.	A
5.	C	12.	A	19.	C
6.	B	13.	C	20.	B
7.	D	14.	D	21.	A

Chapter 12

1.	C	8.	A	15.	A
2.	B	9.	A	16.	B
3.	A	10.	A	17.	B
4.	B	11.	C	18.	D
5.	C	12.	C	19.	A
6.	B	13.	B	20.	D
7.	B	14.	C		

Chapter 13

1.	B	7.	C	13.	C
2.	B	8.	C	14.	A
3.	A	9.	A	15.	D
4.	B	10.	B	16.	D
5.	B	11.	C	17.	B
6.	A	12.	B	18.	A

Chapter 14

1.	D	6.	C	11.	C
2.	C	7.	A	12.	C
3.	B	8.	A	13.	C
4.	A	9.	C	14.	D
5.	B	10.	D	15.	D

Chapter 15

1. D
2. C
3. B
4. A
5. D
6. C
7. D
8. D
9. A
10. B
11. D
12. C
13. B
14. C
15. D
16. D
17. B
18. A
19. C
20. D

Chapter 16

1. C
2. C
3. C
4. B
5. D
6. A
7. D
8. C
9. B
10. B
11. C
12. D
13. C
14. C
15. B
16. B
17. C
18. D
19. A

Chapter 17

1. D
2. B
3. D
4. A
5. D
6. C
7. C
8. A
9. D
10. D
11. C
12. A
13. B
14. B
15. D
16. A
17. A
18. B
19. C
20. D

Chapter 18

1. D	9. D	17. D
2. A	10. B	18. D
3. D	11. C	19. C
4. B	12. D	20. A
5. C	13. C	21. B
6. A	14. B	22. C
7. C	15. D	
8. D	16. B	

Chapter 19

1. C	8. D	15. A
2. B	9. D	16. B
3. A	10. B	17. A
4. B	11. B	18. B
5. D	12. A	19. B
6. A	13. B	20. C
7. C	14. B	

Addendum

1. B	8. B	15. B
2. D	9. A	16. D
3. A	10. C	17. C
4. C	11. D	18. A
5. A	12. C	19. B
6. A	13. B	
7. A	14. A	

PRACTICE END-OF-COURSE EXAM

The following practice exam includes 100 multiple-choice questions that cover key topics from chapters in this textbook. After reading each question, select the most accurate response. You may use the answer sheet provided at the end of this exam to indicate your answers.

QUESTIONS

1. A couple lists their home with Acme Realty and are given a single agent brokerage notice. The couple doesn't want unannounced people knocking on their door and asked that no company yard sign be placed in the front yard. In this situation:
   a. a listing gives the company a legal right to install the sign, so the sign can be placed in the yard
   b. the agent should explain the importance of the yard sign to the couple, and then install it
   c. the agent should talk to the couple about the sign. If the couple won't change their mind, the company must obey or withdraw from the listing
   d. Acme Realty must give the couple the no brokerage relationship notice and continue with the listing procedures

2. A property owner qualifies for a 50% homestead on her residence in Clearwater, Florida. She is 78 years of age and is permanently disabled. Her husband is deceased. What is the cumulative tax exemption on her residence?
   a. $25,000
   b. $25,500
   c. $26,000
   d. $30,500

3. Max is, the only broker for his firm. His license is temporarily suspended. Which of the following best describes what will happen to the licensees registered to work under Max's supervision?

   a. The licenses will be canceled.
   b. The licenses will be placed in involuntarily inactive status.
   c. The licenses of the associates will not be affected.
   d. The licenses will be temporarily suspended.

4. According to Florida law, when a real estate license is suspended, the license becomes:

   a. ineffective
   b. canceled
   c. involuntarily inactive
   d. null and void

5. A broker prepares a comparative market analysis (CMA) for a neighbor and subsequently charges the neighbor for the service.

   a. It is illegal to charge for a CMA.
   b. The broker must have an appraisal license.
   c. This was legal if the CMA followed the Uniform Standards of Professional Appraisal Practice.
   d. The broker's action was legal.

6. A property owner asks her friend to appraise her home. Her friend works as a sales associate for Informal Realty.

   a. The sales associate must follow the Uniform Standards of Professional Appraisal Practice (USPAP).
   b. Only brokers can perform appraisals without an appraisal license.
   c. The sales associate can't do this unless she is a licensed appraiser.
   d. The sales associate can complete the appraisal, but cannot charge for the service.

7. A licensed attorney lives in Alabama. He refers a client wishing to purchase a Florida home to a broker in Pensacola. The broker was appreciative of the referral and sent the attorney a very nice gift.

   a. The broker didn't share the commission, so this is legal.
   b. This is legal because the gift went to an attorney.
   c. The broker violated Florida real estate laws.
   d. It would have been legal if the attorney practiced in Florida.

8. The process whereby a developer gives land in a subdivision to the municipality is referred to as:

   a. dedication
   b. accommodation
   c. follow-up
   d. legal requirement

9. In order to apply for a real estate license in Florida, an applicant:

   a. must declare residency in Florida
   b. has to be a U.S. citizen
   c. cannot have an active license in another state
   d. must disclose any encounter with the law required in the application

10. A Floridian owns two time-shares that she seldom uses. She proceeds to advertise them in the classified ads in the *Miami Herald*. Which of the following would be correct?

    a. Time-shares are not real property, so no license is required.
    b. The time-share owner doesn't need a license to do this.
    c. The time-shares must be sold through a real estate company.
    d. Time-shares are real property, so a license is required.

11. Ian received his sales associate license last year. Now he wants to open a real estate company. This requires a broker's license. Which of the following statements is true?

    a. Ian cannot apply to be a broker until his initial license has been renewed.
    b. Ian must complete the 45-hour post-license course before his first renewal cycle.
    c. Anyone can apply to be a broker at any time.
    d. When Ian completes a minimum number of transactions, his application will be considered.

12. Ben has held a sales associate license for 4 years. His real estate license expired 14 months ago involuntarily inactive. In order for Ben to be active again, which of the following is correct?

    a. Ben must take FREC Course I.
    b. Ben can pay a late fee and a renewal fee to regain his license.
    c. If Ben takes a 14-hour continuing education class, he can renew the license.
    d. After he completes a 28-hour FREC-approved course, Ben can reactivate the license.

13. Which of the following duties must a transaction broker provide?

    a. undivided loyalty
    b. limited confidentiality
    c. full disclosure
    d. obedience to all lawful instructions

14. A buyer received a no brokerage relationship notice from a firm. What duties are owed to the buyer?

    a. attornment
    b. limited confidentiality
    c. disclosure of all material facts
    d. obedience

15. When the Florida Real Estate Commission (FREC) changes administrative rules, their power to do this comes from their:

    a. executive powers
    b. quasi-legislative duties
    c. quasi-judicial powers
    d. composite powers

16. A licensee changed her residence from Kenneth City to Largo, but she still works out of her employing broker's office in Pinellas Park. Which of the following is correct?

    a. There is no paperwork required in this situation.
    b. The licensee has 60 days to sign the irrevocable consent to service.
    c. The DBPR must be notified no later than 10 days from the change of address.
    d. The licensee must reregister her employing broker with her new address.

17. The seven persons who serve on the Florida Real Estate Commission:

    a. are employed by the Division of Real Estate
    b. receive $50 per day when on Commission business
    c. are appointed by the secretary of the DBPR
    d. must have brokers' licenses

18. Frank serves as the broker of record for two different real estate companies. Frank:

    a. has multiple licenses
    b. has a group license
    c. has violated F.S. 475
    d. can operate only one business in Florida

19. Shirley operates her brokerage business out of her home. Which of the following is correct?

    a. An office sign is not required for a home office.
    b. An exterior office sign is required.
    c. Shirley's name must be included on an office sign.
    d. Shirley can't operate a business out of her home.

20. Broker associate Jeremy received a check from a buyer after 2 p.m. on Friday as a deposit to be included with an offer. The broker's normal banking day is Monday, but Monday is a legal holiday. However, banks will be open until noon on Saturday. What is true about the deposit?

    a. Jeremy must deposit the check on Saturday before the banks close.
    b. Jeremy must give the check to the broker before the end of Monday.
    c. The deposit must be turned over to the broker and out of Jeremy's hands before the end of Tuesday.
    d. Jeremy has until Wednesday to hand over the check to the broker.

21. The broker places all escrow deposits in an interest-bearing account and transfers the earned interest into his operating account every 2 weeks. What is true about this situation?

    a. Any interest from an escrow account must be distributed to the buyer and seller.
    b. The broker's action is legal if the buyer and seller agreed in writing.
    c. Escrow accounts cannot be interest-bearing accounts.
    d. Only the seller can receive the interest from an escrow account.

22. The broker for Homes Realty Company keeps around $2,000 in the escrow account to pay for the bank charges on the account.

    a. This is legal if the escrow records are current and accurate.
    b. Only the broker can sign checks on the account.
    c. Escrow records must be kept for 4 years.
    d. The broker is guilty of commingling.

23. A broker gives all binder deposits to a Florida attorney to hold. On a recent transaction, the buyer and seller are not going to close and both parties are claiming the buyer's deposit.

    a. The escrow dispute makes no legal demands on the broker.
    b. The broker must notify FREC of the dispute before 30 business days pass.
    c. The broker must notify FREC of the dispute before 15 business days pass.
    d. The broker can return the money to the buyer.

24. One of the settlement procedures available to a broker in an escrow dispute would be hiring a third party to recommend a solution. This procedure is called:
   a. arbitration
   b. mediation
   c. an escrow disbursement order
   d. litigation

25. Which of these activities requires a real estate license?
   a. Joe works for a motel and receives 10% of the room rent for every room he rents after 9 p.m.
   b. Sarah is paid a salary by the condo association for renting vacant condos to vacationers for up to 6-month periods.
   c. Ben leases interests in local businesses to out-of-state investors.
   d. Steele was paid handsomely for helping sell a radio station.

26. Jill purchased a list of rentals, but immediately decided to live with her cousin instead. She asked for a refund, but the realty company that sold her the list refused because the no-refund policy was clearly stated.
   a. Jill has no legal recourse. She should have read the company policy.
   b. The company must refund 100% of the fee charged to Jill.
   c. Refusing to refund the fee is a second-degree misdemeanor.
   d. The realty company can be subject to civil and criminal actions and can be punished administratively by FREC.

27. In a real estate partnership, if the only partner with an active broker's license dies, which of the following is correct?
   a. The partnership has 14 calendar days to appoint a new broker.
   b. The partnership is dissolved and must be reformed.
   c. The partnership's registration is automatically canceled.
   d. There's no legal requirement for a general partner to be an active broker.

28. A broker is going to open a new real estate business as a sole proprietorship. She's chosen the name Good Deal Realty as the business name. She:
   a. must advertise that she is doing business as Good Deal Realty
   b. must register the business name with FREC
   c. must file her business plan with the Florida Department of State
   d. cannot use a trade name for a sole proprietorship

29. A seller is refusing to pay a broker a legally owed commission. The broker can:
    a. ask for an escrow disbursement order
    b. place a lien on the seller's property
    c. withhold the escrow deposit until the seller pays the commission
    d. file a lawsuit in a civil court

30. One difference between a general partnership and a limited partnership is:
    a. a limited partnership can't be a real estate business
    b. limited partners can participate in the business
    c. limited partners cannot hold a real estate license
    d. limited partners can be associates

31. Following a formal complaint, an agreement reciting the punishment is entered into between a licensee and DRE attorneys. This agreement is called a:
    a. final order
    b. stipulation
    c. probable cause determination
    d. writ of supersedes

32. In the seven-step complaint process, the person who issues a summary suspension is the:
    a. florida real estate chair
    b. administrative law judge
    c. secretary of the DBPR
    d. appeals court judge

33. A complaint filed against a licensee must:
    a. be in writing
    b. not be anonymous
    c. involve Florida real estate laws
    d. have occurred in Florida

34. As a result of a visit from a Division of Real Estate auditor, Sure Fire Realty received a citation. The broker is sure the citation is an error. How can she remedy this?
    a. She has 10 days to request an informal hearing.
    b. The citation must be paid, and then can be disputed.
    c. She has 15 days to report the error to the DBPR.
    d. She must dispute the citation in writing within 30 days.

35. A broker followed an escrow disbursement order and gave the escrow funds to the seller as ordered. The buyer then successfully sued the broker in a civil court and was granted a monetary judgment. Because of the legal entanglement, and a judgment against the broker, what will happen to the broker's license?

    a. The license will be automatically suspended.
    b. The license may be revoked.
    c. No action will be taken against the broker.
    d. The DBPR will initiate an investigation.

36. Five people were damaged in a land investment scam. The broker who was responsible for the damages had an active license at the time. Each of the five was awarded $100,000 by the courts, but the broker can't pay the judgments. How much can these persons collect from the Real Estate Recovery Fund?

    a. FREC will not award any payments in this case.
    b. Each person can collect $50,000 from the Real Estate Recovery Fund.
    c. They will have to split $50,000.
    d. The payout from the fund will be limited to $150,000.

37. The money held in the Real Estate Recovery Fund originates from:

    a. administrative fines collected from licensees
    b. a trust that is funded by the legislature
    c. money set aside from the DRE's budget
    d. fees added to the issuing of real estate licenses

38. Which of the following is a protected class under the federal Fair Housing Act?

    a. age
    b. religion
    c. marital status
    d. receipt of income from public-assistance programs

39. When a prospective buyer applies for a loan with a lender for the purchase of a new home, the law that states lenders must give the borrower the Loan Estimate of closing costs is the:

    a. Real Estate Settlement Procedures Act
    b. Consumer Credit Protection Act (Truth in Lending)
    c. Equal Credit Opportunity Act
    d. Sherman and Clayton Fair Trade Acts

40. A small portion of a lot fell into a bordering stream and was carried away by the rising waters. The loss of the land is termed:

   a. accretion
   b. alluvion
   c. erosion
   d. reliction

41. The officers and directors of a real estate corporation who are active in the real estate business become licensed:

   a. by filing the appropriate paperwork with the Florida Department of State
   b. in the same manner as other real estate licensee applicants
   c. automatically through the licensing and registration of the corporation
   d. by being appointed or elected to the corporation's board of directors

42. Ann left her farm to her cousin for as long as her uncle lives; when the uncle dies, Ann's son will own it. Ann's son now has a:

   a. reversionary estate
   b. remainder estate
   c. life estate
   d. joint estate

43. The seller removed a corner bookcase before the closing papers were signed. The wall is damaged where the bookcase was removed, and the floor is a different color where the bookcase stood. Courts would likely rule the bookcase:

   a. was personal property and belonged to the seller
   b. could be removed because it wasn't mentioned in the contract
   c. was a fixture because it was adapted to fit in a corner
   d. was a fixture because it left damage when it was moved

44. Dan and Jack combined their assets to buy some property together. Dan put up less money and only has a one-third share. According to these facts, the property is owned as a:

   a. joint tenancy
   b. tenancy by the entirety
   c. tenancy in common
   d. holdover estate

45. Cooperatives, a form of residential ownership organized as a corporation, are regulated by the:

   a. Florida Real Estate Commission
   b. Division of Florida Land Sales, Condominiums, and Mobile Homes
   c. Division of Real Estate
   d. Department of Housing and Urban Development

46. Minnie is married to Ralph and they live in Minnie's homestead. Minnie has children from a previous marriage, but she has no children with Ralph. If Minnie dies intestate:

   a. her husband, Ralph, will own the homestead
   b. Minnie's children will own the home by descent
   c. Ralph will receive a life estate; the children are vested remaindermen
   d. Minnie's children and Ralph will be tenants in common

47. Dave signed a contract to purchase a new condominium in downtown Tampa from a developer. Unfortunately, Dave immediately regretted the purchase. Which of the following best applies to Dave's situation?

   a. Dave has 14 days to cancel the purchase in writing.
   b. Dave must cancel the purchase before three business days pass.
   c. A signed contract is legally binding.
   d. Dave can cancel, but must forfeit his binder deposit.

48. What governmental power is the right to take private property when it is needed for a public purpose?

   a. police power
   b. eminent domain
   c. adverse possession
   d. constructive notice

49. Bobby's land is being taken for a new extension to the highway and he doesn't want to give the land up. Bobby:

   a. can go to court to sue over the illegal taking
   b. can file an injunction to stop the taking
   c. has no recourse or options available
   d. can sue in court over the price he is being paid

50. A valid deed:
    a. must be signed by a competent grantee and grantor
    b. is signed by a competent grantor and two witnesses
    c. must be recorded to be legal
    d. must be notarized

51. A deed that contains no warranties whatsoever, not even a claim of ownership, is a:
    a. quitclaim deed
    b. bargain and sale deed
    c. special warranty deed
    d. general warranty deed

52. Which section is due east of Section 14, T2N, R3W?
    a. Section 13
    b. Section 15
    c. Section 16
    d. Section 11

53. Which legal description contains 2.5 acres?
    a. the SW ¼ of the SE ½ and the NE ¼ of the NW ¼ of Section 8
    b. the SW ¼ of the SE ¼ of the NE ¼ of the NW ¼ of Section 6
    c. the SW ¼ of the SW ¼ of the SW ¼ of Section 36
    d. the N ½ of the SW ¼ of the SW ¼ of the NE ¼ of Section 4

54. What is the most critical feature of a metes and bounds legal description?
    a. the accurate description of a corner monument
    b. the accuracy of the "calls"
    c. an accurate point of beginning
    d. Understanding compass directions

55. The law that requires any contract that conveys a part or whole interest in real property to be considered enforceable must be in writing is the:
    a. Statute of Frauds
    b. statute of limitations
    c. Florida Statute 475
    d. Chapter 61J2, FAC

56. Which of these contracts is an exception to the Statute of Frauds?
   a. a listing agreement for more than one year
   b. an option contract
   c. a sale contract
   d. a listing agreement for one year or less

57. The statute of limitations for a parol contract is:
   a. 3 years
   b. 4 years
   c. 5 years
   d. 10 years

58. Once a seller has signed a listing contract, law requires:
   a. the listing must be placed in the multiple-listing service before five business days pass
   b. the seller must be given a copy of the listing before 24 hours pass
   c. the broker is due a commission regardless of who sells the property
   d. the broker must accept any offer that conforms to the listing agreement

59. Four real estate companies have a listing from the seller. This listing is a(n):
   a. exclusive agency listing
   b. exclusive right of sale listing
   c. open listing
   d. net listing

60. Before the showing of a home that was built in the 1960s, the prospective buyers:
   a. must sign the lead-based paint disclosure
   b. must have the property inspected for lead-based paint
   c. must receive an EPA pamphlet describing the dangers of lead in paint
   d. must receive the required inspection report from the sellers

61. Which of the following is a requirement for a legal contract?
   a. signatures of both parties
   b. mutual assent
   c. receipt of a binder deposit
   d. acknowledgment

62. In a lien theory state the:
    a. mortgagor holds title while the mortgagee holds a lien
    b. mortgagee holds the title
    c. mortgage is the legal evidence of the debt
    d. mortgage creates a contract for deed

63. In an adjustable-rate mortgage, the portion of the interest rate that represents the lender's expenses and profit is termed the:
    a. index
    b. rate cap
    c. annual percentage rate (APR)
    d. margin

64. In a level-payment fixed-rate mortgage the portion of the payment that:
    a. pays interest never changes
    b. amortizes the loan gradually decreases with each payment
    c. pays principal gradually increases with each payment
    d. pays interest gradually increases with each payment

65. According to the Department of Veteran Affairs, a VA loan:
    a. is not a government-insured loan
    b. requires a minimum 3% cash investment
    c. can be a direct loan from the VA
    d. is only available for veterans

66. In order to qualify for an FHA loan the:
    a. housing expense ratio cannot exceed 29%
    b. interest rate cannot exceed 7%
    c. borrower must obtain a certificate of eligibility
    d. borrower must pay a one-time upfront insurance premium

67. The action by the Federal Reserve System to influence the cost of money in the economy and the amount of money available is the:
    a. open-market operations
    b. inflation rate
    c. monetary policy
    d. discount rate

68. Which of the following happens when the Federal Reserve purchases U.S. Treasury securities?

    a. the supply of money increases
    b. the supply of money decreases
    c. interest rates increase
    d. the cost of money is unchanged

69. When a title company prepares a Closing Disclosure, the unpaid property taxes:

    a. are charged to the seller only
    b. appear as a credit to the seller and a debit to the buyer
    c. appear as a debit to the seller and a credit to the buyer
    d. are charged to the buyer only

70. How is the binder deposit entered on the Closing Disclosure?

    a. debit the seller and the credit buyer
    b. credit the seller and debit the buyer
    c. debit to the buyer only
    d. credit to the buyer only

71. In any exchange of property ownership in Florida, the documentary stamp tax on the deed:

    a. is paid annually to the state
    b. is based on the entire purchase price
    c. is always charged to the buyer
    d. depends on the financing terms

72. A buyer paid $200,000 for a house. The $200,000 is the property's:

    a. cost
    b. price
    c. value
    d. assessment

73. The majority of savings associations and thrift institutions are regulated by:

    a. the Federal Reserve System
    b. the Office of Thrift Supervision
    c. individual states
    d. the Government National Mortgage Association

74. A lender charged 6.5% interest plus 6 points for a conventional 30-year loan. What is the approximate yield on the loan?

   a. 6.75%
   b. 7%
   c. 7.25%
   d. 7.50%

75. All three approaches to estimating the value of real property utilize:

   a. assemblage
   b. the principle of substitution
   c. the principle of conformity
   d. the law of diminishing returns

76. Which of the following variables below is subtracted to derive the net operating income?

   a. other income
   b. property tax
   c. mortgage payment
   d. IRS tax

77. An appraiser estimated that the pool Jude paid $40,000 to install increased the value to Jude's home by approximately $25,000. This is an example of:

   a. external obsolescence
   b. an over-improvement
   c. functional obsolescence
   d. straight-line depreciation

78. When estimating the value of property, the cost depreciation approach to value:

   a. uses the law of increasing and diminishing returns
   b. relies on the principle of anticipation
   c. never depreciates land
   d. adjustments are made to the comparable properties

79. The approach to value most relevant to estimating the value of a vacant lot in a subdivision is usually the:

   a. sales comparison approach
   b. cost depreciation approach
   c. income capitalization approach
   d. straight-line approach

80. You live in a semitropical climate zone and you read that adding insulation to the attic will reduce the electric bill. What part of the government would you look to when deciding the insulation R values recommended for your locale?
    a. Florida Department of Agriculture and Consumer Services
    b. the Department of Energy
    c. Local Code Enforcement Agency
    d. Environmental Protection Agency

81. A window type that swings out to open is a:
    a. fixed window
    b. jalousie window
    c. hopper window
    d. casement window

82. Which expense can a homeowner deduct when calculating taxable income?
    a. maintenance costs for the home
    b. repairs to the roof
    c. mortgage interest paid on a second home
    d. property insurance on a principal residence

83. Joseph has experienced a hardship due to zoning requirements on his residential lot. He can go to the zoning board of adjustment and request a:
    a. special exception
    b. variance
    c. zoning change for his lot
    d. permit for a nonconforming use

84. An appraiser adjusts the value of a property because of traffic noise from a nearby street. This is an example of:
    a. physical deterioration
    b. functional obsolescence
    c. the principle of anticipation
    d. external obsolescence

85. Which of the following is an advantage of investing in real property?
    a. a local market
    b. liquidity
    c. leverage
    d. risk

86. A type of investment in real property that is organized like a mutual fund and offers liquidity to the investor is a(n):

   a. ostensible partnership
   b. joint venture
   c. limited liability partnership
   d. real estate investment trust

87. When examining an economic base study, an example of an area service industry would be a:

   a. citrus sorting facility
   b. branch bank
   c. film project
   d. tomato packing plant

88. A corner grocery store was the legal use of a lot. The city changed the zoning to residential. What is true in this situation?

   a. The lot's use must be changed.
   b. The store's owner can ask for a variance.
   c. The grocery store is a nonconforming use.
   d. The store's owner must be compensated.

89. The portion of Florida's Growth Management Act that requires that electricity and drinking water must be available before a building permit can be issued is the:

   a. concurrency provision
   b. infrastructure provision
   c. comprehensive plan
   d. zoning requirement

90. Members of the local planning commission generally:

   a. are elected by the local communities
   b. serve for a term of four years
   c. cannot serve more than two consecutive terms
   d. are appointed, unpaid community members

91. The Smiths signed a contract to purchase a home for $72,500. They gave the broker a $7,500 deposit that the broker is holding in escrow. They are assuming a mortgage for $59,760. The sellers will take back a new second mortgage for $3,640. Calculate the taxes to the state on this transaction.

   a. $733.53
   b. $736.33
   c. $736.68
   d. $737.03

92. An investor is analyzing a property with an effective gross income of $850,000 and the operating expenses, including reserves for replacements of $112,000, add up to $530,000. Capitalization rates for competing similar properties are 12%. What should the investor pay for the property?

    a. $1,733,334
    b. $2,666,667
    c. $4,416,667
    d. $7,416,667

93. A duplex is scheduled to close on April 12. The seller collected the rent for April on the first of the month amounting to $525 per unit. According to the sale contract, the buyer is due the rental income for the day of closing. Calculate the proration.

    a. $385 debit to the seller; $385 credit to the buyer
    b. $665 debit to the seller; $665 credit to the buyer
    c. $385 credit to the seller, $385 debit to the buyer
    d. $665 credit to the seller, $665 debit to the buyer

94. The owners sold their home for $234,300, which gave them a 10% profit over their original cost. What did they originally pay for the home?

    a. $195,250
    b. $208,527
    c. $210,870
    d. $213,000

95. An investor purchased an apartment complex for $320,000. There are 10 units that rent for $750 monthly. Land represents 20% of the value. Calculate the annual depreciation. Round to the nearest dollar.

    a. $90,000
    b. $11,635
    c. $9,309
    d. $6,564

96. The seller agreed to pay a 6% commission to the listing broker. The broker will split the commission at 50% with a cooperating broker. The listing sales associate gets 70% of her broker's share; the selling sales associate gets 30% of her broker's share. What was the size of the check of the sales associate who sold the property for $146,000?

    a. $1,314
    b. $2,628
    c. $3,066
    d. $8,760

97. A building purchased 5 years ago was valued at $270,000. The useful economic life of the building is 25 years. Use the straight-line method of depreciation to calculate the building's current depreciated value.

    a. $54,000
    b. $67,500
    c. $202,500
    d. $216,000

98. Van has qualified for a homestead exemption. The city tax rate is 9.6 mills; the county tax rate is 8.5 mills; the school board tax rate is 8.4 mills. The assessed value of Van's home is $285,500. How much will Van save as a result of declaring homestead?

    a. $7,565.75
    b. $1,250.25
    c. $662.50
    d. $65.00

99. A developer purchased four 120-foot lots for $48,000 each and divided them into six lots of equal front footage. The developer sold the lots for $500 per front foot. Calculate the developer's percent of profit.

    a. 9%
    b. 10.2%
    c. 15.5%
    d. 25%

100. In order to obtain a new mortgage loan of $62,000, a buyer agreed to pay all of the state transfer taxes on the new loan. Calculate the tax owed to the state.

    a. $124
    b. $216
    c. $341
    d. $434

ANSWER SHEET
PRACTICE EXAM

Score: _____

Wrong Ways to mark answers:

RIGHT WAY to mark answers:

●

1. Ⓐ Ⓑ Ⓒ Ⓓ
2. Ⓐ Ⓑ Ⓒ Ⓓ
3. Ⓐ Ⓑ Ⓒ Ⓓ
4. Ⓐ Ⓑ Ⓒ Ⓓ
5. Ⓐ Ⓑ Ⓒ Ⓓ
6. Ⓐ Ⓑ Ⓒ Ⓓ
7. Ⓐ Ⓑ Ⓒ Ⓓ
8. Ⓐ Ⓑ Ⓒ Ⓓ
9. Ⓐ Ⓑ Ⓒ Ⓓ
10. Ⓐ Ⓑ Ⓒ Ⓓ
11. Ⓐ Ⓑ Ⓒ Ⓓ
12. Ⓐ Ⓑ Ⓒ Ⓓ
13. Ⓐ Ⓑ Ⓒ Ⓓ
14. Ⓐ Ⓑ Ⓒ Ⓓ
15. Ⓐ Ⓑ Ⓒ Ⓓ
16. Ⓐ Ⓑ Ⓒ Ⓓ
17. Ⓐ Ⓑ Ⓒ Ⓓ
18. Ⓐ Ⓑ Ⓒ Ⓓ
19. Ⓐ Ⓑ Ⓒ Ⓓ
20. Ⓐ Ⓑ Ⓒ Ⓓ

21. Ⓐ Ⓑ Ⓒ Ⓓ
22. Ⓐ Ⓑ Ⓒ Ⓓ
23. Ⓐ Ⓑ Ⓒ Ⓓ
24. Ⓐ Ⓑ Ⓒ Ⓓ
25. Ⓐ Ⓑ Ⓒ Ⓓ
26. Ⓐ Ⓑ Ⓒ Ⓓ
27. Ⓐ Ⓑ Ⓒ Ⓓ
28. Ⓐ Ⓑ Ⓒ Ⓓ
29. Ⓐ Ⓑ Ⓒ Ⓓ
30. Ⓐ Ⓑ Ⓒ Ⓓ
31. Ⓐ Ⓑ Ⓒ Ⓓ
32. Ⓐ Ⓑ Ⓒ Ⓓ
33. Ⓐ Ⓑ Ⓒ Ⓓ
34. Ⓐ Ⓑ Ⓒ Ⓓ
35. Ⓐ Ⓑ Ⓒ Ⓓ
36. Ⓐ Ⓑ Ⓒ Ⓓ
37. Ⓐ Ⓑ Ⓒ Ⓓ
38. Ⓐ Ⓑ Ⓒ Ⓓ
39. Ⓐ Ⓑ Ⓒ Ⓓ
40. Ⓐ Ⓑ Ⓒ Ⓓ

41. Ⓐ Ⓑ Ⓒ Ⓓ
42. Ⓐ Ⓑ Ⓒ Ⓓ
43. Ⓐ Ⓑ Ⓒ Ⓓ
44. Ⓐ Ⓑ Ⓒ Ⓓ
45. Ⓐ Ⓑ Ⓒ Ⓓ
46. Ⓐ Ⓑ Ⓒ Ⓓ
47. Ⓐ Ⓑ Ⓒ Ⓓ
48. Ⓐ Ⓑ Ⓒ Ⓓ
49. Ⓐ Ⓑ Ⓒ Ⓓ
50. Ⓐ Ⓑ Ⓒ Ⓓ
51. Ⓐ Ⓑ Ⓒ Ⓓ
52. Ⓐ Ⓑ Ⓒ Ⓓ
53. Ⓐ Ⓑ Ⓒ Ⓓ
54. Ⓐ Ⓑ Ⓒ Ⓓ
55. Ⓐ Ⓑ Ⓒ Ⓓ
56. Ⓐ Ⓑ Ⓒ Ⓓ
57. Ⓐ Ⓑ Ⓒ Ⓓ
58. Ⓐ Ⓑ Ⓒ Ⓓ
59. Ⓐ Ⓑ Ⓒ Ⓓ
60. Ⓐ Ⓑ Ⓒ Ⓓ

61. Ⓐ Ⓑ Ⓒ Ⓓ
62. Ⓐ Ⓑ Ⓒ Ⓓ
63. Ⓐ Ⓑ Ⓒ Ⓓ
64. Ⓐ Ⓑ Ⓒ Ⓓ
65. Ⓐ Ⓑ Ⓒ Ⓓ
66. Ⓐ Ⓑ Ⓒ Ⓓ
67. Ⓐ Ⓑ Ⓒ Ⓓ
68. Ⓐ Ⓑ Ⓒ Ⓓ
69. Ⓐ Ⓑ Ⓒ Ⓓ
70. Ⓐ Ⓑ Ⓒ Ⓓ
71. Ⓐ Ⓑ Ⓒ Ⓓ
72. Ⓐ Ⓑ Ⓒ Ⓓ
73. Ⓐ Ⓑ Ⓒ Ⓓ
74. Ⓐ Ⓑ Ⓒ Ⓓ
75. Ⓐ Ⓑ Ⓒ Ⓓ
76. Ⓐ Ⓑ Ⓒ Ⓓ
77. Ⓐ Ⓑ Ⓒ Ⓓ
78. Ⓐ Ⓑ Ⓒ Ⓓ
79. Ⓐ Ⓑ Ⓒ Ⓓ
80. Ⓐ Ⓑ Ⓒ Ⓓ

81. Ⓐ Ⓑ Ⓒ Ⓓ
82. Ⓐ Ⓑ Ⓒ Ⓓ
83. Ⓐ Ⓑ Ⓒ Ⓓ
84. Ⓐ Ⓑ Ⓒ Ⓓ
85. Ⓐ Ⓑ Ⓒ Ⓓ
86. Ⓐ Ⓑ Ⓒ Ⓓ
87. Ⓐ Ⓑ Ⓒ Ⓓ
88. Ⓐ Ⓑ Ⓒ Ⓓ
89. Ⓐ Ⓑ Ⓒ Ⓓ
90. Ⓐ Ⓑ Ⓒ Ⓓ
91. Ⓐ Ⓑ Ⓒ Ⓓ
92. Ⓐ Ⓑ Ⓒ Ⓓ
93. Ⓐ Ⓑ Ⓒ Ⓓ
94. Ⓐ Ⓑ Ⓒ Ⓓ
95. Ⓐ Ⓑ Ⓒ Ⓓ
96. Ⓐ Ⓑ Ⓒ Ⓓ
97. Ⓐ Ⓑ Ⓒ Ⓓ
98. Ⓐ Ⓑ Ⓒ Ⓓ
99. Ⓐ Ⓑ Ⓒ Ⓓ
100. Ⓐ Ⓑ Ⓒ Ⓓ

ANSWERS TO PRACTICE END-OF-COURSE EXAM

1. C. A principal's legal instructions must be obeyed. Acme must explain the consequences of having no sign and if Paul won't change the instructions, Acme must obey or withdraw from the listing.
2. C. Add $500 for widow and $500 for nonveteran permanent disability to $25,000. Age doesn't qualify for an exemption unless Millie lives in a low-income household and the city or/and the county has granted additional exemptions for those circumstances.
3. B. When the license of the only broker for a firm is no longer active, the licenses of the associates registered as the broker's employees will be involuntarily inactive.
4. A. A suspended license will become effective after the suspension expires; therefore, a suspended license is ineffective.
5. D. There is nothing in Florida statutes that prevents charging for CMAs.
6. A. Real estate licensees can perform appraisals without an appraisal license, but must know and follow USPAP.
7. C. A licensee cannot compensate any unlicensed person for a referral.
8. A. A gift of land by a private individual to a local government when the land will serve a public purpose is dedication.
9. D. Statements A, B, and C are false. Only the last statement is true. When filling out an application for a real estate license, the applicant must disclose within the application any encounter(s) with the law.
10. B. Time-shares are real property; however a license is not required to sell your own property.
11. B. No sales associate can apply for a broker's license unless the 45-hour post-license class has been completed.
12. D. Any person holding a valid license that has been expired for more than 12 months but less than 24 months can complete a required 28-hour course and reactivate the license.
13. B. Only a transaction broker owes customers limited confidentiality. A single agent broker owes principals the other duties listed.
14. C. From this list, only disclosure of all material facts is owed to customers who have received the no brokerage disclosure notice.

15. B. FREC's power to write rules that become part of Florida statutes (Chapter 61J2) are quasi-legislative powers.
16. C. The DBPR must be informed of any change in a mailing address before 10 days pass.
17. B. Commissioners are appointees, not employees, and receive no salary; they are paid $50 per day plus expenses when on Commission business.
18. A. A broker who serves as the broker for more than one real estate business in Florida holds multiple Florida broker's licenses.
19. C. A realty business from your home is legal if the zoning permits this. All offices must display the office sign. It can be an exterior or an interior sign. The sign must include the name of a broker of record for the firm.
20. C. A binder deposit must be out of an associate's hands before the end of the next business day, which would be Tuesday.
21. B. The escrow account can be interest bearing and the broker can keep the interest if the buyer and seller agreed to these actions in writing.
22. D. A broker can place up to $1,000 of personal or other funds in an escrow account to pay for the bank charges. More than $1,000 makes the broker guilty of commingling.
23. A. When a broker gives the escrow deposit to a Florida attorney or a Florida title company to hold, the broker is relieved of any further actions regarding the deposits.
24. B. The procedure described is mediation.
25. C. Joe works for a transient occupancy facility and doesn't need a license. Sarah's salary and the short rental periods are license exemptions. The sales of radio and television stations are exempted from license requirements. Out of this list, only Ben must have a real estate license.
26. D. Violating the laws regarding the selling of rental lists is a first-degree misdemeanor. The required refund was 75% of the fee. The action made the company subject to civil, criminal, and administrative punishment.
27. A. When the active broker in a real estate partnership dies, resigns, or is terminated, in order to maintain the registration of that partnership they have 14 calendar days to substitute the old party with a new party possessing an active broker's license.
28. B. Brokers only have to register the trade name with FREC.
29. D. The only option open to a broker in this situation is to sue the seller.
30. D. A limited partnership can be a real estate business in Florida. Limited partners cannot participate in the business, and only contribute money or property. Because of this requirement, associates can be limited partners.
31. B. The question refers to a stipulation—after a formal complaint was issued in the complaint process this is one of the three possible elections available to the licensee.

32. C. A summary, or emergency, suspension is issued by the secretary of the DBPR.
33. A. Anonymous complaints are considered; the complaint need not involve real estate and does not have to be located in Florida. However, the DRE will only consider written complaints.
34. D. A citation can be disputed in writing within 30 days of receipt.
35. C. The broker followed legal procedures, and there will be no action against the license.
36. C. The maximum amount that will be paid from the Real Estate Recovery Fund for one transaction is $50,000.
37. D. The Real Estate Recovery Fund is funded from fees added to the issuing of new and renewed licenses.
38. B. In this list, only religion is a protected status in housing.
39. A. It is the Real Estate Settlement Procedures Act (RESPA).
40. C. A loss of the land mass due to the action of water is termed erosion.
41. B. Everybody must qualify for a license by demonstrating knowledge of real estate laws and fulfilling all application requirements.
42. B. The son is the remainderman and has a remainder estate until the uncle dies, at which time the son will own the farm fee simple.
43. D. Courts have ruled that if damage occurred when an item was removed, the item was a fixture and part of the real property.
44. C. If there are unequal interests in the property, the estate must be a tenancy in common.
45. B. The Division of Florida Land Sales, Condominiums, and Mobile Homes regulates all multiple ownership properties, such as cooperatives.
46. C. Florida law will give a surviving spouse whose name is not on the deed of a homestead a life estate in the property. Any children of Minnie's, whether by Ralph or not, will be vested remaindermen who will own the home when Ralph dies.
47. A. A buyer has 15 days to cancel the purchase of a condo from a developer. The cancelation must be in writing. The law states the buyer's money must be returned.
48. B. Eminent domain gives the government the right to take land from a private owner as long as the land is taken for a public purpose.
49. D. While Bobby can't stop the taking, he can ask for a condemnation hearing to protest the price the government is paying.
50. B. Florida law does not require a deed to be recorded to be legal. Courts have ruled actual notice and constructive notice are equal under the law. Notarization is not a deed requirement; it is a requirement for instruments that are placed in the public records. The grantee never signs. However, the grantor must be competent and two witnesses to the grantor's signature must sign as well.

51. A. The quitclaim deed is the simplest deed and contains no warranties at all.
52. A. When numbering the sections in a township, east is to the right. Section 13 is due east of Section 14.
53. B. A ¼ of a ¼ of a ¼ of a ¼ of a section contains 2.5 acres.
54. C. An accurate point of beginning (POB) is the most critical feature of a metes and bounds legal description. If you don't start in the right place, you will not describe the boundaries.
55. A. The Statute of Frauds states that in order for a contract that conveys an interest in real property to be enforceable, the contract must be in writing. Of course, there are three exceptions to the Statute of Frauds.
56. D. One of the three exceptions to the Statute of Frauds (oral contracts that Florida courts will enforce) is an oral listing agreement for 1 year or less.
57. B. The statute of limitations states that any oral (parol) contract that has not been completed before 4 years pass is null and void.
58. B. Sellers who sign written listings must receive a copy of the listing within 24 hours of the signing.
59. C. When several companies have the listing and the seller has reserved the right to sell the property without paying a commission, this describes an open listing.
60. C. No inspection is required for the presence of lead-based paint in residential sales and leases for properties built before 1978. However, before being shown such a property for sale or lease, prospective buyers or lessees must receive the EPA pamphlet regarding the dangers of lead in paint. The lead-based paint disclosure isn't signed unless the buyers are going to make an offer.
61. B. Only the seller signs option contracts, not both parties; consideration for a contract can be good rather than valuable; acknowledgment (notarization) is not required; but there must be an offer and an acceptance, which is mutual assent.
62. A. The note is the legal evidence of the debt. In a lien theory state such as Florida, the buyer (mortgagor) owns the property and the lender (mortgagee) holds a lien.
63. D. The margin or spread is the percentage added to the index to cover the lender's expenses and any profit on the loan.
64. C. The part of the payment that pays back (amortizes) the loan gradually increases with each payment.
65. C. The VA has the power to make direct loans where lenders for VA loans are not available otherwise. The other statements are false.
66. D. The current housing expense ratio for an FHA loan is 31%. The FHA doesn't set interest rates. The FHA loan is a government-insured loan and the borrower must pay an upfront mortgage insurance premium (MIP).

67. C. The Fed's obligation to influence the money supply and the cost of funds is the monetary policy.
68. A. When the Fed buys U.S. Treasury securities, money is released into the economy.
69. C. Unpaid property taxes are entered on the closing statement as a debit to the seller and a credit to the buyer.
70. D. On the closing statement, the binder deposit appears as a credit to the buyer only.
71. B. The documentary stamp tax on the deed is a one-time charge to the state based on the entire purchase price and by custom is charged to the seller.
72. B. The $200,000 is the price paid. Assessment is the value for tax purposes. Cost is how much money it took to create the property. From this information, we can't know what the value is.
73. B. Most savings associations and thrift institutions belong to the Federal Home Loan Bank System and are regulated by the Office of Thrift Supervision.
74. C. Six points will increase the yield to the lender by approximately 6/8 of 1%. The fraction 6/8 equals 0.75. Add 0.75 to 6.5 to result in 7.25%.
75. B. The principle of substitution is the basis of all three approaches to estimating the value of real property.
76. B. Other income is *added* in the calculation. Mortgage payments and IRS taxes are subtracted after the NOI is calculated. Only the property tax, a part of the operating expenses, is subtracted when calculating the NOI.
77. B. The cost of the pool is $40,000; the value of the pool is $25,000. When an improvement adds less value to the property than the improvement's cost, the result is an over-improvement.
78. C. The cost depreciation approach to value never depreciates the land.
79. A. The vacant lot in a subdivision is a residential property. The sales comparison approach to value is preferred in estimating the value of residential properties.
80. B. The Department of Energy recommends insulation R values for different parts of the country.
81. D. A casement window swings out.
82. C. Out of this list, only the interest portion of mortgage payments on a second home is tax deductible.
83. B. When zoning creates a hardship for an individual landowner, the owner can ask for a variance.
84. D. A decrease in value due to conditions outside the property line is external obsolescence.

85. **C.** Leverage, the use of borrowed funds to capture a stream of income, is an advantage of property investment.
86. **D.** The statement describes a real estate investment trust (REIT).
87. **B.** A service industry is where the local people go for some service.
88. **C.** A use that was legal before the zoning was changed is a legally nonconforming use and can continue.
89. **A.** The concurrency provision of the Growth Management Act requires all infrastructure must be in place before new building can occur.
90. **D.** Planning commissioners are generally appointed, unpaid members who are serving to benefit their community.
91. **D.** Deed: $72,500 ÷ 100 × $0.70 = $507.50. Note: $59,760 ÷ 100 = 597.6 = 598 × $0.35 = $209.30. Note: $3,640 ÷ 100 = 36.4 = 37 × $0.35 = $12.95.

    New mortgage: $3,640 × $0.002 = $7.28. Total = $737.03. (Documentary stamp taxes are calculated for every unit of $100; any additional portion of $100, no matter how small, counts for another $100 unit.)
92. **B.** EGI $850,000 − OE $530,000 = $320,000 NOI. Price = NOI ÷ Capitalization Rate. $530,000 ÷ 0.12 = $2,666,667.
93. **B.** Total rent is $1,050. Buyer gets 19 days of the rent. $1,050 ÷ 30 days = $35 per day × 19 days = $665 rent due to buyer.
94. **D.** The sale price received represents 110% of the purchase price. $234,300 ÷ 1.10 = $213,000.
95. **C.** Improvements are 80% of the value. Depreciation of residential investment properties is based on 27.5 years. $320,000 × 0.80 = $256,000. $256,000 ÷ 27.5 years = $9,309.
96. **A.** $146,000 × 0.06 = $8,760. $8,760 × 0.50 = $4,380. $4,380 × 0.30 = $1,314.
97. **D.** $270,000 ÷ 25 years = $10,800 depreciation per year. $10,800 × 5 years = $54,000. $270,000 − $54,000 = $216,000.
98. **C.** Add the mills: 9.6 + 8.5 + 8.4 = 26.5 mills = $0.0265. $25,000 × 0.0265 = $662.50.
99. **D.** $48,000 × 4 lots = $192,000 paid. 4 lots × 120 feet = 480 feet × $500 = $240,000 sale price. $240,000 − $192,000 = $48,000 profit. $48,000 ÷ $192,000 = 0.25 or 25% profit.
100. **C.** A new mortgage has two instruments—the mortgage and the note—that are subject to the state transfer tax. Note: $62,000 ÷ 100 = 620 × $0.35 = $217.00. New mortgage $62,000 × $0.002 = $124 intangible tax. $217 + $124 = $341.

EXAMPLE REAL ESTATE FORMS

DISCLOSURE FORMS

IMPORTANT NOTICE

FLORIDA LAW REQUIRES THAT REAL ESTATE LICENSEES PROVIDE THIS NOTICE TO POTENTIAL SELLERS AND BUYERS OF REAL ESTATE.

You should not assume that any real estate broker or salesperson represents you unless you agree to engage a real estate licensee in an authorized brokerage relationship, either as a single agent or as a transaction broker. You are advised not to disclose any information you want to be held in confidence until you make a decision on representation.

TRANSACTION BROKER NOTICE

FLORIDA LAW REQUIRES THAT REAL ESTATE LICENSEES OPERATING AS TRANSACTION BROKERS DISCLOSE TO BUYERS AND SELLERS THEIR ROLES AND DUTIES IN PROVIDING A LIMITED FORM OF REPRESENTATION.

As a transaction broker, (insert name of Real Estate Firm and its Associates) provides to you a limited form of representation that includes the following duties:

1. Dealing honestly and fairly;
2. Accounting for all funds;
3. Using skill, care, and diligence in the transaction;
4. Disclosing all known facts that materially affect the value of residential real property and are not readily observable to the buyer;
5. Presenting all offers and counteroffers in a timely manner, unless a party has previously directed the licensee otherwise in writing;
6. Limited confidentiality, unless waived by a party. This limited confidentiality will prevent disclosure that the seller will accept a price less than the asking or listed price, that the buyer will pay a price greater than the price submitted in a written offer, of the motivation of any party for selling or buying property, that a seller or buyer will agree to financing terms other than those offered, or of any other information requested by a party to remain confidential; and
7. Any additional duties that are entered into by this or by separate written agreement.

Limited representation means that a buyer or seller is not responsible for the acts of the licensee. Additionally, parties are giving up their rights to the undivided loyalty of the licensee. This aspect of limited representation allows a licensee to facilitate a real estate transaction by assisting both the buyer and the seller, but a licensee will not work to represent one party to the detriment of the other party when acting as a transaction broker to both parties.

Seller or (buyer)

_____   _____
Signature   Date

_____   _____
Signature   Date

DISCLOSURE OF INFORMATION ON LEAD-BASED PAINT AND/OR LEAD-BASED PAINT HAZARDS

IMPORTANT NOTICE

FLORIDA LAW REQUIRES THAT REAL ESTATE LICENSEES PROVIDE THIS NOTICE TO POTENTIAL SELLERS AND BUYERS OF REAL ESTATE.

You should not assume that any real estate broker or salesperson represents you unless you agree to engage a real estate licensee in an authorized brokerage relationship, either as a single agent or as a transaction broker. You are advised not to disclose any information you want to be held in confidence until you make a decision on representation.

SINGLE AGENT NOTICE

FLORIDA LAW REQUIRES THAT REAL ESTATE LICENSEES OPERATING AS SINGLE AGENTS DISCLOSE TO BUYERS AND SELLERS THEIR DUTIES.

As a single agent, (insert name of Real Estate Entity and its Associates) owe to you the following duties:

1. Dealing honestly and fairly;
2. Loyalty;
3. Confidentiality;
4. Obedience;
5. Full disclosure;
6. Accounting for all funds;
7. Skill, care, and diligence in the transaction;
8. Presenting all offers and counteroffers in a timely manner, unless a party has previously directed the licensee otherwise in writing; and
9. Disclosing all known facts that materially affect the value of residential real property and are not readily observable.

Seller or (buyer)
_____   _____
Signature   Date

_____   _____
Signature   Date

IMPORTANT NOTICE

FLORIDA LAW REQUIRES THAT REAL ESTATE LICENSEES PROVIDE THIS NOTICE TO POTENTIAL SELLERS AND BUYERS OF REAL ESTATE.

You should not assume that any real estate broker or salesperson represents you unless you agree to engage a real estate licensee in an authorized brokerage relationship, either as a single agent or as a transaction broker. You are advised not to disclose any information you want to be held in confidence until you make a decision on representation.

NO BROKERAGE RELATIONSHIP NOTICE

FLORIDA LAW REQUIRES THAT REAL ESTATE LICENSEES WHO HAVE NO BROKERAGE RELATIONSHIP WITH A POTENTIAL SELLER OR BUYER DISCLOSE THEIR DUTIES TO SELLERS AND BUYERS.

As a real estate licensee who has no brokerage relationship with you, (insert name of Real Estate Entity and its Associates) owe to you the following duties:

1. Dealing honestly and fairly;
2. Disclosing all known facts that materially affect the value of residential real property which are not readily observable to the buyer; and
3. Accounting for all funds entrusted to the licensee.

Seller or (buyer)
_____   _____
Signature   Date

_____   _____
Signature   Date

Source: Federal Register/Vol. 61, No. 45/Wednesday, March 6, 1996/Rules and Regulations.

FLORIDA LAW ALLOWS REAL ESTATE LICENSEES WHO REPRESENT A BUYER OR SELLER AS A SINGLE AGENT TO CHANGE FROM A SINGLE AGENT RELATIONSHIP TO A TRANSACTION BROKERAGE RELATIONSHIP IN ORDER FOR THE LICENSEE TO ASSIST BOTH PARTIES IN A REAL ESTATE TRANSACTION BY PROVIDING A LIMITED FORM OF REPRESENTATION TO BOTH THE BUYER AND THE SELLER. THIS CHANGE IN RELATIONSHIP CANNOT OCCUR WITHOUT YOUR PRIOR WRITTEN CONSENT.

As a transaction border,:_____ (insert name of Real Estate Firm and its Associates) provides to you a limited form of representation that includes the following duties:

1. Dealing honestly and fairly;
2. Accounting for all funds;
3. Using skill, care, and diligence in the transaction;
4. Disclosing all known facts that materially affect the value of residential real property and are not readily observable to the buyer;
5. Presenting all offers and counteroffers in a timely manner, unless a party has previously directed the licensee otherwise in writing;
6. Limited confidentiality, unless waived by a party. This limited confidentiality will prevent disclosure that the seller will accept a price less than the asking or listed price, that the buyer will pay a price greater than the price submitted in a written offer, of the motivation of any party for selling or buying property, that a seller or buyer will agree to financing terms other than those offered, or of any other information requested by a party to remain confidential; and
7. Any additional duties that are entered into by this or by separate written agreement.

Limited representation means that a buyer or seller is not responsible for the acts of the licensee. Additionally, parties are giving up their rights to the undivided loyalty of the licensee. This aspect of limited representation allows a licensee to facilitate a real estate transaction by assisting both the buyer and the seller, but a licensee will not work to represent one party to the detriment of the other party when acting as a transaction broker to both parties.

_____ I agree that my agent may assume the role and duties of a transaction broker. [must be initialed or signed]

Disclosure of Information on Lead-Based Paint and/or Lead-Based Paint Hazards

Lead Warning Statement
Every purchaser of any interest in residential real property on which a residential dwelling was built prior to 1978 is notified that such property may present exposure to lead from lead-based paint that may place young children at risk of developing lead poisoning. Lead poisoning in young children may produce permanent neurological damage, including learning disabilities, reduced intelligence quotient, behavioral problems, and impaired memory. Lead poisoning also poses a particular risk to pregnant women. The seller of any interest in residential real property is required to provide the buyer with any information on lead-based paint hazards from risk assessments or inspections in the seller's possession and notify the buyer of any known lead-based paint hazards. A risk assessment or inspection for possible lead-based paint hazards is recommended prior to purchase.

Seller's Disclosure
(a) Presence of lead-based paint and/or lead-based paint hazards (check (i) or (ii) below):
    (i)—— Known lead-based paint and/or lead-based paint hazards are present in the housing (explain).
_____
    (ii)——Seller has no knowledge of lead-based paint and/or lead-based paint hazards in the housing.
(b) Records and reports available to the seller (check (i) or (ii) below):
    (i)——Seller has provided the purchaser with all available records and reports pertaining to lead-based paint and/or lead-based paint hazards in the housing (list documents below).
_____
    (ii)—— Seller has no reports or records pertaining to lead-based paint and/or lead-based paint hazards in the housing.

Purchaser's Acknowledgment (initial)
(c)——Purchaser has received copies of all information listed above.
(d)——Purchaser has received the pamphlet *Protect Your Family from Lead in Your Home*.
(e)——Purchaser has (check (i) or (ii) below):
    (i)—— received a 10-day opportunity (or mutually agreed upon period) to conduct a risk assessment or inspection for the presence of lead-based paint and/or lead-based paint hazards; or
    (ii)—— waived the opportunity to conduct a risk assessment or inspection for the presence of lead-based paint and/or lead-based paint hazards.

Agent's Acknowledgment (initial)
(f)——Agent has informed the seller of the seller's obligations under 42 U.S.C. 4852d and is aware of his/her responsibility to ensure compliance.

Certification of Accuracy
The following parties have reviewed the information above and certify, to the best of their knowledge, that the information they have provided is true and accurate.

_____ _____ _____ _____
Seller   Date   Seller   Date

_____ _____ _____ _____
Purchaser   Date   Purchaser   Date

_____ _____ _____ _____
Agent   Date   Agent   Date

Disclosure of Information on Lead-Based Paint and/or Lead-Based Paint Hazards

Lead Warning Statement
Housing built before 1978 may contain lead-based paint. Lead from paint, paint chips, and dust can pose health hazards if not managed properly. Lead exposure is especially harmful to young children and pregnant women. Before renting pre-1978 housing, lessors must disclose the presence of known lead-based paint and/or lead-based paint hazards in the dwelling. Lessees must also receive a federally approved pamphlet on lead poisoning prevention.

Lessor's Disclosure
(a) Presence of lead-based paint and/or lead-based paint hazards (Check (i) or (ii) below):
 (i)—— Known lead-based paint and/or lead-based paint hazards are present in the housing (explain).

 _____

 (ii)——Lessor has no knowledge of lead-based paint and/or lead-based paint hazards in the housing.
(b) Records and reports available to the lessor (Check (i) or (ii) below):
 (i)—— Lessor has provided the lessee with all available records and reports pertaining to lead-based paint and/or lead-based paint hazards in the housing (list documents below).

 _____

 (ii)——Lessor has no reports or records pertaining to lead-based paint and/or lead-based paint hazards in the housing.

Lessee's Acknowledgment (initial)
(c)——Lessee has received copies of all information listed above.
(d)——Lessee has received the pamphlet *Protect Your Family from Lead in Your Home*.

Agent's Acknowledgment (initial)
(e)—— Agent has informed the lessor of the lessor's obligations under 42 U.S.C. 4852d and is aware of his/her responsibility to ensure compliance.

Certification of Accuracy
The following parties have reviewed the information above and certify, to the best of their knowledge, that the information they have provided is true and accurate.

_____	_____	_____	_____
Lessor	Date	Lessor	Date
_____	_____	_____	_____
Lessee	Date	Lessee	Date
_____	_____	_____	_____
Agent	Date	Agent	Date

IRREVOCABLE CONSENT TO SERVICE FORM

Department of Business & Professional Regulation

Charlie Crist, Governor
Holly Benson, Secretary

Division of Real Estate
Thomas O'Bryant, Director
400 West Robinson Street, N801
Orlando, Florida 32801-1757

Phone: 407.481.5662
Fax: 407.317.7245
www.MyFlorida.com/dbpr
www.MyFloridaLicense.com

IRREVOCABLE CONSENT TO SERVICE

I agree, as the holder of a Florida Real Estate license, to submit to the jurisdiction of the Department of Business and Professional Regulation and the Division of Administrative Hearings, which agreement is irrevocable.

I agree, as the holder of a Florida Real Estate license, that the Director of the Division of Real Estate and his/her successors in office shall receive service of all legal process issued against me in any administrative or civil action or proceeding in this state, and process so served shall be valid and binding, which agreement is irrevocable. I further agree to file with the Division of Real Estate an address (shown below) where a copy of the process served upon the Division Director is to be sent by registered mail, and that I will keep said address current.

_____
Name (Please Print)   License #

_____
Number   Street Address   City   State   Zip

_____(Signature)

STATE OF _____

COUNTY OF _____

The foregoing instrument was acknowledged before me this _____ day of _____, 20____,

_____
by: Signature of Notary Public--State of Florida (Out of State Notary Acceptable)

_____
(Print, Type, or Stamp Commissioned Name of Notary Public)

Personally Known _____ Or Produced Identification _____

Type of Identification Produced _____

Forward Form to:
Florida Department of Business and Professional Regulation
1940 North Monroe Street
Tallahassee, Florida 32399

Source: Florida Department of Business and Professional Regulation (http://www.myflorida.com/dbpr/re/index.html).

EXCLUSIVE RIGHT-OF-SALE LISTING AGREEMENT–COOP

Date:_____

Re: Any Property, Florida (the "Unit")

To:

In consideration for the work you are presently doing and are going to do in the future on our behalf, we hereby appoint and grant _____ ("Broker") the sole "exclusive right-to-sell" the proprietary lease and shares of stock allocated to the above referenced apartment/unit. This shall include but not be limited to (i) the outright sale of the Unit; (ii) by sale of the Corporation/Entity that is the registered owner of the shares and proprietary lease or by any other disposition method.

We understand and you have fully disclosed that an "exclusive right-to-sell" means that if we the owner find a buyer, you the Broker find a buyer or another outside broker not within your employ finds a buyer and/or any other person finds a buyer, the agreed commission will be due to you the Broker in either of the cases above.

The terms of this agreement are as follows:

1. This agreement shall be effective as of _____("Effective Date").
   It shall continue in full force and effect for the earlier of one (1) year from the Effective Date or closing of sale.

2. Broker is authorized to offer the _____ shares for sale at a price of $_____ and to represent that the monthly maintenance charge is $_____.

3. If the shares and the proprietary lease are sold pursuant to this agreement, Seller agrees to pay Broker and Broker agrees to accept a commission equal to six (6%) percent of the total sales price and/or any other valuable consideration received by us. This commission will be due and payable by certified check or attorney's escrow check, at closing, in full and without setoff of any kind.

4. Broker will offer the Unit through your own organization and direct as well as oversee its sale. Seller shall receive from Broker a monthly report of all pertinent developments.

5. Seller hereby authorizes Broker to solicit the cooperation of other licensed real estate brokers who will act as agents for the prospective buyers, and to work with them on a cooperating basis. In the event another licensed real estate broker is involved in the transaction, you will share the commission with such broker and in no event will the commission paid by Seller exceed six (6%) per cent of the sale price as outlined in paragraph #3 herein.

6. Seller agrees that during the life of this agreement, Seller will refer all inquiries, including but not limited to the Cooperative, concerning the sale of the Unit to Broker.

7. Within ten (10) days after the expiration of this listing, Broker shall deliver to Seller a list of names of persons who inspected the premises during athe listing term. If within one (1) year after the expiration of the listing term a contract is signed to sell the premises to a person contained on the list, Broker shall be entitled to a commission provided for in paragraph #3 herein.

8. This agreement shall bind and benefit the personal representatives, successors, assigns of the parties. This agreement may not be changed, rescinded or modified except in writing, signed by both parties.

9. In the event Seller becomes legally entitled to retain any deposit paid to Seller pursuant to a signed contract of sale, by a person introduced during the term of this agreement, Seller agrees to pay Broker six (6%) per cent of that amount to Broker. This payment shall be non-refundable.

10. Seller warrants and represents to Broker that Seller is in fact the owner of the shares and proprietary lease covering the Unit and that Seller has marketable title to the Unit.

    If the above is in accordance with your understanding, please indicate your acceptance on the signature line provided below.

    Sincerely,

    _____
    Broker:

    Agreed & Accepted:

    _____
    Seller:

Source: Parker Madison Partners, Inc., New York, New York. Reprinted with permission.

RESIDENTIAL SALE AND PURCHASE CONTRACT: CONDOMINIUMS

THIS FORM HAS BEEN APPROVED BY THE FLORIDA ASSOCIATION OF REALTORS® AND THE FLORIDA BAR

Contract For Sale And Purchase
FLORIDA ASSOCIATION OF REALTORS® AND THE FLORIDA BAR

1* **PARTIES:** _____ ("Seller"),
2* and _____ ("Buyer"),
3 hereby agree that Seller shall sell and Buyer shall buy the following described Real Property and Personal Property (collectively "Property")
4 pursuant to the terms and conditions of this Contract for Sale and Purchase and any riders and addenda ("Contract"):
5 **I. DESCRIPTION:**
6* (a) Legal description of the Real Property located in _____ County, Florida: _____
7* _____
8* (b) Street address, city, zip, of the Property: _____
9 (c) Personal Property includes existing range(s), refrigerator(s), dishwasher(s), ceiling fan(s), light fixture(s), and window treatment(s) unless
10 specifically excluded below.
11* Other items included are: _____
12* _____
13* Items of Personal Property (and leased items, if any) excluded are: _____
14* _____
15* **II. PURCHASE PRICE** (U.S. currency): .... $ _____
16 **PAYMENT:**
17* (a) Deposit held in escrow by _____ ("Escrow Agent") in the amount of (checks subject to clearance) $ _____
18* Escrow Agent's address: _____ Phone: _____
19* (b) Additional escrow deposit to be made to Escrow Agent within _____ days after Effective Date in the amount of ...... $ _____
20* (c) Financing in the amount of ("Loan Amount") see Paragraph IV below .... $ _____
21* (d) Other .... $ _____
22 (e) Balance to close by cash, wire transfer or LOCALLY DRAWN cashier's or official bank check(s), subject
23* to adjustments or prorations .... $ _____
24 **III. TIME FOR ACCEPTANCE OF OFFER AND COUNTEROFFERS; EFFECTIVE DATE:**
25 (a) If this offer is not executed by and delivered to all parties OR FACT OF EXECUTION communicated in writing between the parties on or
26* before _____, the deposit(s) will, at Buyer's option, be returned and this offer withdrawn. **Unless other-**
27 wise stated, the time for acceptance of any counteroffers shall be 2 days from the date the counteroffer is delivered.
28 (b) The date of Contract ("Effective Date") will be the date when the last one of the Buyer and Seller has signed or initialed this offer or the
29 final counteroffer. If such date is not otherwise set forth in this Contract, then the "Effective Date" shall be the date determined above for
30 acceptance of this offer or, if applicable, the final counteroffer.
31 **IV. FINANCING:**
32* ❏ (a) This is a cash transaction with no contingencies for financing;
33* ❏ (b) This Contract is contingent on Buyer obtaining written loan commitment which confirms underwriting loan approval for a loan to purchase
34* the Property ("Loan Approval") within _____ days (if blank, then 30 days) after Effective Date ("Loan Approval Date") for (CHECK ONLY
35* ONE): ❏ a fixed; ❏ an adjustable; or ❏ a fixed or adjustable rate loan, in the Loan Amount (See Paragraph II.(c)) at an initial interest rate not to
36* exceed _____%, and for a term of _____ years. Buyer will make application within _____ days (if blank, then 5 days) after Effective Date.
37 **BUYER:** Buyer shall use reasonable diligence to: obtain Loan Approval; **notify Seller in writing of receipt of Loan Approval by Loan Approval**
38 **Date**; satisfy terms of the Loan Approval; and close the loan. Loan Approval which requires a condition related to the sale of other property shall
39 not be deemed Loan Approval for purposes of this subparagraph. Buyer shall pay all loan expenses. Buyer authorizes the mortgage broker(s) and
40 lender(s) to disclose information regarding the conditions, status, and progress of loan application and Loan Approval to Seller, Seller's attorney,
41 real estate licensee(s), and Closing Agent.
42 **SELLER:** If Buyer does not deliver to Seller written notice of Loan Approval by Loan Approval Date, Seller may thereafter cancel this Contract by
43 delivering written notice ("Seller's Cancellation Notice") to Buyer, but not later than seven (7) days prior to Closing. Seller's Cancellation Notice shall
44 notify Buyer that Buyer has three (3) days to deliver to Seller written notice waiving this Financing contingency, or the Contract shall be cancelled.
45 **DEPOSIT(S) (for purposes of this Financing Paragraph IV(b) only):** If Buyer has used reasonable diligence but does not obtain Loan Approval
46 by Loan Approval Date, and thereafter either party elects to cancel this Contract, the deposit(s) shall be returned to Buyer. If Buyer obtains Loan
47 Approval or waives this Financing contingency, and thereafter the Contract does not close, then the deposit(s) shall be paid to Seller; provided how-
48 ever, if the failure to close is due to: (i) Seller's failure or refusal to close or Seller otherwise fails to meet the terms of the Contract, or (ii) Buyer's lender
49 fails to receive and approve an appraisal of the Property in an amount sufficient to meet the terms of the Loan Approval, then the deposit(s) shall be
50 returned to Buyer.
51* ❏ (c) Assumption of existing mortgage (see rider for terms); or
52* ❏ (d) Purchase money note and mortgage to Seller (see Standards B and K and riders; addenda; or special clauses for terms).
53* **V. TITLE EVIDENCE:** At least _____ days (if blank, then 5 days) before Closing a title insurance commitment with legible copies of instruments listed as
54 exceptions attached thereto ("Title Commitment") and, after Closing, an owner's policy of title insurance (see Standard A for terms) shall be obtained by:
55* **(CHECK ONLY ONE):** ❏ (1) Seller, at Seller's expense and delivered to Buyer or Buyer's attorney; or
56* ❏ (2) Buyer at Buyer's expense.
57* **(CHECK HERE):** ❏ If an abstract of title is to be furnished instead of title insurance, and attach rider for terms.
58* **VI. CLOSING DATE:** This transaction shall be closed and the closing documents delivered on _____ ("Closing"), unless
59 modified by other provisions of this Contract. In the event of extreme weather or other conditions or events constituting "force majeure", Closing will be
60 extended a reasonable time until: (i) restoration of utilities and other services essential to Closing, and (ii) availability of Hazard, Wind, Flood, or Homeowners'
61* insurance. If such conditions continue more than _____ days (if blank, then 14 days) beyond Closing Date, then either party may cancel this Contract.

FAR/BAR-8   Rev. 9/07   © 2007   Florida Association of REALTORS® and The Florida Bar   All Rights Reserved   Page 1 of 4

62 **VII. RESTRICTIONS; EASEMENTS; LIMITATIONS:** Seller shall convey marketable title subject to: comprehensive land use plans, zoning, restrictions,
63 prohibitions and other requirements imposed by governmental authority; restrictions and matters appearing on the plat or otherwise common to the subdivi-
64 sion; outstanding oil, gas and mineral rights of record without right of entry; unplatted public utility easements of record (located contiguous to real property
65 lines and not more than 10 feet in width as to the rear or front lines and 7 1/2 feet in width as to the side lines); taxes for year of Closing and subsequent years;
66 and assumed mortgages and purchase money mortgages, if any (if additional items, see addendum); provided, that there exists at Closing no violation of the
67* foregoing and none prevent use of the Property for _____ purpose(s).
68 **VIII. OCCUPANCY:** Seller shall deliver occupancy of Property to Buyer at time of Closing unless otherwise stated herein. If Property is intended
69 to be rented or occupied beyond Closing, the fact and terms thereof and the tenant(s) or occupants shall be disclosed pursuant to Standard F.
70 If occupancy is to be delivered before Closing, Buyer assumes all risks of loss to Property from date of occupancy, shall be responsible and liable
71 for maintenance from that date, and shall be deemed to have accepted Property in its existing condition as of time of taking occupancy.
72 **IX. TYPEWRITTEN OR HANDWRITTEN PROVISIONS:** Typewritten or handwritten provisions, riders and addenda shall control all printed pro-
73 visions of this Contract in conflict with them.
74* **X. ASSIGNABILITY:** (CHECK ONLY ONE): Buyer ❑ may assign and thereby be released from any further liability under this Contract; ❑ may
75* assign but not be released from liability under this Contract; or ❑ may not assign this Contract.
76 **XI. DISCLOSURES:**
77 (a) The Property may be subject to unpaid special assessment lien(s) imposed by a public body ("public body" does not include a
78 Condominium or Homeowners' Association). Such liens(s), if any, whether certified, confirmed and ratified, pending, or payable in installments,
79* as of Closing, shall be paid as follows: ❑ by Seller at closing ❑ by Buyer (if left blank, then Seller at Closing). If the amount of any
80 assessment to be paid by Seller has not been finally determined as of Closing, Seller shall be charged at Closing an amount equal to the
81 last estimate or assessment for the improvement by the public body.
82 (b) Radon is a naturally occurring radioactive gas that when accumulated in a building in sufficient quantities may present health risks to per-
83 sons who are exposed to it over time. Levels of radon that exceed federal and state guidelines have been found in buildings in Florida.
84 Additional information regarding radon or radon testing may be obtained from your County Public Health unit.
85 (c) Mold is naturally occurring and may cause health risks or damage to property. If Buyer is concerned or desires additional information
86 regarding mold, Buyer should contact an appropriate professional.
87 (d) Buyer acknowledges receipt of the Florida Energy-Efficiency Rating Information Brochure required by Section 553.996, F.S.
88 (e) If the Real Property includes pre-1978 residential housing then a lead-based paint rider is mandatory.
89 (f) If Seller is a "foreign person" as defined by the Foreign Investment in Real Property Tax Act, the parties shall comply with that Act.
90 (g) **BUYER SHOULD NOT EXECUTE THIS CONTRACT UNTIL BUYER HAS RECEIVED AND READ THE HOMEOWNERS' ASSOCIA-
91 TION/COMMUNITY DISCLOSURE.**
92 (h) PROPERTY TAX DISCLOSURE SUMMARY: BUYER SHOULD NOT RELY ON THE SELLER'S CURRENT PROPERTY TAXES AS THE AMOUNT
93 OF PROPERTY TAXES THAT THE BUYER MAY BE OBLIGATED TO PAY IN THE YEAR SUBSEQUENT TO PURCHASE. A CHANGE OF OWNER-
94 SHIP OR PROPERTY IMPROVEMENTS TRIGGERS REASSESSMENTS OF THE PROPERTY THAT COULD RESULT IN HIGHER PROPERTY TAXES.
95 IF YOU HAVE ANY QUESTIONS CONCERNING VALUATION, CONTACT THE COUNTY PROPERTY APPRAISER'S OFFICE FOR INFORMATION.
96 **XII. MAXIMUM REPAIR COSTS:** Seller shall not be responsible for payments in excess of:
97* (a) $_____ for treatment and repair under Standard D (if blank, then 1.5% of the Purchase Price).
98* (b) $_____ for repair and replacement under Standard N not caused by Wood Destroying Organisms (if blank, then 1.5% of the Purchase Price).
99* **XIII. HOME WARRANTY:** ❑ Seller ❑ Buyer ❑ N/A will pay for a home warranty plan issued by _____
100* at a cost not to exceed $_____
101 **XIV. RIDERS; ADDENDA; SPECIAL CLAUSES: CHECK** those riders which are applicable AND are attached to and made part of this Contract:
102* ❑ CONDOMINIUM ❑ VA/FHA ❑ HOMEOWNERS' ASSN. ❑ LEAD-BASED PAINT ❑ COASTAL CONSTRUCTION CONTROL LINE
103* ❑ INSULATION ❑ "AS IS" ❑ EVIDENCE OF TITLE (SOUTH FLORIDA CONTRACTS) ❑ Other Comprehensive Rider Provisions ❑ Addenda
104* Special Clause(s): _____
105* _____
106* _____
107* _____
108 **XV. STANDARDS FOR REAL ESTATE TRANSACTIONS ("Standards"):** Buyer and Seller acknowledge receipt of a copy of Standards A
109 through Y on the reverse side or attached, which are incorporated as part of this Contract.
110 **THIS IS INTENDED TO BE A LEGALLY BINDING CONTRACT. IF NOT FULLY UNDERSTOOD, SEEK THE ADVICE OF AN ATTORNEY PRIOR TO SIGNING.**
111 THIS FORM HAS BEEN APPROVED BY THE FLORIDA ASSOCIATION OF REALTORS® AND THE FLORIDA BAR.
112 Approval does not constitute an opinion that any of the terms and conditions in this Contract should be accepted by the parties in a particular transac-
113 tion. Terms and conditions should be negotiated based upon the respective interests, objectives and bargaining positions of all interested persons.
114 AN ASTERISK(*) FOLLOWING A LINE NUMBER IN THE MARGIN INDICATES THE LINE CONTAINS A BLANK TO BE COMPLETED.

115* _____   _____   _____   _____
116 (BUYER)   (DATE)   (SELLER)   (DATE)
117* _____   _____   _____   _____
118 (BUYER)   (DATE)   (SELLER)   (DATE)
119* Buyers' address for purposes of notice _____   Sellers' address for purposes of notice _____
120* _____   _____
121* _____ Phone   _____ Phone
122 **BROKERS:** The brokers (including cooperating brokers, if any) named below are the only brokers entitled to compensation in connection with
123 this Contract:
124* Name: _____   _____
125   Cooperating Brokers, if any   Listing Broker

FAR/BAR-8   Rev. 9/07   © 2007   Florida Association of REALTORS® and The Florida Bar   All Rights Reserved   Page 2 of 4

STANDARDS FOR REAL ESTATE TRANSACTIONS

A. TITLE INSURANCE: The Title Commitment shall be issued by a Florida licensed title insurer agreeing to issue Buyer, upon recording of the deed to Buyer, an owner's policy of title insurance in the amount of the purchase price, insuring Buyer's marketable title to the Real Property, subject only to matters contained in Paragraph VII and those to be discharged by Seller at or before Closing. Marketable title shall be determined according to applicable Title Standards adopted by authority of The Florida Bar and in accordance with law. Buyer shall have 5 days from date of receiving the Title Commitment to examine it, and if title is found defective, notify Seller in writing specifying defect(s) which render title unmarketable. Seller shall have 30 days from receipt of notice to remove the defects, failing which Buyer shall, within 5 days after expiration of the 30 day period, deliver written notice to Seller either: (1) extending the time for a reasonable period not to exceed 120 days within which Seller shall use diligent effort to remove the defects; or (2) requesting a refund of deposit(s) paid which shall be returned to Buyer. If Buyer fails to so notify Seller, Buyer shall be deemed to have accepted the title as it then is. Seller shall, if title is found unmarketable, use diligent effort to correct defect(s) within the time provided. If, after diligent effort, Seller is unable to timely correct the defects, Buyer shall either waive the defects, or receive a refund of deposit(s), thereby releasing Buyer and Seller from all further obligations under this Contract. If Seller is to provide the Title Commitment and it is delivered to Buyer less than 5 days prior to Closing, Buyer may extend Closing so that Buyer shall have up to 5 days from date of receipt to examine same in accordance with this Standard.

B. PURCHASE MONEY MORTGAGE; SECURITY AGREEMENT TO SELLER: A purchase money mortgage and mortgage note to Seller shall provide for a 30 day grace period in the event of default if a first mortgage and a 15 day grace period if a second or lesser mortgage; shall provide for right of prepayment in whole or in part without penalty; shall permit acceleration in event of transfer of the Real Property; shall require all prior liens and encumbrances to be kept in good standing; shall forbid modifications of, or future advances under, prior mortgage(s); shall require Buyer to maintain policies of insurance containing a standard mortgagee clause covering all improvements located on the Real Property against fire and all perils included within the term "extended coverage endorsements" and such other risks and perils as Seller may reasonably require, in an amount equal to their highest insurable value; and the mortgage, note and security agreement shall be otherwise in form and content required by Seller, but Seller may only require clauses and coverage customarily found in mortgages, mortgage notes and security agreements generally utilized by savings and loan institutions or state or national banks located in the county wherein the Real Property is located. All Personal Property and leases being conveyed or assigned will, at Seller's option, be subject to the lien of a security agreement evidenced by recorded or filed financing statements or certificates of title. If a balloon mortgage, the final payment will exceed the periodic payments thereon.

C. SURVEY: Buyer, at Buyer's expense, within time allowed to deliver evidence of title and to examine same, may have the Real Property surveyed and certified by a registered Florida surveyor. If the survey discloses encroachments on the Real Property or that improvements located thereon encroach on setback lines, easements, lands of others or violate any restrictions, Contract covenants or applicable governmental regulations, the same shall constitute a title defect.

D. WOOD DESTROYING ORGANISMS: "Wood Destroying Organisms" (WDO) shall be deemed to include all wood destroying organisms required to be reported under the Florida Structural Pest Control Act, as amended. Buyer, at Buyer's expense, may have the Property inspected by a Florida Certified Pest Control Operator ("Operator") within 20 days after the Effective Date to determine if there is any visible active WDO infestation or visible damage from WDO infestation, excluding fences. If either or both are found, Buyer may within said 20 days (1) have cost of treatment of active infestation estimated by the Operator; (2) have all damage inspected and cost of repair estimated by an appropriately licensed contractor; and (3) report such cost(s) to Seller in writing. Seller shall cause the treatment and repair of all WDO damage to be made and pay the costs thereof up to the amount provided in Paragraph XII(a). If estimated costs exceed that amount, Buyer shall have the option of canceling this Contract by giving written notice to Seller within 20 days after the Effective Date, or Buyer may elect to proceed with the transaction and receive a credit at Closing equal to the amount provided in Paragraph XII(a). If Buyer's lender requires an updated WDO report, then Buyer shall, at Buyer's expense, have the opportunity to have the Property re-inspected for WDO infestation and have the cost of active infestation or new damage estimated and reported to Seller in writing at least 10 days prior to Closing, and thereafter, Seller shall cause such treatment and repair to be made and pay the cost thereof; provided, Seller's total obligation for treatment and repair costs required under both the first and second inspection shall not exceed the amount provided in Paragraph XII (a).

E. INGRESS AND EGRESS: Seller warrants and represents that there is ingress and egress to the Real Property sufficient for its intended use as described in Paragraph VII hereof and title to the Real Property is insurable in accordance with Standard A without exception for lack of legal right of access.

F. LEASES: Seller shall, at least 10 days before Closing, furnish to Buyer copies of all written leases and estoppel letters from each tenant specifying the nature and duration of the tenant's occupancy, rental rates, advanced rent and security deposits paid by tenant. If Seller is unable to obtain such letter from each tenant, the same information shall be furnished by Seller to Buyer within that time period in the form of a Seller's affidavit, and Buyer may thereafter contact tenant to confirm such information. If the terms of the leases differ materially from Seller's representations, Buyer may terminate this Contract by delivering written notice to Seller at least 5 days prior to Closing. Seller shall, at Closing, deliver and assign all original leases to Buyer.

G. LIENS: Seller shall furnish to Buyer at time of Closing an affidavit attesting to the absence, unless otherwise provided for herein, of any financing statement, claims of lien or potential lienors known to Seller and further attesting that there have been no improvements or repairs to the Real Property for 90 days immediately preceding date of Closing. If the Real Property has been improved or repaired within that time, Seller shall deliver releases or waivers of construction liens executed by all general contractors, subcontractors, suppliers and materialmen in addition to Seller's lien affidavit setting forth the names of all such general contractors, subcontractors, suppliers and materialmen, further affirming that all charges for improvements or repairs which could serve as a basis for a construction lien or a claim for damages have been paid or will be paid at the Closing of this Contract.

H. PLACE OF CLOSING: Closing shall be held in the county wherein the Real Property is located at the office of the attorney or other closing agent ("Closing Agent") designated by the party paying for title insurance, or, if no title insurance, designated by Seller.

I. TIME: Calendar days shall be used in computing time periods except periods of less than six (6) days, in which event Saturdays, Sundays and state or national legal holidays shall be excluded. Any time periods provided for herein which shall end on a Saturday, Sunday, or a legal holiday shall extend to 5:00 p.m. of the next business day. **Time is of the essence in this Contract.**

J. CLOSING DOCUMENTS: Seller shall furnish the deed, bill of sale, certificate of title, construction lien affidavit, owner's possession affidavit, assignments of leases, tenant and mortgagee estoppel letters and corrective instruments. Buyer shall furnish mortgage, mortgage note, security agreement and financing statements.

K. EXPENSES: Documentary stamps on the deed and recording of corrective instruments shall be paid by Seller. All costs of Buyer's loan (whether obtained from Seller or third party), including, but not limited to, documentary stamps and intangible tax on the purchase money mortgage and any mortgage assumed, mortgagee title insurance commitment with related fees, and recording of purchase money mortgage to Seller, deed and financing statements shall be paid by Buyer. Unless otherwise provided by law or rider to this Contract, charges for related closing services, title search, and closing fees (including preparation of closing statement), shall be paid by the party responsible for furnishing the title evidence in accordance with Paragraph V.

L. PRORATIONS; CREDITS: Taxes, assessments, rent, interest, insurance and other expenses of the Property shall be prorated through the day before Closing. Buyer shall have the option of taking over existing policies of insurance, if assumable, in which event premiums shall be prorated. Cash at Closing shall be increased or decreased as may be required by prorations to be made through day prior to Closing, or occupancy, if occupancy occurs before Closing. Advance rent and security deposits will be credited to Buyer. Escrow deposits held by mortgagee will be credited to Seller. Taxes shall be prorated based on the current year's tax with due allowance made for maximum allowable discount, homestead and other exemptions. If Closing occurs at a date when the current year's millage is not fixed and current year's assessment is available, taxes will be prorated based upon such assessment and prior year's millage. If current year's assessment is not available, then taxes will be prorated on prior year's tax. If there are completed improvements on the Real Property by January 1st of year of Closing, which improvements were not in existence on January 1st of prior year, then taxes shall be prorated based upon prior year's millage and at an equitable assessment to be agreed upon between the parties; failing which, request shall be made to the County Property Appraiser for an informal assessment taking into account available exemptions. A tax proration based on an estimate shall, at request of either party, be readjusted upon receipt of current year's tax bill.

M. (RESERVED - purposely left blank)

N. INSPECTION AND REPAIR: Seller warrants that the ceiling, roof (including the fascia and soffits), and exterior and interior walls, and foundation of the Property do not have any visible evidence of leaks, water damage, or structural damage and that dockage, seawalls, septic tank, pool, all appliances, mechanical items,

FAR/BAR-8   Rev. 9/07   © 2007   Florida Association of REALTORS® and The Florida Bar   All Rights Reserved   Page 3 of 4

STANDARDS FOR REAL ESTATE TRANSACTIONS (CONTINUED)

heating, cooling, electrical, plumbing systems, and machinery are in Working Condition. The foregoing warranty shall be limited to the items specified unless otherwise provided in an addendum. Buyer may inspect, or, at Buyer's expense, have a firm or individual specializing in home inspections and holding an occupational license for such purpose (if required), or by an appropriately licensed Florida contractor, make inspections of, those items within 20 days after the Effective Date. Buyer shall, prior to Buyer's occupancy but not more than 20 days after Effective Date, report in writing to Seller such items that do not meet the above standards as to defects. Unless Buyer timely reports such defects, Buyer shall be deemed to have waived Seller's warranties as to defects not reported. If repairs or replacements are required to comply with this Standard, Seller shall cause them to be made and shall pay up to the amount provided in Paragraph XII (b). Seller is not required to make repairs or replacements of a Cosmetic Condition unless caused by a defect Seller is responsible to repair or replace. If the cost for such repair or replacement exceeds the amount provided in Paragraph XII (b), Buyer or Seller may elect to pay such excess, failing which either party may cancel this Contract. If Seller is unable to correct the defects prior to Closing, the cost thereof shall be paid into escrow at Closing. For purposes of this Contract: (1) "Working Condition" means operating in the manner in which the item was designed to operate; (2) "Cosmetic Condition" means aesthetic imperfections that do not affect the Working Condition of the item, including, but not limited to: pitted marcite or other pool finishes; missing or torn screens; fogged windows; tears, worn spots, or discoloration of floor coverings, wallpaper, or window treatments; nail holes, scratches, dents, scrapes, chips or caulking in ceilings, walls, flooring, fixtures, or mirrors; and minor cracks in floors, tiles, windows, driveways, sidewalks, or pool decks; and (3) cracked roof tiles, curling or worn shingles, or limited roof life shall not be considered defects Seller must repair or replace, so long as there is no evidence of actual leaks or leakage or structural damage, but missing tiles will be Seller's responsibility to replace or repair.

O. RISK OF LOSS: If, after the Effective Date, the Property is damaged by fire or other casualty ("Casualty Loss") before Closing and cost of restoration (which shall include the cost of pruning or removing damaged trees) does not exceed 1.5% of the Purchase Price, cost of restoration shall be an obligation of Seller and Closing shall proceed pursuant to the terms of this Contract and if restoration is not completed as of Closing, restoration costs will be escrowed at Closing. If the cost of restoration exceeds 1.5% of the Purchase Price, Buyer shall either take the Property as is, together with the 1.5% or receive a refund of deposit(s) thereby releasing Buyer and Seller from all further obligations under this Contract. Seller's sole obligation with respect to tree damage by casualty or other natural occurrence shall be the cost of pruning or removal.

P. CLOSING PROCEDURE: The deed shall be recorded upon clearance of funds. If the title agent insures adverse matters pursuant to Section 627.7841, F.S., as amended, the escrow and closing procedure required by this Standard shall be waived. Unless waived as set forth above the following closing procedures shall apply: (1) all closing proceeds shall be held in escrow by the Closing Agent for a period of not more than 5 days after Closing; (2) if Seller's title is rendered unmarketable, through no fault of Buyer, Buyer shall, within the 5 day period, notify Seller in writing of the defect and Seller shall have 30 days from date of receipt of such notification to cure the defect; (3) if Seller fails to timely cure the defect, all deposits and closing funds shall, upon written demand by Buyer and within 5 days after demand, be returned to Buyer and, simultaneously with such repayment, Buyer shall return the Personal Property, vacate the Real Property and reconvey the Property to Seller by special warranty deed and bill of sale; and (4) if Buyer fails to make timely demand for refund, Buyer shall take title as is, waiving all rights against Seller as to any intervening defect except as may be available to Buyer by virtue of warranties contained in the deed or bill of sale.

Q. ESCROW: Any Closing Agent or escrow agent (collectively "Agent") receiving funds or equivalent is authorized and agrees by acceptance of them to deposit them promptly, hold same in escrow and, subject to clearance, disburse them in accordance with terms and conditions of this Contract. Failure of funds to clear shall not excuse Buyer's performance. If in doubt as to Agent's duties or liabilities under the provisions of this Contract, Agent may, at Agent's option, continue to hold the subject matter of the escrow until the parties hereto agree to its disbursement or until a judgment of a court of competent jurisdiction shall determine the rights of the parties, or Agent may deposit same with the clerk of the circuit court having jurisdiction of the dispute. An attorney who represents a party and also acts as Agent may represent such party in such action. Upon notifying all parties concerned of such action, all liability on the part of Agent shall fully terminate, except to the extent of accounting for any items previously delivered out of escrow. If a licensed real estate broker, Agent will comply with provisions of Chapter 475, F.S., as amended. Any suit between Buyer and Seller wherein Agent is made a party because of acting as Agent hereunder, or in any suit wherein Agent interpleads the subject matter of the escrow, Agent shall recover reasonable attorney's fees and costs incurred with these amounts to be paid from and out of the escrowed funds or equivalent and charged and awarded as court costs in favor of the prevailing party. The Agent shall not be liable to any party or person for misdelivery to Buyer or Seller of items subject to the escrow, unless such misdelivery is due to willful breach of the provisions of this Contract or gross negligence of Agent.

R. ATTORNEY'S FEES; COSTS: In any litigation, including breach, enforcement or interpretation, arising out of this Contract, the prevailing party in such litigation, which, for purposes of this Standard, shall include Seller, Buyer and any brokers acting in agency or nonagency relationships authorized by Chapter 475, F.S., as amended, shall be entitled to recover from the non-prevailing party reasonable attorney's fees, costs and expenses.

S. FAILURE OF PERFORMANCE: If Buyer fails to perform this Contract within the time specified, including payment of all deposits, the deposit(s) paid by Buyer and deposit(s) agreed to be paid, may be recovered and retained by and for the account of Seller as agreed upon liquidated damages, consideration for the execution of this Contract and in full settlement of any claims; whereupon, Buyer and Seller shall be relieved of all obligations under this Contract; or Seller, at Seller's option, may proceed in equity to enforce Seller's rights under this Contract. If for any reason other than failure of Seller to make Seller's title marketable after diligent effort, Seller fails, neglects or refuses to perform this Contract, Buyer may seek specific performance or elect to receive the return of Buyer's deposit(s) without thereby waiving any action for damages resulting from Seller's breach.

T. CONTRACT NOT RECORDABLE; PERSONS BOUND; NOTICE; COPIES: Neither this Contract nor any notice of it shall be recorded in any public records. This Contract shall bind and inure to the benefit of the parties and their successors in interest. Whenever the context permits, singular shall include plural and one gender shall include all. Notice and delivery given by or to the attorney or broker representing any party shall be as effective as if given by or to that party. All notices must be in writing and may be made by mail, personal delivery or electronic media. A legible facsimile or electronic (including "pdf") copy of this Contract and any signatures hereon shall be considered for all purposes as an original.

U. CONVEYANCE: Seller shall convey marketable title to the Real Property by statutory warranty, trustee's, personal representative's, or guardian's deed, as appropriate to the status of Seller, subject only to matters contained in Paragraph VII and those otherwise accepted by Buyer. Personal Property shall, at the request of Buyer, be transferred by an absolute bill of sale with warranty of title, subject only to such matters as may be otherwise provided herein.

V. OTHER AGREEMENTS: No prior or present agreements or representations shall be binding upon Buyer or Seller unless included in this Contract. No modification to or change in this Contract shall be valid or binding upon the parties unless in writing and executed by the parties intended to be bound by it.

W. SELLER DISCLOSURE: There are no facts known to Seller materially affecting the value of the Property which are not readily observable by Buyer or which have not been disclosed to Buyer.

X. PROPERTY MAINTENANCE; PROPERTY ACCESS; REPAIR STANDARDS; ASSIGNMENT OF CONTRACTS AND WARRANTIES: Seller shall maintain the Property, including, but not limited to lawn, shrubbery, and pool in the condition existing as of Effective Date, ordinary wear and tear and Casualty Loss excepted. Seller shall, upon reasonable notice, provide utilities service and access to the Property for appraisal and inspections, including a walk-through prior to Closing, to confirm that all items of Personal Property are on the Real Property and, subject to the foregoing, that all required repairs and replacements have been made, and that the Property has been maintained as required by this Standard. All repairs and replacements shall be completed in a good and workmanlike manner, in accordance with all requirements of law, and shall consist of materials or items of quality, value, capacity and performance comparable to, or better than, that existing as of the Effective Date. Seller will assign all assignable repair and treatment contracts and warranties to Buyer at Closing.

Y. 1031 EXCHANGE: If either Seller or Buyer wish to enter into a like-kind exchange (either simultaneous with Closing or deferred) with respect to the Property under Section 1031 of the Internal Revenue Code ("Exchange"), the other party shall cooperate in all reasonable respects to effectuate the Exchange, including the execution of documents; provided (1) the cooperating party shall incur no liability or expense related to the Exchange and (2) the Closing shall not be contingent upon, nor extended or delayed by, such Exchange.

FAR/BAR-8 Rev. 9/07 © 2007 Florida Association of REALTORS® and The Florida Bar All Rights Reserved Page 4 of 4

Source: Florida Association of REALTORS©. Reprinted with permission.

RESIDENTIAL SALE AND PURCHASE CONTRACT

Residential Sale and Purchase Contract
FLORIDA ASSOCIATION OF REALTORS®

1* **1. SALE AND PURCHASE:** _____ ("Seller")
2* and _____ ("Buyer")
3 agree to sell and buy on the terms and conditions specified below the property described as:
4* Address: _____
5* _____ County: _____
6* Legal Description: _____
7* _____ Tax ID No: _____
8 together with all existing improvements and attached items, including fixtures, built-in furnishings, major appliances (including
9* but not limited to range(s), refrigerator(s), dishwasher(s), washer(s), and dryer(s), ___ (#) ceiling fans (if left blank, all ceiling fans),
10 light fixtures, attached wall-to-wall carpeting, rods, draperies and other window treatments as of Effective Date. The only other
11* items included in the purchase are: _____
12* _____
13* _____
14* The following attached items are excluded from the purchase: _____
15* _____
16 The real and personal property described above as included in the purchase is referred to as the "Property." Personal property listed
17 in this Contract is included in the purchase price, has no contributory value and is being left for **Seller's** convenience.

18   **PRICE AND FINANCING**
19* **2. PURCHASE PRICE:** $_____ payable by **Buyer** in U.S. currency as follows:
20*   (a) $_____   Deposit received (checks are subject to clearance) on _____, _____ by
21*   _____ for delivery to _____ ("Escrow Agent")
22   *Signature*   *Name of Company*
23*   (Address of Escrow Agent) _____
24*   (Phone # of Escrow Agent) _____
25*   (b) $_____   Additional deposit to be delivered to Escrow Agent by _____,
26*   _____ or _____ days from Effective Date. (10 days if left blank)
27*   (c) _____   Total financing (see Paragraph **3** below) (express as a dollar amount or percentage) _____
28*   (d) $_____   Other: _____
29*   (e) $_____   Balance to close (not including **Buyer's** closing costs, prepaid items and prorations). All funds paid
30   at closing must be paid by locally drawn cashier's check, official bank check, or wired funds.

31* **3. FINANCING:** (Check as applicable) ❑ **(a) Buyer** will pay cash for the Property with no financing contingency.
32*   ❑ **(b) Buyer** will apply for new ❑ conventional ❑ FHA ❑ VA financing specified in paragraph 2(c) at the prevailing interest rate and
33 loan costs based on **Buyer's** creditworthiness (the "Financing") within _____ days from Effective Date (5 days if left blank) and
34 provide **Seller** with either a written Financing commitment or approval letter ("Commitment") or written notice that **Buyer** is unable to
35 obtain a Commitment within _____ days from Effective Date (the earlier of 30 days after the Effective Date or 5 days prior to Closing
36 Date if left blank) ("Commitment Period"). **Buyer** will keep **Seller** and Broker fully informed about loan application status, progress
37 and Commitment issues and authorizes the mortgage broker and lender to disclose all such information to **Seller** and **Broker**. If,
38 after using diligence and good faith, **Buyer** is unable to provide the Commitment and provides **Seller** with written notice that **Buyer** is
39 unable to obtain a Commitment within the Commitment Period, either party may cancel this Contract and **Buyer's** deposit will be
40 refunded. **Buyer's** failure to provide **Seller** with written notice that **Buyer** is unable to obtain a Commitment within the Commitment
41 Period will result in forfeiture of **Buyer's** deposit(s). Once **Buyer** provides the Commitment to **Seller**, the financing contingency is
42 waived and **Seller** will be entitled to retain the deposits if the transaction does not close by the Closing Date unless (1) the Property
43 appraises below the purchase price and either the parties cannot agree on a new purchase price or **Buyer** elects not to proceed, (2)
44 the property related conditions of the Commitment have not been met (except when such conditions are waived by other provisions
45 of this Contract), or (3) another provision of this Contract provides for cancellation.

46   **CLOSING**
47 **4. CLOSING DATE; OCCUPANCY:** Unless the Closing Date is specifically extended by the **Buyer** and **Seller** or by any other provision in
48 this Contract, the Closing Date shall prevail over all other time periods including, but not limited to, inspection and financing periods. This
49 Contract will be closed on _____, _____ ("Closing Date") at the time established by the closing agent, by which time **Seller**
50 will (a) have removed all personal items and trash from the Property and swept the Property clean and (b) deliver the deed, occupancy
51 and possession, along with all keys, garage door openers and access codes, to **Buyer**. If on Closing Date insurance underwriting is
52 suspended, **Buyer** may postpone closing up to 5 days after the insurance suspension is lifted. If this transaction does not close for any
53 reason, **Buyer** will immediately return all **Seller**-provided title evidence, surveys, association documents and other items.
54* **Buyer** (____) (____) and **Seller** (____) (____) acknowledge receipt of a copy of this page, which is Page 1 of 8 Pages.
FAR-9 4/07 © 2007 Florida Association of REALTORS®   All Rights Reserved

5. **CLOSING PROCEDURE; COSTS:** Closing will take place in the county where the Property is located and may be conducted by mail or electronic means. If title insurance insures **Buyer** for title defects arising between the title binder effective date and recording of **Buyer's** deed, closing agent will disburse at closing the net sale proceeds to **Seller** and brokerage fees to Broker as per Paragraph 19. In addition to other expenses provided in this Contract, **Seller** and **Buyer** will pay the costs indicated below.

(a) **Seller Costs:**
Taxes and surtaxes on the deed
Recording fees for documents needed to cure title
Other: _____
Seller will pay up to $_____ or _____% (1.5% if left blank) of the purchase price for repairs to warranted items (**"Repair Limit"**); and up to $_____ or _____% (1.5% if left blank) of the purchase price for wood-destroying organism treatment and repairs (**"WDO Repair Limit"**); and up to $_____ or _____% (1.5% if left blank) of the purchase price for costs associated with closing out open permits and obtaining required permits for unpermitted existing improvements (**"Permit Limit"**).

(b) **Buyer Costs:**
Taxes and recording fees on notes and mortgages
Recording fees on the deed and financing statements
Loan expenses
Lender's title policy
Inspections
Survey
Flood insurance, homeowner insurance, hazard insurance
Other: _____

(c) **Title Evidence and Insurance: Check (1) or (2):**
❑ **(1)** The title evidence will be a Paragraph 10(a)(1) owner's title insurance commitment. ❑ **Seller** will select the title agent and will pay for the owner's title policy, search, examination and related charges or ❑ **Buyer** will select the title agent and pay for the owner's title policy, search, examination and related charges or ❑ **Buyer** will select the title agent and **Seller** will pay for the owner's title policy, search, examination and related charges.
❑ **(2) Seller** will provide an abstract as specified in Paragraph 10(a)(2) as title evidence. ❑ **Seller** ❑ **Buyer** will pay for the owner's title policy and select the title agent. **Seller** will pay fees for title searches prior to closing, including tax search and lien search fees, and **Buyer** will pay fees for title searches after closing (if any), title examination fees and closing fees.

(d) **Prorations:** The following items will be made current (if applicable) and prorated as of the day before Closing Date: real estate taxes, interest, bonds, assessments, association fees, insurance, rents and other current expenses and revenues of the Property. If taxes and assessments for the current year cannot be determined, taxes shall be prorated on the basis of taxes for the preceding year as of the day before Closing Date and shall be computed and readjusted when the current taxes are determined with adjustment for exemptions and improvements. If there are completed improvements on the Property by January 1 of the year of the Closing Date, which improvements were not in existence on January 1 of the prior year, taxes shall be prorated based on the prior year's millage and at an equitable assessment to be agreed upon by the parties prior to Closing Date, failing which, request will be made to the County Property Appraiser for an informal assessment taking into consideration available exemptions. If the County Property Appraiser is unable or unwilling to perform an informal assessment prior to Closing Date, **Buyer** and **Seller** will split the cost of a private appraiser to perform an assessment prior to Closing Date. Nothing in this paragraph shall act to extend the Closing Date. This provision shall survive closing.

(e) **Special Assessment by Public Body:** Regarding special assessments imposed by a public body, **Seller** will pay (i) the full amount of liens that are certified, confirmed and ratified before closing and (ii) the amount of the last estimate of the assessment if an improvement is substantially completed as of Effective Date but has not resulted in a lien before closing, and **Buyer** will pay all other amounts. If special assessments may be paid in installments ❑ **Buyer** ❑ **Seller** (if left blank, **Buyer**) shall pay installments due after closing. If **Seller** is checked, **Seller** will pay the assessment in full prior to or at the time of closing. Public body does not include a Homeowner Association or Condominium Association.

(f) **Tax Withholding: Buyer** and **Seller** will comply with the Foreign Investment in Real Property Tax Act, which may require **Seller** to provide additional cash at closing if **Seller** is a "foreign person" as defined by federal law.

(g) **Home Warranty:** ❑ **Buyer** ❑ **Seller** ❑ **N/A** will pay for a home warranty plan issued by _____ at a cost not to exceed $_____. A home warranty plan provides for repair or replacement of many of a home's mechanical systems and major built-in appliances in the event of breakdown due to normal wear and tear during the agreement period.

PROPERTY CONDITION

6. **INSPECTION PERIODS: Buyer** will complete the inspections referenced in Paragraphs 7 and 8(a)(2) by _____, _____ (the earlier of 10 days after the Effective Date or 5 days prior to Closing Date if left blank) ("Inspection Period"); the wood-destroying organism inspection by _____, _____ (at least 5 days prior to closing, if left blank); and the walk-through inspection on the day before Closing Date or any other time agreeable to the parties; and the survey referenced in Paragraph 10(c) by _____, _____ (at least 5 days prior to closing if left blank).

Buyer (____) (____) and **Seller** (____) (____) acknowledge receipt of a copy of this page, which is Page 2 of 8 Pages.
FAR-9   4/07   © 2007   Florida Association of REALTORS®   All Rights Reserved

7. REAL PROPERTY DISCLOSURES: Seller represents that **Seller** does not know of any facts that materially affect the value of the Property, including but not limited to violations of governmental laws, rules and regulations, other than those that **Buyer** can readily observe or that are known by or have been disclosed to **Buyer**.

    (a) Energy Efficiency: Buyer acknowledges receipt of the energy-efficiency information brochure required by Section 553.996, *Florida Statutes*.

    (b) Radon Gas: Radon is a naturally occurring radioactive gas that, when it has accumulated in a building in sufficient quantities, may present health risks to persons who are exposed to it over time. Levels of radon that exceed federal and state guidelines have been found in buildings in Florida. Additional information regarding radon and radon testing may be obtained from your county public health unit. **Buyer** may, within the Inspection Period, have an appropriately licensed person test the Property for radon. If the radon level exceeds acceptable EPA standards, **Seller** may choose to reduce the radon level to an acceptable EPA level, failing which either party may cancel this Contract.

    (c) Flood Zone: Buyer is advised to verify by survey, with the lender and with appropriate government agencies which flood zone the Property is in, whether flood insurance is required and what restrictions apply to improving the Property and rebuilding in the event of casualty. If the Property is in a Special Flood Hazard Area or Coastal High Hazard Area **and** the buildings are built below the minimum flood elevation, **Buyer** may cancel this Contract by delivering written notice to **Seller** within 20 days from Effective Date, failing which **Buyer** accepts the existing elevation of the buildings and zone designation of the Property.

    (d) Homeowners' Association: If membership in a homeowners' association is mandatory, an association disclosure summary is attached and incorporated into this Contract. **BUYER SHOULD NOT SIGN THIS CONTRACT UNTIL BUYER HAS RECEIVED AND READ THE DISCLOSURE SUMMARY.**

    (e) PROPERTY TAX DISCLOSURE SUMMARY: BUYER SHOULD NOT RELY ON THE **SELLER'S** CURRENT PROPERTY TAXES AS THE AMOUNT OF PROPERTY TAXES THAT **BUYER** MAY BE OBLIGATED TO PAY IN THE YEAR SUBSEQUENT TO PURCHASE. A CHANGE OF OWNERSHIP OR PROPERTY IMPROVEMENTS TRIGGERS REASSESSMENTS OF THE PROPERTY THAT COULD RESULT IN HIGHER PROPERTY TAXES. IF YOU HAVE ANY QUESTIONS CONCERNING VALUATION, CONTACT THE COUNTY PROPERTY APPRAISER'S OFFICE FOR FURTHER INFORMATION.

    (f) Mold: Mold is part of the natural environment that, when accumulated in sufficient quantities, may present health risks to susceptible persons. For more information, contact the county indoor air quality specialist or other appropriate professional.

    (g) Coastal Construction Control Line: If any part of the Property lies seaward of the coastal construction control line as defined in Section 161.053 of the Florida Statutes, **Seller** shall provide **Buyer** with an affidavit or survey as required by law delineating the line's location on the Property, unless **Buyer** waives this requirement in writing. The Property being purchased may be subject to coastal erosion and to federal, state, or local regulations that govern coastal property, including delineation of the coastal construction control line, rigid coastal protection structures, beach nourishment, and the protection of marine turtles. Additional information can be obtained from the Florida Department of Environmental Protection, including whether there are significant erosion conditions associated with the shoreline of the Property being purchased.

❏ **Buyer** waives the right to receive a CCCL affidavit or survey.

8. MAINTENANCE, INSPECTIONS AND REPAIR: Seller will keep the Property in the same condition from Effective Date until closing, except for normal wear and tear ("Maintenance Requirement") and repairs required by this Contract. **Seller** will provide access and utilities for **Buyer's** inspections. **Buyer** will repair all damages to the Property resulting from the inspections, return the Property to its pre-inspection condition and provide **Seller** with paid receipts for all work done on Property upon its completion. If **Seller** is unable to complete required repairs or treatments or meet the Maintenance Requirement prior to closing, **Seller** will give **Buyer** a credit at closing for the cost of the repairs and maintenance **Seller** was obligated to perform. At closing, **Seller** will assign all assignable repair and treatment contracts to **Buyer** and provide **Buyer** with paid receipts for all work done on the Property pursuant to the terms of this Contract. At closing, **Seller** will provide **Buyer** with any written documentation that all open permits have been closed out and that **Seller** has obtained required permits for improvements to the Property.

    (a) Warranty, Inspections and Repair:

        (1) Warranty: Seller warrants that non-leased major appliances and heating, cooling, mechanical, electrical, security, sprinkler, septic and plumbing systems, seawall, dock and pool equipment, if any, are and will be maintained in working condition until closing; that the structures (including roofs, doors and windows) and pool, if any, are structurally sound and watertight; and that torn or missing screens and missing roof tiles will be repaired or replaced. **Seller** warrants that all open permits will be closed out and that **Seller** will obtain any required permits for improvements to the Property prior to Closing Date. **Seller** does not warrant and is not required to repair cosmetic conditions, unless the cosmetic condition resulted from a defect in a warranted item. **Seller** is not obligated to bring any item into compliance with existing building code regulations unless necessary to repair a warranted item. "Working condition" means operating in the manner in which the item was designed to operate and "cosmetic conditions" means aesthetic imperfections that do not affect the working condition of the item, including pitted marcite; tears, worn spots and discoloration of floor coverings/wallpapers/window treatments; nail holes, scratches, dents, scrapes, chips and caulking in bathroom ceiling/walls/flooring/tile/fixtures/mirrors; cracked roof tiles; curling or worn shingles; and minor cracks in floor tiles/windows/driveways/sidewalks/pool decks/garage and patio floors.

        (2) Professional Inspection: Buyer may, at **Buyer's** expense, have warranted items inspected by a person who specializes in and holds an occupational license (if required by law) to conduct home inspections or who holds a Florida license to repair and maintain the items inspected ("professional inspector"). **Buyer** must, within 5 days from the end of the Inspection Period, deliver written notice of any items that are not in the condition warranted and a copy of the portion of

Buyer (_____) (_____) and **Seller** (_____) (_____) acknowledge receipt of a copy of this page, which is Page 3 of 8 Pages.
FAR-9   4/07   © 2007   Florida Association of REALTORS®   All Rights Reserved

inspector's written report dealing with such items to **Seller**. If **Buyer** fails to deliver timely written notice, **Buyer** waives **Seller's** warranty and accepts the items listed in subparagraph (a) in their "as is" conditions, except that **Seller** must meet the maintenance requirement.

(3) Repair: Seller will obtain repair estimates and is obligated only to make repairs necessary to bring warranted items into the condition warranted, up to the Repair Limit. **Seller** may, within 5 days from receipt of **Buyer's** notice of items that are not in the condition warranted, have a second inspection made by a professional inspector and will report repair estimates to **Buyer**. If the first and second inspection reports differ and the parties cannot resolve the differences, **Buyer** and **Seller** together will choose, and equally split the cost of, a third inspector, whose written report will be binding on the parties. If the cost to repair warranted items equals or is less than the Repair Limit, **Seller** will have the repairs made in a workmanlike manner by an appropriately licensed person. If the cost to repair warranted items exceeds the Repair Limit, either party may cancel this Contract unless either party pays the excess or **Buyer** designates which repairs to make at a total cost to **Seller** not exceeding the Repair Limit and accepts the balance of the Property in its "as is" condition.

(4) Permits: Seller shall close out any open permits and remedy any violation of any governmental entity, including but not limited to, obtaining any required permits for improvements to the Property, up to the Permit Limit, and with final inspections completed no later than 5 days prior to Closing Date. If final inspections cannot be performed due to delays by the governmental entity, Closing Date shall be extended for up to 10 days to complete such final inspections, failing which, either party may cancel this Contract and **Buyer's** deposit shall be refunded. If the cost to close out open permits or to remedy any violation of any governmental entity exceeds the Permit Limit, either party may cancel the Contract unless either party pays the excess or **Buyer** accepts the Property in its "as is" condition and **Seller** credits **Buyer** at closing the amount of the Permit Limit.

(b) Wood-Destroying Organisms: "Wood-destroying organism" means arthropod or plant life, including termites, powder-post beetles, oldhouse borers and wood-decaying fungi, that damages or infests seasoned wood in a structure, excluding fences. **Buyer** may, at **Buyer's** expense, have the Property inspected by a Florida-licensed pest control business to determine the existence of past or present wood-destroying organism infestation and damage caused by infestation. If the inspector finds evidence of infestation or damage, **Buyer** will deliver a copy of the inspector's written report to **Seller** within 5 days from the date of the inspection. If **Seller** previously treated the Property for the type of wood-destroying organisms found, **Seller** does not have to treat the Property again if (i) there is no visible live infestation, and (ii) **Seller** transfers to **Buyer** at closing a current full treatment warranty for the type of wood-destroying organisms found. Otherwise, **Seller** will have 5 days from receipt of the inspector's report to have reported damage estimated by a licensed building or general contractor and corrective treatment estimated by a licensed pest control business. **Seller** will have treatments and repairs made by an appropriately licensed person at **Seller's** expense up to the WDO Repair Limit. If the cost to treat and repair the Property exceeds the WDO Repair Limit, either party may pay the excess, failing which either party may cancel this Contract by written notice to the other. If **Buyer** fails to timely deliver the inspector's written report, **Buyer** accepts the Property "as is" with regard to wood-destroying organism infestation and damage, subject to the maintenance requirement.

(c) Walk-through Inspection/Reinspection: Buyer, and/or **Buyer's** representative, may walk through the Property solely to verify that **Seller** has made repairs required by this Contract, has met the Maintenance Requirement and has met contractual obligations. If **Buyer**, and/or **Buyer's** representative, fails to conduct this inspection, **Seller's** repair obligations and Maintenance Requirement will be deemed fulfilled.

9. RISK OF LOSS: If any portion of the Property is damaged by fire or other casualty before closing and can be restored by the Closing Date or within 45 days after the Closing Date to substantially the same condition as it was on Effective Date, **Seller**, will, at **Seller's** expense, restore the Property and deliver written notice to **Buyer** that **Seller** has completed the restoration, and the parties will close the transaction on the later of: (1) Closing Date; or, (2) 10 days after **Buyer's** receipt of **Seller's** notice. **Seller** will not be obligated to replace trees. If the restoration cannot be completed in time, **Buyer** may cancel this Contract and **Buyer's** deposit shall be refunded, or **Buyer** may accept the Property "as is", and **Seller** will credit the deductible and assign the insurance proceeds, if any, to **Buyer** at closing in such amounts as are (i) attributable to the Property and (ii) not yet expended in restoring the Property to the same condition as it was on Effective Date.

TITLE

10. TITLE: Seller will convey marketable title to the Property by statutory warranty deed or trustee, personal representative or guardian deed as appropriate to **Seller's** status.

(a) Title Evidence: Title evidence will show legal access to the Property and marketable title of record in **Seller** in accordance with current title standards adopted by the Florida Bar, subject only to the following title exceptions, none of which prevent residential use of the Property: covenants, easements and restrictions of record; matters of plat; existing zoning and government regulations; oil, gas and mineral rights of record if there is no right of entry; current taxes; mortgages that **Buyer** will assume; and encumbrances that **Seller** will discharge at or before closing. **Seller** will, at least 2 days prior to closing, deliver to **Buyer Seller's** choice of one of the following types of title evidence, which must be generally accepted in the county where the Property is located (specify in Paragraph **5(c)** the selected type). **Seller** will use option (1) in Palm Beach County and option (2) in Miami-Dade County.

(1) A title insurance commitment issued by a Florida-licensed title insurer in the amount of the purchase price and subject only to title exceptions set forth in this Contract.

(2) An existing abstract of title from a reputable and existing abstract firm (if firm is not existing, then abstract must be certified as correct by an existing firm) purporting to be an accurate synopsis of the instruments affecting title to the

Buyer (____) (____) and **Seller** (____) (____) acknowledge receipt of a copy of this page, which is Page 4 of 8 Pages.
FAR-9   4/07   © 2007   Florida Association of REALTORS®   All Rights Reserved

Property recorded in the public records of the county where the Property is located and certified to Effective Date. However, if such an abstract is not available to **Seller**, then a **prior owner's title policy** acceptable to the proposed insurer as a base for reissuance of coverage. **Seller** will pay for copies of all policy exceptions and an update in a format acceptable to **Buyer's** closing agent from the policy effective date and certified to **Buyer** or **Buyer's** closing agent, together with copies of all documents recited in the prior policy and in the update. If a prior policy is not available to **Seller** then (1) above will be the title evidence. Title evidence will be delivered no later than 10 days before Closing Date.

(b) Title Examination: **Buyer** will examine the title evidence and deliver written notice to **Seller**, within 5 days from receipt of title evidence but no later than Closing Date, of any defects that make the title unmarketable. **Seller** will have 30 days from receipt of **Buyer's** notice of defects ("Curative Period") to cure the defects at **Seller's** expense. If **Seller** cures the defects within the Curative Period, **Seller** will deliver written notice to **Buyer** and the parties will close the transaction on Closing Date or within 10 days from **Buyer's** receipt of **Seller's** notice if Closing Date has passed. If **Seller** is unable to cure the defects within the Curative Period, **Seller** will deliver written notice to **Buyer** and **Buyer** will, within 10 days from receipt of **Seller's** notice, either cancel this Contract or accept title with existing defects and close the transaction.

(c) Survey: **Buyer** may, at **Buyer's** expense, have the Property surveyed and deliver written notice to **Seller**, within 5 days from receipt of survey but no later than closing, of any encroachments on the Property, encroachments by the Property's improvements on other lands or deed restriction or zoning violations. Any such encroachment or violation will be treated in the same manner as a title defect and **Buyer's** and **Seller's** obligations will be determined in accordance with subparagraph **(b)** above.

MISCELLANEOUS

11. EFFECTIVE DATE; TIME; FORCE MAJEURE:
(a) Effective Date: The "Effective Date" of this Contract is the date on which the last of the parties initials or signs and delivers the final offer or counteroffer. **Time is of the essence for all provisions of this Contract.**

(b) Time: All time periods will be computed in business days (a "business day" is every calendar day except Saturday, Sunday and national legal holidays). If any deadline falls on a Saturday, Sunday or national legal holiday, performance will be due the next business day. All time periods will end at 5:00 p.m. local time (meaning in the county where the Property is located) of the appropriate day.

(c) Force Majeure: **Buyer** or **Seller** shall not be required to perform any obligation under this Contract or be liable to each other for damages so long as the performance or non-performance of the obligation is delayed, caused or prevented by an act of God or force majeure. An "act of God" or "force majeure" is defined as hurricanes, earthquakes, floods, fire, unusual transportation delays, wars, insurrections and any other cause not reasonably within the control of the **Buyer** or **Seller** and which by the exercise of due diligence the non-performing party is unable in whole or in part to prevent or overcome. All time periods, including Closing Date, will be extended (not to exceed 30 days) for the period that the force majeure or act of God is in place. In the event that such "act of God" or "force majeure" event continues beyond the 30 days in this sub-paragraph, either party may cancel the Contract by delivering written notice to the other and Buyer's deposit shall be refunded.

12. NOTICES: All notices shall be in writing and will be delivered to the parties and Broker by mail, personal delivery or electronic media. Except for the notices required by Paragraph 3 of this Contract, **Buyer's failure to deliver timely written notice to Seller**, when such notice is required by this Contract, regarding any contingencies will render that contingency null and void and the Contract will be construed as if the contingency did not exist. Any notice, document or item delivered to or received by an attorney or licensee (including a transaction broker) representing a party will be as effective as if delivered to or by that party.

13. COMPLETE AGREEMENT: This Contract is the entire agreement between **Buyer** and **Seller**. Except for brokerage agreements, no prior or present agreements will bind Buyer, Seller or Broker unless incorporated into this Contract. Modifications of this Contract will not be binding unless in writing, signed or initialed and delivered by the party to be bound. Signatures, initials, documents referenced in this Contract, counterparts, and written modifications communicated electronically or on paper will be acceptable for all purposes, including delivery, and will be binding. Handwritten or typewritten terms inserted in or attached to this Contract prevail over preprinted terms. If any provision of this Contract is or becomes invalid or unenforceable, all remaining provisions will continue to be fully effective. **Buyer** and **Seller** will use diligence and good faith in performing all obligations under this Contract. This Contract will not be recorded in any public records.

14. ASSIGNABILITY; PERSONS BOUND: Buyer may **not** assign this Contract without **Seller's** written consent. The terms "**Buyer**," "**Seller**," and "**Broker**" may be singular or plural. This Contract is binding on the heirs, administrators, executors, personal representatives and assigns (if permitted) of **Buyer**, **Seller** and Broker.

DEFAULT AND DISPUTE RESOLUTION

15. DEFAULT: (a) Seller Default: If for any reason other than failure of **Seller** to make **Seller's** title marketable after diligent effort, **Seller** fails, refuses or neglects to perform this Contract, **Buyer** may choose to receive a return of **Buyer's** deposit without waiving the right to seek damages or to seek specific performance as per Paragraph 16. **Seller** will also be liable to Broker for the full amount of the brokerage fee. **(b) Buyer Default:** If **Buyer** fails to perform this Contract within the time specified, including timely payment of all deposits, **Seller** may choose to retain and collect all deposits paid and agreed to be paid as liquidated damages or to seek specific performance as

Buyer (____) (____) and Seller (____) (____) acknowledge receipt of a copy of this page, which is Page 5 of 8 Pages.
FAR-9 4/07 © 2007 Florida Association of REALTORS® All Rights Reserved

per Paragraph **16**; and Broker will, upon demand, receive 50% of all deposits paid and agreed to be paid (to be split equally among Broker) up to the full amount of the brokerage fee.

16. DISPUTE RESOLUTION: This Contract will be construed under Florida law. All controversies, claims and other matters in question arising out of or relating to this transaction or this Contract or its breach will be settled as follows:

(a) **Disputes concerning entitlement to deposits made and agreed to be made: Buyer** and **Seller** will have 30 days from the date conflicting demands are made to attempt to resolve the dispute through **mediation**. If that fails, Escrow Agent will submit the dispute, if so required by Florida law, to Escrow Agent's choice of arbitration, a Florida court or the Florida Real Estate Commission ("FREC"). **Buyer** and **Seller** will be bound by any resulting award, judgment or order. A broker's obligation under Chapter 475, FS and the FREC rules to timely notify the FREC of an escrow dispute and timely resolve the escrow dispute through mediation, arbitration, interpleader or an escrow disbursement order, if the broker so chooses, applies to brokers only and does not apply to title companies, attorneys or other escrow companies.

(b) **All other disputes: Buyer** and **Seller** will have 30 days from the date a dispute arises between them to attempt to resolve the matter through mediation, failing which the parties will resolve the dispute through neutral binding **arbitration** in the county where the Property is located. The arbitrator may not alter the Contract terms or award any remedy not provided for in this Contract. The award will be based on the greater weight of the evidence and will state findings of fact and the contractual authority on which it is based. If the parties agree to use discovery, it will be in accordance with the Florida Rules of Civil Procedure and the arbitrator will resolve all discovery-related disputes. Any disputes with a real estate licensee or firm named in Paragraph **19** will be submitted to arbitration only if the licensee's broker consents in writing to become a party to the proceeding. This clause will survive closing.

(c) **Mediation and Arbitration; Expenses:** "Mediation" is a process in which parties attempt to resolve a dispute by submitting it to an impartial mediator who facilitates the resolution of the dispute but who is not empowered to impose a settlement on the parties. Mediation will be in accordance with the rules of the American Arbitration Association ("AAA") or other mediator agreed on by the parties. The parties will equally divide the mediation fee, if any. "Arbitration" is a process in which the parties resolve a dispute by a hearing before a neutral person who decides the matter and whose decision is binding on the parties. Arbitration will be in accordance with the rules of the AAA or other arbitrator agreed on by the parties. Each party to any arbitration will pay its own fees, costs and expenses, including attorneys' fees, and will equally split the arbitrators' fees and administrative fees of arbitration.

ESCROW AGENT AND BROKER

17. ESCROW AGENT: Buyer and **Seller** authorize Escrow Agent to receive, deposit and hold funds and other items in escrow and, subject to clearance, disburse them upon proper authorization and in accordance with Florida law and the terms of this Contract, including disbursing brokerage fees. The parties agree that Escrow Agent will not be liable to any person for misdelivery of escrowed items to **Buyer** or **Seller**, unless the misdelivery is due to Escrow Agent's willful breach of this Contract or gross negligence. If Escrow Agent interpleads the subject matter of the escrow, Escrow Agent will pay the filing fees and costs from the deposit and will recover reasonable attorneys' fees and costs to be paid from the escrowed funds or equivalent and charged and awarded as court costs in favor of the prevailing party. All claims against Escrow Agent will be arbitrated, so long as Escrow Agent consents to arbitrate.

18. PROFESSIONAL ADVICE; BROKER LIABILITY: Broker advises **Buyer** and **Seller** to verify all facts and representations that are important to them and to consult an appropriate professional for legal advice (for example, interpreting contracts, determining the effect of laws on the Property and transaction, status of title, foreign investor reporting requirements, the effect of property lying partially or totally seaward of the coastal construction control line, etc.) and for tax, property condition, environmental and other specialized advice. **Buyer** acknowledges that Broker does not reside in the Property and that all representations (oral, written or otherwise) by Broker are based on **Seller** representations or public records. **Buyer agrees to rely solely on Seller, professional inspectors and governmental agencies for verification of the Property condition, square footage and facts that materially affect Property value. Buyer** and **Seller** respectively will pay all costs and expenses, including reasonable attorneys' fees at all levels, incurred by Broker and Broker's officers, directors, agents and employees in connection with or arising from **Buyer's** or **Seller's** misstatement or failure to perform contractual obligations. **Buyer** and **Seller** hold harmless and release Broker and Broker's officers, directors, agents and employees from all liability for loss or damage based on **(1) Buyer's** or **Seller's** misstatement or failure to perform contractual obligations; **(2)** Broker's performance, at **Buyer's** and/or **Seller's** request, of any task beyond the scope of services regulated by Chapter 475, F.S., as amended, including Broker's referral, recommendation or retention of any vendor; **(3)** products or services provided by any vendor; and **(4)** expenses incurred by any vendor. **Buyer** and **Seller** each assume full responsibility for selecting and compensating their respective vendors. This paragraph will not relieve Broker of statutory obligations. For purposes of this paragraph, Broker will be treated as a party to this Contract. This paragraph will survive closing.

19. BROKERS: The licensee(s) and brokerage(s) named below are collectively referred to as "Broker." **Instruction to Closing Agent: Seller** and **Buyer** direct closing agent to disburse at closing the full amount of the brokerage fees as specified in separate brokerage agreements with the parties and cooperative agreements between the brokers, except to the extent Broker has retained such fees from the escrowed funds. In the absence of such brokerage agreements, closing agent will disburse brokerage fees as indicated below. This paragraph will not be used to modify any MLS or other offer of compensation made by **Seller** or listing broker to cooperating brokers.

Buyer (_____) (_____) and **Seller** (_____) (_____) acknowledge receipt of a copy of this page, which is Page 6 of 8 Pages.
FAR-9   4/07   © 2007   Florida Association of REALTORS®   All Rights Reserved

354* _____ _____
355 *Selling Sales Associate/License No.*   *Selling Firm/Brokerage Fee: ($ or % of Purchase Price)*

356* _____ _____
357 *Listing Sales Associate/License No.*   *Listing Firm/Brokerage fee: ($ or % of Purchase Price)*

358   **ADDENDA AND ADDITIONAL TERMS**
359 **20. ADDENDA:** The following additional terms are included in the attached addenda and incorporated into this Contract (check if
360 applicable):
361* ❏ A. Condo. Assn.   ❏ H. As Is w/Right to Inspect   ❏ O. Interest-Bearing Account   ❏ V. Prop. Disclosure Stmt.
362* ❏ B. Homeowners' Assn.   ❏ I. Inspections   ❏ P. Back-up Contract   ❏ W. FIRPTA
363* ❏ C. Seller Financing   ❏ J. Insulation Disclosure   ❏ Q. Broker - Pers. Int. in Prop. ❏ X. 1031 Exchange
364* ❏ D. Mort. Assumption   ❏ K. Pre-1978 Housing Stmt. (LBP) ❏ R. Rentals   ❏ Y. Additional Clauses
365* ❏ E. FHA Financing   ❏ L. Insurance   ❏ S. Sale/Lease of Buyer's Property
366* ❏ F. VA Financing   ❏ M. Housing Older Persons   ❏ T. Rezoning   ❏ Other_____
367* ❏ G. New Mort. Rates   ❏ N. Lease purchase/Lease option ❏ U. Assignment   ❏ Other_____

368* **21. ADDITIONAL TERMS:** _____
369* _____
370* _____
371* _____
372* _____
373* _____
374* _____
375* _____
376* _____
377* _____
378* _____
379* _____
380* _____
381* _____
382* _____
383* _____
384* _____
385* _____
386* _____
387* _____
388* _____
389* _____
390* _____
391* _____
392* _____
393* _____
394* _____
395* _____
396* _____
397* _____
398* _____
399* _____
400* _____
401* _____
402* _____
403* _____
404* _____
405* _____
406* _____
407* _____
408* _____
409* _____

410* **Buyer** (____) (____) and **Seller** (____) (____) acknowledge receipt of a copy of this page, which is Page 7 of 8 Pages.
     FAR-9   4/07   © 2007   Florida Association of REALTORS®   All Rights Reserved

411 This is intended to be a legally binding contract. If not fully understood, seek the advice of an attorney prior to signing.

412 **OFFER AND ACCEPTANCE**
413* (**Check if applicable:** ❏ **Buyer** received a written real property disclosure statement from **Seller** before making this Offer.)
414 **Buyer** offers to purchase the Property on the above terms and conditions. Unless this Contract is signed by **Seller** and a copy
415* delivered to **Buyer** no later than _____ ❏ a.m.❏ p.m. on _____, _____, this offer will be revoked
416 and **Buyer's** deposit refunded subject to clearance of funds.

417 **COUNTER OFFER/REJECTION**
418* ❏ **Seller** counters **Buyer's** offer (to accept the counter offer, **Buyer** must sign or initial the counter offered terms and deliver a copy
419 of the acceptance to **Seller**. Unless otherwise stated, the time for acceptance of any counteroffers shall be 2 days from the
420* date the counter is delivered. ❏ **Seller** rejects **Buyer's** offer.

421* Date: _____ Buyer: _____
422*   Print name: _____

423* Date: _____ Buyer: _____
424* Phone: _____ Print name: _____
425* Fax: _____ Address: _____
426* E-mail: _____   _____

427* Date: _____ Seller: _____
428*   Print name: _____

429* Date: _____ Seller: _____
430* Phone: _____ Print name: _____
431* Fax: _____ Address: _____
432* E-mail: _____   _____

433* **Effective Date:** _____ (The date on which the last party signed or initialed and delivered the final offer or counteroffer.)

434* **Buyer** (____) (____) and **Seller** (____) (____) acknowledge receipt of a copy of this page, which is Page 8 of 8 Pages.

The Florida Association of REALTORS and local Board/Association of REALTORS make no representation as to the legal validity or adequacy of any provision of this form in any specific transaction. This standardized form should not be used in complex transactions or with extensive riders or additions. This form is available for use by the entire real estate industry and is not intended to identify the user as a REALTOR. REALTOR is a registered collective membership mark that may be used only by real estate licensees who are members of the National Association of REALTORS and who subscribe to its Code of Ethics.

The copyright laws of the United States (17 U.S. Code) forbid the unauthorized reproduction of blank forms by any means including facsimile or computerized forms.
FAR-9   4/07   © 2007   Florida Association of REALTORS®   All Rights Reserved

Source: Florida Association of REALTORS©. Reprinted with permission.

GLOSSARY

CHAPTER 1

absentee owner investors who own income-producing properties who do not have the time or the expertise to devote to a project.

appraisal an opinion of value that is based upon certain facts as of a given date.

appraiser hired for the purpose of valuing a property.

business opportunities means and includes a business, business opportunity, and goodwill of an existing business, or any one or combination thereof when the transaction or business includes an interest in real property.

comparative market analysis (CMA) an opinion of value by examining recently sold properties, listings of properties currently on the market, and previous expired-listing information. It is never referred to as an appraisal.

broker price opinion (BPO) an estimate of value usually provided in written form.

dedication private property given by an owner for the public's use.

farm areas (target market) residential properties consisting of four or fewer units intended for dwelling purposes to include up to 10 acres of agricultural property.

follow-up checking on new and existing clientele.

Multiple Listing Service (MLS) allows the member licensee to access available properties for sale or lease by creating certain parameters of search.

property management the real estate sector whose business is dealing with the management of real property.

real estate brokerage the business of matching buyers with sellers and tenants with landlords.

special purpose property properties that are not income producing or used for owner occupant use

subdivision plat map a visual rendering of the proposed development. Streets, building lots, water, sewer, and public utilities are often the subject of the rendering.

Uniform Standards of Professional Appraisal Practice (USPAP) dictates how appraisers must accomplish their assignments.

CHAPTER 2

adjudication withheld means that the person is placed on probation; if probation is successfully completed, the conviction is not entered into the records.

broker any person, corporation, partnership, limited liability partnership, or limited liability company that performs a real estate act for another, in exchange for or in anticipation of compensation or other valuable consideration.

broker associate a person who is licensed and is otherwise qualified as a real estate broker but, rather than forming his/her own business, chooses to work under the name and supervision of another broker.

caveat emptor the Latin term for "let the buyer beware."

compensation a payment or something given of value.

expungement destruction or sealing of a previous criminal record.

Florida resident Rule 61J2-26.002 defines a Florida resident as anyone who has resided in Florida continuously for four calendar months or more within a calendar year. This definition would also include one's intent to reside for four calendar months or more within a calendar year.

license/registration state permission to operate as a real estate agent.

nolo contendere/no contest means the person does not dispute the charges but does not admit any guilt.

prima facie evidence a legal term that can be defined as valid on its face value unless proven to be invalid.

real estate services rendering of services for which a real estate license is required.

sales associate a person associated with a licensed real estate broker who assists in performing services offered by the broker. A sales associate is licensed to work for, and act as a representative of, the broker.

CHAPTER 3

active/inactive is where the licensee is free to be actively engaged in real estate activities as defined by the FREC.

canceled a license that is canceled is considered void.

cease to be in force licenses that are issued but cease to be in force when notification has not been received by the FREC as a result of a change of address or a change of the licensee's association occurs.

group license an owner-developer who owns property in the name of several entities may submit proof that such entities are so connected or affiliated that ownership is essentially held by the same individual(s). Any sales associate or broker associate working for the owner-developer may be issued a group license. The licensee is considered to hold one license and to be working for one employer.

involuntarily inactive involuntary inactive status occurs automatically when a licensee fails to renew his/her license in a timely manner.

license authority voided a licensee chooses to no longer conduct real estate activities or merely because the licensee did not complete his/her required continuing education to renew the license and same expires.

multiple licenses any broker who holds more than one broker's license at one time is termed as a holder licenses.

null and void having no legal effect.

voluntarily inactive when a licensee holds a valid real estate license but chooses not to engage actively in the practice of real estate.

CHAPTER 4

agent any person who transacts business activities on behalf of another (usually for a fee).

caveat emptor Latin for "let the buyer beware."

consent to transition gives rise to the need for a licensee to change his/her relationship with a principal; therefore, the consent to transition form is used to apprise a principal of the agent's need to transition to another authorized form of agency relationship. Prior to any transition on the part of a licensee, the written consent of the principal is required.

customer the third party in a transaction who is owed fair and honest dealing.

dealing at arm's length any transaction where buyers and sellers or landlords and tenants have no relationship to each other.

designated sales associate the broker may designate one sales associate to act as a single agent for the buyer and a different sales associate to act as a single agent for the seller. Both buyer and seller must have assets of $1 million or more and must execute documents evidencing same.

dual agent a relationship in which the agent represents both the buyer (or lessee) and the seller (or lessor) within the same transaction. In Florida this relationship is illegal.

fiduciary any agent under an agency relationship who is granted a position of the highest form of trust and owes a party fiduciary responsibilities.

general agent a general agent is authorized to act for the principal in a specific business or trade (i.e., management company under a property management agreement with the owner).

limited representation the broker does not represent either party in a fiduciary capacity as a single agent. Rather, the broker provides a limited form of nonfiduciary representation to the buyer, seller, or both.

nonrepresentation principal the broker is not obligated to provide the fiduciary duties that a broker owes to a principal under a single agency relationship. The broker must provide fair and honest dealing.

residential sale the sale of improved land used as one- to four-family dwelling units, the sale of unimproved land intended for use as one- to four-family dwelling units, and/or the sale of farm/agricultural land of up to 10 acres.

single agent a licensee represents either a buyer or a seller but never both within the same transaction.

special agent the agency relationship authorizing the agent to perform a narrow and specific range of duties concerning an act or transaction (i.e., a broker under a listing agreement with the principal).

subagency an outside broker (not in the employ of the listing broker) procures the buyer or tenant but owes fiduciary responsibilities to only the seller or landlord rather than to the buyer or tenant.

transaction broker a broker who provides limited non-fiduciary representation to one or both parties to the transaction.

CHAPTER 5

arbitration when parties who are unable to agree among themselves seek the assistance of a third party (one or more arbitrators) who formulates a decision that is binding on all the parties involved.

blind ad any advertisement that does not include the brokerage firm name is called a blind ad.

commingle the mixing of funds belonging to others with the broker's personal funds or business funds.

conflicting demands demands made upon the escrowed funds when two parties (such as a buyer and a seller) do not agree as to how the funds should be disbursed.

conversion when the broker unlawfully takes funds belonging to others for his/her own personal use.

corporation a legal person/entity organized under the laws of Florida or another state. A corporation may include one or more people.

deposit money or other valuable consideration belonging to others placed with an escrow agent.

earnest money a deposit paid by a prospective buyer to show his/her intention to go through with the sale.

escrow (trust) account established to hold the funds of others that have been entrusted to the broker.

escrow disbursement order (EDO) the instructions given by the FREC to the licensee to distribute the funds to one party or the other. The FREC may or may not issue an EDO.

general partnership is formed when two or more partners comprise the business entity.

good-faith doubt when the broker questions or doubts the parties' willingness and desire to transact business.

interpleader when the broker deposits the escrowed funds with the courts and petitions the courts to decide on the appropriate disbursement.

kickback undisclosed secret profit.

limited liability company basically hybrids of corporations and partnerships. A limited liability company has full liability protection to the same degree as a corporation and profit that is not subject to double taxation. Rather, like partnerships, limited liability companies enjoy profit that is taxed once.

limited liability partnership a partner is not liable for negligent acts committed by another partner. A partner is, however, liable for his/her own negligent acts.

limited partnership is created with one or more general partners and one or more limited partners.

litigation when parties enter into a lawsuit and petition the courts to decide the outcome of a dispute

mediation when parties who are unable to agree among themselves seek the assistance of a third party (a mediator) for the purpose of providing a recommended nonbinding solution.

ostensible partnership an entity that appears to be a partnership but is not a real partnership. The parties act like a partnership exists, when in fact, one does not. Because ostensible partnerships are deceitful, such entities are prohibited.

professional association (PA) requires membership where use of the name or insignia represents that person is a member.

point of contact information the method by which the brokerage firm or licensee may be contacted, such as e-mail address, mailing address, street address, phone number and/or fax number.

sole proprietorship is a business where the sole owner is the individual licensee.

trade name a fictitious name other than one's own name used to conduct one's business.

CHAPTER 6

breach of trust failure to carry out fiduciary duties.

citation identifies a violation and the penalty required.

complaint an allegation to a violation of a rule or law.

concealment to hide from being discovered.

conversion legal term for stealing.

culpable negligence failure to carry out fiduciary duties.

formal complaint lists the charges set forth against the respondent licensee. The licensee then has a prescribed period of time to either accept or reject the charges set forth within the complaint.

fraud performing an act intended to deceive.

legally sufficient a complaint containing facts concerning allegations that if they were true, a rule, regulation, or statute has been violated.

mediation form of alternative dispute resolution and a recommended solution provided by a third person to the opposing parties.

misrepresentation false act or statement.

moral turpitude conduct that is contradictory to society and results in a crime.

notice of noncompliance identifies the violation of law and describes steps the licensee must take to comply with the law. If the licensee fails to comply, disciplinary procedures may proceed.

probable cause defined as reasonable grounds for charging and prosecuting a licensee.

recommended order at the conclusion of a formal hearing, the administrative law judge will issue a recommended order to the FREC. The recommended order includes case findings, a conclusion, and the recommended penalty.

stipulation settlement of penalty.

subpoena order requiring someone to appear in court or an order for the producing of records.

summary (emergency) suspension emergency action taken against a license to protect the public against future repeated offenses while determination is made as to charges and penalties.

CHAPTER 7

blockbusting also referred to as panic selling, is the illegal practice of inducing owners to sell their properties by using information about changes or expected changes in the makeup of the neighborhood.

familial status families with children under the age of 18 and pregnant women.

handicapped status persons with either a physical and/or mental disability (1988 amendment added this protected class.

property report necessary disclosure that a developer of 25 lots or more must make to purchasers when selling residential property (required under ILSA).

public accommodation any facility that serves the general public.

redlining the practice of discriminating when making loans in a neighborhood because of the makeup of the neighborhood in terms of race, color, religion, national origin, or sex.

steering refers to the practice of influencing potential buyers to buy only in certain areas or neighborhoods on the basis of race, color, religion, sex, or national origin.

CHAPTER 8

community development districts an alternative means to municipal creation, management, and financing of infrastructure necessary to the creation and use of supporting community development.

condominium a form of individual fee ownership of a unit within a multifamily development property.

cond-op a hybrid of condominiums and cooperatives.

cooperative a form of community ownership. Title to the land, building, and all other improvements to the property are held by the cooperative. The cooperative is organized as a not-for-profit corporation.

declaration of condominium the instrument used to create the condominium.

estate for years is a lease that has a specified starting and ending date. In spite of its name, it does not necessarily have to be for more than 1 year. It can be for any duration—as little as 1 day to many years.

estate in land the degree, quantity, nature, and extent of one's interest in the land

exempt property personal property that a spouse is automatically entitled to when the other spouse dies.

fee simple estate is the most comprehensive and simplest form of property ownership; it is ownership in land itself.

fixture when permanently attached to the real property, a fixture becomes a part of the real property via utility and permanence of the object to the property.

freehold estate is commonly known as ownership interest in land (the fee).

homeowners association a domestic corporation formed and charged with the responsibilities for the operation of a community

homestead is to ensure that families with unsecured debts cannot be removed from their homestead as a result of a forced sale of the property. It is also a tax exemption to an owner of a primary residence.

joint tenancy two or more persons who hold title as joint tenants. The primary distinguishing characteristic of joint tenancy is the fact that it carries the rights of survivorship.

land the ground and all permanent attachments.

leasehold estate nonfreehold estates or estates less than freehold are also called leasehold estates. This applies to any property that is leased by a tenant.

life estate estates that are held for a lifetime (but not longer) are not inheritable and therefore may not be willed to heirs.

personal property includes all other property other than real property. Personal property is also known as chattel or personalty. If it is moveable, it is personal property.

proprietary lease an occupancy agreement granted to a shareholder in a cooperative that conveys rights of occupancy to the respective unit.

prospectus a formal legal document, which is required by and filed with the Securities and Exchange Commission, that provides details about an investment offering for sale to the public.

real property (real estate) land and all things attached to and affixed to it.

remainderman the third party named to receive the fee simple estate.

right of survivorship the right of a surviving party to the property of a deceased party.

separate property an individual dwelling unit (like a unit in a condominium) for which the owner receives a deed

tenancy at sufferance occurs when a tenant remains in possession beyond his/her legal tenancy without the consent of the landlord/lessor.

tenancy at will lease that has no expiration date but may be terminated at any time by either the tenant or the landlord upon serving a prescribed or statutory notice.

tenancy by the entireties reserved solely for husband and wife relationships.

tenancy in common when two or more persons hold title to property where the unity of possession is required; unlike joint tenancy, each tenant holds a separate title to his/her undivided interest within that subject property.

time-share a method of dividing up and selling a living unit for a specified period each year.

Time-shares are almost exclusively resort-type properties, such as hotels, condominiums, townhouses, villas, recreational vehicle parks, and campgrounds.

CHAPTER 9

abstract of title is a full summary of all instruments affecting the title to a property, such as deeds, wills, grants, and a statement of all liens and encumbrances affecting the property and their present status.

acknowledgment in a sale, acknowledgment is when the grantor (seller) must acknowledge his/her signature to the grantee (buyer). This is achieved by the grantor signing the deed before a notary public.

actual notice specific knowledge based on what you have actually seen, heard, read, or observed.

adverse possession a lawful taking of another's property based on specific conditions and requirements; usually a private taking.

alienation title transferred between parties.

assignment the transfer of all rights that in a lease the tenant (assignor) holds in the property and gives to another (assignee).

chain of title allows interested parties to research the public records for the purposes of identifying the correct owner of record.

condemnation a municipality's process that takes private property.

constructive notice based on a presumption that the records and property have been inspected.

deed an instrument that is used to convey and transfer the ownership interest in real property from one or more parties to another. A deed is used to convey any fee estate, any life estate, or certain easements.

deed restrictions are enforceable restrictions on the ownership of private property that are contained in deeds.

easement also known as a right of way, easement is the right to use or occupy the property of another in a limited way.

eminent domain a public taking of private property through the process known as condemnation.

encroachment an unauthorized intrusion of a building, fixture, or other improvement on the land of another.

escheat when no existence of a valid will or remaining heirs to accept the property of a decedent, the property goes to the state.

further assistance obligates the grantor to perform any acts necessary to protect the title being conveyed to the grantee.

general warranty deed also called the full covenant and warranty deed, the most common form of deed. It provides the greatest guarantee about the title being conveyed.

graduated lease a lease in which the tenant pays a fixed rent for an initial period, but the rent increases at specific intervals thereafter

grantee the buyer or recipient of a grant.

granting clause the words grant and convey, either alone or in combination, are commonly used in the conveyance. Another name for the words of conveyance is the granting clause.

grantor the seller or the giver of the grant.

gross lease where the tenant pays a fixed monthly or annual rent only and the property owner is responsible for all costs associated with the running of the property.

ground lease a long-term lease of land. It is usually the subject of development.

habendum clause found in most deeds, but not required, it is the clause that contains the type of estate being granted. The habendum clause describes the extent of interest being transferred.

lien a legal claim or charge for the repayment of debt/owing that one person has upon the property of another. It is used as security for repayment of a debt.

net lease the tenant pays a fixed monthly rent, plus some or all of the expenses associated with the property, such as taxes, insurance, utilities, etc. The landlord pays only those expenses not paid by the tenant.

percentage lease leases commonly used for retail establishments in shopping malls. The landlord receives a percentage of the gross sales of the business as part or all of the rent.

quiet enjoyment deals with the issue of title and/or rights associated with the granted estate.

quitclaim deed a deed that contains no warranties to title, either expressed or implied. It can be defined to be an instrument of release (as it may apply to any claim).

seisen covenant in which the grantor warrants that he/she is the owner of the property and that he/she has the right to convey the property

sublease a further letting of space where the original tenant becomes the sub-landlord in relationship to the subsequent tenant known as the sub-tenant.

testate when a person dies but has a valid enforceable will

title the sum of all facts or evidence of ownership.

warranty forever ensures that the grantor will bear the expense of defending the title against the claims of others.

CHAPTER 10

base line under the Government Rectangular System east/west lines are intersected by principal meridians (north/south lines), thus creating townships.

benchmark permanent reference markers are also referred to as benchmarks.

check the 24-mile square that is achieved through the intersecting guide meridians.

datum position from which a distance or distances can be measured while datum lines are horizontal lines that aid in measuring heights and depths.

government (rectangular) survey system a method of legal property description established by Congress in the mid to late 1780s.

legal description a description of property that is used for the purpose of transferring title is called a legal description.

lot and block a block is the largest unit within a subdivision. Each block is subdivided into individual lots that houses are built on.

metes and bounds metes means distance and bounds means direction. The metes and bounds method is the oldest method of legal description.

monument is an object that is used to define a corner of a parcel of property.

point of beginning (POB) a term used in a metes and bounds description that must always begin at a point of beginning. The point of beginning is identified as the POB on the plat and is usually marked by an iron pin placed by the surveyor.

principal meridian each principal meridian (north/south lines) is intersected by only one base line. Throughout the United States, there are 36 different intersecting principal meridians and base lines.

range a range runs north and south.

section one of 36 units contained within a township. Each section measures 1 mile square. Each section within a township is represented by a number from 1-36.

survey a report that a purchaser of real property may request that shows and uncovers the boundaries of the property, as well as any encroachments in adjoining neighboring properties.

terminus where a metes and bounds description ends (back at the point of beginning)

township intersection of a **tier.**

township line (tier) lines that are drawn every 6 miles north and south of a base line thereby forming east and west parcels of land.

CHAPTER 11

assignment is the transfer of one's interest in a executory contract to another person.

attorney-in-fact is someone who has been granted power of attorney limited to a specific transaction named in a document. A contract entered into by an attorney-in-fact is valid when the power of attorney has been properly granted. The party need not be an attorney.

bilateral contract is one in which both parties promise to give up something or to perform in such a manner as required by the agreement. A promise is exchanged for a promise.

competent having the ability and capacity to enter into a binding and enforceable contract

contract an agreement between two parties

culpable negligence acting recklessly without thinking about the risk of one's actions to others.

exclusive agency listing seller appoints one agent to transact business on their behalf with the intent of achieving a successful conclusion (the sale of the property).

exclusive right to sell listing the seller appoints one agent to transact business on their behalf with the intent of achieving a successful conclusion (the sale of the property).

fraud intentionally or unintentionally attempting to deceive another for personal profit.

liquidated damages sales contracts may include a statement that if the buyer breaches the contract, the seller may demand forfeiture of the earnest money deposit as liquidated damages.

meeting of the minds a requirement of a valid contract is mutual agreement or mutuality. This is sometimes called a meeting of the minds or offer and acceptance. This means that there must be a mutual agreement on the provisions of the contract.

net listing seller is seeking a stated amount as the final purchase price.

novation is a substitution of a new contract for an old contract or substitution of a new party for an old party under an existing contract. Novation is also a means of general release from previous contractual obligations.

open listing properties that are for sale by owner (FSBO).

option contract a unilateral contract in real estate that gives someone the right but not the obligation to buy a property.

Statute of Frauds requires that all contracts involving either the purchase of or sale of any parcel of real property must be in writing to be deemed enforceable.

Statute of Limitations a specific time period for an innocent party to take action to remedy the breach of contract.

unenforceable a contract that cannot be enforced in a court of law. An unenforceable contract is valid until challenged in court.

unilateral contract a contract that only one party promises to give up something. A promise is exchanged for some act or performance by the other party.

valid contract a contract that is legally sufficient and meets all the essential requirements of the law to create a contract between two or more persons.

void contract a contract that is not recognized legally and has no legal effect. From its inception, the agreement lacks one or more of the necessary essential requirements for the creation of a valid and enforceable contract.

voidable contract a contract that is capable of being voided by one of the parties to the contract. It is binding on one party to the contract only and is valid until action is taken by one party to make it void.

CHAPTER 12

acceleration clause a clause in the mortgage agreement that allows the lender to demand full and immediate payment (accelerate the payment) if the borrower fails to meet all terms of the promissory note.

assumption when a new borrower assumes the obligation under an existing loan.

blanket mortgage the single large principal payment necessary to retire the loan at the end of the loan's term. This is known as a balloon payment.

buy-down a long-term mortgage offered by a third party, as a builder or developer, to lower interest rates for a buyer in the early years of the loan.

deed in lieu of foreclosure commonly referred to as a friendly foreclosure where the borrower avoids foreclosure by signing the property over to the lender. This is done using the deed in lieu of foreclosure.

defeasance clause right of the mortgagor (borrower) to defeat the lien held by the mortgagee/lender by fulfilling all the terms and conditions of the loan.

discount points represent 1% of the borrowed amount that is paid upfront as a fee by the borrower to the lender.

due on sale clause commonly referred to as the alienation clause, it permits the mortgagee to call in the note if the mortgagor transfers the property either through sale or gift. It is used to prohibit the assumption of the mortgage loan by a buyer or the use of a wraparound mortgage.

equity the difference between the market value of a property and the principal balance on any loans against it. At the time of purchase, equity is equal to the down payment.

escrow account established by a broker for holding funds on behalf of the broker's principal or some other person until the consummation or termination of a transaction.

estoppel certificate document that is completed by a *borrower* to acknowledge the full amount of the debt that the borrower owes.

hypothecation a mortgage provides security for a note through a process called hypothecation. Hypothecation means that the real property is put up as security for a loan without surrendering possession of the property.

interest the money paid for the privilege of using the lender's principal (payment of rent for the use of another's money).

land development loan a form of construction financing/acquisition financing

lien theory in a lien theory state, the legal title remains in the possession of the borrower while the mortgage held by the lender creates a lien on the title in favor of the lender.

lis pendens a notice of lis pendens is filed that informs the public that there is a legal action pending.

loan origination fee commonly associated as being a processing or servicing fee for arranging the financing over and above the cost of discount points.

loan servicing business that mirrors that of property management services.

loan-to-value ratio amount of loan (in percentage terms) that a lender would be willing to loan to a borrower on real property.

mortgage the instrument that places the property (by the borrower) as collateral for securing the repayment of the loan.

mortgagee the lender is called the mortgagee because the lender is the one to whom the mortgage (collateral or security) is given/conveyed.

mortgagor the borrower is called the mortgagor because the borrower gives/conveys the mortgage (collateral or security) to the lender.

note legal agreement between a buyer and lender.

novation represents a substitution of a new agreement for an old agreement.

partial release clause allows the owner to sell off lots and have the lender remove the lien for the sold parcel.

PITI monthly payments made for *P*rincipal, *I*nterest, *T*axes, and *I*nsurance.

prepayment clause provides the borrower with the ability to prepay the outstanding principal balance (in part or in whole), either with or without a penalty.

prepayment penalty when the borrower prepays the outstanding principal balance in part or in whole at any time; however, there is a preprescribed penalty for prepayment.

promissory note the instrument whereby the borrower promises to repay money borrowed from the lender

receivership clause preserving the property's condition during the foreclosure process.

right to reinstate mortgagor/borrower has the right to accelerate the maturity of the note by paying all the past due amounts on the mortgage.

satisfaction of mortgage acts as the instrument or vehicle that ultimately allows for the removal of the lender's previous lien.

short sale any sale where the note loan balance is greater than the property value at time of sale or at the time of a foreclosure sale

statutory equity of redemption a period of time given to a borrower after foreclosure to repay the debt and take back ownership of the property.

subject to the mortgage the direct opposite of assumption. In a subject to the mortgage transaction, the buyer is not assuming the loan, but merely making the payments associated with that loan. In order for this arrangement to occur, the existing loan must not contain a due on sale clause.

subordination agreement the clause within a lease that states that the rights of the leasehold interest are secondary to that of a previous or subsequent lien or interest in the real property. A subordination clause is a major requirement by all lenders on income-producing property.

takeout commitment the construction loan is paid off when permanent financing is obtained on the property. The permanent financing is commonly referred to as the takeout loan.

title theory a financing theory involving a three-party two-instrument loan transaction secured by real property. The parties are referred to as trustor (property owner/borrower), trustee (neutral third party appointed by both the borrower and the lender to hold the naked title), and beneficiary (lender). The instruments are referred to as the note and trust deed or deed of trust.

CHAPTER 13

adjustable rate mortgage (ARM) any loan that, over the term of the loan, periodically allows the lender (under prescribed terms) to raise or lower the interest rate.

amortized mortgage a mortgage in which each installment payment is constant over the life of the loan.

balloon payment payment of the remaining balance after a partially amortized loan reaches maturity.

biweekly mortgage a mortgage in which the borrower makes payments every two weeks as opposed to once a month.

conforming loan for loans sold to Fannie Mae (Federal National Mortgage Association [FNMA]) or Freddie Mac, the guidelines developed by Freddie Mac must be used in making a conventional loan. These guidelines are often called the FNMA/FHLMC guidelines, because they are used by Fannie Mae as well. Any loan approved under these guidelines is called a conforming loan.

disintermediation occurs when depositors withdraw their savings in order to achieve higher yielding returns on invested capital within alternative investment vehicles. Disintermediation results in a scarcity of money available for mortgages.

home equity loan a loan that consider only the equity portion a property owner has in a property; previously used to fund home improvement and/or credit debt consolidation.

intermediation occurs when thrift institutions (commercial banks and savings associations) receive inflows of money into savings accounts. The purpose on the part of the depositor is to achieve high-yielding returns on the investment. These savings in turn are used to invest in larger investment projects. Intermediation results in funds being available for mortgages.

index one of the two items used to determine the rate of an ARM; either Treasury notes or London Interbank Offer Rate

level payment plan mortgage an amortized mortgage

lifetime cap one of the caps inherent in an ARM loan; the maximum, not to exceed rate of the loan over the life of the loan

margin one of the two items used to determine the rate of an ARM; percentage above the margin representing the lender's profit for originating the loan

mortgage broker one who brings together borrowers and lenders for a fee, usually based on a percentage of the loan.

mortgage fraud when a prospective borrower lies on his/her loan application to improve the securing of getting a loan.

mortgage loan originator anyone who works with a borrower to obtain a mortgage loan

mortgage insurance premium (MIP) policy established to protect a lender from a situation where the borrower can't make his/her mortgage payments.

negative amortization when the balance owed increases with every payment

package mortgage any loan that includes both real and personal property as the lender's held collateral

partially amortized (balloon) mortgage any loan whose entire borrowed principal loan balance cannot be retired at time of maturity by the monthly payments of principal and interest

payment cap a limit on the amount the monthly payment can increase during the adjustment period

periodic cap one of the caps inherent in an ARM loan; the limitation on the amount that the interest rate can increase during any adjustment period

purchase money mortgage (PMM) commonly referred to as seller financing.

reverse annuity loan a loan available for retirees or the elderly in the form of a home mortgage.

teaser rate the rate used to attract borrowers by offering a below-market initial interest rate

UFMIP up-front mortgage insurance premium; payment required by the FHA at closing

CHAPTER 14

arrears periodic payments that are paid at the end of the payment period rather than before.

credit money that is received by someone from someone else.

debit a payment by someone to someone else.

level payment plan a type of loan whose monthly payment amount remains the same throughout the loan.

preclosing inspection a final walk-through inspection just prior to the date of closing.

principal original amount of investment or borrowed amount.

profit amount realized on an investment over and above the original invested amount.

prorate in real property closings, the process of determining the cost to the appropriate party of an item that will be paid or received by the buyer or by the seller. It is always based on how long each party will own the property.

CHAPTER 15

buyer's market occurs when there are more sellers than there are buyers.

demand means that someone has a desire to own or use the property.

household defined by the U.S. Census Bureau as a space designed for dwelling purposes occupied by one or more persons.

seller's market occurs when there are more buyers than there are sellers or available product.

situs a Latin-derived term used to describe a legal fixed location.

supply (as it pertains to real property) the amount of housing stock of properties available for sale or for lease.

transitioning market type of market in which conditions tend to resemble a tug-of-war between the buyer and seller

vacancy rate generally quoted as a percentage figure as opposed to numbers representing available product. Rising vacancy rates indicate a buyer's market while lower rates indicate a seller's market.

CHAPTER 16

appraisal is a formal estimation of the value of real property as of a given date.

assemblage refers to the process of combining two or more adjacent properties into one larger tract of land.

automated valuation model (AVM) a database service that provides real estate property valuations to the real estate industry

comparative market analysis (CMA) analysis to determine marketing pricing.

cost-depreciation approach an appraisal approach that determines an appropriate price for property based on the current cost of reproduction or replacement of the improvements

curable when remediation of a defect results in equal or greater value to the overall property through its utility as opposed to the cost of making the correction. A defect is considered curable if it is economically feasible to correct the problem.

depreciation is a loss of value of any kind resulting from functional obsolescence (outdated layout, lighting, columns, etc.), physical deterioration (usually representative of poor maintenance and preventive maintenance programs), and/or economic/external obsolescence (declining neighborhoods, adverse zoning changes, interest rates, etc.).

economic life the expected period of time during which a property is useful to the average owner.

effective age based on the property's condition and use at the time of examination

federally related transaction any transaction that includes or involves a financial institution insured or regulated by the federal government.

gross rent multiplier (GRM) another form of analysis within the income approach used informally in selected applications involving income-producing property. Its primary use is for an investor who is evaluating several properties and wants a simple and quick way to eliminate some properties from consideration before doing formal price determinations.

highest and best use the legal and feasible use that generates the highest possible land value attributable to that use.

income (capitalization) approach a valuation method appraisers and real estate investors use to estimate the value of income-producing real estate.

incurable when fixing a problem is beyond the homeowner's control.

market value the most probable price that a property should bring in a competitive and open market.

overimprovement the cost to upgrade a property whereby the upgrade does not produce a corresponding increase in the overall property value.

plottage refers to any increase in value for a tract of land formed by combining two or more parcels.

principle of substitution the premise for all three approaches to appraisals. It suggests that a smart investor would not pay more for a property with equal utility that they could purchase for less.

progression states that the value of a lower valued property is increased if it is located among properties of higher value.

reconciliation in every appraisal that is conducted, the three approaches to valuation are applied. It is only within the reconciliation step of the appraisal process that one of the three approaches is given weight over the other two to determine the appraiser's final estimate of value.

regression a principle of appraisal that states that the value of a higher valued property is decreased if it is located among properties of lower value.

replacement cost the cost to replace the improvements of the subject property with another building that performs the same function and utility but is not an exact replica of the subject property. It is used in the cost approach to appraisal.

reproduction cost the cost to produce an exact replica of the original subject property, using the same materials and construction techniques as the original. It is used in the cost approach to appraisal.

sales comparison approach also referred to as the market data approach, it is based on a comparison of the subject property (the property being appraised) to similar properties that have recently sold. As with other approaches to appraisal, it assumes the basic principle of substitution in the purchase of real property.

situs a Latin term used in legal documents to describe the location of a property

subject property the property being appraised.

Uniform Standards of Professional Appraisal Practice (USPAP) identifies the procedures an appraiser must follow while performing appraisal services. Appraisers must always conform to the Uniform Standards of Professional Appraisal Practice (USPAP).

valuation an impartial estimate or opinion of the value of a parcel of property. It is based on specific data that can be used to support and defend the estimate or opinion of value.

CHAPTER 17

appreciation increased values derived during the property holding period (that is, appreciation).

asset something that bears value, real or personal property that has value.

basis amount attributable to the property (which is usually the purchase price or adjusted purchase price) by the Internal Revenue Service for the purpose of calculating during holding or at point of sale.

capital gain difference between the property's cost basis and the sales price after deducting the cost of sale and adding to the cost basis any capital improvements made to the property during the holding period.

cash flow receipts less payments from income activities over a period of time.

equity the difference between the market value of a property and the unpaid balance of any loans on that property. Equity increases (builds up) as any loan is paid down and as the property appreciates.

going concern value the value of a business that is expected to continue as an operating entity is called the going concern value.

goodwill refers to an intangible asset that usually reflects the business's name recognition, the business's customer base, and the business's employees.

leverage the use of borrowed funds with the anticipation of earning substantial profits not only on the investment but also on the borrowed funds.

liquidation analysis the process of estimating the assets, liabilities, and amount the business could be sold for in the event the business is terminated or goes bankrupt.

liquidity the ability to convert an asset into cash by selling it. An asset that can be readily sold and converted to cash is considered liquid. For example, stocks are considered liquid assets. Real property is not considered liquid.

personal property anything not categorized as real property—that is, the item is movable.

risk the profit on the investor's invested capital (represents investor profit, return on investment).

tax shelter an investment that results in tax advantages is sometimes referred to as a tax shelter.

CHAPTER 18

ad valorem a Latin term that means "according to valuation."

assessment limitation payments that are made at the end of the payment period rather than at the beginning. Arrears is also used in the context of past due amounts when payment is due in advance and same has not been tendered.

assessed value the value of a property established for the purpose of determining taxes.

capital gains gains from sale of real property that is taxable.

community development districts particular government jurisdictions that are affected by improvements made with special assessment taxes

exempt property subject to taxation, but the owner is not obligated to pay all (or part) of the taxes.

installment sale a means of financing where the seller receives payment for the property over a period of years. In this situation, the seller can avoid paying the entire amount of taxes on any gain from the sale in the year the sale took place. Rather, the seller can postpone the payment of taxes to future years, when the installment payments are actually received.

immune properties not subject to taxation (government buildings).

just value the fair market value of the property.

like-kind exchange transaction or series of transactions that allow for the disposal of an asset and the acquisition of another replacement asset without generating a current tax liability from the sale of the first asset.

mill one mill equals 1/1,000 of one dollar. (One mill also equals 1/10 of one cent.)

special assessment taxes levied to fund a specific project that benefits only some of the citizens in a government jurisdiction.

tax rate the rate that a taxpayer's income tax payment or property tax payment is predicated on.

taxable income the net income that is subject to taxation.

taxable value the taxable value of the property is calculated by subtracting the exemption from the assessed value.

CHAPTER 19

asbestos natural fiber material that was previously used as a fire retardant material in modern day construction.

buffer zone a strip of land that varies in size from community to community and acts as a separator between two zones.

building codes set the allowable minimum standards for construction of improvements on real property. They are established under the government's police powers.

building inspection conducted by representatives of local building departments to establish construction conformance with filed plans and specifications on new construction as well as code compliance on existing construction.

building permits grant permission to construct improvements and are issued by local government.

certificate of occupancy issued to a property owner by the local building department stating that the property conforms to all current building codes and may be occupied

concurrency the Florida Growth Management Act of 1985 also has a concurrency provision. According to this provision, sufficient infrastructure (sewer, water, and transportation systems) must exist before new development is permitted.

environmental impact statement any development in Florida that will affect residents in more than one county is referred to as a development of regional impact. An environmental impact statement must be prepared to address the impact that the project may or will have on the environment and its neighboring communities.

health ordinance local codes designed to address and regulate the maintenance and sanitation of public areas.

nonconforming use the existing use (residential, commercial, agricultural, light industrial) of a parcel of real property that is zoned for a more limited or other use in the city or county's general plan.

planned unit development type of development that incorporates a variety of different yet compatible land uses.

R-value the thickness of construction insulation material; measures the retention of heat and resistance to cold

special exception a property owner may also be granted a special exception, which allows a specific use for a specific property.

special flood hazard area an area designated as having susceptibility to flooding.

variance permission for an exemption to some of the specific requirements within a zoning classification. Variances when granted allow for a deviation from the allowed zoning.

zoning ordinance the principal mechanism of public land use control. Through zoning ordinances, the government and local municipalities can regulate permitted uses for land, type, size, and height of structures built on the land, open-air requirements in relation to site improvement, density factors that will dictate the project size and occupancy of the land, and location of structures on the land such as setback requirements.

ADDENDUM

asbestos natural fiber material that was previously used as a fire retardant material in modern day construction.

chemical contamination occurs when a supply of drinking water is contaminated by pesticides and fertilizers used in farming, leaking underground storage tanks, hazardous toxic waste dumps, or mining.

corner lot sits at the intersection of two streets. The lot has frontage along both streets. (Frontage refers to the length of the property that abuts the street.)

cul-de-sac lot located at the end of a cul-de-sac (a dead-end street with a circular turnaround). They are part of subdivisions. Because of the curved turnaround, these lots are often irregular in shape; that is, they are tapered with a smaller frontage but larger backyards.

double-hung window consists of two sashes, both of which slide vertically allowing the window to be opened at the top and bottom.

flag lot is shaped like a flag on a flagpole. Often, a flag lot is located behind another lot. The flagpole portion of the lot is the access road or driveway that runs along the front lot to the street. The flag portion of the lot is the square or rectangular lot that is located behind the front lot.

green building construction that lowers the impact on the environment.

insulation materials used for the purpose of keeping the heat out of the home as it is in cold climates to keep the heat in the home.

interior lot surrounded by other lots on three sides (left, right, and rear). The interior lot has frontage on just one street.

key lot surrounded by many other lots. Often, a key lot is an extremely deep lot. The side yard abuts the rear of many different properties that are located on a street that runs perpendicular to the street where the key lot is located.

R value the standard method to rate the effectiveness of insulation materials is the R value. The R stands for resistance to heat flow. The higher the R value for a particular insulation material, the better the insulation effect.

shingles exterior coverings that are typically flat and rectangular shaped that overlap one another

T lot a type of interior lot that is located at the end of a T intersection.

toxic waste waste material that can cause death, injury, or birth defects to living creatures.

underground storage tanks used to store chemicals, gasoline, or other petroleum products.

urea-formaldehyde foam insulation foam insulation that emitted formaldehyde gas when it was previously used in many older homes before its usage was sharply curtailed by HUD.

zero lot line residential lot construction where the improvement is constructed up to or very close to the property line.

INDEX

A

Abandonment, easement, 235
Absentee owners, 6, 14
Abstract of title, 228
Accelerated depreciation, 540–1, 550–1
Acceleration clause, 311, 321
Acceptance, 223, 293
Accountability, 84–5, 93, 95, 97
Accretion, 184
Accrued depreciation, 470, 609
A certiorari proceeding, 524
Acknowledgment, 220, 227–8, 229
Acres, 263, 264, 612
Active income, 208–9, 531–2
Active license, 60–1
"Active with Contract" status, 399
Actual eviction, 175, 244
Actual notice, 229
Additional rent, 512
Address, change of, 121–2
Address requirements, DRE, 66
Adjudication withheld, 31
Adjustable rate mortgage (ARM), 342
Adjusted basis, 542
Adjusted net operating income (ANOI), 537–8
Adjustment
   in appraisal, 464–5
   in CMA, 489–90
Administrative complaint, 137–8
Administrative law judge (ALJ), 138
Administrative penalties, 143–8
Ad valorem taxes, 521–9
Ad valorem tax liens, 247
Adverse possession, 219, 234, 235
Advertising, 166, 376–7
After-tax cash flow (ATCF), 537
Age-life method, 470
Agency coupled with an interest, 82
Agency relationships, 78–9
   designated sales associate, 100–1
   determined by broker, 91
   discipline, 101–2
   disclosure requirements, 92
   dual, 78–9, 87
   fiduciary relationships, 82–7
   nonrepresentation, 96–8
   principal, 90–1
   record keeping and retention, 102
   responsibilities to customer, 88–91
   single agent, 94–6
   statutory and common law, 80
   subagency, 87–8
   termination of, 102–4
   transaction broker, 92–4
   transitions between, 99–100
   types of, 80–2
Agents
   defined, 78, 88, 90
   role of, 6–8, 12
   types of, 80–2
Agreement, on contract, 273, 278–80
Agricultural property, 2, 10, 506–7, 527, 563
Air-conditioning systems, 587–8
Air lots, 204
Air rights, 183
Alienation, 218–19
Alienation (due on sale) clause, 311–12, 317, 319, 354, 362
Allodial system, 181–2
Alluvion, 184
Alternative documentation, 371
Alternative Minimum Tax (AMT), 550
Amendment I (Property Tax), 522–3
Americans with Disabilities Act (ADA), 168–9
Amortization schedule, 374
Amortized mortgages, 335–6
Amount invested, 387–9
Amount realized, 541
Amperes (amps), 589
Annual debt service (ADS), 537
Annual fiscal budget, 528–9
Annual percentage rate (APR), 377
Anticipation, principle of, 457–8
Appeal process, 139–40
Applications
   licensing, 33–6
   loan, 401, 403–4
Appraisal, 2, 6, 15–17
   adjustment process, 464–5
   automated valuation model, 496
   of business, 514, 516
   versus CMA, 16–17, 452–3

as contingency, 401–2
cost-depreciation approach, 465–70, 477, 490–1
FHA loans, 353–4
gross rent multiplier, 476
income approach, 470–5, 477
reconciliation, 465, 476–7
regulation of, 448–9, 450–2
report, 465
sales comparison approach, 462–5, 477
steps in process, 463–5
terminology related to, 460–2
underwriting, 371
VA loans, 359–60
value, 453–60
Appraisal fee, 373–4
Appraisal Foundation, 449
Appraisal Qualifications Board (AQB), 449
Appraisal Standards Board (ASB), 449
Appraisal Subcommittee (ASC), 449
Appraiser, 15, 450
Appreciation, 502, 508
Appurtenances, 223
Arbitration, 117
Architect, 5
Architectural styles, 601–2
Area, calculating, 261, 607
Area preference, 443
Area variance, 565
Armed Forces members
    licensure of, 47, 59, 63–4
    termination of lease by, 174
Arm's length transaction, 86
Arrears, 410
Articles of incorporation, 126
Asbestos, 569, 593
"As is" provision, 290–1
Assemblage, 461
Assessed value, 521–2, 523–4
Assessment limitation, 523
Assets, 368–9, 503

Assignment
    contract, 281, 282
    lease, 245
    mortgage, 316
Associations, 128–9
Assumption, of mortgage, 317
    changing loan balance, 318–19
    on closing statements, 429
    contingency clauses, 401
    conventional loans, 342
    FHA loans, 354
    methods of, 361–6
Attorney fees, 374
Attorneys
    escrow accounts held by, 113
    licensing exemptions for, 38, 39, 47, 51
    role in real estate business, 4
Attorneys-in-fact, 274
Automated valuation model (AVM), 496

B

Backfill, 596
Background check procedure, 33–4
Back-up contract, 293
Balance of loan, 318–19, 362–3, 393–5
Balconies, 207
Balloon framing, 590, 591
Balloon payment, 343
Bargain and sale deed, 225
Base industry, 559
Base lines, 258
Basements, 598
Base rent, 512
Basis, 502, 542
Bearing wall, 582
Before-tax cash flow (BTCF), 537, 613
Benchmarks, 265
Beneficiary, 303, 304
Bilateral contract, 276
Bill of sale, 221

Binder, 293
Biweekly mortgage, 343
Blanket mortgage, 311–12
Blind advertising, 110–11, 143
Blind individuals exemption, 526
Blockbusting, 160, 161–2, 163–4
Board of Realtors, 168
Bonds, 305–6
Book value, 516
Boot, 546
Branch offices, 110
Breach of contract, 244, 284–5
Breach of trust, 145
Bridge loans, 331
Broker
    agency relationships, 91
    change of address, 121–2
    expertise of, 119
    handling of deposits, 112
    licensing for, 30, 39–41, 48, 64, 122
    policy manuals, 120
    post-license education, 44–5
    role of, 6–8
Brokerage, 2, 5
    advertising, 110–12
    versus business brokerage, 513–14
    business of, 9–11
    change of employer, 121
    fiduciary relationship, 9
    nonfiduciary relationship, 8
    officers/directors of, 129
    offices, 109–10
    professions involved in, 6–8
    property group types, 11–12
    records, in market analysis, 486
    registered business entities, 122–9
    sales process, 12–13
    specialization, 8
    trade names, 109, 129
Broker associates, 30, 39–41, 48–9, 64
Broker price opinion (BPO), 17, 451, 453

Buffer zone, 564, 568
Builders acre, 597
Building codes, 564
Building code violation disclosure, 293
Building inspections, 564
Building permits, 564
Bundle of rights, 189–90, 217
Business brokerage, 6, 10, 513–16
Business entities, 122–9
Business environment, 559
Businesses, sale of, 514–16
Business Improvement Districts (BIDs), 530
Business opportunities, 507
Business property, 538–41, 542–3
Business risk, 503, 511
Business taxes, 550–1
Buy-down, 315
Buyer broker agreements, 287
Buyers, qualifying. *See* Underwriting
Buyer's market, 441–2, 460
Bylaws, 206

C

Calculations. *See* Math problems
Canceled licenses, 62
Capital gains, 502, 541–5, 547–8
Capitalization, 389–93, 471–2, 475, 502, 608–9
Capital loss, 502
Capital recapture, 508
Capital risk, 503
Care, 85, 93, 95, 97
Carpenter ants, 572, 591
Casement window, 583, 584
Cash break-even ratio (CBR), 610–11
Cash flow, 501, 502, 609
Cash investment, FHA loans, 350–1
Cash-on-cash return, 611
Cash to control, loan assumption with, 319, 363
Casualty losses, 535

Caveat emptor, 27, 78, 86
C corporations, 126
Cease to be in force, 62
Central air-conditioning, 587
Certificate of title, 228
Certificates of occupancy, 564
Certified appraisal reports, 451
Certified general appraiser, 450
Certified public accountant (CPA), 4
Certified residential appraiser, 450
Chain of title, 222, 228
Chapter 163, 557–8, 560
Chapter 190, 213
Chapter 404, 570
Chapter 455, 58–60
Chapter 475, 92, 113, 185, 451–2
Chapter 61J2-20, 68–71
Chapter 720, 211–13
Chattel, 185
Check, 258, 612
Chemical contamination, 571, 594–5
Child tax credit (CTC), 549
Circuit breaker, 589
Citations, 134–5, 143–4
City planning. *See* Urban planning
Civil penalties, 149
Civil Rights Act of 1866, 156, 158
Civil Rights Act of 1964, 156–7, 168
Civil Rights Act of 1968, 157–60
Closing agent, 405
Closing costs
  FHA loans, 352
  income tax deductions, 533
  legislation related to, 376–8
  types of, 372–5
  VA loans, 358
Closing day, 407–8
Closing disclosure, 378, 406
Closing process
  loan assumption, 365
  loan processing, 403–4
  preparation for closing, 405–7
  prorated expenses, 407–15

  sales contract to closing phase, 399–402
Closing sales contract, 13
Closing statements
  debits and credits, 423–31
  items to account for, 415–21
  purpose of, 423
  state transfer taxes, 421–3
Club plan, time-shares, 211
Code of Ethics, NAR, 168
Commercial acre, 596
Commercial banks, 331
Commercial easements, 233
Commercial property, 2, 3, 5, 505–7, 563
Commercial transaction, 9, 10
Commingling, 113–14, 141
Commissions
  calculating, 383–7
  fixing, 119–20
  formulas for, 606
Committee's deed, 226
Common areas, 203, 204, 210
Common charges, 205–6
Common law, 80
Community association manager (CAM), 15
Community development district (CDD), 213, 530
Community ownership, 203
  CDDs, 213
  condominiums, 203–7
  cooperatives, 207–9
  homeowners associations, 211–13
  PUDs, 210
  time-share, 210–11
Community property, 197, 200
Company records, 486
Comparables, 463, 464–5, 488–9
Comparable sales analysis, 514, 516
Comparative market analysis (CMA), 451
  versus appraisal, 16–17, 452–3, 477, 484
  fair market value, 484–5

gathering data, 485–7
steps in process, 487–90
Compass directions, 256–7
Compensation, 6–7, 14, 27, 69–70, 119–20
Competent grantor, 221
Competent parties, 273–4, 280
Competition, principle of, 459
Complaint process
  appeal process, 139–40
  final order, 139
  formal complaint, 137–8
  formal or informal hearing, 138
  investigation, 134–6
  probable cause panel, 136–7
  Statute of Limitations, 270
Comprehensive Environmental Response, Compensation, and Liability Act (CERCLA), 572–3
Comprehensive plans, 558, 560–1
Computations, 382–3. *See also* Math problems
Concealment, 145
Conciliation agreement, 167
Concurrency, 561
Concurrent ownership, 197–201
Condemnation, 219, 234, 235, 244, 564
Condominiums, 203–7, 208–9, 210, 292
Cond-ops, 209
Conduit, 597
Confidentiality, 85, 94, 95
Conflicting demands, 115–18
Conforming loans, 334, 367
Conformity, principle of, 460
Consent to Transition to Transaction Broker form, 99
Consideration, 222, 272–3
Construction, 3, 18–19, 576–7
  architectural styles, 601–2
  framing, 590–1
  insulation, 584–5
  joists, 583
  local regulations, 577
  lot types, 577–9
  material types, 581–2
  mechanical systems and equipment, 585–9
  roofs, 579–81
  terminology related to, 596–600, 603
  walls, 582–3
  windows, 583–4
Construction loans, 316, 441
Constructive eviction, 175, 244
Constructive notice, 229
Consulting, 3
Consumer, 88
Consumer Credit Protection Act, 376–7
Consumer preferences, 439–40
Contesting property taxes, 523–4
Contingencies, sales contracts, 400–2
Continuing education, 44–7
Contract for deed, 320–1
Contract rent, 243
Contracts, 269
  breach of, 284–5
  classifications of, 275–8
  enforceable, 170–1
  enforcement requirements, 271–5
  important to real estate, 285–96
  negotiation, 278–80
  preparation of, 270, 274–5
  real estate considerations, 297–8
  in sales process, 13
  Statute of Frauds, 269–70
  termination of, 281–4
  valid, 270–5
  void, 271
  voidable, 271, 280, 283
Control right, 190, 217
Conventional loans
  adjustable rate, 342
  assumption, 342
  biweekly, 343
  characteristics of, 340
  down payments, 344–5
  formulas for, 611
  HECM, 345–6
  home equity, 345
  interest rates, 341–2
  package, 343–4
  partially amortized, 343
  payment cap, 343
  PMI payments, 346–8
  prepayment, 342
  teaser rate, 343
  types of, 340–1
Conversion, 114, 141
Conveyance, 206, 222
Cooling systems, 587–8
Cooperative Act, 208
Cooperatives, 207–9, 292
Co-ownership, 197–201
Corner lot, 577, 579
Corporate tax liens, 247
Corporate tax rate, 550
Corporations, 125–6, 199, 274
Corporation sole, 127
Correction lines, 258, 259–60
Cost-depreciation approach, 465–71, 477, 490–1, 514, 516
Cost factors, replacement cost pricing, 492–3
Costs. *See also* Closing costs
  cost problems, 395–6
  versus value, 455
Cost to repair, 495
Counteroffer, 278
County property appraiser, 521–2, 523–4
Covenants, 224, 225, 226–7, 309–10
Crawl space, 598
Credit history, 370
Credit report fee, 374
Credits, on closing statements, 423–31
Credit unions, 331
Criminal penalties, 149
Crops, as property, 186–7
Cubic foot method, 467
Cul-de-sac lots, 578, 579
Culpable negligence, 145, 298

Culvert, 600
Curable defects, 469
Curtesy, 193
Customer, 88–91
Custom homes, 19

D

Damages, 284
Datum, 255
Dealing at arm's length, 86
Debits, on closing statements, 423–31
Debt ratios, 368, 369
Debt service, 537
Debt service coverage ratio (DSCR), 610
Decay, wood, 572, 591
Deciduous tree, 597
Decimals, 382
Declaration of condominium, 206
Dedication, 19
Deductions, tax, 533–5, 538–41
Deed in lieu of foreclosure, 323
Deed of trust, 303, 304
Deed restrictions, 220, 221, 235
Deeds, 218, 220–1
    clauses, 226–7
    preparation of, 227–8
    requirements of valid, 221–4
    types of, 224–6
Default, 321–4, 511
Defeasance clause, 310, 312
Defects, disclosure of, 290–1
Deficiency judgment, 248–9, 250, 322–3
Delinquent property tax, 531
Delivery, of deed, 223
Demand
    market response to, 434–5
    principle of supply and, 459–60
    role in value, 437–40, 455–6, 457
Demised premises, maintenance of, 171

Department of Business and Professional Regulation (DBPR), 26
    checking applications for errors, 34
    citations, 143
    complaint process, 135–6, 137
    divisions of, 57–8, 60
    as official reporter, 70
    power and duties of, 59
Department of Housing and Urban Development (HUD), 162, 167
Department of Veterans Affairs (VA) loans, 317, 355–61, 370
Deposits
    on closing statements, 418, 426
    handling of, 112–15, 171–3
Depreciation, 476–7
    accelerated, 540–1, 550–1
    accrued, 470, 609
    replacement cost pricing, 494–5
    tax deductions for, 539–41
    types of, 468–70
Descent, transfer by, 219–20
Destruction
    contract termination by, 284
    lease termination by, 244
Development, 3, 18–19
Developments of regional impact, 566
Diminishing and increasing returns, 460
Directors, of real estate firms, 129
Disabilities, housing laws related to, 168–9
Disability exemption, 526
Disciplinary action
    procedures for, 134–5
    types of, 101–2, 142–9
Disciplinary guidelines, FREC, 144–8
Disclosure
    of defects, 290–1
    environmental hazard, 595–6

    exemptions to, 92
    in fiduciary relationships, 84
    homeowners associations, 211–13
    by licensees, 291–3
    in nonrepresentation relationship, 97–8
    property tax, 292, 523
    requirements, 92
    responsibilities to customer, 89
    in single agent relationships, 95–6
    under TILA/RESPA, 377–8
    under TILA/TILSRA, 315–16
    in transaction broker relationship, 93
    when transitioning to other agency relationship, 99
Discount points, 314–15, 338–9
    calculating dollar amount of, 606
    closing costs, 374–5
    federal income tax deductions, 535
    FHA loans, 352
    VA loans, 358
Discount rate, 328
Discrimination. *See* Fair housing laws
Disintermediation, 329
Disposition right, 190, 217
Disputes, escrow account, 115–18
Distribution panel, 589
Division of Administrative Hearings (DOAH), 138
Division of Real Estate (DRE), 26, 57
    address requirements, 66
    change of address, 121–2
    change of employer, 121
    complaint process, 134
    functions of, 66–7
    license renewal, 46
    organizational structure, 65–6
Doctrine of laches, 285

Doctrine of prior appropriation, 184
Documentation, underwriting, 370-1
Dodd-Frank Wall Street Reform and Consumer Protection Act, 406
Domestic corporation, 126
Dominant estate, 232
Do Not Call Registry, 111
Double-hung window, 583, 584
Double taxation, 125-6
Dower, 193
Down payments, 312, 344-5, 350-1, 357, 369
Drywall, 597
Dual agency relationships, 78-9, 87
Dual heating system, 587
Due diligence investigation, 596
Due on sale clause. *See* Alienation clause
Duress, 280

E

Earnest money, 112, 288-9, 400, 426
Easement appurtenant, 232
Easement in gross, 232-3
Easements, 232-6
Economic (external) obsolescence, 469, 494-5
Economic characteristics, 436-41
Economic growth, 437, 440-1
Economic life, 470
Economic rent, 243
Education
    legal updates, 51-2
    license renewal, 44-7
    pre-license, 37, 38, 39-40
    proprietary real estate schools, 65
Effective age, 470
Effective gross income (EGI), 473, 474, 475, 536
80/20 rule, 208-9

Elective share, 201
Electrical system, 589
Electric heating systems, 586
Elevation drawing, 597
Eminent domain, 219, 234, 235, 564
Employer, change of, 121
Employment contracts, 285-7
Encroachments, 236
Encumbrances
    covenant against, 224, 225, 227
    liens, 245-51
    transfer of title with, 251
Energy-efficiency disclosure, 292
Energy efficiency ratio (EER), 597
Enforceable contracts, 170-1, 271
Engineers, 5
Enjoyment right, 189, 217
Enroachments, 236
Entitlement, VA loans, 357, 361
Environmental disclosure statement, 596
Environmental hazards, 568-73, 591-6
Environmental impact statement, 566
Environmental Impact Study (EIS), 567
Environmental Protection Agency (EPA), 292
Equal Credit Opportunity Act (ECOA), 168, 376
Equal housing opportunity posters, 162
Equitable title, 217-19, 288, 289-90
Equity, 312, 345, 503, 509
Equity dividend rate (EDR), 611, 613
Equity financing, 313
Erosion, 184
Escalation clauses, 512
Escheat, 219
Escrow accounts
    disputes and disposition of funds, 115-18
    FHA loans, 352

    held by title company or attorney, 113
    loan assumption, 365
    management of, 113-15, 289
    PITI, 314
    purpose of, 112
    VA loans, 359
Escrow disbursement order (EDO), 115-16
Estate at sufferance, 196, 237
Estate at will, 195-6, 237
Estate for years, 195, 236-7
Estate/inheritance tax liens, 247
Estate in land, 182
Estate in severalty, 197
Estates, 182
    created by leases, 236-7
    freehold, 190-4
    nonfreehold or less than freehold, 194-6
Estate tax exemption, 550
Estoppel certificate, 316-17
Ethics, 17, 168, 297-8
Eviction process, 175-6, 244
Examinations, licensing, 38-9, 40-1, 60-3
Exceptions and reservations clause, 223
Excess from sale, 323
Exclusion of capital gains, 543-4
Exclusion right, 190, 217
Exclusive agency listing, 286-7
Exclusive right to sell listing, 286
Exculpation clause, 322, 323
Executed contract, 270, 277
Executory contract, 278
Exempt income, 531, 532
Exemptions
    continuing education requirements, 47
    disclosure requirements, 92
    fair housing laws, 158
    homestead, 193, 202
    licensing, 38, 49-51, 63
    zoning ordinance, 565-6

Exempt property, 201, 525-7
Expediters, 5
Experience requirement, broker license, 40-1
Expiration
　easement, 235
　of lease, 244
　of time, on contracts, 283
Expressed contract, 275
Expungement, 31
Exterior wall covering, 582-3
External economic influences, 512

F

Fair and honest practice, 93, 95, 97
Fair Housing Act of 1968, 157-60
Fair housing laws
　additional regulations, 168-70
　enforcement of, 167
　major provisions of, 155-60
　violations, 160-7
Fair market value, 484-5, 521
False advertising, 110-11
Familial status, 157
Fannie Mae, 333, 337, 367-9
Fans, ventilation by, 587-8
Farm areas, 10, 506-7
Farming, 8
Fasteners, 582
Federal Deposit Insurance Corporation (FDIC), 328-9, 450-1
Federal Financial Institutions Examination Council (FFIEC), 449
Federal government, role of, 19-20
Federal Home Loan Bank System (FHLB), 328
Federal Home Loan Mortgage Corporation (FHLMC), 334, 366-9
Federal Housing Administration (FHA) loans, 317, 337
　formulas for, 611-12
　loan programs, 348-55
　underwriting guidelines, 369

Federal housing laws. *See* Fair housing laws
Federal income tax
　categories of income, 531-2
　deductions, 533-5, 538-41
　installment sales, 545
　real estate exchanges, 545-6
　taxable income, 537-8
　tax on sale of property, 541-5
Federal income tax liens, 247, 249, 250
Federal Institutions Reform, Recovery, and Enforcement Act (FIRREA), 448-9
Federally related mortgage loan, 406
Federally related transactions, 16, 448, 450-1, 452
Federal National Mortgage Association (FNMA), 333, 337, 367-9
Federal Reserve Regulation Z, 376-7
Federal Reserve System (the Fed), 328
Federal telephone solicitation laws, 297
Fee, in property ownership, 181, 191, 238
Fees. *See also* Closing costs
　fixing, 119-20
　licensure, 33, 60
　property management, 14
　referral, 120
　for service, as provided, 7
Fee simple estate, 191-2
Feudal system, 181
Fiduciary relationships, 82-3, 90, 94-5
Final order, 70, 139, 144
Financial analysis of investments, 513
Financial reporting, 2, 14
Financial risk, 511
Financing, 3, 6, 17-18, 441, 486-7. *See also* Mortgages

Fines, 149
Fingerprinting, 34, 35
Fire insurance policy, 365
First-degree misdemeanors, 101, 149
First mortgage, 307, 308
Fixed closing costs, 373-4
Fixed operating expenses, 474, 536-7
Fixed window, 584
Fixing commissions or fees, 119-20
Fixtures, 186-9
Flag lot, 578, 579
Flashing, 597, 600
Flat fee arrangements, 7
Flood insurance, 404
Flood zones, 567-8
Florida Brokerage Relationship Disclosure Act, 78, 87, 92
Florida Building Code, 564
Florida Building Energy-Efficiency Rating Act, 292
Florida Condominium Act, 205, 206, 292
Florida Cooperative Act, 292
Florida Fair Housing Act, 162, 170
Florida Fictitious Name Act, 51
Florida Growth Management Act, 557, 558
Florida Homeowners Association Act, 211-13
Florida housing laws, 170-6
Florida law 61J2-14.008, 113
Florida Real Estate Appraisal Board, 16
Florida Real Estate Commission (FREC), 27, 34, 56
　administrative penalties, 143
　authority of, 140
　courses, 32, 38, 39-40
　disciplinary guidelines, 144-8
　duties and powers of, 72-3
　escrow disbursement orders, 115-16
　final order, 139

functions of, 66–8
licensure fees, 33
meetings and minutes, 71–2
membership, 68–70, 71
organization and operation of, 68–71
probable cause panel, 136–7
revocation/suspension of license, 142
Rule 61j2-3.009(2), 51
violations resulting in disciplinary action, 140–1
Florida real estate law, 25–9
Florida Realtors, 20
Florida Realtors/Florida Bar Residential Contract for Sale or Purchase, 275, 290
Florida resident, 35, 42
Florida Residential Landlord and Tenant Act, 170–6, 245
Florida Statutes, 28–9, 32, 47–8. *See also specific chapters*
Florida telephone solicitation laws, 297
Florida Time-Share Act, 211
Footing, 598, 600
Foreclosure, 321–3
Foreign corporation, 126
Foreign earnings, under Tax Reform Act of 2018, 551
Formal complaint, 137–8
Formal contracts, 278
Formaldehyde gas, 592–3
Formal hearing, 138
Formulas, 606–13
For sale by owner (FSBO), 287
Foundations, 598
Fractions, 382
Framing, 590–1
Fraud, 141, 279, 298, 375
Freddie Mac, 334, 366–9
Freehold estates, 190–4
Friendly foreclosure, 323
Frontage, 577
Fructus industriales, 186–7
Fructus naturales, 186

Fuel types, 586–7
Full covenant and warranty deed, 224
Functional obsolescence, 469, 494, 495
Funding fee, VA loans, 358, 375
Further assistance, 227
Fuse, 589

G

Gable roof, 579, 580
Gains, 541
Gambrel roof, 579, 580
General agency, 81, 82
General liens, 248, 249–50
General partnerships, 123–4
General warranty deed, 224
Ginnie Mae, 333–4
Going concern value, 514
Good consideration, 273
Good-faith doubt, 116–17
Good repair, covenant of, 309
Goodwill, 514
Governmental controls, 436
Government National Mortgage Association (GNMA), 333–4
Government survey system, 257–64
Graduated lease, 241–2
Graduated payment loan (GPM) program, FHA, 349
Grandfather clause, 566, 568
Grantee, 220, 221–2, 223
Granting clause, 222, 310
Grantor, 220, 221–2, 223
Green Belt law exemption, 527
Green building, 591
Grievance process, property taxes, 523–4
Gross lease, 239, 240
Gross rent multiplier (GRM)/gross rent income (GIM) technique, 476
Ground lease, 241
Groundwater hazards, 568–9, 570, 571, 594–5

Group license, 64
Growth cycle, 437, 440–1
Guarantees
 deed, 224
 VA loans, 356–7
Guardian's deed, 226
Guide meridians, 258

H

Habendum clause, 222, 224
Handicapped status, 157
Hazard insurance, 404, 409
Hazardous wastes, 570, 595
Header, 598
Head of household filing status, 549
Healthcare, under Tax Reform Act of 2018, 549
Health ordinances, 564–5
Heating systems, 585–7
Heat pumps, 587
Heavy manufacturing, 506
Heirs, rightful, 219
Heterogeneous property, 436
Highest and best use, 436, 458–9, 463–4
High-rise construction, 557
Hip roof, 579, 580
Holding naked title, 303
Home equity conversion mortgage (HECM), 345–6
Home equity loans, 345
Homeowner association, 205, 292
Homeowner's insurance, 404, 409
Homestead exemption, 522, 525–6
Homestead protection, 194
Homestead status, 193, 201–2
Honesty, 93, 95, 97
Horizontal sliding window, 583
Hot air heating systems, 585, 586
Hotel properties, 506
Hot water system, 588–9
House Bill 927, 52
Household trends, 437–8
Housing expense ratio, 351

Housing laws, 170–6. *See also* Fair housing laws
Hurricane anchors, 582
Hurricane clips, 581
Hypothecation, 246, 302

I

Illiquidity, 510
Immediate expensing, 550–1
Immobility, 434
Immune properties, 525–7
Implied contract, 276
Improper listings, 164–5
Inactive license, 60–1
Income
   capitalization, 472
      FHA guidelines, 369
      Freddie Mac guidelines, 367–8
   from investment property, 535–7
   relation to demand, 438
   in value problems, 390–3
Income capitalization approach, 470–5, 477, 514, 516
Income tax rate (ITR), 538. *See also* Federal income tax
Incurable defects, 469
Indestructibility of land, 435
Index, and ARM rate, 342
Index lease, 239, 242
Industrial property, 3, 5, 10, 506, 507, 563
Ineffective licenses, 62–3
Inflation, 508–9, 511
Inflation gauge, Tax Reform Act of 2018, 549
Informal contracts, 278
Informal hearing, 138
Informal reference, 255
Inheritance tax liens, 247
Innocent landowner defense, 572–3, 596
Innocent misrepresentation, 279–80
Innocent party, 284
Insane persons, 274

Inspections, 401, 407
Installment sales, 545
Installment sales contract, 217–18, 296, 320–1
Insulation, 584–5
Insurance
   covenant of, 309
   FHA loan, 348–55
   in loan processing, 404
   PITI, 314
   private mortgage, 313, 340, 346–8
   title, 230–1, 373, 402
Insurance companies, as lenders, 332
Insured conventional loans, 340
Intangible tax, 422
Intentional misrepresentation, 279
Interest, 313, 314, 393–5, 535, 606
Interest-bearing accounts, 114–15
Interest deduction, under Tax Reform Act of 2018, 551
Interest-rate risk, 511
Interest rates
   conventional loans, 341–2
   FHA loans, 352
   in loan problems, 393–5
   property investment analysis, 513
   relation to demand, 438–9
   VA loans, 357–8
Interim loans, 331, 441
Interior lot, 578, 579
Intermediation, 329
Internet advertising, 111
Interplead motion, 117–18
Interstate Land Sales Full Disclosure Act (ILSA), 169–70
Interval ownership format, timeshares, 210–11
Intoxicated persons, 274
Investigation, 134–6
Investment
   analysis of, 512–13
   business brokerage, 513–16
   deductions on, 538–41

   goals of, 508–11
   income from, 535–7
   licensee as expert in, 503–4
   math problems, 387–9
   taxable income from, 537–8
   tax on sale of property, 541–5
   terminology related to, 501–3
   types of, 504–7
Investment risk, 503
Involuntary alienation, 219
Involuntary inactive status, 47, 61–2
Involuntary liens, 249, 250
IRA withdrawal, 533–4
Irrevocable consent to service form, 35
Itemized deductions, 549–50

J

Jalousie window, 584
Johnson v. Davis, 89, 290
Joint tenancy, 197, 198–9
Joint ventures, 128
Joists, 581, 583
Jones v. Mayer, 156, 158
Judgment liens, 248, 250
Judicial foreclosure, 321–2
Junior mortgage, 307, 308
Just value, 521

K

Key lot, 578, 579
Kickbacks, 120
Knob, 600

L

Laches, 285
Land
   acquisition of, 18–19
   availability of, 441
   estimating value of, 464, 491
   indestructibility of, 435
   versus site, 459
Land contract, 320–1
Land development loans, 316, 372
Landlords, 171–6, 195, 238

Land use controls, 562–4
Law, statutory and common, 80
Law of agency, 78–9
Laws, licensing
    historical purposes of, 25–7
    important statutes and rules, 28–30
    state, 25–6, 28–9, 47–8, 58–60
    updates to, 51–2
Layaway plans, 296, 320
Lead-based paint disclosure, 291–2
Lead contamination, 570–1, 593–4
Leasehold, in property ownership, 181, 191, 238
Leasehold estates, 195–6, 236–7
Leases, 9–10
    assignment and subletting, 245
    basic principles of, 237–8
    contract versus economic rent, 243
    covering residential dwelling units, 171–6
    essentials of valid, 243–4
    estates in land, 236–7
    estoppel certificate, 317
    novation, 320
    property investment analysis, 512
    security deposits, 243
    termination of, 244–5
    types of, 238–42
Legal descriptions
    in deed, 222
    government survey system, 257–64
    informal reference, 255
    metes and bounds, 255–7
    purpose of, 254–5
    recorded subdivision plat maps, 264–5
Legally competent parties, 273–4, 280
Legally nonconforming use, 566
Legally registered brokerage entities, 122–7
Legally sufficient, 134
Legal objective of contract, 273
Legal title, 217, 289
Lenders, 329–32, 403–4
Lessee, 195, 238
Lessor, 195, 238
Level payment plan mortgage, 336, 428
Leverage, 501–2, 509, 612
License authority voided, 62
Licenses, personal, 234
Licensing
    applications for, 33–6
    appraiser, 450
    authority to prepare contracts, 274–5
    broker and broker associate, 39–41, 48–9
    examinations for, 38–9, 40–1, 60–3
    fair housing law violations, 163–7
    federal, 29–30
    fees for, 33, 60
    general provisions, 30–7
    historical purposes of laws for, 25–7
    important statutes and rules, 28–30
    individuals exempt from, 49–51
    information included on license, 43
    issuance/expiration periods, 63
    leasehold, 238
    license categories, 30, 64–5
    license law infractions, 140–1
    mutual recognition agreements, 41–3
    pre-license course regulations, 37
    public record, 37
    Real Estate Recovery Fund, 149–51
    registrations versus licenses, 43–4, 122
    renewal, 44–7, 63–4
    revocation/suspension, 142
    for sales associates, 38–9, 49
    state examinations, 38–9
    state laws, 25–6, 28–9, 47–8, 58–60
    statuses, 60–3
    third-degree felonies, 149
    unauthorized practice of law, 51
Liens, 245–6
    categories of, 249–50
    priority of, 250–1
    transfer of encumbered title, 251
    types of, 246–9
Lien theory, 305–8
Life estates, 190, 192–4
Lifetime caps, ARM loans, 342
Light manufacturing, 506
Like-kind exchange, 545
Limited liability companies, 126–7
Limited liability partnerships, 127
Limited partnerships, 124–5
Limited representation, 92–3
Linkage, 513
Liquidated damages, 284, 285
Liquidation analysis, 514, 516
Liquidity, 503
Liquidity risk, 511
Lis pendens, 229, 321, 323
Listing contracts/agreements, 285–7
Listings, improper, 164–5
Litigation, 117–18
Littoral rights, 183, 184
Loan applications, 401, 403–4
Loan balance, 318–19, 362–3, 393–5
Loan charges, closing statements, 419–20
Loan constant, 502, 613
Loan estimate, 377
Loan insurance programs, FHA, 348–55
Loan originating/financing, 6
Loan origination fees, 315–16, 355, 428
Loan problems, 393–5

Loan processing, 403–4
Loans. *See* Mortgages; *specific loan types*
Loan servicing, 313
Loan-to-value ratio (LTV), 339
   versus borrower equity, 312–13
   conventional loans, 340
   FHA loans, 351–2
   formulas for, 609–10
   loan assumption, 364
   VA loans, 360
Loan transfer fee, 365
Local government, 20
Local planning agency, 559–60
Local property taxes, 535. *See also* Property taxes
Local regulations, 577
Location, 434, 443, 461, 513
Location adjustments, 464
Loft buildings, 506
Long-term capital gains tax, 547
Long-term gain, 502
Long-term loans, 441
Lot and block survey method, 264–5
Lot coverage, 563
Lot size, 562
Lot types, 577–9
Loyalty, 83–4, 95, 97

M

Maintenance fee, 207
Mansard roof, 579, 580
Manufacturing properties, 2, 506
Margin, and ARM rate, 342
Marginal release, 303
Margin of safety, 611
Marketable title, 228
Market analysis. *See* Comparative market analysis
Market conditions, 441–3, 460, 510
Market data approach, 462–5
Market price, 455
Market risk, 511

Market value, 455, 521
Master plans, 558, 560–1
Materials
   construction, 581–2
   relation to supply, 441
Mathematical formulas, 606–13
Math problems
   commission problems, 384–7
   cost problems, 395–6
   investment problems, 387–9
   loan problems, 393–5
   price problems, 396–8
   value problems, 389–93
Maximum loan amount, 351–2, 371–2
Maximum term, 352, 357
Mechanical systems and equipment, 585–9
Mechanic's lien, 248, 251
Mediation, 117, 144
Meeting of the minds, 273
Merger, easement, 235
Metes and bounds descriptions, 255–7
Mezzanine financing, 313
Miles, 612
Mill rate, 528–9
Minorities. *See* Fair housing laws
Minors, 274
Misleading advertising, 110–11
Misrepresentation, 141, 279–80
Mistakes, in contracts, 280
Mixed-use property, 2, 506, 507, 563–4
Modified gross lease, 239, 242
Mold, 571
Money supply, 328
Monthly housing obligations ratio, 368, 369
Monthly total obligations ratio, 368, 369
Monument, 256
Moral turpitude, 141
Mortgage bond financing, 375
Mortgage brokers, 330–1, 332

Mortgage companies, 330
Mortgagee, 306
Mortgagee's title insurance, 231
Mortgage fraud, 375
Mortgage insurance premium (MIP), 348, 350
Mortgage interest, prorating, 409, 410
Mortgage interest deduction, 549
Mortgage liens, 246
Mortgage loan originator, 330
Mortgage markets, 329–35
Mortgages, 302. *See also specific mortgage types*
   availability of, 438–9
   clauses, 310–12
   closing costs, 372–5
   on closing statements, 419
   common features, 312–17
   contingency clauses, 401
   default, 321–4
   discounting, 338–9
   essential elements of, 308–10
   formulas for, 611–12
   history of, 335–7
   income tax deductions, 533, 535
   lien theory, 305–8
   processing of, 403–4
   purchasing mortgaged property, 317–21
   relation to supply, 441
   title theory, 302–4
   underwriting, 366–72
Mortgagor, 306
Motel properties, 506
Multiple licenses, 64–5
Multiple listing services (MLSs), 20, 297, 399, 485
Municipal bonds, 332
Mutual agreement
   on contract, 273, 278–80
   lease termination by, 244
   to termination of contract, 282
Mutual recognition agreements, 41–3

N

Naked title, 303, 304
National Association of REALTORS® (NAR), 20–1, 168
National Flood Insurance Program (NFIP), 567–8
Natural breakeven, 240
Natural gas, 586, 587
Natural monuments, 256
Negative amortization, 343
Neighborhood observation, 486
Net lease, 239–40
Net listing, 287
Net operating income (NOI), 473, 474–5, 536–7
Net worth, 368–9
No Brokerage Relationship Notice disclosure form, 98
No document loans, 375
Nolo contendere/no contest plea, 33–4
Nonbearing wall, 582
Nonconforming loans, 334
Nonconforming use, 566, 568
Nonfreehold estates, 194–6
Non-homestead property assessment cap, 523
Nonjudicial foreclosure, 303, 323
Nonpayment of property taxes, 531
Nonrecognition orders, 449
Nonrecourse loans, 249, 322–3
Nonrepresentation, 96–8
Nonresidential property, 505
Nonresidential transactions, 100
Nonresident license applications, 35–6
Nonstandardized property, 436
Notary public, 220, 228, 229
Notes, 302, 305–7, 311. *See also* Mortgages
Notice of noncompliance, 134–5, 136, 144
Novation, 281–2, 319–20
Null and void licenses, 62

O

Obedience, 84, 95
Offers, 278–9
Office buildings, 505
Officers, real estate firm, 129
Older persons, housing for, 160–1
Open listings, 277, 287
Open-market operations, 328
Operating expense ratio (OER), 610
Operating expenses (OE), 473, 474, 475, 536–8, 609
Operational duties, property management, 2, 14
Operation of law, 283–4
Option contracts, 277, 294–5
Oral contracts, 269
OR and EE rule, 21, 306
Origination fee, 373, 533
Ostensible partnerships, 125
Other income (OI), 473, 536
Overimprovement, 460, 469
Owners associations, 205, 292
Ownership. *See* Community ownership; Property ownership
Owner's title insurance, 231

P

Package mortgage, 343–4
Panic selling. *See* Blockbusting
Parcel numbers, 264–5
Parol contract, 269
Part 323, FDIC rules, 450–1
Partially amortized loans, 343
Partial release clause, 311–12
Partitioning of ownership, 200–1
Partnerships, 123–5
Party wall easement, 233
Passive income, 208–9, 532
Pass-through income, 551
Payment cap, 343
Penalties, 101, 143–9
Percentage lease, 240–1
Percentages, 383
Percolation test, 598–9

Periodic caps, ARM loans, 342
Permanent monuments, 256
Permanent reference marker (PRM), 265
Personal easement in gross, 233, 234
Personal exemptions for taxes, 549
Personal property, 183, 185, 514
Personal property exemption, 523
Personal representative deed, 226
Physical adjustments, 464
Physical characteristics, 183–4, 434–6
Physical deterioration, 468, 494, 495
Pitch, roof, 579
PITI (principal, interest, taxes, and insurance), 314
Planned unit development (PUD), 210, 567
Planning. *See* Urban planning
Plants, as property, 186–7
Platform framing, 590, 591
Plat maps, 206, 264–5, 559–60
Plot plan (plot map), 600
Plottage, 461
Plumbing systems, 588
Point of beginning (POB), 255, 256
Point of contact information, 111
Police powers, 562, 564
Policy manuals, broker, 120
Population trends, 437–8
Portfolio income, 532
Portfolio lenders, 334
Possession right, 189–90, 217
Post-and-beam framing, 590, 591
Post-and-beam roofing, 581
Post-license education, 44–7
Potable water, 600
Potential gross income (PGI), 473, 536
Power-of-sale clause, 303
Preclosing inspection, 407
Preferences, relation to demand, 439–40

Pre-license education, 37, 38, 39–40
Prepayment
 on closing statements, 426–7
 conventional loans, 342
 FHA loans, 355
Prepayment clause, 310
Prepayment penalty, 310
Prescription, easement, 234, 235
Price
 calculating, 383–4
 commission problems, 384–7
 math problems, 396–8
 relation to demand, 437
Price fixing, 119–20
Price levels, 442
Price to control, loan assumption with, 318–19, 363
Pricing property, 451, 452–3. *See also* Appraisal; Comparative market analysis
Prima facie evidence, 43
Primary mortgage market, 329–32, 333
Principal, 88, 90–1, 121, 314, 383
Principal meridians, 258
Priority of liens, 250–1
Private grant, 234
Private lenders, 331
Private mortgage insurance (PMI), 313, 340, 346–8
Probable cause panel, 68, 136–7
Probation, 145
Processing FHA loans, 352
Procuring cause, contracts, 297
Professional associations (PAs), 121
Professional organizations, 20–1
Professional reporting services, 485–6
Profit, 383, 387–9
Progression, 461
Promissory notes, 305–6, 311
Property descriptions. *See* Legal descriptions
Property investment. *See* Investment

Property management, 2, 6, 14–15, 510
Property ownership. *See also* Community ownership
 bundle of rights, 189–90, 217
 concurrent, 197–201
 deeds, 218
 historic perspective on, 181–2
 partitioning of, 200–1
 personal property, 185
 real property, 182–5
 sole, 196–7
 special interests, 201–2
 title, 217–20, 228–31
 transfer of, 218–20
Property pricing, 451, 452–3. *See also* Appraisal; Comparative market analysis
Property report, 169
Property taxes
 ad valorem, 521–9
 amendment on, 522–3
 disclosure of, 292, 523
 formulas for, 608
 grievance process, 523–4
 immune and exempt properties, 525–7
 nonpayment of, 531
 payment of, 529
 prorating, 408, 410–15
 special assessment, 521, 530
Proprietary lease, 207
Proprietary real estate schools, 65
Prorated expenses, 407–10
 formulas for, 607
 property taxes, 410–15
 time methods, 414–15, 416–17
Prospectus, condominiums, 206
Public accommodations, 156
Public records, 37, 228
Public utility revenues, 521
Purchase money mortgage (PMM), 331, 338, 363, 375
Purchase price, 606
Purchasing-power risk, 511
Pyramid roof, 580

Q

Qualifying ratios, FHA loans, 351
Quantity survey method, 467–8, 492
Quiet enjoyment clause, 224, 227
Quitclaim deed, 225

R

Radon gas, 291, 569–70, 592
Rafters, 581, 600
Ranges, 258–60
Rate of capitalization, 390–3, 472, 475
Rate of commission, 384–7
Rate of return, 387–9, 508
Ratios, 383
Reactivation education, 47
Real estate business, 1–4. *See also specific areas of real estate*
 professions relying on, 4–5
 role in economy, 4
 services requiring licensure, 48
 specialty areas of, 5–6
Real Estate Education and Research Foundation, 73
Real estate exchanges, 545–6
Real estate finance. *See* Financing
Real estate organizations, 121
Real Estate Recovery Fund, 149–51
Real Estate Settlement and Procedures Act (RESPA), 315–16, 377–8, 406–7
Real property/real estate, 182–3
 bundle of rights, 189–90
 economic characteristics, 436–41
 federal income tax and, 533–5
 fixtures, 186–9
 physical characteristics, 434–6
 physical components of, 183–4
 tax on sale of, 541–5
 types of, 504–7
Real property taxes. *See* Property taxes
Receivership clause, 321
Reciprocity, in licensure, 43

Recommended order, 138
Reconciliation, in appraisal, 465, 476–7
Reconveyance deed, 303, 304
Recordation, title, 230
Recorded subdivision plat maps, 264–5
Recording fee, 374
Record keeping and retention, 102
Recourse loans, 249, 322–3
Redlining, 167
Reentry, covenant of, 310
Referral fees, 120
Registered trainee appraiser, 450
Registration
    versus licensing, 43–4, 122
        permitted business entities, 122–9
    of proprietary real estate schools, 65
Regression, 461
Regular documentation, 371
Release, easement, 235
Reliction, 184
Remainderman, 193
Removal, covenant against, 309
Renewal, license, 44–7, 63–4
Rental lists, 118–19
Rent paid in advance, handling of, 171–3
Rent per square foot, 609
Repair, cost to, 495
Repairs, as contingency, 401
Replacement cost pricing, 466–8, 490–5
Report, appraisal, 465
Reproduction cost, 466, 490
Rescission of contract, 283, 284
Reservation, easement, 234, 235
Reserve requirements, 328
Reserves for replacements, 474–5
Resident, 35, 42
Residential brokerage, 4
Residential dwelling units, leases covering, 171–6

Residential Lead-Based Paint Hazard Reduction Act, 594
Residential property, 2, 3, 5, 504–5, 507, 535, 562
Residential sale, 92
Residential transaction, 8, 9, 10
Resource Conservation and Recovery Act (RCRA), 570
Retail property, 505–6
Retail sector, 438, 442
Retirement plans, under Tax Reform Act of 2018, 550
Return on investment (ROI), 508
Reverse annuity loans, 372
Reverse mortgage, 345–6
Review process, investment, 512
Revocation, 62, 142
Ridgeboard, 600
Rightful heirs, 219
Right of first refusal, 295
Right of rescission, 169–70, 206–7
Rights. *See also specific rights*
    bundle of, 189–90, 217
    leasehold estates, 195
    of survivorship, 198, 200
Right to reinstate, 311
Right-to-use format, time-shares, 210
Riparian rights, 183, 184
Risk, 503, 510–11, 513
Roofs, 579–81
Rural housing loans, 372
R-value, 564
R value, 585, 600, 603

S

Safety risk, 511
Sale of business, 514–16
"Sale Pending" sign, 399
Sales
    real estate, 9–10
    tax on, 541–5
Sales associates
    in brokerage, 109
    change of employer, 121
    compensation, 119–20

    designated, 100
    expertise of, 119
    handling of deposits, 112
    licensing for, 30–2, 38–9, 49, 64
    post-license education, 44
    role of, 7
    steps associated with sales, 12–13
Sales commissions, 383–7
Sales comparison approach, 462–5, 477, 490
Sales contracts, 287–90, 399–402
Sales process, 12–13
Sale subject to lease, 245
Sales volume, 443
Sandwich lease, 242, 282
Sashes, 603
Satisfaction of mortgage, 307
Save Our Homes (SOH), 522, 523
Savings and loan associations (S&Ls), 330, 332
Scarcity, role in value, 456, 457
Secondary mortgage market, 332–5
Second-degree misdemeanors, 101, 149
Second mortgage, 308, 354, 363, 419
Section 203(b) loan program, FHA, 348–9, 350–5
Section 245 GPM program, FHA, 349
Sections, 260, 262–3, 612
Secured note, 302, 305, 307
Security deposits, 171–3, 174, 243, 302
Seisin, 227
Seller financing, 331, 375
Seller's market, 441–2, 460
Senior housing, 160–1
Senior mortgage, 307, 308
Separate property, 203, 204
Septic tanks, 569, 588
Service industry, 559
Servient estate, 232–3
Setbacks, 562

Settlement statements. *See* Closing statements
Severalty, 197
Sewers, 588
Shakes, 603
Sheathing materials, 581, 582–3
Shed roof, 579, 580
Shells, 603
Sheriff's sale, 322
Shingles, 581, 603
Short sales, 323–4
Short-term capital gains tax, 547–8
Short-term gain, 502
Short-term loans, 441
Shutters, 582
Signage, for brokerage, 109–10
Signage control, 560
Sill, 600
Single agent relationship, 9, 94–6
Single-hung window, 583, 584
Single-purpose properties, 465
Site, 459
Site plan approval, 560
Situs, 443, 461
Skilled labor, relation to supply, 440–1
Slab-on-grade foundation, 598
Slabs, 603
Slate, 603
Soil, toxic waste in, 570
Soil pipe, 600
Solar energy, 586
"Sold" sign, 399
Sole ownership, 196–7
Sole plate, 603
Sole proprietorships, 123
Special agency, 81–2
Special assessment taxes, 247, 521, 530
Special exception, 566
Special Flood Hazard Areas (SFHAs), 568
Special ownership interests, 201–2
Special purpose deeds, 226
Special purpose properties, 3–4, 465, 563

Special warranty deed, 225
Specific liens, 250
Specific performance, 284, 285
Speculative homes, 19
Square foot method, 467, 492–4
Standard Deduction, 548
State and Local (Property) Tax Deduction (SALT), 549
State fair housing law, 162, 170
State government, 20
State housing laws, 170–6
State licensing laws, 25–6, 28–9, 47–8, 58–60
State licensure examination, 38–9
State taxes. *See* Property taxes
State transfer taxes, 421–3, 607–8
Statute of Frauds, 220, 238, 269–70
Statute of Limitations, 270
Statutory equity of redemption, 323
Statutory law, 80
Statutory liens, 249
Statutory life estates, 193–4
Stay of enforcement, 140
Steam heat, 586
Steering, 159, 161, 165–6
Stipulation, 137
Straight-line method of depreciation, 540
Straw buyers, 375
Structural damage, 571–2
Structural pest control report, 428
Studs, 603
Subagency, 87–8
Subdivision, 3, 18–19, 169, 577–9
Subdivision plat map, 19, 264–5, 559–60
Subject property, 462, 488
Subject to the mortgage transactions, 317–18
Subletting, 242, 245, 282
Subordination agreements, 308
Subpoenas, 136
Substitution, principle of, 458, 484–5
Subsurface rights, 183

Summary emergency suspension order, 139
Superfund Amendments and Reauthorization Act, 572, 596
Supply, 434–5, 440–1, 459–60
Surface rights, 183, 184
Surveys, 265, 374, 402. *See also* Legal descriptions
Surviving spouse exemption, 526
Survivorship, rights of, 198, 200
Suspension of license, 142
Sustainability, 591
Swing loans, 331

T

Takeout commitment, 316, 441
Taking subject to existing loan, 361
Taxable income, 537–8
Taxable value, 525–6
Taxation. *See also* Federal income tax; Property taxes; Tax Reform Act of 2018
    covenant to pay taxes, 309
    double, 125–6
    80/20 rule, 208–9
    federal income, 531–5, 541–6
    formulas for, 607–8
    homestead exemption, 202
    investment advantages, 509
    PITI, 314
    state transfer taxes, 421–3, 607–8
    types of, 520–1
Tax certificates, 531
Tax Cuts and Jobs Act. *See* Tax Reform Act of 2018
Tax deed, 226
Tax deferred, 545
Tax liens, 246–7, 250
Tax rates, 528, 544–5
Tax Reform Act of 2018, 546–7
    business taxes, 550–1
    capital gains tax, 547–8
    child tax credit, 549
    head of household filing status, 549

health insurance coverage, 549
inflation gauge, 549
itemized deductions, 549–50
personal exemptions, 549
Standard Deduction, 548
Tax shelter, 503
T-bar
commission problems, 384–7
investment problems, 387–9
loan problems, 393–5
value problems, 389–93
Teaser rate, 343
Telephone solicitation laws, 297
Temporary shelters, 110
Tenancy at sufferance, 196, 237, 245
Tenancy at will, 195–6, 245
Tenancy by the entireties, 197, 199–200
Tenancy in common, 197, 199
Tenants, 173–6, 195, 238
Termination of agency, 102–4
Termination of contracts, 281–4
Termination of easements, 235–6
Termination of employment, 121
Termination of lease, 174–6, 244–5
Termites, 402, 571–2, 591
Terraces, 207
Testate, 218
Third-degree felonies, 149
Thrift institutions, 329
Tiers, 258–60
TILA-RESPA, 315–16, 377–8, 406–7
"Time is of the essence", 285
Time limits, contracts, 283, 293
Title, 228–31. *See also* Deeds
equitable, 217–19, 288, 289
legal, 217, 289
naked, 303, 304
transfer of, 218–20, 251
Title closing, 407
Title company, 5, 113
Title insurance, 230–1, 373, 402
Title opinion, 228
Title theory, 302–4

Title X, 594
T lot, 578, 579
Torrens land titles, 230
Total debt service ratio, 368, 369
Total monthly expense ratio, 351
Township lines, 259
Townships, 258–9, 262, 612
Toxic waste, 570, 595
Tract homes, 19
Trade fixtures, 188–9
Trade names, 109, 129
Transactional adjustments, 464
Transactional residential property, 504
Transaction brokers, 8, 92–4
Transferability, role in value, 456, 457
Transfer of title, 218–20, 251
Transitioning market, 442
Trees, as property, 186–7
Triggering terms, 376–7
Trusses, 580–1, 603
Trust deed, 303, 304
Trustee, 303, 304
Trustor, 303, 304
Trusts, 128
Truth in Lending Act (TILA), 315–16, 376–8, 406–7
Truth-in-millage (TRIM) notice, 529

U

Unauthorized practice of law, 51, 102, 119
"Under Contract" status, 399
Underground storage tanks, 570, 594
Underwriting
appraisal, 371
credit history, 370
documentation, 370–1
FHA guidelines, 369
Freddie Mac guidelines, 366–9
maximum loan amount, 371–2
purpose of, 366
reverse annuity loans, 372

rural housing loans, 372
VA guidelines, 370
Undue influence, 280
Unenforceable contracts, 271
Uniform Residential Appraisal Report, 478–83
Uniform Standards of Professional Appraisal Practice (USPAP), 15, 16, 17, 451, 452
Uniform Vendor and Purchaser Risk Act, 284
Unilateral contract, 276–7
Unincorporated associations, 128–9
Uninsured casualty losses, 535
Unintentional misrepresentation, 279–80
United States Code, 29
Unities of joint tenancy, 198, 200
Unit-in-place method, 467–8, 492
Universal agency, 80–1, 82
Unpaid taxes, 531
Unsecured note, 302, 305, 307
Unused development rights, 183–4
Upside down status, 324
Urban planning
appeals and exemptions, 565–6
building codes, 564
comprehensive plans, 558, 560–1
developments of regional impact, 566
Environmental Impact Study, 567
flood zones, 567–8
health ordinances, 564–5
history of, 556–8
local planning agency, 559–60
planned unit development, 567
process of, 558–60
zoning ordinances, 562–4
Urea-formaldehyde foam insulation, 593
Use/enjoyment right, 189, 217
User taxes, 521
Use variance, 566
Utility, role in value, 456, 457

V

Vacancy and collection (V&C), 473, 536
Vacancy rates, 434–5, 442–3, 460
Vacating leased premises, 174–6
Vacation, easement, 235
Valid contracts, 270–5
VA loans, 317, 355–61, 370
Valuable consideration, 272
Valuation, 454, 456, 496. *See also* Appraisal
Value
   ad valorem taxes, 521–2, 523–4
   capitalization, 472
   concept of, 453–5
   elements of, 455–7
   math problems, 389–93
   principles of, 457–60
   taxable, 525–6
   terminology related to, 460–2
Value Adjustment Board, 524
Variable closing costs, 373
Variable lease, 241–2
Variable operating expenses, 474, 537
Variances, 565–6, 568
Ventilation by fans, 587–8
Veterans, FHA program for, 349
Victorian roof, 580
Voidable contract, 271, 280, 283
Void contract, 271
Void licenses, 62
Volts, 589
Voluntary alienation, 218
Voluntary inactive status, 61
Voluntary liens, 249, 250
Voluntary life estates, 193

W

Wall construction, 582–3
Warehousing, 506
Warm air heating systems, 585, 586
Warranty deed, 365
Warranty forever covenant, 227
Water heating systems, 585, 586
Water rights, 183
Water supply, 568–9, 570, 571, 588
Weights, in CMA, 490
Will, property conveyed by, 218
Window air-conditioning units, 587
Windows, 583–4
Wood-destroying organisms, 571–2, 591
Writ of supersedes, 140
Written contracts, 269, 278

Y

Yield calculation, 612
Yield maintenance, 310

Z

Zero lot line, 578, 579
Zoning Board of Adjustment, 565
Zoning ordinances
   appeals and exemptions, 565–6
   categories of, 562–4
   comprehensive plans, 558, 560–1
   history of, 556–8